Practical Cookery

11TH EDITION

John Campbell David Foskett Victor Ceserani

HODDER
EDUCATION
PART OF HACHETTE LIVRE UK

Orders: please contact Bookpoint Ltd, 130 Milton Park, Abingdon, Oxon OX14 4SB. Telephone: (44) 01235 827720. Fax: (44) 01235 400454. Lines are open from 9.00 – 5.00, Monday to Saturday, with a 24-hour message answering service. You can also order through our website www.hoddereducation.co.uk.

British Library Cataloguing in Publication Data
A catalogue record for this title is available from the British Library

ISBN: 978 0340 94837 8

First Published 2008
Impression number   10 9 8 7 6 5 4 3 2
Year   2014 2013 2012 2011 2010 2009 2008

Cover photo © Tim Imrie/Photolibrary
Typeset by Fakenham Photosetting Ltd, Fakenham, Norfolk
Illustrations by Richard Morris
Printed in Italy for Hodder Education, part of Hachette Livre UK, 338 Euston Road, London NW1 3BH.

Contents

Conversion tables

Weights and measures

Metric	Approx. Imperial equivalent
5 g	¼ oz
10 g	½ oz
25 g	1 oz
50 g	2 oz
75 g	3 oz
100 g	4 oz
125 g	5 oz
150 g	6 oz
175 g	7 oz
200 g	8 oz
225 g	9 oz
250 g	10 oz
275 g	11 oz
300 g	12 oz
325 g	13 oz
350 g	14 oz
375 g	15 oz
400 g	16 oz
1 kg	2 lb
125 ml	¼ pt
250 ml	½ pt
375 ml	¾ pt
500 ml	1 pt
750 ml	1½ pt
1 litre	2 pt (1 qt)
2 litres	2 qt
4.5 litres	1 gal
0.5 cm	¼ in
1 cm	½ in
2 cm	1 in
4 cm	1½ in
5 cm	2 in
6 cm	2½ in
8 cm	3 in
10 cm	4 in
12 cm	5 in
15 cm	6 in
16 cm	6½ in
18 cm	7 in
30 cm	12 in
45 cm	18 in

Spoons and cups

	Metric
1 teaspoon (tsp)	5 ml
1 dessertspoon (dsp)	10 ml
1 tablespoon (tbsp)	15 ml
¼ cup	60 ml
⅓ cup	80 ml
½ cup	125 ml
1 cup	250 ml

Oven temperatures

	°C	Gas regulo	°F
slow (cool)	110	¼	225
	130	½	250
	140	1	275
	150	2	300
	160	3	325
moderate	180	4	350
	190	5	375
	200	6	400
hot	220	7	425
	230	8	450
very hot	250	9	475

Acknowledgements

We are most grateful to the following for their assistance in preparing this edition of *Practical Cookery*:

The staff at the Vineyard at Stockcross, especially Peter Eaton for his meticulous testing and Olly Rouse not only for his assistance with the text of the book but also for his support during the filming process.

Dipna Anand and the staff of the Brilliant Restaurant, Southall.

Alexia Chan, Paul Cherry, Deborah Edwards and Laura DeGrasse at Hodder Education, and Lynn Brown and Rick Jackman.

Adrian Moss of Instructional Design Ltd for producing and creating the videos which accompany this book and the associated teacher resources.

Sam Bailey for the photography.

Jenny Arthur, nutrition consultant, for the nutritional analysis, Dr Jenny Poulter, Jane Cliff and Pat Bacon for their work on previous editions.

Russums Catering Clothing and Equipment.

Compass Group UK.

Special thanks to Russell Hume Ltd for sponsoring the butchery videos, and in particular to Pat Herlihy, Operations Director, and Terry Connelly, Sales Account Manager. Russell Hume are meat, game and poultry specialists and national suppliers of meat, game and poultry products to hotels, restaurants, pubs and event caterers. They are committed to quality and service nationwide and have 90 years' experience, with managers who have over 20 years' experience in the meat trade.

Introduction to the eleventh edition

The purpose of this book is to provide a sound foundation of professional cookery for all levels of students of catering.

The following points are important:

- to develop a professional attitude and appearance, acquire skills and behave in a professional manner;
- to develop knowledge and understanding of all commodities regarding cost, quality and use;
- to understand the methods of cooking and be able to produce a variety of dishes for various types of establishment;
- to understand recipe balance and be able to produce dishes of the required quality, colour, consistency, seasoning, flavour, temperature, quantity and presentation;
- with experience, to develop recipes using original ideas;
- to understand the principles of healthy eating and basic nutrition;
- to fully understand the essential necessity for healthy, hygienic and safe procedures at all times in the storage, preparation, cooking and serving of food.

These books may also assist you in your career: *The Theory of Catering* and *Advanced Practical Cookery*.

As the world is getting 'smaller' due to factors such as fast transport and tourism, modern cuisine uses a wide variety of ingredients from all over the world. This has led to an intermix of cuisine cultures, for example a fusion of western and eastern styles; traditional European cuisine has blended with Oriental, and so on. This may be described as 'eclectic' cuisine, which is the deriving of ideas, tastes and styles from various sources and which originated in Australia. This development enables chefs to be creative and this has been demonstrated by the many restaurants and food service outlets taking this approach.

However, to be creative, chefs must understand and acquire the basic skills of practical professional cookery. These skills and underpinning knowledge must be formed from the subject knowledge – 'the body of knowledge' upon which every discipline relies as the source from which concepts, models and theories develop.

In practical professional cookery it is the basic principles, procedures and classical dishes that originate from the traditional French kitchen, further developed by master chefs such as Carême and Escoffier. The chefs in the traditional French kitchen were the first to practise fusion cuisine as ingredients were brought from different countries, together with different recipes and methods, which these chefs refined to suit the various types of customer. Therefore, fusion or eclectic cuisine is not new but, with globalisation, that is the bringing together of countries, peoples, cultures and cuisines, chefs have been enabled to be more creative and innovative.

Basic skills and recipes are fundamental as these provide the framework for all the essential underpinning knowledge for a successful career in professional cookery that will allow individuals to gain employment across continents.

This book provides an invaluable foundation for acquiring basic professional skill and knowledge and in this edition we have attempted to balance the traditional with the modern in the illustrations.

The decision to use metric weights and measures was taken after consultation with catering colleges.

There is no such thing as unhealthy food but there are unfortunately unhealthy eating habits that in many cases lead to obesity followed by ill-health and premature death.

It is because of national concern with the alarming increase in cases of obesity, particularly with the young, that we invited Jenny Arthur to develop the nutritional analysis for some of the new recipes.

Analysis for the nutrients has been performed using the computer software CompEat Pro Version 5.8.0 (2002). This holds the UK integrated databases of McCance & Widdowson's *The Composition of Foods 6th Summary Edition* and associated supplements, RSC.

Weights and measures were used as given in the text unless mentioned as a single item e.g. an egg,

and in such cases information derived from *Food Portion Sizes, 3rd Edition*, Dept of Environment, Fisheries and Rural Affairs.

Where appropriate, the edible portion of the recipe ingredient was used; there were instances where the waste produced in the recipe would have distorted the nutritional values e.g. whole chicken as part of the recipe, but only the wing and leg quarters were used.

Vegetable oil was used as the first choice of oil unless specified otherwise, and butter was used as the first choice over margarine. Semi-skimmed milk is used as first choice milk unless otherwise specified.

Picture credits

The authors and publisher would like to thank the following for permission to reproduce copyright illustrative material:

Sam Bailey for the photos at the beginning of each chapter and for figures 1.2, 1.3, 2.5, 2.7, 3.3–3.5, 4.1–4.11, 4.13, 4.14, 5.3, 5.5, 5.6, 6.1–6.5, 7.5–7.7, 7.11, 7.13–7.16, 7.18, 7.19, 8.6–8.9, 8.16, 8.22–8.25, 8.33, 9.8–9.17, 10.2–10.4, 10.6–10.15, 11.1–11.5, 11.7–11.11, 12.1, 12.3–12.13, 13.4–13.11, 14.1–14.5, 14.7, 14.9–14.23, 14.25–14.31, 14.33–14.37, 14.39, 14.40, 14.44, 14.49–14.54, 15.1, 17.9, 20.3, 20.5, 21.1 and 23.1.

The British Potato Council for figure 13.1.

Compass Group UK for figures 2.15, 17.1, 17.2, 17.7, 17.10, 17.12, 17.13, 20.1 and 20.7.

The Meat and Livestock Commission for figures 8.5, 8.13, 8.18–8.20 and 8.27–8.32.

Richard Morris for figures 8.1–8.4, 8.10–8.12, 8.14, 8.17, 8.21, 8.26, 8.34, 9.1 and 9.3.

Adrian Moss for figures 2.1–2.4, 2.6, 2.8–2.14, 3.1, 3.2, 4.12, 5.1, 5.2, 5.4, 7.1–7.4, 7.8–7.10, 7.12, 7.17, 8.15, 9.2, 9.4–9.7, 10.1, 10.5, 11.6, 12.2, 14.6, 14.8, 14.24, 14.32, 14.38 and 14.41–14.43.

Oxford Designers and Illustrators for figures 9.18, 13.2, 13.3, 16.1, 16.3, 16.9–16.11, 17.3, 17.4, 17.8, 17.11, 18.3, 18.5–18.8, 19.1 and 20.2.

Russums Catering Clothing and Equipment for figures 17.14, 20.4 and 20.6.

Crown copyright material is reproduced with the permission of the Controller of HMSO and the Queen's Printer for Scotland.

HODDER
EDUCATION
The Expert Choice

What does 'the expert choice' mean for you?

We work with more examiners and experts than any other publisher

- Because we work with more experts and examiners than any other publisher, the very latest curriculum requirements are built into this course and there is a perfect match between your course and the resources that you need to succeed. We make it easier for you to gain the skills and knowledge that you need for the best results.

- We have chosen the best team of experts – including the people that mark the exams – to give you the very best chance of success; look out for their advice throughout this book: this is content that you can trust.

Welcome to Dynamic Learning

Dynamic Learning is a simple and powerful way of integrating this text with digital resources to help you succeed, by bringing learning to life. Whatever your learning style, Dynamic Learning will help boost your understanding. And our Dynamic Learning content is updated online so your book will never be out of date.

1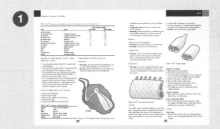

- Complete digital copy of the entire book on-screen, with zoom function and access to photographs and diagrams so that you can use them in your studies.

2 Test your knowledge with a quiz

 View a short video

 Boost your understanding through interactive activities, web links and extension material

- These icons appear throughout the book. They mean that extra material is available on the digital page.

More direct contact with teachers and students than any other publisher

- We talk with more than 100 000 students every year through our student conferences, run by Philip Allan Updates. We hear at first hand what you need to make a success of your studies and build what we learn into every new course. Learn more about our conferences at **www.philipallan.co.uk**

- Our new materials are trialled in classrooms as we develop them, and the feedback built into every new book or resource that we publish. You can be part of that. If you have comments that you would like to make about this book, please email us at: **feedback@hodder.co.uk**

More collaboration with Subject Associations than any other publisher

- Subject Associations sit at the heart of education. We work closely with more Associations than any other publisher. This means that our resources support the most creative teaching and learning, using the skills of the best teachers in their field to create resources for you.

More opportunities for your tutors to stay ahead than with any other publisher

- Through our Philip Allan Updates Conferences, we offer tutors access to Continuing Professional Development. Our focused and practical conferences ensure that your tutors have access to the best presenters, teaching materials and training resources. Our presenters include experienced teachers, Chief and Principal Examiners, leading educationalists, authors and consultants. This course is built on all of this expertise.

❸

- Key preparation techniques and recipes are presented by 2-star Michelin chef, John Campbell, in 52 video films.

❹ Extra material, including more videos, is available on the Network Edition

- Also available is the Network Edition. If your college has purchased this edition, look out for even more resources where you see this icon.

To start up Dynamic Learning now, make sure that your computer has an active broadband connection to the internet and insert the disk into your DVD-ROM drive. Dynamic Learning should run automatically if you have 'Auto Run' enabled. Full installation instructions are printed on the disk label.

Basic system requirements for your Student Edition: **PC** Windows 2000 (SP4), XP SP2 (Home & Pro), Vista; **PC (Server)** Windows 2000 and 2003; **Mac** Mac OS X 10.3 or 10.4; G4, G5 or Intel processor. Dynamic Learning is not currently Leopard-compatible: see the website for latest details. Up to 1.4Gb hard disc space per title. Minimum screen resolution 1024 x 768. Sound card. A fast processor (PC, 1GHz; Mac, 1.25 GHz) and good graphics card. Copyright restrictions mean that some materials may not be accessible from within the Dynamic Learning edition. Full details of your single-user licence can be found on the disk under 'Contents'.

You can find out more at **www.dynamic-learning.co.uk**

How to access Chapters 16 to 24

The following chapters are designed to support your study towards a Level 2 NVQ or VRQ.

They are provided on the DVD-ROM as PDF files which you can read on-screen or print out.

16 Investigating the hospitality and catering industry

VRQ Unit 201 Investigate the catering and hospitality industry

17 Food safety, hygiene and security

NVQ Unit 501 (1GEN1) Maintain a safe, hygienic and secure working environment

NVQ Unit 603 (2GEN3) Maintain food safety when storing, preparing and cooking food
VRQ Unit 202 Food safety in catering

18 Health and safety

NVQ Unit 501 (1GEN1) Maintain a safe, hygienic and secure working environment

VRQ Unit 203 Health and safety in catering and hospitality

19 Teamwork

NVQ Unit 504 (1GEN4) Contribute to effective teamwork

20 Kitchen operations, costs and menu planning

VRQ Unit 205 Kitchen operations, costs and menu planning

21 Applying workplace skills

VRQ Unit 206 Applying workplace skills

22 Kitchen documentation and ordering stock

NVQ Unit 602 (2GEN2) Order stock

NVQ Unit 671 (2P&C1) Complete kitchen documentation

23 Cook-chill and cook-freeze

NVQ Unit 634 (2FC8) Cook-chill food

NVQ Unit 635 (2FC9) Cook-freeze food

24 Setting up and closing a kitchen

NVQ Unit 672 (2P&C2) Set up and close a kitchen

chapter 1

HEALTHY EATING

Unit 204   **Healthier food and special diets**

Unit 648 (2FPC13) Prepare, cook and finish healthier dishes

Demonstrate knowledge of balanced diets

Underpinning knowledge
The candidate will be able to:
1 Identify sources of current government nutritional guidelines
2 Explain the intentions of current government nutritional guidelines
3 Explain the importance of good health
4 Explain the principles of a balanced diet throughout life stages
5 Describe good practice that will ensure the preservation of the nutritional value of food throughout preparation, cooking and service of food
6 List sources where the nutritional values of food items can be found

Plan special diets

Practical skills
The candidate will be able to:
1 Produce menu items suitable for special diets

Underpinning knowledge
The candidate will be able to:
1 List types of special diet
2 Explain the main features of special diets
3 Describe the practices to be considered when preparing, cooking and serving special diets

Why healthy eating is important

With more and more people eating outside the home, caterers are in a strong position to influence customers.

The need to provide healthier menu options

Nearly 24 million adults in the UK today are overweight or obese. Levels of obesity have trebled in England over the past 20 years and are still on the increase. Figures for Scotland are similar and Wales has one of the worst health records in Europe.

Healthy eating is not just about reducing obesity, however. Research work carried out at the Royal Marsden Hospital suggests that a third of all cancers are caused by poor diet. Diet can be linked to bowel cancer, stomach and lung cancer, high blood pressure, diabetes, osteoporosis and tooth decay. Eating a balanced nutritional diet can protect us from these illnesses. Caterers should therefore be informed on healthy eating, and chefs should provide a range of healthy menu options.

What is healthy eating?

Food, nutrition and exercise are crucial to our health and well-being. There is no doubt that making the right choices of food and drink, combined with taking regular exercise, can protect against many western 'killer diseases' like coronary heart disease and cancer. There are also lots of immediate benefits and really positive results in keeping slim for life.

The picture presented in the media may seem confusing, but scientists are united on what makes for a healthy style of eating; unfortunately,

however, many myths still prevail. Contrary to popular opinion it is not about taking chips off the menu or sticking to salad, but simply eating more bulky, filling foods, piling on the fruit and vegetables, and eating less of the high-fat sugary foods. Some of the greatest dishes and most exciting cuisines in the world are based on these principles (e.g. paella, biryani, Chinese vegetables stir-fried with noodles, sushi and rice, couscous, and cannelloni stuffed with ricotta and spinach).

Table 1.1 Summing up healthy eating

What it is about	What it is not about	Immediate benefits
Filling up on bread, pasta, rice and potatoes	Cutting down on food	Better weight control
Eating more fruit and vegetables	Going hungry	Improved self-esteem
Eating a little less of some food items	Depriving yourself of treats	Looking and feeling better
Enjoying good food	Spending more money on food	Feeling fitter, with more energy
Making small, gradual changes	Not enjoying food	Enjoying a wide variety of foods
Knowing more about food	'Brown and boring food'	Not buying expensive 'diet' products
Altering food shopping patterns	Just salads	Knowing that changes made today will have long-term benefits
Feeling satisfied and good about food	Making major changes	
	Going on a 'special diet'	

The balance of good health

There are no 'good' or 'bad' foods – it is the overall balance of the diet that matters. How people choose to put together meals and snacks with drinks will determine whether their style of eating is healthy or not. In practice – as noted above – this means having a variety of foods, basing meals on starchy foods and eating at least five portions of fruit and vegetables a day. The balance to strive for is illustrated in a nationally recognised model (see Figure 1.1), which emphasises that people should consume:

- **more starchy foods** (e.g. cereals, breads, pasta, potatoes, rice)
- **more fruit and vegetables** (aiming for five portions per day)
- **moderate amounts of food from the milk and dairy, and meat, fish and alternative proteins groups** – as a guideline, two to three portions from each group per day
- **very small amounts of foods containing fats and sugars, and drinks containing sugars**, selecting lower-fat options where possible; in

addition, foods that are high in salt should be restricted.

 Further information

Information on the portions of different types of foods that make up a healthy diet is given in the *Balance of Good Health* leaflet, which is available from the Food Standards Agency (FSA). It can be downloaded as a PDF file from the FSA's website at: www.food.gov.uk/multimedia/pdfs/bghbooklet.pdf.

Translating this into practice means:

- bigger portions of starchy foods, vegetables and fruit with meals
- getting more energy (kcals) from starchy carbohydrate and less from fatty and sugary foods
- there is scope for the occasional treat
- aiming to achieve this balance over a period of days, not necessarily at every meal
- often making very small changes to favourite meals.

The eatwell plate

FOOD STANDARDS AGENCY
food.gov.uk

Use the eatwell plate to help you get the balance right. It shows how much of what you eat should come from each food group.

Fruit and vegetables

Bread, rice, potatoes, pasta and other starchy foods

Meat, fish, eggs, beans and other non-dairy sources of protein

Foods and drinks high in fat and/or sugar

Milk and dairy foods

Figure 1.1 ✎ The eatwell plate. Use the eatwell plate to help you get the balance right. It shows how much of what you eat should come from each food group

Nutrients from food

Healthy eating is about selecting certain foods that provide the nutrients that are needed by the body in different amounts. If people choose foods in the proportions shown in the FSA's *Balance of Good Health* leaflet (mentioned above) then they should obtain all the nutrients they need in the quantities that promote good health. Nutrients perform different functions in the body and you can find out more about this in any basic nutrition textbook. Table 1.2 summarises some of the key nutritional terms you will encounter, plus the current guidance for health.

Table 1.2 Key nutritional terms and current guidance for health

Foods provide . . .	For health . . .
Energy is locked up in food and comes from carbohydrate, fat, protein and alcohol. It is measured in calories or joules, which are so tiny they are usually expressed in kilocalories (kcals) or kilojoules (kJ).	Balance energy intake through food with energy output through activity. This helps control body weight. Specific figures for energy intakes are given in the government's report on Dietary Reference Values.
Fat is a very concentrated source of energy. The same weight of pure fat has over twice as much energy as sugar or starch. Fat is present in foods in two main types: saturated fat in foods from animal sources like butter, cheese, meat and milk, and fatty meats; unsaturated fat in foods from plants (e.g. oils, nuts and seeds) and oily fish (e.g. tuna, salmon, mackerel) sources.	To cut down on fat intake, particularly the saturated type – aiming for 30–35 per cent energy from fat. It is the saturated fat that pushes up blood cholesterol, which is why it is important to switch to foods containing unsaturated types of fat. For example, using oils instead of butter or lard in recipes, incorporating more oily fish like salmon and mackerel plus white meats into menu planning.
Carbohydrate may be one of two types: sugars, which occur naturally in certain foods like fruit and honey but are added to many manufactured foods, particularly confectionery, cakes and biscuits; starches, found naturally in filling foods like bread, breakfast cereals, rice, pasta and potatoes.	We should aim for 50 per cent of our energy from starch and cut back on sugars.
Fibre is the 'roughage' in plant foods and is great for the digestive system. Good sources include all wholegrain cereals, pulses, fruits, vegetables and nuts.	On current estimates we all eat around 20 g dietary fibre per day. The healthy goal is around 30 g per day.
Protein is the 'body-building' nutrient found in animal foods like meat, fish, cheese and eggs, but also in vegetable sources including cereals (e.g. pasta, breakfast cereals, bread) pulses and nuts.	Protein requirements are often overestimated. For example, adults need only between 35 and 50 g of protein per day. This can be provided by a 100 g portion of chicken plus a carton of yoghurt and 200 g of baked beans.
Vitamins and minerals are needed in minute amounts for many bodily processes. Since the body cannot make these essential micronutrients, they have to be provided by the diet.	Recommended daily amounts for 9 vitamins and 11 minerals are given in the Government's report on Dietary Reference Values.
Salt is sodium chloride, which is involved in maintaining the body's water balance. Sodium is a type of mineral; sodium chloride is added to many manufactured foods and in particularly high amounts in cured and snack foods.	There is now stronger evidence that the high intakes of salt in this country (estimated at about 8 g per day) can lead to high blood pressure. The goal is around 4 g of salt per day.

The chef's role

Chefs have a vital role in making healthy eating an exciting reality for us all. Customer trends show that many people are looking for healthier options within menus, particularly if they eat away from home every day. Healthy eating is one of the major consumer trends to emerge over the past decade and represents an important commercial opportunity for caterers across the UK. This is not a passing fad; healthy eating is here to stay.

As well as escalating consumer demand, some sectors of catering have strict requirements relating to health and nutrition. For example, by law, school caterers have to provide meals that meet a minimum nutritional standard. Often there are health-related specifications for workplace catering contracts because employers feel they have a commitment to the health of their staff.

Chefs can be highly influential in the health arena. The amount of ingredients and the proportion in which they are used, plus careful choice of cooking and service methods, can make an enormous difference to the nutritional content of a dish or meal. Research has shown that the most effective approach to healthy catering is to make small changes to popular dishes. This may involve the following measures.

- Small shifts in portion sizes (e.g. Figure 1.2) or adding a bread roll or jacket potato to a meal. This yields more starch in proportion to fat (effectively diluting the fat).
- Subtle modifications to recipes for composite dishes. For instance, making a pizza with a thicker base and adding mushrooms and roasted peppers topped with less mozzarella but adding a sprinkling of Parmesan for flavour. Omitting the salt, but relying on the Parmesan, black pepper and chopped oregano to add flavour.

This is where chefs are vital in developing healthier recipes that work. The skill in all this is deciding when and where dishes can be modified without losing quality. Some highly traditional dishes are best left alone whilst subtle changes can be made to others with no loss in texture, appearance or flavour (e.g. Figure 1.3). The

Figure 1.2   A healthy portion size: navarin of lamb

Figure 1.3   A traditional dish made healthier: Mexican bean pot and salad

'Healthy eating tips' throughout the recipe sections can help in making some of these changes. In summary the key to healthier catering is to:

- make small changes to best-selling items
- increase the amount of starchy foods
- increase the amount of fruit and vegetables
- increase the fibre content of dishes where it is practical and acceptable
- reduce fat in traditional recipes
- change the type of fat used
- select healthier ways to prepare dishes and be adventurous
- be moderate in the use of sugar and salt.

Note: take care when providing nutritional information on menus as there may be a danger of making misleading claims, which could break the law. If unsure, take advice.

Special diets

Vegetarian/vegan and other ethical diets

Vegetarians do not eat meat or fish, or any type of dish made with or containing the products of animals. Check for vegetarians who:

- occasionally eat fish and/or meat – semi-vegetarian or demi-vegetarian
- do not eat milk and dairy products – ovo-vegetarian
- do not eat eggs – lacto-vegetarian
- do not eat any food of animal origin (including honey, dairy products and eggs); such people are known as vegans (note that vegetables, fruits, grains, legumes, pasta made without eggs, soya products and other products of plants are acceptable)
- eat only fruit, nuts and berries – frutarian or fructarian.

Religious diets

Adherents of the religions listed below do not eat the following foods.

- **Hindu:** meat, fish or eggs (orthodox Hindus are usually strict vegetarians; less strict Hindus may eat lamb, poultry and fish, but definitely not beef as cattle have a deep religious meaning – milk, however, is highly regarded).
- **Jewish:** pork, pork products, shellfish and eels, meat and milk served at the same time or cooked together; strict Jews eat only Kosher meat; milk and milk products are usually avoided at lunch and dinner (but are acceptable at breakfast).
- **Muslim:** pork, meat that is not halal (slaughtered according to custom), shellfish and alcohol (even when used in cooking).
- **Rastafarian:** all processed foods, pork, fish without fins (eels), alcohol, coffee, tea.
- **Sikh:** beef, pork, lamb, poultry and fish may be acceptable to Sikh men; Sikh women tend to avoid all meat.

Medical diets

For medical reasons, the people on the special diets below do not eat the foods listed.

- **Dairy/milk free:** milk, butter, cheese, yoghurt and any prepared foods that include milk products (check label).
- **Diabetes:** dishes that are high in sugar and/or fat (low-calorie sweeteners can be used to sweeten desserts).
- **Gluten free:** wheat, wholemeal, wholewheat and wheatmeal flour, wheat bran, rye, barley and oats (some doctors say oats are permitted, the Coeliac Society advises against) and any dishes made with these, including pasta, noodles, semolina, bread, pastries, some yoghurts (e.g. muesli), some cheese spreads, barley-based drinks, malted drinks, beer, some brands of mustard, proprietary sauces made with flour (use cornflour to thicken; rice, potato, corn and sage are also acceptable).
- **Low cholesterol and saturated fat:** liver, egg yolks and shellfish (which are high in cholesterol), beef, pork and lamb (which contain saturated fats), butter, cream, groundnut oil, margarine (use oils and margarines labelled high in polyunsaturated fats).
- **Low fat:** any food that contains fat, or has been fried or roasted.
- **Low residue:** wholemeal bread, brown rice and pasta, fried and fatty foods.
- **Low salt:** foods and dishes that have had salt added in the cooking or processing (including smoked and cured fishes and meats, and hard cheeses) or contain monosodium glutamate.
- **Nut allergy:** nuts, blended cooking oils and margarine (since these may include nut oil; use pure oils or butter) and any dishes containing these (check label).

chapter 2

METHODS OF COOKERY

This section underpins all the practical units for both NVQ and VRQ.

Practical skills
The candidate will be able to:
1 Demonstrate the skills required to carry out each different method of cookery
2 Prepare the various ingredients according to the method of cookery
3 Use each appropriate method of cookery as required by the recipe
4 Apply the quality checks required to ensure that the dish is cooked successfully using the method of cookery
5 Demonstrate safe, hygienic working practices for each method of cookery

Underpinning knowledge
The candidate will be able to:
1 Identify the appropriate method of cookery for the list of ingredients and the dish requirements
2 State the principles underpinning each method of cookery
3 Explain the quality points to assess for each method of cookery
4 State the cooking time for a range of ingredients using each method of cookery
5 Evaluate the differences between each method of cookery using different ingredients
6 Explain the health and safety procedures to be followed when using each method of cookery

Why we apply cooking methods

This chapter looks at the different ways in which food may be cooked. The basis of all cooking is the application of heat, which may be transferred to food by the processes of convection, conduction and radiation. Once food is in contact with heat the theory behind the heat transfer is called molecular conduction or thermal energy, which translates into one molecular layer conducting the heat to the next.

Food is cooked to make it more palatable and digestible, to develop or add flavour, to make it safe to eat, to improve its aesthetic appeal and add variety to the diet.

A chef has a variety of basic methods of cookery from which to choose. These may incorporate methods of cooking that use moist heat (using liquids such us water, stock and milk) or dry heat (without the use of liquids to cook the food).

The principles of cooking food

The cooking of food involves heating it in a variety of ways to make it more palatable. The heat to cook the food comes from a variety of sources, including electric elements or hotplates; gas flame from a stove or grill; the heat from a conventional oven; and heat generated by a microwave oven or in the case of *sous vide* the heat from the cooking medium is outside the bag (this is a similar approach to the classic method of cookery called *en papillote*.

Heat is transferred to the food and cooking medium (the fat, water, stock or milk) by means of convection, conduction and radiation. It must be remembered that most foods are cooked by a combination of at least two of the processes of transferring heat, not just one. For example, a basic sponge will be cooked by heat directly reflecting from the oven walls (**radiation**), heat circulating in the air of the oven (**convection**), and heat transferred from the cake tin/tray to the cake mixture (**conduction**).

Convection

When food is cooked through the convection process, the heat passes through another medium – either liquid or gas. When liquids or gases are heated, the heat is distributed throughout the cooking medium and food by convection currents. For example, in baking, the air in the oven gradually heats up until the heat is transferred to the product being baked.

When food is boiled, the water (the cooking medium) is gradually heated by the process of convection. Once the water is heated, it transfers the heat to the food. The same principle applies to deep-frying, except that oil is the cooking medium.

Cooking equipment that uses the process of convection to cook food includes deep-fryers, stockpots, steamers, boilers, poachers, cooking pots and ovens. Methods of cooking by convection include poaching, boiling, stewing, braising, baking and roasting.

Conduction

Conduction is the process in which heat is transferred to the food by direct contact with the cooking vessel (e.g. pot, pan, solid top). The heat passes through a solid or from one solid to another. For food to be cooked by conduction, it must be in direct contact with a heated item. This process relies on the use of good conductors, which allow the heat to transfer through them to the food. Metals are generally good conductors of heat, which is why the cooking equipment in a commercial kitchen is mostly metallic.

Cooking equipment that uses the process of conduction to cook food includes brat pans, solid grill plates and stove hotplates. Methods of cooking by conduction include stir-frying, shallow-frying and sautéing or searing.

Radiation

Radiation is the process of heat transference directly onto the food being cooked. The heat is transferred by electromagnetic waves, such as microwaves and infrared waves. These waves go directly to the food being cooked, and any object in the path of the rays will also become hot, such as a salamander.

When food is microwaved, the cooking process is due to the action of electromagnetic waves produced from the magnetron in the microwave oven; these electromagnetic rays cause the food molecules to vibrate; this is called molecular disturbance and the friction cause by the vibration creates steam from the water present and thus cooks the food. Infrared waves are produced from the grill. These waves cause the food, which is located close to the heat source, to first heat then cook. Cooking equipment that uses the process of radiation to cook food includes microwaves, salamanders, grills and toasters. Methods of cooking by radiation include grilling, toasting, baking and microwaving.

Moist heat or dry heat can be used to cook food in this way. The decision as to which cooking method to choose depends on the desired end result of the cooked product. For example, a boneless chicken breast fillet will taste and appear very different if it is poached in chicken stock, rather than being chargrilled, or crumbed and shallow-fried.

The effect of heat on food

Protein

Protein is coagulated by heat. The process is gradual – for example, when heat is applied to egg white it thickens, becomes opaque and then firm. Overheating will harden the protein, making it tough, unpalatable and shrunken. This characteristic coagulation of protein when heated is employed in its use as a coating for deep- and shallow-fried foods and in the development of crust in bread, formed by the protein gluten in wheat.

Carbohydrates

Moist heat on starch causes the starch grains to soften and swell. Near boiling point the cellulose framework bursts, releasing the starch, which thickens the liquid.

Dry heat causes the starch to change colour from creamy white to brown and, after prolonged heat, it will carbonise and burn. Water is given off during heating and the starch on the surface is changed to dextrin, a form of sugar, as in toast.

Moist heat causes sugar to dissolve in water – more rapidly in hot water than in cold. On heating it becomes syrup; on further heating it colours then caramelises and will eventually turn to carbon and ash.

Dry heat causes sugar to caramelise quickly and burn.

Fats

Fats melt to oils when heated. Water is given off with a bubbling noise as heating continues. When all the water has been driven off, a faint blue haze appears; further heating will result in smoking and burning. The unpleasant smell of burning fat is caused by the presence of fatty acids.

Vitamins

Vitamin A and *carotene* are insoluble in water so they are not lost by moist methods of cooking, such as boiling and steaming, or by soaking. For this reason boiled vegetables contain the same amount of carotene as raw vegetables.

Vitamin D is not destroyed by heat or lost by solubility.

Thiamine (vitamin B1) is very soluble in water and about 50 per cent will dissolve in the cooking liquid. High temperatures (e.g. in pressure cooking) destroy vitamin B1, and alkali (e.g. baking powder) will cause some destruction.

Riboflavin (vitamin B2) is soluble in water and will dissolve out in the cooking liquid; some is lost in normal cooking but more losses occur in pressure cooking.

Nicotinic acid (niacin) is soluble in water and dissolves to some extent in the cooking liquid. It is stable in the presence of heat but is easily oxidised, which means that the chemical process of the product is adversely affected by taking in oxygen.

Vitamin C is lost or destroyed very easily in cooking and care must be taken to preserve it as much as possible. It is soluble in water and is easily dissolved in cleaning and cooking water; therefore vegetables containing vitamin C should not be soaked in water and cooking liquid should be made use of. It is best to cook in small quantities and as quickly as possible as vitamin C is destroyed by heat. Raw fruit and vegetables contain most vitamin C.

Vitamin C oxidises (see nicotinic acid) to form a substance that is useless to the body; to minimise oxidation cook with a lid on; also food containing vitamin C should only be stored for short periods and must be used as fresh as possible. There is an enzyme present with vitamin C in foods which, once the cells of the plant are damaged by bruising or cutting, begins to destroy the vitamin by oxidising it. The optimum, or most favourable, condition for destruction of the enzyme is between 65 and 88°C so if the vegetable is put into boiling water the enzyme activity will quickly be destroyed.

Ways of cooking food

The following ways of cooking food are described in the sections below:

- boiling
- poaching
- steaming
- stewing/casserole
- braising
- sous vide
- baking
- roasting
- pot roasting (*poêlé*)
- tandoori
- grilling (griddling)
- frying (shallow and deep)
- paper bag (*en papillotte*)
- microwave.

Boiling

Definition

Boiling is the method of cooking in which food is immersed in a liquid and cooked at 100°C. To do this, foods are fully immersed in boiling water and then the water is returned to a rapid boil. Sometimes it is necessary to reduce the temperature a little and maintain it at the simmering point. If this is done, it is important to keep the water moving, or what is commonly known as 'rolling'.

Boiling is one of the most common ways used to cook vegetables in commercial cookery. However, for large-scale operations, the steaming process is preferred for blanching vegetables as this is more productive. Vegetables are often boiled to be served as a side dish, or as part of a main dish. They may also be parboiled to be used later as part of another method of cooking. For example, potatoes may be parboiled and then later roasted or deep-fried.

Before boiling any food, it is important to ensure that all pieces of food that are going into

Figure 2.1 Boiling a crab

the same pot are of similar size or density so that they finish cooking at the same time. Foods that require different cooking times should not be cooked together. For example, the cooking time of potato is longer than that of cauliflower. It is important to be familiar with the cooking times of different vegetables for this reason.

The size of the cooking pot selected needs to be relative to the amount of food being cooked. As common sense dictates, large amounts of food need large pots. You should use enough water to entirely cover the food throughout its cooking time. Again, this amount is relative to the amount of food being cooked; be mindful that if you were to immerse green vegetables in the boiling cooking medium, the amount of liquid used needs to be sufficient not to be affected too much by the food being placed in the pan – the aim is to achieve a very small drop in the temperature of the liquid (or even no drop at all) as this helps maintain the vitamins and colour in the green vegetables.

When you make stock, you should bring the ingredients to the boil from a cold start, which aids in the removal of impurities. These impurities can be removed when the scum is skimmed off regularly during the cooking process.

Purpose

The purpose of boiling is to cook food so that it is:

- pleasant to eat, with an agreeable flavour
- of a suitable texture, tender or slightly firm according to the food
- easy to digest and safe to eat.

Methods

There are two ways of boiling:

1 place the food into boiling liquid, reboil, then reduce the heat for gentle boiling to take place, this is known as simmering
2 cover food with cold liquid, bring to the boil, then reduce heat to allow food to simmer.

Effects of boiling

Gentle boiling helps to break down the tough fibrous structure of certain foods that would be less tender if cooked by other methods. When boiling meats for long periods the soluble meat extracts are dissolved in the cooking liquid. Cooking must be slow in order to give time for the connective tissue in tough meat to be changed into soluble gelatine, so releasing the fibres and making the meat tender. If the connective tissue gelatinises too quickly the meat fibres fall apart and the meat will be tough and stringy. Gentle heat will ensure coagulation of the protein without hardening.

Advantages of boiling

- Older, tougher, cheaper joints of meat and poultry can be made palatable and digestible.
- It is appropriate for large-scale cookery and is economic in terms of fuel use.
- Nutritious, well-flavoured stock can be produced.
- It is labour saving, as boiling needs little attention.

(a) The advantages of food started slowly in cold liquid, brought to the boil and allowed to boil gently are that it:
- helps to tenderise the fibrous structure (meat), extracts starch (vegetable soups) and flavour from certain foods (stocks)
- can avoid damage to foods that would lose their shape if added to boiling liquid, e.g. whole fish.

(b) Adding food to boiling liquid:
- is suitable for green vegetables as maximum colour and nutritive value are retained, provided boiling is restricted to the minimum time
- seals in the natural juices, as with meat.

Temperature and time control

Temperature must be controlled so that the liquid is brought to the boil, or reboil, then adjusted in order that gentle boiling takes place until the food is cooked to the required degree. Stocks, soups and sauces must only simmer, pasta should be cooked only until it is slightly firm (al dente), meat and poultry should be well cooked and tender; vegetables should not be overcooked.

Although approximate cooking times are given for most foods, the age, quality and size of various foods will nevertheless affect the cooking time required.

General rules

- Select pans that are neither too small nor too large.
- When cooking in boiling liquid ensure there is sufficient liquid and that it is at boiling point before adding food.
- Frequently skim during the cooking.
- Simmer whenever possible so as to minimise evaporation, maintain the volume of liquid and minimise shrinkage.

Health and safety

When people work with large amounts of hot or boiling water, occupational health and safety becomes an important issue to consider. With large pots of hot water you must be aware of their presence and do everything possible to avoid hazardous behaviour.

- When pots of boiling liquids are on stoves, make sure that handles are turned in so that sleeves or hands will not be caught on them.
- When you place food items into boiling water, you should gently lower them into the water to prevent splashing and scalding.
- Reduce the risk of splashes by ensuring that the cooking vessel is large enough to allow water to cover the food, as well as large enough to allow extra space above the water when it boils.
- When removing the lid, tilt it away from your face, to allow the steam to escape safely.

Poaching

Definition

Poaching is the cooking of food in a liquid at just below boiling point. For most foods, the poaching liquid is heated first. When the desired temperature is reached, the prepared food is lowered into the barely simmering liquid, and allowed to cook in the gentle heat.

Unlike boiling, with poaching there should be no sign of the liquid moving, except for the occasional bubble rising to the surface. Poaching is a slow and very gentle method of cooking, most suitable for delicate foods such as eggs and fish. A health benefit of poaching is that foods can be cooked in water alone, which is excellent for reduced-fat diets.

During poaching, foods usually retain their shape, but after cooking their appearance can be a little pale. Poached foods are often accompanied by a sauce, usually made from the poaching liquid, especially in the case of oven-poached white fish.

Poaching media

Milk

Fish fillets such as smoked haddock may be poached in milk. However, milk is used mainly for poaching foods suitable for desserts. Meringue quenelles are made from a light meringue mixture that is poached gently in milk, and served with poached or stewed fruit.

Figure 2.2 Poaching fish

Stock

Different foods may be poached using different stocks. The stock should be suited to the food. For example, fish fillets can be poached in fish stock, and chicken breast fillets in chicken stock. You can also poach poultry and fish in a rich vegetable stock.

Stock syrup

Freshly squeezed or commercially prepared fruit juice is used to make the stock syrup in which to poach fresh or dried fruit. The syrup may also contain sugar to form the syrup. The stock syrup selected needs to relate to the food being poached. For example, apricots poached in a stock liquid based on apricot nectar would be suitable.

Court bouillon

Court bouillon is a poaching liquid that must first be prepared. It contains water and an acid (wine, vinegar or lemon juice). The acid in the water acts to stabilise the protein of the food being poached. This is especially important for protein foods that are soft in texture, such as eggs. Vegetables, herbs, spices and sugar may also be added to make the court bouillon.

Purpose

The purpose of poaching is to cook food so that it is:

- easy to digest
- of a suitable, tender texture
- safe and pleasant to eat because, where appropriate, an agreeable sauce is made with the cooking liquid.

Methods

There are two ways of poaching: shallow and deep.

1 *Shallow poaching.* Foods to be cooked by this method, such as cuts of fish and chicken, are cooked in the minimum of liquid – that is, water, stock, milk or wine. The liquid should never be allowed to boil but kept at a temperature as near to boiling point as possible. To prevent the liquid boiling, bring to the boil on top of the stove and complete the cooking in a moderately hot oven, approximately 180°C.
2 *Deep poaching.* Eggs are cooked in approximately 8 cm (3 inches) of gently simmering water. (The practice of poaching eggs in individual shallow metal pans over boiling water is cooking by steaming.) Whole fish (e.g. salmon), slices of fish on the bone (e.g. turbot), grilled cod and salmon, and whole chicken may be deep poached.

Figure 2.3 Poaching eggs

Effects of poaching

Poaching helps to tenderise the fibrous structure of the food, and the raw texture of the food becomes edible by chemical action.

Temperature and time control

- Temperature must be controlled so that the cooking liquid does not fall below, or exceed, the correct degree required: *shallow poaching* is cooking at just below simmering point (and may be carried out in an oven); *deep poaching* is just below gentle simmering.
- Time is important so that the food is neither undercooked, therefore unpalatable, nor overcooked, when it will break up and also lose nutritive value.
- The various types and qualities of food will affect both the time and temperature needed to achieve successful poaching.

Health and safety

Although poaching temperatures are not quite as dangerous as boiling temperatures, the liquid involved is still very hot and can cause serious burns or scalds if it makes contact with human skin. Therefore, as with boiling liquids, you need to be aware of the presence of hot liquids, and ensure that handles cannot be caught on sleeves or passing hands. When you lower food items into the poaching liquid, you should do so carefully to prevent splashes that can cause burns and scalds.

Steaming

Steaming is another moist heat method of cooking. Food is cooked in the steam produced by

Figure 2.4 ✎ Putting food into a steamer

a boiling liquid (rather than placing the food itself in the boiling liquid). Steaming relies on the steam produced being under pressure. The amount of pressure produced is determined by the type of equipment used.

Methods of steaming

Atmospheric steaming
With atmospheric steaming, steam may be produced by placing water in the bottom of a saucepan and bringing it to a rapid boil. Food is kept in cooking vessels placed above the boiling water. The steam from the boiling water heats the vessel, and thus the enclosed food.

High-pressure steaming
Steaming can also be carried out in high-pressure steamers, such as pressure cookers. These steamers work on the principle that higher pressure will produce higher temperatures, causing the food to cook faster. Steam enters the cooking chamber and builds up pressure. A safety valve is used to control the amount of pressure that builds up. The highest pressure that the unit is allowed to go to is predetermined and preset.

Combination steaming
Steaming can also be carried out in an oven. A 'combi' oven, which is how it is referred to in the industry, combines dry heat and steam in the oven chamber; this helps to add a little moisture to the cooking process, however for this method of cookery our focus will be on the steaming element of the 'combi' oven. As most modern ovens are convected with aid of a fan, once water vapour is added to the oven's chamber, steam is created; with the added facility of a fan the steam is

distributed more evenly and quickly; although still only at 100°C, it will cook more quickly than in a conventional oven. Be mindful, though, that when choosing a method of cookery, the cooking time may have to be adjusted if using a combi oven.

Purpose
The purpose of steaming food is to cook it so that it is:

- easy to digest
- of an edible texture, pleasant and safe to eat
- as nutritious as possible (steaming minimises nutritive loss).

Effects of steaming
When food is steamed its structure and texture is changed by chemical action and it becomes edible. The texture will vary according to the type of food, type of steamer and degree of heat; sponges and puddings are lighter in texture if steamed rather than baked.

Advantages of steaming
These include:

- retention of goodness (nutritional value)
- makes some foods lighter and easy to digest, e.g. suitable for invalids
- low-pressure steaming reduces risk of overcooking protein
- high-pressure steaming enables food to be cooked or reheated quickly because steam is forced through the food, thus cooking it rapidly
- labour-saving and suitable for large-scale cookery
- high-speed steamers used for 'batch' cooking enable the frequent cooking of small quantities of vegetables throughout the service, keeping vegetables freshly cooked, retaining colour, flavour and nutritive value
- with steamed fish, the natural juices can be retained by serving with the fish or in making the accompanying sauce
- steaming is economical on fuel as a low heat is needed and a multitiered steamer can be used.

Temperature and time control

For high-pressure steaming, foods should be placed in the steamer when the pressure gauge indicates the required degree of pressure. This will ensure that the necessary cooking temperature has been reached.

Cooking times will vary according to the equipment used, and the type, size and quality of food to be steamed. Manufacturers' instructions are an essential guide to successful steaming.

Cleaning

The inside of the steamer, trays and runners are washed in hot detergent water, rinsed and dried. Where applicable the water-generating chamber should be drained, cleaned and refilled. Door controls should be lightly greased occasionally and the door left slightly open to allow air to circulate when the steamer is not in use.

Before use check that the steamer is clean and safe to use. Any fault must be reported immediately.

Metal containers (sleeves and basins) may be thoroughly cleaned with kitchen paper or a clean cloth; other containers must be washed in hot detergent water, rinsed in hot water and dried. Containers are stored in closed cupboards.

Specific points

Meat and sweet pudding basins must be greased, then, after being filled, efficiently covered with greased greaseproof or silicone paper and foil to prevent moisture penetrating and resulting in a soggy pudding.

Health and safety

During the steaming process, boiling water is used in the bottom of individual steamers. Thus the same rules of safety as those for boiling need to be followed. The steam created under these conditions is very dangerous, as its temperature is higher than boiling point and there is a high risk of injury due to burning and scalding.

There are several safety precautions that must be followed to avoid the risk of injury. You should make sure that you know how to use all specialised equipment, and you should use it with great care. The pressure in high-pressure steamers must be checked continually to avoid accidents, and you should allow the pressure to return to the correct level before opening doors or removing pressure cooker lids. When opening commercial steamers, allow time for the pressure to return to normal first, then stand well away from the door, avoiding the full impact of the release of the steam.

Stewing/casserole

Stewing is a cooking method that is nearly identical to braising but generally involves smaller pieces of meat, and hence a shorter cooking time.

The term **casserole** refers to both a baking dish and the ingredients it contains. A 'casserole dish' usually refers to a deep, round, ovenproof container with handles and a tight-fitting lid. It can be made of glass, metal, ceramic or any other heatproof material. A casserole's ingredients can include meat, vegetables, beans, rice and anything else that might seem appropriate. Often a topping such as cheese or breadcrumbs is added for texture and flavour.

Stewing is a slow, gentle, moist heat method of cooking in which the food is completely covered by a liquid. The stew is cooked on top of the stove, and both the food and the sauce are served together. Stewing may also be done in the oven, in an ovenproof dish with a lid. This is referred to as a casserole. Stewing is a nutritious method of cooking, as both the liquid and the food are eaten. This means that any vitamins and minerals leached into the cooking liquid are not lost. Stews also have little wastage, shrinkage and loss of flavour, and they reheat easily.

Before stewing, meat needs to be trimmed of fat, the skin should be removed from chicken, and vegetables should be well washed (peel them only if necessary). For meat and other animal protein stews, a mirepoix of vegetables is usually added to stews for flavour, colour and nutritional value. The preparation of these vegetables into mirepoix should be completed before the cooking process begins. To ensure even cooking, all meat, chicken and vegetables for the stew need to be cut into even sizes, usually about 3 cm. Because fish can break up during cooking, it should be cut into larger portions.

Meat may be marinated before cooking. Placing meats in a marinade helps to soften the tougher cuts of meat, preserves and adds flavour to the stew. The most common marinade is red wine. Other alcohol or acidic liquids, such as white wine, vinegar and lemon juice, may also be used as part of a marinade. Other flavouring agents – such as soy sauce, herbs and spices – can also be added to a marinade. The liquid selected for the stew needs to be related to the product being stewed. Fruit is usually stewed in fruit juice or syrup; vegetables in vegetable stock; and meat, chicken and fish in meat, chicken and fish stock, respectively. A meat stew usually uses a good brown stock. Alcohol, such as wine or sherry, may be added to the liquid for flavour, especially when stewing red meat. Sufficient liquid needs to be added to the stew to allow for evaporation.

Once the food is cut to the desired size, and the liquid to be used is determined, the cooking process may begin. With most meat and vegetable stews, the food needs to be seasoned (tossed in flour with pepper and dried herbs). The seasoned food is shallow-fried in a small amount of hot fat, usually oil or lard. Frying browns the food on the surface, which will add colour and flavour to the stew. It must be remembered not to use too much fat, as the result will be a greasy stew. To deglaze the pan, the meat juices that have been browned in the pan should be removed when the liquid is added.

If marinated meat is used, the meat must be well drained from the liquid, otherwise it may splatter when placed into hot fat for the shallow-frying process. Once the liquid has been added, and the pan deglazed, the stew is brought to simmering point. The pan should be covered and kept at that point for the remaining cooking time, usually about two to three hours (see page 234 for more information on meat cookery).

The stew should be checked occasionally to ensure that not too much liquid has evaporated and that nothing is sticking to the bottom of the pan. The cooking time will depend on the type and amount of food to be stewed. The liquid may be thickened with a thickening agent, such as flour, before cooking begins, or water-diluted arrowroot, later in the cooking process. Thickening may also be a result of the cooking process. The liquid may reduce enough during the cooking time. It may also thicken as a result of the ingredients of the stew. In Irish stew, for example, both the process of cooking and the breaking down of the starch in the potatoes will thicken the liquid. Remember that the stewing process is meant to be a slow, gradual process. If it is hurried, and cooked at higher temperatures, the food may toughen, dry out or become stringy. The process also needs to be slower to allow the flavours to be released. During the cooking process, the flavours from the meat are released into the liquid, and the flavours of the liquid and other added flavourings are absorbed by the meat. It is this slow process of the two-way transference of flavour that forms the base of a tasty stew. Tougher cuts of meat are used for stewing, as they are more economical. These cuts also often have more flavour. Due to the long cooking times, more tender cuts of meat will tend to dry out in stews. During the cooking time, the heat and the liquid act to convert the collagen of the meat to gelatine, thus making it more tender. The meat fibres also soften and separate, allowing the meat to 'melt in the mouth'. When stewing fruit, flavours and pectin from the fruit are released into the cooking liquid, making it quite flavoursome. The pectin also causes the liquid to thicken slightly.

Purpose

Because stewing is both economical and nutritious, cheaper cuts of meat and poultry, which would be unsuitable for roasting and grilling, can be made tender and palatable. Stewing also produces an acceptable flavour, texture and eating quality.

Methods of stewing

All stews have a thickened consistency achieved by:

- the unpassed ingredients in the stew, such as Irish stew (see page 255)

- thickening of the cooking liquor, such as white stew (*blanquette*) (see page 255)
- cooking in the sauce, such as brown stew (*navarin*) (see page 253).

Stewed foods can be cooked in a covered pan on the stove or in a moderate oven.

Effects of stewing

In the slow process of cooking in gentle heat, the connective tissue in meat and poultry is converted into a gelatinous substance so that the fibres fall apart easily and become digestible. The protein is coagulated without being toughened. Unlike boiling, less liquid is used and the cooking temperature is approximately 5°C lower.

See also 'effects of boiling' (page 11) as this section also applies to stewing.

Advantages

- The meat juices that escape from the meat during cooking are retained in the liquid, which is part of the stew.
- Correct slow cooking results in very little evaporation.
- Nutrients are conserved.
- Tough goods are tenderised.
- It is economical in terms of labour because foods can be cooked in bulk.

Temperature and time control

- Temperature control is essential to the slow cooking required for efficient stewing; therefore, the liquid must barely simmer.
- A tight-fitting lid is used to retain steam, which helps maintain temperature and reduce evaporation.
- Time will vary according to the quality of the food used.
- The ideal cooking temperature for stewing on top of the stove is approximately 82°C (simmering temperature); for cooking in the oven it is 170°C.

Care and cleanliness

Thoroughly wash equipment with hot detergent water, rinse with hot water and dry. Moving parts

of large-scale equipment should be greased occasionally. Store pans upside-down on clean racks. Check that handles are not loose and that copper pans are completely tinned. Report any faults with large equipment.

General rules

- Stews should not be over-thickened. The sauce should be light in consistency; therefore, correct ratios of thickening agents are essential.
- Adjustments to the consistency should be made as required during cooking.
- Overcooking causes: (a) evaporation of liquid; (b) breaking up of the food; (c) discolouration; and (d) spoilage of flavour.

Health and safety

Large stews on stovetops need to be placed carefully to avoid splashes and spills. Stews must simmer continually as they cook, so they become very hot. Because you will need to stir stews regularly, the risk of burns and scalds increases. When you lift the lid from a pan, lift it away from you to avoid burning yourself. When using brat pans, care needs to be taken when stirring the large quantity of hot, semi-liquid food.

Braising

Definition

Braising is a moist heat method of cooking larger pieces of food, on the stovetop or in the oven,

Figure 2.5   Braised shank of lamb, with mashed potatoes and glazed carrots

where the liquid only half covers the food. Whole joints, chicken, game meat or fowl and vegetables can all be braised. Tougher cuts of meat and other foods are also suitable for braising. With braising, food is cooked very slowly, using very low temperatures, in a pan with a tightly fitting lid. A combination of steaming and stewing cooks the food. Food is usually cooked in very large pieces and carved before serving.

Whole joints or large pieces of red meat and pork, and the tougher cuts of meat, are suitable for cooking using the braising method. Furred game, such as hare and rabbit, taste very good when they are braised, as does most feathered game, such as pheasant, duck and goose.

The cooking process

Once the food is sealed and browned, or blanched, the braising process may start. For meat-based braises, a layer of browned mirepoix is placed on the base of the pan. The sealed and browned meat is then placed over the vegetables. During the cooking process, the vegetables protect the protein food from contact with the base of the pan. If it does come in contact, it may cause the meat to become tough and dry. The layer of mirepoix also acts as a method of steaming the meat.

The liquid for braising is usually a stock, but it may also be water, wine or beer. The braising liquor needs to be suitable for the product being braised. A good brown beef stock is often used for braised beef, for example. It is added to the braising pan so that it only half covers the food being braised.

Once the liquid is added, a heavy, tightly fitting lid needs to be placed on the cooking pan. The lid keeps the moisture in the pan and around the food, and creates steam. Moisture must not be allowed to escape, otherwise a dry, tough product may result. This moist heat method of cooking helps to soften and separate the meat fibres, and converts collagen to gelatine. If you are using the oven for braising, it is usually set at 150°C to ensure that the cooking process is gentle and slow. The food should be basted occasionally with the braising liquor.

While the meat is cooking, the meat juices are released into the liquid. The flavour of the liquid also assists in flavouring the meat, thus producing an interchange of flavours. The braising liquid contains many nutrients, which are retained in this method of cooking. In many cases, this liquid is reduced and made into a sauce to accompany the food being braised.

Vegetables are braised in vegetable stock or vegetable juice. Braising liquors need to be discarded after cooking, due to the strong flavours that they take on. If a sauce is required, such as a demi-glace, cream or warm emulsion, it should be made separately. Braised vegetables may also be filled with other foods such as pulses, rice, nuts, meat and other vegetables, and then braised. Non-meat-filled braised vegetables are popular with vegetarians, as they add variety and extra nutrition. Many different combinations and fillings can be used, such as cabbage rolls stuffed with rice and braised in tomato juice. The length of time for braising will be determined by the type, amount and size of the food being cooked. You will know when meat is cooked by inserting a metal skewer into it. If there is only slight resistance, the meat is cooked.

Once the braising is complete, the liquid is strained from the food. For all foods other than vegetables, this liquid may then be made into a sauce. This may be done in one of two ways. The sauce may either be heated and allowed to reduce, or thickened with a thickening agent. The thickening agent may be either cornflour, arrowroot or *beurre manié*. If the sauce is too thick after the braising process, stock may be added.

Purpose

The purpose of braising is:

- to give variety to the menu and the diet
- to make food tender, digestible, palatable and safe to eat
- to produce and enhance flavour, texture and eating quality.

Methods of braising

There are two methods: brown braising, used, for

example, for joints and portion-sized cuts of meat; and white braising, used, for example, for vegetables and sweetbreads.

Brown braising

- Joints such as beef and venison are marinated and may be larded, then sealed quickly by browning on all sides in a hot oven or in a pan on the stove. Sealing the joints helps retain flavour and nutritive value, and gives a good brown colour. Joints are then placed on a bed of root vegetables in a braising pan, with the liquid and other flavourings, covered with a lid and cooked slowly in the oven.
- Cuts (steaks, chops, liver). The brown braising of cuts of meat is similar to that of joints.

White braising

Used, for example, with celery, cabbage and sweetbreads. Foods are blanched, refreshed and then cooked on a bed of root vegetables with white stock in a covered container in the oven.

Effects of braising

Cooking by braising causes the breakdown of the tissue fibre in the structure of certain foods, which softens the texture, thus making it tender and edible. The texture is also improved by being cooked in the braising liquid.

Advantages

- Tougher, less expensive meats and poultry can be used.
- Maximum flavour and nutritional value are retained.
- Variety of presentation and flavour is given to the menu.

Temperature and time control

- Slow cooking is essential for efficient braising; the liquid must barely simmer.
- To reduce evaporation and maintain temperature, use a tight-fitting lid.
- Time needed for braising will vary according to the quality of the food.
- Ideal oven temperature for braising is 160°C.

General rules

These are the same as for stewing. However, if the joint is to be served whole, the lid is removed three-quarters of the way through cooking. The joint is then frequently basted to give a glaze for presentation.

Health and safety

During cooking, the contents of the braising pan, and the *braisière* itself, become extremely hot. Whenever removing the pot from the oven or lifting the lid, heavy oven cloths need to be used. When removing the lid, lift it away from you to allow the steam to escape, and to avoid being burnt or scalded. Because the contents can become extremely hot, extreme care needs to be taken to prevent splashing when stirring.

Sous vide

Sous vide is a professional cooking method that employs plastic oxygen barriers and precise temperature controls to reduce oxidisation and extend the useable shelf life of inventory by diminishing contact with aerobic bacteria. The result is a final product with superior texture, amplified flavours and enhanced visual qualities.

History of sous vide

Preparing food at low temperatures in sealed vessels is one of the oldest forms of cooking. Early civilisations used clay pots to simmer tough meats in China, whole pigs were slowly roasted underground in Hawaii, and corn husks were tossed onto glowing embers in Mexico. One of the most traditional French preparation methods, cooking *en papillote*, involves packaging food in a parchment paper envelope. The development of stable, high-temperature, food-safe plastic films in the late 1960s made it possible to develop the concept of *sous vide* cooking.

The *sous vide* method of preserving and cooking in laminated plastic film sachets is generally credited to the chef Georges Pralus. Pralus discovered *sous vide* cooking in 1967 while trying to reduce shrinkage on a foie gras terrine at

Restaurant Troisgros in Roanne, France. He discovered that, by packaging the *foie gras* in a vacuum-sealed plastic pouch and submersing it in a heated water bath with precisely controlled temperatures, he could reduce shrinkage from 40 per cent to 5 per cent. In addition to the reduced product loss, Pralus discovered that the sensory properties of the food were significantly enhanced. The plastic film formed a barrier that prevented the loss of flavour notes through evaporation, and the low temperature minimised the destruction of protein structures, preserving natural textures.

Applications for *sous vide* techniques are split into two general categories: centralised manufacturing plants, which fabricate hundreds of thousands of high-quality meals under factory conditions intended for later reheating; and small-scale restaurants and hotels, generally producing meal components for uninterrupted in-house usage.

Operational benefits of sous vide in restaurants

One of the biggest benefits sous vide brings to the restaurant business is operational efficiency. Vacuum packaging inventory and preparing complete single-serving meals one or two days in advance can reduce food costs and streamline kitchen operations, especially during busy service periods. Properly labelled portions are easily retrieved from chilled storage, and may be quickly reheated if more guests appear, or efficiently conserved if fewer guests than expected arrive.

Standardised recipes may be used, enhancing consistency and providing guests with an excellent-quality meal, regardless of line cooking skills. Since several meals can be pasteurised or regenerated in the same bath, clean-up is reduced, and fewer pots and pans are used. Fire is eliminated, lowering the kitchen's ambient air temperature and reducing cooling costs.

Health and safety

Dangers of *sous vide* in an unregulated environment
A good chef normally always smells a product before cooking to ensure freshness. When cooking

in a sealed plastic sachet, it is impossible to detect good or bad smells. Contrary to popular belief, vacuum packaging does not inhibit the growth of all bacteria. The anaerobic conditions, together with the relatively low-temperature heat treatment of sous vide cooking creates an atmosphere in which the most deadly food-borne pathogen, Clostridium botulinum, thrives.

It is imperative to carefully monitor, document and control the preparation and packaging conditions within the kitchen. If improperly handled, the following conditions can exacerbate normal bacterial growth and spoilage.

- The reduced oxygen packaging extends the shelf life by retarding aerobic micro-organisms, but can facilitate the growth of anaerobic pathogens such as *Clostridium botulinum*, *Clostridium perfringens*, *Bacillus cereus* and *Listeria monocytogenes*.
- Sufficient cooling must be rigorously applied to prevent bacterial reproduction at all stages of preparation, storage and regeneration. While pathogenic contamination is inevitable with all food products, the reduced oxygen packaging used with *sous vide* presents a potentially ideal environment for bacterial reproduction. With rigorous application of proper food-handling procedures, the risk of food-borne illness may be virtually eliminated. *Sous vide* is a technique that should only be used by trained professionals who can maintain hygienic, precise conditions on a consistent basis.

Addressing food safety issues with proper handling procedures
By identifying critical control points and establishing hurdles to microbial growth, all the safety concerns related to vacuum packaging and *sous vide* cooking may be virtually eliminated.

- Only the freshest, highest-quality ingredients must be used when preparing *sous vide* packages. This can significantly lower initial microbial levels, extending shelf life and product freshness.
- It is also critical to calibrate equipment on a daily basis and quality-check all seals and packages for leaks.

- Raw packets must not be stored for more than two days before pasteurisation above 60°C, and must be cooled below 3°C within two hours.
- Pasteurised inventory should be stored below 3°C and consumed or frozen within a specified time period.
- The date and time of packaging, pasteurisation and expiration must be documented and labelled on the package.

Chilled *sous vide* items must be stored within walk-in coolers in covered pans with alternating layers of ice in order to maintain strict temperature control. Walk-ins are typically accessed several times per hour, which can bring the ambient temperature – and everything inside – as high as 14°C. Since *sous vide* bags are packaged and hermetically sealed, there is no certain way of knowing the core temperature of the packaged product unless it is buried in ice at all times.

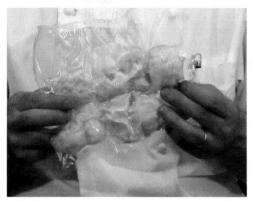

Figure 2.6 Food in a vacuum sealed bag

Conclusion

Sous vide technology is a thoroughly modern application of an ancient, cross-cultural cooking practice: applying long, slow heat to enhance flavours while preserving texture. Industrial food producers have embraced *sous vide* as a safe, effective method of packaging wholesome, minimally processed food with superior sensory characteristics. Restaurants have been slower to adopt the technology, due to the complexity of the technique, a lack of training and the cost of the equipment.

Fresh *sous vide* handling procedures, mostly used in high-end restaurants; emphasise control over the organoleptic properties of the final product. Pasteurisation times are kept relatively short to maintain texture and sensory properties at the expense of long storage intervals.

The hermetically sealed plastic bags form oxygen barriers, which slow the growth of aerobic bacteria, delaying spoilage. While this is certainly a benefit, the downside is that anaerobic bacteria may thrive under the right conditions. Unfortunately, the most deadly food-borne illness, botulism, is carried by anaerobic bacteria. Because of this, foods must be of the highest quality and handled within strictly maintained temperature ranges according to HACCP procedures.

Sous vide cooking brings multiple benefits to restaurants in the form of increased service efficiency and lowered food costs. Preserving inventory in vacuum sealed bags is an excellent way of extending the shelf life of a product, provided proper handling procedures are followed.

Baking

Definition

Baking is the cooking of food with dry heat in an oven; steam plays a big part in this method of cookery (see 'The principles of cooking food' on page 8). All products that are baked contain water. This, once heated, will create steam. Steam is an important and integral part of the baking process, however it is essential to evenly space the products that are being cooked to ensure that, when the heat is applied and the water starts to evaporate from the product, there are reasonable gaps between the items to ensure that baking is not taken over by steaming. The product to be baked requires enough room to bake efficiently without steaming; utilisation of full trays is also of paramount importance as this will save time and energy costs.

There are several different types of baking, as described below.

- *Dry baking*: in a pre-heated oven, when steam rises due to the water content of the food; this steam combines with the dry heat of the oven to cook the food (e.g. cakes, pastry, baked jacket potatoes).
- *Baking with increased humidity:* when baking certain foods, such as bread, oven humidity is increased by placing a bowl of water or injecting steam into the oven, thus increasing the water content of the food and so improving the eating quality.
- *Baking with heat modification:* placing food, such as baked egg custard, in a bain-marie (tray of water) modifies the heat so that the food cooks more slowly and doesn't overheat; in the case of egg custard it also lessens the possibility of the egg mixture overcooking.

The chemical action caused by the effect of heat on certain ingredients, such as yeast and baking powder, changes the raw structure of many foods to an edible texture (e.g. pastry, cakes). However, different ingredients, methods of mixing and the type of product required will lead to a host of variations.

Figure 2.7 An oven

Purpose

The purpose of baking is:

- to make food digestible, palatable and safe to eat
- to create visual appeal through colour and texture, and to produce an enjoyable eating quality
- to lend variety to the menu.

Methods

Note: Ovens must be preheated prior to baking.

- *Dry baking*: when baking, steam arises from the water content of the food; this steam combines with the dry heat of the oven to cook the food (e.g. cakes, pastry, baked jacket potatoes).
- *Baking with increased humidity:* when baking certain foods, such as bread, the oven humidity is increased by placing a bowl of water or injection steam into the oven, thus increasing the water content of the food and so improving eating quality.
- *Baking with heat modification:* placing food in a container of water (bain-marie), such as baked egg custard, modifies the heat so that the food cooks more slowly, does not overheat and lessens the possibility of the egg mixture overcooking.

Effects of baking

Chemical action caused by the effect of heat on certain ingredients, such as yeast and baking powder, changes the raw structure of many foods to an edible texture (pastry, cakes). However, different ingredients, methods of mixing and types of product required will cause many variations.

Advantages of baking

- A wide variety of sweet and savoury foods can be produced.
- Bakery products yield appetising goods with visual appeal and mouth-watering aromas.
- Bulk cooking can be achieved with uniformity of colour and degree of cooking.
- Baking ovens have effective manual or automatic temperature controls.
- There is straightforward access for loading and removal of items.

Temperature and time control

- Ovens must always be heated to the required temperature before the food is added.
- In general-purpose ovens, shelves must be placed according to the food being cooked, because the hotter part of the oven is at the top. With convection ovens the heat is evenly distributed.
- Accurate timing and temperature control are

essential to baking. The required oven temperature must be reached before each additional batch of goods is placed in the oven. This is known as 'recovery time'.

General rules

- Always preheat ovens so that the required cooking temperature is immediately applied to the product, otherwise the product will be spoiled.
- Accuracy is essential in weighing, measuring and controlling temperature.
- Trays and moulds must be correctly prepared.
- Minimise the opening of oven doors as draughts may affect the quality of the product, and the oven temperature is reduced.
- Utilise oven space efficiently.
- Avoid jarring of products (fruit cake, sponges, soufflés) before and during baking as the quality may be affected.

Health and safety

It is essential to use thick, dry oven cloths when removing trays from the oven. (Baking trays need to be kept level in the oven otherwise, if liquids are being baked, an uneven product will result.) Trays should not be overloaded. Oven doors should not be opened too quickly as there is likely to be a lot of steam present and this may burn your face. (Opening the oven door too quickly may also adversely affect the presentation of products such as Yorkshire puddings and soufflés.)

Roasting

Definition

Roasting is cooking in dry heat with the aid of fat or oil in an oven or on a spit. Radiant heat is the means of cooking when using a spit; oven roasting is a combination of convection and radiation.

Purpose

The purpose of roasting is to cook food so that it is tender, easy to digest, safe to eat and palatable. It also gives variety to the menu and the diet.

Methods

- Placing prepared foods (meat, poultry) on a rotating spit over or in front of fierce radiated heat.
- Placing prepared foods in an oven with either: applied dry heat; forced air-convected heat; convected heat combined with microwave energy.

To prevent the base of the product burning or overcooking, whole joints and large pieces of meat and fish are placed on what is commonly known as a trivet. A trivet can consist of chopped vegetable (larger than mirepoix – not dissimilar to braising) or can be made up from the bones or skeleton of the product you are roasting.

During the cooking process the product must be basted regularly with the cooking medium, fat or oil, and any other juices that may leach from the product; this will help keep the food moist and aid in the caramelisation of the finished product; it will also enhance the visual appeal of the dish.

Effects of roasting

The surface protein of the food is sealed by the initial heat of the oven, thus preventing the escape of too many natural juices. When the food is lightly browned, the oven temperature is reduced to cook the inside of the food without hardening the surface.

Advantages

- Good-quality meat and poultry is tender and succulent when roasted.
- Meat juices issuing from the joint can be used for gravy and to enhance flavour.
- Both energy and oven temperature can be controlled.
- Ovens with transparent doors enable cooking to be observed.
- Access, adjustment and removal of items is straightforward.
- Minimal fire risk.

The roasting and low-temperature cooking of meat

To follow on from the text earlier, explaining how proteins and collagen react under heat, this section describes a combination of traditional methods and the new low-temperature cooking approach. Low-temperature cooking respects the protein and collagen content of the meat group. The meat groups are loosely split in to two categories:

1 *primal* (the muscle groups that are worked less), and
2 *secondary* (the muscle groups that are worked more, found predominantly towards the front of the animal and the leg joints).

The general rule of thumb is: the more work the muscle group does the more collagen present in the meat. It is the presence of collagen that offers a tough mouth-feel. For example, fillet of beef (from a primal muscle group) does very little work and therefore offers a very tender mouth-feel when cooked to medium; however if the cooking temperature is such that the proteins shrink quickly, the liquid will be forced out through shrinkage, rendering the meat dry, and basically leaving protein mass with very little moisture. The more work the muscle group does – for example, rump or rib (from secondary muscle groups) – the higher the collagen content and the joint will offer a more 'chewy' mouth-feel when cooked to medium. When cooking secondary joints it is the collagen the cook should focus on. For muscle groups with a high collagen content the temperature that should be applied to allow breakdown is above the 'gastronomic protein shrink' point; this means that all liquid in the protein will invariably be lost and the collagen will take over. Collagen will start to break down for gastronomic purposes at 60°C and is totally lost above 92°C; so slowing the cooking process down retains the internal basting properties of the collagen, leaving the meat supple, flavoursome and, above all, not dry.

This is an offset to the tenderness vs flavour debate, as the more tender the joint is – for example, fillet – the less flavour it will tend to offer. Indeed the mouth-feel is perhaps the most tender but the offset is that the flavour is at the low end. It is down to the skill of the chef to decide what joint best suits the desired result: is it a Sunday roast or fine dining main course, will it be cooked quickly or slowly, will it be served with sauce or not? All these are determining factors when choosing the correct joint to roast, whether it be a single portion or large joint to carve for the whole table.

When using low-temperature cooking the whole process slows down for the simple reason that the temperature is lower. The science behind cooking meats is a simple concept called molecular conduction or thermal energy; this translates into each layer of molecules conducting heat from the outside in: if the temperature on the outside is very hot it will take a short time to achieve a desired core temperature, producing a progressive degree of cooking from the outside through to the core; if things are slowed down – for example, setting the oven temperature to 57°C – through the same process of thermal energy the core will eventually reach 57°C but it will take a little longer to afford the same degree of cooking throughout the whole piece of meat. This method of cookery is very easy to control as the speed of cooking is slower, therefore the chances of overcooking are slim.

There are many way to achieve a more controlled cooking medium – *sous vide*, for example, which is perhaps the most efficient way of slow cooking. Another alternative is to set the oven to a temperature closer to the core temperature required (turn the fan off if it is convected heat as this will otherwise dry out the meat).

Using Table 2.1, you can successfully adjust cooking times and temperature according to yield to get the best result from the joint you are cooking. Below are some guidelines to achieve a good roasted result by balancing the breakdown of collagen in respect of the protein matter.

- First, to achieve roasted flavours from the Maillard reaction the joint must reach a temperature of 140°C for the roasted flavours to be released; this is what is called browning; it

Figure 2.1 ✎ Temperature guidelines

Meat temperature	Doneness	Meat qualities	Proteins	Collagen	Protein-bound water
50°C	Rare	Becoming firmer Becoming opaque	The proteins begin to coagulate		Escape and accumulation accelerate
55°C	Medium rare	Resilient to touch Less slick, more fibrous Releases juice when cut Opaque, lighter red	Myosin coagulated		
60°C	Medium	Begins to shrink Losing resilience Exudes juice Red fades to pink	Other fibre proteins denature, coagulate	Collagen sheaths shrink, squeeze cells	Flows from cells under collagen pressure
65°C	Medium well	Continues to shrink Little resilience Less free juice Pink fades to grey-brown			
70°C	Well	Continues to shrink Stiff Little free juice Grey-brown		Begins to dissolve	Flow ceasing
90°C		Fibres more easily separated from each other		Dissolving rapidly	

can be done at the start of the cooking process or at the end.

- The more collagen in the joint the longer it will need to be cooked to slowly break this down, but while respecting the protein mass.
- Fat self-bastes the meat while cooking, so be mindful of trimming off too much as this will render the meat dry if cooked for a prolonged period.

Roasting of beef 1 (fillet)

As fillet has very little collagen the respect here needs to be afforded to the protein mass; as this will start to shrink at 50°C, at 55°C for the myosin protein and up to 60°C for the rest of the protein mass, this temperature range is what you should work within. A good balance between the 10° range is 58°C; at this temperature there is enough heat in the meat to move it away from its 'raw' state, but not so that it shrinks all the proteins, leaving ample moisture in the meat to offer a good supple mouth-feel.

Roasting of beef 2 (sirloin standard size whole or half (3–7 kg))

As sirloin has more collagen in it than fillet – as it has contracted and relaxed more times than the fillet – it is therefore a little tougher. Set the oven to 200°C; while the oven is coming up to temperature seal the outside of the sirloin quickly to initiate the Maillard reaction, then place in the oven and set the timer for 15 minutes.

Once the timer has gone off remove from the oven and re-set the oven to 60°C. Once the oven has reached this temperature place the joint in the oven and cook for about 50 minutes (depending on size). To ensure that the joint is cooked through, insert a temperature probe if the oven is fitted with one and follow the instructions in the manufacturer's manual; alternatively periodically probe until the core reaches 60°C. The finished product will have approx half an inch of roasted edge and a pink and tender centre; as it has been finished at 60°C there is no need to let it rest.

Spit roasting

- Skill and techniques can be displayed to the customer.
- Continual basting with the meat juice over the carcass or joint on the revolving spit gives a distinctive flavour, depending on the fuel used (e.g. wood, charcoal).

Temperature and time control

- Ovens must be preheated.
- Oven temperature and shelf settings in recipes must be followed.
- Shape, size, type, bone proportion and quality of food will affect the cooking time.
- Meat thermometers or probes can be inserted to determine the exact temperature in the centre of the joint.

Table 2.2 gives approximate cooking times. For internal temperature of meat, see Table 2.3.

Health and safety

It is essential to use thick, dry oven cloths when removing trays from the oven. Trays should not be overloaded. Oven doors should not be opened too quickly as there is likely to be a lot of steam present and this may burn your face. Care should be taken when removing the product from the oven as a joint, say, may have released a lot of fat and this may splash when removing the tray, and could cause burns and/or scalds. When basting the product be mindful of the likelihood of hot fat splashing.

Low-temperature roasting

Low-temperature roasting will keep meat juicy and tender provided that the oven temperature is strictly controlled by using a digital meat thermometer. This allows the meat to cook slowly until the centre reaches a certain temperature, at which point it is ready. The meat needs to be browned all over in a frying pan over a high heat with a little oil brushed over the lean surfaces until a crust has formed; then transfer to a roasting tray or ovenproof dish.

Set the digital meat thermometer to the required temperature (see Table 2.3) and insert the probe horizontally into the centre of the meat. Place the meat into a pre-heated oven with the cord pinned through the door and the main unit outside the oven. When the meat reaches the set temperature an alarm will sound. Stop the alarm and remove the joint from the oven.

The oven must be preheated to 80°C and, in order to maintain the temperature, the oven door must be kept closed. Beef, lamb, pork, veal, venison and poultry can be cooked by this method.

Table 2.2 Approximate cooking times for different meat types

	Approximate cooking times	Degree of cooking
beef	15 minutes per ½kg and 15 minutes over	underdone
lamb	20 minutes per ½kg and 20 minutes over	cooked through
lamb	15 minutes per ½kg and 15 minutes over	cooked pink
mutton	20 minutes per ½kg and 20 minutes over	cooked through
veal	20 minutes per ½kg and 25 minutes over	cooked through
pork	25 minutes per ½kg and 25 minutes over	thoroughly cooked

Table 2.3 ✎ Guide to internal core temperatures

Beef (rare)	50°C
Beef (medium)	55°C
Beef (well done)	60°C
Lamb	55°C
Pork	60–65°C
Veal	60°C
Venison	60°C

Notes

Most boneless cuts of meat are suitable for low-temperature cooking. Those with minimal fat cover are suitable as they experience less shrinkage and will give better serving yields. The thickness of the meat will affect the cooking time. Thick, chunky pieces will take longer than thin cuts of the same weight. To keep a joint warm for up to an hour turn the oven to an internal temperature of 60°C.

Slow roasting: example recipe

Slow roast pork belly

	4	10
pork belly	1.2 kg	3 kg

1 Pre-heat oven to 150°C.
2 Season pork with salt and pepper.
3 Place on a rack in a large roasting tray, skin side up.
4 Roast for 3–3.5 hours, then remove from tray.
5 Pour off excess fat and make a gravy.
6 Carve into thick slices and serve with apple sauce, sage and onion dressing and a suitable potato and vegetable.

Sourcing good-quality meat

Transparency is the latest approach to menu writing: naming the breed of livestock and, in some cases, stating on the menu the passport number, date of kill and for how long the meat has been hung. This represents a good start in terms of getting back to the farming culture we had in the 1960s, however the understanding of an animal, it history and what each joint can offer from the breed is just as important as showcasing the breed on your menu.

This understanding will not only give you an indication of what breed can best offer you, the cook, the joint that matches your outcome perfectly – for example, pure Charolais offers a great fillet of beef, however for some chefs the sirloin better suits their needs when it is taken from a Charolais cross – the marbling differs in the sirloin and the fillet. It is such understanding that helps chefs realise that there is more than one type of fillet, sirloin etc., and many and varied different results.

ⓘ **Further information**

To find out more about Charolais beef, which is of exceptionally good quality, refer to the following websites:
www.theworldwidegourmet.com/meat/beef/charolais.htm
www.baldwinbeef.com/

Pot roasting

Definition

Pot roasting (*poêlé*) is cooking on a bed of root vegetables in a covered pan. This method retains the maximum flavour of all ingredients.

Method

Place the food on a bed of roots and herbs, coat generously with butter or oil, cover with a lid and cook in an oven.

Figure 2.8 ✎ Pot roasting chicken on a bed of root vegetables

General rules

- Select pans that are neither too large nor too small.
- Use the vegetables and herbs with a good stock as a base for the sauce.

Tandoori cooking

Definition

Tandoori cooking is by dry heat in a clay oven called a tandoor. Although the heat source is at the base of the oven, the oven heat is evenly distributed because of the clay, which radiates heat evenly.

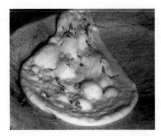

Figure 2.9 ✎ Naan bread cooking in a tandoor

Method

Meat (small cuts and small joints), poultry (small cuts and whole chickens) and fish, such as prawns, are usually placed vertically in the oven. No fat or oil is used. The food is cooked quickly and the flavour is similar to that of barbecued food. Oven temperatures reach 375°C. Depending on the type, foods may be marinated for 20 minutes to two hours before being cooked and, in some cases, they may be brushed with the marinade during cooking.

Naan – a flat, leavened bread – is slapped onto the inside walls of a tandoor and cooks alongside other skewered foods. If a traditional tandoor is not available, then an oven, grill rotisserie or barbecue can be used provided the basic rules and principles of tandoori cooking are applied. However, as the spices for a tandoori marinade should be well cooked at a high temperature, then the spices in this case should be briefly cooked briefly over a fierce heat before being added to the marinade.

Advantages

- The distinctive flavour of tandoori-cooked food comes from both the marinade and the cooking process.
- Marinating tenderises and also adds flavour to foods.
- Colour change may occur depending on the spices used: a red colouring agent is used in some marinades, also onions, garlic, herbs, spices and oil, wine or lemon juice.

Grilling

Definition

This is a fast method of cookery from radiant heat, sometimes known as broiling. Grilled foods can be cooked:

- over heat (charcoal, barbecues, gas or electric heated grills/griddles)
- under heat (gas or electric salamanders (overfired grills))
- between heat (electrically heated grill bars or plates).

Grilling over heat

Grill bars must be preheated and brushed with oil prior to use, otherwise food will stick to them. The bars should char the food on both sides to give the distinctive appearance and flavour of grilling. Most foods are started on the hottest part of the grill and moved to the cooler part. The thickness of the food and the heat of the grill will determine the cooking time.

Figure 2.10 Grilling steaks

Grilling under heat/salamander

Salamanders (sometimes called overfired grills) should be preheated and the bars greased. Steaks, chops and items that are likely to slip between the grill bars may be cooked under the salamander.

Food items that are difficult to handle because they may easily break up may be placed in between a well-greased, centre-hinged, double wire grid with a handle, making it both easy and swift to cook food such as whole sole and whole plaice.

The salamander can also be used for browning, gratinating and glazing certain dishes. Because of the speed of the cooking there is maximum retention of nutrients and flavour. Grilling in this way is suitable only for certain cuts of best-quality meat; inferior meats would be tough and inedible.

Grilling between heat

This is grilling between electrically heated grill bars or plates, and is applied to small cuts of meat.

Degrees of cooking grills	Appearance of juice issuing from the meat when pressed
rare	red and bloody
underdone	reddish pink
just done	pink
well done	clear

Barbecuing (see page 273)

This is grilling on preheated, greased bars over a fierce heat (gas, charcoal or wood). When using solid fuel, the flames and smoke must be allowed to die down before placing food on the bars, otherwise the food will be tainted and spoiled. Certain foods, such as brochettes or chicken, may be marinated before cooking. Other foods (e.g. pork spare ribs) are brushed liberally with a barbecue sauce on both sides during cooking.

Effects of grilling

Because of the speed of cooking there is maximum retention of nutrients and flavour. As mentioned above, grilling is suitable for only certain cuts of best-quality meat, and inferior meat will turn out tough and inedible. The effect of fierce heat on the surface of the meat rapidly coagulates and seals the surface protein, thus helping to retain the meat juices. Grilled meats lose less of their juices than meat cooked by any other method provided they are not pierced with a fork while cooking.

Advantages

- Speed of grilling enables food to be cooked quickly to order.
- Charring foods gives a distinctive appearance and improves flavour.
- Control of cooking is aided because food is visible while it is being grilled.
- Variety is given to menu and diet.
- Grills may be situated in view of the customer.

General rules for efficient grilling

- Smaller, thinner items require cooking quickly.
- Seal and colour food on the hot part of the grill,

then move to a cooler part to complete cooking.
- Slow cooking results in the food drying out.
- Basting of food and oiling of bars prevents dryness.
- Tongs are used for turning and lifting cutlets and steaks. Palette knives and slices are used for turning and lifting tomatoes, mushrooms and whole or cut fish from trays.

Health and safety

Tongs should be used for turning and lifting cutlets and steaks. Slicers should be used for turning and lifting tomatoes, mushrooms, and whole or cut fish. When reaching over to, say, turn a steak at the back of the grill, be mindful of the heat coming up from underneath, which may burn the base of the forearm. If there is an oil marinade for the meat or fish, ensure that it is well drained as placing a product with excessive oil on it may be a fire hazard if moved directly from the marinating container to the grill.

Shallow-frying

Definition

Shallow-frying is the cooking of food in a small quantity of preheated fat or oil in a shallow pan or on a flat surface (griddle plate).

Figure 2.11 ✎ Shallow-frying fish

Purpose

The purpose of shallow-frying is:

- to give variety to the menu and the diet by making food palatable, digestible and safe to eat
- to brown food, giving it a different colour and an interesting and attractive flavour.

Methods

There are four methods of frying using a shallow amount of fat or oil: shallow-fry; sauté; griddle; stir-fry.

Using clarified butter for shallow-frying
Butter is melted and the fat is then carefully strained off, leaving behind the liquid. Clarified butter has a higher burning point and will not burn so easily as unclarified butter. This makes it more suitable for shallow-frying; for this reason, clarified butter should always be used if the shallow-fried food is required to be cooked in butter.

Food is cooked in a small amount of fat or oil in a frying pan or sauté pan. The presentation side of the food should be fried first, as this side will have the better appearance because the fat is clean, then turned so that both sides are cooked and coloured. This applies to small cuts of fish, meat and poultry, also small whole fish (up to 400 g). Eggs, pancakes and certain vegetables are cooked by this method. The term *meunière* refers to shallow-fried fish, which is passed through seasoned flour, shallow-fried and finished with lemon juice, nut-brown butter and chopped parsley.

Sauté
Tender cuts of meat and poultry are cooked in a sauté or frying pan. After the food is cooked on both sides it is removed from the pan, the fat is discarded and the pan deglazed with stock or wine. This then forms an important part of the finished sauce.

Sauté is also used when cooking, for example, potatoes, onions or kidneys, when they are cut into slices or pieces and tossed (*sauter* means to jump or toss) in hot shallow fat or oil in a frying pan until golden brown and cooked.

Griddle
Foods can be cooked on a griddle (a solid metal plate); hamburgers, sausages or sliced onions can be placed on a lightly oiled, preheated griddle and turned frequently during cooking. Pancakes may be cooked this way but are turned only once.

Stir-fry

Vegetables, strips of fish, meat and poultry can be fast-fried in a wok or frying pan in a little fat or oil.

Figure 2.12 Stir-frying

Effects of shallow-frying

The high temperature used in shallow-frying produces almost instant coagulation of the surface protein of the food and prevents the escape of the natural juices. Some of the frying medium will be absorbed by the food being fried, which will change its nutritional content.

Advantages

Shallow-frying is a quick method of cooking prime cuts of meat and poultry as suitable fats or oils can be raised to a high temperature without burning. As the food is in direct contact with the fat, it cooks rapidly.

Temperature and time control

This is particularly important as all shallow-fried foods should have an appetising golden-brown colour on both sides. This can only be achieved by careful control of the temperature, which should initially be hot; the heat is then reduced and the food turned when required.

General rules

- When shallow-frying continuously over a busy period, prepare and cook in a systematic way.
- Pans should be cleaned after every use.

Health and safety

- Select the correct type and size of pan: not too small, as food, such as fish, will not brown evenly and may break up; not too large, as areas not covered by food will burn and spoil the flavour of the food being cooked.
- Always keep sleeves rolled down as splashing fat may burn the forearm.
- Avoid being splashed by hot fat when placing food in the pan – add it carefully, away from you.
- Use a thick, clean, dry cloth when handling pans.
- Move pans carefully in case they jar and tip fat onto the stove.

Deep-frying

Definition

Although oils and lards are 'wet', deep-frying is classified as a dry method of cookery. This is because it has a drying effect on the food. To deep-fry food, small, tender pieces of food are totally immersed in hot fat or oil, and cooked quickly. The heat of the oil penetrates the food and cooks it. The food is usually coated to protect it from the high temperatures of the fat. With this method, the food is mainly cooked by convection of heat through the frying medium. It is also cooked by conduction when the hot fat cooks the surface of the food.

When we think of deep-fried foods, we tend to think first of fish and chips, which are probably the most popular kind of fried food. However, many things can be deep-fried, such as any small pieces of tender foods, such as lean meat, chicken fillets, whole or filleted fish, cheese and vegetables.

Most deep-fried foods need to be coated in a batter to protect them from the effects of the extremely high temperature of the fat or oil. Fatty foods are not suitable to be deep-fried; if the fat from these foods enters the frying medium used it must be able to withstand very high temperatures.

The fat chosen will be determined by availability, the type of food being cooked, temperatures required, and the desired taste. The cooking medium will take on the flavour of the food being cooked, so strongly flavoured foods should be deep-fried last, or in separate deep-fryers. The role of the frying medium is to conduct heat, add flavour and richness to the food, and act as a lubricant. Cooking mediums suitable for deep-frying are oil, butter and animal fats, such as lard. A mixture of oil and butter can also be used but the butter would need to be clarified before it is added to the oil.

In most cases, food needs to be cut into small portions before deep-frying. The pieces should be uniform in size and thickness to give an even cooking result. Some foods – especially thick pieces of vegetables such as potatoes – may be parboiled and deep-fried later before serving. This is often done in fish and chip shops, where large quantities of chips need to be partially cooked and left to wait before deep-frying.

Once food is prepared, and coated if necessary, the deep-frying process may begin. The commercial deep-fryer or the cooking pot needs to be filled with the frying medium. Commercial fryers usually have a mark to indicate the required fat level. For safety reasons, these levels should be strictly adhered to, as excess oil may bubble over the top of the deep-fryer when the food is placed into it. If there is no indicator, or a cooking pot is used, the container should be filled between half and two-thirds full. This is because the moisture of the food causes the fat to bubble and rise when food is immersed.

If solid fats are used for the cooking medium, they need to be melted at lower temperatures. This prevents the outside surfaces from burning before the entire amount is melted. It is important to ensure that the fat in the deep-fryer is at the correct temperature. If you are using commercial deep-fryers, the temperature may be thermostatically set. This ensures that the food is cooked at an even temperature throughout the entire cooking process. Thermostatically controlled deep-fryers are the best sort to use. There is greater control over the temperature, and they are much safer. If you are using a large saucepan on a stovetop, it is a little more difficult to determine the temperature. When it is close to deep-frying temperature, the fat gets quite still, and a slight steam can be seen above it. This can be difficult to determine, however, and if the hot fat is left too

long after this point, it may quickly reach flashpoint and ignite.

The frying medium should be at the correct temperature before the food is added. If it is too high, the outside of the food will burn while the inside stays raw. It will also cause the food to dry out and toughen. If the temperature of the frying medium is too low, the food will soak in extra fat, and become greasy and unpalatable. Correct cooking time depends on the:

- quantity of food being cooked
- size, shape and density of food
- water content of the food
- ratio of fat to food
- recovery time of the deep-fryer after the food is placed in the fryer.

When food is placed in the deep-fryer, if the frying medium starts to foam, it may be lifted to allow the temperature to readjust. If it is obvious that there is too much food in the frying medium, remove excess and fry in batches. Food may be turned with a spider during the frying process, to assist with even cooking. It is finished when it is a golden-brown colour. Some commercial deep-fryers feature a 'cool zone'. This is a section at the front base of the fryer where crumbs and food particles collect, thus ensuring that they are not continually overcooked. This would cause the fat to go off quicker, giving it a rancid taste. These food particles can easily be removed when the fat is cool.

It should be noted that different kinds of coatings require different cooking techniques. Crumbed food should be chilled before frying to assist in the staying power of the crumb mixture during frying. Excess crumbs should be shaken off, and the surface should be patted to ensure the coating remains in contact. Excess crumb may cause a build-up in the frying medium, resulting in the need to replace the fat sooner. During the cooking process, residues of crumbs need to be skimmed regularly using a spider. This will help the cooking medium last longer. When food is battered, time should be given for the excess batter to drain from the food, and then it needs to be lowered carefully into the frying medium.

Very cold or frozen food should not be allowed to defrost as this can result in a very soggy deep-fried product. Also, frozen food needs to be placed into the hot cooking medium in smaller quantities. This is because the temperature of the cooking medium will quickly reduce, and it needs to be given time to return to the correct temperature.

Figure 2.13 ✐ Deep-frying fish

Purpose

The purpose of deep-frying is:

- to cook appetising foods of various kinds, thus giving variety to the diet and the menu
- to produce food with an appetising golden-brown colour, that is crisp, palatable and safe to eat.

Methods

Conventional deep-fried foods, with the exception of potatoes, are coated with either milk and flour, egg and crumbs, batter or pastry to:

- protect the surface of the food from intense heat
- prevent the escape of moisture and nutrients
- modify the rapid penetration of the intense heat.

The food is carefully placed into deep preheated oil or fat, fried until cooked and golden brown, drained well and served.

Partial deep-frying is known as blanching and this method may be used with chipped potatoes. The purpose is to partly cook in advance of service and to complete the cooking to order. With certain types of potato this gives an eating quality of a floury inside and crisp exterior to the chips.

Effects of deep-frying

Deep-frying items coated with milk or egg seals the surface by coagulation of the protein, with the minimum absorption of fat. However, the interior may be raw, as in apple fritters, and will require to be cooked first. An already-cooked interior, as in croquette potatoes, needs only to be heated through. The coating (batter, etc.) needs to be cooked thoroughly. With uncoated items, such as chipped potatoes, the food absorbs a large amount of fat, thus affecting its texture and nutritional content.

The effect of deep-frying on the structure of the item being cooked will vary according to the nature of the food.

Advantages

- Blanching, or partial cooking, enables certain foods to be held for cooking later, which helps during busy service and saves time.
- Coating enables a wide variety of foods to be cooked by this method.
- Foods can be cooked quickly and handled easily for service.
- Coated foods are quickly sealed, thus preventing the enclosed food becoming greasy.

Temperature and time control

With deep fat frying it is essential for fat temperatures to be maintained at the correct degree. When quantities of food are continuously being fried, after the removal of one batch the temperature of the fat must be allowed to recover before the next batch is cooked. If this is not done the food will be pale and insipid in appearance and soggy to eat.

Timing is important: if thicker pieces of food are being cooked, the temperature must be lowered to allow for sufficient cooking time otherwise the food will be overcoloured and undercooked. The reverse is also true: the smaller the pieces of food the hotter the frying temperature and the shorter the cooking time.

Table 2.5 ✒ Oil temperatures

Type	Approximate flash-point (°C)	Smoke point (°C)	Recommended frying temp (°C)
finest quality vegetable oils	324	220	180
finest vegetable fat	321	220	180
high-class vegetable oil	324	204	180
pure vegetable fat	318	215	180
pure vegetable oil	330	220	170–182
finest quality maize oil	315	224	180
finest fat	321	202	180
finest quality dripping	300	165	170–180
finest natural olive oil	270–273	148–165	175

General rules

Never overfill fryers with fat or oil or food to be cooked.

- When using free-standing fryers without a thermometer never allow smoke to rise from the fat; this will give a disagreeable taste and smell to food being fried.
- The normal frying temperature is between 175°C and 195°C; this is indicated by a slight heat haze rising from the fat.
- Do not attempt to fry too much food at one time.
- Allow fat to recover its heat before adding the next batch of food.
- Ensure a correct oil/fat ratio to food. If too much food is cooked in too little fat, even if the initial temperature of the fat is correct, the effect of a large amount of food will reduce the temperature drastically and spoil the food.
- Reduce frying temperatures during slack periods to conserve fuel.
- Restrict holding time to a minimum – fried foods soon lose their crispness.
- Oil and fat should be strained after use, otherwise remaining food particles will burn when the fat is next heated thus spoiling the appearance and flavour of the food.
- Always cover oil or fat when not in use to prevent oxidation.
- Systematic preparation and cooking are essential.

Health and safety

Deep-frying can be a very dangerous method of cooking, especially if people are not correctly trained. Only trained people should use deep-fryers. Hot fat has the ability to cause serious burns, either through spills or accidents. Remember that commercial deep-fryers have built-in safety features, such as thermostatic controls and fat-level indicators. From a safety point of view, these safety features make commercial fryers preferable to pots on stoves.

Before using a deep-fryer, know how to put out a fat fire. Remember: oil and water do not mix. To put out a fat fire, you should cover the pot or fryer with a lid to suffocate the fire then use the correct fire extinguisher and use it correctly, or use a fire blanket. Fire extinguishing equipment should be kept nearby. Always keep a close watch over a deep-fryer and never leave it unattended. This also means keeping an eye on the temperature of the deep-fryer. If it is too high, the fat may easily ignite and cause a fire. Never allow fat to reach the smoke point: smoke indicates that the hot oil is near its flashpoint, a very hazardous situation. Do not move a deep-fryer that is either on or still hot. Avoid sudden movements around deep-fryers, as items may be bumped or dropped into the hot fat. Stand back when placing food into the frying medium to help avoid steam and splash burns. Avoid putting your face, arms or hands over the deep-fryer.

Paper bag cooking

Known as *en papillotte*, this is a method of cookery in which food is tightly sealed in oiled greaseproof paper or foil so that no steam escapes during cooking, and maximum natural flavour and nutritive value is retained.

Thick items of food, such as veal chops or red mullet, may be partly and quickly precooked, usually by grilling or shallow-frying, then finely cut vegetables, herbs and spices can be added. The bags are sealed tightly, placed on a lightly greased tray and cooked in a hot oven. When cooked, the food is served in the bag and opened by or in front of the customer.

Figure 2.14 ✒ Cooking *en papillotte*

See the section on vacuum cooking in *The Theory of Catering* (by Professor David Foskett and Victor Ceserani, 11th edition, published by Hodder Arnold, 2007).

Microwave cooking

Definition

This is a method of cooking and reheating food using electromagnetic waves in a microwave oven powered by electricity. The microwaves are similar to those that carry television signals from the transmitter to the receiver but are at a higher frequency. The microwaves activate the water molecules or particles of food and agitate them, causing heat by friction, which cooks or reheats the food.

Figure 2.15 ✒ Microwave cooking

Purpose

- Raw, preprepared or precooked foods are cooked quickly and made palatable and digestible.
- Foods are safer to eat, particularly reheated foods, because the total food is heated at the same time.

Application

Microwave cooking can be used for cooking raw food, reheating cooked food and defrosting frozen foods.

Advantages

- A saving of between 50 and 70 per cent over conventional cooking times on certain foods.
- A quick way to cook and reheat foods.
- A fast method of defrosting foods.
- Economical in terms of: electricity – less energy required; labour – less washing up as foods can be cooked in serving dishes.
- Hot meals can be available 24 hours a day and completely operated on a self-service basis, thereby increasing consumer satisfaction and reducing costs.
- Food is cooked in its own juices so flavour and goodness are retained.
- Minimises food shrinkage and drying out.
- When used with conventional cooking methods, production can be more flexible.

Disadvantages

- Not suitable for all foods.
- Limited oven space restricts use to small quantities.

- Many microwave ovens do not brown food, although browning elements are available within certain models.
- Not all containers are suitable for use in microwave ovens.
- Microwaves can penetrate only 5 cm (1.5 inches) into food (from all sides).

Points for special attention

- Correct selection of cooking and time controls according to the manufacturer's instructions is essential.
- Certain foods must be removed when underdone to finish cooking, so standing time is important; during this time fish, for example, turns from opaque to flaky, scrambled eggs turn creamy. Tender, crisp vegetables do not need to stand.
- Baked potatoes and whole unpeeled apples must have their skin pierced in order to release pressure and prevent them bursting.
- Eggs must not be cooked in their shells or they will burst.
- Cover foods when possible to reduce condensation and spluttering.

Factors that affect efficient cooking

- Only use suitable containers: glass, china, plastic. Only use metal or foil if the particular cooker has been developed to take metal without causing damage. For best results use straight-sided, round, shallow containers.
- Even-shaped items cook uniformly; arrange uneven-shaped items with the thickest part to the outside of the dish.
- Keep food as level as possible; do not pile into mounds.
- Allow sufficient space to stir or mix.
- Turn items, such as corn on the cob, during cooking because dense items take longer to cook than porous items.
- Foods with a high water content cook faster than those that are drier.
- Most foods should be covered when cooked in a microwave oven. Microwave clingfilm is available to cover food.

Safety

- Should the door seal be damaged, do not use the oven. This should be reported to the employer immediately.
- Do not operate the oven when it is empty.
- Remember to pierce foods and cover foods that are likely to burst.
- Regular inspection is essential and manufacturers' instructions must be followed.

Supplementary information

When preparing food for microwave heating, bear in mind the following points.

- Certain foods and container materials absorb energy at a faster rate than others and, as a result, are heated more quickly.
- The lower the starting temperature of the food, the longer it will take to heat.
- The denser the food, the longer it will take to heat.
- The thicker or deeper the food, the more awkward it is to heat (i.e. there is an ideal microwave depth of penetration for each food item).
- The shape of the food is an influence (i.e. in a ring shape, liquids in taller containers instead of low flat ones, composite meals in a compact, even mass).
- The weight or quantity of items influences the overall heating times.
- A cover is an important aid to faster heating, greater moisture retention and reduced cleaning up afterwards.
- Frozen, dense or larger amounts of food benefit by being heated in stages with rest intervals.

Foods that are not suitable for microwave cookery

You cannot deep-fry items in a microwave, boil eggs in their shells or make Yorkshire pudding, bake items such as choux pastry goods or make meringues.

However, although deep-frying is not possible because the temperature of the cooking fat can't be controlled, microwaving breadcrumbed fish in a tablespoon of oil will give a similar result. Eggs cooked in their shells would burst because of the build-up of pressure inside the shell, but scrambled, poached and fried eggs (in a browning dish) are successful. Yorkshire pudding, éclairs and meringues cannot be cooked by microwave because it is impossible to achieve a crispy crust while maintaining a soft interior. Meringue toppings, for example on a lemon meringue pie, can however be microwaved.

Microwaves tend to cook more round the edges of the food than in the centre, so that 'stirrable' foods will cook more evenly. The pattern of the microwaves is sometimes uneven, with the result that some parts will not cook as quickly as others. To test whether an oven has 'hot' or 'cold' spots, quarter-fill approximately nine microwave suitable glasses or bowls with cold water. Spread them out evenly on the oven shelf and switch on the oven at full power. The hottest spot is where the water boils first. This test will enable the chef to place the dishes in the best position in the oven. Small items or dishes should be arranged in a circle and be turned individually during the cooking, even when the oven has a turntable.

Dishes that cannot be stirred should be rotated a quarter turn three times during cooking. Should the edges of the food become cooked while the centre is still raw, this can be remedied by securing small pieces of microwave clingfilm over the parts that are ready. Another way of ensuring even cooking for 'unstirrable' dishes is to choose even-shaped round or square containers and arrange the food in them to a uniform thickness. It is desirable to keep to a depth of 4–5 cm. The shape and consistency of foods are very important when deciding on how best to cook them. Items with skin, such as jacket potatoes, tomatoes and peppers, must be pierced or scored with a knife, otherwise the steam created inside will burst the skins and food particles will spatter all over the cavity. Eggs are similarly affected and even the yolks of poached eggs should be lightly pricked. Kidney and liver, although usually cooked after slicing, have a thin covering of membrane. Any 'popping' sounds that are heard will be these membranes splitting, but if the dishes are lightly covered, all will be well. Other 'popping' foods are those containing bones – which act as tunnels storing up the pressure so that the food alongside spits – and poultry with the skin on. Boilable pouches behave in the same way. The plastic must be slashed on top and it is prudent to put the bag on a plate as it will become difficult to handle when it is hot and soft.

Always cover food that is to be cooked moist, such as stews and conventionally boiled foods. Clingfilm is suitable to cover with but it must be applied loosely. The clingfilm must be removed carefully, pulling it towards you, to avoid being scalded by the escaping steam. When cooking food in a considerable quantity of liquid that will require stirring, only cover three-quarters, so that you are able to stir through the gap – it is not possible to replace clingfilm covering during cooking.

Undercook rather than overcook because overcooking cannot be remedied and reheating must be taken into account. For food safety reasons, a thermometer should be used for high-risk foods, especially meat and poultry, and when reheating foods.

Foods containing sugar and fat

Sugar heats slowly at first and then suddenly becomes very hot very quickly and will burn in the microwave oven if left for too long. Sugar attracts microwaves and, when dissolved in liquid, will heat even more rapidly. Fat also attracts microwaves. Therefore good effects can be obtained by brushing food with fat or oil to achieve a crispy result.

Standing time

Cooking may continue after the oven is switched off and the food removed. During this period the heat spreads evenly throughout the food. Dense and large pieces of food, therefore, such as joints of meat and chicken, need to stand for 10–15 minutes after being taken out of the oven.

am stock

Chicken stock

Veal stock

Mushroom nage

Crab stock

Vegetable nage

Shellfish nage

STOCKS, SOUPS AND SAUCES

VRQ

Unit 207   **Prepare and cook stocks, soups and sauces**

NVQ

Unit 636 (2FPC1)   **Prepare, cook and finish basic hot sauces**
Unit 637 (2FPC2)   **Prepare, cook and finish basic soups**
Unit 638 (2FPC3)   **Make basic stock**

Prepare and cook stocks

Practical skills
The candidate will be able to:
1 Demonstrate the correct use of equipment to prepare, cook and store stocks
2 Prepare ingredients for making stock
3 Cook different types of stocks (fresh)
4 Apply quality points to each stage of the process
5 Demonstrate safe and hygienic practices
6 Evaluate the finished product

Underpinning knowledge
The candidate will be able to:
1 Identify different types of stock
2 State the uses of stock
3 Explain the quality points in preparing and cooking stocks
4 Identify the preparation principles for stocks
5 Explain why different stocks require different cooking times
6 State the cooking times of different stocks
7 Identify the cooking and chilling principles for stocks
8 Identify correct storage procedures for stock

Prepare and cook soups

Practical skills
The candidate will be able to:
1 Demonstrate the correct use of equipment to prepare, cook and store soups
2 Prepare ingredients for making soup according to recipe or dish requirements
3 Cook different types of soup
4 Demonstrate finishing methods and present with appropriate accompaniments
5 Apply quality points to each stage of the process
6 Demonstrate safe and hygienic practices
7 Evaluate the finished product

Underpinning knowledge
The candidate will be able to:
1 Identify the different types of soup
2 Explain the quality points in preparing and cooking soups
3 Identify preparation and cooking principles for soups
4 Identify appropriate finishing methods and accompaniments for soup

Prepare and cook sauces

Practical skills
The candidate will be able to:
1 Demonstrate the correct use of equipment to prepare, cook and store sauces
2 Prepare ingredients for making sauces according to recipe and dish requirements
3 Produce different types of sauces
4 Demonstrate finishing methods
5 Apply quality points to each stage of the process
6 Demonstrate safe and hygienic practices
7 Evaluate the finished product

Underpinning knowledge
The candidate will be able to:
1 Identify different types of sauces
2 Identify sauce and dish combinations
3 Explain the purpose of sauces
4 Explain the quality points in preparing and cooking sauces
5 Identify the preparation/cooking principles for sauces
6 Describe the skills needed to check and finish sauces
7 Identify correct storage procedures for sauces

Stocks, soups and sauces

Health, safety and hygiene

For information on maintaining a safe and secure working environment, a professional and hygienic appearance, and clean food production areas, equipment and utensils, as well as food hygiene, please refer to Chapters 17 and 18. Additional health and safety points are as follows.

- After stock, sauces, gravies and soups have been rapidly cooled they should be stored in a refrigerator at a temperature below 5°C.
- If they are to be deep-frozen they should be labelled and dated, and stored below −20°C to −18°C.

- When taken from storage they must be boiled for at least 2 minutes before being used.
- They must not be reheated more than once.
- Ideally, stocks should be made fresh daily and discarded at the end of the day.
- If stocks are not given the correct care and attention, particularly with regard to the soundness of the ingredients used, they can easily become contaminated and a risk to health.
- Never store a stock, sauce, gravy or soup above eye level as this could lead to an accident by someone spilling the contents over themselves.

Stocks

Stock is the basis of all meat sauces, soups and purées. It is really just the juice of meat extracted by long and gentle simmering, or the infusion/transfer of flavour from an ingredient such as fish, vegetables or shellfish. In making stock, it should be remembered that the object is to draw the goodness out of the materials and into the liquor, imparting the desired level of flavour and other elements that are important to the end product, whether it be a soup, sauce or perhaps a reduction.

Stock is a liquid that contains some of the soluble nutrients and flavours of food that, as mentioned above, are extracted by prolonged and gentle simmering (with the exception of fish stock – see recipe 3); such liquid is the foundation of soups, sauces and gravies. Stocks are the foundation of many important kitchen preparations; for this reason, the greatest possible care should be taken in their production, and stocks, bouillons and nages should not be used as a culinary 'washing machine'. Respect is the greatest ingredient one can afford a stock.

Key points to remember when making stocks

- Unsound meat or bones and decaying vegetables will give stock an unpleasant flavour and cause it to deteriorate quickly.
- Scum should be removed; otherwise it will boil into the stock and spoil the colour and flavour.
- Fat should be skimmed off, otherwise the stock will taste greasy.
- Stock should always simmer gently; if it is allowed to boil quickly, it will evaporate and go cloudy/milky.
- Salt should not be added to stock.
- When making chicken stock the bones will need to be soaked first to remove the blood that is in the cavity.
- If stock is to be kept, strain it and cool quickly, then place it in the refrigerator.

1 Stock (white or brown)

Cal	Cal	Fat	Sat Fat	Carb	Sugar	Protein	Fibre
4 KJ	1 kcal	0.0 g	0.0 g	0.2 g	00.2 g	00.0 g	0.0 g

The general proportion of ingredients and methods for all stocks (except fish stock – recipe 3) is to use 2 kg of bones for 4½ litres of stock.

	4½ litres	10 litres
raw meaty bones	1 kg	2½ kg
water	5 litres	10½ litres
onion, carrot, celery, leek	400 g	1½ kg
bouquet garni		
peppercorns	8	16

1 Chop the bones into small pieces, and remove any fat or marrow.
2 Place the bones in a large stock pot, cover with cold water and bring to the boil.
3 Wash off the bones under cold water, then clean the pot.
4 Return the bones to the cleaned pot, add the water and reboil.
5 Skim as and when required, wipe round inside the pot and simmer gently.
6 After 2 hours, add the washed, peeled whole vegetables, bouquet garni and peppercorns.
7 Simmer for 6–8 hours. Skim, strain and, if to be kept, cool quickly and refrigerate.

For brown stocks
1 Chop the beef bones and brown well on all sides either by placing in a roasting tin in the oven, or carefully browning in a little fat in a frying pan.
2 Drain off any fat and place the bones in a stock pot.
3 Brown any sediment that may be in the bottom of the tray, deglaze (swill out) with ½ litre of boiling water, simmer for a few minutes and add to the bones.
4 Add the cold water, bring to the boil and skim. Simmer for 2 hours.
5 Wash, peel and roughly cut the vegetables, fry in a little fat until brown, strain and add to the beef pieces.
6 Add the bouquet garni and peppercorns.
7 Simmer for 6–8 hours. Skim and strain.

Note: A few squashed tomatoes and washed mushroom trimmings can also be added to brown stocks to improve flavour, as can a calf's foot and/or a knuckle of bacon. This will also increase the viscosity of the stock.

2 Reduced veal stock for sauce

Cal	Cal	Fat	Sat Fat	Carb	Sugar	Protein	Fibre
8 KJ	2 kcal	0.0 g	0.0 g	0.5 g	0.4 g	00.0 g	0.0 g

Makes 4½ litres

veal bones	4 kg
calves' feet, split lengthways	2
water	4 litres
carrots	400 g
onions	200 g
celery	100 g
tomatoes	1 kg
mushrooms	200 g
bouquet garni	1 large
unpeeled cloves of garlic (optional)	4

1 Brown the chopped bones and calves' feet (split lengthways) on a roasting tray in the oven.
2 Place the browned bones in a stock pot, cover with cold water and bring to simmering point.

3 Roughly chop the carrots, onions and celery. Using the same roasting tray and the fat from the bones, brown them off.
4 Drain off the fat, add vegetables to the stock and deglaze the tray.
5 Add the quartered tomatoes, chopped mushrooms, bouquet garni and garlic (if desired). Simmer gently for 4–5 hours. Skim frequently.
6 Strain the stock into a clean pan and reduce until a light consistency is achieved.

HEALTHY EATING TIP
• Drain off all the fat before deglazing the tray. Skim all fat from the stock as it simmers, and the fat from the finished product.

3 Fish stock

Makes 2 litres

fish bones, no heads, gills or roe (turbot, sole and brill bones are best)	5 kg
olive oil	100 ml
onions, finely chopped	3
leeks, finely chopped	3
celery sticks, finely chopped	3
fennel bulb, finely chopped	1
dry white wine	350 ml
parsley stalks	10
sprigs of thyme	3
white peppercorns	15
lemons, finely sliced	2

1 Wash off the bones in cold water for 1 hour. Heat the olive oil in a pan that will hold all the ingredients, leaving a 3 cm gap at the top for skimming.
2 Add all the vegetables and sweat off without colour for 3 minutes.
3 Add the fish bones and sweat for a further 3 minutes.
4 Next add the white wine and water to cover. Bring to a simmer, skim off the impurities, and add the herbs, peppercorns and lemon. Turn off the heat.
5 Infuse for 25 minutes, then pass into another pan and reduce by half. The stock is now ready for use.

4 Crab stock

Makes 2 litres (when reduced)

crab shells, smashed	2 kg
prawns, with shells still on	1.5 kg
corn oil	50 ml
brandy (optional)	200 ml
Pernod (optional)	100 ml
carrots, peeled and chopped for mirepoix	250 g
leeks, prepared and chopped for mirepoix	250 g
celery, chopped for mirepoix	150 g
garlic cloves, smashed	2
shallot, peeled and sliced	180 g
tomato paste	150 ml
fish stock	2.5 litres
small sprig of thyme	
bay leaf	1

1 Roast the shells in the oil and deglaze with the brandy and Pernod (or, if not using these, some of the stock).
2 In a separate pan roast the vegetables then add the tomato paste, stock and herbs, add the roasted shells and the prawns, and simmer for 20 minutes.
3 Turn off the heat and allow to infuse for 30 minutes. Pass, and reduce by half. The stock is now ready for use.

5 Game stock

Makes 3 litres

game bones (e.g. duck, squab, rabbit, venison)	2 kg
white onion, peeled and cut into quarters	1
carrots, large, peeled and cut into quarters	2
celery, cut into quarters	1
leek, cut into quarters	1
red wine	500 ml
small sprig of thyme	
garlic cloves	4
fresh bay leaf	½
juniper berries, slightly crushed	6
peppercorns	6
water, cold	6 litres

1 Preheat the oven to 175°C. Place all ingredients, excluding the juniper berries, peppercorns and water, in a large roasting tray

2 Place the bones on a rack to allow the roasting juices to be caught in an 'aromat tray' below, and roast in the oven for 30 minutes.
3 When the bones are completely roasted and have taken on a dark golden-brown colour, remove them from the oven.
4 Place all ingredients in a large pot and cover with the cold water.
5 Place the pot onto the heat and bring to a simmer, then immediately skim all the fat that rises to the surface. Keep just under a simmer, making sure there is as little movement as possible, in order to create more of an infusion than a stock.
6 Skim continuously. Leave to infuse/cook for 12 hours then pass through a fine sieve into a clean container. Place in the chiller until cold and then in the refrigerator overnight.
7 The next day, reduce down rapidly until you have about 3 litres or a quarter remaining.

6 White chicken stock

Makes 3 litres

chicken carcass/wings	5 kg
onions, peeled	1½
carrots, peeled	2
cloves of garlic, crushed	2
leeks, washed and blemishes removed	1
celery sticks	2
bay leaf	1
sprigs of thyme, small	1
whole white peppercorns	5 g
water, cold	7 litres

1 Remove any excess fat from the chicken carcasses and wash off under cold water.

2 Place all the bones into a pot that will hold all the ingredients, leaving 5 cm at the top to skim.
3 Add all the other ingredients and cold water, and bring to a simmer; immediately skim all the fat that rises to the surface.
4 Turn the heat off and allow the bones and vegetables to sink. Once this has happened turn the heat back on, skim and bring to just under a simmer, making as little movement as possible to create more of an infusion than a stock. Skim continuously.
5 Leave to simmer (infuse) for 12 hours then pass through a fine sieve into a clean pan; reduce down rapidly, until you have about 3 litres remaining.

Note: Alternatively follow recipe 1 (white stock) using chicken; the cooking time can be reduced to 6–8 hours, or even to as little as 4 hours if required. Remember that the reduced cooking time will yield a weaker product.

Fungi stock

White or brown fungi stock can be made using the vegetable stock recipes in Chapter 11 (pages 440 and 441), adding 200–400 g white mushrooms, stalks and trimmings (all well washed) for white fungi stock. For brown fungi stock, use the brown vegetable stock recipe, adding 200–400 g open or field mushrooms, stalks and trimmings (all well washed).

Jus

7 Beef jus

mushrooms, finely sliced	750 g
butter	100 g
shallots, finely sliced	350 g
beef trim, diced	350 g
sherry vinegar	100 ml
red wine	700 ml
chicken stock	500 ml
lamb or beef jus	1 litre

1 Caramelise the mushrooms in foaming butter, strain then put aside in pan.
2 Caramelise the shallots in foaming butter, strain then put aside in pan.
3 In another pan, caramelise the beef trim until golden brown.
4 Place the mushrooms, shallots and beef trim in one of the pans. Deglaze the other two pans with the vinegar, add to the pan with the beef, shallots and mushrooms in it.
5 In a separate pan reduce the wine by half and add to the main pan.
6 Add the stock and jus then reduce to sauce consistency.
7 Pass through a sieve, then chill and store until needed.

8 Chicken jus

This jus is used with rich, red game meat, e.g. version and wild boar. These meats lend themseleves to a sweet note, counter-balancing the bitter treacle note.

chicken stock	300 ml
lamb jus	300 ml
chicken wings, chopped small	300 g
oil	
vegetable oil	60 ml
shallots, sliced	100 g
butter	
tomatoes, chopped	200 g
white wine vinegar	40 ml
Cabernet Sauvignon vinegar (not home-made)	75 ml
tarragon	3 g
chervil	3 g

1 Put the jus and stock in a pan and reduce to 400 ml.
2 Roast the chicken wings in oil until slightly golden.
3 Add the shallots and butter, and cook until a good colour is achieved (do not allow the butter to burn).
4 Strain off the butter and return the bones to the pan, deglaze with the tomatoes and vinegar.
5 Ensure the bottom of the pan is clean. Add the reduced stock/jus and simmer for 15 minutes.
6 Pass through a sieve then reduce to sauce consistency.
7 Remove from the heat and infuse with the aromats for 5 minutes.
8 Pass through a chinois and then muslin cloth.

9 Lamb jus

	Makes 2 litres
thyme	bunch
bay leaves, fresh	4
garlic	2 bulbs
red wine	1 litre
lamb bones	20 kg
veal bones	10 kg
white onions, peeled	6
large carrots, peeled	8
celery sticks	7
leeks	4
tomato purée	6 tbsp

1 Pre-heat the oven to 175°C. Place the herbs, garlic and the wine in a large, deep container. Place all the bones on to a roasting rack on top of the container of herbs and wine, and roast in the oven for 50–60 minutes. When the bones are completely roasted and have taken on a dark golden-brown appearance, remove from oven.
2 Place all the ingredients in a large pot and cover with cold water. Put the pot onto the heat and bring to the simmer; immediately skim all fat that rises to the surface.
3 Turn the heat off and allow the bones and vegetables to sink. Once this has happened, turn the heat back on and bring to just under a simmer, making as little movement as possible to create more of an infusion than a stock.
4 Skim continuously. Leave to infuse for 12 hours then pass through a fine sieve, place in the blast chiller until cold and then in the refrigerator overnight. Next day, reduce down rapidly, until you have about 2 litres remaining.

10 Red wine jus

shallots, sliced	150 g
butter	50 g
garlic, halved	10 g
Cabernet Sauvignon vinegar	100 ml
red wine	250 ml
chicken stock	350 ml
lamb or beef jus	250 ml
bay leaves	2
sprig of thyme	1

1 Caramelise the shallots in foaming butter until golden, adding the garlic at the end.
2 Strain through a colander and then put back into the pan and deglaze with the vinegar.
3 Reduce the red wine by half along with the stock and jus, at the same time as colouring the shallots.
4 When everything is done, combine and simmer for 20 minutes.
5 Pass through a sieve and reduce to sauce consistency.
6 Infuse the aromats for 5 minutes.
7 Pass through muslin cloth and store until needed.

11 Oxtail jus

oxtail braising liquor	400 ml
chicken stock	300 ml
onions, for mirepoix	80 g
celery, for mirepoix	60 g
carrots, for mirepoix	40 g
leeks, for mirepoix	20 g
Cabernet Sauvignon vinegar	120 ml
oxtail bones, chopped small	250 g
red wine, reduced to 125 ml	250 ml

1 Reduce the braising liquor and stock to 350 ml.
2 Roast the mirepoix in a pan until a good colour is achieved. Deglaze with the vinegar.
3 Roast the bones in a separate pan until a good colour is achieved,
4 Mix the mirepoix into the bones, then add the reduced wine.
5 Add stocks and simmer for 35 minutes.
6 Pass through a chinois and reduce to sauce consistency.
7 Pass through a muslin cloth and store until needed.

12 Treacle jus

This jus is used with rich, red game meat, e.g. venison and wild boar. These meats lend themselves to a sweet note, counter-balancing the bitter treacle note.

onions	60 g
carrots	90 g
celery	60 g
leeks	35 g
garlic clove	½
chicken stock	250 ml
lamb jus	250 ml
squab bones, cut into small pieces	400 g
Merlot vinegar	60 ml
red wine	400 ml
treacle	90 g
sherry vinegar	10 ml

1 Roast the vegetables from hard to soft until a golden colour is achieved, then add the stock and jus. Reduce to 250 ml.
2 Roast the bones in a separate pan until golden in colour, then deglaze with the Merlot vinegar.
3 In a separate pan, reduce the wine to 200 ml.
4 Add the wine and jus to the bones, then add this combination to the vegetable pan and simmer for 15 minutes.
5 Pass through a sieve and then reduce quickly to a sauce consistency.
6 Add the treacle, checking as you go until the desired taste is acquired.
7 Pass through muslin cloth.
8 Add the sherry vinegar to clean the sauce and help cut through the rich and bitter notes of the treacle, then chill.

13 Venison jus

onions	60 g
carrots	40 g
celery	30 g
leeks	25 g
chicken stock	500 g
lamb jus	500 g
venison bones, cut into small pieces	450 g
Merlot vinegar	50 ml
red wine	150 g
gin	100 ml
bay leaf	1
juniper berries	3

1 Roast the vegetables from hard to soft until a golden colour is achieved, then add the stock and jus. Reduce to 750 ml.

2 Roast the bones in a separate pan until a good colour, then deglaze with the vinegar and remove from the heat.

3 Reduce the wine in another pan to 200 ml, then add to the pan with the bones in it.

4 Take the pan with the jus and vegetables in it and add to the pan with the bones in it. Bring to the boil and simmer for 20 minutes.

5 Pass through a sieve and reduce quickly to sauce consistency.

6 Finish with the gin mixture (gin, bay leaf, juniper berries) by bringing it to the boil for 3 minutes and then adding it to the reduced sauce.

7 Pass through muslin cloth to remove any sediment, and chill.

14 Jerez sauce

lamb jus	300 ml
chicken stock	200 ml
shallots	200 g
mushrooms	300 g
garlic	5 g
sprigs of thyme	3
Xeres vinegar	60 ml
red wine, reduced to 300 ml	500 ml

1 Reduce the lamb jus and chicken stock to sauce consistency.

2 Caramelise the shallots and mushrooms separately until golden brown. Strain off the fat then deglaze with the Xeres vinegar.

3 Place the stock, shallots, mushrooms, garlic and thyme in one pan.

4 Add the red wine, bring to the boil and simmer for 10 minutes.

5 Pass through muslin cloth to remove any sediment and chill.

Glazes

A glaze is a stock, fond or nage that has been reduced, allowing a high percentage of water to be removed through boiling, thus permitting the concentration of solids and flavour to increase. This yields an intense sauce that should be used sparingly to finish a dish; alternatively, it can be refrigerated or frozen and added to a weak stock to give it the vibrant boost it may need.

When cooking predominantly meat stocks, be mindful that they will contain collagen. This is the main fibrous component of skin, tendons,

connective tissue and bones. Thermal denaturation (the breakdown of the current structure) occurs between 60 and 104°C – the higher the temperature, the more collagen will be extracted into the cooking medium. If you have cooked at the higher end (e.g. boiling) the collagen content of the sauce will be high, giving you a viscous sauce earlier in the reduction process; due to the thickness of such a sauce, it is impossible to reduce it further without burning.

If the collagen extraction is medium, the sauce will reduce more as the viscosity stage will be reached later in the reduction process, giving the sauce more flavour as the water content is less.

When making a glaze ensure that the base stock used at the start has a medium extraction of collagen. This will yield a more flavoursome result and the glaze will be less 'claggy'.

Glazes should be used sparingly as they are very powerful and hold a high degree of residual salt.

Sauces

Preparing and cooking sauces

A sauce is a liquid that has been thickened by either:

- *beurre manié* (kneaded butter)
- egg yolks
- roux
- cornflour, arrowroot or starch
- cream and/or butter added to reduced stock
- rice (in the case of some shellfish bisques)
- reducing cooking liquor or stock.

We will take a closer look at some of these below.

All sauces should be smooth, glossy in appearance, definite in taste and light in texture; the thickening medium should be used in moderation.

Beurre manié

Beurre manié is used chiefly for fish sauces. This a paste made from equal quantities of soft butter and flour then added to a simmering liquid while whisking continuously to prevent lumping.

Egg yolks

This is commonly known in the trade as a liaison and is traditionally used to thicken a classic velouté (**see recipes 17 and 18**). Both egg yolks and cream are mixed together and added to the sauce/velouté off the boil; this mixture is intended to thicken, however it is essential to keep stirring it as, otherwise, the eggs will curdle. Once thickening is achieved the sauce/velouté must be removed and served immediately. *The liquid must not be allowed to boil or simmer.*

Egg yolks are used in mayonnaise, hollandaise and custard sauces. Refer to the appropriate recipe, though, as the yolks are used in a different manner for each sauce.

Cornflour, arrowroot or starch

Cornflour, arrowroot or starch (such as potato starch) is used for thickening gravy and sauces. These are diluted with water, stock or milk, then stirred into the boiling liquid, allowed to reboil for a few minutes and then strained. For large-scale cooking and economy, flour may be used.

Roux

A roux is a combination of fat and flour, which are cooked together. There are three degrees to which a roux may be cooked (white, blond and brown) and one 'modern' approach known as 'continental' roux style.

A boiling liquid should never be added to a hot roux as the result may be lumpy and the person making the sauce may be scalded by the steam produced. If allowed to stand for a time over a moderate heat a sauce made with a roux may become thin due to a chemical change (dextrinisation) in the flour.

White roux
This is used for white (béchamel) sauce and soups. Equal quantities of margarine or butter and flour are cooked together without colouring for a few minutes, to a sandy texture. Alternatively, use polyunsaturated vegetable margarine or make a roux with vegetable oil, using equal quantities of oil to flour. This does give a slack roux but enables the liquid to be incorporated easily.

Blond roux
This is used for veloutés, tomato sauce and soups. Equal quantities of margarine, butter or vegetable oil and flour are cooked for a little longer than a white roux, but without colouring, to a sandy texture.

Brown roux

This was traditionally used for brown (espagnole) sauce and soups and is slightly browned in the roux-making process. It is not commonly used today.

Continental roux

This is a very easy and straightforward thickening agent that can be frozen and used as a quick thickener during service or à la minute.

Mix equal quantities of flour and vegetable oil together to a paste and place in the oven at 140°C. Cook the mixture, mixing it in on itself continually until a biscuit texture is achieved. Remove and allow to cool to room temperature. When it is cool enough to handle form into a sausage shape using a double layer of cling film. Chill, then freeze.

To use, remove from the freezer and shave a little off the end of the log. Whisk it into the boiling sauce (as the flour is already cooked it is not necessary to add it slowly to prevent lumping as this will not occur). Once the desired thickness has been achieved, pass and serve.

Other sauces

- Vegetables or fruit purées are known as a cullis (coulis). No other thickening agent is used.
- Blood was traditionally used in recipes such as jugged hare, but is used rarely today.
- Cooking liquor from certain dishes and/or stock can be reduced to give a light sauce.

Other thickening agents for sauces

Thickening sauces with sauce flour

Sauce flour is a specially milled flour that does not require any addition of fat to prevent it from going lumpy. Sauces may be thickened using this flour. It is useful when making sauces for those on a low-fat diet.

Basic sauce recipes

15 Béchamel sauce (white sauce)

Cal	Cal	Fat	Sat Fat	Carb	Sugar	Protein	Fibre
7228 KJ	1721 kcal	120.3 g	59.5 g	124.8 g	48.6 g	42.5 g	3.6 g

This is a basic white sauce made from milk and a white roux.

	1 litre	4.5 litres
margarine, oil or butter	100 g	400 g
flour	100 g	400 g
milk	1 litre	4½ litres
1 onion, studded with clove		

1 Melt the margarine or butter in a thick-bottomed pan.
2 Add the flour and mix in.
3 Cook for a few minutes over a gentle heat without colouring.
4 Remove from the heat to cool the roux.
5 Gradually add the warmed milk and stir until smooth.
6 Add the onion, studded with a clove.
7 Allow to simmer for 30 minutes.
8 Remove the onion, pass the sauce through a conical strainer.
9 Cover with a film of butter or margarine to prevent a skin forming.

HEALTHY EATING TIP

- Try using a 'soft' margarine and semi-skimmed milk.
- Some cornflour milk could be used to extend the sauce and reduce the fat content.

* Using whole milk/hard margarine, for 1 litre. Using skimmed milk/hard margarine, this recipe provides, for 1 litre: 5884 kJ/1401 kcal Energy; 83.3 g Fat; 36.1 g Sat Fat; 127.8 g Carb; 51.6 g Sugar; 43.5 g Protein; 3.6 g Fibre

16 Béchamel sauce (reduced fat)

Cal 302 KJ	Cal 73 kcal	Fat 1.8 g	Sat Fat 1.1 g	Carb 10.9 g	Sugar 4.8 g	Protein 4.2 g	Fibre 0.3 g

milk	500 ml
sauce flour	40 g
seasoning	

HEALTHY EATING TIP
- Try using yoghurt or fromage frais.

1 The milk may be first infused with a studded onion clouté, carrot and a bouquet garni. Allow to cool.
2 Place the milk in a suitable saucepan, gradually whisk in the sauce flour. Bring slowly to the boil until the sauce has thickened.
3 Season, simmer for approximately 5–10 minutes. Use as required.

Table 3.1 Other sauces made from basic white sauce (quantities given are for ½ litre, 8–12 portions)

Sauce	Served with	Additions per ½ litre
anchovy	poached or fried or boiled fish	1 tbsp anchovy essence
egg	poached fish or boiled fish	2 hard-boiled eggs, diced
cheese or mornay sauce	fish or vegetables	50 g grated cheese, 1 egg yolk; mix well in boiling sauce, remove from heat; strain if necessary but do not allow to reboil
onion	roast lamb or mutton	100 g chopped or diced onions cooked without colour either by boiling or sweating in butter
soubise	roast lamb or mutton	As for onion sauce but passed through a strainer
parsley	poached or boiled fish and vegetables	1 tbsp chopped parsley
cream	poached fish and boiled vegetables	Add cream, milk, natural yoghurt or fromage frais to give the consistency of double cream
mustard	grilled herrings	Add diluted English or continental mustard to make a fairly hot sauce

17 Velouté (chicken, veal, fish, mutton)

Cal 4594 KJ	Cal 1094 kcal	Fat 82.6 g	Sat Fat 35.4 g	Carb 79.0 g	Sugar 1.6 g	Protein 13.3 g	Fibre 3.6 g	*

This is a basic white sauce made from white stock and a blond roux.

	1 litre	4.5 litres
margarine, butter or oil	100 g	400 g
flour	100 g	400 g
stock (chicken, veal, fish, mutton) as required	1 litre	4½ litres

1 Melt the fat or oil in a thick-bottomed pan.
2 Add the flour and mix in.
3 Cook out to a sandy texture over gentle heat without colouring.
4 Allow the roux to cool.
5 Gradually add the boiling stock.
6 Stir until smooth and boiling.
7 Allow to simmer for approximately 1 hour.
8 Pass it through a fine conical strainer.

Note: A velouté sauce for chicken, veal or fish dishes is usually finished with cream and, in some cases, also egg yolks. The finished sauce should be of a light consistency, barely coating the back of a spoon.

Sauce suprême is a chicken velouté flavoured with 25 g of mushroom trimmings finished with a liaison of 1 egg yolk and 60 ml of cream and 2–3 drops of lemon juice.

HEALTHY EATING TIP

• Make sure all the fat has been skimmed from the stock before adding it to the roux.

* Using hard margarine, for 1 litre. Using sunflower oil instead, this recipe provides, for 1 litre: 5304 kJ/1263 kcal Energy; 101.5 g Fat; 13.3 g Sat Fat; 78.9 g Carb; 1.5 g Sugar; 13.2 g Protein; 3.6 g Fibre

Table 3.2 ✎ Sauces made from veloutés (quantities given are for ½ litre, 8–12 portions)

Sauce	Served with	Additions per ½ litre
caper	boiled leg of mutton	2 tbsp capers
aurore	poached or boiled chicken, poached eggs	25 g mushroom trimmings, 60 ml cream, 1 egg yolk, 2–3 drops lemon juice, 1 tbsp tomato purée
mushroom	poached or boiled chicken, sweetbreads	as for aurore, but substitute for the tomato purée 100 g well-washed, sliced, sweated white button mushrooms after straining the velouté, simmer for 10 minutes, then add egg yolk and cream
ivory	poached or boiled chicken	as for mushroom but add a little meat glaze for an ivory colour

18 Fish velouté

Cal 4850 KJ	Cal 1144 kcal	Fat 90.4 g	Sat Fat 39.0 g	Carb 77.8 g	Sugar 1.6 g	Protein 9.5 g	Fibre 3.6 g

	1 litre	2.5 litres
margarine or butter	100 g	250 g
flour	100 g	250 g
fish stock	1 litre	2½ litres

1 Prepare a blond roux using the margarine or butter and flour.
2 Gradually add the stock, stirring continuously until boiling point is reached.
3 Simmer for approximately 1 hour.
4 Pass through a fine conical strainer.

Note: This will give a thick sauce that can be thinned down with the cooking liquor from the fish for which the sauce is intended.

HEALTHY EATING TIP
- Make sure all the fat has been skimmed from the stock before adding it to the roux.

Espagnole

This is a traditional brown sauce made from brown roux and brown stock, simmered for several hours and skimmed frequently to produce a refined sauce. Because of the lengthy, time-consuming process and a move away from heavy flour-based sauces, in many kitchens a reduced veal stock (see recipe 2) is used as a base for most brown sauces.

Demi-glace

Demi-glace is used as the base for a number of derivative sauces. Current practice in most kitchens is to use either stock reduced sauce, jus-lié or a commercially produced powder- or granule-based product.

Sauces made from demi-glace or stock-reduced base

19 Red wine sauce (sauce bordelaise)

Cal 95 KJ	Cal 23 kcal	Fat 0.1 g	Sat Fat 0.0 g	Carb 5.1 g	Sugar 3.8 g	Protein 0.6 g	Fibre 0.7 g

	4 portions	10 portions
shallots, chopped	50 g	125 g
red wine	125 ml	300 ml
mignonette pepper	pinch	pinch
thyme	sprig	sprig
bay leaf	1	1
demi-glace, jus-lié or stock-reduced base	250 ml	625 ml

1 Reduce the shallots, red wine, pepper, thyme and bay leaf.
2 Place the reduction in a small sauteuse.
3 Allow to boil until reduced to a quarter.
4 Add the demi-glace. Simmer for 20–30 minutes.
5 Correct the seasoning. Pass through a fine strainer.

Note: This sauce traditionally included poached beef marrow, either: in dice, poached and added to the sauce; or cut in slices, poached and placed on meat before being sauced over. It may be served with fried steaks.

20 Chasseur sauce (sauce chasseur)

Cal	Cal	Fat	Sat Fat	Carb	Sugar	Protein	Fibre
227 KJ	55 kcal	5.3 g	2.5 g	1.4 g	1.2 g	0.5 g	0.5 g

	4 portions	10 portions
butter, margarine or oil	25 g	60 g
shallots, chopped	10 g	25 g
garlic clove, chopped (optional)	1	1
button mushrooms, sliced	50 g	125 g
white wine (dry)	60 ml	150 ml
tomatoes, skinned, deseeded, diced	100 g	250 g
demi-glace, jus-lié or reduced stock	250 ml	625 ml
parsley and tarragon, chopped		

1 Melt the butter in a small sauteuse.
2 Add the shallots and cook gently for 2–3 minutes without colour.
3 Add the garlic and the mushrooms, cover and cook gently for 2–3 minutes.
4 Strain off the fat.
5 Add the wine and reduce by half. Add the tomatoes.
6 Add the demi-glace; simmer for 5–10 minutes.
7 Correct the seasoning. Add the tarragon and parsley.

Note: May be served with fried steaks, chops, chicken, etc.

HEALTHY EATING TIP
- Use an unsaturated oil (sunflower or olive). Lightly oil the pan and drain off any excess after the frying is complete. Skim the fat from the finished dish.
- Season with the minimum amount of salt.

21 Pepper sauce (sauce poivrade)

Cal	Cal	Fat	Sat Fat	Carb	Sugar	Protein	Fibre
247 KJ	60 kcal	5.3 g	2.5 g	2.6 g	2.0 g	0.5 g	0.6 g

	4 portions	10 portions
margarine, butter or oil	25 g	60 g
onions	50 g	125 g
carrots	50 g	125 g
celery	50 g	125 g
bay leaf	1	1
sprig of thyme		
white wine	2 tbsp	5 tbsp
vinegar	2 tbsp	5 tbsp
mignonette pepper	5 g	12 g
demi-glace, jus-lié or reduced stock	250 ml	625 ml

1 Melt the fat or oil in a small sauteuse.
2 Add the vegetables and herbs (mirepoix) and allow to brown.
3 Pour off the fat.
4 Add the wine, vinegar and pepper.
5 Reduce by half. Add the demi-glace.
6 Simmer for 20–30 minutes. Correct the seasoning.
7 Pass through a fine conical strainer.

Note: Usually served with joints or cuts of venison.

HEALTHY EATING TIP
- Use an unsaturated oil (sunflower or olive). Lightly oil the pan and drain off any excess after the frying is complete. Skim the fat from the finished dish.
- Season with the minimum amount of salt.

22 Italian sauce (sauce italienne)

Cal 258 KJ	Cal 63 kcal	Fat 5.6 g	Sat Fat 2.6 g	Carb 1.3 g	Sugar 1.2 g	Protein 1.8 g	Fibre 0.4 g

	4 portions	10 portions
margarine, oil or butter	25 g	60 g
shallots, chopped	10 g	25 g
mushrooms, chopped	50 g	125 g
demi-glace, jus-lié or reduced stock	250 ml	625 ml
lean ham, chopped	25 g	60 g
tomatoes, skinned, de-seeded, diced	100 g	250 g
parsley, chervil and tarragon, chopped		

1 Melt the fat or oil in a small sauteuse.
2 To make a duxelle, add the shallots and cook gently for 2–3 minutes, then add the mushrooms and cook gently for a further 2–3 minutes.
3 Add the demi-glace, ham and tomatoes.
4 Simmer for 5–10 minutes. Correct the seasoning. Add the chopped herbs.

Note: Usually served with fried cuts of veal, lamb or chicken.

HEALTHY EATING TIP
• Use an unsaturated oil (sunflower or olive). Lightly oil the pan and drain off any excess after the frying is complete.
• Trim as much fat as possible from the ham.
• The ham is salty, so do not add more salt; flavour will come from the herbs.
• Skim all fat from the finished sauce.

23 Brown onion sauce (sauce lyonnaise)

Cal 240 KJ	Cal 58 kcal	Fat 5.2 g	Sat Fat 2.5 g	Carb 2.3 g	Sugar 1.7 g	Protein 0.3 g	Fibre 0.4 g

	4 portions	10 portions
margarine, oil or butter	25 g	60 g
onions, sliced	100 g	250 g
vinegar	2 tbsp	5 tbsp
demi-glace, jus-lié or reduced stock	250 ml	625 ml

1 Melt the fat or oil in a sauteuse.
2 Add the onions, cover with a lid.
3 Cook gently until tender and golden in colour.
4 Remove the lid and colour lightly.
5 Add the vinegar and completely reduce.
6 Add the demi-glace, simmer for 5–10 minutes.
7 Skim and correct the seasoning.

Note: May be served with burgers, fried liver or sausages.

HEALTHY EATING TIP
• Use an unsaturated oil (sunflower or olive). Lightly oil the pan and drain off any excess after the frying is complete. Skim the fat from the finished dish.
• Season with the minimum amount of salt.

24 Madeira sauce (sauce Madère)

Cal	Cal	Fat	Sat Fat	Carb	Sugar	Protein	Fibre
43 KJ	10 kcal	0.1 g	0.0 g	1.6 g	1.2 g	0.3 g	0.4 g

	4 portions	10 portions
demi-glace, jus-lié or reduced stock	250 ml	625 ml
Madeira wine	2 tbsp	5 tbsp
butter	25 g	60 g

1 Boil the demi-glace in a small sauteuse.
2 Add the Madeira; reboil. Correct the seasoning.
3 Pass through a fine conical strainer. Gradually mix in the butter.

Note: May be served with braised ox tongue or ham. Dry sherry or port wine may be substituted for Madeira and the sauce renamed accordingly.

25 Piquant sauce (sauce piquante)

Cal	Cal	Fat	Sat Fat	Carb	Sugar	Protein	Fibre
197 KJ	48 kcal	5.1 g	3.3 g	0.3 g	0.3 g	0.0 g	0.0 g

	4 portions	10 portions
vinegar	60 ml	150 ml
shallots, chopped	50 g	125 g
demi-glace, jus-lié or reduced stock	250 ml	625 ml
gherkins, chopped	25 g	60 g
capers, chopped	10 g	25 g
chervil, tarragon and parsley, chopped	½ tbsp	1½ tbsp

1 Place the vinegar and shallots in a small sauteuse and reduce by half.
2 Add the demi-glace; simmer for 15–20 minutes.
3 Add the rest of the ingredients. Skim and correct the seasoning.

Note: May be served with made-up dishes, sausages and grilled meats.

26 Robert sauce (sauce Robert)

Cal	Cal	Fat	Sat Fat	Carb	Sugar	Protein	Fibre
229 KJ	56 kcal	2.6 g	1.0 g	7.2 g	6.8 g	0.6 g	0.2 g

	4 portions	10 portions
margarine, oil or butter	20 g	50 g
onions, finely chopped	10 g	25 g
vinegar	60 ml	150 ml
demi-glace, jus-lié or reduced stock	250 ml	625 ml
English or continental mustard	1 level tbsp	2½ level tbsp
caster sugar	1 level tbsp	2½ level tbsp

1 Melt the fat or oil in a small sauteuse. Add the onions.
2 Cook gently without colour. Add the vinegar and reduce completely.
3 Add the demi-glace; simmer for 5–10 minutes.

4 Remove from the heat and add the mustard diluted with a little water and the sugar; do not boil. Skim and correct the seasoning.

Note: May be served with fried sausages and burgers, or grilled pork chops.

HEALTHY EATING TIP

• Use an unsaturated oil (sunflower or olive). Lightly oil the pan and drain off any excess after the frying is complete. Skim the fat from the finished dish.
• Season with the minimum amount of salt.

27 Charcutière sauce (sauce charcutière)

Proceed as for Robert sauce (recipe 26), but at the end add 25 g sliced or julienne of gherkins.

Miscellaneous sauces

28 Curry sauce (sauce kari)

Cal 1092 KJ	Cal 260 kcal	Fat 14.1 g	Sat Fat 4.1 g	Carb 30.3 g	Sugar 19.9 g	Protein 4.9 g	Fibre 4.1 g	*

	4 portions	10 portions
onion, chopped	50 g	125 g
clove of garlic	½	½
oil, butter or margarine	10 g	25 g
flour	10 g	25 g
curry powder	5 g	12 g
tomato purée	5 g	12 g
stock	375 ml	1 litre
apple, chopped	25 g	60 g
chutney, chopped	1 tbsp	2 tbsp
desiccated coconut	5 g	12 g
sultanas	10 g	25 g
ginger root		
or	10 g	25 g
ground ginger	5 g	12 g
salt		

1 Gently cook the onion and garlic in the fat in a small sauteuse without colouring.
2 Mix in the flour and curry powder. Cook gently to a sandy mixture.
3 Mix in the tomato purée, cool.
4 Gradually add the boiling stock and mix to a smooth sauce.

5 Add the remainder of the ingredients; season with salt, and simmer for 30 minutes. Skim and correct the seasoning.

Note: This sauce has a wide range of uses, with prawns, shrimps, vegetables, eggs, and so on. For use with poached or soft-boiled eggs it may be strained and for all purposes it may be finished with 2–3 tbsp cream or natural yoghurt. For a traditional recipe the curry powder would be replaced by either curry paste or a mixture of freshly ground spices such as turmeric, cumin, allspice, fresh ginger, chilli and clove.

HEALTHY EATING TIP
• Use a small amount of an unsaturated oil (e.g. sunflower or olive) to fry the onion and garlic.
• Add the minimum amount of salt, tasting first – there is already lots of flavour from the spices, ginger, etc.

* Using sunflower oil, for 4 portions

29 Roast gravy (jus rôti)

Cal	Cal	Fat	Sat Fat	Carb	Sugar	Protein	Fibre	*
504 KJ	120 kcal	10.0 g	1.3 g	1.8 g	0.0 g	5.6 g	0.0 g	

	4 portions	10 portions
raw veal bones or beef and veal trimmings	200 g	500 g
stock or water	500 ml	1½ litres
onions	50 g	125 g
celery	25 g	60 g
carrots	50 g	125 g

1 Chop the bones and brown in the oven, or brown in a little oil on top of the stove in a frying pan. Drain off all the fat.
2 Place the bones in a saucepan with the stock or water.
3 Bring to the boil, skim and allow to simmer.
4 Add the lightly browned vegetables, which may be fried in a little fat in a frying pan or added to the bones when partly browned.
5 Simmer for 1½–2 hours.
6 Remove the joint from the roasting tin when cooked.
7 Return the tray to a low heat to allow the sediment to settle.
8 Carefully strain off the fat, leaving the sediment in the tin.
9 Return the joint to the stove and brown carefully; deglaze with the brown stock.
10 Allow to simmer for a few minutes.
11 Correct the colour and seasoning. Strain and skim off all fat.

Note: For preference use beef bones for roast beef gravy and the appropriate bones for lamb, veal, mutton and pork.

HEALTHY EATING TIP
• Use an unsaturated oil (sunflower or olive). Lightly oil the pan and drain off any excess after the frying is complete.
• Season with the minimum amount of salt.

* Using sunflower oil, for 4 portions

30 Thickened gravy (jus-lié)

Thickened gravy is made:

1 by simmering roast gravy with the addition of a little tomato purée, a few mushroom trimmings and a pinch of thyme for 10–15 minutes; then lightly thicken by stirring in to the simmering gravy some arrowroot diluted in cold water; reboil, simmer for 5–10 minutes and pass through a strainer.
2 by using reduced veal stock (see recipe 2).

Variations
Add a little rosemary, thyme or lavender.

31 Bread sauce

Cal	Cal	Fat	Sat Fat	Carb	Sugar	Protein	Fibre
318 KJ	77 kcal	3.8 g	2.3 g	7.6 g	4.6 g	3.8 g	0.1 g

	4 portions	10 portions
semi-skimmed milk	375 ml	1 litre
onion, small, studded with a clove	1	2
fresh white breadcrumbs	25 g	60 g
salt, cayenne pepper		
butter	10 g	25 g

1 Infuse the simmering milk with the studded onion for 15 minutes.
2 Remove the onion, mix in the breadcrumbs. Simmer for 2–3 minutes.

3 Season, correct the consistency.
4 Add the butter on top of the sauce to prevent a skin forming.
5 Mix well when serving.

Note: Served with roast chicken, turkey and roast game.

HEALTHY EATING TIP
• Use semi-skimmed milk and the minimum amount of salt.

32 Tomato sauce (sauce tomate) (1)

Cal	Cal	Fat	Sat Fat	Carb	Sugar	Protein	Fibre	*
931 KJ	221 kcal	12.5 g	51 g	20.2 g	11.5 g	8.5 g	2.9 g	

	4 portions	10 portions
margarine, butter or oil	10 g	25 g
onions (for mirepoix)	50 g	125 g
carrots (for mirepoix)	50 g	125 g
celery (for mirepoix)	25 g	60 g
bay leaf (for mirepoix)	1	3
bacon scraps (optional)	10 g	25 g
flour	10 g	25 g
tomato purée	50 g	125 g
stock	375 ml	1 litre
clove garlic	½	2
salt, pepper		

1 Melt the fat or oil in a small sauteuse.
2 Add the vegetables and herbs (mirepoix) and bacon scraps, and brown slightly.
3 Mix in the flour and cook to a sandy texture. Allow to colour slightly.

4 Mix in the tomato purée, allow to cool.
5 Gradually add the boiling stock, stir to the boil.
6 Add the garlic, season. Simmer for 1 hour.
7 Correct the seasoning and cool.
8 Pass through a fine conical strainer.

Note: This sauce has many uses, served with pasta, eggs, fish, meats, and so on. The amount of tomato purée used may need to vary according to its strength. The sauce can also be made without using flour by adding 400 g of fresh fully ripe tomatoes or an equivalent tin of tomatoes for 4 portions.

* Using hard margarine, for 4 portions. Using butter, this recipe provides for 4 portions: 936 kJ/223 kcal Energy; 12.6 g Fat; 6.7 g Sat Fat; 20.2 g Carb; 11.5 g Sugar; 8.5 g Protein; 2.9 g Fibre

33 Tomato sauce *(sauce tomate)* (2)

carrots	90 g
celery	30g
clove garlic	½
vegetable oil	25 g
butter	25 g
thyme	1 g
bay leaf	½
tomato purée	12 g
plum tomatoes	200 g
chicken stock	750 g
juniper berries	2
cream	75 g
gastric (50/50 sherry vinegar and sugar)	5 g

1 Sweat the carrots, celery and garlic in the oil and butter.
2 Add the thyme, bay and tomato purée.
3 Cook for 5 minutes.
4 Add the tomatoes.
5 Cook for 5 minutes.
6 Add the chicken stock and juniper berries, reduce by a third.
7 Finish with the cream, bring to the boil and blitz (purée or liquidise). Season with salt and gastric.

Note: Gastric (or gastrique) is made by reducing 100 ml sherry vinegar and 35 g caster sugar to a light caramel. It is used in hot sauces made with fruit.

34 Pesto

	4 portions	10 portions
fresh basil leaves	4 small bunches	10 small bunches
garlic clove, chopped	1	2–3
salt, to taste		
pine nuts, lightly toasted	1 tbsp	2½ tbsp
Parmesan cheese, grated	2 tbsp	5 tbsp
extra virgin olive oil		

1 Put the basil leaves, garlic, salt and pine nuts into a mortar (or use a food processor) and pound into a smooth paste.
2 Place in a bowl, mix in the cheese and sufficient olive oil to make a sauce-like consistency.

Note: Pesto is a green basil sauce used in some pasta dishes, salads and fish dishes.

Salsa

Salsa is the Spanish word for a sauce. A wide variety of ingredients can be used and chunky mixtures made to serve with grilled or fried fish, meat and poultry dishes.

35 Tomato and cucumber salsa

Cal	Cal	Fat	Sat Fat	Carb	Sugar	Protein	Fibre
202 KJ	49 kcal	4.3 g	0.7 g	2.0 g	2.0 g	0.6 g	0.7 g

ripe, chopped tomatoes	400 g
cucumber, chopped	½
spring onions	6
fresh basil, chopped	1 tbsp
fresh parsley, chopped	1 tbsp
olive oil	3 tbsp
lemon or lime (juice of)	1
salt and pepper	

1 In a large bowl, mix all the ingredients together.
2 Correct seasoning and serve.

HEALTHY EATING TIP

- Rely on the herbs for flavour with the minimum amount of salt.
- Extra vegetables can be added and the salsa used liberally with grilled fish or chicken. Rice could be served or the salsa used to fill a tortilla.

Note: This recipe may be varied by using any chopped salad ingredients and fresh herbs (e.g. tarragon, chervil). Do not be afraid to experiment.

36 Salsa verde

Cal	Cal	Fat	Sat Fat	Carb	Sugar	Protein	Fibre	*
281 KJ	69 kcal	7.5 g	1.1 g	0.2 g	0.1 g	0.1 g	0.0 g	

mint	1 tbsp	⎫ coarsely
parsley	3 tbsp	⎬ chopped
capers	3	⎭
garlic clove (optional)	1	
Dijon mustard	1 tsp	
lemon juice	½	
extra virgin olive oil	120 ml	
salt		

1 In a large bowl, mix all the ingredients together and check the seasoning. Serve with grilled fish.

* Per tablespoon

37 Avocado and coriander salsa

Cal	Cal	Fat	Sat Fat	Carb	Sugar	Protein	Fibre
361 KJ	87 kcal	8.6 g	1.4 g	1.8 g	1.4 g	0.8 g	1.0 g

ripe avocado, peeled and diced	1
ripe tomatoes, peeled, deseeded and diced	3
shallot, peeled and cut into rings	1
fresh coriander, chopped	1 tsp
pine kernels, toasted	10 g
cucumber, diced	25 g
lemon or lime (juice)	1
virgin olive oil	3 tbsp
salt and pepper to taste	

1 In a large bowl, mix all the ingredients together, check seasoning and serve.

Variations

- Peeled, de-stoned, diced mango in place of avocado
- 1 tsp finely chopped garlic or garlic juice
- 1 tsp finely chopped red chilli
- tbsp of finely chopped lemon grass
- 25 g chopped red onion in place of shallot

HEALTHY EATING TIP

- Although avocado is rich in fat, it is unsaturated fat and therefore healthier.
- Try using the salsa to fill a tortilla, and add grilled fish or chicken to make a healthy meal.

Butter as a sauce

Clarified butter

Clarified butter is butter that has been melted and skimmed. After that, the fat element of the butter is carefully poured off, leaving the milky residue behind. This gives a clear fat that can reach higher temperatures than normal butter without burning, but that can also be used to nap over steamed vegetables, or poached or grilled fish.

Beurre noisette

Beurre noisette basically translates to 'nut butter', and its flavour comes from the caramelisation of the milk element in the butter solids. It is achieved by placing diced hard butter into a moderately hot pan and bringing to a foam (a good indication that it is ready). While it is foaming under heat, the milk element is cooking in the fat, which creates a popping/cracking sound. This is due to the water mixing with the fat – not too dissimilar to the deep-frying of moist products. When this cracking/popping stops, this means that there is no more liquid in the fat and all the proteins have now caramelised, yielding that nutty flavour. Like clarified butter, this can be served with poached or steamed vegetables and fish, but the classic use is with shallow-fried fish. If you take the butter a little further, however, and almost burn the sediment, then add a little vinegar, this is called black butter and is traditionally served with skate.

Beurre fondu/emulsion

This is basically an emulsion between fat and liquid – for example, melted butter emulsified with any nage described above will give you a slightly thicker sauce that can be used to coat vegetables or fish. However, to intensify the flavour, if you were to add a *beurre noisette* to the pan or your cooking medium was clarified butter, you could start cooking the product in the pan with the fat. Once it is half cooked, arrest the cooking by adding a nage and then bring quickly to the boil. Through this boiling process the fat and the stock will become emulsified, which gives an emulsified sauce made in the pan, but with the cooking juices also added.

38 Hollandaise sauce (sauce hollandaise)

Cal	Cal	Fat	Sat Fat	Carb	Sugar	Protein	Fibre	*
6789 KJ	1616 kcal	176.2 g	107.9 g	0.1 g	0.1 g	7.3 g	0.0 g	

	4 portions	10 portions
crushed peppercorn reduction (optional)	6	15
vinegar	1 tbsp	2½ tbsp
egg yolks	2	5
butter or good-quality oil	200 g	500 g
salt, cayenne, to taste		

1 Place the peppercorns and vinegar in a small sauteuse or stainless steel pan and reduce to one-third. Strain off.
2 Add 1 tbsp cold water, allow to cool.
3 Mix in the yolks with a whisk.
4 Return to a gentle heat and, whisking continuously, cook to a sabayon (this is the cooking of the yolks to a thickened consistency, like cream, sufficient to show the mark of the whisk).
5 Remove from the heat and cool slightly.
6 Whisk in gradually the melted warm butter until thoroughly combined.
7 Correct the seasoning. If reduction is not used, add a few drops of lemon juice.
8 Pass through a muslin, tammy cloth or fine conical strainer.
9 The sauce should be kept at only a slightly warm temperature until served.
10 Serve in a slightly warm sauceboat.

Notes: The cause of hollandaise sauce curdling is either because the butter has been added too quickly or because of excess heat, which will cause the albumen in the eggs to harden, shrink and separate from the liquid.

Should the sauce curdle, place a teaspoon of boiling water in a clean sauteuse and gradually whisk in the curdled sauce. If this fails to reconstitute the sauce, then place an egg yolk in a clean sauteuse with 1 dessertspoon of water. Whisk lightly over a gentle heat until slightly thickened. Remove from the heat and gradually add the curdled sauce, whisking continuously. To stabilise the sauce during service, 60 ml thick béchamel may be added before straining (see page 51).

To reduce the risk of salmonella infection pasteurised egg yolks may be used. Do not keep the sauce for longer than 2 hours before discarding. This applies to all egg-based sauces.

Served with hot fish (e.g. salmon, trout, turbot) and vegetables (e.g. asparagus, cauliflower, broccoli). Variations (e.g. béarnaise) can be found in recipe 39.

HEALTHY EATING TIP

- This recipe is obviously high in saturated fat (butter, egg yolk).
- Add the minimum of salt and consider it to be a treat.
- The fat is proportionally reduced when served with grilled or baked fish and plenty of potatoes and other vegetables.

* For four portions

39 Béarnaise sauce (1)

	Makes 500 g
shallots, chopped	50 g
tarragon	10 g
peppercorns, crushed	12
white wine vinegar	3 tbsp
egg yolks	6
melted butter	325 g
salt and cayenne pepper	
chervil and tarragon to finish, chopped	

1 Place the shallots, tarragon, peppercorns and vinegar in a small pan and reduce to one-third.
2 Add 1 tablespoon of cold water and allow to cool. Add the egg yolks.
3 Put on a bain-marie and whisk continuously to a sabayon consistency.
4 Remove from the heat and gradually whisk in the melted butter.

5 Add seasoning. Pass through muslin or a fine chinois.
6 To finish, add the chopped chervil and tarragon.
7 Store in an appropriate container at room temperature.

Note: Egg-based sauces should not be kept warm for more than 2 hours. After this time, they should be thrown away, but are best made fresh to order.
Variations
- Choron sauce: 200 g tomato concassée, well dried. Do not add the chopped tarragon and chervil to finish.
- Foyot or valois sauce: 25 g warm meat glaze.
- Paloise sauce: this sauce is made as for béarnaise using chopped mint stalks in place of the tarragon in the reduction. To finish, add chopped mint instead of the chervil and tarragon.

40 Béarnaise sauce (2)

Cal	Cal	Fat	Sat Fat	Carb	Sugar	Protein	Fibre
1728 KJ	420 kcal	45.2 g	27.2 g	0.6 g	0.5 g	2.6 g	0.0 g

	4–6 portions
shallots, chopped	10 g
peppercorns, crushed	6
tarragon	5 g
tarragon vinegar	1 tbsp
egg yolks	3
butter or good-quality oil	200 g
sprig chervil, chopped	

1 Make a reduction with the shallots, peppercorns, tarragon stalks and vinegar.
2 Proceed as for hollandaise sauce (recipe 38).
3 After passing, add the chopped tarragon leaves and chervil.

Note: This is usually served with grilled meat and fish, e.g. Chateaubriand grillé, sauce béarnaise. This sauce should be twice as thick as hollandaise.

41 Smitaine sauce (sauce smitaine)

Cal 254 KJ	Cal 62 kcal	Fat 6.0 g	Sat Fat 3.8 g	Carb 1.2 g	Sugar 1.1 g	Protein 0.8 g	Fibre 0.0 g	*

butter or margarine	25 g
onion, finely chopped	50 g
white wine	60 ml
sour cream	½ litre
seasoning	
juice of ½ of a lemon	

1 Melt the butter or margarine in a sauteuse and cook the onion without colour.
2 Add the white wine and reduce by half.
3 Add the sour cream and season lightly, reduce by one-third.
4 Pass through a fine strainer and finish with the lemon juice.

* Per tablespoon

42 Melted butter (beurre fondu)

Cal 388 KJ	Cal 94 kcal	Fat 10.3 g	Sat Fat 6.5 g	Carb 0.1 g	Sugar 0.1 g	Protein 0.1 g	Fibre 0.0 g	*

	4 portions	10 portions
butter	200 g	500 g
water or white wine	2 tbsp	5 tbsp

Method 1
1 Boil the butter and water together gently until combined, then pass through a fine strainer.

Method 2
1 Melt the butter in the water and carefully strain off the fat, leaving the water and sediment in the pan.

Note: Usually served with poached fish and certain vegetables (e.g. blue trout, salmon; asparagus, sea kale). For butter sauce see pages 63 and 185. For compound butter sauces see below.

* Per tablespoon

Compound butter sauces

Compound butters are made by mixing the flavouring ingredients into softened butter, which can then be shaped into a roll 2 cm in diameter, placed in wet greaseproof paper or foil, hardened in a refrigerator and cut into ½ cm slices when required.

- *Parsley butter*: chopped parsley and lemon juice.
- *Herb butter*: mixed herbs (chives, tarragon, fennel, dill) and lemon juice.
- *Chive butter*: chopped chives and lemon juice.
- *Garlic butter*: garlic juice and chopped parsley or herbs.
- *Anchovy butter*: few drops anchovy essence.
- *Shrimp butter*: finely chopped or pounded shrimps.
- *Garlic*: mashed to a paste.
- *Mustard*: continental-type mustard.
- *Liver pâté*: mashed to a paste.

Compound butters are served with grilled and some fried fish, and with grilled meats.

Flavoured oils

Flavoured oils are used to enhance certain types of food and dishes, especially pasta, fish and salads.

43 Walnut oil

olive or walnut oil	500 ml
walnuts, finely crushed	75 g
Parmesan cheese	75 g
salt, to taste	
mill pepper	

1 Mix all the ingredients together and bottle until required.

44 Basil oil

fresh basil	25 g
oil	200 ml
salt, to taste	
mill pepper	

Note: Basil extract can be used in place of fresh basil; 50 g of grated Parmesan or Gorgonzola cheese may also be added to the basil oil.

1 Blanch and refresh the basil, purée with the oil.
2 Allow to settle overnight and decant.
3 Store in bottles with a sprig of blanched basil.

45 Garlic oil

vegetable, sunflower, soya and olive oil	250 ml
garlic, chopped and crushed	3 tbsp

1 Heat the oil in a suitable pan, add the crushed garlic, heat until the garlic is golden, allow to cool, add to the oil, store and use as required.

46 Sundried tomato oil

olive oil	500 ml
sundried tomatoes	75 g
salt, to taste	
mill pepper	

1 Reconstitute the tomatoes in the olive oil.
2 Lightly warm the oil/tomatoes and purée in a liquidiser.
3 Add the mill pepper and salt.
4 Store in a bottle until required.

47 Mint oil

	Makes 150 ml
mint	100 g
oil	150 ml
salt	3 tbsp

1 Blanch the mint for 30 seconds.
2 Refresh and squeeze the water out.
3 Place in a blender and slowly add the oil.
4 Allow to settle overnight and decant into bottles.

Note: Uses include lamb dishes, salads and fish dishes.

48 Lemon oil

	Makes 250 ml
lemons, rind	3 (no pith – the whitish layer between skin and fruit)
lemon grass stick, cut lengthways and chopped into 2 cm strips	1
grapeseed oil	250 ml
olive oil	2 tbsp

1 Place all the ingredients into a food processor and pulse the mix until the lemon peel and grass are approximately 3 mm thick.
2 Allow to stand for two days. Decant and store in the fridge until ready for use (or you could freeze for longer if you wish).

49 Lemon and horseradish oil

	Makes 250 ml
lemons, rind	3 (no pith – the whitish layer between skin and fruit)
lemon grass stick, cut lengthways and chopped into 2 cm strips	1
grapeseed oil	250 ml
olive oil	2 tbsp
freshly grated horseradish	50 g

1 Place all the ingredients into a food processor, excluding the horseradish, and pulse the mix until the lemon peel and grass are approx 3 mm thick.
2 Add the horseradish and allow to stand for two days. Decant and store in the refrigerator until ready for use (or you can freeze for longer if you wish).

Note: Uses include fish dishes and salads.

50 Herb oil

	Makes 200 ml
picked flat leaf parsley	25 g
chives	10 g
picked basil leaves	10 g
picked spinach	100 g
corn oil	250 ml

1 Blanch all the herbs and spinach for 1½ minutes.
2 Drain well, place with the oil in a liquidiser and blitz for 2½ minutes. Pass and decant when rested.

Note: Uses include salads, salmon micuit and other fish dishes.

51 Vanilla oil

	Makes 200 ml
vegetable oil	200 ml
vanilla pods, whole	5
vanilla pods, used	2
vanilla extract	50 ml

1 Warm the oil to around 60°C, add the vanilla in its various forms and infuse, scraping all the seeds into the oil. Store in a plastic bottle.

Note: Uses include salads, salmon micuit and other fish dishes.

52 Smoked oil

	Makes 200 ml
vegetable chippings	200 ml
wood chippings	200 g
oil	200 ml

1 Place all the chippings into a pan and start to smoke. Once you see a little smoke rising, remove from the heat.
2 Place the oil into a bowl and then put this bowl into the pan. Cover with a damp cloth and allow the smoking process to proceed for 30 minutes, using the residual heat in the pan.
3 When ready, allow the oil to cool then store.

Note: Uses include fish dishes and salads.

53 Parsley oil

	Makes 200 ml
picked flat leaf parsley	75 g
picked spinach	50 g
corn oil	250 ml

1 Blanch the parsley and spinach for 1½ minutes, drain well and place with the oil in a liquidiser.
2 Liquidise for 2½ minutes, place in the fridge and allow the sediment to settle overnight.
3 The next day, decant when rested and use.

Note: Uses include fish and meat dishes.

Soups

The history of soup

'Our modern word 'soup' derives from the Old French words *sope* and *soupe*. The French word was used in England in the form of 'sop' at the end of the Middle Ages and, fortunately, has remained in the English language in its original form and with much of its original sense.

'Fortunately' because it is clear that nowadays a 'sop' is not a 'soup'. The distinction is important. When cooks in the Middle Ages spoke of 'soup', what they and the people for whom they were cooking really understood was a dish comprising primarily a piece of bread or toast soaked in a liquid or over which a liquid had been poured. The bread or toast was an important, even vital, part of this dish. It was a means by which the diner could consume the liquid efficiently by sopping it up. The bread or toast was, in effect, an alternative to using a spoon. Soups were important in the medieval diet, but the dish that the cook prepared was often a sop that consisted of both nutritious liquid and the means to eat it. The meal at the end of a normal day was always the lighter of the two meals of the day, and the sop appears to have had an important place in it. In fact it was precisely because of the normal inclusion of a sop in this end-of-the-day meal that it came to be called 'souper' or 'supper'.

Originally soup was basic sustenance and in most houses it would be a one-pot meal that would consist of scrag ends of meat, vegetables, pulses and roots, which would be left cooking for a while to extract lots of flavour. Soups can almost be classified as a lighter style of stew, but basically a soup was a meal in itself, with a generous chunk of bread and a warm hearth to enjoy it by. These hearty soups are still with us today – for example, Scotch broth, minestrone, bouillabaisse, pea and ham, chowder, and many more – some of which are explained below.

More sophisticated dining concepts have altered the role of soups and more restaurant chefs are offering a lighter slant to the soup approach. Classically, 15 or 20 years ago most soups were thickened by either purée or by roux, the latter seemed to be most used. Nowadays the approach is lighter with a reduction in flour and fat, offering a most sophisticated dish.

There are many ways to classify soup, whether it be a classic velouté thickened with a liaison, a purée of lentils with ham hock stock or a broth with a clear liquid; even the crystal clarity of consommé still graces our modern restaurant tables. However, the fundamental foundation of today's dining is a lighter and more sophisticated approach. Therefore, a combination of the above, with a careful approach to thickening, will yield a modern and up-to-date soup.

The principles of soup making

Though the perfection of soups can take experience, the basic principles of soup-making are quite simple to follow.

Most soup-making begins by preparing a stock (see above) made by the slow simmering of vegetables with seasonings, then straining the liquid. Stock can come in as many variations as there are meats (e.g. chicken, beef, turkey, veal, fish, lobster).

The underlying flavours of a broth's foundation ingredients are enhanced by the herbs and seasonings added. In many cases, this flavour base begins by preparing a mixture of flavouring elements cooked in a little fat or oil; because of their aromatic properties and flavours, most soups begin this phase with a combination of onion, garlic, leeks and carrots (this is called a mirepoix) or aromats.

The resulting broth is the foundation of all soups. From this point meat, fish, vegetables, fruits, seasonings, fats like butter or cream, and vegetables or dried pulses are added in countless variations to create the wealth of soups available today.

Health-conscious eaters should look for clear broth soups containing vegetables, beans and lean protein like chicken, fish or lean beef. Italian minestrone, bouillabaisse and gazpacho are excellent choices, and cream-based soups can often be adapted to fit a more healthful menu.

Types of soup

- **Bisque:** a very rich soup with a creamy consistency; usually made of lobster or shellfish (crab, shrimp, etc.).
- **Bouillabaisse:** a Mediterranean fish soup/stew, made of multiple types of seafood, olive oil, water, and seasonings like garlic, onions, tomato and parsley.
- **Chowder:** a hearty North American soup, usually with a seafood base.
- **Consommé:** a definitively clear double or triple broth (broth added to another broth) with a meat, rather than bone, base; consommé is painstakingly strained to make it clear.
- **Dashi:** the Japanese equivalent of consommé; made of giant seaweed, or *konbu*, dried bonito and water.
- **Gazpacho:** a Spanish tomato-vegetable soup served ice cold.
- **Minestrone:** an Italian vegetable-based soup.
- **Potage:** a French term referring to a thick soup.
- **Puréed soup:** a soup of vegetable base that has been puréed in a food mill or blender; typically altered after milling with the addition of broth, cream, butter, sour cream or coconut milk.
- **Velouté:** a velvety French sauce made with stock; synonymous with soup in many cases and thickened with a liaison (see thickenings, below).
- **Vichyssoise:** a simple, flavourful puréed potato and leek soup, thickened with the potato itself. Traditionally this is leek and potato soup, if served hot a little cream or crème fraiche may be added to give a richness to the soup; however, served cold, it is classified as vichyssoise and if fat is added to this preparation the dish would leave a fatty residue on the palate and offer a less than clear mouth feel.

Soups may be served for luncheon, dinner, supper and snack meals. A portion is usually between 200 and 250 ml, depending on the type of soup and the number of courses to follow.

Table 3.3 ✎   Guide to soups, their preparation and presentation

Soup classification	Base	Passed or unpassed?	Finish	Example
clear	stock	strained	usually garnished	consommé
broth	stock cut vegetables	unpassed	chopped parsley	Scotch broth minestrone
purée	stock fresh vegetables pulses	passed	croutons	lentil soup potato soup
velouté	blond roux vegetables stock	passed	liaison of yolk and cream	velouté of chicken
cream	stock and vegetables vegetable purée and béchamel velouté	passed	cream, milk or yoghurt	cream of vegetable cream of fresh pea cream of tomato
bisque	shellfish fish stock	passed	cream	lobster soup
miscellaneous (soups that are not classified under the above headings), e.g. chowders			mulligatawny mussel	Recipes will be found in Advanced Practical Cookery*

* *Advanced Practical Cookery: A Textbook For Education and Industry* (4th edn) by John Campbell, David Foskett and Victor Ceserani, Hodder, 2006

54 Clear soup (consommé) (basic recipe)

Cal	Cal	Fat	Sat Fat	Carb	Sugar	Protein	Fibre
126 KJ	30 kcal	0.0 g	0.0 g	1.8 g	0.0 g	5.6 g	0.0 g

	4 portions	10 portions
chopped or minced beef	200 g	500 g
salt, to taste		
egg whites	1–2	3–5
cold white or brown		
beef stock	1 litre	2½ litres
mixed vegetables		
(onion, carrot, celery, leek)	100 g	250 g
bouquet garni		
peppercorns	3–4	8–10

1 Thoroughly mix the beef, salt, egg white and a quarter of the cold stock in a thick-bottomed pan.
2 Peel, wash and finely chop the vegetables.
3 Add to the beef with the remainder of the stock, the bouquet garni and the peppercorns.
4 Place over a gentle heat and bring slowly to the boil, stirring occasionally.
5 Allow to boil rapidly for 5–10 seconds. Give a final stir.
6 Lower the heat so that the consommé is simmering very gently.
7 Cook for 1½–2 hours without stirring.
8 Strain carefully through a double muslin.
9 Remove all fat, using both sides of 8 cm square pieces of kitchen paper.
10 Correct the seasoning and colour, which should be a delicate amber.
11 Degrease again, if necessary. Bring to the boil and serve.

Note: A consommé should be crystal clear. The clarification process is caused by the albumen of the egg white and meat coagulating, rising to the top of the liquid and carrying other solid ingredients. The remaining liquid beneath the coagulated surface should be gently simmering. Cloudiness is due to some or all of the following:

- poor-quality stock
- greasy stock
- unstrained stock
- imperfect coagulation of the clearing agent
- whisking after boiling point is reached, whereby the impurities mix with the liquid
- not allowing the soup to settle before straining
- lack of cleanliness of the pan or cloth
- any trace of grease or starch.

HEALTHY EATING TIP

- This soup is fat free!
- Keep the salt to a minimum and serve as a low-calorie starter for anyone watching their weight.

Variations

- Consommés are varied in many ways by altering the flavour of the stock (chicken, chicken and beef, game, etc.), also by the addition of numerous garnishes (julienne or brunoise of vegetables – shredded savoury pancakes or pea-sized profiteroles) added at the last moment before serving, or small pasta.
- Cold, lightly jellied consommés, served in cups, with or without garnish (diced tomato), may be served in hot weather.

Figure 3.1 Mixing the ingredients for consommé

Figure 3.2 Clarification of consommé

55 Chicken consommé

onion	150 g
carrot	100 g
oil	
celery	100 g
leek	50 g
chicken wings, chopped small	1 kg
Noilly Prat	350 ml
thyme	2 g
bay leaf	1
water	2 litres

1 Sprinkle the onion and carrot lightly with oil and roast until a light brown.
2 Add celery and leek, and roast lightly.
3 In a separate tray roast the chicken wings until well browned.
4 Deglaze with the Noilly Prat and reduce.
5 Add the vegetables, herbs and water. Simmer for 15 minutes.
6 Cover with a lid and allow to infuse for 30 minutes.
7 Correct the seasoning, strain, skim and clarify.

56 Mutton broth

Cal 410 KJ	Cal 100 kcal	Fat 4.5 g	Sat Fat 2.0 g	Carb 8.5 g	Sugar 2.8 g	Protein 6.8 g	Fibre 1.0 g

	4 portions	10 portions
scrag end of mutton	200 g	500 g
water, or mutton or lamb stock	1 litre	2½ litre
barley	25 g	60 g
vegetables (carrot, turnip, leek, celery, onion), chopped	200 g	500 g
bouquet garni		
salt, pepper		
chopped parsley		

1 Place the mutton, free from fat, in a saucepan and cover with cold water.
2 Bring to the boil, immediately wash off under running water.
3 Clean the pan, replace the meat, cover with cold water, bring to the boil and skim.
4 Add the washed barley, simmer for 1 hour.
5 Add the vegetables, bouquet garni and seasoning.
6 Skim when necessary; simmer until tender for approximately 30 minutes.
7 Remove the meat, allow to cool and cut from the bone, remove all fat and cut the meat into neat dice the same size as the vegetables; return to the broth.
8 Correct the seasoning, skim off all the fat, add the chopped parsley and serve.

HEALTHY EATING TIP

- Remove all fat from the meat and skim any fat from the finished dish.
- Use only a small amount of salt.
- There are lots of healthy vegetables in this dish and the addition of a large bread roll will increase the starchy carbohydrate.

Variations

- *Scotch broth:* use beef stock in place of mutton. Barley and vegetable garnish is the same as for mutton broth.
- *Chicken broth:* use chicken stock, garnish with rice and vegetables.

57 Pulse soup (basic recipe) with croutons

Cal	Cal	Fat	Sat Fat	Carb	Sugar	Protein	Fibre	*
728 KJ	177 kcal	1.3 g	0.2 g	32.0 g	3.3 g	11.3 g	3.6 g	

	4 portions	10 portions
pulses (soaked overnight if necessary)	200 g	500 g
white stock or water	1½ litres	3¾ litres
onions, chopped	50 g	125 g
carrots, chopped	50 g	125 g
bouquet garni		
knuckle of ham or bacon (optional)	50 g	125 g
salt, pepper		
Croutons		
slice stale bread	1	2½
butter, margarine or oil	50 g	125 g

1 Pick and wash the pulse (if pre-soaked, change the water).
2 Place in a thick-bottomed pan; add the stock or water, bring to the boil and skim.
3 Add the remainder of ingredients, season lightly.
4 Simmer until tender; skim when necessary.
5 Remove the bouquet garni and ham.
6 Liquidise and pass through a conical strainer.
7 Return to a clean pan and reboil; correct the seasoning and consistency.
8 Serve accompanied by ½ cm diced bread croutons shallow-fried in butter.

Note: Any type of pulse can be made into soup – for example, split green and yellow peas, haricot beans and lentils. Serve accompanied by ½ cm diced bread croutons shallow-fried in butter or oil.

HEALTHY EATING TIP
- The fat and salt are reduced if the ham is omitted.
- Try lightly brushing the stale bread with olive oil and oven baking with garlic and herbs. Alternatively, serve with sippets.

* 1 portion (no croutons). 1 portion (with croutons) provides: 1223 kJ/291 kcal Energy; 111.7 g Fat; 6.8 g Sat Fat; 36.5 g Carb; 3.6 g Sugar; 12.1 g Protein; 3.8 g Fibre
Variations
Variations can be made with the addition of:
- chopped fresh herbs (parsley, chervil, tarragon, coriander, chives, etc.)
- spice(s) (e.g. garam masala)
- crisp lardons of bacon
- toasted sippets.

58 Cream of green pea soup (crème St Germain)

Cal	Cal	Fat	Sat Fat	Carb	Sugar	Protein	Fibre
1356 KJ	323 kcal	23.6 g	12.8 g	19.6 g	8.0 g	9.3 g	8.3 g

	4 portions	10 portions
onion	25 g	60 g
leek	25 g	60 g
celery	25 g	60 g
butter, margarine or oil	25 g	60 g
water or white stock	500 ml	1½ litres
peas, fresh (shelled) or frozen	250 ml	625 ml
sprig of mint		
bouquet garni		
thin béchamel	500 ml	1½ litres
cream, natural yoghurt or fromage frais	60 ml	150 ml

Figure 3.3 Cream of green pea soup

1 Sweat the onion, leek and celery in the butter.
2 Moisten with water or stock and bring to the boil.
3 Add the peas, mint and bouquet garni, and allow to boil for approximately 5 minutes.
4 Remove the bouquet garni, add the béchamel and bring to the boil.
5 Remove from the heat and liquidise or pass through a sieve. Skim off any fat.
6 Correct seasoning, pass through medium strainer.
7 Finish with cream, natural yoghurt or fromage frais.

Note: Fresh or frozen peas can be used.

Variations

Variations can be made with the addition of:
- a garnish of 25 g cooked and washed tapioca, added at the same time as the cream
- a garnish of 25 g cooked and washed vermicelli and julienne of sorrel cooked in butter
- natural yoghurt, skimmed milk or non-dairy cream may be used in place of cream
- see also the variations listed under pulse soup (recipe 57).

HEALTHY EATING TIP
- Use an unsaturated oil (sunflower or olive). Lightly oil the pan and drain off any excess after the frying is complete.
- Season with the minimum amount of salt.

59 Potato soup (purée parmentier)

Cal 1063 KJ	Cal 253 kcal	Fat 15.7 g	Sat Fat 9.8 g	Carb 26.1 g	Sugar 2.1 g	Protein 3.6 g	Fibre 2.9 g	*

	4 portions	10 portions
butter, margarine or oil	25 g	60 g
onion	50 g	125 g
white of leek	50 g	125 g
white stock or water	1 litre	2½ litres
peeled potatoes	400 g	1½ kg
bouquet garni		
salt, pepper		
parsley, chopped		
Croutons		
slice stale bread	1	3
butter, margarine or oil	50 g	125 g

1 Melt the butter or margarine in a thick-bottomed pan.
2 Add the peeled and washed sliced onion and leek, cook for a few minutes without colour with the lid on.
3 Add the stock, the peeled, washed and sliced potatoes and the bouquet garni. Season.
4 Simmer for approximately 30 minutes. Remove the bouquet garni, skim off all fat.
5 Liquidise or pass the soup firmly through a sieve then pass through a medium conical strainer.
6 Return to a clean pan, reboil, correct the seasoning and consistency, and serve.
7 Sprinkle with chopped parsley. Serve fried or toasted croutons separately.

HEALTHY EATING TIP
- Use an unsaturated oil (sunflower or olive). Lightly oil the pan and drain off any excess after the frying is complete.
- Season with the minimum amount of salt.
- Serve with toasted croutons.

* *Using butter*

60 Potato and watercress soup (purée cressonnière)

Ingredients as for potato soup (recipe 59) plus a small bunch of watercress.

1 Pick off 12 neat leaves of watercress, plunge into a small pan of boiling water for 1–2 seconds. Refresh under cold water immediately; these leaves are to garnish the finished soup.

2 Add the remainder of the picked and washed watercress, including the thin stalks, to the soup at the same time as the potatoes.
3 Finish as for potato soup.

61 Leek and potato soup (potage de poireaux et pommes)

Cal	Cal	Fat	Sat Fat	Carb	Sugar	Protein	Fibre	*
531 KJ	126 kcal	5.3 g	3.3 g	16.7 g	6.3 g	3.9 g	4.2 g	

	4 portions	10 portions
leeks, trimmed and washed	400 g	1½ kg
butter, margarine or oil	25 g	60 g
white stock	750 ml	2 litres
bouquet garni		
potatoes	200 g	½ kg
salt, pepper		

1 Cut the white and light green of leek into ½ cm paysanne.
2 Slowly cook in the butter in a pan with the lid on until soft, but without colouring.
3 Add the stock, the bouquet garni and the potatoes cut into ½ cm paysanne, 2 mm thick, and season with salt and pepper.
4 Simmer until the leeks and potatoes are cooked – approximately 15 minutes.

Note: This soup can be enriched by adding 25–50 g of butter and 1/16 litre of cream and stirring, just before serving.

HEALTHY EATING TIP
• Use an unsaturated oil (sunflower or olive). Lightly oil the pan and drain off any excess after the frying is complete.
• Season with the minimum amount of salt.
• Try using natural yoghurt or fromage frais to finish the soup.

* Using butter

62 Chive and potato soup (vichyssoise)

Cal	Cal	Fat	Sat Fat	Carb	Sugar	Protein	Fibre	*
949 KJ	228 kcal	15.0 g	9.3 g	20.3 g	3.2 g	4.1 g	1.8 g	

	4 portions	10 portions
butter, margarine or oil	25 g	60 g
onions, peeled, washed and sliced	50 g	125 g
white of leek, washed and sliced	50 g	125 g
potatoes, peeled, washed and sliced	400 g	1½ kg
white stock	1 litre	2½ litres
bouquet garni		
salt, pepper		
cream	125–250 ml	500 ml
chives, chopped		

1 Melt the butter, margarine or oil in a thick-bottomed pan.
2 Add the onion and leek, cook for a few minutes without colour, with the lid on.

3 Add the stock, potatoes and bouquet garni. Season.
4 Simmer for approximately 30 minutes. Remove the bouquet garni, skim.
5 Liquidise or pass the soup firmly through a sieve, then through a medium conical strainer.
6 Return to a clean pan and reboil; correct the seasoning and consistency, skim off any fat.
7 Finish with cream and garnish with chopped chives, either raw or cooked in a little butter. Usually served chilled.

HEALTHY EATING TIP

- Use an unsaturated oil (sunflower or olive). Lightly oil the pan and drain off any excess after the frying is complete.
- Season with the minimum amount of salt.
- Try using natural yoghurt or fromage frais to finish the soup.

* Using 200 ml single cream

63 Gazpacho

	4 portions	10 portions
plum tomatoes, ripe	2½ kg	6.25 kg
white onion, roughly chopped	1	2
cucumber, peeled and roughly chopped	1	2
garlic clove, crushed	½	1
red peppers, peeled and deseeded	550 g	1.3 kg
salt	40 g	80 g
cayenne pepper	2 g	5 g
Chardonnay vinegar or white wine vinegar	6 g	15 g
sugar (to taste, depending on season)	30 g	75 g

1 Mix all the ingredients together and leave to marinate overnight in the fridge.
2 Next day, blitz the ingredients in a food processor and strain through a chinois.
3 Discard the remaining pulp into a colander lined with muslin (this is to catch the extra juices that will come from the pulp).
4 The juices from the pulp can be used to thin out the gazpacho until it reaches the correct consistency.
5 Check seasoning. Store in the refrigerator.

64 Tomato soup (potage de tomates)

Cal	Cal	Fat	Sat Fat	Carb	Sugar	Protein	Fibre	*
1150 KJ	274 kcal	21.3 g	11.2 g	17.1 g	3.7 g	4.6 g	1.0 g	

	4 portions	10 portions
butter, margarine or oil	50 g	125 g
bacon trimmings, optional	25 g	60 g
onion, diced	100 g	250 g
carrot, diced	100 g	250 g
flour	50 g	125 g
tomato purée	100 g	250 g
stock	1½ litres	3½ litres
bouquet garni		
salt, pepper		
Croutons		
slice stale bread	1	3
butter	50 g	125 g

1 Melt the butter, margarine or oil in a thick-bottomed pan.
2 Add the bacon, onion and carrot (mirepoix) and brown lightly.
3 Mix in the flour and cook to a sandy texture.
4 Remove from the heat, mix in the tomato purée.
5 Return to heat. Gradually add the hot stock.
6 Stir to the boil. Add the bouquet garni, season lightly.
7 Simmer for approximately 1 hour. Skim when required.
8 Remove the bouquet garni and mirepoix.
9 Liquidise or pass firmly through a sieve, then through a conical strainer.

10 Return to a clean pan, correct the seasoning and consistency. Bring to the boil.

11 Serve fried or toasted croutons separately.

Note: If a slight sweet/sour flavour is required, reduce 100 ml vinegar and 35 g caster sugar to a light caramel and mix into the completed soup. This is known as gastric or gastrique, and is prepared by heating the ingredients together until the mix has nearly evaporated.

HEALTHY EATING TIP

• Use soft margarine or sunflower/olive oil in place of the butter.
• Serve with toasted croutons.
• Use the minimum amount of salt – there is plenty in the bacon.

* *Using hard margarine*
Variations
Variations can be made with the addition of:
• juice and lightly grated zest of 1–2 oranges
• tomato concassée
• cooked rice
• chopped fresh coriander, basil or chives
• 200 g peeled, sliced potatoes with the stock.

65 Tomato soup *(crème de tomates fraiche)* (using fresh tomatoes)

1 Prepare the soup as for recipe 64, using 1 litre stock.

2 Substitute 1–1½ kg fresh fully ripe tomatoes for the tomato purée.

3 Remove the eyes from the tomatoes, wash them well, and squeeze them into the soup after the stock has been added and has come to the boil.

4 If colour is lacking, add a little tomato purée soon after the soup comes to the boil.

Note: Flour may be omitted from recipe if a thinner soup is required.

66 Cream of tomato soup *(crème de tomates)*

1 Prepare the soup as for recipe 64, using 1 litre stock.

2 When finally reboiling the finished soup, add ½ litre of milk or ⅛ litre of cream or yoghurt.

HEALTHY EATING TIP

• Use semi-skimmed milk and finish with natural yoghurt or fromage frais.

67 Roasted red pepper and tomato soup

Cal	Cal	Fat	Sat Fat	Carb	Sugar	Protein	Fibre	Salt
983 KJ	235 kcal	16.8 g	7.1 g	18.3 g	16.4 g	3.6 g	4.5 g	2.1 g

(To serve 4 or 10 people)

	4	10
red peppers	4	10
tomatoes	400 g	1.25 kg
butter, margarine or oil	50 g	125 g
onion, chopped	100 g	250 g
carrot	100 g	250 g
stock	500 ml	1.5 litres
	(2 tbsp)	(5 tbsp)
basil	25 g	75 g

1 Core and de-seed the peppers and halve the tomatoes.
2 Lightly sprinkle with oil and place on a tray into a hot oven or under a grill until the pepper skins are blackened.
3 Allow the peppers to cool in a plastic bag.
4 Remove the skins and slice the flesh.
5 Place the fat or oil in a pan, add the onions and carrots and fry gently for five minutes.
6 Add stock, peppers and tomatoes, bring to the boil.
7 Simmer for 30 minutes, correct seasoning and blend in a food processor until smooth.
8 Add crème fraîche and basil leaves torn into pieces and serve with croutons.

68 Brown onion soup *(soupe à l'oignon)*

Cal	Cal	Fat	Sat Fat	Carb	Sugar	Protein	Fibre	*
197 KJ	827 kcal	9.7 g	5.8 g	20.4 g	8.1 g	0.3 g	3.1 g	

Figure 3.4 ✎ French onion soup

	4 portions	10 portions
onions	600 g	1.5 kg
butter or margarine	25 g	65 g
clove of garlic, chopped (optional)	1	3
flour, white or wholemeal	10 g	25 g
brown stock	1 litre	2.5 litres
salt, mill pepper		
flute (French loaf)	½	1
grated cheese	50 g	125 g

1 Peel the onions, halve and slice finely.
2 Melt the butter in a thick-bottomed pan, add the onions and garlic, and cook steadily over a good heat until cooked and well browned.
3 Mix in the flour and cook over a gentle heat, browning slightly.
4 Gradually mix in the stock, bring to the boil, skim and season.
5 Simmer for approximately 10 minutes until the onion is soft. Correct the seasoning.
6 Pour into an earthenware tureen or casserole, or individual dishes.
7 Cut the flute into 2 cm diameter slices and toast on both sides.
8 Sprinkle the toasted slices of bread liberally over the top of the soup.
9 Sprinkle with grated cheese and brown under the salamander.
10 Place on a dish and serve.

* Using butter

69 Mushroom soup (crème de champignons)

Cal	Cal	Fat	Sat Fat	Carb	Sugar	Protein	Fibre	*
712 KJ	170 kcal	11.8 g	5.2 g	12.6 g	3.0 g	3.8 g	1.6 g	

	4 portions	10 portions
onion, leek and celery, sliced	100 g	250 g
margarine or oil	50 g	125 g
flour	50 g	125 g
white stock (preferably chicken)	1 litre	2½ litre
white mushrooms	200 g	500 g
bouquet garni		
salt, pepper		
milk (or cream)	125 ml or 60 ml cream	300 ml or 150 ml cream

1 Gently cook the sliced onions, leek and celery in the margarine or oil in a thick-bottomed pan without colouring.
2 Mix in the flour and cook over a gentle heat to a sandy texture without colouring.
3 Remove from the heat and cool slightly.
4 Gradually mix in the hot stock. Stir to the boil.
5 Add the well-washed, chopped mushrooms, the bouquet garni and season.
6 Simmer for 30–45 minutes. Skim when needed.
7 Remove the bouquet garni. Pass through a sieve or liquidise.
8 Pass through a medium strainer. Return to a clean saucepan.
9 Reboil, correct the seasoning and consistency; add the milk or cream.

Note: Natural yoghurt, skimmed milk or non-dairy cream may be used in place of dairy cream. A garnish of thinly sliced mushrooms may be added. Wild mushrooms may also be used.

HEALTHY EATING TIP
- Use soft margarine or sunflower/olive oil in place of the butter.
- Use the minimum amount of salt.
- The least fatty option is to use semi-skimmed milk and yoghurt or fromage frais in place of the cream.

* Using hard margarine

70 Chicken soup (crème de volaille or crème reine)

Cal	Cal	Fat	Sat Fat	Carb	Sugar	Protein	Fibre	*
836 KJ	199 kcal	13.6 g	6.2 g	14.0 g	4.2 g	5.9 g	1.0 g	

	4 portions	10 portions
onion, leek and celery	100 g	250 g
butter, margarine or oil	50 g	125 g
flour	50 g	125 g
chicken stock	1 litre	2½ litres
bouquet garni		
salt, pepper		
milk or cream	250 ml or 125 ml	625 ml or 300 ml
cooked dice of chicken (garnish)	25 g	60 g

1 Gently cook the sliced onions, leek and celery in a thick-bottomed pan, in the butter, margarine or oil without colouring.
2 Mix in the flour; cook over a gentle heat to a sandy texture without colouring.
3 Cool slightly; gradually mix in the hot stock. Stir to the boil.
4 Add the bouquet garni and season.
5 Simmer for 30–45 minutes; skim when necessary. Remove the bouquet garni.
6 Liquidise or pass firmly through a fine strainer.
7 Return to a clean pan, reboil and finish with milk or cream; correct the seasoning.
8 Add the chicken garnish and serve.

Note: Natural yoghurt, skimmed milk or non-dairy cream may be used in place of dairy cream. Add cooked small pasta or sliced mushrooms for variations.

HEALTHY EATING TIP
- Use soft margarine or sunflower/olive oil in place of the butter.
- Use the minimum amount of salt.
- The least fatty option is to use semi-skimmed milk and yoghurt or fromage frais in place of the cream.

* Using hard margarine

71 Vegetable soup (purée de légumes)

Cal	Cal	Fat	Sat Fat	Carb	Sugar	Protein	Fibre	*
1106 KJ	263 kcal	20.7 g	11.1 g	17.2 g	3.7 g	3.1 g	2.8 g	

	4 portions	10 portions
mixed vegetables (onion, carrot, turnip, leek, celery)	300 g	1 kg
butter, margarine or oil	50 g	125 g
flour	25 g	60 g
white stock	1 litre	2½ litres
potatoes, sliced	100 g	300 g
bouquet garni		
salt, pepper		
Croutons		
slice stale bread	1	3
butter	50 g	125 g

1 Peel, wash and slice all the vegetables (except the potatoes).
2 Cook gently in the butter or margarine in a covered pan, without colouring.
3 Mix in the flour and cook slowly for a few minutes without colouring; cool slightly.

4 Mix in the hot stock. Stir and bring to the boil.
5 Add the sliced potatoes and bouquet garni. Season. Simmer for 30–45 minutes; skim when necessary. Remove the bouquet garni.
6 Liquidise or pass through a sieve and then through a medium strainer.
7 Return to a clean pan and reboil; correct the seasoning and the consistency.
8 Serve with croutons separately.

Note: For variations see pulse soup (recipe 57).

HEALTHY EATING TIP
- Use soft margarine or sunflower/olive oil in place of the butter.
- Serve with toasted croutons and the minimum amount of salt.

* Using hard margarine

72 Cream of vegetable soup (crème de légumes)

Ingredients and method are as for vegetable soup (recipe 71). Either replace ½ litre stock with ½ litre béchamel; or finish with milk or ⅛ litre cream (see note in recipe 70), simmer for 5 minutes and serve as for vegetable soup.

73 Basic soup recipe for purées

Cal 601 KJ	Cal 143 kcal	Fat 4.4 g	Sat Fat 4.4 g	Carb 11.4 g	Sugar 1.8 g	Protein 1.9 g	Fibre 0.0 g	*

	4 portions	10 portions
onions, leek and celery, sliced	100 g	250 g
other suitable vegetables,* sliced	200 g	500 g
butter, margarine or oil	50 g	125 g
flour	50 g	125 g
white stock or water	1 litre	2½ litres
bouquet garni		
salt, pepper		

* Suitable vegetables include Jerusalem artichokes, cauliflower, celery, leeks, onions, parsnips, turnips and fennel

1 Gently cook all the sliced vegetables in the fat under a lid, without colour.
2 Mix in the flour and cook slowly for a few minutes without colour. Cool slightly.
3 Gradually mix in the hot stock. Stir to the boil.
4 Add the bouquet garni and season.
5 Simmer for approximately 45 minutes; skim when necessary.

6 Remove the bouquet garni; liquidise or pass firmly through a sieve and then through a medium strainer.
7 Return to a clean pan, reboil, and correct the seasoning and consistency.

Note: For cream soups see the note in recipe 70.

Variations
● Add a little spice, sufficient to give a subtle background flavour, e.g. garam masala with parsnip soup.
● Just before serving add a little freshly chopped herb(s), e.g. parsley, chervil, tarragon, coriander.

HEALTHY EATING TIP

• Use an unsaturated oil (sunflower or olive) to lightly oil the pan. Drain off any excess after the frying is complete and skim the fat from the finished dish.
• Season with the minimum amount of salt.
• Try using more vegetables to thicken the soup in place of the flour.

Using hard margarine

74 Basic soup for creams

Suitable vegetables as for basic soup for purées (recipe 73).

As basic recipe but in place of ½ litre stock use ½ litre thin béchamel or use ⅛–½ litre less stock and finish with ½ litre milk or ⅛ litre of cream.

75 Asparagus soup (crème d'asperges)

Cal	Cal	Fat	Sat Fat	Carb	Sugar	Protein	Fibre	*
1515 KJ	361 kcal	25.3 g	11.9 g	27.1 g	8.1 g	7.7 g	2.5 g	

	4 portions	10 portions
onion, sliced	50 g	125 g
celery, sliced	50 g	125 g
butter, oil or margarine	50 g	125 g
flour	50 g	125 g
white stock (preferably chicken)	1 litre	2½ litres
asparagus stalk trimmings	200 g	500 g
or		
tin of asparagus	150 g	325 g
bouquet garni		
salt, pepper		
milk or cream	250 ml or 125 ml	625 ml or 300 ml

1 Gently sweat the onions and celery, without colouring, in the butter or margarine.
2 Remove from the heat, mix in the flour, return to a low heat and cook out, without colouring, for a few minutes. Cool.
3 Gradually add the hot stock. Stir to the boil.
4 Add the well-washed asparagus trimmings, or the tin of asparagus, and bouquet garni. Season.
5 Simmer for 30–40 minutes then remove bouquet garni.
6 Liquidise and pass through a strainer.
7 Return to a clean pan, reboil, correct seasoning and consistency.
8 Add the milk or cream and serve.

Note: See the note in recipe 70.

HEALTHY EATING TIP

• Use an unsaturated oil (sunflower/olive) to lightly oil the pan. Drain off any excess after the frying is complete and skim the fat from the finished dish.
• Season with the minimum amount of salt.
• Milk with a little cornflour can be added to achieve the desired consistency.

* Using hard margarine. Using butter, 1 portion provides: 919 kJ/223 kcal Energy; 13.1 g Fat; 8.0 g Sat Fat; 18.9 g Carb; 8.8 g Sugar; 8.4 g Protein; 2.5 g Fibre

76 Roasted butternut squash soup

Cal	Cal	Fat	Sat Fat	Carb	Sugar	Protein	Fibre	*
923 KJ	220 kcal	12.0 g	3.5 g	19.6 g	13.1 g	9.9 g	2.8 g	

	4 portions	10 portions
butternut squash, peeled and deseeded	600 g	2 kg
olive oil	2 tbsp	5 tbsp
onion, finely chopped	100 g	250 g
garlic (optional), finely chopped	1 clove	2 cloves
bacon, back rashers, in small pieces	4	10
chicken or vegetable stock	625 ml	1½ litres
salt, pepper		
cream or thick natural yoghurt	6 tbsp	15 tbsp

1 Cut the squash into thick pieces, place on a lightly oiled baking sheet and roast for 20–25 minutes in a hot oven until the flesh is soft and golden brown.
2 Sweat the onions and garlic without colouring (approx. 5 minutes).
3 Add the bacon and lightly brown.
4 Add the roasted squash, pour in the stock, bring to the boil and simmer for 20 minutes.
5 Allow to cool, then liquidise or blend until smooth.
6 Season lightly, add yoghurt or cream, reheat gently and serve.

HEALTHY EATING TIP

- Use an unsaturated oil (sunflower or olive) and lightly oil the pan to sweat the garlic and onions. Drain off any excess fat after cooking the bacon.
- Use low-fat yoghurt to reduce the fat.
- Add a little cornflour to stabilise the yoghurt before adding to the soup.

Variation
Add 3–4 saffron strands soaked in 1 tbsp hot water at point 4.

77 Minestrone

Cal	Cal	Fat	Sat Fat	Carb	Sugar	Protein	Fibre	*
1115 KJ	265 kcal	22.9 g	5.8 g	11.9 g	4.2 g	3.8 g	4.1 g	

Figure 3.5 Minestrone soup

	4 portions	10 portions
mixed vegetables (onion, leek, celery, carrot, turnip, cabbage)	300 g	750 g
butter, margarine or oil	50 g	125 g
white stock or water	½ litre	2 litres
bouquet garni		
salt, pepper		
peas	25 g	60 g
French beans	25 g	60 g
spaghetti	25 g	60 g
potatoes	50 g	125 g
tomato purée	1 tsp	3 tsp
tomatoes, skinned, deseeded, diced	100 g	250 g
fat bacon	optional	
chopped parsley	50 g	125 g
clove garlic	1	2½

1 Cut the peeled and washed mixed vegetables into paysanne.
2 Cook slowly without colour in the oil or fat in the pan with a lid on.
3 Add the stock, bouquet garni and seasoning; simmer for approximately 20 minutes.
4 Add the peas and the beans cut into diamonds and simmer for 10 minutes.
5 Add the spaghetti in 2 cm lengths, the potatoes cut into paysanne, the tomato purée and the tomatoes, and simmer gently until all the vegetables are cooked.
6 Meanwhile finely chop the fat bacon, parsley and garlic, and form into a paste.
7 Mould the paste into pellets the size of a pea and drop into the boiling soup.
8 Remove the bouquet garni, correct the seasoning.
9 Serve grated Parmesan cheese and thin toasted flute (French loaf) slices separately.

HEALTHY EATING TIP

- Use an unsaturated oil (sunflower or olive) to lightly oil the pan. Drain off any excess after the frying is complete and skim the fat from the finished dish.
- Season with the minimum amount of salt as the bacon and cheese are high in salt.

* *Using sunflower oil*

Chowders

Chowders are American-style fish soups, usually made from shellfish. The most popular is clam chowder.

78 New England clam chowder

Cal 1109 KJ	Cal 269 kcal	Fat 14.9 g	Sat Fat 7.7 g	Carb 24.5 g	Sugar 2.5 g	Protein 14.9 g	Fibre 1.8 g	*

8 portions

salt pork, cut into ½ cm dice	100 g
onion, finely chopped	100 g
cold water	625 ml
potatoes, cut into ½ cm dice	1 kg
fresh trimmed clams, or 2 × 200 g tins, and their juices	400 g
cream	375 ml
thyme, crushed or chopped	1/8 tsp
salt, white pepper	
butter	25 g
paprika	

1 Dry-fry the pork in a thick-bottomed saucepan for about 3 minutes, stirring constantly until a thin film of fat covers the bottom of the pan.

2 Stir in the chopped onion and cook gently until a light golden brown.

3 Add the water and potatoes, bring to the boil and simmer gently until the potatoes are cooked but not mushy.

4 Add the chopped clams and their juice, the cream and thyme, and heat until almost boiling. Season with salt and pepper.

5 Correct the seasoning, stir in the softened butter and serve, dusting each soup bowl with a little paprika.

Note: The traditional accompaniment is salted cracker biscuits. An obvious variation would be to use scallops in place of clams.

* Using bacon or salt pork

79 Red lentil soup

Cal 1807 KJ	Cal 432 kcal	Fat 71.4 g	Sat Fat 43.9 g	Carb 6.7 g	Sugar 1.5 g	Protein 5.3 g	Fibre 1.5 g	Salt 2.2 g

approximately 10 portions

For the ham hock	
	1 ham hock 800 g
onion, peeled	½
whole carrot, peeled	1
For the soup	
baby shallots	3
leek	½
stick celery	½
oil	100 ml
red lentils	500 g
cooking liquid from the hock	
milk, cream or crème fraiche	300 ml

1 Place the ham hock, onion and carrot in a pan and cover with water (approx. 3 l).

2 Bring to the boil and then turn down to a slow simmer. (To test that the hock is cooked the centre bone will slide out in one smooth motion.)

3 Slice the shallots, leek and celery into 1 cm dice.

4 Heat a pan with about 100 ml of oil, add the vegetables and cook until they are slightly coloured; add the lentils and cover them with the ham stock.

5 Bring to the boil then turn the heat down to a very slow simmer.

6 Cook until all the lentils have broken down.

7 Allow to cool for 10 minutes and then purée until smooth.

8 Correct the consistency as necessary, and finish with boiled milk, cream or crème fraiche.

80 Watercress soup

	4 portions	10 portions
oil	80 ml	200 ml
potatoes, chopped	240 g	600 g
leeks, chopped	90 g	240 g
shallots, chopped	120 g	300 g
garlic cloves (optional)	1	2
vegetable nage	1 litre	2½ litres
horseradish sauce	¾ tsp	1½ tbsp
spinach, picked and washed	300 g	750 g
watercress (½ stalk removed)	150 g	375 g

1 Heat 50 ml of the oil in a thick-bottomed pan.
2 Add the potatoes and cook without colour for 2 minutes.
3 Add the leeks, shallots and garlic, and cook for a further 4 minutes without colour.
4 Add the nage and horseradish, bring to the boil and simmer for 6 minutes, then remove from the stove.
5 Heat a clean pan, add the remainder of the oil and shock/wilt the spinach and watercress in a hot pan until the bitterness of the watercress is well rounded.
6 Add this to the liquid mix, liquidise until smooth and very green, pass through a conical strainer (not a chinois).
7 Allow to cool, then store.

81 Pea velouté

	4 portions	10 portions
frozen peas	400 g	1 kg
vegetable oil	4 ml	10 ml
shallots, chopped	1	2
milk	200 ml	500 ml
double cream	40 ml	100 ml
butter	40 g	100 g

1 Blanch the peas in a small pan of boiling water for 3 minutes, then drain.
2 Heat the oil in large saucepan and cook the shallots without letting them colour.
3 Add the peas to this pan, and cook for a further 2–3 minutes, again without colouring.
4 Add the milk, bring to a simmer and cook until the peas are tender.
5 Cool the mixture slightly, then transfer to a food processor and liquidise until very smooth – this may take a while. At this point, the soup can be cooled completely then stored in an airtight container in the refrigerator until ready to serve.
6 Add the cream and butter just before serving.

82 Squash/pumpkin velouté

Cal	Cal	Fat	Sat Fat	Carb	Sugar	Protein	Fibre	Salt	*
2883 KJ	689 kcal	71.4 g	43.9 g	6.7 g	1.5 g	5.3 g	1.5 g	3.0 g	

	4 portions	10 portions
shallots, sliced	1	3
butter	320 g	800 g
clove garlic, sliced (optional)	½	1
large squash or pumpkin 300 g, flesh diced	1	2
Parmesan, grated	30 g	70 g
truffle oil	1 tbsp	2 tbsp
salt, pepper		
chicken stock	400–600 ml	1–1½ litres

1 Sweat the shallots in 200 g butter, without colour, until cooked and soft.
2 Add the garlic, squash, Parmesan and truffle oil. Correct the seasoning and cook for 5 minutes.
3 Add the chicken stock, bring to the boil, simmer for 5 minutes.
4 Blitz, pass, correct seasoning, then blast chill if to be stored.

* Using acorn squash and olive oil

Mixed vegetable
salad

Terrine (page 99)

us salad
67)

chapter 4

COLD PREPARATION

NVQ

Unit 650 (2FPC15)   **Prepare and present food for cold preparation**

To prepare, cook and present a range of cold dishes, hors d'oeuvre, main dishes and salads

Practical skills
The candidate will be able to:
1. Demonstrate the correct use of equipment to prepare, cook and present cold dishes
2. Choose the appropriate ingredients
3. Prepare, cook and serve a range of hors d'oeuvre, salads and cold dishes
4. Demonstrate safe and hygienic practices
5. Evaluate the finished product

Underpinning knowledge
The candidate will be able to:
1. Identify the preparation methods needed to produce a range of cold dishes, salads and hors d'oeuvre
2. State the quality points needed to assess cold preparations
3. Explain the different preparation methods
4. Identify the various ingredients required to produce a range of cold dishes
5 Explain the various cooking methods and chilling principles used in preparing and serving cold dishes
6. Identify the correct storage procedures required when preparing a range of cold preparations

Cold food preparation (hors d'oeuvre, salads, cooked/cured/prepared foods)

Cold food is popular in every kind of food service operation for at least three good reasons:

1 **Visual appeal:** when the food is attractively displayed, carefully arranged and neatly garnished, the customers can have their appetites stimulated by seeing exactly what is being offered.
2 **Efficiency:** cold food can be prepared in advance, allowing a large number of people to be served in a short space of time. Self-service is also economic in terms of staffing.
3 **Adaptability:** if cold food is being served from a buffet, the range of foods can be simple or complex and wide-ranging, depending on the type of operation.

Cold foods can either be pre-plated or served from large dishes and bowls. In both cases presentation is important: the food should appear fresh, neatly arranged and not over-garnished.

Health, safety and hygiene

For information on maintaining a safe and secure working environment, a professional and hygienic appearance, and clean food production areas, equipment and utensils, as well as food hygiene, please refer to Chapters 17 and 18. Additional health and safety points are as follows.

- Where possible use plastic gloves when handling food.
- Keep unprepared and prepared food under refrigeration at a temperature not exceeding 4–5°C. Refrigeration will not kill the bacteria that are present in the foods, but does help to prevent their growth.
- Whenever possible, the food on display to the public should be kept under refrigeration and the temperature should be checked to ensure that it is being maintained at a safe level.
- Where customers are viewing the food closely, ideally it should be displayed behind a sneeze screen.
- Dishes prepared in advance should be covered with film and refrigerated at 1–3°C to prevent them drying out.
- Personal, food and equipment hygiene of the highest order must be observed with all cold work.

Cold preparations

Definition

The preparation of raw and/or cooked foods into a wide variety of cold items.

Purpose

The purpose of these dishes is:

- to add variety to the menu and diet by preparing food that has eye appeal, and is palatable and digestible
- to produce a variety of flavours and textures, and provide food that is particularly suitable for hot weather
- to prepare food that can be conveniently wrapped to take away.

Cold food characteristics

- Its appearance must be clean and fresh. Its presentation should be appealing to the eye – neither too colourful nor over-decorative – therefore stimulating the appetite.
- Its nutritional value is provided due to the mixture of raw and cooked foods.

Techniques associated with cold preparation

- **Peeling:** the removal of the outer skin of fruit or vegetables using a peeler or small knife, according to the thickness of the skin.
- **Chopping:** cutting into very small pieces (e.g. parsley, onions).
- **Cutting:** using a knife to divide food into the required shapes and sizes.
- **Carving:** cutting meat or poultry into slices.
- **Seasoning:** the light addition of salt, pepper and possibly other flavouring agents.
- **Dressing:** this can either mean an accompanying salad dressing, such as vinaigrette, or the arrangement of food for presentation on plates, dishes or buffets.
- **Garnishing:** the final addition to the dish, such

as lettuce, quarters of tomato and sliced cucumber added to egg mayonnaise.
- **Marinade:** a richly spiced pickling liquid used to give flavour and to assist in tenderising meats such as venison. Simple marinades (e.g. olive oil with herbs or soy sauce with herbs and/or spices) can be used with cuts of fish, chicken or meat.

Equipment

Bowls, tongs, whisks, spoons, and so on, as well as food processors, mixing machines and blenders are used with cold preparations.

Preparation for cold work

Well-planned organisation is essential to ensure adequate pre-preparation (*mise-en-place*), so that foods are assembled with a good work flow and are ready on time. Before, during and after assembling, and before final garnishing, foods must be kept in a cool place, cold room or refrigerator so as to minimise the risk of food contamination. Garnishing and final decoration should take place as close to the serving time as possible.

General rules

- Be aware of the texture and flavour of many raw foods that can be mixed together or combined with cooked foods (e.g. coleslaw, meat salad).
- Understand what combination of foods – for example, salads – is best suited to be served with other foods, such as cold meat or poultry.
- Develop simple artistic skills that require the minimum of time for preparation and assembly.
- Provide an attractive presentation of food at all times.
- Because of the requirements of food safety, cold foods are often served straight from the refrigerator. This is an error because, at refrigerator temperature, food flavours are not at their best. Individual portions should be

removed from refrigeration and allowed to
stand at room temperature for 5–10 minutes
before serving.

Types of hors d'oeuvre

The choice of a wide variety of foods,
combination of foods and recipes is available for
preparation and service as hors d'oeuvre and
salads. hors d'oeuvre can be divided into three
categories:

1 single cold food items (smoked salmon, pâté,
   melon, etc.)
2 a selection of well-seasoned cold dishes
3 well-seasoned hot dishes.

hors d'oeuvre may be served for luncheon, dinner
or supper, and the wide choice, colour appeal and
versatility of the dishes make many items and
combinations of items suitable for snacks and
salads at any time of day.

Salads may be served as an accompaniment to
hot and cold foods and as dishes in their own
right. They can be served for lunch, tea, high tea,
dinner, supper and snack meals. Salads may be
divided in two sections:

Figure 4.1 Salads may be served as an
accompaniment to hot and cold foods
and as dishes in their own right

1 simple, using one ingredient
2 mixed, or composite, using more than one
   ingredient.

Some salads may form part of a composite hors
d'oeuvre. Accompaniments include dressings and
cold sauces.

Dressings, cold sauces, chutneys and relishes

Salad dressings

These dressings may be varied by the addition of
other ingredients. Salads should be lightly dressed
or the dressing offered separately to give the
customer the choice.

1 Vinaigrette

Cal 1740 KJ	Cal 415 kcal	Fat 45.5 g	Sat Fat 6.3 g	Carb 0.5 g	Sugar 0.1 g	Protein 0.6 g	Fibre 0.0 g	*

	4–6 portions
olive oil, according to taste	3–6 tbsp
French mustard	1 tsp
vinegar	1 tbsp
salt, mill pepper, to taste	

Combine all the ingredients together.

** Using 3 tbsp oil, for 4–6 portions. Using 6 tbsp oil,
this recipe provides for 4–6 portions: 3439 kJ/415 kcal*

*Energy; 90.5 g Fat; 12.6 g Sat Fat; 0.5 g Carb; 0.1 g
Sugar; 0.6 g Protein; 0.0 g Fibre*

Variations
Variations to vinaigrette include:
- English mustard in place of French mustard
- chopped herbs (chives, parsley, tarragon, etc.)
- chopped hard-boiled egg
- other good-quality oils, e.g. sesame seed or walnut
- different flavoured vinegars or lemon juice.

2 Leek and mushroom vinaigrette

olive oil	250 ml
balsamic vinegar	50 ml
lemon juice	1 tbsp
shallot, freshly chopped	1
mushrooms, diced and cooked	100 g
seasoning	
leek julienne, blanched	100 g

1 Mix together the olive oil, vinegar and lemon juice.
2 Add the chopped shallot, mushrooms and seasoning.
3 Season further to taste.
4 Add the blanched julienne of leek.

Note: This vinaigrette is ideally served with terrine of bacon, spinach and mushrooms (see recipe 28).

3 Thousand Island dressing

Cal	Cal	Fat	Sat Fat	Carb	Sugar	Protein	Fibre	*
15065 KJ	3584 kcal	378.0 g	56.5 g	10.2 g	9.8 g	16.1 g	1.8 g	

4–6 portions

salt, pepper	
Tabasco	3–4 drops
vinegar	125 ml
oil	375 ml
red pimento, chopped	50 g
green pimento, chopped	50 g
parsley, chopped	
hard-boiled eggs, sieved	2
tomato ketchup (optional)	2 tbsp

1 Place the salt, pepper, Tabasco and vinegar in a basin.
2 Mix well. Mix in the oil.
3 Add the chopped pimentos and parsley.
4 Mix in the sieved hard-boiled eggs.
5 Mix in ketchup if desired.

* For 4–6 portions

Cold sauces

4 Mayonnaise sauce

Cal	Cal	Fat	Sat Fat	Carb	Sugar	Protein	Fibre	*
10030 KJ	2388 kcal	26.2 g	38.9 g	0.3 g	0.1 g	6.8 g	0.0 g	

8 portions

egg yolks, pasteurised	2
vinegar	2 tsp
salt, ground white pepper	
English or continental mustard	⅛ tsp
corn oil	250 ml
boiling water	1 tsp (approx.)

1 Place the yolks, vinegar and seasoning in a bowl and whisk well.
2 Gradually pour on the oil very slowly, whisking continuously.

3 Add the boiling water, whisking well. Correct the seasoning.

Notes: This is a basic cold sauce and has a wide variety of uses, particularly in hors d'oeuvre dishes. It should always be available on any cold buffet. Because of the risk of salmonella food poisoning it is strongly recommended that pasteurised egg yolks are used.

If, during the making of the sauce, it should become too thick, then a little vinegar or water may be added. Mayonnaise will turn or curdle for several reasons:

- if the oil is added too quickly
- if the oil is too cold
- if the sauce is insufficiently whisked
- if the yolk is stale and therefore weak.

The method used to rethicken a turned mayonnaise is either:

- by taking a clean basin, adding 1 teaspoon boiling water and gradually whisking in the curdled sauce, or

- by taking another yolk thinned with half a teaspoon of cold water whisked well, then gradually whisking in the curdled sauce.

Many ingredients can be used to vary mayonnaise, such as fresh herbs, garlic juice, Parmesan or blue cheese, red pepper purée and chopped sundried tomatoes. Lemon juice may be used in place of vinegar.

For 8 portions

5 Andalusian sauce (sauce andalouse)

Add to ¼ litre of mayonnaise, 2 tbsp tomato juice or ketchup and 1 tbsp pimento cut into julienne. Makes ¼ litre. May be served with cold salads.

6 Green sauce (Sauce verte)

	8 portions
spinach, tarragon, chervil, chives, watercress	50 g
mayonnaise	250 ml

1 Pick, wash, blanch and refresh the green leaves. Squeeze dry.
2 Pass through a very fine sieve. Mix with the mayonnaise.

Note: May be served with cold salmon or salmon trout.

7 Tartare sauce (sauce tartare)

Cal	Cal	Fat	Sat Fat	Carb	Sugar	Protein	Fibre
938 KJ	228 kcal	24.8 g	3.6 g	0.3 g	0.3 g	0.7 g	0.1 g

	8 portions
mayonnaise	250 ml
capers, chopped	25 g
gherkins	50 g
sprig of parsley, chopped	

HEALTHY EATING TIP
- Proportionally reduce the fat by adding some low-fat yoghurt.

Combine all the ingredients.

Note: This sauce is usually served with deep-fried fish.

8 Remoulade sauce (sauce remoulade)

Cal	Cal	Fat	Sat Fat	Carb	Sugar	Protein	Fibre	*
938 KJ	228 kcal	24.8 g	3.6 g	0.3 g	0.3 g	0.8 g	0.1 g	

Prepare as for tartare sauce, adding 1 teaspoon of anchovy essence and mixing thoroughly. Makes 1/8 litre.

Note: This sauce may be served with fried fish. It can also be mixed with a fine julienne of celeriac to make an accompaniment to cold meats, terrines, etc. (see Figure 4.2).

* *Using gherkins*

Figure 4.2 Celeriac remoulade (recipe 59)

9 Horseradish sauce (sauce raifort)

Cal	Cal	Fat	Sat Fat	Carb	Sugar	Protein	Fibre	*
1807 KJ	430 kcal	43.8 g	27.8 g	6.0 g	5.0 g	3.6 g	2.1 g	

	8 portions
horseradish	25 g
vinegar or lemon juice	1 tbsp
salt, pepper	
cream or crème fraiche, lightly whipped	125 ml

1 Wash, peel and rewash the horseradish. Grate finely.
2 Mix all the ingredients together.

Note: Serve with roast beef, smoked trout, eel or halibut.

* *For 8 portions*

10 Mint sauce

Cal	Cal	Fat	Sat Fat	Carb	Sugar	Protein	Fibre	*
204 KJ	49 kcal	0.0 g	0.0 g	11.3 g	11.3 g	1.5 g	1.8 g	

	8 portions
mint	2–3 tbsp
caster sugar	1 tsp
vinegar	125 ml

1 Chop the washed, picked mint and mix with the sugar.
2 Place in a china basin and add the vinegar.
3 If the vinegar is too sharp dilute it with a little water.

Note: Serve with roast lamb. A less acid sauce can be produced by dissolving the sugar in 125 ml boiling water and, when cold, adding the chopped mint and 1–2 tablespoon vinegar to taste.

* *For 8 portions*

Chutneys and relishes

Chutneys are made from a variety of ingredients, usually fruit, preserved in sugar and acid after careful cooking. They are flavoured with a range of spices. Chutneys are served as an accompaniment to terrines and pâtés, salads, cold meats, poultry, game and cheese. They may also accompany a traditional curry (e.g. mango chutney).

Relishes are similar to chutneys except they are generally smoother and do not always contain as much sugar.

Fruits and vegetables for use in relishes and chutneys must be unblemished and well washed. Good-quality vinegars must be used at 4 per cent acetic acid.

When making chutneys and relishes, never use copper or unsealed cast iron pans; the acid in the preserve will damage the metal, and the colour and flavour of the ingredients.

There are a great many types of chutney and plenty of scope for experimentation for those interested.

Figure 4.3 Cheese and crackers with beetroot chutney

11 Tomato chutney

	Makes 1 litre
tomatoes, peeled	1.5 kg
onions, finely chopped	450 g
brown sugar	300 g
malt vinegar	375 ml
mustard powder	1½ tsp
cayenne pepper	½ tsp
coarse salt	2 tsp
mild curry powder	1 tbsp

1 Peel and coarsely chop the tomatoes, then combine with the remaining ingredients in a large heavy-duty saucepan.
2 Stir over heat without boiling until the sugar dissolves. Simmer uncovered, stirring occasionally until the mixture thickens (about 1½ hours).
3 Place in hot, sterilised jars. Seal while hot.

12 Rhubarb and tomato chutney

	Makes approximately 2 kg
rhubarb	1 kg
olive oil	1 tbsp
black mustard seeds	1½ tbsp
ground cumin	1½ tbsp
ground cloves	½ tsp
ground coriander	1½ tbsp
tomatoes, peeled, coarsely chopped	2 kg
onions, finely chopped	400 g
coarse salt	1 tsp
garlic cloves, chopped	2
raisins	400 g
brown sugar	200 g
malt vinegar	250 ml

1 Peel the rhubarb, cut into 2 cm pieces, then set aside.
2 Heat the oil in a large heavy-duty saucepan, add the seeds and spices, sweat for 2–3 minutes.
3 Add the tomatoes, onion, salt, garlic, raisins, sugar and vinegar.
4 Stir over heat without boiling until the sugar dissolves. Simmer uncovered, stirring occasionally, for approximately 35 minutes, until mixture thickens.
5 Stir in the rhubarb, simmer for 5–10 minutes until tender.
6 Pour the hot chutney into sterilised jars. Seal while hot.

13 Pear chutney

	Makes approximately 5 kg
white wine vinegar	900 g
demerara sugar	900 g
ginger, brunoise	125 g
onion, diced	375 g
nutmeg	5 g
saffron	0.25 g
cinnamon	5 g
golden sultanas	375 g
tomato concassée	750 g
pears, diced	2000 g

1 Make a thick syrup with the white wine vinegar and the sugar.
2 Add the ginger, onion, nutmeg, saffron, cinnamon, sultanas and concassée, and reduce to a thick syrup.
3 Add the diced pears and reduce again to a sticky consistency.
4 Cool the chutney and then store in a kilner jar.

14 Fig and apple chutney

	Makes 1.5 kg
Bramley apples	800 g
onion, diced	80 g
dried fig	200 g
white wine vinegar	100 g
English mustard	20 g
sultanas	200 g
cayenne pepper	1 g
sugar	100 g

1 Dice the apple into 2 x 2 cm pieces.
2 Add the rest of the ingredients into a pan and then cover with clingfilm.
3 Cook on a low heat for 2 hours to slowly release the juices; this will also help it cook out.
4 Once all the liquid has gone, blitz and then store in a kilner jar.

15 Apricot chutney

	Makes 1.4 kg
red wine vinegar	250 g
demerara sugar	250 g
ginger, fine brunoise	30 g
onion, diced	125 g
nutmeg	0.1 g
saffron	0.1 g
vanilla pod	½
tomato concassée	250 g
dried apricot, cut into 6	500 g
lemon juice	2 g
lemon zest	6 g
szechuan pepper	5 turns on pepper mill
black mill pepper	10 turns on pepper mill
moscatel vinegar	20 g

1 Make a thick syrup with the red wine vinegar and the sugar.
2 Add the ginger, onion, nutmeg, saffron, vanilla and tomato concassée and reduce again to a thick syrup.
3 Add the apricots and reduce again.
4 Cool the chutney and, once cold, add the rest of the ingredients.

16 Beetroot relish

	Makes 1.75 litres
beetroots, peeled and chopped coarsely	1 kg
onions, finely chopped	800 g
caster sugar	225 g
coarse salt	1 tbsp
ground allspice	1 tsp
malt vinegar	500 ml
plain flour	1 tbsp

1 Mix the chopped beetroot and onion together, add the sugar, salt, allspice and 375 ml of the vinegar to a large saucepan. Bring to the boil and simmer for 30 minutes.
2 Mix the flour with the remaining vinegar, whisk together well. (Make sure it is smooth and does not contain any lumps.) Add to the beetroot mixture. Stir until all is well blended and thickens.
3 Place in hot sterilised jars. Seal while still hot.

17 Date and tamarind relish

	Makes 625 ml
boiling water	500 ml
dried tamarind	75 g
olive oil	2 tsp
black mustard seeds	2 tsp
cumin seeds	2 tsp
fresh dates, stoned and chopped	500 g
malt vinegar	60 ml

1 In a suitable bowl, pour the boiling water over the tamarind and allow to stand for 30 minutes.
2 Strain the liquid, press to extract all moisture, discard the tamarind.
3 Heat the oil in a suitable saucepan, cook the mustard seeds until they pop, add the cumin seeds, stir in the dates, tamarind liquid and vinegar, bring to the boil. Simmer for 5 minutes until almost dry.
4 Purée in a processor until smooth.
5 Place the hot relish into hot sterilised jars. Seal while hot.

Single-food hors d'oeuvre

Serve hors d'oeuvre with bread or toast, butter separately. Add a salad garnish.

18 Oysters

Oysters should be kept, covered with damp seaweed, in boxes or barrels in a cold room or refrigerator to keep them moist and alive. The shells should be tightly shut to indicate freshness. The oysters should be opened carefully with a special oyster knife so as to avoid scratching the inside shell, then turned and arranged neatly in the deep shell and served on a bed of crushed ice on a plate. They should not be washed unless gritty, and the natural juices should always be left in the deep shell.

Accompaniments include brown bread and butter, and lemon. It is usual to serve six oysters as a portion.

Oysters are available when there is an 'r' in the month.

19 Caviar

This is the fresh, salted roe of the sturgeon, a very expensive imported commodity usually served in its original tin or jar, in a timbale of crushed ice. One spoonful – 25 g – represents a portion.

20 Smoked salmon

Cal	Cal	Fat	Sat Fat	Carb	Sugar	Protein	Fibre
149 KJ	36 kcal	1.1 g	0.3 g	0.0 g	0.0 g	6.4 g	0.0 g

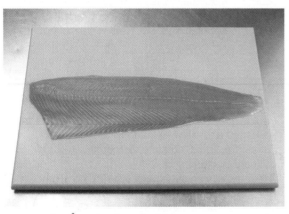

Before service, a side of smoked salmon must be carefully trimmed to remove the dry outside surface. All bones must be removed; a pair of pliers is useful for this. The salmon is carved as thinly as possible on the slant and neatly dressed, overlapping, on a plate or dish, decorated with sprigs of parsley 35–50 g per portion.

Accompaniments include brown bread and butter, and lemon.

Note: Other smoked fish served as hors d'oeuvre include halibut, eel, conger eel, trout, mackerel, herring (buckling), cod's roe and sprats.

Figure 4.4 Side of smoked salmon

HEALTHY EATING TIP

- Oily fish (e.g. salmon, trout, mackerel, rollmops, sprats) are high in omega-3 fatty acids, which are beneficial for health.

21 *Foie gras*

This is a ready-prepared delicacy made from goose liver, and it may be served in its original dish. If tinned, it should be chilled thoroughly, removed from the tin and cut into 1 cm slices.

Alternatively, *foie gras* may be cut into thick slices, lightly fried on both sides in a dry pan, served on a bed of salad leaves (lightly dressed with vinaigrette), and served accompanied by freshly toasted brioche or bread.

22 Salami and assorted cooked or smoked sausages

These are ready-bought sausages usually prepared from pork by specialist butchers. Most countries have their own specialities, and a variety of them is exported. They are thinly sliced and either served individually or an assortment may be offered. Mortadella, garlic sausage and zungenwurst are other examples of this type of sausage.

Terrines and pâté

A slice of terrine served with a suitable garnish (e.g. a small tossed salad dressed with vinaigrette and chopped fresh herbs) makes an ideal first course, or a small portion can form part of an hors d'oeuvre selection.

Figure 4.5 Suckling pig terrine with toast and golden raisin and pear chutney

23 Liver pâté (pâté de foie)

Cal	Cal	Fat	Sat Fat	Carb	Sugar	Protein
213 KJ	896 kcal	19.1 g	8.5 g	0.7 g	0.1 g	9.8 g

	4 portions	10 portions
liver (chicken, pig, calf, lamb, etc.)	100 g	250 g
butter, oil or margarine	25 g	62 g
onion, chopped	10 g	25 g
clove garlic		
sprigs of parsley, thyme, chervil	1	2
fat pork	50 g	125 g
salt, pepper		
fat bacon	25 g	62 g

1 Cut the liver into 2 cm pieces.
2 Toss quickly in the butter in a frying pan over a fierce heat for a few seconds with the onion, garlic and herbs.
3 Allow to cool.
4 Pass, with the pork, twice through a mincer. Season.

5 Line an earthenware terrine with wafer-thin slices of fat bacon.
6 Place the mixture into the terrine. Cover with fat bacon.
7 Stand in a tray half full of water and bring to simmering point.
8 Cook in a moderate oven for 1 hour.
9 When quite cold, cut into ½ cm slices and serve on lettuce leaves. Usually served accompanied with freshly made toast.

Note: This is a typical home-made preparation often seen on the menu as pâté maison.

HEALTHY EATING TIP

• Use an unsaturated oil (sunflower or olive). Lightly oil the pan and drain off any excess after the frying is complete.
• The bacon is high in salt so very little (or no) added salt is necessary.

24 Tartare of smoked haddock

Cal	Cal	Fat	Sat Fat	Carb	Sugar	Protein	Fibre
1471 KJ	354 kcal	28.8 g	5.3 g	4.8 g	1.6 g	19.5 g	2.9 g

	4 portions	10 portions
smoked haddock, free from bone and skin, diced	150 g	300 g
cucumber, peeled, seeded and finely diced	50 g	125 g
new potatoes, cooked and diced	50 g	125 g
parsley, chopped		
mayonnaise, cream or natural yoghurt	60 ml	125 ml
salt, cayenne		
avocado, fully ripe	2	5
lemon juice		
plum tomatoes, peeled, deseeded and diced	50 g	125 g
mixed salad, vinaigrette dressing	50 g	125 g

1 Mix the haddock, cucumber, potatoes, parsley and mayonnaise. Season lightly.
2 Place into moulds, set into centre of plates, remove moulds.
3 Peel the avocados, cut in halves, remove stones, slice and sprinkle lightly with lemon juice to prevent discoloration.
4 Arrange the avocado in a fan around the base of the tartare.
5 Sprinkle the tomato around the plates.
6 Garnish the tops with lightly dressed salad and serve.

HEALTHY EATING TIP

• Try using half mayonnaise and half natural yogurt/fromage frais.
• The smoked haddock is high in salt, so no added salt is necessary.
• Serve with bread or toast, butter optional.

Variations
Layers of creamed horseradish and tomato chutney can be placed in the tartare. Sieved hard-boiled egg can be sprinkled on. A few chives can be used as garnish.

25 Tapenade

Tapenade is a provençale dish consisting of puréed or finely chopped black olives, capers, anchovies and olive oil. It may also contain garlic, herbs, tuna, lemon juice or brandy. Its name comes from the provençale word for capers: *tapeno*. It is popular food in the South of France, where it is generally eaten as an hors d'oeuvre, spread on toast.

1 Mix all the ingredients together, adding the olive oil to make a paste.

2 For a smoother texture, place garlic, lemon juice, capers and anchovies into a food processor and process until a smooth texture. Add the olives and parsley, and sufficient oil to form a smooth paste.
3 Season, if required.
4 Garnish with a sprinkle of roast cumin and chopped red chilli.
5 Serve chilled.

26 Haddock and smoked salmon terrine

Cal	Cal	Fat	Sat Fat	Carb	Sugar	Protein	Fibre
563 KJ	133 kcal	3.4 g	0.7 g	0.1 g	0.1 g	25.7 g	0.1 g

	4 portions	10 portions
smoked salmon	140 g	350 g
haddock fillets, skinned	320 g	800 g
salt, pepper		
eggs, lightly beaten	1	2
crème fraiche	40 ml	105 ml (7 tbsp)
capers	3 tbsp	7 tbsp
green or pink peppercorns	1 tbsp	2 tbsp

1 Grease a 1 litre loaf tin with oil; alternatively, line with clingflim.
2 Line the tin with thin slices of smoked salmon. Let the ends overhang the mould. Reserve the remaining salmon until needed.
3 Cut two long slices of haddock the length of the tin and set aside.
4 Cut the rest of the haddock into small pieces. Season all the haddock with salt and pepper.
5 In a suitable basin, combine the eggs, crème fraiche, capers, and green or pink peppercorns. Add the pieces of haddock.
6 Spoon the mixture into the mould until one-third full. Smooth with a spatula.
7 Wrap the long haddock fillets in the reserved smoked salmon. Lay them on top of the layer of the fish mixture in the terrine.

8 Fill with the remainder of the haddock and crème fraiche mixture.
9 Smooth the surface and fold over the overhanging pieces of smoked salmon.
10 Cover with tin foil, secure well.
11 Cook in a water bath (bain-marie) of boiling water. Place in the oven at 200°C for approximately 45 minutes, until set.
12 Remove from oven and bain-marie. Allow to cool. Do not remove foil cover.
13 Place heavy weights on top and leave in refrigerator for 24 hours.
14 When ready to serve, remove the weights and foil. Remove from mould.
15 Cut into thick slices, serve on suitable plates with a dill mayonnaise and garnished with salad leaves and fresh dill.

Note: As an alternative to haddock, use halibut or Arctic bass.

HEALTHY EATING TIP
• Season with the minimum amount of salt.
• Offer the customer the mayonnaise separately.
• Serve with a warm bread or rolls (butter optional).

27 Terrine of chicken and vegetables

Cal	Cal	Fat	Sat Fat	Carb	Sugar	Protein	Fibre
930 KJ	226 kcal	17.3 g	9.4 g	2.0 g	1.8 g	15.5 g	0.9 g

8–10 portions

carrots, turnips and swedes, peeled and cut into 7 mm dice	50 g of each
broccoli, small florets	50 g
baby corn, cut into 7 mm rounds	50 g
French beans, cut into 7 mm lengths	50 g
chicken (white meat only), minced	400 g
egg whites	2
double cream	200 ml
salt, mill pepper	

1 Blanch all the vegetables individually in boiling salted water, ensuring that they remain firm. Refresh in cold water, and drain well.
2 Blend the chicken and egg whites in a food processor until smooth. Turn out into a large mixing bowl and gradually beat in the double cream.
3 Season with salt and mill pepper, and fold in the vegetables.
4 Line a lightly greased 1-litre terrine with clingfilm.
5 Spoon the farce into the mould and overlap the clingfilm.
6 Cover with foil, put the lid on and cook in a bain-marie in a moderate oven for about 45 minutes.
7 When cooked, remove the lid and leave to cool overnight.

HEALTHY EATING TIP

- Keep the added salt to a minimum.
- Serve with plenty of salad vegetables and bread or toast (optional butter or spread).

28 Terrine of bacon, spinach and mushrooms

Cal	Cal	Fat	Sat Fat	Carb	Sugar	Protein	Fibre	*
1436 KJ	347 kcal	30.4 g	7.2 g	1.2 g	1.0 g	17.0 g	1.4 g	

12 portions

collar of bacon	1 kg
carrot	1
onion clouté	1
bouquet garni	1
celery	2 sticks
peppercorns	8
fresh spinach	500 g
butter	50 g
mushrooms (preferably morels)	200 g

1 If necessary soak the bacon overnight. Drain.
2 Place the bacon in cold water, bring to the boil, add the carrot, onion, bouquet garni, celery and peppercorns.
3 Poach until tender.
4 Pick some large leaves of spinach to line the terrine, blanch the leaves, refresh and drain.
5 Lightly cook the rest of the spinach gently, refresh, drain and shred.
6 Alternatively shred the spinach raw, quickly cook in butter, drain and then blast chill.
7 Cook the mushrooms in a little butter, chill well, season.
8 When cool, remove the bacon from the cooking liquor, chop into small pieces.
9 Line the terrine with clingfilm, then the spinach leaves. Layer with bacon, mushrooms and spinach. Cover with spinach leaves and clingfilm. Wait for 12 hours or overnight.
10 When ready, turn out, slice and serve on plates, with leek and mushroom vinaigrette (see recipe 2) served separately.

HEALTHY EATING TIP

- Soaking the bacon overnight will remove some of the salt.
- Use only a little butter to cook the mushrooms.
- Use a minimum amount of salt to season the vinaigrette.
- Serve with warm bread rolls, butter optional.

* *Using common mushrooms*

29 Duck and chicken terrine

Cal	Cal	Fat	Sat Fat	Carb	Sugar	Protein	Fibre	*
1444 KJ	347 kcal	22.4 g	9.5 g	0.6 g	0.3 g	35.8 g	0.1 g	

Figure 4.6 Duck and chicken terrine

6–8 portions

chicken breasts	2 large, approx. 150 g
duck breasts	1 large, approx. 150 g
chicken livers, trimmed	100 g
brandy	62 ml
rosemary leaves, finely chopped	¼ tsp
bay leaf	1
orange zest	2 dried strips
seasoning	
streaky bacon	10–12 slices
Mousse	
port	100 ml
brandy	62 ml
shallots, finely chopped	25 g
garlic, crushed and chopped	2 cloves
chicken livers	100 g
egg	1
butter	50 g

1 Carefully prepare the chicken breasts, removing all the sinews.
2 Slice each chicken breast into two and the duck breast into four.
3 Prepare the chicken livers, remove all traces of green.
4 Marinade the chicken livers, and duck and chicken breasts in the brandy, rosemary, bay leaf and orange zest, and season. Allow to marinade in a refrigerator for 24 hours.

5 Prepare the mousse. In a saucepan reduce the port and brandy with the shallot and garlic until almost dry. Place in a food processor with the chicken livers and purée until smooth.
6 Add the egg and butter, and purée until smooth and light.
7 Place through a fine sieve.
8 Prepare a terrine mould (15 cm x 6 cm), lining it with the slices of streaky bacon (leaving the ends hanging over the edge, ready to be folded over the top of the terrine in step 14, below).
9 Place a layer of mousse in the bottom of the terrine.
10 Place on top one piece of chicken and one piece of duck.
11 Cover with another layer of mousse and then another piece of chicken and duck.
12 Cover with mousse again, then all the remaining chicken livers.
13 Layer up with the remaining chicken, duck and mousse, alternating the position of the dark and light meats each time to create a mosaic effect.
14 Finish with the last of the mousse, fold the streaky bacon over, then wrap the clingfilm over the top.
15 Cover with foil and cook in an oven in a bain-marie of water or in a combination oven with steam injection – 150°C – for approximately 1¼ hours, until the blade of a small knife comes out warm from the centre.
16 When the terrine is cooked, transfer to a bain-marie of cold water or a blast chiller. First, press down the foil, then place a sheet of foil-covered cardboard on top of the terrine, and weigh down with a 500 g weight during chilling.
17 Keep refrigerated until required.
18 Serve sliced, garnished with salad leaves and a suitable chutney, and warm brioche.

HEALTHY EATING TIP

• Reduce the fat content by removing the skin from the chicken and duck breasts.

* 1 of 6 portions. 1 of 8 portions provides: 1083 kJ/260 kcal Energy; 16.6 g Fat; 7.1 g Sat Fat; 0.4 g Carb; 0.2 g Sugar; 26.9 g Protein; 0.1 g Fibre

30 Potted meats

Cal	Cal	Fat	Sat Fat	Carb	Sugar	Protein	Fibre	*
1160 KJ	280 kcal	23.8 g	14.5 g	0.2 g	0.2 g	16.4 g	0.0 g	

cooked meat e.g. beef, salt beef,
or tongue, venison, chicken   200 g
salt, pepper and mace
clarified butter   100 g

1 Using an electric blender or chopper reduce the meat, seasoning and 85 g of the butter to a paste.
2 Pack firmly into an earthenware or china pot and refrigerate until firm.
3 Cover with 1 cm of clarified butter and refrigerate.
4 Serve with a small tossed green salad and hot toast.

Note: Chicken can also be combined in equal quantities with the other meats, e.g. chicken and ham.

HEALTHY EATING TIP
• Keep added salt to a minimum.
• Serve with plenty of salad vegetables and bread or toast (optional butter or spread).

* 1 of 4 portions

31 Potted shrimps

Potted shrimps are freshly cooked and peeled shrimps mixed with warmed butter and a little spice, chiefly mace, served in small dishes. Ready prepared commercially potted shrimps are available. Potted shrimps have a better flavour when served warm, accompanied by thin toast or brown bread and butter.

Fruits and juices

32 Grapefruit *(pamplemousse)*

These are halved crosswise, not through the stalk, and the segments individually cut with a small knife, then chilled. Serve with a maraschino cherry in the centre. The common practice of sprinkling with caster sugar is incorrect, as some customers prefer their grapefruit without sugar. Serve half a grapefruit per portion in a coupe. Grapefruit may also be served hot, sprinkled with rum and demerera sugar.

HEALTHY EATING TIP
• This, and the following fruit dishes and juices, contribute to the recommended five portions of fruit and vegetables per day. Include them as often as possible on the menu.

33 Grapefruit cocktail

Figure 4.7 ✐ Preparation of yellow and pink grapefruit and an orange, in four steps

The fruit should be peeled with a sharp knife in order to remove all the white pith and yellow skin. Cut into segments and remove all the pips. The segments and the juice should then be dressed in a cocktail glass or grapefruit coupe and chilled. A cherry may be added. Allow ½–1 grapefruit per head.

Variations
- *Grapefruit and orange cocktail*, allowing half an orange and half a grapefruit per head.
- *Orange cocktail*, using oranges in place of grapefruit.
- *Florida cocktail* – a mixture of grapefruit, orange and pineapple segments.

34 Avocado pear (l'avocat)

Figure 4.8  Preparation of an avocado pear

The pears must be ripe (test by pressing gently – the pear should give slightly).

1 Cut in half length-wise. Remove the stone.
2 Serve garnished with lettuce accompanied by vinaigrette (see recipe 1) or variations on vinaigrette.

Note: Avocado pears are sometimes filled with shrimps or crabmeat bound with a shellfish cocktail sauce or other similar fillings, and may be served hot or cold using a variety of fillings and sauces. Avocados may also be halved lengthwise, the stone removed, the skin peeled and the flesh sliced and fanned on a plate. Garnish with a simple or composed salad. Allow half an avocado per portion.

HEALTHY EATING TIP
• Serve with plenty of salad vegetables and bread or toast (optional butter or spread).

35 Fruit cocktail

This is a mixture of fruits, such as apples, pears, pineapples, grapes and cherries, washed, peeled and cut into neat segments or dice, and added to a syrup – 100 g sugar to ¼ litre water – and the juice of half a lemon. Neatly place in cocktail glasses and chill. Allow ½ kg unprepared fruit for four portions, 1½ kg for ten. Variations include a tropical fruit cocktail, which uses a variety of tropical fruits, such as mango, passion fruit, lychees, pineapple and kiwi fruit.

36 Melon cocktail

The melon, which must be ripe, is peeled, then cut into neat segments or dice, or scooped out with a parisienne spoon, dressed in cocktail glasses and chilled. A little liqueur, such as crème de menthe or maraschino, may also be added. Allow approximately half a melon for four portions, 1½ for ten.

37 Chilled melon

Cal	Cal	Fat	Sat Fat	Carb	Sugar	Protein	Fibre
82 KJ	20 kcal	0.0 g	0.0 g	4.7 g	4.7 g	0.6 g	0.9 g

1 Cut the melon in half, remove the pips and cut it into thick slices.
2 Cut a piece off the skin so that the slice will stand firm, and serve on crushed ice.

Note: Use caster sugar and ground ginger as accompaniments. Allow approximately half a honeydew or cantaloupe melon for four portions.

38 Tropical fruit plate (without accompaniment)

See page 585.

39 Fruit juices

These can be bought ready prepared but may be made from the fresh fruit (e.g. pineapple, orange or grapefruit).

40 Tomato juice (jus de tomate)

Cal	Cal	Fat	Sat Fat	Carb	Sugar	Protein	Fibre
74 KJ	18 kcal	0.0 g	0.0 g	3.5 g	3.5 g	1.1 g	0.0 g

1 Fresh ripe tomatoes must be used. Wash them, remove the eyes, then liquidise and pass them through a strainer.
2 Serve the juice in cocktail glasses, chilled.

Note: Offer Worcester sauce when serving. Use ½ kg tomatoes for four portions, 1¼ kg for ten.

Seafood

41 Shellfish cocktails: crab, lobster, shrimp, prawn (*cocktail de crabe, homard, crevettes, crevettes roses*)

Cal	Cal	Fat	Sat Fat	Carb	Sugar	Protein	Fibre
966 KJ	230 kcal	21.0 g	3.2 g	0.6 g	0.6 g	00.0 9.6	0.3 g

Figure 4.9 ✎ Shellfish cocktail

	4 portions	10 portions
lettuce	½	1½
prepared shellfish	100–150 g	250–350 g
shellfish cocktail sauce (see recipe 42)	125 ml	300 ml

1 Wash, drain well and finely shred the lettuce, avoiding long strands. Place about 2 cm deep in cocktail glasses or dishes.
2 Add the prepared shellfish: crab (shredded white meat only); lobster (cut in 2 cm dice); shrimps (peeled and washed); prawns (peeled, washed and, if large, cut into two or three pieces).
3 Coat with sauce.
4 Decorate with an appropriate piece of the content, such as a prawn with the shell on, the tail removed, on the edge of the glass of a prawn cocktail.

42 Shellfish cocktail sauce

Cal	Cal	Fat	Sat Fat	Carb	Sugar	Protein	Fibre
889 KJ	216 kcal	22.7 g	14.2 g	1.9 g	1.9 g	1.2 g	0.1 g

Method 1

	4 portions	10 portions
egg yolk, pasteurised	1	3
vinegar	1 tsp	2½ tsp
salt, pepper, mustard		
olive oil or sunflower oil	5 tbsp	8 tbsp
tomato juice or ketchup to taste		
Worcester sauce (optional)	2–3 drops	6–8 drops

1 Make the mayonnaise with the egg yolk, vinegar, seasonings and oil.
2 Combine with the tomato juice and Worcester sauce (if using).

Method 2

	4 portions	10 portions
lightly whipped cream or unsweetened non-dairy cream	5 tbsp	12 tbsp
tomato juice or ketchup to taste	3 tbsp	8 tbsp
salt, pepper		
lemon juice	a few drops	

1 Mix all the ingredients together.

Note: Fresh or tinned tomato juice, or diluted tomato ketchup, may be used for both the above methods, but the use of tinned tomato purée gives an unpleasant flavour.

HEALTHY EATING TIP
• Keep added salt to a minimum.
• Extend the high-fat mayonnaise with low-fat yoghurt to proportionally reduce the fat content.

43 Soused herring or mackerel

Cal	Cal	Fat	Sat Fat	Carb	Sugar	Protein	Fibre	*
2419 KJ	576 kcal	44.5 g	9.4 g	3.0 g	3.0 g	41.0 g	1.1 g	

	4 portions	10 portions
herrings or mackerel	2	5
salt, pepper		
button onions	25 g	60 g
carrots, peeled and fluted	25 g	60 g
bay leaf	½	1½
peppercorns	6	12
thyme	1 sprig	2 sprigs
vinegar	60 ml	150 ml

1 Clean, scale and fillet the fish.
2 Wash the fillets well and season with salt and pepper.
3 Roll up with the skin outside. Place in an earthenware dish.
4 Peel and wash the onion. Cut the onion and carrots into neat, thin rings.

5 Blanch for 2–3 minutes.
6 Add to the fish with the remainder of the ingredients.
7 Cover with greaseproof paper and cook in a moderate oven for 15–20 minutes.
8 Allow to cool, place in a dish with the onion and carrot.
9 Garnish with picked parsley, dill or chives.

HEALTHY EATING TIP
• Serve with plenty of salad vegetables and bread or toast (optional butter or spread).
• Keep the added salt to a minimum.

* For 4 portions

44 Smoked mackerel mousse

Cal	Cal	Fat	Sat Fat	Carb	Sugar	Protein	Fibre	*
1192 KJ	289 kcal	27.5 g	10.7 g	0.4 g	0.4 g	9.8 g	0.0 g	

	4 portions	10 portions
smoked mackerel, free from bone and skin	200 g	500 g
optional seasoning: pepper, chopped parsley, fennel or chervil, 1 tbsp tomato ketchup, two ripe tomatoes free from skin and pips		
double cream (or non-dairy cream)	90 ml	250 ml

1 Ensure that the mackerel is completely free from skin and bones.
2 Liquidise with the required seasoning.
3 Three-quarter whip the cream.

4 Remove mackerel from liquidiser and fold into the cream. Correct the seasoning.
5 Serve in individual dishes accompanied with hot toast.

Note: This recipe can be used with smoked trout or smoked salmon trimmings. It can also be used for fresh salmon, in which case 50 g of cucumber can be incorporated with the selected seasoning.

HEALTHY EATING TIP
• Serve with plenty of salad vegetables and bread or toast (optional butter or spread).
• Use the minimum amount of salt.

* Using double cream

Assorted hors d'oeuvre

The following recipes may be served in four ways, unless otherwise indicated:

1 as a single hors d'oeuvre (first course)
2 as part of a composite hors d'oeuvre
3 as a main course, when it will be suitably garnished with salad items

4 as an accompaniment to a main course.

The relevant numbers are included in the recipe titles.

45 Egg mayonnaise (oeuf mayonnaise) (1, 2 or 3)

Cal	Cal	Fat	Sat Fat	Carb	Sugar	Protein	Fibre
763 KJ	182 kcal	15.7 g	3.4 g	2.4 g	2.4 g	8.1 g	1.6 g

Figure 4.10 Egg mayonnaise

To cook hard-boiled eggs, place the eggs in boiling water; reboil and simmer for 8–10 minutes. Refresh until cold.

As part of a selection for hors d'oeuvre
Cut the hard-boiled eggs in quarters or slices, dress neatly and coat with mayonnaise.

As an individual hors d'oeuvre
Allow one hard-boiled egg per portion, cut in half and dress on a leaf of lettuce; coat with mayonnaise, and garnish with quarters of tomatoes and slices of cucumber.

As a main dish
Allow two hard-boiled eggs per portion, cut in halves and dress on a plate, coat with mayonnaise sauce. Surround with a portion of lettuce, tomato, cucumber, potato salad, beetroot or coleslaw.

Note: When started in cold water cook for 12 minutes. If the eggs are overcooked, iron in the yolk and sulphur compounds in the white are released to form the blackish ring (ferrous sulphide) around the yolk. This will also occur if the eggs are not refreshed immediately they are cooked.

HEALTHY EATING TIP
• Thin the mayonnaise to coat the eggs.
• Serve with plenty of bread or toast and salad garnish (offer butter separately).

46 Seafood and French bean salad with roasted garlic mustard vinaigrette (1)

Cal 3465 KJ	Cal 839 kcal	Fat 81.7 g	Sat Fat 12.3 g	Carb 6.9 g	Sugar 4.3 g	Protein 19.6 g	Fibre 1.0 g	*

	4 portions	10 portions
prawns, cooked, shelled, de-veined	8	20
mussels, large cooked, de-bearded	8	20
scallops, poached, sliced	4	10
lobster, cooked	4 slices	10 slices
artichoke bottoms	2	5
French beans, blanched	100 g	250 g
tarragon, chopped	1 tbsp	2½ tbsp
mixed leaves, e.g. raddiccio, rocket, lamb's lettuce, watercress		
Roasted garlic mustard vinaigrette		
seasoning		
garlic bulb ⎫ roasted	1	2½
milk ⎬ garlic	250 ml	625 ml
olive oil ⎭ purée	6 tbsp	312 ml
Dijon mustard	1 tsp	2½ tsp
rice wine vinegar	2 tbsp	5 tbsp
olive oil	6 tbsp	15 tbsp

1 First prepare the roasted garlic purée. Peel the garlic bulb, simmer in the milk for 10 minutes. Drain, discard the milk. Place the garlic in a small roasting tray, add the olive oil.

2 Bake in a hot oven at 180°C until the garlic is soft. This will take approximately 1 hour.
3 Once soft, purée until smooth.
4 Mix in the Dijon mustard, rice vinegar and the olive oil, season. The vinaigrette is now ready to use.
5 Prepare the salad by carefully tossing together the seafood, artichoke bottoms, French beans and tarragon.
6 Sprinkle with the vinaigrette, then season.
7 Serve on a bed of mixed leaves, drizzle the plate with some additional vinaigrette.

Note: Other types of seafood may also be included (such as shrimps, scallops, squid, oysters) or some of those listed omitted. Asparagus, mushrooms and mangetout may also be included in the salad.

HEALTHY EATING TIP
- Keep the amount of added salt to a minimum.
- Serve with a large portion of starchy carbohydrate – bread or new potatoes.

* *Using approx 170 g lobster meat*

47 Potato salad *(salade de pommes de terre)* (2, 4)

Cal 2013 KJ	Cal 479 kcal	Fat 34.9 g	Sat Fat 5.1 g	Carb 40.0 g	Sugar 1.3 g	Protein 4.0 g	Fibre 2.6 g	*

	4 portions	10 portions
potatoes, cooked	200 g	500 g
vinaigrette	1 tbsp	2½ tbsp
onion or chive (optional), chopped	10 g	25 g
mayonnaise or natural yoghurt	125 ml	300 ml
salt, pepper		
parsley or mixed fresh herbs, chopped		

1 Cut the potatoes into ½–1 cm dice; sprinkle with vinaigrette.
2 Mix with the onion or chive, add the mayonnaise and correct the seasoning. (The onion may be blanched to reduce its harshness.)
3 Dress neatly and sprinkle with chopped parsley or herbs.

Note: This is not usually served as a single hors d'oeuvre or main course. Potato salad can also be made by dicing raw peeled or unpeeled potato, cooking them – preferably by steaming (to retain shape) – and mixing with vinaigrette while warm. Variations include the addition of two chopped hard-boiled eggs, or 100 g of peeled dessert apple mixed with lemon juice, or a small bunch of picked watercress leaves. Potatoes may be cooked with mint and allowed to cool with the mint. Cooked small new potatoes can be tossed in vinaigrette with chopped fresh herbs (e.g. mint, parsley, chive).

Using mayonnaise, for 4 portions

48 Vegetable salad (Russian salad) (salade de légumes (salade russe)) (2)

Cal	Cal	Fat	Sat Fat	Carb	Sugar	Protein	Fibre	*
1566 KJ	373 kcal	35.0 g	5.2 g	10.1 g	8.2 g	5.0 g	11.9 g	

	4 portions	10 portions
carrots	100 g	250 g
turnips	50 g	125 g
French beans	50 g	125 g
peas	50 g	125 g
vinaigrette	1 tbsp	2–3 tbsp
mayonnaise or natural yoghurt	125 ml	300 ml
salt, pepper		

1 Peel and wash the carrots and turnips, cut into ½ cm dice or batons.
2 Cook separately in salted water, refresh and drain well.
3 Top and tail the beans, and cut into ½ cm dice; cook, refresh and drain well.
4 Cook the peas, refresh and drain well.
5 Mix all the well-drained vegetables with vinaigrette and then mayonnaise.
6 Correct the seasoning. Dress neatly.

HEALTHY EATING TIP
- Try half mayonnaise and half natural yoghurt.
- Season with the minimum amount of salt.

Using mayonnaise, for 4 portions

49 Fish salad (salade de poisson) (1, 2, 3)

Cal	Cal	Fat	Sat Fat	Carb	Sugar	Protein	Fibre	*
978 KJ	233 kcal	13.5 g	3.0 g	1.5 g	1.4 g	26.4 g	1.3 g	

	4 portions	10 portions
cooked fish, free from skin and bone	200 g	500 g
hard-boiled egg	1	2–3
cucumber (optional)	50 g	125 g
lettuce	½	1
parsley or fennel, chopped		
salt, pepper		
vinaigrette	1 tbsp	2–3 tbsp

1 Flake the fish. Cut the egg and cucumber into ½ cm dice.
2 Finely shred the lettuce. Mix ingredients together, add the parsley.
3 Correct the seasoning. Mix with the vinaigrette.
4 May be decorated with lettuce, anchovies and capers.

HEALTHY EATING TIP
- Use salt sparingly.

For 4 portions

50 Meat salad (salade de viande) (1, 2, 3)

Cal	Cal	Fat	Sat Fat	Carb	Sugar	Protein	Fibre	*
1616 KJ	385 kcal	15.2 g	4.8 g	2.7 g	2.5 g	26.4 g	1.3 g	

	4 portions	10 portions
lean meat, cooked	200 g	500 g
gherkins	25 g	60 g
French beans, cooked	50 g	125 g
tomatoes	50 g	125 g
onion or chives		
(optional), chopped	5 g	12 g
vinaigrette	1 tbsp	2½ tbsp
chopped parsley or mixed		
fresh herbs		
salt, pepper		

1 Cut the meat, gherkins and beans into ½ cm dice.

2 Skin the tomatoes, deseed and cut into ½ cm dice.
3 Mix with remainder of the ingredients, blanching the onions if required.
4 Correct the seasoning. Dress neatly.
5 Decorate with lettuce leaves, tomatoes and fans of gherkins.

Note: Well-cooked braised or boiled meat is ideal for this salad.

HEALTHY EATING TIP
• The 'balance' of this dish is improved with less meat, more vegetables and a light dressing.

For 4 portions

51 Beetroot

1 Wash and cook the beetroot in a steamer or in gently simmering water until tender (test by skinning). Cool and peel.

2 Cut into ½ cm dice or ½–1 cm batons.
3 Serve plain, or with vinegar or sprinkled with vinaigrette, but not as a main course.

52 Beetroot salad (salade de betterave) (2)

Cal	Cal	Fat	Sat Fat	Carb	Sugar	Protein	Fibre
134 KJ	32 kcal	2.0 g	0.3 g	3.2 g	3.1 g	0.7 g	0.9 g

	4 portions	10 portions
cooked beetroot,		
neatly cut or sliced	200 g	500 g
onion or chive (optional),		
chopped	10 g	25 g
vinaigrette		
parsley, chopped	1 tbsp	2½ tbsp

1 Combine all the ingredients except the parsley, blanching the onion if required.
2 Dress neatly. Sprinkle with the chopped parsley.

Note: Variations include the addition of 60–120 ml mayonnaise or natural yoghurt in place of vinaigrette (150–200 ml for 10 portions).

53 Cucumber

1 Peel the cucumber if desired.
2 Cut into thin slices and dress neatly.
3 Lightly dress with vinaigrette or serve separately.

Note: Not to be served as a single hors d'oeuvre or main course.

HEALTHY EATING TIP

• All vegetable-based salads are a healthy way to start a meal.
• Add the minimum amount of salt.

54 Cucumber salad (salade de concombres) (2, 4)

Cal	Cal	Fat	Sat Fat	Carb	Sugar	Protein	Fibre
91 KJ	22 kcal	2.0 g	0.3 g	1.0 g	0.9 g	0.4 g	0.3 g

	4 portions	10 portions
cucumber	½	1¼
vinaigrette	1 tbsp	2½ tbsp
parsley or mixed fresh herbs, chopped		

1 Peel and slice the cucumber.
2 Sprinkle with the vinaigrette and parsley.

Note: To remove indigestible juices from the cucumber, slice and lightly sprinkle with salt. Allow the salt to draw out the water for approximately 1 hour, wash well under cold water and drain. This will make the cucumber limp. Alternatively, cucumber may be sliced into ½ cm dice and bound with mayonnaise or yoghurt.

55 Tomato (tomate)

1 Wash, remove the eyes, slice thinly or cut into segments.
2 Dress neatly.

Note: If of good quality, the tomatoes need not be skinned.

56 Tomato salad (salade de tomates) (1, 2)

Cal	Cal	Fat	Sat Fat	Carb	Sugar	Protein	Fibre	*
394 KJ	94 kcal	6.6 g	1.1 g	6.7 g	6.6 g	3.5 g	3.9 g	

	4 portions	10 portions
tomatoes	200 g	500 g
lettuce	¼	½
vinaigrette	1 tbsp	2½ tbsp
onion or chives (optional), chopped	10 g	25 g
parsley or mixed fresh herbs, chopped		

1 Peel the tomatoes if required. Slice thinly. Arrange neatly on lettuce leaves.
2 Sprinkle with the vinaigrette, onion (blanched if required) and parsley.

Variation
Alternate slices of tomato and mozzarella with basic dressing or a little balsamic vinegar.
Use finely sliced shallots instead of onions.

* For 4 portions

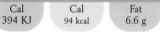

57 Tomato and cucumber salad (salade de tomates et concombres) (1, 2, 3)

Cal	Cal	Fat	Sat Fat	Carb	Sugar	Protein	Fibre
112 KJ	27 kcal	2.0 g	0.3 g	1.9 g	1.8 g	0.5 g	0.6 g

	4 portions	10 portions
tomatoes	2	5
cucumber	½	½
vinaigrette	1 tbsp	2½ tbsp
parsley or mixed fresh herbs, chopped		

1 Alternate slices of tomato and cucumber.
2 Sprinkle with the vinaigrette and parsley.

58 Rice salad (salade de riz) (2, 4)

Cal	Cal	Fat	Sat Fat	Carb	Sugar	Protein	Fibre	*
906 KJ	216 kcal	6.9 g	1.1 g	34.6 g	3.3 g	5.9 g	8.3 g	

	4 portions	10 portions
tomatoes	100 g	250 g
rice, cooked	100 g	250 g
peas, cooked	50 g	125 g
vinaigrette	1 tbsp	2½ tbsp
salt, pepper		

1 Skin and deseed the tomatoes; cut into ½ cm dice.
2 Mix with the rice and peas.
3 Add the vinaigrette and correct the seasoning.

HEALTHY EATING TIP
• This dish is high in starchy carbohydrate and can be varied with different/additional vegetables.
• Lightly dress with vinaigrette and add salt sparingly.

For 4 portions

59 Celeriac remoulade (2, 3)

Cal	Cal	Fat	Sat Fat	Carb	Sugar	Protein	Fibre
938 KJ	228 kcal	3.9 g	3.9 g	2.0 g	1.6 g	1.1 g	1.9 g

	4 portions	10 portions
celeriac	200 g	500 g
lemon	½	1
English or continental mustard	1 level tsp	2½ level tsp
salt, pepper		
mayonnaise, cream or natural yoghurt	125 ml	300 ml

1 Wash and peel the celeriac. Cut into fine julienne.
2 Combine with remoulade juice (lemon, mustard, seasoning) and the remainder of the ingredients.

Note: Other uses are as an accompaniment to pâté or terrine either as above or mixed with remoulade sauce (recipe 8).

After cutting into julienne, the celeriac may be sprinkled with suet and then squeezed, to draw out and remove excess liquid. It should then be lightly washed and squeezed to remove the suet.

HEALTHY EATING TIP
• Try using some natural yoghurt in place of mayonnaise/cream.

60 French bean salad (*salade de haricots verts*) (2)

Cal 125 KJ	Cal 30 kcal	Fat 1.9 g	Sat Fat 0.3 g	Carb 2.5 g	Sugar 1.2 g	Protein 0.9 g	Fibre 2.0 g

	4 portions	10 portions
French beans, cooked	200 g	500 g
vinaigrette	1 tbsp	3 tbsp
salt, pepper		

Combine all the ingredients.

HEALTHY EATING TIP

• Add salt sparingly.

61 Niçoise salad (1, 2, 3)

Cal 867 KJ	Cal 207 kcal	Fat 9.6 g	Sat Fat 1.5 g	Carb 25.0 g	Sugar 4.9 g	Protein 6.9 g	Fibre 9.9 g	*

	4 portions	10 portions
tomatoes	100 g	250 g
French beans, cooked	200 g	500g
diced potatoes, cooked	100 g	250g
salt, pepper		
vinaigrette	1 tbsp	2½ tbsp
anchovy fillets	10 g	25 g
capers	5 g	12 g
stoned olives	10 g	25 g

1 Peel the tomatoes, deseed and cut into neat segments.
2 Dress the beans, tomatoes and potatoes neatly.
3 Season with salt and pepper. Add the vinaigrette.
4 Decorate with anchovies, capers and olives.

HEALTHY EATING TIP

• Lightly dress with vinaigrette.
• The anchovies are high in salt, so no added salt is necessary.

* For 4 portions

62 Waldorf salad (1, 2, 3)

1 Dice celery or celeriac and crisp russet apples.
2 Mix with shelled and peeled walnuts, and bind with mayonnaise.
3 Dress on quarters or leaves of lettuce (may also be served in hollowed-out apples).

HEALTHY EATING TIP

• Try using some yoghurt in place of the mayonnaise, which will proportionally reduce the fat.
• Keep added salt to a minimum.

63 Haricot bean salad (salade de haricots blancs) (2)

Cal	Cal	Fat	Sat Fat	Carb	Sugar	Protein	Fibre
278 KJ	66 kcal	2.1 g	0.4 g	9.0 g	0.7 g	3.3 g	3.1 g

	4 portions	10 portions
haricot beans, cooked	200 g	500 g
vinaigrette	1 tbsp	2½ tbsp
parsley, chopped		
onion, chopped and		
blanched if required, or		
chives (optional)	15 g	40 g
salt, pepper		

Combine all the ingredients.

Note: This recipe can be used for any type of dried bean (see page 507).

HEALTHY EATING TIP
- Lightly dress with vinaigrette and add salt sparingly.

64 Three-bean salad (2)

Cal	Cal	Fat	Sat Fat	Carb	Sugar	Protein	Fibre	
1849 KJ	440 kcal	8.7 g	1.1 g	63.4 g	6.3 g	30.9 g	36.0 g	*

Use 200 g (500 g for 10 portions) of three different dried beans (e.g. red kidney, black-eyed, flageolet). Proceed as for recipe 63.

* For 4 portions

65 Lentil and goats' cheese salad (1)

Cal	Cal	Fat	Sat Fat	Carb	Sugar	Protein	Fibre
907 KJ	216 kcal	9.2 g	4.1 g	22.8 g	10.5 g	11.9 g	4.5 g

	4 portions	10 portions
puy lentils	100 g	250 g
bay leaf	1	3
spring onions, finely chopped	4	10
red pepper, finely chopped	1	3
chopped parsley	1 tbsp	3 tbsp
cherry tomatoes sliced in half	400 g	1 kg
rocket leaves	200 g	500 g
goats' cheese	100 g	250 g
Dressing		
olive oil	1 tbsp	2½ tbsp
balsamic vinegar	1 tbsp	2½ tbsp
clear honey	2 tbsp	5 tbsp
garlic clove, crushed and		
chopped	1	3

1 Rinse the lentils and place in a saucepan. Add the bay leaf, cover with water, bring to the boil, simmer for 20–30 minutes until tender.
2 Drain and then place in a bowl. Add the spring onions, red pepper, parsley and cherry tomatoes, mix well.
3 For the dressing, whisk together in a bowl the oil, vinegar, honey and garlic, and stir into the lentils. Serve on a bed of rocket, with the goats' cheese sprinkled over.

HEALTHY EATING TIP
- This dish provides a healthy, balanced starter.

66 Coleslaw (2, 4)

Cal 2514 KJ	Cal 599 kcal	Fat 59.0 g	Sat Fat 8.8 g	Carb 11.7 g	Sugar 11.4 g	Protein 5.9 g	Fibre 7.2 g

	4 portions	10 portions
white or Chinese cabbage	200 g	500 g
carrot	50 g	125 g
onion (optional)	25 g	60 g
mayonnaise, natural yoghurt or fromage frais	125 ml	300 ml

1 Trim off the outside leaves of the cabbage.
2 Cut into quarters. Remove the centre stalk.
3 Wash the cabbage, shred finely and drain well.
4 Mix with a fine julienne of raw carrot and shredded raw onion. To lessen the harshness of raw onion, blanch and refresh.

5 Bind with mayonnaise, natural yoghurt or vinaigrette.

HEALTHY EATING TIP
- Replace some or all of the mayonnaise with natural yoghurt and/or fromage frais.
- Add salt sparingly.

* *Using mayonnaise, for 4 portions*

67 Couscous salad with roasted vegetables and mixed herbs (1, 2, 3, 4)

Cal 1248 KJ	Cal 300 kcal	Fat 12.5 g	Sat Fat 1.7 g	Carb 42.2 g	Sugar 8.6 g	Protein 6.6 g	Fibre 3.8 g

	4 portions	10 portions
couscous	250 g	625 g
balsamic vinegar	1 tbsp	2½ tbsp
olive oil	3 tbsp	8 tbsp
lemon juice	¼ lemon	1 lemon
seasoning		
fresh mint, chopped	½ tsp	1¼ tsp
fresh coriander, chopped	½ tsp	1¼ tsp
fresh thyme, chopped	½ tsp	1¼ tsp
roasted vegetables (see page 503)		

1 Prepare the roasted vegetables as per page 503.
2 Place the couscous in a suitable bowl and gently pour over 300 ml of boiling water (750 ml for 10 portions).
3 Stir well, cover and leave to stand for 5 minutes.
4 Separate the grains with a fork.

5 Add the balsamic vinegar, olive oil, lemon juice and seasoning.
6 Mix well, stir in the chopped herbs.
7 Finish by adding the roasted vegetables.
8 Serve in a suitable bowl or use individual plates.

Note: For plated service, arrange the couscous neatly in the centre of the plate, arrange the roasted vegetables around, then garnish with fresh herbs.

HEALTHY EATING TIP
- Use an unsaturated oil and lightly brush the vegetables when roasting.
- Use the minimum amount of salt.

68 Florida salad (salade Florida) (1, 4)

	4 portions	10 portions
oranges	2	5
lettuce, round or cos	1	2½
double cream	250 ml	625 ml
lemon, juice of	½	1½

1 Remove the orange zest with a peeler.
2 Cut into fine julienne.
3 Blanch for 2–3 minutes, then refresh.
4 Peel the oranges and remove all the white skin.

5 Cut into segments between the white pith and remove all the pips.
6 Dress the lettuce in a bowl, keeping it in quarters if possible.
7 Arrange 3 or 4 orange segments in each portion.
8 Sprinkle with a little orange zest.
9 Serve an acidulated cream dressing separately (cream mixed with a few drops of lemon juice).

Note: Allow ¼ lettuce and ½ large orange per portion.

Greek-style hors d'oeuvre

All vegetables *à la grecque* are cooked in the following liquid.

	4 portions	10 portions
water	250 ml	625 ml
olive oil	60 ml	150 ml
lemon, juice of	1	1½
bay leaf	½	1
sprig of thyme		
peppercorns	6	18
coriander seeds	6	18
salt		

HEALTHY EATING TIP
• All these vegetable dishes offer a healthy way to start a meal.

69 Artichokes (artichauts à la grecque) (2)

Cal	Cal	Fat	Sat Fat	Carb	Sugar	Protein	Fibre	*
585 KJ	142 kcal	15.1 g	2.1 g	1.1 g	0.7 g	0.9 g	0.0 g	

1 Peel and trim six artichokes for 4 portions (15 for 10).
2 Cut the leaves short. Remove the chokes.
3 Blanch the artichokes in water with a little lemon juice for 10 minutes.

4 Refresh the artichokes. Place in cooking liquid. Simmer for 15–20 minutes.
5 Serve cold in a ravier with a little of the unstrained cooking liquid.

* Not all liquid included

70 Cauliflower (chou-fleur à la grecque) (2)

Cal	Cal	Fat	Sat Fat	Carb	Sugar	Protein	Fibre
687 KJ	167 kcal	15.8 g	2.3 g	2.9 g	2.5 g	3.3 g	0.0 g

1 Trim and wash one medium cauliflower for 4 portions (2½ for 10).
2 Break into small sprigs about the size of a cherry.
3 Blanch for approximately 5 minutes and refresh.
4 Simmer in the cooking liquor for 5–10 minutes. Keep the cauliflower slightly undercooked and crisp.
5 Serve cold with unstrained cooking liquor.

71 Onions (button) (oignons à la grecque) (2)

Cal	Cal	Fat	Sat Fat	Carb	Sugar	Protein	Fibre
634 KJ	154 kcal	15.1 g	2.2 g	4.2 g	3.0 g	0.7 g	0.7 g

1 Peel and wash 200 g button onions for 4 portions (500 g for 10).
2 Blanch for approximately 5 minutes and refresh.
3 Place onions in the cooking liquor. Simmer until tender.
4 Serve cold with unstrained cooking liquor.

HEALTHY EATING TIP
• Use salt sparingly in the cooking liquid. Do not serve too much liquid with the finished dish.

72 Leeks (poireaux à la grecque) (2)

Cal	Cal	Fat	Sat Fat	Carb	Sugar	Protein	Fibre	*
264 KJ	639 kcal	60.0 g	8.4 g	19.3 g	19.3 g	7.6 g	16.4 g	

1 Trim and clean ½ kg leeks for 4 portions (1¼ kg for 10).
2 Tie into a neat bundle.
3 Blanch for approximately 5 minutes and refresh.
4 Cut into 2 cm lengths and place in a shallow pan.
5 Cover with the cooking liquor. Simmer until tender.
6 Serve cold with unstrained cooking liquor.

* For 4 portions

73 Mushrooms (champignons à la grecque) (2)

Cal	Cal	Fat	Sat Fat	Carb	Sugar	Protein	Fibre
587 KJ	142 kcal	15.2 g	2.2 g	0.4 g	0.3 g	1.1 g	0.6 g

1 Allow 200 g of small, cleaned, white button mushrooms for 4 portions.
2 Cook gently in the cooking liquor for 3 to 4 minutes.
3 Serve cold with the unstrained liquor.

Portuguese-style hors d'oeuvre

All the vegetables prepared in the Greek style may also be prepared in the Portuguese style. They are prepared and blanched in the same way then cooked in the following liquid.

	4 portions	10 portions
onion, chopped	1	2½
olive oil	1 tbsp	2½ tbsp
tomatoes	400 g	1¼ kg
garlic	1 clove	1½ cloves
bay leaf	½	3
parsley, chopped		
sprig of thyme		
tomato purée	25 g	60 g
salt, pepper		

1 Sweat the onion in the oil.
2 Skin and deseed the tomatoes. Chop roughly.
3 Add to the onion with the remainder of the ingredients.
4 Correct the seasoning.
5 Add the vegetables (depending on selection) and simmer until tender, with the exception of cauliflower, which should be left crisp.
6 Serve hot or cold with the unstrained cooking liquor.

Salad leaves and vegetables

As these are eaten raw they may contain live food-poisoning bacteria and must be thoroughly washed to remove any soil. Watercress, as the name suggests, is grown in water and, as there is always the danger that the water may have been polluted, it must also be washed thoroughly in clean water.

74 Celery (céleri)

Trim and thoroughly wash the celery. Remove any discoloured outer stalks. If the celery is thick ribbed, peel off the outer until smooth. Serve stalks whole or cut into strips.

75 Chicory (endive belge)

Trim off the root end. Cut into 1 cm lengths, wash well and drain.

76 Curled chicory (endive frisée)

Thoroughly wash and trim off the stalk. Drain well.

77 Lettuce and iceberg lettuce *(laitue)*

Trim off the root and remove the outside leaves. Wash thoroughly and drain well. The outer leaves can be pulled off and the hearts cut into quarters.

78 Cos lettuce *(laitue romaine)*

Trim off the root end and remove the outside leaves. Wash thoroughly and drain well. Cut into quarters.

79 Mustard and cress

Trim off the stalk ends of the cress. Wash well and lift out of the water so as to leave the seed cases behind. Drain well.

80 Radishes *(radis)*

The green stems should be trimmed to about 2 cm long, and the root end cut off. Wash well, drain and dress neatly.

81 Rocket

A small-leafed, sharp, peppery-tasting salad. Trim, wash well and drain.

82 Watercress *(cresson)*

Trim off the stalk ends, discard any discoloured leaves, thoroughly wash and drain.

83 Mixed salad (salade panachée)

Neatly arrange in a salad bowl. A typical mixed salad would consist of lettuce, tomato, cucumber, watercress, radishes, etc. Almost any kind of salad vegetable can be used. Offer a vinaigrette separately (see recipe 1).

Figure 4.11 ✒ Mixed salad (individual portion)

84 Green salad (salade verte)

Any of the green salads – lettuce, cos lettuce, lamb's lettuce (also known as corn salad or mâche), curled chicory – or any combination of green salads may be used, and a few leaves of radicchio. Neatly arrange in a salad bowl; serve with vinaigrette separately (see recipe 1).

85 French salad (salade française)

The usual ingredients are lettuce, tomato and cucumber, but these may be varied with other salad vegetables, in some cases with quarters of egg. A vinaigrette made with French mustard (French dressing) should be offered.

Cold fish dishes

Cooking and presentation of cold fish

86 Fish cooking liquid (court bouillon)

	4 portions	10 portions
water	1 litre	2½ litres
salt	10 g	25 g
carrots, sliced	50 g	125 g
bay leaf	1	2
parsley stalks	2–3	5–8
vinegar	60 ml	150 ml
peppercorns	6	15
onions, sliced	50 g	125 g
sprig of thyme		

1 Simmer all the ingredients for 30–40 minutes.
2 Pass through a strainer, use as required.

87 Salmon

Salmon may be obtained in varying weights from 3½–15 kg: ½ kg uncleaned salmon yields 2–3 portions. Size is an important consideration, depending on whether the salmon is to be cooked whole or cut into darnes. A salmon of any size may be cooked whole. When required for darnes, a medium-sized salmon will be more suitable.

Figure 4.12 ✎ Salmon prepared for poaching

88 Cooking of a whole salmon

1 Scrape off all scales with the back of a knife.
2 Remove all gills and clean out the head.
3 Remove the intestines and clear the blood from the backbone.
4 Trim off all fins. Wash well.
5 Place in a salmon kettle, cover with cold court bouillon (see recipe 86).
6 Bring slowly to the boil, skim, then simmer gently.
7 Allow the following approximate simmering times:

- 3½ kg – 15 minutes
- 7 kg – 20 minutes
- 10½ kg – 25 minutes
- 14 kg – 30 minutes.

Note: Always allow the salmon to remain in the court bouillon until cold.

89 Cold salmon

Cal 1794 KJ	Cal 427 kcal	Fat 33.6 g	Sat Fat 6.0 g	Carb 1.3 g	Sugar 1.2 g	Protein 29.9 g	Fibre 0.7 g

Figure 4.13 ✒ Dressed cold salmon

	8–10 portions
salmon, cleaned	1¼ kg
court bouillon (recipe 86)	1 litre
cucumber	½
large lettuce	1
tomatoes	200 g
mayonnaise (see recipe 4) or green sauce (see recipe 6)	250 ml

1 Cook the salmon in the court bouillon, either whole or cut into 4 or 8 darnes.
2 Allow to cool thoroughly in the cooking liquid to keep it moist. Divide a whole salmon into eight even portions; for darnes, remove centre bone and cut each darne in half, if required.
3 Except when whole, remove the centre bone, the skin and brown surface, and dress neatly on a flat dish.
4 Peel and slice the cucumber and neatly arrange a few slices on each portion.
5 Garnish with quarters of lettuce and quarters of tomatoes.
6 Serve the sauce or mayonnaise in a sauceboat separately.

Presentation of a whole salmon

If a cooked salmon is to be presented and served cold from the whole fish, the procedure is as follows.

- Carefully remove the skin and the dark layer under the skin (which is cooked blood). The now bared salmon flesh should be perfectly smooth.
- Make sure the salmon is well drained and place it on to the serving dish or board.

- The salmon is now ready for decorating and garnishing. Keep this to the minimum and avoid over-covering the fish and the dish. Neatly overlapping thin slices of cucumber (the skin may be left on or removed), quartered tomatoes (which can be peeled and neatly cut), small pieces of hearts of lettuce can, if artistically set out, give a quick, neat-looking, appetising appearance. Remember, time is money and there is no justification for spending a lot of time cutting fiddly little pieces of many different items to form patterns that often look untidy once the first portion has been cut.

Figure 4.14 ✏ Garnished portion of hot salmon

The typical meats or poultry for cold presentation are roast beef, boiled or honey roast ham or gammon, roast chicken or turkey, and boiled ox tongue. These are available as leftover joints from previous hot meals, cooked specially for cold service or bought in ready cooked from suppliers. The various ways of presentation and service are:

- sliced from whole joints on the bone in front of the customer (in which case all bones that may hinder carving must be removed first)
- sliced from boned joints, which in some cases may be rolled and stuffed (also in front of the customer)
- pre-sliced in the kitchen, in which case the meat or poultry should be cut as close to service time as possible, otherwise it will start to dry and curl up; pre-sliced meats or poultry can be neatly cut, dressed with the slices overlapping each other, placed on to large dishes or individual plates, covered with clingfilm and kept under refrigeration; when large numbers of plated meals have to be prepared, plate rings can be used and the plates stacked in sensible-sized numbers.

When joints of meat, hams, tongue or turkeys are cooked fresh for serving cold, this is usually done the day before. After cooking they are allowed to cool (the hams are left in the cooking liquor) and then kept under refrigeration overnight.

When roast chickens are required for serving cold, ideally they should be cooked 1–2 hours before service, left to cool (not in the refrigerator) and then carved as required. In this way, the meat remains moist and succulent. Chickens can then be cut into eight pieces and the excess bones removed before serving.

When any meats or poultry are required for a cold buffet, the joint can be presented whole with 2–3 slices cut, laid overlapping from the base of the joint, on a suitably sized dish. The two rear sides of the joint can then be garnished (if required) with two small, neatly placed bunches of watercress dressed so that only leaves show. If a little more colour is required, then a tulip-cut tomato or two may be added. It is a mistake to over-garnish any cold dishes.

If the cut surface of any joint begins to look dry, a thin slice should be removed and discarded before cutting any slices for service or presenting the joint on a cold buffet.

Ham should not be confused with gammon. A gammon is the hind leg of a baconer weight pig and is cut from a side of bacon. A ham is the hind leg of a porker pig and is cut round from the side of pork with the aitch bone, and usually cured by dry salting. Ham is boiled and can be served hot or cold. Certain imported hams (Parma ham, Bayonne and Ardennes) are sliced thinly and eaten raw, generally as an hors d'oeuvre. In order to carve the ham efficiently it is necessary to remove the aitch bone after cooking. Traditional English hams include York and Bradenham.

Pre-prepared pâtés or terrines are available in a wide variety of types and flavourings, which include liver (chicken, duck, etc.), poultry and game. Pâtés are usually cooked enclosed in a thin layer of bacon fat, or they may be enclosed in hot water pastry within a special mould.

Pâtés and terrines must be kept under refrigeration at all times and should never be allowed to stand in a warm kitchen or dining room because they are easily contaminated by food poisoning bacteria. For service, the pâté or

terrine can be displayed whole with one or two slices cut, or cut in slices and dressed on plates. If in either case these are to be on display to the customer, then the display counter or cabinet must be refrigerated.

Fish and vegetable pâtés and terrines are also available. When serving meat, poultry or game pâtés, a simple garnish of a fan of gherkin and a little salad is sufficient.

The use of plastic gloves when cold foods are being handled will reduce the risk of pâté contamination. See pages 100–104 for pâté and terrine recipes.

90 Chicken salad

	4 portions	10 portions
lettuce, washed	1	2–3
cooked chicken, free from skin and bone	1 x 1½ kg	2 x 2kg
tomatoes	400 g	1½ kg
hard-boiled egg	1	5
anchovies	10 g	25 g
olives	4–8	10–20
capers	5 g	12 g
vinaigrette (see recipe 1)	4 tbsp	10 tbsp

1 Remove heart from the lettuce. Shred the remainder. Place in a salad bowl.
2 Cut the chicken into neat pieces and place on the lettuce.

3 Decorate with quarters of tomato, hard-boiled egg, anchovies, olives, quartered heart of the lettuce and capers.
4 Serve accompanied with vinaigrette.

HEALTHY EATING TIP
- The anchovies, capers and olives will contribute a considerable amount of salt, so no added salt is necessary.
- Serve with plenty of starchy carbohydrate and additional salad vegetables.

91 Raised pork pie/hot water paste

Hot water paste

	4 portions	10 portions
strong plain flour	250 g	500 g
salt		
lard or margarine (alternatively use 100 g lard and 25 g		
butter or margarine)	125 g	300 g
water	125 ml	300 ml

1 Sift the flour and salt into a basin. Make a well in the centre.
2 Boil the fat with the water and pour immediately into the flour.
3 Mix with a wooden spoon until cool.
4 Mix to a smooth paste and use while still warm.

Raised pork pie

	4 portions	10 portions
shoulder of pork, without bone	300 g	1 kg
bacon	100 g	250 g
allspice (or mixed spice) and chopped sage	½ tsp	1½ tsp
salt, pepper		
bread soaked in milk	50 g	125 g
stock or water	2 tbsp	5 tbsp
In addition		
eggwash		
stock, hot	125 ml	375 ml
gelatine	5 g	12.5 g
picked watercress and salad to serve		

1 Cut the pork and bacon into small even pieces and combine with the rest of the main ingredients.
2 Keep one-quarter of the paste warm and covered.
3 Roll out the remaining three-quarters and carefully line a well-greased raised pie mould.
4 Add the filling and press down firmly.
5 Roll out the remaining pastry for the lid, and eggwash the edges of the pie.
6 Add the lid, seal firmly, neaten the edges, cut off any surplus paste; decorate if desired.
7 Make a hole 1 cm in diameter in the centre of the pie; brush all over with eggwash.
8 Bake in a hot oven (230–250°C) for approximately 20 minutes.
9 Reduce the heat to moderate (150–200°C) and cook for 1½–2 hours in all.
10 If the pie colours too quickly, cover with greaseproof paper or foil. Remove from the oven and carefully remove tin. Eggwash the pie all over and return to the oven for a few minutes.
11 Remove from the oven and fill with approximately 125 ml of good hot stock in which 5 g of gelatine has been dissolved.
12 Serve when cold, garnished with picked watercress and offer a suitable salad.

HEALTHY EATING TIP

• The paste, pork and bacon result in a high-fat dish. Serve with plenty of potato, rice or pasta and a large salad to proportionally reduce the fat.
• Little or no added salt is needed – there is plenty in the bacon.

92 Veal and ham pie

Cal	Cal	Fat	Sat Fat	Carb	Sugar	Protein	Fibre
607 KJ	144 kcal	4.5 g	1.5 g	3.8 g	0.8 g	22.4 g	0.1 g

	4 portions	10 portions
ham or bacon	150 g	375 g
salt, pepper		
hard-boiled egg	1	2
lean veal	250 g	625 g
parsley and thyme	½ tsp	1 tsp
lemon, grated zest of	1	2
stock or water	2 tbsp	5 tbsp
bread soaked in milk	50 g	125 g
hot water paste (recipe 91)		

Proceed as for raised pork pie (recipe 91). Place the shelled egg in the centre of the mixture. Serve when cold, garnished with picked watercress and offer a suitable salad.

HEALTHY EATING TIP

• The paste and bacon result in a high-fat dish. Serve with plenty of potato, rice or pasta and a large salad to proportionally reduce the fat.
• Little or no added salt is needed – there is plenty in the bacon.

Pickles

Vegetables to be pickled are usually brined (unless they are to be used in a chutney or similar mixture, then it is not necessary). Brining removes the surplus water that would otherwise dilute the vinegar and make it too weak to act as a preservative.

Dry brining is used for watery vegetables such as cucumbers, marrows and tomatoes. Place the prepared vegetables in a deep bowl, sprinkle salt between the layers, allowing about ½ tsp salt per each 500 g. Cover and leave overnight.

Wet brining is used for cauliflower, onions, etc. Allow 50 g salt to 500 ml water (sufficient for about ½ kg vegetables), place the prepared vegetables in a deep bowl, cover with the brine and leave overnight. Root vegetables such as artichokes, and sometimes beetroot, are cooked in half-strength brine until tender. After brining, rinse and drain the vegetables.

Spiced vinegar is used to cover most simple pickles; the vinegar used for this – and for all pickles – must be of high quality, with an acetic acid content of not less then 6 per cent. Brewed malt vinegar is most commonly used, but for onions, cauliflower and other light-coloured vegetables, white vinegar may be used.

93 Spiced vinegar

vinegar	1 litre
blade mace	5 g
allspice	5 g
cloves	5 g
stick cinnamon	5 g
peppercorns	6
root ginger (for hot pickle)	5 g

Tie the spices in muslin, place them in a covered pan with the vinegar and heat slowly to boiling point. Remove from the heat, stand for 2 hours, then remove bag.

94 Pickled red cabbage

Remove the outer leaves of the cabbage and shred the rest finely. Place in a deep bowl, sprinkle each layer with dry salt and leave for 24 hours. Rinse and drain, cover with spiced vinegar and leave for a further 24 hours, mixing occasionally. Pack and cover.

95 Mixed pickle

Prepare the vegetables, with the exception of the marrow (see note below for suggested vegetables to use), and soak them in brine for 24 hours. Peel the marrow, remove the seeds and cut into small squares, sprinkle and salt, and let it stand for 12 hours. Drain the vegetables, pack them into jars, and cover with cold spiced vinegar (see recipe 93). Cover the jars and allow the pickle to mature for at least a month before use.

Note: The following make a good mixture: cauliflower, cucumber, green tomatoes, onions and marrow.

Scrambled eggs
(recipe 1)

Hard-boiled eggs
(recipe 5)

Fried eggs
(recipe 8)

Plain omelette
(recipe 13)

Poached eggs
(recipe 10)

chapter 5

EGG DISHES

VRQ

Unit 212   **Prepare and cook rice, pasta, grains and egg dishes**

NVQ

Unit 643 (2FPC8)   **Prepare, cook and finish basic egg dishes**

Prepare and cook eggs

Practical skills
The candidate will be able to:
1 Use the correct type and amount of eggs for the dish specification
2 Demonstrate the correct use of tools and equipment to prepare egg dishes
3 Prepare and cook eggs according to dish specifications
4 Demonstrate control of the cooking process to obtain the required quality
5 Assemble and finish the dish in line with dish/customer requirements
6 Evaluate finished egg dishes
7 Demonstrate safe and hygienic practices

Underpinning knowledge
The candidate will be able to:
1 Identify types of eggs and their use
2 Identify sauces and additions for egg dishes
3 Identify the appropriate tools and equipment to prepare egg dishes
4 Identify preparation and cooking methods for eggs
5 Describe the cooking process and adjustments necessary for egg dishes
6 Describe the skills needed to check and finish to specification
7 State the correct holding, serving and storage procedures for eggs

Eggs

Types of egg

Hens' eggs are almost exclusively used for cookery but eggs from turkeys, geese, ducks, guinea fowl, quail and gulls are also edible.

Quails' eggs are used in a variety of ways: for example, as a garnish to many hot and cold dishes; as a starter or main course, such as a salad of assorted leaves with hot wild mushrooms and poached quail eggs, or tartlet of quail eggs on chopped mushrooms coated with hollandaise sauce.

Sizes

Hens' eggs are graded in four sizes: small, medium, large and very large, as shown in Table 5.1.

Table 5.1 Hens' egg sizes

Very large	73 g+	Size 0
		Size 1
Large	63–73 g	Size 1
		Size 2
		Size 3
Medium	53–63 g	Size 3
		Size 4
		Size 5
Small	53 g and under	Size 5
		Size 6
		Size 7

Purchasing and quality

The size of the eggs does not affect their quality, but it does affect their price. Eggs are tested for quality, then weighed and graded. When buying eggs the following points should be noted.

- The eggshell should be clean, well shaped, strong and slightly rough.
- When eggs are broken there should be a high proportion of thick white to thin white. If an egg is kept, the thick white gradually changes into thin white, and water passes from the white into the yolk.
- The yolk should be firm, round (not flattened) and of a good even colour. As eggs are kept the yolk loses strength and begins to flatten, water evaporates from the egg and is replaced by air.

Food value

Eggs are useful as a main dish as they provide the energy, fat, minerals and vitamins needed for growth and repair of the body. The fat in the egg yolk is high in saturated fat. The egg white is made up of protein and water (see recipe 14 – egg white omelette).

Salmonella

Hens can pass salmonella bacteria into their eggs and thus cause food poisoning. To reduce this risk, pasteurised eggs may be used where appropriate (e.g. in omelettes, scrambled eggs).

Storage

Store in a cool but not too dry place – 0–5°C is ideal – where the humidity of the air and the amount of carbon dioxide present are controlled. Eggs will keep for up to nine months under these conditions.

Because eggshells are porous the eggs will absorb any strong odours; therefore, they should not be stored near strong-smelling foods such as onions, fish and cheese.

Pasteurised eggs are washed, sanitised and then broken into sterilised containers. After combining the yolks and whites they are strained, pasteurised – that is, heated to 63°C for 1 minute – then rapidly cooled.

Health, safety and hygiene

- Eggs should be stored in a cool place, preferably under refrigeration.
- Eggs should be stored away from possible contaminants, such as raw meat, fish and strong-smelling foods.
- Stocks should be rotated: first in, first out.
- Hands should be washed before and after handling eggs.
- Cracked eggs should not be used.
- Preparation surfaces, utensils and containers should be cleaned regularly and always cleaned between preparation of different dishes.
- Egg dishes should be consumed as soon as possible after preparation or, if not for immediate use, refrigerated.

Versatility

Fried, scrambled, poached and boiled eggs, and omelettes are mainly served at breakfast. A variety of dishes may be served for lunch, high tea, supper and snacks.

Egg dishes

1 Scrambled eggs (basic recipe) (oeufs brouillés)

Cal 1105 KJ	Cal 263 kcal	Fat 22.9 g	Sat Fat 8.7 g	Carb 0.5 g	Sugar 0.5 g	Protein 13.9 g	Fibre 0.0 g	*

	4 portions	10 portions
eggs	6–8	15–20
milk (optional)	2 tbsp	5 tbsp
salt, pepper		
butter or oil	50 g	125 g

1 Break the eggs in a basin, add milk (if using), lightly season with salt and pepper and thoroughly mix with a whisk.
2 Melt half the butter in a thick-bottomed pan, add the eggs and cook over a gentle heat, stirring continuously until the eggs are lightly cooked.
3 Remove from the heat, correct the seasoning and mix in the remaining butter. (A tablespoon of cream may also be added at this point.)
4 Serve in individual egg dishes.

Note: If scrambled eggs are cooked too quickly or for too long the protein will toughen, the eggs will discolour because of the iron and sulphur compounds being released, and syneresis (separation of water from the eggs) will occur. This means that they will be unpleasant to eat. The heat from the pan will continue to cook the eggs after it has been removed from the stove; therefore, the pan should be removed from the heat just before the eggs are cooked. Scrambled eggs can be served on a slice of freshly buttered toast with the crust removed.

HEALTHY EATING TIP
- Try to keep the butter used in cooking to a minimum and serve on unbuttered toast.
- Garnish with a grilled tomato.

* Using hard margarine

2 Eggs in cocotte (basic recipe) *(oeufs en cocotte)*

Cal	Cal	Fat	Sat Fat	Carb	Sugar	Protein	Fibre
534 KJ	127 kcal	11.2 g	5.2 g	0.0 g	0.0 g	6.8 g	0.0 g

	4 portions	10 portions
butter	25 g	60 g
eggs	4	10
salt, pepper		

1 Butter the appropriate number of egg cocottes.
2 Break an egg carefully into each and season.
3 Place the cocottes in a sauté pan containing 1 cm water.
4 Cover with a tight-fitting lid, place on a fierce heat so that the water boils rapidly.
5 Cook for 2–3 minutes until the eggs are lightly set, then serve.

Variations
Variations include:
- half a minute before the cooking is completed, add 1 tsp of cream to each egg and complete the cooking
- when cooked, add 1 dsp of jus-lié to each egg
- place diced cooked chicken mixed with cream in the bottom of the cocottes; break the eggs on top of the chicken and cook
- as above, using tomato concassée in place of chicken.

3 Boiled eggs *(oeufs à la coque)*

Cal	Cal	Fat	Sat Fat	Carb	Sugar	Protein	Fibre	*
340 KJ	81 kcal	6.0 g	1.9 g	0.0 g	0.0 g	6.8 g	0.0 g	

Allow 1 or 2 eggs per portion.

Method 1 (soft)
1 Place the eggs in cold water and bring to the boil.
2 Simmer for 2–2½ minutes, then remove from the water.
3 Serve at once in an egg cup.

Method 2 (medium soft)
1 Plunge the eggs in boiling water, then reboil.
2 Simmer for 4–5 minutes.

Note: Boiled eggs are always served in the shell.

* *Using 1 egg per portion*

4 Soft-boiled eggs *(oeufs mollets)*

Cal	Cal	Fat	Sat Fat	Carb	Sugar	Protein	Fibre	*
1052 KJ	251 kcal	18.9 g	8.7 g	8.0 g	3.3 g	12.5 g	1.2 g	

1 Plunge the eggs into boiling water, then reboil.
2 Simmer for 4½–5 minutes. Refresh immediately.
3 Remove the shells carefully.
4 Reheat when required for 30 seconds in hot salted water.

Note: All the recipes given for poached eggs (recipe 10) can also be applied to soft-boiled eggs.

* *Using 1 egg per portion*

5 Hard-boiled eggs *(oeufs durs)*

1 Plunge the eggs into a pan of boiling water.
2 Reboil and simmer for 8–10 minutes.
3 Refresh until cold under running water.

Note: If high temperatures or a long cooking time are used to cook eggs, iron in the yolk and sulphur compounds in the white are released to form an unsightly blackish ring around the yolk. Stale eggs will also show a black ring round the yolk.

6 Hard-boiled eggs with mushroom and cheese sauce (oeufs Chimay)

Cal 679 KJ	Cal 162 kcal	Fat 12.0 g	Sat Fat 3.8 g	Carb 0.0 g	Sugar 0.0 g	Protein 13.5 g	Fibre 0.0 g	*

	4 portions	10 portions
hard-boiled eggs	4	10
shallots, chopped	10 g	25 g
butter, margarine or oil } duxelle	10 g	25 g
mushrooms	100 g	250 g
parsley or other fresh herbs, chopped		
salt, pepper		
mornay sauce (see page 52)	250 ml	625 ml
grated Parmesan cheese		

1 Cut the eggs in halves lengthwise.
2 Remove the yolks and pass them through a sieve.
3 Place the whites in an earthenware serving dish.
4 Prepare the duxelle by cooking the chopped shallot in the butter without colouring, add the well-washed and finely chopped mushroom or mushroom trimmings, cook for 3–4 minutes.

5 Mix the yolks with the duxelle and parsley, and correct the seasoning.
6 Spoon or pipe the mixture into the egg white halves.
7 Cover the eggs with mornay sauce, sprinkle with grated Parmesan cheese and brown slowly under a salamander or in the top of a moderate oven, and serve.

HEALTHY EATING TIP
- Serve with French bread or toast and a green salad.
- There is plenty of salt in the cheese, so additional salt is not necessary.

Using 2 eggs per portion

7 Hard-boiled eggs with cheese and tomato sauce (oeufs aurore)

1 Proceed as for recipe 6, using béchamel in place of the mornay sauce.
2 Add a little tomato sauce or tomato purée to the béchamel to give it a pinkish colour.
3 Mask the eggs, sprinkle with grated cheese.
4 Gratinate under the salamander.

HEALTHY EATING TIP
- Serve with French bread or toast and a green salad.
- There is plenty of salt in the cheese, so additional salt is not necessary.

8 Fried eggs (oeufs frits)

Cal	Cal	Fat	Sat Fat	Carb	Sugar	Protein	Fibre	*
536 KJ	128 kcal	31.0 g	9.8 g	0.0 g	0.0 g	7.6 g	0.0 g	

1 Allow 1 or 2 eggs per portion.
2 Melt a little fat in a frying pan. Add the eggs.
3 Cook gently until lightly set. Serve on a plate or flat dish.

Note: To prepare an excellent fried egg it is essential to use a fresh high-quality egg, to maintain a controlled low heat and use a high-quality fat (butter or oil, such as sunflower oil).

* Fried in sunflower oil

Figure 5.1   Starting to fry an egg

9 Fried eggs and bacon (oeufs au lard)

Cal	Cal	Fat	Sat Fat	Carb	Sugar	Protein	Fibre	*
536 KJ	128 kcal	10.7 g	4.1 g	0.0 g	0.0 g	7.6 g	0.0 g	

1 Allow 2–3 rashers of bacon per portion. Remove the rind and bone.
2 Fry in a little fat or grill on both sides, on a flat tray under the salamander. Dress neatly around the fried egg.

Note: Fried eggs may also be served with grilled or fried tomatoes, mushrooms, sauté potatoes, sausage, black pudding, fried bread etc., as ordered by the customer.

HEALTHY EATING TIP

• The fat can be reduced by serving the eggs with grilled tomatoes and mushrooms, baked beans and unbuttered toast.

* Fried in butter

10 Poached eggs (oeufs pochés)

Cal	Cal	Fat	Sat Fat	Carb	Sugar	Protein	Fibre
358 KJ	85 kcal	6.4 g	2.0 g	0.0 g	0.0 g	6.8 g	0.0 g

High-quality fresh eggs should be used for poaching because they have a large amount of thick white and consequently less of a tendency to spread in the simmering water. Low-quality eggs are difficult to manage because the large quantity of thin white spreads in the simmering water.

A well-prepared poached egg has a firm tender white surrounding the slightly thickened unbroken yolk. The use of a little vinegar (an acid) helps to set the egg white, so preventing it from spreading; it also makes the white more tender and whiter. Too much malt vinegar will discolour and give the eggs a strong vinegar flavour; white vinegar may be used.

1 Carefully break the eggs one by one into a pan of vinegar water (approx. 15 per cent acidulation) and make sure the water is at a gentle boil.
2 Simmer until lightly set, for approximately 3–3½ minutes.
3 Remove carefully with a perforated spoon into a bowl of ice water.
4 Trim the white if necessary.
5 Reheat, when required, by placing into hot salted water for approximately ½–1 minute.
6 Remove carefully from the water using a perforated spoon.
7 Drain on a cloth and use as required.

HEALTHY EATING TIP
• Serve with a thick slice of wholegrain bread or unbuttered toast.

Figure 5.2 Poached eggs

11 Poached eggs with cheese sauce (oeufs pochés mornay)

Cal	Cal	Fat	Sat Fat	Carb	Sugar	Protein	Fibre
1177 KJ	280 kcal	19.1 g	8.7 g	15.2 g	3.4 g	12.8 g	0.8 g

	4 portions	10 portions
eggs	4	10
short paste tartlets		
or	4	10
half slices of buttered		
toast	4	10
mornay sauce (page 52)	250 ml	625 ml

1 Cook eggs as for poached eggs (recipe 10).
2 Place tartlets or toast in an earthenware dish (the slices of toast may be halved, cut in rounds with a cutter, crust removed).
3 Add the hot, well-drained eggs.
4 Completely cover with the sauce, sprinkle with grated Parmesan cheese, brown under the salamander and serve.

HEALTHY EATING TIP
• No added salt is necessary as there is plenty in the cheese.
• Grilled tomatoes could be served to accompany this dish.

Variations
Variations include:
• *florentine* – poached eggs on a bed of leaf spinach and finished as for mornay
• *curried* – poached eggs on a bed of cooked rice coated with a strained curry sauce (page 58)
• *Washington* – on a bed of sweetcorn coated with suprême sauce (page 53) or cream.

12 Scotch eggs

Cal	Cal	Fat	Sat Fat	Carb	Sugar	Protein	Fibre
2094 KJ	499 kcal	39.9 g	11.4 g	18.4 g	0.6 g	18.0 g	1.0 g

	4 portions	10 portions
hard-boiled eggs	4	10
sausage meat	300 g	1 kg
flour	25 g	60 g
beaten egg	1	3
breadcrumbs	50 g	125 g

1 Completely cover each egg with sausage meat.
2 Pass it through the flour, beaten egg and breadcrumbs. Shake off any surplus crumbs.
3 Deep-fry to a golden brown in a moderately hot fat.
4 Drain well, cut in halves and serve hot or cold.

Hot: garnish with fried or sprig parsley, and a sauceboat of suitable sauce, such as tomato (page 60).

Cold: garnish with salad in season and a sauceboat of salad dressing (page 91).

HEALTHY EATING TIP
• Make sure the fat is hot so that less fat will be absorbed into the food during cooking.
• Drain the cooked scotch eggs on kitchen paper.

13 Omelettes (basic recipe) (omelette nature)

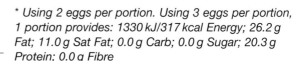

Cal 990 KJ	Cal 236 kcal	Fat 20.2 g	Sat Fat 9.1 g	Carb 0.0 g	Sugar 0.0 g	Protein 13.6 g	Fibre 0.0 g	*

eggs, per portion	2–3
salt, pepper	
butter, margarine or oil	10 g

1 Allow 2–3 eggs per portion.
2 Break the eggs into a basin, season lightly with salt and pepper.
3 Beat well with a fork, or whisk until the yolks and whites are thoroughly combined and no streaks of white can be seen.
4 Heat the omelette pan; wipe thoroughly clean with a dry cloth.
5 Add the butter; heat until foaming but not brown.
6 Add the eggs and cook quickly, moving the mixture continuously with a fork until lightly set; remove from the heat.
7 Half fold the mixture over at right angles to the handle.
8 Tap the bottom of the pan to bring up the edge of the omelette.
9 With care, tilt the pan completely over so as to allow the omelette to fall into the centre of the dish or plate.
10 Neaten the shape if necessary and serve immediately.

HEALTHY EATING TIP
• Use salt sparingly and serve with plenty of starchy carbohydrate and vegetables or salad.

* Using 2 eggs per portion. Using 3 eggs per portion, 1 portion provides: 1330 kJ/317 kcal Energy; 26.2 g Fat; 11.0 g Sat Fat; 0.0 g Carb; 0.0 g Sugar; 20.3 g Protein; 0.0 g Fibre

Variations
Variations to omelettes can easily be made by adding the required ingredient that the guest or dish may require. For example:
• *fine herbs* (chopped parsley, chervil and chives)
• *mushroom* (cooked, sliced, wild or cultivated)
• *cheese* (25 g grated cheese added before folding)
• *tomato* (incision made down centre of cooked omelette, filled with hot tomato concassée; served with tomato sauce)
• *bacon* (grill and then julienne into small strips and fold in at the end).

Figure 5.3 Tomato omelette

14 Egg white omelette

Being prepared and cooked without the egg yolks means that this is almost fat free. The whites are three-quarter whipped, lightly seasoned and then cooked as for any other omelette, folded or flat, garnished or served plain.

15 Spanish omelette

This omelette has tomato concassée, cooked onions, diced red pimento and parsley added, and is cooked and served flat. Many other flat omelettes can be served with a variety of ingredients. A flat omelette is made as for a basic omelette (recipe 13) up to point 7; then sharply tap the pan on the stove to loosen the omelette and toss it over as for a pancake.

16 Jam omelette

This omelette is made omitting salt and pepper. When the eggs are almost set, a tablespoon of warmed jam is added. The omelette is then folded, placed on the serving dish or plate, liberally sprinkled with icing sugar and branded with a red hot iron to caramelise the sugar. (This is illustrated below.)

Figure 5.4 ✐ Making an omelette

Figure 5.5 ✐ Jam omelette

Figure 5.6 ✐ Spanish omelette

Summer vegetable risotto
(see page 164)

...caroni cheese
...ipe 6)

Chestnut gnocchi
(see page 159)

chapter 6

PASTA AND RICE

VRQ

Unit 212   **Prepare and cook rice, pasta, grains and egg dishes**

NVQ

Unit 639 (2FPC4) **Prepare, cook and finish basic rice dishes**

Prepare and cook rice

Practical skills
The candidate will be able to:
1 Use the correct type and amount of rice for the dish specification
2 Pick over and wash the rice
3 Demonstrate the correct use of tools and equipment to prepare rice dishes
4 Prepare and cook rice according to dish specifications
5 Demonstrate control of the cooking process to obtain the required quality
6 Assemble and finish the dish in line with dish/customer requirements
7 Evaluate finished rice dishes
8 Demonstrate safe and hygienic practices

Underpinning knowledge
The candidate will be able to:
1 Identify types of rice and the appropriate cooking method
2 Identify suitable equipment to prepare rice dishes
3 Describe preparation methods for rice
4 Describe the cooking process and adjustments necessary for rice dishes
5 Describe the skills needed to check and finish the dish to specification
6 State the correct holding and storage procedures for rice and rice dishes

Unit 640 (2FPC5) Prepare, cook and finish basic pasta dishes

Prepare and cook pasta

Practical skills

The candidate will be able to:

1 Use the correct type and amount of pasta for the dish specification
2 Demonstrate the correct use of tools and equipment to prepare and cook pasta dishes
3 Prepare and cook pasta according to dish specifications
4 Demonstrate control of the cooking process to obtain the required quality
5 Assemble and finish the dish in line with dish/customer requirements
6 Evaluate finished pasta dishes
7 Demonstrate safe and hygienic practices

Underpinning knowledge

The candidate will be able to:

1 Identify types of pasta and appropriate cooking methods
2 Identify sauces and additions used with pasta
3 Identify suitable equipment to prepare pasta dishes
4 Identify preparation and cooking methods for pasta
5 Describe the cooking process and adjustments necessary for pasta dishes
6 Describe the skills needed to check and finish to dish specification
7 State the correct holding and storage procedures for pasta and pasta dishes

Pasta

The history of pasta

The history of pasta is linked with the history of wheat farming. Wheat has been farmed for at least the last 10,000 years, and there is a good chance that a form of pasta was consumed somewhere in the Middle East in that period.

The popular *'history' of pasta* suggests that it was brought back from China by Marco Polo, This is factually incorrect. The *real history of pasta* records that the Ancient Romans were eating pasta a good thousand years before Marco Polo was born. The famous Roman chef, Apicius, makes reference to a form of pasta ribbons in his first-century cookbook.

Other historical records show that pasta-making equipment was probably used by the Etruscans, and that pasta itself may have come to Italy from Ancient Greece.

We have to wait until the twelfth century for the next specific mention of pasta, when Guglielmo di Malavalle makes reference to macaroni being served at a banquet.

The history of dried pasta probably starts with the Sicilians, and was rapidly adopted by other Italian states as the perfect food for taking on the long naval voyages that merchants and traders depended on.

The history of lasagne starts with a book by Fr Bartolomeo Secchi, which makes reference to long pasta, hollow pasta and pasta soup noodles.

During the sixteenth century pasta was still very much a luxury food. Although it was now being produced commercially, the durum wheat required was expensive, and as result pasta tended to be eaten only by the wealthy.

Pasta finally became a regular part of the national Italian diet in the seventeenth century. The ready availability of simple pasta home-manufacturing machines, coupled with the mass farming of durum wheat, meant that home-made pasta was both practical and economical.

The first large-scale pasta manufacturer was Buitoni, established in 1827. Buitoni still exists today, but is no longer an independent company being part of the Nestlé group.

Mass-produced pasta is now available all over the world, but any respectable Italian chef will still prefer to make his own, or buy from a reputable smaller company.

Food value

Durum wheat has a 15 per cent protein content, which makes it a good alternative to rice and potatoes for vegetarians. Pasta also contains carbohydrates in the form of starch, which gives the body energy. Eating more pasta is in line with the recommendation to 'eat more starchy carbohydrates'.

Storage

Dry pasta can be stored almost indefinitely if kept in a tightly sealed package or a covered container in a cool, dry place.

If cooked pasta is not to be used immediately, drain and rinse thoroughly with cold water. If the pasta is left to sit in water, it will continue to absorb water and become mushy. When the pasta is cool, drain and toss lightly with salad oil to prevent it from sticking and drying out. Cover tightly and refrigerate or freeze. Refrigerate the pasta and sauce separately or the pasta will become soggy. To reheat, put pasta in a colander and immerse in rapidly boiling water just long enough to heat through. Do not allow the pasta to continue to cook. Pasta may also be reheated in a microwave.

Preparation

Bring plenty of water (at least 3.8 litres for every 585 g of dry pasta) to a rolling boil. Add about 1 tbsp of salt per 4 litres of water, if desired. Add the pasta in small quantities to maintain the rolling boil. Stir frequently to prevent sticking. Do not cover the pan. Follow package directions for cooking time. Do not overcook. Pasta should be 'al dente' (meaning literally 'to the tooth' – tender, yet firm). It should be slightly resistant to the bite, but cooked through. Drain pasta to stop the cooking action. Do not rinse unless the recipe specifically says to do so. For salads, drain and rinse pasta with cold water.

About dried pasta

There are an almost infinite number of types of pasta asciutta, especially if you include all the regional variations. Almost 90 per cent of the pasta eaten in Italy is dried, the remainder being home-made. A rule of thumb for cooking dried pasta and portion weights is 80–100 g per portion as a starter course and, if larger portions are required, increase accordingly; traditionally pasta is eaten predominantly as a starter

Most types of dried pasta will cook perfectly well in under 10 minutes. The cooking times on British packaging are often grossly overstated. Spaghetti that has been stored too long and is over-dry may take longer and you might not want to eat the result.

Allow between 500 ml and 1 litre of water per person – the more the better. The reason for this is that the water should always be at a fiercely rolling boil. The more water you have in proportion to pasta the quicker it will return to the boil after the pasta is added. This means fast cooking and better-textured pasta.

Some recipe books suggest you add a little oil to the water when cooking pasta. This has no benefit; it was a method of storage in restaurants when the pasta (predominantly spaghetti) was pre-cooked and a little oil was added to the reheating water to prevent sticking due to the exposure of starch on the spaghetti.

Tortellini and its history

Tortellini literally means 'navel of Venus' (the Roman goddess of love, the Greek equivalent of Aphrodite) and derives from its shape. As legend would have it, Venus and Jupiter were planning to get together one night. When Venus checked into an inn, the chef found out. He went to her room,

peeped through the keyhole and saw Venus laying there, half-naked in bed on her back. When the chef saw her navel, he was inspired to rush to the kitchen to create a stuffed pasta that looked like it, and thus arose the legend of the famous tortellina (tortellini is plural). About the size of a 10 pence piece, this is a round, wrinkled pasta filled with cheese most of the time and, of course, other variant ingredients like meat.

Types of pasta and sauces

There are basically four types of pasta, each of which may be plain, or flavoured with spinach or tomato:

1 dried durum wheat pasta
2 egg pasta
3 semolina pasta
4 wholewheat pasta.

Examples of sauces to go with pasta include:

- tomato sauce
- cream, butter or béchamel-based
- rich meat sauce
- olive oil and garlic
- soft white or blue cheese
- pesto (see page 61).

Pasta cooking with cheese

Examples of cheeses used in pasta cooking include those described below.

Parmesan

The most popular hard cheese for use with pasta, ideal for grating. The flavour is best when it is freshly grated. If bought ready grated, or if it is grated and stored, the flavour deteriorates.

Pecorino

A strong ewes' milk cheese, sometimes studded with peppercorns. Used for strongly flavoured dishes, it can be grated or thinly sliced.

Ricotta

Creamy-white in colour, made from the discarded whey of other cheeses. It is widely used in fillings for pasta such as cannelloni and ravioli, and for sauces.

Mozzarella

Traditionally made from the milk of the water buffalo, mozzarella is pure white and creamy, with a mild but distinctive flavour, and usually round or pear-shaped. It will keep for only a few days in a container half-filled with milk and water.

Gorgonzola or Dolcelatte

Distinctive blue cheeses that can be used in sauces.

Ingredients for pasta dishes

The following are some examples of ingredients that can be used in pasta dishes. The list is almost endless, but can include:

smoked salmon	prawns
shrimps	mussels
scallops	tongue
lobster	chicken livers
tuna fish	smoked ham
crab	mustard and cress
anchovies	parsley
cockles	rosemary
avocado	basil
mushrooms	tarragon
tomatoes	fennel
onions	chives
courgettes	spring onions
peas	marjoram
spinach	pine nuts
chillies	walnuts
peppers	stoned olives

broad beans	capers
broccoli	cooked, dried
sliced sausage	beans
salami	eggs
ham	grated lemon zest
bacon	saffron
beef	grated nutmeg
chicken	sultanas
duck	balsamic vinegar

Summary: cooking pasta

- Always cook pasta in plenty of gently boiling salted water.
- Stir to the boil. Do not overcook.
- If not to be used immediately, refresh and reheat carefully in hot salted water when required. Drain well in a colander.
- With most pasta, freshly grated cheese (Parmesan) should be served separately.
- Allow 50 g dry weight as a first course; 100 g as a main course.
- When cooking fresh pasta add a little oil to the water to prevent the pieces sticking together.

Figure 6.1   Pasta machine

Pasta dishes

1 Fresh egg pasta dough (1)

strong flour	400 g
salt	
eggs, beaten	4 × medium
olive oil as required	approx. 1 tbsp

1 Sieve the flour and salt, shape into a well. Pour the beaten eggs into the well.
2 Gradually incorporate the flour and only add oil to adjust to required consistency. The amount of oil will vary according to the type of flour and the size of the eggs used.
3 Pull and knead the dough until it is of a smooth, elastic consistency.
4 Cover the dough with a dampened cloth and allow to rest in a cool place for 30 minutes.
5 Roll out the dough on a well-floured surface to a thickness of ½ mm, or use a pasta rolling machine.
6 Trim the sides and cut the dough as required using a large knife.

Note: If using a pasta rolling machine, divide the dough into three or four pieces. Pass each section by hand through the machine, turning the rollers with the other hand. Repeat this five or six times, adjusting the rollers each time to make the pasta thinner.

Fresh egg pasta requires less cooking time than dried pasta. When cooking fresh pasta, the addition of a few drops of olive oil in the water will help prevent the pasta pieces from sticking together. Fresh egg pasta not for immediate use must be stored in a cool, dry place. If fresh egg pasta is to be stored, it should be allowed to dry, then kept in a clean, dry container or bowl in a cool dry store.

Variations
- *Spinach:* add 75–100 g finely puréed, dry, cooked spinach to the dough.
- *Tomato:* add 2 tbsp of tomato purée to the dough.
- *Other flavours used include:* beetroot, saffron and black ink from squid.
- *Wholewheat pasta:* use half wholewheat and half white flour.

2 Fresh egg pasta dough (2)

pasta flour	700 g
whole eggs	4
egg yolks	12

1 Place all the ingredients into a food processor and mix quickly until a wet crumb mix appears; this should take no more than 30–45 seconds.
2 Tip the mix out on to a clean surface; this is where the working of the pasta begins.
3 The pasta dough may feel wet at this stage, however the working of the gluten will take the moisture back in to the dry mass, leaving a velvety-smooth finish that is malleable and easy to work; most of this process should be carried out using a pasta machine.
4 Rest the dough for 30 minutes and then it is ready to use.

3 Spaghetti with tomato sauce (spaghetti alla pomodoro)

Cal	Cal	Fat	Sat Fat	Carb	Sugar	Protein	Fibre	*
1672 KJ	400 kcal	17.2 g	9.4 g	50.0 g	10.2 g	11.8 g	4.0 g	

	4 portions	10 portions
spaghetti	100 g	250 g
butter (optional) or		
olive oil	25 g	60 g
tomato sauce (page 60)	250 ml	625 ml
salt, mill pepper		
tomato concassée		
(optional)	100 g	250 g
fresh basil, to serve		
grated cheese, to serve		

HEALTHY EATING TIP
- Use very little or no salt as there is already plenty from the cheese.
- Reduce or omit the added butter and serve with a large green salad.

* Using hard margarine

1 Plunge the spaghetti into a saucepan containing boiling salted water. Allow to boil gently.
2 Stir occasionally with a wooden spoon. Cook for approximately 12–15 minutes.
3 Drain well in a colander. Return to a clean, dry pan.
4 Mix in the butter and add the tomato sauce. Correct the seasoning.
5 Add the tomato concassée and 4–5 leaves of fresh basil torn into pieces with your fingers, and serve with grated cheese.

4 Spaghetti bolognaise (spaghetti alla bolognese)

Cal	Cal	Fat	Sat Fat	Carb	Sugar	Protein	Fibre	*
3188 KJ	760 kcal	32.3 g	5.6 g	83.4 g	10.4 g	39.0 g	9.6 g	

	4 portions	10 portions
butter or oil	20 g	50 g
onion, chopped	50 g	125 g
clove garlic, chopped	1	2
lean minced beef or tail		
end fillet (see note),		
cut into 3 mm dice	400 g	1 kg
jus-lié or demi-glace	125 ml	300 ml
tomato purée	1 tbsp	2½ tbsp
marjoram or oregano	⅛ tsp	¼ tsp
mushrooms, diced	100 g	250 g
salt, mill pepper		
spaghetti	100 g	250 g

1 Place half the butter or oil in a sauteuse.
2 Add the chopped onion and garlic, and cook for 4–5 minutes without colour.
3 Add the beef and cook, colouring lightly.

Figure 6.2 Spaghetti bolognaise with tossed salad

4 Add the jus-lié or demi-glace, the tomato purée and the herbs.
5 Simmer until tender.
6 Add the mushrooms and simmer for 5 minutes. Correct the seasoning.
7 Meanwhile, cook the spaghetti in plenty of boiling salted water.
8 Allow to boil gently, stirring occasionally with a wooden spoon.
9 Cook for approximately 12–15 minutes. Drain well in a colander.
10 Return to a clean pan containing the rest of the butter or oil (optional).
11 Correct the seasoning.
12 Serve with the sauce in centre of the spaghetti.
13 Serve grated cheese separately.

Note: There are many variations on bolognaise sauce – e.g. substitute lean beef with pork mince, or use a combination of both; add 50 g each of chopped carrot and celery; add 100 g chopped pancetta or bacon.

HEALTHY EATING TIP

• Use an unsaturated oil (sunflower or olive). Lightly oil the pan and drain off any excess after the frying is complete. Skim the fat from the finished dish.
• Season with the minimum amount of salt.
• Try using more pasta and extending the sauce with tomatoes.
• Serve with a large green salad.

* *Using sunflower oil, for 4 portions*

5 Bolognese sauce (alternative recipe)

	4 portions	10 portions
olive oil	1 tbsp	2½ tbsp
beef mince and pork mince	270 g	700 g
onion, chopped	½	1
mushrooms, sliced	100 g	250 g
carrots, peeled and cut as for paysanne	1	2
red wine	75 ml	180 ml
beef stock or meat stock, reduced	100 ml	250 ml
tomato purée	1 tbsp	2 tbsp
Tabasco sauce (optional)	½ tsp	1 tsp
salt and freshly ground black pepper, to taste		
fresh parsley, chopped	2 tbsp	5 tbsp
fresh chives, chopped, to garnish		

1 Heat the olive oil in a frying pan, over a medium heat.
2 Add the beef and pork mince and the chopped onion, and pan-fry for 4–6 minutes, stirring well, until the mince has browned and the onion has softened.
3 Add the mushrooms and carrots, and cook for a further minute, before adding the red wine, beef stock and tomato purée.

4 Add the Tabasco and season to taste (optional).
5 Add the chopped parsley and cook for 2–4 minutes more, to allow the wine and stock to reduce a little.
6 When mixing the pasta into the sauce, first drain the water thoroughly from the pasta then place into the bolognese sauce.
7 Toss well, to evenly coat, then spoon into a serving bowl.
8 Garnish with the chopped chives, to serve (optional).

Figure 6.3 Macaroni cheese (recipe 6)

6 Macaroni cheese

Cal	Cal	Fat	Sat Fat	Carb	Sugar	Protein	Fibre	*
7596 KJ	1808 kcal	116.6 g	64.2 g	136.6 g	26.6 g	60.0 g	6.8 g	

	4 portions	10 portions
macaroni	100 g	250 g
butter or oil, optional	25 g	60 g
grated cheese	100 g	250 g
thin béchamel	500 ml	1¼ litre
diluted English or		
continental mustard	¼ tsp	1 tsp
salt, mill pepper		

1 Plunge the macaroni into a saucepan containing plenty of boiling salted water.
2 Allow to boil gently and stir occasionally with a wooden spoon.
3 Cook for approximately 15 minutes and drain well in a colander.
4 Return to a clean pan containing the butter.
5 Mix with half the cheese, and add the béchamel and mustard. Season.
6 Place in an earthenware dish and sprinkle with the remainder of the cheese.
7 Brown lightly under the salamander and serve.

Note: Macaroni may also be prepared and served as for any of the spaghetti dishes.

HEALTHY EATING TIP
- Half the grated cheese could be replaced with a small amount of Parmesan (more flavour and less fat).
- Use semi-skimmed milk for the béchamel. No added salt is necessary.)

Variations
Variations include the addition of cooked, sliced mushrooms, diced ham, sweetcorn, tomato, and so on.

* *For 4 portions*

7 Noodles

Cal	Cal	Fat	Sat Fat	Carb	Sugar	Protein	Fibre	*
2246 KJ	534 kcal	18.4 g	4.8 g	77.8 g	1.6 g	19.4 g	3.6 g	

	4 portions	10 portions
flour	100 g	250 g
salt		
olive or other vegetable oil	1 tsp	3 tsp
egg and egg yolk	1 & 1	3 & 3

Noodles are usually bought ready prepared but may be made as follows.

1 Sieve the flour and salt. Make a well.
2 Add the oil and eggs. Mix to a dough.
3 Knead well until smooth. Leave to rest.
4 Roll out to a thin rectangle 45 × 15 cm.
5 Cut into ½ cm strips. Leave to dry.

Note: For wholemeal noodles use 50 g wholemeal flour and 50 g strong flour. Semolina is a good dusting agent to use when handling this paste. The noodles are cooked in the same way as spaghetti and may be served as for any of the spaghetti recipes. The most popular method of serving them is with butter (as in the next recipe).

* *Using white flour and olive oil, for 4 portions. Using wholemeal flour and olive oil, this recipe provides for 4 portions: 2116 kJ/504 kcal Energy; 19.2 g Fat; 4.8 g Sat Fat; 65.8 g Carb; 2.2 g Sugar; 22.6 g Protein; 8.6 g Fibre*

8 Noodles with butter

Cal 796 KJ	Cal 191 kcal	Fat 12.3 g	Sat Fat 7.1 g	Carb 18.0 g	Sugar 0.6 g	Protein 3.1 g	Fibre 0.7 g	*

	4 portions	10 portions
noodles	100 g	250 g
salt, mill pepper		
a little grated nutmeg		
butter or sesame oil	50 g	125 g

1 Cook the noodles in plenty of gently boiling salted water.
2 Drain well in a colander and return to the pan.
3 Add the seasoning and butter, and toss carefully until mixed.
4 Correct the seasoning and serve.

Note: Noodles may also be used as a garnish with meat and poultry dishes (e.g. braised beef).

HEALTHY EATING TIP
• Keep the added salt to a minimum.

* *Using margarine*

Noodles (oriental style)

Noodles are probably the world's oldest fast food; they are versatile and quick to cook. They may be steamed, boiled, pan-fried, stir-fried or deep-fried. A staple food in the Far East, their popularity is spreading rapidly in the West.

Noodles are high in starch (carbohydrate). They provide some protein, especially those made from hard wheat and beans. The addition of egg also increases noodles' protein content.

Examples of the nutritional content of some noodles are given in Table 6.1.

Table 6.1 🥄 Nutritional content of noodles

100 g dry weight	Calories	Carbohydrate	Protein	Fat	Sodium/salt
rice sticks	380	88%	6%	0	
rice vermicelli	363	85.5%	7.3%	0	
egg noodles	341	70%	11%	1.9%	0.8%
wheat noodles	308	60% + fibre 10%	12.5%	2%	0.8%
bean thread	320	65%	20%	0	
pasta	350	75%	11.5%	0.3%	

Source: Chapman, 1998

9 Rice noodles

Cal 1059 KJ	Cal 253 kcal	Fat 3.2 g	Sat Fat 0.0 g	Carb 50.1 g	Sugar 0.0 g	Protein 4.0 g	Fibre 1.3 g	*

rice flour	125 g
strong wheat flour	125 g
vegetable oil	tbsp
salt	1 tsp
water	

1 Mix the flour with the oil and salt, and just enough water to form a soft, sticky dough. Knead the mixture until it becomes elastic and cohesive.

Note: The measurements given for flour above are a rough guide only. Due to the lack of gluten in rice flour, it is necessary to substitute approx. 25–50 per cent of rice flour with strong wheat flour.

10 Rice noodles salad with duck and orange

Cal	Cal	Fat	Sat Fat	Carb	Sugar	Protein	Fibre
937 KJ	224 kcal	8.1 g	2.0 g	22.8 g	2.4 g	14.4 g	0.5 g

	4 portions	10 portions
rice noodles	100 g	250 g
vegetable oil	1 tbsp	2½ tbsp
spring onions	4	10
coriander leaves, chopped	2 tbsp	5 tbsp
mint leaves, chopped	1 tbsp	2½ tbsp
duck breast, cooked and thinly sliced in julienne	200 g	500 g
lime juice	½	1
orange juice	1 tbsp	2½ tbsp
orange segments (garnish)	8	20

1 Cook the noodles in boiling salted water until done, then refresh and drain.
2 Add the remaining ingredients (except the orange segments), mix well and season.

3 Serve on suitable individual plates garnished with orange segments and coriander leaves. Finish with Thai coconut dressing (see next recipe).

HEALTHY EATING TIP
- Keep the amount of added salt throughout to a minimum.
- Serve with a large portion of mixed leaves.

11 Thai coconut dressing

Cal	Cal	Fat	Sat Fat	Carb	Sugar	Protein	Fibre
83 KJ	20 kcal	0.1 g	0.1 g	3.7 g	3.0 g	0.5 g	0.0 g

coconut milk	125 ml
rice vinegar	62 ml
chilli purée	1 tbsp
garlic, chopped	1 clove
lime juice	2 tbsp
palm sugar	1 tsp
Nnm pla (fish sauce)	optional
seasoning	

1 Mix all ingredients together, then chill.

12 Penne and mangetout

Cal	Cal	Fat	Sat Fat	Carb	Sugar	Protein	Fibre	*
3035 KJ	724 kcal	37.7 g	22.8 g	80.3 g	5.9 g	20.9 g	5.4 g	

	4 portions	10 portions
penne	400 g	1 kg
cream cheese	150 g	375 g
Gorgonzola	75 g	180 g
single cream	2–3 tbsp	3–7 tbsp
mangetout	400 g	1 kg
butter	50 g	125 g
salt and black mill pepper		

1 Cook the pasta in plenty of boiling salted water.
2 Blend the cream cheese, Gorgonzola and cream in a pan over a low heat, to a smooth sauce. If the sauce is too thick, thin with a little water from the pasta.
3 Cook the mangetout in boiling salted water for 1–2 minutes, keeping them slightly firm.

4 Drain the pasta, add the butter, then the sauce and finally the mangetout.
5 Season, finishing with freshly ground black pepper. If desired, a few thin strips of red pepper may be added for decoration.

Note: Macaroni or rigatoni may be used in place of penne.

HEALTHY EATING TIP
• The sauce is high in fat and salt, so additional butter and salt is not necessary.
• For a lower-fat version, use a 'light' cream cheese.
• Serve with a large green salad.

* Using 2.5 tbsp single cream

13 Green fettuccine with ham and creamy cheese (fettucine verdi in salsa cremona)

Cal	Cal	Fat	Sat Fat	Carb	Sugar	Protein	Fibre
3183 KJ	760 kcal	42.2 g	25.4 g	76.3 g	2.7 g	23.7 g	3.1 g

	4 portions	10 portions
green fettuccine or other pasta	400 g	1¼ kg
cream cheese, mashed	200 g	500 g
single cream	2 tbsp	5 tbsp
Parmesan cheese, grated	50 g	125 g
salt, pepper		
melted butter	50 g	125 g
lean cooked ham, cut into thick julienne	100 g	250 g

1 Cook the fettuccine in plenty of boiling salted water.
2 Mix the cream cheese, cream, Parmesan, salt and pepper.
3 Drain the fettuccine and return to the pan.
4 Mix in the butter and cheese mixture. Add the ham. Toss and serve.

HEALTHY EATING TIP
• This sauce is high in fat and salt, so additional butter and salt is not necessary.
• For a lower-fat version, use a 'light' cream cheese.
• Serve with a large green salad.

Stuffed pasta

Examples of stuffed pasta include the following.

- **Agnolini** are small half-moon shapes usually filled with ham and cheese or minced meat.
- **Cannelloni** are squares of pasta, poached, refreshed, dried and stuffed with a variety of fillings (e.g. ricotta cheese and spinach), rolled and finished with an appropriate sauce.
- **Cappelletti**, shaped like little hats, are usually filled as agnolini, and are available dried.
- **Ravioli** are usually square with serrated edges. A wide variety of fillings can be used (fish, meat, vegetarian, cheese, etc.).
- **Ravolini**, or 'little ravioli', are made half the size of ravioli.
- **Tortellini**, a slightly larger version of cappelletti, are also available in dried form.
- **Tortelloni** is a double-sized version of tortellini.

Pasta that is to be stuffed must be rolled as thinly as possible. The stuffing should be pleasant in taste and plentiful in quantity. The edges of the pasta must be thoroughly sealed otherwise the stuffing will seep out during poaching.

All stuffed pasta should be served in or coated with a suitable sauce and, depending on the type of recipe, may be finished 'au gratin' by sprinkling with freshly grated Parmesan and browning lightly under the salamander.

Stuffings

The examples of stuffing for pasta in Table 6.2 are for 400 g pasta. The list is almost endless as every district in Italy has its own variations and, with thought and experimentation, many more can be produced.

Table 6.1 🔪 Examples of pasta stuffings

cooked minced chicken	200 g
minced ham	100 g
butter	25 g
2 yolks or 1 egg	
grated cheese	25 g
pinch of grated nutmeg	
salt and pepper, fresh white breadcrumbs	25 g
cooked dry spinach, puréed	200 g
ricotta cheese	200 g
butter	25 g
nutmeg	
salt and pepper	
cooked minced lean pork	200 g
cooked minced lean veal	200 g
butter	25 g
grated cheese	25 g
2 yolks or 1 egg	
fresh white breadcrumbs	25 g
salt and pepper	

pinch of chopped marjoram	
ricotta cheese	150 g
grated Parmesan	
1 egg	75 g
nutmeg	
salt and pepper	
minced cooked meat	200 g
spinach, cooked	100 g
onion, chopped and cooked	50 g
oregano	
salt, pepper	
chopped cooked fish	200 g
chopped cooked mushrooms	100 g
chopped parsley	
anchovy paste	

14 Ravioli

Cal	Cal	Fat	Sat Fat	Carb	Sugar	Protein	Fibre
1027 KJ	249 kcal	9.4 g	1.4 g	38.9 g	0.8 g	4.8 g	1.6 g

	4 portions	10 portions
flour	200 g	500 g
salt		
olive oil	35 ml	150 ml
water	105 ml	250 ml
fresh egg pasta (recipe 1 or 2)		
can also be used		

1 Sieve the flour and salt. Make a well. Add the liquid.
2 Knead to a smooth dough. Rest for at least 30 minutes in a cool place.
3 Roll out to a very thin oblong: 30 cm × 45 cm.
4 Cut in half and eggwash.
5 Place the stuffing in a piping bag with a large plain tube.

6 Pipe out the filling in small pieces, each about the size of a cherry, approximately 4 cm apart, on to one half of the paste.
7 Carefully cover with the other half of the paste and seal, taking care to avoid air pockets.
8 Mark each with the back of a plain cutter.
9 Cut in between each line of filling, down and across with a serrated pastry wheel.
10 Separate on a well-floured tray.
11 Poach in gently boiling salted water for approximately 10 minutes. Drain well.
12 Place in an earthenware serving dish.
13 Cover with 250 ml jus-lié, demi-glace or tomato sauce.
14 Sprinkle with 50 g grated cheese.
15 Brown under the salamander and serve.

Modern method of making ravioli

1 Cut the pasta sheets into discs approximately 6 cm across and 3 mm thick.
2 Roll the discs in a pasta machine to form ovals 1 mm thick.
3 Place the ovals on a board and fill the centre with the required filling.

4 Egg wash, mould the pasta into shape around the filling and allow to dry.
5 Trim with scissors and nip the rim. Cook as required.

15 Cannelloni (1)

Cal	Cal	Fat	Sat Fat	Carb	Sugar	Protein	Fibre	*
1823 KJ	435 kcal	20.3 g	5.6 g	44.2 g	4.3 g	21.6 g	4.1 g	

Use the same ingredients as for ravioli dough (recipe 14).

1 Roll out the paste as for ravioli.
2 Cut into squares approximately 6 cm × 6 cm.
3 Cook in gently boiling salted water for approximately 10 minutes. Refresh in cold water.
4 Drain well and lay out singly on the table. Pipe out the filling across each.
5 Roll up like sausage rolls. Place in a greased earthenware dish.

6 Add 250 ml demi-glace, jus-lié or tomato sauce.
7 Sprinkle with 25–50 g grated cheese.
8 Brown slowly under the salamander or in the oven, then serve.

Note: a wide variety of fillings may be used, such as those given for ravioli.

* 1 portion with beef

16 Cannelloni (2)

Cal 6292 KJ	Cal 1504 kcal	Fat 123.2 g	Sat Fat 57.9 g	Carb 89.8 g	Sugar 33.0 g	Protein 71.5 g	Fibre 11.1 g	Salt 3.6 g	*

	4 portions	10 portions
onion, finely chopped	1	2
Italian olive oil	8 tbsp	20 tbsp
minced beef	500 g	1¼ kg
salt and freshly ground black pepper, to taste		
ricotta cheese	700 g	1¾ kg
mascarpone cheese	150 g	375 g
pinch of grated nutmeg		
Parmesan cheese, grated	200 g	500 g
Parmesan shavings	100 g	250 g
fresh pasta sheets (15 g each) (approx. 13 × 10 cm)	16–20	40–60
Italian tinned chopped tomatoes	15	40 approx.
handful (approx. 15) fresh basil leaves		
double cream	160 ml	400 ml
extra virgin olive oil	4 tbsp	10 tbsp

1 Preheat the oven to 200°C.
2 Gently fry the onion in olive oil until golden.
3 Add the minced beef, and season with salt and freshly ground black pepper, to taste. Cook for 10–15 minutes.
4 Allow meat to cool.
5 Mix the cooked meat with the ricotta cheese, mascarpone, nutmeg and Parmesan in a large clean bowl.
6 Taste the mixture and then season with salt and freshly ground black pepper.
7 Take a sheet of pasta and, at one end, place two heaped tablespoons of meat mix.

8 Gently roll the pasta to achieve a filled tube shape.
9 Place in a deep-sided baking tray. Repeat the process until the baking tray is full and the pasta sheets are all used up.
10 Pour over the chopped tomatoes. Top with the basil, drizzle over the cream and season with salt and freshly ground black pepper.
11 Finally, drizzle the extra virgin olive oil on top and bake for approximately 20 minutes. For the first 10 minutes cover with foil, then remove.
12 To serve, place three cannelloni on a plate and top with shaved Parmesan, and (if you like) serve with a glass of Italian medium red wine.

* *Using cream cheese instead of mascarpone*

Figure 6.4 Cannelloni

17 Leek cannelloni with lemon thyme and ricotta

Cal 2964 KJ	Cal 708 kcal	Fat 40.2 g	Sat Fat 23.3 g	Carb 63.9 g	Sugar 16.5 g	Protein 26.9 g	Fibre 5.8 g

	4 portions	10 portions
butter	50 g	125 g
leeks	800 g	2 kilo
garlic cloves, crushed and chopped	2	5
lemon thyme leaves	2 tsp	5 tsp
water	2 tsp	5 tsp
ricotta cheese	250 g	625 g
salt, pepper		
fresh pasta dough (see page 146)	12 sheets (approx. 250 g)	30 sheets (approx. 625 g)
fresh tomato sauce (see page 60)	500 ml	1¼ litres
cheese sauce (see page 52)	500 ml	1¼ litres

1 Melt the butter in a suitable pan, add the leeks cut into julienne, garlic and chopped lemon thyme leaves, and the water to prevent from browning. Sweat until tender.
2 Allow to cool, then drain, add the ricotta cheese and season.
3 Cook the pasta sheets – 6 × 6 cm – in boiling water for approximately 3–5 minutes.
4 Refresh and drain well.
5 Spoon the leek filling along one short edge of each sheet and roll up. Arrange the cannelloni seam side down on top of the tomato sauce.
6 Mask with cheese sauce, place in a hot oven to glaze and reheat the cannelloni. Serve immediately.

Note: The cheese sauce may be made with Cheddar, Parmesan, Gruyère or Beaufort.

HEALTHY EATING TIP

- Sweat the leeks in a little sunflower oil and drain before adding the ricotta.
- Use half Cheddar and a small amount of Parmesan to reduce the fat content of the cheese sauce.

18 Pumpkin tortellini with brown butter balsamic vinaigrette

Cal 1744 KJ	Cal 417 kcal	Fat 24.6 g	Sat Fat 9.0 g	Carb 43.2 g	Sugar 4.1 g	Protein 8.2 g	Fibre 3.0 g

	4 portions	10 portions
small pumpkin	1	2½
olive oil	1 tbsp	2½ tbsp
ground cinnamon	½ tsp	1¼ tsp
ground nutmeg	¼ tsp	¾ tsp
caster sugar	1 tsp	1½ tsp
seasoning		
ravioli paste (2)		
egg	1	2
butter	50 g	125 g
shallots, finely chopped	25 g	62 g
balsamic vinegar	2 tbsp	5 tbsp
spinach leaves	100 g	250 g
sage, chopped	1 tbsp	2½ tbsp

1 First prepare the pumpkin filling. Cut in half and scoop out the seeds.
2 Place in a roasting tray. Sprinkle with olive oil, cinnamon and nutmeg. Add a little water to the pan. Roast the pumpkin at 200°C for approximately 45 minutes, until tender.
3 Remove from the oven, allow to cool, scrape out the flesh. Purée the flesh with the sugar in a food processor until smooth, then season.
4 To make the tortellini, roll out the ravioli paste into ⅛ cm thick sheets. Cut the pasta sheets into 8 cm squares.
5 Place 1 teaspoon of the pumpkin filling in the centre of each square. Lightly brush two sides of the pasta with beaten egg and fold the pasta in half, creating a triangle. Join the two ends of the long side of the triangle to form the tortellini, eggwash the seam and firmly press the ends together to seal.

6 Cook the tortellini in boiling salted water for 3–4 minutes until al dente.

7 To prepare the vinaigrette, cook the butter until nut brown, remove from the heat, add the shallots and balsamic vinegar, then season.

8 Place the washed spinach leaves in a pan with one-third of the vinaigrette and quickly wilt the spinach. Season.

9 To serve, place the wilted spinach in the centre of the plates. Arrange the well-drained tortellini on the spinach. Spoon the vinaigrette around the plates. Finish with a sprinkling of fresh sage.

HEALTHY EATING TIP

• Lightly brush the pumpkin with olive oil when roasting.
• Keep the amount of added salt to a minimum throughout.

Figure 6.5 Pumpkin tortellini with brown butter balsamic vinaigrette

19 Lasagne (1)

Cal	Cal	Fat	Sat Fat	Carb	Sugar	Protein	Fibre
2416 KJ	575 kcal	28.7 g	11.4 g	56.1 g	10.0 g	26.7 g	5.8 g

	4 portions	10 portions
lasagne	200 g	500 g
oil	1 tbsp	3 tbsp
thin strips of streaky bacon	50 g	125 g
onion, chopped	100 g	250 g
carrot, chopped	50 g	125 g
celery, chopped	50 g	125 g
minced beef	200 g	500 g
tomato purée	50 g	125 g
jus-lié or demi-glace	375 ml	1 litre
clove garlic	1	1½
salt, pepper		
marjoram	½ tsp	1½ tsp
sliced mushrooms	100 g	250 g
béchamel sauce	250 ml	600 ml
Parmesan or Cheddar cheese, grated	25 g	125 g

1 This recipe can be made using 200 g of ready-bought lasagne or it can be prepared fresh using 200 g flour noodle paste (see recipe 7). Wholemeal lasagne can be made using noodle paste made with 100 g wholemeal flour and 100 g strong flour.

2 Prepare the noodle paste and roll out to 1 mm thick.

3 Cut into 6 cm squares.

4 Allow to rest in a cool place and dry slightly on a cloth dusted with flour.

5 Whether using fresh or ready-bought lasagne, cook in gently simmering salted water for approximately 10 minutes.

6 Refresh in cold water, then drain on a cloth.

7 Gently heat the oil in a thick-bottomed pan, add the bacon and cook for 2–3 minutes.

8 Add the onion, carrot and celery, cover the pan with a lid and cook for 5 minutes.

9 Add the minced beef, increase the heat and stir until lightly brown.

10 Remove from the heat and mix in the tomato purée.

11 Return to the heat, mix in the jus-lié or demi-glace, stir to boil.

12 Add the garlic, salt, pepper and marjoram, and simmer for 15 minutes. Remove the garlic.

13 Mix in the mushrooms, reboil for 2 minutes, then remove from the heat.

14 Butter an ovenproof dish and cover the bottom with a layer of the meat sauce.

15 Add a layer of lasagne and cover with meat sauce.
16 Add another layer of lasagne and cover with the remainder of the meat sauce.
17 Cover with the béchamel.
18 Sprinkle with cheese, cover with a lid and place in a moderately hot oven at 190°C for approximately 20 minutes.
19 Remove the lid, cook for a further 15 minutes and serve in the cleaned ovenproof dish.

Notes: See also vegetarian lasagne (page 444). Fillings for lasagne can be varied in many ways. Tomato sauce may be used instead of jus-lié.

Traditionally, pasta dishes are substantial in quantity but because they are so popular they are also sometimes requested as lighter dishes. Obviously the portion size can be reduced but other variations can also be considered.

For example, freshly made pasta cut into 8–10 cm rounds or squares, rectangles or diamonds, lightly poached or steamed, well drained and placed on a light tasty mixture (e.g. a tablespoon of mousse of chicken, or fish or shellfish, well-cooked dried spinach flavoured with toasted pine nuts and grated nutmeg, duxelle mixture) using just the one piece of pasta on top or a piece top and bottom. A light sauce should be used (e.g. a measure of well-reduced chicken stock with a little skimmed milk, blitzed to a froth just before serving, pesto sauce, a drizzle of good-quality olive oil, or a light tomato sauce). The dish can be finished with a suitable garnish (e.g. lightly fried wild or cultivated sliced mushrooms).

HEALTHY EATING TIP
- Use an unsaturated oil (sunflower or olive). Lightly oil the pan and drain off any excess after the frying is complete. Skim the fat from the finished dish.
- Season with the minimum amount of salt.
- The fat content can be proportionally reduced by increasing the ratio of pasta to sauce and thinning the béchamel.

20 Lasagne (2)

Cal	Cal	Fat	Sat Fat	Carb	Sugar	Protein	Fibre	Salt
5038 KJ	1204 kcal	65.0 g	30.7 g	89.8 g	33.0 g	71.5 g	11.1 g	2.7 g

	4 portions	10 portions
Sauce		
olive oil	3 tbsp	7 tbsp
onion, finely chopped	50 g	125 g
garlic cloves, chopped	2	5
plum tomatoes, peeled and roughly chopped	3 kg	7½ kg
Meatballs		
lean ground beef	250 g	625 g
lean ground pork	250 g	625 g
fennel seeds	2 tsp	5 tsp
large egg	1	3
salt and black pepper to taste		
Pasta assembly		
dried lasagne sheets	300 g	750 g
fresh ricotta	450 g	1125 g
balls hand-rolled mozzarella, sliced 60 g each	4	10
grated Parmesan	150 g	375 g

1 Warm the oil in a large pot and stir in onion and garlic. When the onion is softened (about 10 minutes), add the peeled tomatoes and their juice. Break up the tomatoes as the sauce cooks.
2 While the sauce is cooking, mix the beef, pork, fennel, egg, salt and pepper together and form into meatballs a little smaller than golf balls.
3 When the sauce boils, add the meat balls. Let sit before stirring to harden meatballs. Bring to a hard boil, then lower flame and cook, partially covered for 1 hour, stirring deep in the pot from time to time. When finished, remove meatballs and chop into small pieces.
4 Cook the lasagne in an abundance of boiling water. When not quite al dente, stop cooking, drain and lay each sheet on a damp towel in preparation for assembling.
5 Pre-heat oven to 185°C and, taking a baking dish about 5 cm deep, coat the bottom of the dish sparingly with tomato sauce.
6 Line with layer of lasagne. Dot with ricotta and slices of mozzarella. Sprinkle lightly with grated Parmesan, spread with sauce, then add the chopped meatballs. Repeat the layers in same order, ending the top layer with pasta. Spread this last layer with tomato sauce and grated Parmesan.
7 Cover pan with aluminium foil and bake in a pre-

heated oven at 175°C for 15 minutes. Remove foil and cook for an additional 30 minutes. Cool slightly before serving.

8 Serve with a crisp green salad and home-made garlic bread.

21 Gnocchi parisienne (choux paste)

Cal	Cal	Fat	Sat Fat	Carb	Sugar	Protein	Fibre	*
1433 KJ	000 kcal	25.0 g	11.8 g	19.5 g	3.3 g	10.7 g	0.8 g	

	4 portions	10 portions
water	125 ml	300 ml
margarine or butter	50 g	125 g
salt		
flour, white or wholemeal	60 g	150 g
eggs	2	5
cheese, grated	50 g	125 g
béchamel (thin)	250 ml	625 ml
salt, pepper, to season		

1 Boil the water, margarine or butter, and salt in a saucepan. Remove from the heat.
2 Mix in the flour with a wooden spoon. Return to a gentle heat.
3 Stir continuously until the mixture leaves the sides of the pan.
4 Cool slightly. Gradually add the eggs, beating well. Add half the cheese.
5 Place in a piping bag with ½ cm plain tube.
6 Pipe out in 1 cm lengths into a shallow pan of gently simmering salted water. Do not allow to boil.
7 Cook for approximately 10 minutes. Drain well in a colander.
8 Combine carefully with béchamel. Correct the seasoning.
9 Pour into an earthenware dish.
10 Sprinkle with the remainder of the cheese.
11 Brown lightly under the salamander and serve.

Note: Gnocchi may be used to garnish goulash or navarin in place of potatoes.

HEALTHY EATING TIP
• No added salt is necessary because of the presence of the cheese.

* *Using hard margarine*

22 Gnocchi romaine (semolina)

Cal	Cal	Fat	Sat Fat	Carb	Sugar	Protein	Fibre	*
1066 KJ	254 kcal	12.5 g	6.9 g	27.5 g	7.0 g	9.8 g	0.8 g	

	4 portions	10 portions
milk	500 ml	1½ litre
semolina	100 g	250 g
salt, pepper		
grated nutmeg		
egg yolk	1	3
cheese, grated	25 g	60 g
butter or		
margarine	25 g	60 g
tomato sauce	250 ml	625 ml
(see page 60)		

1 Boil the milk in a thick-bottomed pan.
2 Sprinkle in the semolina, stirring continuously. Stir to the boil.
3 Season and simmer until cooked (approx. 5–10 minutes). Remove from heat.
4 Mix in the egg yolk, cheese and butter.
5 Pour into a buttered tray 1 cm deep.
6 When cold, cut into rounds with a 5 cm round cutter.
7 Place the debris in a buttered earthenware dish.
8 Neatly arrange the rounds on top.
9 Sprinkle with melted butter and cheese.
10 Lightly brown in the oven or under a salamander.
11 Serve with a thread of tomato sauce round the gnocchi.

HEALTHY EATING TIP
• No added salt is necessary because of the presence of the cheese.

* *Using semi-skimmed milk*

23 Gnocchi piemontaise (potato)

Cal	Cal	Fat	Sat Fat	Carb	Sugar	Protein	Fibre	*
1045 KJ	248 kcal	9.7 g	4.7 g	35.2 g	2.1 g	7.2 g	2.1 g	

	4 portions	10 portions
mashed potato	300 g	1 kg
flour, white or wholemeal	100 g	250 g
egg and egg yolk	1	2
butter	25 g	60 g
salt, pepper		
grated nutmeg		
tomato sauce (see page 60)	250 ml	625 ml
grated cheese, to serve		

1 Bake or boil the potatoes in their jackets.
2 Remove the skins and mash with a fork or pass through a sieve.

3 Mix with the flour, egg, butter and seasoning while hot.
4 Mould into balls the size of walnuts.
5 Dust well with flour and flatten slightly with a fork.
6 Poach in gently boiling water until they rise to the surface. Drain carefully.
7 Dress in a buttered earthenware dish, cover with tomato or any other pasta sauce.
8 Sprinkle with grated cheese and brown lightly under the salamander and serve.

HEALTHY EATING TIP
• No added salt is necessary.

* Using white flour

Rice dishes

The history of rice

Rice is a staple in Asia that has a long history. It is a healthy food source that falls into the vegetable category; in China it is eaten alone or with fish. While westernised countries eat rice with meat and even in desserts, the Chinese prefer to eat it as we do bread.

The northern region of China has a very mild climate and therefore does not grow rice. In contrast, the southern region of the country is abundant with rice plantations, which are flooded to help produce this crop. The water level must be maintained at a certain level and remain consistent in subtropical weather for the rice to grow.

The Chinese myth is that rice was sold as a gift to the gods in lieu of animals. It is believed that, after the lands were flooded, all living plants were destroyed; animals were scarce, making hunting difficult. One day, a dog came bounding across a field and, as it approached some Chinese people, they noticed its fur was covered with yellow seeds. Not knowing what these seeds would

produce, they planted them and, as a result, rice grew! Even today, the Chinese have a strong belief that the precious things of life are not pearls or jade, but the five grains – with rice being number one. This grain has fed thousands of people for longer periods than any other grain.

When it comes to cultivated rice, three primary species are grown. The first is O. *Sativa* and the second, O. *Glaberrima*. The first is found in Africa and, while it is the most widely used, it is not cultivated. It is believed that this particular species was developed from other forms approximately 15 million years ago. The third species, O. *Rufipogon*, is grown in China, among other regions.

There is documentation to show that the Buddhist scriptures referred to rice quite often and, again, it was used as an offering to the gods. Initial evidence from archaeologists showed that rice was a valued food dating back as early as 2500 BC during the late Neolithic period in the Yangtze basin.

Even so, in 1966, an archaeologist by the name of Wilhelm G. Solheim II made an important discovery in Southeast Asia. He found pottery shards that had imprints of O. *Sativa* husks and grains. These were discovered in the Korat area of Thailand and, after extensive testing, it was confirmed that these shards dated back to 4000 BC.

The Chinese eventually developed a system of growing rice on farms using puddling soil and then transplanting the seedlings. Today, this system is still widely used in China. The puddling works to break down the internal structure of the soil so it loses little water during the percolation process. The seedlings are then transported once they are one to six weeks old. The transplanting of the rice seedling helps the farmer work the rice field better, thus producing a higher yield. This very process helped to domesticate rice in China.

Rice varieties

A hot, wet atmosphere is required for the cultivation of rice, and it is grown chiefly in India, the Far East, South America, Italy and the southern states of the USA. Rice is the main food crop for about half the world's population. In order to grow, it needs more water than any other cereal crop. There are around 250 different varieties of rice. The main ones are described below.

- **Long-grain:** a narrow, pointed grain that has had the full bran and most of the germ removed so that it is less fibrous than brown rice. Because of its firm structure, which helps to keep the grains separate when cooked, it is suitable for plain boiling and savoury dishes such as kedgeree and curry.
- **Brown grain:** any rice that has had the outer covering removed, but retains its bran and, as a result, is more nutritious and contains more fibre. It takes longer to cook than long-grain rice. The nutty flavour of brown rice lends itself to some recipes, but does not substitute well in traditional dishes such as paella, risotto or puddings.

Many other types of rice are now available, which can add different colours and textures to dishes. Some of these are described below.

- **Short-grain:** a short, rounded grain with a soft texture, suitable for sweet dishes and risotto. *Arborio* is an Italian short-grain rice.
- **Basmati:** a narrow long-grain rice with a distinctive flavour, suitable for serving with Indian dishes. Basmati rice needs to be soaked before being cooked to remove excess starch.
- **Whole-grain rice:** the whole unprocessed grain of the rice.
- **Wild rice:** the expensive seed of an aquatic plant related to the rice family.
- **Precooked instant rice:** par-boiled, ready cooked and boil-in-the-bag rice are similar.
- **Ground rice:** used for milk puddings (see pages 572–73). *Rice flour* can be used for thickening cream soups. *Rice paper* is used for macaroons and nougat.

Storage

Uncooked rice can be stored on the shelf in a tightly sealed container. The shelf life of brown rice is shorter than that of white rice. The bran layers contain oil that can become rancid. Refrigerator storage is recommended for longer shelf life. Washing rice is not necessary; just measure and cook. Cooked rice can be refrigerated for up to seven days or stored in the freezer for six months.

Once cooked, keep hot (above 65°C for no longer than two hours) or cool quickly (within 90 minutes) and keep cool, below 5°C. If this is not done, the spores of *Bacillus cereus* (a bacterium found in the soil) may revert to bacteria and multiply in the cooked rice. Rice is a very useful and versatile carbohydrate. When added to dishes it helps to proportionally reduce the fat content.

24 Plain boiled rice

Cal	Cal	Fat	Sat Fat	Carb	Sugar	Protein	Fibre
37 KJ	90 kcal	0.1 g	0.0 g	20.0 g	0.0 g	1.9 g	0.0 g

	4 portions
rice (dry weight)	100 g

1 Pick and wash the long-grain rice. Add to plenty of boiling salted water.
2 Stir to the boil and simmer gently until tender (approx. 12–15 minutes).

3 Pour into a sieve and rinse well under cold running water, then boiling water. Drain and leave in sieve, placed over a bowl and covered with a cloth.
4 Place on a tray in the hotplate and keep hot.
5 Serve separately in a vegetable dish.

25 Steamed rice

Cal	Cal	Fat	Sat Fat	Carb	Sugar	Protein	Fibre
1277 KJ	305 kcal	1.4 g	0.0 g	63.7 g	0.0 g	7.1 g	0.0 g

	4 portions
rice (dry weight)	100 g

1 Place the washed rice into a saucepan and add water until the water level is 2.5 cm above the rice.
2 Bring to the boil over a fierce heat until most of the water has evaporated.

3 Turn the heat down as low as possible, cover the pan with a lid and allow the rice to complete cooking in the steam.
4 Once cooked, the rice should be allowed to stand in the covered steamer for 10 minutes.

26 Braised or pilaff rice (riz pilaff – Indian pilau)

Cal	Cal	Fat	Sat Fat	Carb	Sugar	Protein	Fibre	*
774 KJ	184 kcal	10.4 g	4.5 g	22.1 g	0.3 g	1.9 g	0.6 g	

	4 portions	10 portions
butter, margarine or oil	50 g	125 g
onion, chopped	25 g	60 g
rice, long grain, white or brown	100 g	250 g
white stock (preferably chicken)	200 ml	500 ml
salt, mill pepper		

1 Place half the butter into a small sauteuse. Add the onion.

2 Cook gently without colouring for 2–3 minutes. Add the rice.
3 Cook gently without colouring for 2–3 minutes.
4 Add twice the amount of stock to rice.
5 Season, cover with buttered paper, bring to the boil.
6 Place in a hot oven (230–250°C) for approximately 15 minutes, until cooked.
7 Remove immediately into a cool sauteuse.
8 Carefully mix in the remaining butter with a two-pronged fork.
9 Correct the seasoning and serve.

Note: It is usual to use long-grain rice for pilaff because the grains are firm, and there is less likelihood of them breaking up and becoming mushy. During cooking the long-grain rice absorbs more liquid, loses less starch and retains its shape as it swells; short or medium grains may split at the ends and become less distinct in outline.

Pilaff may also be infused with herbs and spices such as cardamom.

HEALTHY EATING TIP

- Use an unsaturated oil (sunflower or olive). Lightly oil the pan and drain off any excess after the frying is complete.
- Keep the added salt to a minimum.

Using white rice and hard margarine. Using brown rice and hard margarine, 1 portion provides: 769 kJ/183 kcal Energy; 10.9 g Fat; 4.6 g Sat Fat; 20.7 g Carb; 0.7 g Sugar; 1.9 g Protein; 1.0 g Fibre

27 Braised rice with mushrooms (riz pilaff aux champignons – Indian pilau)

Ingredients are as for braised rice (recipe 26) with the addition of 50–100 g of button mushrooms.

1 Place 25 g butter in a small sauteuse. Add the onion.
2 Cook gently without colour for 2–3 minutes.

3 Add the rice and well-washed, sliced mushrooms.
4 Complete as for braised rice (recipe 26) from step 4.

28 Braised rice with peas and pimento (riz à l'orientale – Indian pilau)

Ingredients and method are as for braised rice (recipe 26) plus 25 g cooked peas and 25 g 1 cm diced pimento carefully mixed in when finishing with butter.

Note: Many other variations of pilaff may be made with the addition of such ingredients as tomato concassée, diced ham, prawns, etc.

29 Braised or pilaff rice with cheese (riz pilaff au fromage – Indian pilau)

Ingredients and method are as for braised rice (recipe 26) with 50–100 g freshly grated cheese added with the butter, before serving.

Risotto demystified

- The whole process, not including heating the stock, should take 30 minutes.
- Arborio is the easiest rice to find.
- Vialone and carnaroli are other Italian types, and each has its adherents.
- Do not attempt to use pudding, patna or Japanese rice, despite their similar appearance to Italian rice.

- A perfect risotto is not a mound of stodgy rice on a plate sitting like a glutinous mound, nor is it a soupy liquid mess lying flat on the plate. It should be just about moundable, fighting to hold its little peaks from collapsing back into the rest.
- All the liquid should be combined with the rice to give a creamy-type consistency. Finish with butter and cream.

30 Risotto with Parmesan (risotto con Parmigiano)

Cal	Cal	Fat	Sat Fat	Carb	Sugar	Protein	Fibre	Salt
2598 KJ	621 kcal	36.2 g	14.1 g	49.9 g	4.2 g	23.0 g	0.3 g	1.4 g

This is the classic risotto. With the addition of saffron and bone marrow it becomes risotto Milanese.

	4 portions	10 portions
chicken stock	1.2 litres	3 litres
butter	80 g	200 g
onion, peeled and finely chopped	½	1
Arborio rice	240 g	600 g
Parmesan, freshly grated	75 g	180 g
salt, pepper		

1 Bring the stock to a simmer, next to where you will cook the risotto. Take a wide, heavy-bottomed pan or casserole, put half the butter in over a medium heat and melt.
2 Add the onion and sweat until it softens and becomes slightly translucent.

HEALTHY EATING TIP
- Use an unsaturated oil (sunflower or olive). Lightly oil the pan and drain off any excess after the frying is complete.
- Additional salt is not necessary.
- Serve with a large salad and tomato bread.

3 Add the rice and stir with a heat-resistant spatula until it is thoroughly coated in butter (about 2 minutes). Then take a soup ladle of hot stock and pour it into the rice.
4 Continue to cook and stir until this liquid addition is completely absorbed (about 3 minutes).
5 Repeat this procedure several times until the rice has swollen and is nearly tender. The rice should not be soft but neither should it be chalky. Taste and wait: if it is undercooked, it will leave a gritty, chalky residue in your mouth.
6 Normally the rice is ready in about 20 minutes after the first addition of stock
7 Add the other half of the butter and half the Parmesan off the heat. Stir these in, season and cover. Leave to rest and swell a little more for 3 minutes. Serve immediately after this in soup plates, with more Parmesan offered separately.

Variations
Risotto variations include:
- *saffron or Milanese-style* – soak ¼ teaspoon saffron in a little hot stock and mix into the risotto near the end of the cooking time
- *seafood* – add any one or a mixture of cooked mussels, shrimp, prawns, etc., just before the rice is cooked; also use half fish stock, half chicken stock
- *mushrooms*.

31 Fried rice

Cal	Cal	Fat	Sat Fat	Carb	Sugar	Protein	Fibre	*
826 KJ	196 kcal	7.4 g	1.1 g	29.9 g	0.3 g	4.3 g	0.2 g	

	4 portions	10 portions
boiled rice (cooked at least 3 hours in advance)	400 g	1 kg
spring onions	2	5
oil	2 tbsp	5 tbsp
egg	1	2½
a pinch of salt		
thick soy sauce	2 tbsp	5 tbsp

1 Separate the rice grains as much as possible.
2 Separate the white and green parts of the onions and cut into small rounds.
3 Heat a wok or thick-bottomed pan over high heat.
4 Add the oil and white spring onions; stir for 30–40 seconds.
5 Beat the egg with oil and salt, then pour into the wok; leave for 6–8 seconds until the egg sets on the bottom but remains runny on top.
6 Add the rice; turn and mix continuously for 3–4 minutes until thoroughly hot.
7 Mix in the soy sauce; if the rice is too hard add a little stock and stir for a few seconds.
8 Add the green spring onion and serve.

HEALTHY EATING TIP
- Use an unsaturated oil (sunflower or olive) to lightly oil the pan.
- Soy sauce adds sodium, so no added salt is needed.

* Using vegetable oil

32 Stir-fried rice

Cal	Cal	Fat	Sat Fat	Carb	Sugar	Protein	Fibre	*
1423 KJ	338 kcal	10.2 g	1.9 g	30.6 g	0.6 g	32.7 g	0.6 g	

Stir-fried rice dishes consist of a combination of cold pre-cooked rice and ingredients such as cooked meat or poultry, fish, vegetables or egg.

1 Prepare and cook meat or poultry in fine shreds; dice and lightly cook any vegetables. Add bean sprouts just before the egg.
2 Place a wok or thick-bottomed pan over fierce heat, add some oil and heat until smoking.
3 Add the cold rice and stir-fry for about 1 minute.
4 Add the other ingredients and continue to stir-fry over fierce heat for 4–5 minutes.
5 Add the beaten egg and continue cooking for a further 1–2 minutes.
6 Correct the seasoning and serve immediately.

HEALTHY EATING TIP
- Use an unsaturated oil (sunflower or olive) to lightly oil the pan.
- Soy sauce adds sodium, so no added salt is needed.

* Using 125 g chicken (average dark and light meat) and 25 g mung beans per portion

33 Saffron and almond basmati rice

Cal 1826 KJ	Cal 499 kcal	Fat 18.0 g	Sat Fat 4.5 g	Carb 60.1 g	Sugar 1.5 g	Protein 8.4 g	Fibre 1.1 g

	4 portions	10 portions
basmati rice	250 g	625 g
sunflower oil	2 tbsp	5 tbsp
vermicelli pasta	40 g	100 g
onion, finely chopped	50 g	125 g
clove of garlic, crushed	1	2
butter or ghee	25 g	62 g
saffron strands	½ tsp	1½ tsp
vegetable stock or water	500 ml	1.25 litres
cardamom pods	6	15
cinnamon stick	1	2½
bay leaves	2	5
flaked almonds, lightly toasted	50 g	125 g

1 Soak the rice in cold water with cover for 30 minutes then drain in a sieve.
2 In a large saucepan, heat half the oil and break in the vermicelli. Stir-fry until brown. Carefully remove, and drain off excess oil.
3 Add the remaining oil, lightly fry the onion and garlic until lightly coloured, add the butter or ghee.

4 Add the rice, stir well and fry for 1 minute.
5 Place the saffron in 2 tablespoons of hot stock for 2 minutes.
6 Add the rest of the stock to the rice.
7 Add the vermicelli, cardamom, cinnamon, bay leaves and saffron, and season.
8 Bring to the boil, cover and simmer until rice is cooked.
9 Remove from heat, allow to stand covered for approximately 3 minutes.
10 Sprinkle and stir in the almonds and serve immediately.

HEALTHY EATING TIP

• Use an unsaturated oil (sunflower or olive). Lightly oil the pan and drain off any excess after the frying is complete.
• Drain the vermicelli on kitchen paper.
• Omit the butter/ghee.

Reference

Chapman, P. (1998) *Pat Chapman's Noodle Book*, Hodder & Stoughton Ltd.

Crab

Lobster

Langoustines

Mussels

Crayfish

Scallops

chapter 7

FISH AND SHELLFISH

VRQ

Unit 211 **Prepare and cook fish and shellfish**

NVQ

Unit 620 (2FP1) Prepare fish for basic dishes
Unit 621 (2FP2) Prepare shellfish for basic dishes

Prepare fish and shellfish

Practical skills
The candidate will be able to:
1 Demonstrate the correct use of tools and equipment to prepare fish and shellfish
2 Demonstrate preparation skills for fish and shellfish according to dish
3 Demonstrate portion control with cuts of fish
4 Apply flavourings to fish and shellfish
5 Line appropriate moulds, basins or shape pastes according to dish specifications
6 Apply coatings to fish and shellfish
7 Demonstrate safe and hygienic practices
8 Undertake correct storage procedures for fish and shellfish

Underpinning knowledge
The candidate will be able to:
1 Identify types of fish and shellfish
2 Explain the quality points of fish and shellfish
3 State the most commonly used cuts of fish
4 Describe methods used to preserve fish and shellfish
5 Describe the advantages and disadvantages of the preservation methods
6 Explain portion sizes/weights for cuts of fish and shellfish for dish requirements
7 State the correct storage procedures and temperatures for fish and shellfish

Unit 627 (2FC1)   Cook and finish basic fish
                  dishes
Unit 628 (2FC2)   Cook and finish basic
                  shellfish dishes

Cook fish and shellfish

Practical skills
The candidate will be able to:
1 Demonstrate the correct use of tools and
   equipment in cooking or use of fresh or
   preserved fish and shellfish
2 Apply appropriate cooking methods and
   principles to fish and shellfish
3 Make appropriate sauces or coulis for fish and
   shellfish
4 Prepare dressings for fish and shellfish dishes
5 Make suitable flavoured butters/oils for fish
   and shellfish dishes

6 Prepare garnishes for fish and shellfish dishes
7 Apply finishing skills to fish and shellfish dishes
8 Assemble dishes according to dish
   specification
9 Evaluate the finished dish/dishes
10 Demonstrate safe and hygienic practices

Underpinning knowledge
The candidate will be able to:
1 Identify tools and equipment used in the
   cooking of fish and shellfish
2 Explain suitable cooking methods for fish and
   shellfish
3 Explain reasons for applying cooking principles
   to fish and shellfish
4 Explain how to determine when fish and shellfish
   are cooked
5 Describe the skills needed to check and finish
   the dish to specification

Fish

Origins

Fish are vertebrates (animals with a backbone) and are split into two primary groups: flat and round. From this they can be split again, into subgroups or secondary groups such as pelagic (oil-rich fish that swim midwater, such as mackerel and herring) and demersal (white fish that live at or near the bottom of the sea, such as cod, haddock, whiting and plaice).

Marine and freshwater fish were a crucial part of man's diet long before prehistoric societies learnt how to cultivate vegetables and domesticate livestock. Fish provided essential proteins and vitamins; they were easy to catch and eat, and predominantly eaten raw.

There are more than 20,000 species of fish in the seas of the world, yet we use only a fraction of the resources available. Undoubtedly certain types are neither edible nor ethical – however, the European market has a dozen types of fish that make up a large percentage of our consumption. The Japanese and, closer to home, the Portuguese are the exceptions to the rule when it comes to utilisation of a high proportion of fish species.

Because of health considerations many people choose to eat fish in preference to meat, and consequently consumption of fish is and has been steadily increasing. This popularity has resulted in a far greater selection becoming available and, due to swift and efficient transport, well over 200 types of fish are on sale throughout the year.

Fish is plentiful in the UK because we are surrounded by water, although overfishing and pollution are having a detrimental effect on supplies of certain fish. Most catches are made off Iceland or Scotland, in the North Sea, Irish Sea and the English Channel. Salmon are caught in certain English and Scottish rivers, and are also extensively farmed. Frozen fish is imported from Scandinavia, Canada and Japan and other countries worldwide; Canada and Japan both export frozen salmon to Britain.

Unfortunately the supply of fish is not unlimited, due to overfishing, so it is now necessary to have fish farms (such as those for trout and salmon, turbot, bass and cod) to supplement natural sources. This is not the only problem: due to contamination by humans, seas and rivers are becoming increasingly polluted, thus affecting both the supply and the suitability of fish – particularly shellfish – for human consumption.

Types or varieties

- **Oily fish** are round in shape (e.g. herring, mackerel, salmon, tuna, sardines).
- **White fish** are round (e.g. cod, whiting, hake) or flat (e.g. plaice, sole, turbot).
- **Shellfish** (see page 213).

Fresh fish is bought by the kilogram, by the number of fillets or whole fish of the weight that is required. For example, 30 kg of salmon could be ordered as 2 × 15 kg, 3 × 10 kg or 6 × 5 kg. Frozen fish can be purchased in 15 kg blocks.

The checklist in the accompanying box summarises the main points to look for when choosing and buying fish.

Checklist for choosing and buying fish

Whole fish
- clear, bright eyes, not sunken
- bright red gills
- scales should not be missing and they should be firmly attached to the skin
- moist skin (fresh fish feels slightly slippery)
- shiny skin with bright natural colouring
- tail should be stiff and the flesh should feel firm
- should have a fresh sea smell and no trace of ammonia

Fillets
- neat, trim fillets with firm flesh
- fillets should be firm and closely packed together, not ragged or gaping
- white fish should have a white translucent colour with no discoloration

Smoked fish
- glossy appearance
- flesh should feel firm and not sticky
- pleasant, smoky smell

Frozen fish
- frozen hard with no signs of thawing
- the packaging should not be damaged
- no evidence of freezer burn (i.e. dull, white, dry patches)

Cooking

Fish is a very economical to prepare as it cooks quickly and thus can actually represent a fuel saving. When cooked, fish loses its translucent look and in most cases takes on an opaque white colour. It will also flake easily and has to be considered as a delicate product after preparation.

Fish easily becomes dry and loses its flavour if overcooked; for this reason, carefully considered methods of cookery need to be applied as certain fish will dry out too quickly before benefiting from the chosen cooking approach. Overcooked and dry fish is to be avoided as it will reduce the eating quality.

Storage

Spoilage is mainly caused by the actions of enzymes and bacteria. Enzymes are present in the gut of the living fish and help convert its food to tissue and energy. When the fish dies, these enzymes carry on working and help the bacteria in the digestive system to penetrate the belly wall and start breaking down the flesh itself. Bacteria exist on the skin and in the fish intestine. While the fish is alive, the normal defence mechanisms of the body prevent the bacteria from invading the flesh. Once the fish dies, however, the bacteria invade the flesh and start to break it down – the higher the temperature the faster the deterioration. Note that although these bacteria are harmless to humans, eating quality is reduced and the smell will deteriorate dramatically.

Fish, once caught, has a shelf life of 10 to 12 days if kept properly in a refrigerator at a temperature of between 0°C and 5°C. If the fish is delivered whole with the innards still in the fish, then gut and wash the cavity well before storage.

Fresh fish

Fresh fish should be used as soon as possible, but it can be stored overnight. Rinse, pat dry, cover with clingfilm and store towards the bottom of the refrigerator.

Ready-to-eat cooked fish, such as 'hot' smoked mackerel, prawns and crab, should be stored on shelves above other raw foodstuffs to avoid cross-contamination.

Food value

Fish is as useful a source of animal protein as meat. The oily fish (sardines, mackerel, herring, salmon, sardines) contain fat-soluble vitamins (A and D) in their flesh and omega-3 fatty acids (these are unsaturated fatty acids that are essential for health). It is recommended that we eat more oily fish.

The flesh of white fish does not contain any fat. Vitamins A and D are only present in the liver (e.g. cod liver or halibut liver oil).

The small bones in sardines, whitebait and tinned salmon provide the human body with calcium/phosphorus.

Owing to its fat content oily fish is not so digestible as white fish and is not suitable for use in cooking for invalids.

Preservation

Freezing

Fish is either frozen at sea or as soon as possible after reaching port. It should be thawed out before being cooked. Plaice, halibut, turbot, haddock, sole, cod, trout, salmon, herring, whiting, scampi, smoked haddock and kippers are available frozen.

Frozen fish should be checked for:

- no evidence of freezer burn
- undamaged packaging
- minimum fluid loss during thawing
- flesh still feeling firm after thawing.

Frozen fish should be stored at −18°C to −20°C. and thawed out overnight in a refrigerator. It should *not* be thawed out in water as this spoils the taste and texture of the fish, and valuable water-soluble nutrients are lost. Fish should not be re-frozen as this will impair its taste and texture.

When freezing a protein-based product, care should be taken with the speed at which the item freezes. The longer a product takes to freeze the larger and more angular the ice crystals become, and they invariably sever the protein strands allowing the liquid contained in them to flow out once it has been defrosted, leaving you with an inferior product. If, however, you freeze quickly the ice crystals are small (remember: quick = small); liquid loss will always be present, but if frozen quickly the loss will be less dramatic

Canning

Oily fish are usually canned. Sardines, salmon, anchovies, pilchards, tuna, herring and herring roe are canned in their own juice (as with salmon), or in oil or tomato sauce.

Salting

In the UK, the salting of fish is usually accompanied by a smoking process.

- Cured herrings are packed in salt.
- Caviar – the slightly salted roe of the sturgeon – is sieved, tinned and refrigerated. Imitation caviar is also obtainable.

Pickling

Herrings pickled in vinegar are filleted, rolled and skewered, and known as rollmops.

Smoking

Fish that is to be smoked may be gutted or left whole. It is then soaked in a strong salt solution (brine) and in some cases a dye is added to improve colour. After this, it is drained, hung on racks in a kiln and exposed to smoke for five or six hours.

Smoked fish should be wrapped up well and kept separate from other fish to prevent the smell and dye penetrating other foods.

Cold smoking takes place at a temperature of no more than 33°C (this is to avoid cooking the flesh). Therefore all cold smoked fish is raw and is usually cooked before being eaten, the exception being smoked salmon.

Hot-smoked fish is cured at a temperature between 70 and 80°C in order to cook the flesh, so does not require further cooking.

Choose fish with a pleasant smoky smell and a bright glossy surface. The flesh should be firm; sticky or soggy flesh means that the fish may have been of low quality or undersmoked.

Note: there is a high salt content in salted, pickled and smoked fish. Added salt is not necessary.

Cooking methods

The following are the main cooking methods used for fish.

En sous vide

This is a well-matched method of cookery for fish as moisture from the flesh is lost very quickly while cooking. *Sous vide* helps eliminate this moisture loss and also isolates it, preventing absorption of outside flavours or liquids and thus offering a truer taste. The dish *escabeche* (cured fish) benefits very well from this method as it helps with the marinating process and distributes the liquor evenly around the fish.

Frying

Frying is probably the most popular method of cooking fish. Described below are the three main types of frying.

Shallow-frying (recipes 14–23)

The fish should be seasoned and lightly coated with flour or crumb before frying, in order to protect it and seal in the flavour. Use a mixture of oil and butter when frying and turn the fish only once during cooking, to avoid it breaking up.

This method is suitable for small whole fish, cuts or fillets that are cooked in oil or fat in a frying pan. The fish are usually coated with flour but semolina, matzo meal, oatmeal or breadcrumbs may also be used. If the frying medium is to be butter, it must be clarified (**see page 30**) otherwise there is a risk that the fish may burn. Oil is the best medium, to which a little butter may be added for flavour.

Deep-frying (recipes 8–13)

The fish should be seasoned and coated before frying, usually with a batter or an egg and breadcrumb mixture. Use a suitable container and heat the oil to 190°C. Test the temperature before cooking the fish. Drain the fish on absorbent paper after cooking.

This is suitable for small whole white fish, cuts and fillets. The fish must be coated to form a surface that prevents penetration of the cooking fat or oil into the fish. Coatings can be either:

- flour, egg and breadcrumbs
- milk and flour
- batter.

For further information, refer to the text on deep-frying on pages 31–35 of Chapter 2.

Any white fish are suitable for deep-frying in batter, including cod, haddock, skate and rock salmon (a term used for catfish, coley, dog-fish and so on when cleaned and skinned). Depending on size the fish may be left whole, or may be portioned or filleted.

Stir-frying (recipes 24–25)

This is a very fast and popular method of cooking. Use a wok or deep frying pan and a high cooking temperature. Food should be cut into thin strips and prepared before cooking begins. This method is very well suited to cooking firm-fleshed fish.

It is suitable for fish fillets cut into finger-sized pieces and quickly fried in hot oil. Finely cut ginger and vegetables (e.g. garlic, shallots, broccoli sprigs, mushrooms and beanshoots) may be added. Soy sauce is often used as a seasoning.

Grilling (recipes 36–47)

Grilling, or griddling, is cooking under radiant heat, and is a fast and convenient method suitable for fillets or small whole fish. When grilling whole fish cut through the thickest part of the fish to allow even cooking. Lightly oil and season fish or fillets and, to avoid breaking, do not turn more than once.

Poaching (recipes 27–34)

Poaching is sometimes referred to as boiling, and is suitable for:

- whole fish (e.g. salmon, trout, bass), and
- certain cuts on the bone (e.g. salmon, turbot, brill, halibut, cod, skate).

In either case, the prepared fish should be completely immersed in the cooking liquid, which can be either water, water and milk, fish stock (for white fish) or a court bouillon (water, vinegar, onion, carrot, thyme, bay leaf, parsley stalks and peppercorns) for oily fish. Most kinds of fish can be cooked in this way and should be poached gently for 5–8 minutes, depending on the thickness of the fish. Whole fish are covered with a cold liquid and brought to the boil then simmered *gently*. Cut fish are usually cooked in a *gently* simmering liquid. The resulting liquid is ideal for use in sauces and soups (although see the note on smoked fish in the next paragraph).

When poaching smoked fish, place in cold, unsalted water and bring to a steady simmer. This liquid will be salty and may not be suitable for reuse.

Roasting (recipes 48–49)

Roasting is a word in common use nowadays and, particularly when describing a method of cookery

in a menu, it is used quite loosely. It is not impossible to roast fish but a fishbone trivet should be used, primarily to prevent the fish frying in the oil or cooking medium and, second, to impart more flavour to the fish while cooking.

This method of cookery, when used with fish, should be quick and used only with thick cuts of fish such as cod, salmon, turbot, sea bass and monkfish. Depending on size, the fish may be roasted whole (e.g. sea bass).

The fish is more usually portioned, skin left on, and lightly seared in hot oil skin side down in a pan, then roasted in a hot oven (230°C) skin side up. Finely sliced vegetables and sprigs of herbs can be added to the roasting tray and, when the fish is cooked and removed, the tray can be deglazed with a suitable wine (usually a dry white) and fish stock to form the basis of an accompanying sauce.

If the fish is skinned after it has been seared a light crust of breadcrumbs mixed with a good oil, butter or margarine, lemon juice, fresh chopped herbs (e.g. parsley, tarragon, chervil, rosemary), a duxelle-based mixture or a light coating of creamed horseradish can be used.

The fish portions may be served with a sauce or salsa, or placed on a bed of creamed or flavoured mashed potato (page 521) with a compound butter sauce (page 65) and quarters of lemon. Examples of this method of cooking include roast cod on garlic mash and roast sea bass flavoured with fennel.

Steaming (recipe 35)

Small whole fish or fillets are good cooked in this way. Flavour can be added by using different cooking liquids, but usually the fish is seasoned. Place it in a steamer, cover it tightly and cook over simmering water for 10–15 minutes, depending on the thickness of the fish or the fillets. If a steamer is not available fish can be steamed between two plates above a pan of boiling water.

Any fish that can be poached or boiled may also be cooked by steaming. This method has a number of advantages.

- It is an easy method of cooking.

- Because it is quick, it conserves flavour, colour and nutrients.
- It is suitable for large-scale cookery.

Fish is prepared as for poaching. Any fish that can be poached or boiled can also be steamed. The liquor from the steamed fish should be strained off, reduced and incorporated into the sauce. Preparation can also include adding finely cut ingredients (e.g. ginger, spring onions, garlic, mushrooms and soft herbs), lemon juice and dry white wine to the fish on the steamer dish before cooking or served with the fish.

Baking (recipes 50–51)

Many fish (whole, portioned or filleted) may be oven-baked. To retain their natural moisture it is necessary to protect the fish from direct heat. There are various ways of preparing fish for baking:

- whole fish (scaled, gutted and washed)
- whole fish stuffed, e.g. a duxelle-based mixture, breadcrumbs, herbs
- wrapped in pastry (puff or filo)
- completely covered with a thick coating of dampened sea salt
- portions of fish can be baked (e.g. cod, hake, haddock).

Then proceed as follows.

1 Place the prepared portions in a greased ovenproof dish, brush with oil and bake slowly, basting frequently. Add herbs (e.g. parsley, rosemary, thyme) and finely sliced vegetables (e.g. mushrooms, onions, shallots).
2 Depending on the size and shape of the fish, 100–150 g thick portions can be cut leaving the skin on (this helps to retain the natural moisture of the fish) and baked skin side up. The fish can then be simply served, e.g. on a bed of creamy or flavoured mashed potato (page 521) with a suitable sauce, such as compound butter (page 65) or a salsa (page 62).

Health, safety and hygiene

For information on maintaining a safe and secure working environment, a professional and hygienic appearance, and clean food production areas, equipment and utensils, as well as food hygiene, please refer to Chapters 17 and 18. Additional health and safety points relating to fish preparation and cookery are as follows.

- Store fresh fish in containers with ice (changed daily) in a refrigerator at a temperature of 1–2°C.
- To avoid the risk of cross-contamination, fish should be stored in a separate refrigerator away from other foods; cooked and raw fish must be kept separate.
- Frozen fish should be stored in a deep-freezer at −18°C. When required, frozen fish should be defrosted in a refrigerator. If the frozen food is removed from the freezer and left uncovered in the kitchen, there is a danger of contamination.
- Smoked fish should be kept in a refrigerator.
- Use the correct colour-coded boards for preparing raw fish, and different ones for cooked fish. Keep the boards clean using fresh disposable wiping cloths.
- Use equipment reserved for raw fish. If this is not possible, wash and sanitise equipment before and immediately after each use.
- Unhygienic equipment, utensils and preparation areas increase the risk of cross-contamination and danger to health.
- Fish offal and bones present a high risk of contamination and must not be mixed or stored with raw prepared fish.
- Wash equipment, knives and hands regularly using a bactericide detergent, or sanitising agent, to kill germs.
- Dispose of all wiping cloths immediately after use. Reused cloths may cause contamination.

Basic fish preparation

Unless otherwise stated, as a guide allow 100 g fish off the bone and 150 g on the bone for a portion.

- All fish should be washed under running cold water before and after preparation.
- Whole fish are trimmed to remove the scales, fins and head using fish scissors and a knife. If the head is to be left on (as in the case of a salmon for the cold buffet), the gills and the eyes are removed.

Gutting

Figure 7.1 ✎ Gutting a red mullet: (a) gutting; (b) cleaning the blood line

Skinning and filleting

Figure 7.2 ✎ Skinning and filleting a plaice: (a) removing the skin; (b) filleting; (c) trimming

Figure 7.3 ✎ Filleting round fish (red mullet)

Boning and trimming

Figure 7.4 🥄 Boning and trimming red mullet: (a) pin boning; (b) trimming; (c) finished portion

If the fish has to be gutted, the following procedure should be used.

- Cut from the vent to two-thirds along the fish.
- Draw out the intestines with the fingers or, in the case of a large fish, use the hook handle of a utensil such as a ladle.
- Ensure that the blood lying along the main bone is removed, then wash and drain thoroughly.
- If the fish is to be stuffed then it may be gutted by removing the innards through the gill slits, thus leaving the stomach skin intact, forming a pouch in which to put the stuffing. When this method is used, care must be taken to ensure that the inside of the fish is clear of all traces of blood.

Filleting of flat fish with the exception of Dover sole

- Using a filleting knife, make an incision from the head to tail down the line of the backbone.
- Remove each fillet, holding the knife almost parallel to the work surface and keeping the knife close to the bone.

Skinning of flat fish fillets with the exception of Dover sole

- Hold the fillet firmly at the tail end.
- Cut the flesh as close to the tail as possible, as far as the skin.
- Keep the knife parallel to the work surface, grip the skin firmly and move the knife from side to side to remove the skin.

Figure 7.5 🥄 Filleting turbot

Figure 7.6 🖊 Preparation of whole Dover sole: (a) scoring the skin; (b) lifting the edge of the skin; (c) pulling back the skin; (d) trimming; (e) finished

Preparation of whole Dover sole

- Hold the tail firmly, then cut and scrape the skin until sufficient is lifted to be gripped.
- Pull the skin away from the tail to the head.
- Both black and white skins may be removed in this way.
- Trim the tail and side fins with fish scissors, remove the eyes, and clean and wash the fish thoroughly.

Preparation of turbot

- Remove the head with a large chopping knife.
- Cut off the side bones.
- Commencing at the tail end, chop down the centre of the backbone, dividing the fish into two halves.
- Divide each half into steak portions (tronçons) as required.
- Alternatively, cut large tronçons at the base of the turbot and then split it down the middle.

Note: Allow approximately 300 g per portion on the bone. A 3½ kg fish will yield approximately 10 portions.

Filleting of round fish

- Remove the head and clean thoroughly.
- Remove the first fillet by cutting along the backbone from head to tail.
- Keeping the knife close to the bone, remove the fillet.
- Reverse the fish and remove the second fillet in the same way, this time cutting from tail to head.

Note: Fish bones may be degored by soaking in water.

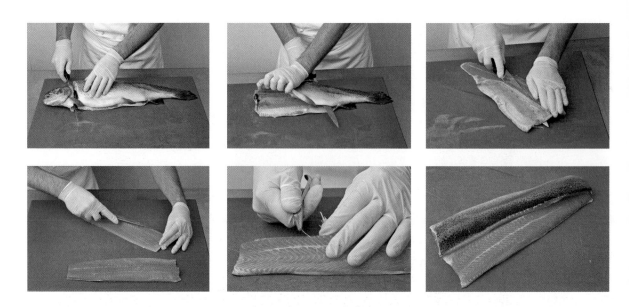

Figure 7.7 Filleting of trout: (a) cutting off the head; (b) cutting down the back; (c) cutting into the flesh to remove the ribcage; (d) trimming; (e) pin boning; (f) finished

Cuts of fish

Steaks

- Thick slices of fish on or off the bone.
- Steaks of round fish (salmon, cod) may be called darnes.
- Steaks of flat fish on the bone (turbot, halibut) may be called tronçons.

Fillets

- Cuts of fish free from bone: a round fish yields two fillets, a flat fish four fillets.

Suprêmes

- Prime cuts of fish without bone and skin (pieces cut from fillets of salmon, turbot, brill, etc.).

Figure 7.8 Darnes of salmon

Figure 7.9 Tronçons of white fish

Figure 7.10 Suprêmes of salmon

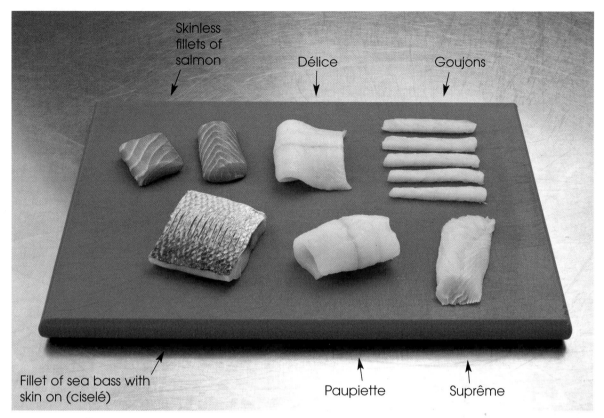

Figure 7.11 Cuts of fish

Goujons

- Filleted fish cut into strips approximately 8 × 0.5 cm.

Paupiettes

- Fillets of fish (e.g. sole, plaice, whiting) spread with a stuffing and rolled.

Plaited

- Also known as *en tresse* – for example, sole fillets cut into three even pieces lengthwise to within 1 cm of the top, and neatly plaited.

Ciseler

- Ciseler means to make slight incisions in the surface of a thick fillet of fish, or on the bone, to allow even cooking.
- The depth of the incisions depends on the size of the fish at the thickest and thinnest points: a balance should be achieved in appearance and cooking time.

181

Fish types

Table 7.1 gives examples of the 200-plus fish types that are available.

Table 7.1 ✏ Examples of fish types available, and suitable cooking methods (O = oily, W = white)

		Baking	Boiling	Deep-frying	Grilling	Poaching	Roasting	Shallow (pan-frying)	Steaming	Stir-frying
Barracuda	O				✓			✓		
Cod	W	✓	✓	✓	✓	✓	✓	✓	✓	
Coley	W		✓	✓	✓			✓		
Dorade (red sea bream)	O	✓			✓			✓		✓
Dover Sole	W			✓	✓	✓		✓		
Emperor bream	O	✓			✓			✓		
Grouper	W				✓		✓	✓		
Haddock	W	✓		✓	✓	✓		✓		
Hake	W	✓			✓	✓		✓		
Halibut	W	✓			✓	✓	✓	✓	✓	✓
Herring	O				✓			✓		
Huss	W			✓	✓	✓		✓		
John Dory	W	✓				✓		✓		
Lemon sole	W	✓		✓	✓	✓		✓		
Mackerel	O	✓			✓	✓				
Marlin	O	✓			✓	✓		✓		
Monkfish	O	✓					✓	✓		✓
Plaice	W	✓		✓	✓			✓		
Red mullet	O	✓			✓		✓	✓		
Red snapper	O	✓			✓	✓		✓		
Salmon	O	✓	✓		✓	✓	✓	✓	✓	✓
Sardines	O				✓			✓		
Sea bass	W	✓			✓	✓		✓	✓	
Shark	W	✓			✓	✓	✓	✓	✓	✓
Skate wings	W		✓	✓		✓		✓		
Swordfish	W	✓			✓			✓		✓
Trout	O	✓			✓			✓		
Tuna	O				✓	✓		✓		✓
Turbot	W	✓	✓	✓	✓	✓	✓	✓		✓
Whitebait	O			✓						

Seasonality and availability of fish

Seasonality

The quality of fish can vary due to local climatic and environmental conditions. Generally, all fish spawn over a period of four to six weeks. During spawning, they use up a lot of their reserves of fat and protein in the production of eggs. This has the effect of making their flesh watery and soft. Fish in this condition are termed 'spent fish'. This takes anything between one and two months, depending on local environmental conditions.

Availability

Naturally, prevailing weather conditions have an enormous bearing on fishing activities. The full range of species may not always be available during stormy weather, for instance.

Methods of cooking fish

To maintain the quality and food safety of fish and shellfish dishes it is advisable to check the internal temperature using a probe. It is recommended that all fish and shellfish should be cooked to an internal temperature of 62°C.

Note: Environmental Health Officers may require higher temperatures.

Table 7.2   Seasonality of fish

	JAN	FEB	MAR	APR	MAY	JUN	JUL	AUG	SEP	OCT	NOV	DEC
Bream					*	*	*					
Brill			*	*	*							
Cod			*	*								
Eel												
Mullet (grey)			*	*								
Gurnard												
Haddock												
Hake			*	*	*							
Halibut				*	*							
Herring												
John Dory												
Mackerel												
Monkfish												
Plaice			*	*								
Red mullet												
Salmon (farmed)												
Salmon (wild)												
Sardines												
Sea bass				*	*							
Sea trout								*	*	*	*	
Skate												
Squid												
Sole (Dover)	*											
Sole (lemon)												
Trout												
Tuna												
Turbot				*	*	*						
Whiting												

Code:
Available
At best

*Spawning and roeing – this can deprive the flesh of nutrients and will decrease the yield.

Fish recipes

Stocks

1 Fish cooking liquid (court bouillon)

	4 portions	10 portions
water	1 litre	2½ litres
salt	10 g	25 g
carrots, sliced	50 g	125 g
bay leaf	1	2
parsley stalks	2–3	5–8
vinegar	60 ml	150 ml
peppercorns	6	15
onions, sliced	50 g	125 g
sprig of thyme		

1 Simmer all the ingredients for 30–40 minutes.
2 Pass through a strainer, use as required.

2 Fish stock, traditional *(fumet de poisson)*

Cal 4 KJ	Cal 1 kcal	Fat 0.0 g	Sat Fat 0.0 g	Carb 0.2 g	Sugar 0.2 g	Protein 0.0 g	Fibre 0.0 g	*

	4½ litres	12 litres
margarine, butter or oil	50 g	125 g
onions, sliced	200 g	500 g
white fish bones (preferably sole, whiting or turbot)	2 kg	4 kg
lemon, juice of	½	1½
peppercorns	8	16
bay leaf	1	2
parsley stalks		
water	4½ litres	12 litres

1 Melt the fat, or heat the oil, in a thick-bottomed pan.
2 Add the onions, the well-washed fish bones and the remainder of the ingredients except the water.
3 Cover with greaseproof paper and a lid; sweat (cook gently without colouring) for 5 minutes.
4 Add the water, bring to the boil, skim and simmer for 20 minutes, then strain. A longer cooking time will spoil the flavour.

Note: There is an alternative recipe for fish stock in Chapter 3, 'Stocks, soups and sauces' (recipe 3).

HEALTHY EATING TIP
• Use an oil rich in unsaturates to lightly oil the pan. Drain off any excess after the frying is complete. Skim the fat from the finished dish.

* *100 ml*

Sauces

3 Sabayon

This is a mixture of egg yolks and a little water whisked to the ribbon stage over gentle heat. The mixture should be the consistency of thick cream. It is added to sauces to assist their glazing.

4 Butter sauce *(beurre blanc)*

	4 portions	10 portions
water	125 ml	300 ml
wine vinegar	125 ml	300 ml
shallots, finely chopped	50 g	125 g
unsalted butter	200 g	500 g
lemon juice	1 tsp	2½ tsp
salt, pepper		

1 Reduce the water, vinegar and shallots in a thick-bottomed pan to approximately 62 ml, and allow to cool slightly.
2 Gradually whisk in the butter in small amounts, whisking continually until the mixture becomes creamy.
3 Whisk in the lemon juice, season lightly and keep warm in a bain-marie.

Note: The sauce may be strained if desired. Variations include adding freshly shredded sorrel or spinach, blanched fine julienne of lemon or lime, or chopped fresh herbs.

HEALTHY EATING TIP
• Use the minimum amount of salt in these sauces.
• Do not use too much sauce with the various fish dishes.

5 White wine sauce *(sauce vin blanc)*

Cal	Cal	Fat	Sat Fat	Carb	Sugar	Protein	Fibre	*
3255 KJ	775 kcal	73.7 g	42.2 g	21.0 g	2.0 g	3.3 g	1.1 g	

	4 portions	10 portions
fish velouté	250 ml	625 ml
dry white wine	2 tbsp	5 tbsp
butter	50 g	125 g
cream	2 tbsp	5 tbsp
salt, cayenne		
few drops of lemon juice		

1 Boil the fish velouté. Whisk in the wine.
2 Remove from the heat.
3 Gradually add the butter. Stir in the cream.
4 Correct the seasoning and consistency, add the lemon juice.
5 Pass through a double muslin or fine strainer.

Note: If the sauce is to be used for a glazed fish dish then 1 egg yolk or 1 tbsp sabayon should be added as soon as the sauce is removed from the heat. (Trade practice sometimes is to whisk in 1 tbsp hollandaise sauce.)

Variations
- Finely sliced button mushrooms and chopped parsley.
- Finely sliced button mushrooms and diced, peeled, and deseeded tomato.

- Picked shrimps.
- A few strands of blanched saffron.

* *4 portions*

6 Shrimp sauce

Cal	Cal	Fat	Sat Fat	Carb	Sugar	Protein	Fibre	*
1381 KJ	332 kcal	22.1 g	10.3 g	20.0 g	0.9 g	14.3 g	0.8 g	

	4 portions	10 portions
fish velouté or béchamel	250 ml	625 ml
salt, cayenne		
pickled shrimps	60 ml	150 ml

1 Boil the fish velouté or béchamel.
2 Correct the seasoning and consistency using fish stock or cream.
3 Pass through double muslin or fine strainer. Mix in the shrimps.

Note: May be served with any poached or steamed fish.

* *Using margarine reduced to half*

7 Balsamic vinegar and olive oil dressing

water	62 ml
olive oil	250 ml
balsamic vinegar	62 ml
sherry vinegar	2 tbsp
caster sugar	½ tsp
seasoning	

1 Whisk all ingredients together. Correct the seasoning.

Note: The amount of balsamic vinegar needed will depend on its quality, age, etc. Add more or less as required.

8 Tomato vinaigrette

	4 portions	10 portions
tomatoes	200 g	500 g
caster sugar	½ tsp	1¼ tbsp
white wine vinegar	1 tbsp	2½ tsp
extra virgin olive oil	3 tbsp	8 tbsp
seasoning		

1 Blanch and deseed the tomatoes, purée in a food processor.
2 Add the sugar, vinegar, olive oil and seasoning, whisk well to emulsify.
3 The vinaigrette should be smooth.

Note: This vinaigrette is used in recipe 17.

Deep-frying

8 Frying batters (pâtes à frire)

Recipe A

	4 portions	10 portions
flour	200 g	500 g
salt		
yeast	10 g	25 g
water or milk	250 ml	625 ml

1. Sift the flour and salt into a basin.
2. Dissolve the yeast in a little of the water.
3. Make a well in the flour. Add the yeast and the liquid.
4. Gradually incorporate the flour and beat to a smooth mixture.
5. Allow to rest for at least 1 hour before using.

Recipe B

	4 portions	10 portions
flour	200 g	500 g
salt		
egg	1	2–3
water or milk	250 ml	625 ml
oil	2 tbsp	5 tbsp

1. Sift the flour and salt into a basin. Make a well. Add the egg and the liquid.
2. Gradually incorporate the flour and beat to a smooth mixture.
3. Mix in the oil. Allow to rest before using.

Recipe C

	4 portions	10 portions
flour	200 g	500 g
salt		
water or milk	250 ml	625 ml
oil	2 tbsp	5 tbsp
egg whites, stiffly beaten	2	5 tbsp

1. As for recipe B, but fold in the egg whites just before using.

Note: Other ingredients can be added to batter (e.g. chopped fresh herbs, grated ginger, garam masala, beer).

Figure 7.12 ✐ Preparation and cooking of deep-fried fish

9 Fried fish in batter

1 Pass the prepared, washed and well-dried fish through flour, shake off the surplus and pass through the batter (see recipe 8).
2 Place carefully away from you into the hot deep-fryer at 175°C until the fish turns a golden-brown. Remove and drain well.
3 Serve with either lemon quarters or tartare sauce.

10 Fried egg and breadcrumbed fish

1 For fish fillets, pass through flour, beaten egg and fresh white breadcrumbs. (Pat the surfaces well to avoid loose crumbs falling into the fat, burning and spoiling both the fat and the fish.)
2 Deep-fry at 175°C, then drain well.
3 Serve with lemon quarters and a suitable sauce (e.g. tartare).

11 Goujons of fish

1 Cut fish fillets (e.g. sole, plaice, salmon) into strips approx. 8 × ½ cm.
2 Prepare, cook and serve as in recipe 9 or 10, above.

12 Fried sole (sole frite)

For fish courses use 200–250 g sole per portion; for main course 300–400 g sole per portion.

1 Remove the black and white skin. Remove the side fins.
2 Remove the head. Clean well.
3 Wash well and drain. Pané and deep-fry at 175°C (347°F).
4 Serve on a dish paper with picked or fried parsley and a quarter of lemon on a flat dish, and with a suitable sauce, such as tartare or anchovy.

13 Whitebait (blanchailles)

Cal 2174 KJ	Cal 525 kcal	Fat 47.5 g	Sat Fat 0.0 g	Carb 5.3 g	Sugar 0.1 g	Protein 19.5 g	Fibre 0.2 g

1 Pick over the whitebait, wash carefully and drain well.
2 Pass through milk and seasoned flour.
3 Shake off surplus flour in a wide-mesh sieve and place fish into a frying-basket.
4 Plunge into very hot fat (195°C).
5 Cook until brown and crisp (approximately 1 minute).
6 Drain well.
7 Season lightly with salt and cayenne pepper.
8 Serve garnished with fried or picked parsley and quarters of lemon.

Note: Allow 100 g per portion.

Shallow- or pan-frying

14 Shallow-frying: basic recipe

1 Prepare, clean, wash and dry the fish well.
2 Pass through flour and shake off all surplus. (If using non-stick pans it is not necessary to flour the fish.)
3 Heat the frying medium in a frying pan.
4 Shallow-fry on both sides (presentation side first), then serve.

Note: Do not overcrowd the pan because this may cause the temperature of the fat to fall and this will affect the efficient cooking of the fish, and perhaps semi-steam it.

Variations
- *À la meunière* (see recipe 15) – when cooked, mask with nut brown butter, lemon juice and chopped parsley.
- As for meunière, with sliced almonds lightly browned in the butter.
- As for meunière, with picked shrimps and finely sliced button mushrooms heated in the butter.
- As for meunière, with a sprinkling of capers and segments of lemon or lime taken from peeled lemons (yellow and white skins removed).
- When cooked, sprinkle with a mixture of grated lemon zest, finely chopped garlic and chopped parsley – known as gremolata.

15 Fish meunière

Cal 1314 KJ	Cal 313 kcal	Fat 24.1 g	Sat Fat 10.3 g	Carb 3.1 g	Sugar 0.0 g	Protein 21.2 g	Fibre 0.1 g

1 Prepare and clean the fish, wash and drain.
2 Pass through seasoned flour, shake off all surplus.
3 Shallow-fry on both sides, presentation side first, in hot clarified butter, margarine or oil.
4 Dress neatly on an oval flat dish or plate/plates.
5 Peel a lemon, removing the peel, white pith and pips.
6 Cut the lemon into slices and place one on each portion.
7 Squeeze some lemon juice on the fish.
8 Allow 10–25 g butter per portion and colour in a clean frying pan to the nut-brown stage (*beurre noisette*).
9 Pour over the fish.
10 Sprinkle with chopped parsley and serve.

Note: Many fish, whole or filleted, may be cooked by this method: for example, sole, sea bass, bream, fillets of plaice, trout, brill, cod, turbot, herring, scampi.

HEALTHY EATING TIP

- Use a small amount of unsaturated oil to fry the fish.
- Use less *beurre noisette* per portion.
- Some customers will prefer the finished dish without the additional fat.

Variations

Variations include the following.

- *Fish meunière with almonds:* as for fish meunière (recipe 15), adding 10 g of almonds cut in short julienne or coarsely chopped into the meunière butter just before it begins to turn brown. This method is usually applied to trout.
- *Fish belle meunière:* as for recipe 15, with the addition of a grilled mushroom, a slice of peeled tomato and a soft herring roe (passed through flour and shallow-fried), all neatly dressed on each portion of fish.
- *Fish Doria:* as for fish meunière (recipe 15) with a sprinkling of small turned pieces of cucumber carefully cooked in 25 g of butter in a small covered pan, or blanched in boiling salted water.

- *Grenobloise:* as for fish meunière (recipe 15), the peeled lemon being cut into segments, neatly dressed on the fish, with a few capers sprinkled over.
- *Bretonne:* as for fish meunière (recipe 15), with a few picked shrimps and cooked sliced mushrooms sprinkled over the fish.

Figure 7.13 ✒ Pan-fried fillets of lemon sole

16 Pan-fried sea bass with rosemary mash and mushrooms

Cal 1183 KJ	Cal 282 kcal	Fat 11.6 g	Sat Fat 3.6 g	Carb 17.3 g	Sugar 0.6 g	Protein 28.2 g	Fibre 1.3 g	*

	4 portions	10 portions
vegetable oil	10 ml	25 ml
salt, pepper		
sea bass portions, skin on	4 × 100 g	10 × 100 g
wild mushrooms, sliced	200 g	600 g
extra virgin olive oil	10 ml	25 ml
rosemary, chopped	pinch	1 tsp
mashed potato, (see page 521)	400 g	1 kg

1 Heat the vegetable oil in a non-stick pan, season and then fry the lemon sole, skin side first, until it has a golden colour and is crispy.
2 Turn the fish over and gently seal without colouring.
3 Remove from the pan (skin side up) and keep warm.
4 Quickly and lightly fry the mushrooms in extra virgin olive oil.
5 Mix the rosemary into the mashed potato.

6 Arrange the potato in the centre of hot plates.
7 Place the fish on top, skin side down.
8 Garnish with the mushrooms and olive oil and serve.

HEALTHY EATING TIP

- Using an unsaturated oil (sunflower or olive), lightly oil the non-stick pan to fry the sole.
- Use a little olive oil to fry the mushrooms.
- Keep added salt to a minimum.
- Serve with plenty of seasonal vegetables and new potatoes.

Variations

- A sauce of light veal or chicken jus flavoured with fennel can be served around the plates.
- If the rosemary is in fresh sprigs it can be used to garnish the dish instead of being put into the potato.

- Girolle or some other wild mushrooms can be used in place of button mushrooms.
- Sautéd leeks, small stewed baby leeks or points of cooked asparagus can be used to garnish the dish and add colour.

Using lemon sole in place of sea bass, and button mushrooms

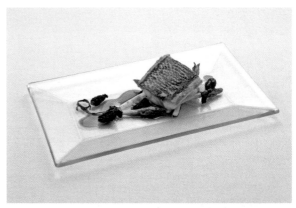

Figure 7.14 ✐ Pan-fried fillet of sea bass on rosemary mash with asparagus, wild mushrooms and reduced veal stock

17 Pan-fried fillet of sea bass with spinach tagliatelle in a tomato vinaigrette*

	4 portions	10 portions
sea bass	4 × 100 g	10 × 100 g
olive oil	2 tbsp	5 tbsp
seasoning		
lemon juice	1	3
seasoned flour		
spinach tagliatelle	100 g	250 g

* *For vinaigrette, see recipe 8*

1 Prepare the tomato vinaigrette (see recipe 8).
2 Cook the spinach tagliatelle fresh and drain.
3 Cook the sea bass as for meunière (see recipe 15).
4 Reheat the tagliatelle in hot olive oil, season and combine with the tomato vinaigrette.
5 Place the tagliatelle onto service plates; lay the sea bass fillets on top.
6 Finish the plates with a cordon of jus-lié of balsamic vinegar and olive oil dressing (hot) (see recipe 7).
7 Decorate with stoned black olives and fresh basil leaves.

Note: Other fish suitable for use with this recipe are sole (lemon and Dover), bream and mullet.

HEALTHY EATING TIP

- Use a small amount of unsaturated oil to fry the fish and half the olive oil when reheating the tagliatelle.
- Increasing the amount of tagliatelle and serving the dish with extra vegetables or salad will proportionally reduce the fat content.

18 Pan-fried fillets of sole with rocket and broad beans

	4 portions	10 portions
trimmed sole fillets	16	40
seasoning		
butter	200 g	500 g
cooked and shelled		
broad beans	250 g	625 g
picked and washed rocket	300 g	750 g
vinaigrette	50 ml	125 ml

1 Heat a little oil in a non-stick pan.
2 Place the fillets of sole on a tray and season on both sides.
3 Place the fish in the pan carefully (presentation side down).
4 Cook for 1 minute on a medium/high heat, and then carefully turn the fish, remove the pan from the heat and allow the residual heat to finish the cooking.

5 Place the sole fillets (4 per portion) on serving plates and keep warm.
6 Place the butter in the cooking pan, heat to the noisette stage, add the broad beans and cook for 30 seconds to 1 minute just to re-heat the beans.
7 Nap the beans, add a little noisette butter over the fish and top with a dressed rocket salad.

Note: This is a very simple and quick dish. Any salad or greens, if they are quickly cooked or lightly dressed, can go with this dish.

When preparing this dish for large numbers, cook for 1 minute and colour one side. Then remove to a buttered baking sheet with cooked side up, ready to reheat for 1 minute in a hot oven.

19 Pan-fried red mullet with artichokes and Swiss chard

	4 portions	10 portions
vegetable oil	100 ml	250 ml
seasoning		
red mullet fillets		
(approx. 120 g each),		
pinned and scaled	4	10
shiitake mushrooms, sliced	8	20
Swiss chard, picked		
and washed (use spinach		
if chard unavailable)	200 g	500 g
green beans, trimmed		
and blanched	200 g	500 g
baby artichokes,		
cooked and trimmed	8	20
fish stock	80 ml	200 ml
crayfish reduction	80 ml	200 ml
soft herbs (chervil,		
chives, dill), washed		
and picked	50 g	125 g
lemon oil	50 ml	125 ml

1 Heat the oil in a non-stick pan, season the red mullet and place skin side down.
2 Seal the skin side for 1 minute only with good colour, remove from the pan and reserve.
3 Add the mushrooms to the pan and hard cook until they become crisp.
4 Add the Swiss chard, green beans and artichokes, and cook for a further minute.
5 Add the fish stock and the reduction. Bring to the boil.
6 Add the fish skin side up and cook for a further minute.
7 Divide the contents of the pan evenly over the serving plate, garnish with the soft herbs and drizzle with lemon oil.

Note: Red mullet has a distinctive and strong fish flavour. Pairing it with Swiss chard, artichokes and shitake mushrooms more than compensates for its bold approach.

20 Pan-fried skate with capers and *beurre noisette*

	4 portions	10 portions
vegetable oil	50 ml	125 ml
seasoning		
skate, skinless fillets		
(approx. 160 g each)	4	10
butter	175 g	450 g
lemons, juice of	2	5
flat parsley, chopped	2 tbsp	5 tbsp
small capers	100 g	250 g

1 Place a skillet on the hottest part of the stove and an empty sauté pan to the side of the stove, achieving a moderate heat (this is for the *beurre noisette*).
2 Ensure the skate wings are fresh, and free from ammonia aromas and skin.

3 Add the vegetable oil to the skillet and place in the seasoned skate wings, cook with colour for 1–2 minutes and then carefully turn; at this point ease the skillet to a cooler point of the stove while the *beurre noisette* cooks.
4 Place the butter in the pan and allow to foam (at this point remove the skate and place in the serving dish).
5 Add the lemon, parsley and capers to the *beurre noisette*, stir well.
6 To finish, nap over the skate wing and serve.

Note: Because skate pass urine through their wings, if they are not super-fresh they will start to smell of ammonia after 3–4 days; this is a key indicator of their freshness.

21 Crispy seared salmon with horseradish foam and caviar

	4 portions	10 portions
salmon fillet steaks,		
skin on, scaled	4 × 140 g	10 × 140 g
vegetable oil		
baby spinach, washed	400 g	1 kg
butter		
spears of asparagus,		
blanched	12	30
garlic cloves, chopped	1	3
caviar (optional)	50 g	125 g
chervil		
Foam		
shallots, sliced	2	5
sprig of thyme	1	3
butter	80 g	200 g
white wine	60 ml	150 ml
double cream	60 ml	150 ml
horseradish, grated	20 g	50 g
lemons, juice of	1	3

1 Place salmon skin side down in a hot pan with a little vegetable oil and cook on a medium heat until two-thirds of the salmon is cooked.
2 For the foam, sweat the shallots and thyme in half the butter, adding white wine after 2 minutes and reduce by half.

3 Add the cream and horseradish, bring to the boil and infuse for 15 minutes off the heat.
4 Pass through a fine chinois and work in the other half of the butter and the lemon juice while the mix is hot (this will stop it from splitting).
5 Wilt the spinach in a little butter, add the asparagus to re-heat and arrange neatly in the centre of each serving dish.
6 Place the seared salmon skin side up on the asparagus and spinach, and finish with a quenelle of caviar. Garnish with chervil.
7 Aerate the foam with a whisk or hand blender to create a light foam.
8 Spoon the foam over the salmon.

Note: This dish can be adapted in many ways by substituting the caviar with avruga caviar to save the expense. Alternatively, if cost is not an issue, why not use smoked salmon (a smaller portion to replace the caviar) and sear that in the same way. The horseradish will be a great foil for this.

1 Place the seared salmon skin side up on the asparagus and spinach and finish with a quenelle of caviar with the foam aerated with a whisk or hand blender to create light foam.

2 Spoon the foam over the salmon.

22 Pan-fried turbot with Alsace cabbage

	4 portions	10 portions
vegetable oil	50 ml	125 ml
seasoning		
turbot fillets		
(approx. 180 g pieces)	4	10
butter	50 g	125 g
lemons for juicing	1	3
Cabbage		
vegetable oil	50 ml	125 ml
butter	50 g	125 g
large (or double the amount small) shallots, finely diced	2	5
cloves garlic, chopped and sprout removed	2	5
large carrot, peeled and thinly sliced	1	3
sprigs thyme	2	5
bay leaf	1	3
savoy cabbage, finely sliced and stalks removed	1	3
water	50 ml	125 ml
fish stock	50 ml	125 ml

Cabbage

1 Place a large pan with a tight-fitting lid over a medium heat. Add the oil and butter heat gently, then add the shallots, garlic and carrot, and cook for 2 minutes without letting them colour.
2 Add the thyme, bay leaf and cabbage to the pan and cook for a further 3 minutes, again without colouring.
3 Pour in the water and fish stock, cover and steam for 3 minutes. If serving immediately, drain, then adjust the seasoning to taste and serve. Otherwise spread the cabbage out thinly on a tray and store covered in the fridge for up to 24 hours.

To finish

1 Heat the oil in a non-stick pan, season the turbot fillets and place in the hot oil presentation side down.
2 When the turbot is golden brown turn in the pan and add the butter.
3 Bring to a light foam, but not noisette.
4 To finish add a squeeze of lemon.
5 Place a mound of cabbage in the centre of the serving plate and top with the turbot.

Note: other white fish can be used in this recipe instead of turbot, e.g. cod or monkfish. It is a great example of bourgeois cooking. Rustication sings out from this dish – really deep flavours, yet so simple!

23 Pan-fried sea bass, asparagus and capers

Cal	Cal	Fat	Sat Fat	Carb	Sugar	Protein	Fibre	Salt	*
3255 KJ	778 kcal	70.0 g	24.4 g	4.0 g	3.4 g	33.8 g	2.9 g	1.3 g	

	4 portions	10 portions
Sea bass		
sea bass, about 160 g, trimmed of scales and bones	4 × 160 g	10 × 160 g
vegetable oil	50 ml	125 ml
butter	50g	125 g
Caper dressing		
fine capers	1 tbsp	2½ tbsp
aged balsamic vinegar	5 tbsp	12 tbsp
lemon oil	5 tbsp	12 tbsp
salt, pepper		
Fennel cream		
bulb fennel	1	2
clove garlic	1	2
vegetable oil	50 ml	125 ml
chicken stock	100 ml	250 ml
whipping cream	100 ml	250 ml
butter	50 g	125 g
Garnish		
asparagus spears	8	20
extra-fine green beans, blanched	100 g	250 g

Caper dressing

In a small bowl, combine all the dressing ingredients, adjust the seasoning to taste and set aside until serving.

Fennel cream

1 Remove the root and stalks from the fennel bulb and trim off any blemishes on the outer leaves.
2 Finely chop the fennel and crush the garlic. Heat the oil in a saucepan, add the fennel and garlic and cook slowly over a moderate heat for 6–7 minutes without letting them colour.
3 Add the fish stock, raise the heat under the pan and boil until reduced by half.
4 Pour in the cream, return to the boil and simmer until reduced by half.
5 Remove the pan from the heat and allow to cool slightly.
6 Transfer the mixture to a food processor and purée until fine. Return the sauce to a clean pan and set aside in a warm place – you need to whisk in the butter just before serving.

To complete

1 Ensure the sea bass is free of bones and scales. Place a large, non-stick frying pan that will accommodate the fish fillets comfortably over a medium-high heat. Add 50 ml vegetable oil.
2 Season the bass on the flesh side and carefully place all the fillets skin side down in the pan. Cook for 2 minutes, then turn and cook for another 1–2 minutes. Add the butter, reduce the heat to very low and allow to rest like this until the fish is just cooked and just firm to the touch.
3 For the garnish, reheat the asparagus and beans in a little butter.
4 Drain the fish and place it on top of the vegetables.
5 Whisk the butter into the fennel cream and garnish the dish with the fennel cream and caper dressing, then serve.

Note: When steaming any fish, be mindful that the fish will cool quicker than a roasted piece of fish.

Using John Dory and olive oil

Stir-frying

24 Hoki stir-fry

Cal	Cal	Fat	Sat Fat	Carb	Sugar	Protein	Fibre
935 KJ	224 kcal	11.1 g	2.1 g	8.8 g	5.8 g	22.6 g	3.8 g

	4 portions	10 portions
hoki fillets	400 g	1 kg
salt, pepper		
five-spice powder	½ tsp	1¼ tsp
carrots	100 g	250 g
mangetout	100 g	250 g
asparagus tips	100 g	250 g
spring onions	4	10
groundnut oil	3 tbsp	8 tbsp
root ginger, grated	1 tsp	2½ tsp
cloves of garlic, chopped	2	5
beansprouts	300 g	750 g
baby sweetcorn	8	20
light soy sauce	2 tbsp	5 tbsp

1 Skin the fillets, cut into goujons (strips – see page 181) and season with salt, pepper and five-spice powder.
2 Cut the carrots in julienne and the mangetout into large strips.
3 Trim the asparagus spears and cut in half crossways. Trim the spring onions and cut them diagonally into 2 cm pieces, keeping the white and green parts separate.

4 Heat the oil in a wok. Add the ginger and garlic. Stir-fry for 1 minute, then add the white part of the spring onions and cook for 1 minute.
5 Add the hoki strips and stir-fry for 2–3 minutes. Add the beansprouts, toss together. Add the carrots, mangetout, asparagus and corn. Continue to stir-fry for 3–4 minutes.
6 Add soy sauce, toss everything together, then stir in the green parts of the spring onions. Serve immediately.

Note: Any firm white fish – such as monkfish, hake or cod – can be used for this stir-fry. The vegetables may be varied according to what is available.

HEALTHY EATING TIP

- Reduce the amount of groundnut oil used for frying.
- No added salt is needed – soy sauce is high in sodium.
- Serve with a large portion of rice or noodles.

25 Seafood stir-fry

Cal 724 KJ	Cal 172 kcal	Fat 4.9 g	Sat Fat 0.8 g	Carb 9.1 g	Sugar 4.9 g	Protein 23.2 g	Fibre 2.1 g

	4 portions	10 portions
small asparagus spears	100 g	250 g
sunflower or groundnut oil	1 tbsp	2½ tbsp
fresh ginger, grated	1 tsp	2½ tsp
leeks, cut into julienne	100 g	250 g
carrots, cut into julienne	100 g	250 g
baby sweetcorn	100 g	250 g
light soy sauce	2 tbsp	5 tbsp
oyster sauce	1 tbsp	2½ tbsp
clear honey	1 tsp	2½ tsp
cooked	400 g	1 kg
assorted		
shellfish		
prawns		
mussels		
scallops		
Garnish		
large cooked prawns	4	10
fresh chives	25 g	62 g

1 Blanch the asparagus for 2 minutes in boiling water, refresh then drain.
2 Heat the oil in a wok, add the ginger, leek, carrots and sweetcorn, stir-fry for 3 minutes without colour.
3 Add the soy and oyster sauce and honey. Stir.
4 Stir in the cooked shellfish and continue to stir-fry for 2–3 minutes until the vegetables are just tender and the shellfish is thoroughly heated through.
5 Add the blanched asparagus and stir-fry for another 1 minute.
6 Serve with fresh cooked noodles garnished with large fresh prawns and chopped chives.

HEALTHY EATING TIP
• No added salt is needed – soy sauce is high in sodium.
• Increasing the ratio of vegetables to seafood will improve the 'balance' of this dish.

Boiling, poaching and steaming

Boiling

26 Boiled turbot, brill, halibut or cod (on the bone)

1 Place the prepared fish into a shallow pan of simmering, lightly salted water containing lemon juice. (The citric acid helps to make the flesh firm and white and gives a gentle flavour.)
2 Allow to simmer gently. The cooking time depends on the thickness of the fish. Do not overcook.
3 Remove with a fish slice, remove black skin, drain and serve.
4 Garnish with picked parsley and plain boiled potatoes, and serve with a suitable sauce (e.g. hollandaise, herb butter, shrimp or mushroom).

Poaching

For further information, refer to page 175 of this chapter or the text on poaching on pages 12–13 of Chapter 2.

27 Poached salmon

1 Place the prepared and washed darnes of salmon in a simmering court bouillon (see page 184) for approximately 5 minutes.
2 Drain well and carefully remove centre bone and outer skin. Ensure that the fish is cleaned of any cooked blood.

3 Serve with a suitable sauce (e.g. hollandaise) or melted herb butter, and thinly sliced cucumber.

Note: Depending on the size of the salmon either a whole or half a darne would be served as a portion.

28 Poached smoked haddock

Cal	Cal	Fat	Sat Fat	Carb	Sugar	Protein	Fibre	Salt
0000 KJ	000 kcal	00.0 g	0.0 g	00.0 g	00.0 g	00.0 g	0.0 g	0.0 g

	4 portions	10 portions
smoked haddock fillets	400–600 g	1.2 kg
milk and water		

1 Cut fillets into even portions, place into a shallow pan and cover with half milk and water.
2 Simmer gently for a few minutes until cooked.
3 Drain well and serve.

Note: This is a popular breakfast dish and is also served as a lunch and a snack dish. For example:

- when cooked, garnish with slices of peeled tomato or tomato concassée, lightly coat with cream, flash under the salamander and serve
- top with a poached egg
- when cooked, lightly coat with Welsh rarebit mixture (page 663), brown under the salamander and garnish with peeled slices of tomato or tomato concassée.

The following three recipes are from the classical repertoire. Although Dover sole fillets are used, any white fish fillets may be prepared and served by the same method. If shallots are used they must be *finely* chopped and sweated in a little butter before use.

The traditional way of making classic fish sauces is to strain off the cooking liquor (after the fish is cooked) and reduce it to a glaze (page 49). Remove the pan from the heat and gradually incorporate small pieces of butter. If the sauce is to be glazed, some lightly whipped double cream can be added.

29 Fillets of fish Duglére (filets de poisson Duglére)

Cal 699 KJ	Cal 167 kcal	Fat 11.6 g	Sat Fat 6.8 g	Carb 1.9 g	Sugar 1.9 g	Protein 11.5 g	Fibre 0.9 g

	4 portions	10 portions
white fish fillets, sweated	400–600 g	1–1.5 kg
butter, for dish and greaseproof paper		
shallots, finely chopped	10 g	25 g
tomatoes concassée	200 g	500 g
pinch parsley, chopped		
salt, pepper		
fish stock	60 ml	150 ml
dry white wine	60 ml	150 ml
lemon, juice of	¼	½
fish velouté	250 ml	600 ml
butter	50 g	125 g

1 Remove the black and white skins and fillet the fish.
2 Wash and drain well.
3 Butter and season an earthenware dish or sauté pan.
4 Sprinkle in the sweated chopped shallots.
5 Add the fillets, which may be folded in two, then add the tomatoes and chopped parsley.

6 Season with salt and pepper.
7 Add the fish stock, wine and the lemon juice.
8 Cover with buttered greaseproof paper.
9 Poach gently in a moderate oven at 150–200°C for 5–10 minutes.
10 Remove the fillets and the garnish, place on a flat dish or in a clean earthenware dish and keep warm.
11 Pass and reduce the cooking liquor in a small sauteuse, add the fish velouté, pass through a fine strainer, then incorporate the butter.
12 Correct the seasoning and consistency.
13 Coat the fillets with the sauce and serve.

HEALTHY EATING TIP
- Keep the added salt to a minimum.
- Sweat the shallots in a small amount of unsaturated oil.
- Reduce or omit the butter when finishing the sauce.

30 Fillets of fish with white wine sauce (filets de poisson vin blanc)

Cal 1421 KJ	Cal 342 kcal	Fat 24.0 g	Sat Fat 12.8 g	Carb 5.8 g	Sugar 0.9 g	Protein 25.9 g	Fibre 0.2 g

	4 portions	10 portions
fillets of white fish	400–600 g	1–1.5 kg
butter, for dish and greaseproof paper		
shallots, finely chopped and sweated	10 g	25 g
fish stock	60 ml	150 ml
dry white wine	60 ml	150 ml
lemon, juice of	¼	½
fish velouté	250 ml	625 ml
butter	50 g	125 g
cream, lightly whipped	2 tbsp	5 tbsp

1 Skin and fillet the fish, trim and wash.
2 Butter and season an earthenware dish.
3 Sprinkle with the sweated chopped shallots and add the fillets of sole.
4 Season, add the fish stock, wine and lemon juice.
5 Cover with buttered greaseproof paper.
6 Poach in a moderate oven at 150–200°C for 7–10 minutes.
7 Drain the fish well; dress neatly on a flat dish or clean earthenware dish.
8 Bring the cooking liquor to the boil with the velouté.
9 Correct the seasoning and consistency, and pass through double muslin or a fine strainer.
10 Mix in the butter then, finally, add the cream.
11 Coat the fillets with the sauce. Garnish with fleurons (puff paste crescents).

HEALTHY EATING TIP

- Keep the added salt to a minimum.
- Reduce the amount of butter and cream added to finish the sauce.
- Less sauce could be added, plus a large portion of potatoes and vegetables.

Variations

Add to the fish before cooking:

- *bonne-femme* – 100 g thinly sliced white button mushrooms and chopped parsley
- *bréval* – as for *bonne-femme* plus 100 g diced, peeled and deseeded tomatoes.

31 Fillets of fish Véronique *(filets de poisson Véronique)*

Cal	Cal	Fat	Sat Fat	Carb	Sugar	Protein	Fibre
1077 KJ	256 kcal	19.3 g	10.7 g	6.9 g	2.1 g	11.8 g	0.4 g

	4 portions	10 portions
fillets of white fish	400–600 g	1–1.5 kg
butter, for dish and greaseproof paper		
shallots, finely chopped	10 g	25 g
fish stock	60 ml	150 ml
dry white wine	60 ml	150 ml
lemon, juice of	¼	½
fish velouté	250 ml	625 ml
butter	50 g	125 g
cream, lightly whipped	2 tbsp	5 tbsp
white grapes, blanched, skinned and pipped	50 g	125 g

1 Prepare and cook as for recipe 30, adding an egg yolk or spoonful of sabayon to the sauce.
2 Glaze under the salamander.
3 Arrange the grapes neatly on the dish.

HEALTHY EATING TIP

- Keep the added salt to a minimum. Reduce the amount of butter and cream added to finish the sauce. Less sauce could be added plus a large portion of potatoes and vegetables.

32 Fillets of fish mornay *(filets de poisson mornay)*

Cal	Cal	Fat	Sat Fat	Carb	Sugar	Protein	Fibre
1309 KJ	315 kcal	19.3 g	9.3 g	5.5 g	0.7 g	29.9 g	0.2 g

	4 portions	10 portions
white fish fillets	500–600 g	1.5 kg
butter, for dish and greaseproof paper		
fish stock	125 ml	300 ml
béchamel sauce	250 ml	625 ml
egg yolk or sabayon	1	3
grated cheese, preferably Gruyère or Parmesan	50 g	125 g
salt, cayenne		
butter	25 g	60 g
cream, lightly whipped	2 tbsp	5 tbsp

1 Prepare the fillets; place in a buttered, seasoned earthenware dish or shallow pan, such as a sauté pan.
2 Add the fish stock, cover with buttered paper.
3 Cook in a moderate oven at 150–200°C for approximately 5–10 minutes.
4 Drain the fish well, place in a clean earthenware or flat dish.
5 Bring the béchamel to the boil, add the reduced cooking liquor, whisk in the yolk and remove from the heat. Add the cheese and correct the consistency. Do not reboil, otherwise the egg will curdle.
6 Correct the seasoning and pass through a fine strainer.
7 Mix in the butter and cream, check the consistency.
8 Mask the fish, sprinkle with grated cheese and gratinate under the salamander.

Variations
Classical variations include:
• *fillets of fish Walewska* – place a slice of cooked lobster on each fish fillet before coating with the sauce; after the dish is browned decorate each fillet with a slice of truffle
• *fillets of fish Florentine* – proceed as for fillets mornay, placing the cooked fish on a bed of well-drained and heated dry leaf spinach.

33 Skate with black butter (raie au beurre noir)

Cal	Cal	Fat	Sat Fat	Carb	Sugar	Protein	Fibre
725 KJ	174 kcal	10.8 g	6.5 g	0.1 g	0.1 g	19.0 g	0.0 g

	4 portions	10 portions
skate wings	400–600 g	1¼ kg
court bouillon (see **page 184**)		
butter	50 g	125 g
vinegar	1 tsp	2½ tsp
parsley, chopped		
capers	10 g	25 g

1 Cut the skate into 4 (or 10) even pieces.
2 Simmer in a court bouillon until cooked (approximately 10 minutes).
3 Drain well, place on a serving dish or plates.
4 Heat the butter in a frying pan until well browned, almost black; add the vinegar, pour over the fish, sprinkle with chopped parsley and a few capers and serve.

Variations
Proceed as for steps 1–3, then drain well and serve on a bed of plain or herb-flavoured mashed potato, accompanied by a compound butter sauce (page 65) or a salsa (page 62).

34 Nage of red mullet with baby leeks

	4 portions	10 portions		4 portions	10 portions
mussels, cooked and out of shell	16	40	celery sticks	2	5
lemons, juice of	2	5	leeks	2	5
baby spinach	200 g	500 g	garlic cloves	1	3
baby leeks	12	30	half white and half pink peppercorns	12	30
spears of baby asparagus	12	30	star anise	1	3
pieces of green beans	24	60	white wine	375 ml	950 ml
red mullet fillets (approx. 120 g each), pinned and scaled	4	10	Noilly Prat	375 ml	950 ml
Nage			chervil	10 g	25 g
large onion	1	3	parsley	10 g	25 g
carrots, peeled	2	5	tarragon	10 g	25 g
			chives, chopped	1 tbsp	3 tbsp

1 In a large pan place the onions, carrots, celery and leeks, which have been cut into 2 cm pieces.
2 Just cover the vegetables with water. Bring to the boil. Simmer for 4–5 minutes. Remove from the heat and add the rest of the ingredients.
3 Cover with clingfilm and allow to cool to room temperature. Place into a plastic container and store in the fridge overnight to develop flavour.
4 Pass through a fine sieve. The resulting nage can be bottled for later use.
5 To finish, place 500 ml of the vegetable nage in a pan, add the mussels, a squeeze of lemon, spinach, baby leeks, asparagus and green beans.
6 Bring to the boil, check the seasoning and retain.

7 Heat a non-stick pan with a little vegetable oil. Season the mullet fillets and cook for one minute on each side (thickness dependent), starting with the skin side down.
8 Divide the vegetable garnish between the bowls. Place the red mullet on top of the vegetable garnish and, returning the pan the mullet was cooked in to the stove, pour in the nage.
9 When the nage has returned to the boil, spoon over the fish and garnish. Serve immediately.

Note: This dish is open to many substitutions of fish and shellfish but one key point to remember is that the nage should not be allowed to overpower the main ingredients.

Steaming

For further information, refer to page 175 of this chapter or the text on steaming on pages 13–15 of Chapter 2.

35 Steamed fish with garlic, spring onions and ginger

Cal	Cal	Fat	Sat Fat	Carb	Sugar	Protein	Fibre	*
468 KJ	112 kcal	3.5 g	0.7 g	1.2 g	0.4 g	18.7 g	0.1 g	

	4 portions	10 portions
white fish fillets, e.g. cod, sole	400 g	1.5 kg
salt		
ginger, freshly chopped	1 tbsp	2½ tbsp
spring onions, finely chopped	2 tbsp	5 tbsp
light soy sauce	1 tbsp	2½ tbsp
garlic cloves, peeled and thinly sliced		
oil	1 tbsp	2½ tbsp

1 Wash and dry the fish well; rub *lightly* with salt on both sides.
2 Put the fish onto plates, scatter the ginger evenly on top.
3 Put the plates into the steamer, cover tightly and steam gently until just cooked (5–15 minutes, according to the thickness of the fish).

4 Remove the plates, sprinkle on the spring onions and soy sauce.
5 Brown the garlic slices in the hot oil and pour over the dish.

Note: This is a Chinese recipe that can be adapted in many ways – for example, replace the spring onions and garlic and use thinly sliced mushrooms, diced tomato (skinned and deseeded), *finely* chopped shallots, lemon juice, white wine, chopped parsley, dill or chervil.

HEALTHY EATING TIP
• Steaming is a healthy way of cooking.
• Serve with a large portion of rice or noodles and stir-fried vegetables.

* *Using 2 cloves of garlic*

Grilling/griddling

For further information, refer to page 175 of this chapter or the text on grilling on pages 28–30 of Chapter 2.

36 Grilled fish steaks (*cod, swordfish, tuna, etc.*)

1 Wash the prepared steaks and dry them well.
2 Pass through flour, shake off surplus and brush with oil.
3 Place on hot grill bars, a griddle or a greased baking sheet if grilling under a salamander. Brush occasionally with oil.

4 Turn the fish carefully and grill on both sides. Do not overcook.
5 Serve with lemon quarters and a suitable sauce (e.g. compound butter or a salsa).

37 Grilled round fish (herring, mackerel, bass, mullet)

1 Descale fish where necessary, using the back of a knife.
2 Remove heads, clean out intestines, trim off all fins and tails using fish scissors. Leave herring roes in the fish.
3 Wash and dry well.

4 Make three light incisions 2 mm deep on either side of fish. This is known as 'scoring' and helps the heat to penetrate the fish.
5 Proceed as for recipe 36, steps 2–5.

Note: Herrings are traditionally served with a mustard sauce. Mackerel may be butterfly filleted and grilled.

38 Grilled fish fillets (sole, plaice, haddock)

1 Remove the black skin from sole and plaice and proceed as for grilled fish steaks (recipe 36).

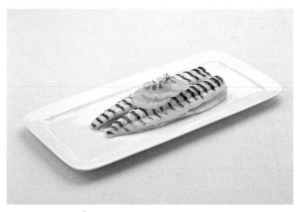

Figure 7.15 ✒ Grilled fillets of lemon sole

39 Grilled whole sole

1 Remove the white and black skin, descale and remove head and side bones with fish scissors.

2 Proceed as for grilled fish steaks (recipe 36) steps 1–5.

40 Grilled salmon

1 Proceed as for grilled fish steaks (recipe 36) steps 1–4.

2 Serve with thinly sliced cucumber and a suitable sauce (e.g. compound butter – see page 65).

41 Griddled monkfish with leeks and Parmesan

Cal 1009 KJ	Cal 239 kcal	Fat 8.3 g	Sat Fat 5.0 g	Carb 1.0 g	Sugar 0.8 g	Protein 40.3 g	Fibre 0.6 g

	4 portions	10 portions
oil		
leeks, finely sliced	100 g	250 g
Parmesan, grated	100 g	250 g
salt, pepper		
prepared monkfish fillets	750 g	1.8 kg
egg white, lightly beaten	2	5
lemons	1	3
mixed salad leaves, to serve		

1 Heat the griddle pan and oil lightly.
2 Cut the leeks into fine julienne with the Parmesan, then season.
3 Cut the monkfish into 1.5 cm thick slices. Dry, dip in the beaten egg white, then in the leek and Parmesan.
4 Place the monkfish on the griddle to cook (approximately 3–4 minutes).
5 Garnish with lemon wedges and mixed leaves.

HEALTHY EATING TIP
- There is no need to add salt – there is plenty in the cheese.
- Serve with a large portion of potatoes and vegetables or salad.

42 Grilled bass with red onion confit

	4 portions	10 portions
red onions, finely chopped	4 medium	9 medium
red wine	250 ml	625 ml
sherry wine vinegar	4 tbsp	10 tbsp
water	4 tbsp	10 tbsp
honey	1 tsp	2½ tsp
butter or margarine	50 g	125 g
tomatoes, peeled, deseeded and finely chopped	10 medium	25 medium
tomato purée (optional)		
bass fillets	4 × 100 g	10 × 100 g
olive oil	4 tbsp	10 tbsp
seasoning		
fresh basil		

1 Place the finely chopped onions, red wine, sherry vinegar and water into a suitable pan and cook until the onions are tender.
2 Add the honey and half the butter, then season.
3 Place the remaining butter into a pan, add the finely chopped tomato flesh, cook to a purée, add a little water if required and a little tomato purée to improve the colour if necessary.
4 Place the fillets of bass through seasoned flour and mark criss-crosses on them with a hot poker to represent a grilling effect (quadrillage).
5 Brush liberally with olive oil and grill until cooked (the fish flakes easily).
6 To serve, place the onion confit on a plate, surround with the tomato purée and place the fillets of bass on top of the confit.
7 Decorate with fresh basil leaves.

Note: John Dory, red snapper, cod and turbot may also be used.

HEALTHY EATING TIP
- Reduce the amount of olive oil used to brush the fish.
- Serve with new potatoes and plenty of vegetables or salad.

43 Grouper with crab and herb crust served on a spicy pepper sauce

Cal 1751 KJ	Cal 422 kcal	Fat 31.8 g	Sat Fat 0.0 g	Carb 7.8 g	Sugar 7.0 g	Protein 26.5 g	Fibre 0.5 g

	4 portions	10 portions
butter or margarine	25 g	62 g
ginger, freshly grated	1 tsp	2½ tsp
white crab meat	100 g	250 g
parsley, chopped	1 tbsp	2½ tbsp
basil, chopped	1 tbsp	2½ tbsp
salt, pepper		
grouper fillets	4 × 100 g	10 × 100 g
oil		
Parmesan, freshly grated	12 g	30 g
Sauce		
butter or margarine	25 g	62 g
vegetable oil	1½ tbsp	3 tbsp
small onion, finely chopped	1	2½
red pepper, deseeded and finely chopped	1	3
small dessert apple, finely chopped	1	3
curry powder	½ tsp	1¼ tsp
saffron	¼ tsp	1 tsp
fish stock	375 ml	1 litre
double cream or crème fraiche	3 tbsp	8 tbsp

1. Heat the butter in a suitable pan, add the ginger and allow to sweat gently for approximately 1 minute.
2. Remove from heat and stir in the crab meat, herbs and seasoning.
3. Season the fish and quickly fry in vegetable oil in a suitable pan on each side for approximately 1 minute.
4. Place on a suitable tray, spread each fillet with the crab mixture and sprinkle with Parmesan.
5. Finish cooking under the grill until the crust is lightly coloured and the fish is cooked through.
6. To prepare the sauce, heat the butter and oil in a suitable pan and sweat the onion without colour.
7. Add the red pepper and allow to sweat for a further 8–10 minutes.
8. Add the apple, curry powder and saffron, stir well and cook for 5 minutes.
9. Add the fish stock, bring to the boil, simmer gently for 20 minutes.
10. Liquidise the sauce, then pass through a fine strainer.
11. Return to a clean saucepan, correct the seasoning and consistency.
12. Finish with cream or crème fraiche.
13. Serve the fillets on a bed of the spicy sauce.

HEALTHY EATING TIP

- No added salt is necessary as Parmesan is added to the crust.
- Use a small amount of an unsaturated oil (olive or sunflower) to fry the fish and the vegetables for the sauce.
- Finish the sauce with low-fat fromage frais. Serve with plenty of potatoes and vegetables.

44 Grilled swordfish and somen noodle salad with cilantro vinaigrette

Cal 2599 KJ	Cal 623 kcal	Fat 42.6 g	Sat Fat 6.1 g	Carb 40.3 g	Sugar 2.7 g	Protein 21.2 g	Fibre 2.5 g	*

	4 portions	10 portions
swordfish fillets	4 × 75 g	10 × 75 g
buckwheat somen noodles	200 g	500 g
romaine lettuce	¼	½
celery, finely diced	50 g	125 g
chopped onion (red)	50 g	125 g
Vinaigrette		
olive oil	70 ml	170 ml
sesame oil	35 ml	85 ml
canola oil	35 ml	85 ml
rice wine	2 tbsp	4½ tbsp
lemon, juice of	½	1
lime, juice of	1	2
fresh ginger, chopped	2 tbsp	5 tbsp
garlic, chopped	1 clove	3 cloves
cilantro leaves	1 tbsp	2½ tbsp
sesame seeds (black)	2 tbsp	5 tbsp
seasoning		

1 Prepare the vinaigrette by placing all the ingredients in a liquidiser, purée until smooth. Season to taste.
2 Season the swordfish fillets, brush with the vinaigrette. Grill for 2 to 3 minutes on each side until cooked. Allow to cool.
3 Cook the noodles in boiling water, refresh and drain. Allow to cool.
4 Shred the lettuce finely, mix with the diced celery and finely chopped red onion. Season with the vinaigrette.
5 Serve by arranging the noodles in the centre of each plate.
6 Place the swordfish fillets on the noodles, season with vinaigrette.
7 Garnish with romaine lettuce. Freshly ground black pepper may be used to finish the dish.

HEALTHY EATING TIP
• Keep added salt to a minimum.
• Adding less vinaigrette to the finished dish can reduce the fat content.

* Using vegetable oil for canola; coriander for cilantro; wheat pasta for buckwheat pasta

45 Fish kebabs

Fish kebabs or brochettes are best made using a firm fish (e.g. salmon, tuna, marlin, turbot). The fish (free from skin and bone) is cut into cubes and can be (a) simply seasoned with salt and pepper or (b) lightly rolled in herbs (e.g. cumin seeds and mustard) or (c) placed in a simple marinade (e.g. olive oil, lemon juice and chopped parsley) for 30 minutes. Other ingredients to be threaded on the skewers can be halves of small, par-boiled new potatoes, cherry tomatoes and mushrooms. The kebabs are lightly brushed with oil and cooked on a fierce grill or barbecue.

Note: See page 216 for scallops, which are suitable for kebabs.

46 Whole sole grilled with traditional accompaniments

	4 portions	10 portions
whole sole, white and black skin removed	4	10
butter for grilling	200 g	500 g
seasoning		
parsley butter	100 g	250 g
lemons, peeled and cut into rondels	1	3

1 Ensure the fish is clean of roe, scales and skin.
2 Place on a buttered grilling tray and rub soft butter in to the flesh.
3 Season and place under the grill.
4 When the butter starts to brown slightly, remove from the grill and turn the fish over carefully using a roasting fork or a long pallet knife.
5 With a spoon, baste the flesh of the uncooked side and continue cooking. Extra care should be taken as the tail end will cook faster than the head end, therefore the gradual reduction in heat towards the front of the grill is where the tail should be cooked.
6 To check whether the fish is done, place your thumb just behind the gill area and you should feel the flesh ease away from the bone.
7 Finish with parsley butter and a wedge of lemon.

Note: This is a classic recipe using slip, Dover or lemon sole. There is no need to modernise it.

47 Grilled salmon, pea soup and quails' eggs

	4 portions	10 portions
Soup		
vegetable oil	50 ml	125 ml
shallots, peeled and sliced	2	5
garlic cloves, crushed	1	3
raw potato, chopped	200 g	500 g
peas	600 g	1½ kg
milk	500 ml	1½ litre
stem of mint	1	3
Salmon		
salmon fillet	4 × 150 g	10 × 150 g
plain flour	25 g	60 g
olive oil	4 tbsp	9 tbsp
To finish		
spinach, washed	200 g	500 g
peas, cooked and crushed	600 g	1½ kg
butter	50 g	125 g
seasoning		
quails' eggs, lightly poached	8	20
first press olive oil		
fresh herbs		

For the soup
1 Heat the oil and add the shallots and garlic, cook without colour for 2 minutes.
2 Then add the potato and cook for a further 2 minutes.
3 Add the peas and milk, bring to the boil and remove from the heat.
4 Add the mint sprig and allow to infuse for 3-4 minutes. Remove and then blitz the soup in a processor.
5 Pass through a strainer and retain.

For the salmon
1 Heat a lower-heat grill ensuring the bars are clean.
2 Lightly oil the bars and then dust the salmon fillet in the flour.
3 Carefully place the salmon fillet on the grill and score.
4 Once sealed rotate the fish 45 degrees and mark, creating a diamond shape.
5 After 2–3 minutes turn the salmon over taking care not to break the flesh.
6 After 2 minutes cooking on the other side check if

cooked by gently pushing your index finger into the centre – the fish should still have a little structure.

To finish

1 Wilt the spinach in a hot pan, add the peas and butter and season.
2 Place the poached eggs in the soup and quickly re-heat.
3 Place a mound of spinach and peas in the centre of a bowl with the salmon on top and 2 quails' eggs per bowl.

Roasting and baking

For further information, refer to pages 175 and 176 of this chapter or the text on roasting and baking on pages 21–26 of Chapter 2.

Roasting

4 Finish the dish with a drizzle of fine olive oil and fresh herbs.

Note: This is a suitable summer dish, light and very seasonal. As an alternative replace the salmon with the salt cod.

Figure 7.16 Grilled salmon, pea soup and quails' eggs

48 Whole roasted red mullet on crushed potatoes with salsa verde

Cal	Cal	Fat	Sat Fat	Carb	Sugar	Protein	Fibre
3120 KJ	750 kcal	55.5 g	6.9 g	21.2 g	3.9 g	42.6 g	4.9 g

	4 portions	10 portions
red mullet	4 × 200 g	10 × 200 g
new potatoes (medium sized)	400 g	1 kg
black olives, stoned and finely chopped	50 g	125 g
plum tomatoes, peeled, deseeded and diced	2	5
chives	25 g	50 g
olive oil		
broad beans	200 g	400 g
diced tomatoes	100 g	250 g
salsa verde (see page 62)		
pak choi, lightly steamed, to finish		

1 Remove the scales, head and intestines, then wash and dry the fish.
2 Cut down both sides of the backbone and carefully remove it.
3 Trim off all fins and excess rib bones, and neaten the tail.

4 Cook the potatoes, drain, cool, peel and crush with a fork.
5 Mix in the olives, plum tomatoes and chives, and season lightly.
6 Lightly season the fish, turn in oil and place on a hot grill to mark.
7 Place on a baking sheet and bake in the oven at 200°C for approx. 5–6 minutes.
8 Arrange the potato in middle of plates, with a ring of broad beans and tomato around it.
9 Place fish on top, coat lightly with warmed salsa and pour a little around it.
10 Garnish with lightly steamed pak choi.

Note: This recipe is adapted from one supplied by Anton Edelmann.

HEALTHY EATING TIP
• Use the minimum amount of salt.
• Brush the fish with a little unsaturated oil before placing on the hot grill.

49 Roast fillet of sea bass with vanilla and fennel

	4 portions	10 portions
sea bass fillets (approx. 160 g each, cut from a 2–3 kg fish) skin on, scaled and pin-boned	4	10
seasoning		
vegetable oil	50 ml	125 ml
Fennel		
bulbs of baby fennel	8	20
vegetable oil	50 ml	125 ml
fish stock	500 ml	1¼ litres
clove of garlic	1	3
Vanilla sauce		
shallots, peeled and sliced	1	3
fish stock	500 ml	1¼ litres
white wine	200 ml	500 ml
vanilla pods	2	5
butter	50 g	125 g
chives, chopped	1 tsp	3 tsp
tomato concassée	100 g	250 g

For the fennel
1 Trim the fennel bulbs well, ensuring they are free from blemishes and root.
2 Heat the oil in a pan, place in the fennel and slightly brown.
3 Add the stock and garlic, bring to the boil and cook until tender.

For the sauce
1 Heat a small amount of vegetable oil in a pan.
2 Place in the shallot and cook without colour, add the stock, white wine and split vanilla, and reduce by two-thirds.
3 Pass through a chinois and reserve for serving.
4 Add the butter and chopped chives.

To finish
1 Pre-heat the oven to 180°C.
2 Heat the oil in a non-stick pan and place the seasoned sea bass fillets in skin side down.
3 Cook for 2 minutes on the stove and then place in the oven for 3 minutes (depending on thickness) still with the skin side down.
4 Meanwhile, reheat the fennel and add the tomato concassée to the sauce.
5 Remove the sea bass from the oven and turn in the pan, finishing the flesh side for 30 seconds to 1 minute.
6 Lay the fennel in the centre of the plate and place the sea bass on top.
7 Finish the dish with the sauce over the bass and around, serve immediately.

Note: A marriage of flavour: vanilla, bass and fennel are made for each other. This fish can also be steamed.

Baking

50 Baked cod with a herb crust

Cal	Cal	Fat	Sat Fat	Carb	Sugar	Protein	Fibre	*
1882 KJ	452 kcal	30.8 g	18.7 g	12.7 g	0.8 g	31.7 g	0.4 g	

	4 portions	10 portions
cod fillets, 100–150 g each	4	10
herb mustard		
fresh breadcrumbs	100 g	250 g
butter, margarine or oil	100 g	250 g
Cheddar cheese, grated	100 g	250 g
parsley, chopped	1 tsp	1 tbsp
salt, pepper		

1 Place the prepared, washed and dried fish on a greased baking tray or ovenproof dish.
2 Combine the ingredients for the herb crust (the mustard, breadcrumbs, butter or oil, cheese, parsley and seasoning) and press evenly over the fish.
3 Bake in the oven at 180°C for approx. 15–20 minutes until cooked and the crust is a light golden-brown.
4 Serve either with lemon quarters or a suitable salsa (page 62) or sauce, e.g. tomato or egg (page 60).

HEALTHY EATING TIP
- Use a little sunflower oil when making the herb crust.
- Cheese is salty – no added salt is needed.
- Serve with a large portion of tomato or cucumber salsa and new potatoes.

* Using mustard powder (1 tsp) for herb mustard

51 Oven-baked marinated cod with bok choi

	4 portions	10 portions
cod fillet (approx. 175 g each) with skin off	4	10
baby bok choi	4	10
red pepper, cut into julienne	1	3
yellow pepper, cut into julienne	1	3
red onion, thinly sliced	1	3
bean sprouts	100 g	250 g
sesame oil	1 tbsp	3 tbsp
vegetable oil	2 tbsp	5 tbsp
soy sauce	1 tbsp	3 tbsp
coriander, chopped	1 tbsp	3 tbsp
Marinade		
soy sauce	100 ml	250 ml
sesame oil	50 ml	125 ml
rice wine	100 ml	250 ml
black bean paste	100 g	250 g

For the marinade
1 Mix all the ingredients together to a smooth consistency.
2 Place the cod fillets in the marinade for 12 hours.
3 After that, remove the fillets and wash off the excess marinade (it is not essential to get it all off).

For the cod
1 Pre-heat the oven to 180°C.
2 Put the cod on a lightly oiled baking tray and place in the oven.
3 Meanwhile heat the oil in a wok (if not available, use a heavy cast pan to retain the heat).
4 Place all the ingredients in the wok/pan excluding the soy and coriander.
5 Cook for 2–3 minutes until cooked but with a bite. Retain and keep warm.
6 Check the cod; it should take between 5 and 6 minutes according to thickness and, if timed well, will be ready when the vegetables are cooked.

7 Place the vegetables in the centre of the serving plate/dish and top with the cod. Any excess juices from the baking tray or the wok/pan may be poured around the fish, then serve.

Note: There is an eastern influence here, which can be adapted to suit a more European palate by changing the marinade to one using lemon and garlic, and using spinach, green beans and even olive to accompany the fish.

Other fish recipes

52 Red mullet ceviche with organic leaves

	4 portions	10 portions
shallots, finely diced	2	5
olive oil	1 tbsp	3 tbsp
white wine vinegar	50 ml	125 ml
fish stock	1 litre	2½ litres
lemons, juice of	1	3
cucumber, diced	2 tbsp	5 tbsp
red mullet fillets (approx. 120 g each), pinned and scaled	4	10
organic salad leaf (5 varieties)	300 g	750 g
vinaigrette	50 ml	125 ml
caviar (optional)	50 g	125 g
Saffron dressing		
water	10 ml	25 ml
saffron		
vegetable oil	50 ml	125 ml
vinegar	10 ml	25 ml

1 Bring the shallots, olive oil, white wine vinegar and fish stock to the boil. Add the lemon and cucumber, and allow to cool at room temperature.
2 Place the red mullet in a container and cover with the liquid. Top with clingfilm to ensure all the air is kept out, capitalising on maximum curing. This will need to remain in the fridge for a minimum of 6 hours.

For the dressing
1 Add water and a pinch of saffron to a pan and bring to the boil.
2 Whisk in the vegetable oil and vinegar.
3 Season.

To finish
1 Mix the dressed leaves lightly in vinaigrette.
2 Place the red mullet carefully on a plate with a little of the curing liquor, shallots and cucumber.
3 Top with the organic salad and finish with the saffron dressing and caviar (if using).

Note: A cured dish always tastes of the true ingredients. Using red mullet, as here, the flavours are bold and earthy, and paired with the saffron it makes a perfect summer starter.

53 Fish kedgeree (cadgery de poisson)

Cal 1974 KJ	Cal 472 kcal	Fat 28.2 g	Sat Fat 15.3 g	Carb 29.3 g	Sugar 4.7 g	Protein 25.7 g	Fibre 1.2 g	*

	4 portions	10 portions
fish (usually smoked haddock or fresh salmon)	400 g	1 kg
rice pilau (see page 162)	200 g	500 g
eggs, hard-boiled	2	5
butter	50 g	125 g
salt, pepper		
curry sauce, to serve (see page 58)	250 ml	625 ml

1 Poach the fish. Remove all skin and bone. Flake.
2 Cook the rice pilaff. Cut the eggs into dice.
3 Combine the eggs, fish and rice, and heat in the butter. Correct the seasoning.
4 Serve hot with a sauceboat of curry sauce.

Note: This dish is traditionally served for breakfast, lunch or supper. The fish used should be named on the menu (e.g. salmon kedgeree).

HEALTHY EATING TIP
- Reduce the amount of butter used to heat the rice, fish and eggs.
- Garnish with grilled tomatoes and serve with bread or toast.

* Using smoked haddock

54 Fish cakes

Cal 1130 KJ	Cal 270 kcal	Fat 13.6 g	Sat Fat 1.9 g	Carb 23.2 g	Sugar 1.1 g	Protein 15.1 g	Fibre 0.8 g	*

	4 portions	10 portions
cooked fish (free from skin and bone)	200 g	500 g
mashed potatoes	200 g	500 g
egg	1	3
salt, pepper		
flour	25 g	60 g
breadcrumbs	50 g	125 g

1 Combine the fish, potatoes and egg, and season.
2 Divide into 4 (or 10) pieces. Mould into balls.
3 Pass through a coating of flour, egg and breadcrumbs.
4 Flatten slightly and neaten with a palette knife.
5 Deep-fry in hot fat (185°C) for 2–3 minutes.

Variations
Other fish can be used – for example, cod, fresh haddock, salmon, or crab (recipe 60).
- Optional extra seasonings are tomato ketchup, fresh chopped herbs (e.g. chervil, dill, parsley, tarragon, chives), anchovy essence, English or continental mustard.
- Coat lightly with flour and shallow-fry.
- Serve with a sauce (e.g. lemon butter, tartare, hollandaise, shrimp or tomato).
- Serve with a little dressed green salad.

HEALTHY EATING TIP
- The fish cakes could be shallow-fried in a small amount of an unsaturated oil, then drained on kitchen paper.

* Using cod

55 Fish pie

Cal 879 KJ	Cal 209 kcal	Fat 12.0 g	Sat Fat 5.3 g	Carb 11.9 g	Sugar 3.2 g	Protein 14.1 g	Fibre 0.9 g

	4 portions	10 portions
béchamel (thin) (see page 51)	250 ml	625 ml
cooked fish (free from skin and bone)	200 g	500 g
mushrooms, cooked and diced	50 g	125 g
egg, hard-boiled and chopped	1	3
parsley, chopped		
salt, pepper		
mashed or duchess potatoes	200 g	500 g
eggwash or milk, to finish		

1 Bring the béchamel to the boil.
2 Add the fish, mushrooms, egg and parsley. Correct the seasoning.
3 Place in a buttered pie dish.
4 Place or pipe the potato on top. Brush with eggwash or milk.
5 Brown in a hot oven or under the salamander and serve.

Note: Many variations can be made to this recipe with the addition of (a) prawns or shrimps, (b) herbs such as dill, tarragon or fennel, (c) raw fish poached in white wine, the cooking liquor strained off, double cream added in place of béchamel and reduced to a light consistency.

HEALTHY EATING TIP

- Keep the added salt to a minimum.
- This is a healthy main course dish, particularly when served with plenty of vegetables.

56 Fish sausages (cervelas de poisson)

Cal 428 KJ	Cal 102 kcal	Fat 1.3 g	Sat Fat 0.3 g	Carb 1.0 g	Sugar 0.9 g	Protein 21.4 g	Fibre 0.7 g	*

fish and/or shellfish	400 g
mushrooms, chopped	50 g
brunoise of skinned red pepper	50 g
fresh parsley, dill or chervil, chopped	25 g
salt, pepper	
sausage skins	

1 Mix all the ingredients.
2 Place the sausage skins in water then hang up and knot one end.
3 Using a forcing bag, stuff the skins with the fish mixture then knot the open end with a piece of string. Pierce skin all over with a needle to prevent bursting.
4 Divide sausage into sections by tying loosely with string.
5 Gently poach the sausages in salted water at no more than 75°C for 15 minutes.
6 With a sharp knife, remove the sausage skins carefully so as not to spoil the shape, drain well on a clean napkin. Serve with a suitable sauce (e.g. white wine) and garnish (e.g. shrimps, mushrooms).

Note: The filling can also be made using a mousseline mixture (see page 128 of *Advanced Practical Cookery*, listed in the References at the end of this chapter). As with meat sausages, the variations of fish sausages that can be produced are virtually endless. Almost any type of fish or shellfish can be used, either chopped or minced. The filling can also be a combination of two or more fish, and additional ingredients can be added (e.g. chopped mushrooms, brunoise of skinned red peppers), a suitable chopped herb (e.g. dill, chervil, parsley) and/or a touch of a spice.

* Using cod

Shellfish

Origins

Shellfish, such as lobsters and crabs, are all invertebrates (i.e. they do not possess an internal skeleton) and are split into two main groups: *molluscs* have either an external hinged double shell (e.g. scallops, mussels) or a single spiral shell (e.g. winkles, whelks), or have soft bodies with an internal shell (e.g. squid, octopus); *crustaceans* have tough outer shells that act like armour, and also have flexible joints to allow quick movement (e.g. crab, lobster).

Choosing and buying

Shellfish are prized for their tender, fine-textured flesh, which can be prepared in a variety of ways, but are prone to rapid spoilage. The reason for this is that they contain quantities of certain proteins, amino acids, which encourage bacterial growth.

To ensure freshness and best flavour it is preferable to choose live specimens and cook them yourself. This is often possible with the expansion of globalisation, air freight and such like, creating a healthy trade in live shellfish.

Bear in mind the following points when choosing shellfish:

- shells should not be cracked or broken
- shells of mussels and oysters should be tightly shut; open shells that do not close when tapped sharply should be discarded
- lobsters, crabs and prawns should have a good colour and be heavy for their size
- lobsters and crabs should have all their limbs.

Table 7.3 Seasonality of shellfish

	JAN	FEB	MAR	APR	MAY	JUN	JUL	AUG	SEP	OCT	NOV	DEC
Crab (brown cock)												
Crab (spider)												
Crab (brown hen)												
Clams												
Cockles												
Crayfish												
Lobster												
Langoustines												
Mussels												
Oysters (rock)												
Oysters (native)												
Prawns												
Scallops												

Code:
Available
At best

Cooking

The flesh of fish and shellfish is different to meat and, as a consequence, their muscle make-up is very different too, making their connective tissue very fragile, the muscle fibres shorter and the fat content relatively low. Generally, care should be taken when cooking and shellfish should be cooked as little as possible, to the point that the protein in the muscle groups just coagulate. Beyond this point the flesh tends to dry out, leading to toughening and a dry texture. Shellfish are known for their dramatic colour changing: from blue/grey to a vibrant orange colour. This is because they contain red and yellow pigments called carotenoids, bound to molecules of protein. The protein bonds obscure the yellow/red pigment and, once heat is applied, the bonds are broken and the vibrant pigmentation revealed.

Storage

All shellfish will start to spoil as soon as they have been removed from their natural environment, therefore the longer shellfish are stored the more they will deteriorate due to the bacteria present (see the guidelines on choosing and buying, above). Best practice would be to cook immediately and store as for cooked fish. Shellfish can be blanched quickly to remove the shell and membrane (especially in lobsters), but they will still need to be stored as for a raw product as they will require further cooking.

Bear in mind the following quality, purchasing and storage points:

- whenever possible, all shellfish should be purchased live so as to ensure freshness
- shellfish should be kept in suitable containers, covered with damp seaweed or damp cloths, and stored in a cold room or refrigerator
- shellfish should be cooked as soon as possible after purchasing.

Shrimps and prawns

These are often bought cooked, either in the shells or peeled. Smell is the best guide to freshness. Shrimps and prawns can be used for garnishes, decorating fish dishes, cocktails, sauces, salads, hors d'oeuvre, omelettes, and snack and savoury dishes. They can also be used for a variety of hot dishes: stir-fries, risotto, curries, etc. Potted shrimps are also a popular dish. Freshly cooked prawns in their shells may also be served cold accompanied by a mayonnaise-based sauce, such as garlic mayonnaise.

King prawns are a larger variety, which can also be used in any of the above ways.

Raw and cooked shrimps and prawns are prepared by having the head, carapace (upper shell), legs, tail section and the dark intestinal vein running down the back removed.

Scampi, salt-water crayfish and Dublin Bay prawns

These are also known as Norway lobster or langoustine and are sold fresh, frozen, raw or cooked. Their tails are prepared like shrimps and they are used in a variety of ways: salads, rice dishes, stir-fries, deep-fried, poached and served with a number of different sauces. They are also used as garnishes to hot and cold fish dishes.

Freshwater crayfish are also known as *écrevisse*. These are small freshwater crustaceans with claws, found in lakes and lowland streams. They are prepared and cooked like shrimps and prawns, and used in many dishes, including soup. They are often used whole to garnish hot and cold fish dishes.

Lobster

Purchasing points

- Purchase alive, with both claws attached, to ensure freshness.
- Lobsters should be heavy in proportion to their size.
- The coral of the hen lobster is necessary to give the required colour for certain soups, sauces and lobster dishes.
- Hen lobsters are distinguished from cock lobsters by their broader tails.

Cooking of lobster

1 Wash then plunge them into a pan of boiling salted water containing 60 ml vinegar to 1 litre water.
2 Cover with a lid, reboil, then allow to simmer for 15–20 minutes according to size.
3 Overcooking can cause the tail flesh to toughen and the claw meat to become hard and fibrous.
4 Allow to cool in the cooking liquid when possible.

214

Cleaning of cooked lobster

1 Remove the claws and the pincers from the claws.
2 Crack the claws and joints and remove the meat.
3 Cut the lobster in half by inserting the point of a large knife 2 cm above the tail on the natural central line.
4 Cut through the tail firmly.
5 Turn the lobster around and cut through the upper shell (carapace).
6 Remove the halves of the sac (which contains grit) from each half. This is situated at the top, near the head.
7 Using a small knife, remove the intestinal trace from the tail and wash if necessary.

Uses

Lobsters are served cold in cocktails, lobster mayonnaise, hors d'oeuvre, salads, sandwiches and in halves on cold buffets. They are used hot in soups, sauces, rice dishes, stir-fry dishes and in numerous ways served in the half shell with various sauces. They are also used to garnish fish dishes.

Crawfish

These are sometimes referred to as 'spiny lobsters', but unlike lobsters they have no claws and their meat is solely in the tail. Crawfish vary considerably in size from 1 to 3 kg; they are cooked as for lobsters and the tail meat can be used in any of the lobster recipes. Because of their impressive appearance crawfish dressed whole are sometimes used on special cold buffets. They are very expensive and are also available frozen.

Crab

Purchasing points

- Buy alive to ensure freshness.
- Ensure that both claws are attached.
- Crabs should be heavy in relation to size.

Cooking

1 Place the crabs in boiling salted water with a little vinegar added.
2 Reboil, then simmer for approximately 12 minutes according to size. These times apply to crabs weighing from ½–2½ kg.
3 Allow the crabs to cool in the cooking liquor.

To dress

Allow 200–300 g unprepared crab per portion

1 Remove large claws and sever at the joints.
2 Remove the flexible pincer from the claw.
3 Crack or saw carefully and remove all flesh.
4 Remove flesh from two remaining joints with the handle of spoon.
5 Carefully remove the soft undershell.
6 Discard the gills (dead man's fingers) and the sac behind the eyes.
7 Scrape out all the inside of the shell and pass through a sieve.
8 Season with salt, pepper, Worcester sauce and a little mayonnaise sauce; thicken lightly with fresh white breadcrumbs.
9 Trim the shell by tapping carefully along the natural line.
10 Scrub the shell thoroughly and leave to dry.
11 Dress the brown meat down the centre of the shell.
12 Shred the white meat, taking care to remove any small pieces of shell.
13 Dress neatly on either side of the brown meat.
14 Decorate as desired, using any of the following: chopped parsley, hard-boiled white and yolk of egg, anchovies, capers, olives.
15 Serve the crab on a flat dish, garnish with lettuce leaves, quarters of tomato and the crab's legs.
16 Serve a vinaigrette or mayonnaise sauce separately.

Uses

Crab meat can be used cold for hors d'oeuvre, cocktails, salads, sandwiches and dressed crab. Used hot, it can be covered with a suitable sauce and served with rice, in bouchées or pancakes, or made into crab fish cakes.

Cockles

Cockles are enclosed in small, attractive, cream-coloured shells. As they live in sand it is essential to purge them by washing well under running cold water and leaving them in cold salted water (changed frequently) until no traces of sand remain.

Cockles can be cooked either by steaming, boiling in unsalted water, on a preheated griddle, or as for any mussel recipe. They should be cooked only until the shells open.

They can be used in soups, sauces, salads, stir-fries and rice dishes, and as garnish for fish dishes.

Mussels

Mussels are extensively cultivated on wooden hurdles in the sea, producing tender, delicately flavoured plump fish. They are produced in Britain and imported from France, Holland and Belgium. French mussels are small, Dutch and Belgian mussels are plumper. The quality tends to vary from season to season.

Purchasing points

- The shells must be tightly closed, indicating the mussels are alive.
- They should be of a good size.
- There should not be an excessive number of barnacles attached.
- They should smell fresh.

Storage

Mussels should be kept in containers, covered with damp seaweed or cloths, and stored in a cold room or refrigerator.

Uses

Mussels can be used for soups, sauces and salads, and cooked in a wide variety of hot dishes.

Cooking

- Scrape the shells to remove any barnacles, etc. Wash well and drain in a colander.
- In a thick-bottomed pan with a tight-fitting lid, place 25 g chopped shallot or onion for each litre of mussels.
- Add the mussels, cover with a lid and cook on a fierce heat for 4–5 minutes until the shells open completely.
- Remove the mussels from the shells, checking carefully for sand, weed, etc.
- Retain the carefully strained liquid for the sauce.

Scallops

There are a number of varieties of scallop:

- great scallops are up to 15 cm in size
- bay scallops are up to 8 cm
- queen scallops, also known as queenies, are small, cockle-sized scallops.

Scallops are found on the seabed and are therefore dirty, so it is advisable to purchase them ready cleaned. If scallops are bought in their shells, the shells should be tightly shut, which indicates they are alive and fresh. The roe (orange in colour) should be bright and moist. Scallops in their shells should be covered with damp seaweed or cloths and kept in a cold room or refrigerator. To remove from the shells, place the shells on top of the stove or in an oven for a few seconds, when they will open and the flesh can then be removed with a knife. Scallops should then be well washed; remove the trail, leaving only the white scallop.

Cooking

Scallops should be only lightly cooked.

- Poach gently for 2–3 minutes in dry white wine with a little onion, carrot, thyme, bay leaf and parsley. Serve with a suitable sauce (e.g. white wine, mornay).
- Lightly fry on both sides for a few seconds in butter or oil in a very hot pan (if the scallops are very thick they can be cut in halves sideways) and serve with a suitable garnish (sliced wild or cultivated mushrooms, or a fine brunoise of vegetables and tomato) and a liquid that need not be thickened (white wine and fish stock, or cream- or butter-mounted sauce).

Fried scallops can also be served hot on a plate of salad leaves.

- Deep-fry, either egg and crumbed or passed through a light batter and served with segments of lemon and a suitable sauce (e.g. tartare).
- Wrap in thin streaky bacon, place on skewers for grilling or barbecuing.

Whelks

The common whelk is familiar around the coast of Britain. It is actually a gastropod, which means it has a large, strong flat foot to move around on. Whelks are also equipped with a think siphon, which is used for breathing and feeling around for food.

British winkles

The main types of British winkle, which can be readily identified on rocky shores, are:

1 small periwinkle – approximately 4 mm
2 rough periwinkle – at least four different subspecies, with the largest reaching 30 mm
3 flat periwinkle.

Oysters

Oysters are bivalve molluscs found near the bottom of the sea in coastal areas. The upper shell (valve) is flattish and attached by an elastic ligament hinge to the lower, bowl-shaped shell. Oysters are high in protein and low in fat; they are rich in zinc and contain many other nutrients such as calcium, iron, copper, iodine, magnesium and selenium.

Size, shape and colour vary considerably. Native oysters are pricier and generally thought of as superior. Pacific or rock oysters tend to have a frillier shell and are smaller, with milder meat.

Purchasing points

- The shells should be clean, bright, tightly closed and unbroken.

Storage

Oysters should be stored at a low temperature and should smell briny fresh. Unopened live oysters can be kept in the fridge covered with wet cloths for two to three days; discard any that open. Do not store in an airtight container or under fresh water as this will cause them to die. Shucked oysters can be kept refrigerated in a sealed container for four to five days.

Shellfish recipes

57 Oysters in their own shells

Serves 4

24 rock or native oysters
1 lemon
To accompany
brown bread and butter
Tabasco or chilli sauce

1 Select only those oysters that are tightly shut and have a fresh smell (category A is best, which means the waters they have grown in are clean).
2 To open an oyster, only the point of the oyster knife is used. Hold the oyster with a thick oven cloth to protect your hand.
3 With the oyster in the palm of your hand, push the point of the knife about 1 cm deep into the 'hinge' between the 'lid' and the body of the oyster.
4 Once the lid has been penetrated, push down. The lid should pop open. Lift up the top shell, cutting the muscle attached to it.
5 Remove any splintered shell from the flesh and solid shell.
6 Return each oyster to its shell and serve on a bed of crushed ice with chilli sauce, brown bread and lemon.

Note: Make sure the oysters have been grown in or fished from clean waters, and take note of the famous rule only to use them when there is an 'r' in the month, although rock oysters are available throughout the year.

Figure 7.17 ✒ Preparation of dressed crab

58 Dressed crab

	Serves 2
crab, cooked and cooled	1 kg
lemon, grated rind and juice	1
fresh parsley, chopped	2 tbsp
mayonnaise	4 tbsp
soft brown breadcrumbs	4 tbsp
Dijon mustard	2 tsp
hard-boiled egg, finely chopped	1

1 Crack open the crab claws and remove the white meat, keeping it as intact as possible, and place into a bowl.
2 Put rest of white meat from claw arms, legs and body into bowl.
3 Add grated lemon rind, half juice, 1 tablespoon of chopped parsley and 3 tablespoons of mayonnaise to the white meat and mix lightly.
4 In a separate bowl, place the breadcrumbs, remaining mayonnaise and lemon juice and the mustard.
5 Scoop out brown meat from shell (discarding the gills and the sac behind the eyes), put into bowl and mix lightly.
6 Wash shell and dry.
7 Use brown meat mixture to fill the two sides of shell and pack the white meat into centre.
8 Sprinkle finely chopped hard-boiled egg and rest of parsley over top for decoration.
9 Serve with lots of brown bread and butter, and a green salad to follow.

Figure 7.18 ✒ Dressed crab (modern)

Figure 7.19 ✒ Dressed crab (traditional)

Note: To ensure freshness, purchase the crab live. When cleaning the cooked crab, ensure that the dead men's fingers (feathery gills) are removed.

59 Crab salad with pink grapefruit

	4 portions	10 portions
Crab		
cooked and picked		
white crab meat	500 g	1¼ kg
coriander, chopped	1 tsp	3 tsp
mayonnaise	50 ml	125 ml
plum tomato concassée	100 g	250 g
grated fresh root ginger	½ tsp	1 tsp
seasoning		
chervil		
Salad		
pink grapefruit in segments	1	3
cooked green beans	100 g	250 g
organic salad leaves	200 g	500 g
honey-lime dressing		
(see recipe 70)		
cooked baby		
artichokes cut into 4	4	10

For the crab
1 Combine all the ingredients, check and adjust the seasoning.
2 Place in a clean bowl and retain in the refrigerator.

For the salad
1 Combine all the ingredients and mix with the dressing.
2 Place in the centre of the serving plate.
3 Top this with 3 quenelles of the crab mix.
4 Finish with the chervil and serve with brown bread and butter, or traditional sour dough bread.

Note: Crab and citrus are always a great contrast for each other; with this recipe pink grapefruit cuts through the richness of the crab well, without being too acidic.

60 Crab cakes with rocket salad and lemon dressing

	4 portions	10 portions
Crab cakes		
shallots, finely chopped	25 g	60 g
spring onions, finely chopped	4	10
fish/shellfish glaze	75 ml	185 ml
crab meat	400 g	1 kg
mayonnaise	75 g	185 g
lemons, juice of	1	3
plum tomatoes skinned, cut into concassée	2	5
wholegrain mustard	1 tsp	3 tsp
seasoning		
fresh white breadcrumbs	200 g	500 g
eggs, beaten with 100 ml of milk	2	5
flour for rolling		
Salad and dressing		
vegetable oil	170 ml	425 ml
white wine vinegar	25 ml	60 ml
lemons, juice of	1	3
seasoning		
washed and picked rocket	250 g	625 g
shaved Reggiano Parmesan	100 g	250 g

To make the crab cakes
1 Mix the shallots, spring onion and the fish glaze with the hand-picked crab meat.
2 Add the mayonnaise, lemon juice, tomato concassée and mustard, check and adjust the seasoning.
3 Allow to rest for 30 minutes in the refrigerator.
4 Scale into 80–90 g balls and shape into discs 1½ cm high, place in the freezer for 30 minutes to harden.
5 When firm to the touch, coat in breadcrumbs using the flour, egg and breadcrumbs.
6 Allow to rest for a further 30 minutes.
7 Heat a little oil in a non-stick pan, carefully place the cakes in and cook on each side until golden brown.

For the salad and dressing

1 Combine the oil, vinegar and lemon juice together, check the seasoning.
2 Place the rocket and Parmesan in a large bowl and add a little dressing, just to coat.
3 Place this in the centre of each plate, top with the crab cakes and serve.

Note: Any excess crab meat can be used up in this recipe – a quick, classic dish. The crab can be exchanged for salmon or most fresh fish trimmings.

61 Potted shrimps

	4 portions	10 portions
butter	100 g	250 g
chives, chopped	2 tbsp	5 tbsp
cayenne pepper to taste		
peeled brown shrimps	600 g	1½ kg
clarified butter	6 tbsp	15 tbsp

1 Put the butter, chives and cayenne pepper in a medium-sized pan and leave to melt over a gentle heat.
2 Add the peeled shrimps and stir over the heat for a couple of minutes until they have heated through, but don't let the mixture boil.
3 Divide the shrimps and butter between 4 small ramekins. Level the tops and then leave them to set in the refrigerator.
4 Spoon over a thin layer of clarified butter and leave to set once more. Serve with plenty of brown toast or crusty brown bread.

Note: A real seaside dish, full of flavour and eaten with plenty of brown bread and butter. Lobster or langoustine can be used – although timings will need to be adapted accordingly. The traditional seasoning for potted shrimps is ground mace.

62 Langoustine and mussel soup

	4 portions	10 portions
raw langoustine tails (large), bodies and claws retained for the stock	20	50
mussels, cleaned	400 g	1 kg
fish stock	300 ml	750 ml
butter	80 g	200 g
fresh bay leaves	2	5
dry white wine	50 ml	125 ml
shallots, chopped	1	3
celery sticks, cut into small dice	1	3
rindless dry-cured unsmoked bacon, cut across into short, fat strips	50 g	125 g
potatoes, peeled and cut into small dice	225 g	560 g
plain flour	20 g	50 g
full-cream milk	300 ml	750 ml
whipping cream	120 ml	300 ml
salt		
freshly ground black pepper		

1 If using raw langoustines, put them into the freezer for 30 minutes to kill them. Then put the langoustines and mussels into a pan and add the stock.
2 Cover, bring to the boil and steam for 2 minutes.
3 Remove from the heat and tip the contents into a colander set over a clean bowl to retain the cooking liquid.
4 Check that all the mussels have opened and discard any that remain closed.
5 Melt about one-third of the butter in a large pan, add the langoustine shells and the bay leaves, cook hard for 1 minute.
6 Add the wine and the reserved cooking liquor and while it is bubbling away, crush the shells to release all their flavour into the cooking liquid.
7 Cook for 10–12 minutes.
8 Meanwhile heat the rest of the butter in a pan, add the shallots, celery and bacon, cook gently until the shallots are soft but not coloured.

9 Add the diced potatoes and cook for 1–2 minutes, stir in the flour, then add the milk and cream.
10 Pass the cooking liquor into a clean pan and add to the roux base, stirring continuously to prevent lumps.
11 When all the stock has been added, cook out until the potatoes are soft.

12 Stir in the langoustines and mussels, and adjust the seasoning if necessary.
13 Ladle into warmed soup plates and serve with traditional sour bread.

Note: Proceed with caution when using both mussels and langoustines as they overcook quickly and this will spoil the eating quality.

63 Poached langoustines with aioli dip

	4 portions	10 portions
raw langoustine tails, large	36	90
Court bouillon		
Carrots	2	5
fennel bulbs	1	3
garlic cloves	2	5
water	1400 ml	3½ litres
white wine	290 ml	725 ml
a few fresh parsley and chervil stalks		
white peppercorns, crushed	3	7
Aioli		
sweet potato (about 250 g each), orange flesh	1	2½
mayonnaise	3 tbsp	7½ tbsp
pinches saffron strands, soaked in a little water	2	5
eggs, boiled and yolks removed and reserved	3	7
crushed garlic	½ tsp	1½ tsp
a little olive oil		
salt and pepper		
lemon, juice of	½	1

For the bouillon
1 Place vegetables in pan and cover with water.
2 Gently bring to the boil and simmer for 5–10 minutes.
3 Add the white wine, parsley, chervil stalks and crushed peppercorns.
4 Cook for a further 10 minutes then leave to stand until cool.
5 Strain out the vegetables and chill the liquid.

For the aioli
1 Pre-heat the oven to 200°C. Bake the sweet potato for about 35–45 minutes or until tender. Peel off the skin and gently crush the flesh.
2 Place sweet potato flesh in a liquidiser, add the mayonnaise, saffron, egg yolks and garlic and blend.
3 Add olive oil to moisten, season and finish with a squeeze of lemon juice.
4 Remove entrails from langoustines by taking the middle segment or tail shell between thumb and forefinger, then twist it and pull.
5 Plunge the langoustines into the simmering court bouillon for 30–40 seconds. Remove and leave to cool naturally. Serve with the aioli.

Note: King or tiger prawns may be used as an alternative.

64 Lobster tail gratin

	4 portions	10 portions
Lobster		
lobster tails (each from a 500–600 g live lobster)	4	10
butter	80 g	200 g
dry sherry	20 ml	50 ml
flour	20 g	50 g
paprika	½ tsp	1 tsp
cream	120 ml	300 ml
seasoning		
Crumb topping		
slices white bread	3	7
cup butter	40 g	100 g
chives, chopped	1 tbsp	2 tbsp
seasoning		

For the crumb topping
1 Remove crust from bread and place in food processor or grate fine.
2 Melt butter in a pan, add the breadcrumbs and cook until brown.
3 Add the chives and salt and pepper. When the lobster meat is returned to the shell sprinkle over.

For the lobster
1 Pre-heat the oven to 190°C.
2 Gently blanch the lobster tails until they are half done, then drain and cool.
3 Remove meat from shells and cut into small pieces, clean and save the shells.
4 Melt butter in a thick-bottomed pan. Stir in sherry and lobster, simmer for 2 minutes.
5 Stir in flour, paprika and cream until thickened, adjust the seasoning then return mixture to shells.
6 Place the filled and topped shells on a baking tray and bake in the oven for 10 minutes.
7 Serve immediately with a green salad or wilted greens.

Note: Cornish or Scottish (native) lobsters are best for this recipe; their Canadian counterparts may be used but the native varieties will yield a better result.

65 Lobster beignets with tomato chutney

	4 portions	10 portions
onion, peeled and chopped	1	2
tomatoes, peeled, seeded and diced as for concassée	1 kg	2½ kg
red wine vinegar	70 g	175 g
cup sugar	50 g	125 g
coriander powder	1 tbsp	2 tbsp
paprika	1 tbsp	2 tbsp
cooked lobster tails	4	10
all-purpose flour	145 g	360 g
fecule (potato starch)	120 g	300 g
active dry yeast	1 tbsp	2½ tbsp
real ale or beer	300 ml	750 ml

For the chutney
1 In a large pot over medium-low heat, warm 1 tablespoon oil.

2 Add onion and cook, stirring occasionally, until tender, 5–10 minutes.
3 Add tomatoes, vinegar, sugar, coriander and paprika; bring to a simmer, stirring occasionally, until thickened, 45–55 minutes.
4 Remove from heat and let cool.
5 Slice lobster meat crosswise into 0.5 cm-thick medallions; keep chilled.
6 In a deep-fry pan, heat oil to 180°C.

For the batter
1 In a bowl, combine the flour, starch, yeast and ½ teaspoon salt; stir to mix. Add beer and stir.
2 Drop a lobster medallion into the batter, coat well and deep-fry until crispy and golden, 2–3 minutes.
3 Fry 3–4 at a time (do not crowd the fryer). Sprinkle beignets lightly with salt and serve hot with chutney.

Note: A quick, hot and spicy bar or terrace dish.

66 Mussels in white wine sauce

	4 portions	10 portions
shallots, chopped	50 g	125 g
parsley, chopped	1 tbsp	2 tbsp
white wine	60 ml	150 ml
strong fish stock	200 ml	500 ml
mussels	2 kg	5 kg
butter	25 g	60 ml
flour	25 g	60 ml
seasoning		

1 Take a thick-bottomed pan and add the shallots, parsley, wine, fish stock and the cleaned mussels.
2 Cover with a tight-fitting lid and cook over a high heat until the shells open.

3 Drain off all the cooking liquor in a colander set over a clean bowl to retain the cooking juices.
4 Carefully check the mussels and discard any that have not opened.
5 Place in a dish and cover to keep warm.
6 Make a roux from the flour and butter; pour over the cooking liquor, ensuring it is free from sand and stirring continuously to avoid lumps.
7 Correct the seasoning and garnish with more chopped parsley.
8 Pour over the mussels and serve.

Note: Classic moules marinière; for an eastern influence why not add a little red chilli and replace the parsley with coriander?

67 Mussels gratin with white wine

Using the recipe above, mix equal quantities of grated Gruyère and fresh breadcrumbs, sprinkle over the dish and gratinate until golden brown under the salamander; alternatively, bake in a moderate to high oven until golden brown on the top.

68 Cockle chowder

	4 portions	10 portions
Cockles		
medium shallots, finely diced	2	5
butter	50 g	125 g
cockles, shells tightly closed	2 kg	5 kg
white wine or vermouth	200 ml	500 ml
Chowder		
vegetable oil	50 ml	125 ml
smoked bacon, cut into 1 cm dice	50 g	125 g
medium onion, cut into 1 cm dice	1	3
medium carrot, cut into 1 cm dice	1	3
garlic cloves, finely chopped	2	5
celery sticks, cut into 1 cm dice	1	3
medium potato, peeled and cut into 1 cm dice	1	3
medium yellow pepper, cut into 1 cm dice	1	3
chicken stock	1 litre	2½ litres
whipping cream	100 ml	500 ml
butter	50 g	125 g
salt and pepper		

For the cockles

1 Take a large saucepan with a tight-fitting lid and place over a medium heat, add the shallots and butter and cook for 1 minute without letting the shallots colour.
2 Add the washed cockles, shake the pan, then add the wine and place the lid on the pan immediately. Leave the cockles to steam for 1–2 minutes so that they open and exude an intense liquor.
3 Remove the lid and make sure all the cockles are open. Remove the pan from the heat and discard any with closed shells.
4 Place a colander over a large bowl, and pour the contents of the pan into the colander, reserving the liquor for the chowder.
5 Allow the cockles to cool. Pick out the meat, check carefully for sand and discard the shells. Store the cockle meat in an airtight container in the fridge until you are ready to serve the chowder.

For the chowder

1 In a large saucepan, heat the oil. When hot, add the bacon and cook for about 5 minutes until crisp and brown.
2 Using a perforated spoon, transfer the bacon onto kitchen paper to drain. Add the onion, carrot, garlic, celery and potato to the saucepan, reduce the heat to medium-low and cook the vegetables for 3–4 minutes without colouring.
3 Add the peppers and cook for 5 minutes. Pour in the reserved liquor from the cockles and the chicken stock.
4 Bring to the boil and simmer for 10 minutes or until the volume of liquid has reduced by about half.
5 Add the cooked bacon and cream, then bring to the boil and reduce for a further 2 minutes until the soup thickens slightly.
6 Just before serving, whisk in the butter.

To finish

1 While the chowder is cooking, carefully remove the meat from the shell, checking for sand, and place in a clean pan.
2 Combine the chowder base and the cockle meat together, reheat carefully and serve.

Note: Cockles are very understated shellfish. Usually pickled and served as a seaside treat in a poly tub, they are as good as mussels or clams and can be used in their respective recipes.

69 Scallops with caramelised cauliflower

	4 portions	10 portions
raisins	100 g	250 g
capers	100 g	250 g
water	180 ml	450 ml
sherry vinegar	1 tbsp	2 tbsp
grated nutmeg		
salt and cayenne pepper		
butter	30 g	75 g
head of cauliflower, sliced into ½ cm-thick pieces	½	1
large hand-dived scallops (roe removed)	12	30

1 In a small saucepan, cook the raisins and capers in the water until the raisins are plump, about 5 minutes.
1 Pour mixture into blender and add the vinegar, nutmeg, salt and pepper, blend just until smooth.
2 Set sauce aside.
3 In a sauté pan, heat butter and cook the cauliflower until golden on both sides. To prevent cauliflower from burning, if necessary, add about 1 tablespoon of water to pan during cooking. Set cauliflower aside.
4 In a separate pan, sauté the scallops in a little butter, about 1½ minutes on each side. To serve, place 3 scallops on each plate, top with cauliflower and finish with the caper-raisin emulsion.

Note: When using scallops, always use hand-dived scallops as first choice as dredged scallops are sometimes unethically sourced. You will pay a bit more for the hand-dived variety but the difference is certainly worth it.

70 Seared scallop salad with honey-lime dressing

	4 portions	10 portions
Honey-lime dressing		
limes, juice of	⅔	⅚
honey, or to taste	25 g	60 g
white wine or rice vinegar	1 tbsp	2 tbsp
seasoning		
Seared scallops		
grapeseed or peanut oil	50 ml	125 ml
chopped mangetout, red pepper and courgette cut into thin strips	500 g	1250 g
mixed greens (such as pea shoots, watercress, baby spinach or escarole)	400 g	1 kg
large scallops (roe removed)	12	30

For the dressing
1 In a non-reactive bowl whisk together the lime juice, honey, vinegar and salt until the honey is completely incorporated. Taste and adjust accordingly. Set aside.

For the seared scallops
1 Heat oil in a large cast-iron or non-stick pan over medium-high heat.
2 Place the vegetable strips into pan and quickly sauté
3 Arrange on the plate and top with the salad leaves.
4 Clean the pan and add a little more butter, sear the scallops very quickly until golden.

Note: The lime is a great foil here, with the acidity cutting effectively through the sweetness of the scallops.

71 Scallop ceviche with organic leaves

This recipe should be made one day prior to serving.

	4 portions	10 portions
large scallops (roe removed)	12	30
limes, juice of	2	5
oranges, juice of	1	3
lemons, grated rind	1	3
limes, grated rind	1	3
orange	1	1
salt and freshly cracked pepper to taste		
orange liqueur	2 tbsp	5 tbsp
vinaigrette	50 ml	125 ml
organic leaves (5 varieties)	500 g	1¼ kg

1 Slice the raw scallops thinly (laterally into 3) and lay on a clean non-reactive tray.
2 Mix all the other ingredients (except the organic leaves) and pour evenly over the scallops.
3 Leave covered in the refrigerator overnight. (The acid in the citrus juice will cook/cure the scallops.)
4 To serve, arrange the scallops in a circle form (9 slices), dress the leaves and arrange in the centre of the scallops.
5 Drizzle any excess cure/dressing around the scallops and serve.

Note: Only the freshest scallops can be used for this recipe as the slightest taint of age will dominate and spoil the dish.

72 Seafood in puff pastry *(bouchées de fruits de mer)*

Cal	Cal	Fat	Sat Fat	Carb	Sugar	Protein	Fibre	Salt	*
1327 KJ	316 kcal	17.6 g	3.1 g	28.9 g	1.1 g	12.2 g	1.2 g	1.2 g	

	4 portions	10 portions
button mushrooms	50 g	125 g
butter	25 g	60 g
lemon, juice of	¼	½
cooked lobster, prawns, shrimps, mussels, scallops	200 g	500 g
white wine sauce (see page 185)	125 ml	300 ml
chopped parsley		
salt, pepper		
bouchée cases (see page 629)	4	10
picked parsley, to garnish		

1 Peel and wash the mushrooms, cut into neat dice.
2 Cook in butter with the lemon juice.
3 Add the cooked shellfish (mussels, prawns, shrimps left whole, the scallops and lobster cut into dice).
4 Cover the pan with a lid and heat through slowly for 3-4 minutes.
5 Add the white wine sauce and chopped parsley, and correct the seasoning.
6 Meanwhile warm the bouchées in the oven or hot plate.
7 Fill the bouchées with the mixture and place the lids on top.
8 Serve garnished with picked parsley.

Note: Vol-au-vents can be prepared and cooked as puff pastry cases (see page 629). The filling is prepared as above and dressed similarly.

HEALTHY EATING TIP
• The white wine sauce is seasoned, so added salt is not required.
• Serve with a salad garnish.

* Fried in peanut oil

73 Lobster thermidor (homard thermidor)

Cal	Cal	Fat	Sat Fat	Carb	Sugar	Protein	Fibre	*
1973 KJ	475 kcal	35.8 g	19.5 g	10.8 g	1.1 g	28.1 g	0.4 g	

	4 portions	10 portions
lobsters, cooked	2	5
butter	25 g	60 g
shallots, finely chopped	12 g	30 g
dry white wine	60 ml	150 ml
English mustard, diluted	½ tsp	1 tsp
parsley, chopped		
mornay sauce		
(see recipe 32)	¼ litre	⅝ litre
Parmesan cheese, grated	25 g	60 g
picked parsley, to garnish		

1 Remove the lobsters' claws and legs.
2 Carefully cut the lobsters in halves lengthwise. Remove the meat.
3 Discard the sac and remove the trail from the tail.
4 Wash the halves of shell and drain on a baking sheet.
5 Cut the lobster meat into thick escalopes.
6 Melt the butter in a sauteuse, add the chopped shallots and cook until tender, without colour.
7 Add the white wine to the shallots and allow to reduce to a quarter of its original volume.
8 Mix in the mustard and chopped parsley.

9 Add the lobster slices, season lightly with salt, mix carefully and allow to heat slowly for 2–3 minutes. If this part of the process is overdone the lobster will become tough and chewy.
10 Meanwhile, spoon a little of the warm mornay sauce into the bottom of each lobster half-shell.
11 Neatly add the warmed lobster pieces and the juice in which they were reheated. If there is an excess of liquid it should be reduced and incorporated into the mornay sauce.
12 Coat the half lobsters with the remaining mornay sauce, sprinkle with the Parmesan and place under a salamander until golden-brown. Serve garnished with picked parsley.

HEALTHY EATING TIP

• Use a small amount of unsaturated oil (olive or sunflower) to cook the lobster.
• Use little or no salt as the cheese will provide the necessary seasoning.

* Using mornay sauce as per recipe 32

74 Chinese stir-fry whelks with beansprouts and mushrooms

Cal	Cal	Fat	Sat Fat	Carb	Sugar	Protein	Fibre	Salt	*
515 KJ	123 kcal	8.5 g	1.0 g	3.1 g	1.0 g	4.8 g	0.7 g	1.2 g	

	4 portions	10 portions
whelks, shelled	200g	500g
vegetable oil	3 tbsp	7 tbsp
cloves of garlic, chopped	3	7
fresh ginger, finely chopped	15g	40g
chilli, finely chopped	¼ tsp	¾ tsp
button mushrooms	100g	250g
pak choi, coarsely chopped	50g	125g
beansprouts	50g	125g
oyster sauce	2 tbsp	5 tbsp
soy sauce	½ tbsp	1 tbsp
dry sherry	2 tbsp	5 tbsp

1 Slice the whelks thinly
2 Heat the oil in a wok. Add the garlic, ginger and chilli, and stir-fry for 30 seconds.
3 Add the whelks and stir-fry for a further minute.

4 Add the mushrooms, stir-fry for 30 seconds, then add the pak choi and the beansprouts, and stir-fry for 30 seconds.
5 Add the oyster sauce, soy sauce and sherry, and cook for 1 more minute.
6 Serve immediately with steamed rice or fresh noodles.

Note: Other types of seafood can be used in place of whelks, or a combination – for example, whelks and winkles, prawns, shrimps.
*Using Chinese cabbage in place of pak choi

References

Campbell, J., Foskett, D. and Ceserani, V. (2006) *Advanced Practical Cookery: A Textbook For Education and Industry* (4th edn). London: Hodder.

Liver

Fillet

Entrecôte
steak

Kidney

xtail

Sirloin

Rump

chapter 8

MEAT

Prepare meat and offal

Practical skills
The candidate will be able to:
1 Demonstrate the correct use of tools and equipment to prepare meat and offal
2 Demonstrate preparation skills for meat and offal according to dish specification
3 Demonstrate portion control with cuts of meat and offal
4 Apply flavourings to joints/cuts of meat and offal
5 Line appropriate moulds/basins or shape pastes according to dish specifications
6 Apply coatings to cuts of meat and types of offal
7 Demonstrate safe and hygienic practices
8 Undertake correct storage procedures for meat and offal

Underpinning knowledge
The candidate will be able to:
1 Identify types of meat and offal
2 Explain the quality points of meat and offal
3 State the most commonly used joints and cuts of meat and offal
4 Describe methods used for preservation of meat and offal
5 Describe the advantages/disadvantages of preservation methods

6 Explain portion sizes/weights of meat and offal
7 State the correct temperature for storing meat and offal

Cook meat and offal

Practical skills
The candidate will be able to:
1 Select correct tools and equipment used in the cooking and/or use of fresh/preserved meat and offal
2 Apply appropriate cooking methods and principles to meat and offal
3 Make sauces, coulis, gravies and jus for meat and offal dishes
4 Prepare dressings for meat and offal dishes
5 Make appropriate flavoured butters/oils for meat and offal dishes
6 Prepare garnishes for meat and offal dishes

7 Apply finishing skills to meat and offal dishes
8 Assemble dishes according to dish specifications
9 Demonstrate safe and hygienic practices
10 Evaluate the finished dish/dishes

Underpinning knowledge
The candidate will be able to:
1 Identify tools and equipment used in the cooking of meat and offal
2 Explain suitable cooking methods for joints or cuts of meat and offal
3 Explain reasons for applying cooking principles to meat and offal
4 Explain how to determine when meat and offal are cooked
5 Describe the skills needed to check and finish the dish to specification

Meats

The structure of meat

To cook meat properly it is important to understand its structure.

- Meat comprises fibres bound by connective tissue.
- Connective tissue (elastin) is yellow and collagen white.
- Yellow tissue needs to be removed.
- Small fibres are present in tender cuts and young animals.
- Coarser fibres are present in tougher cuts and older animals.
- Fat assists in providing flavour, and moistens meat in roasting and grilling.
- Tenderness, flavour and moistness are increased if meat is hung after slaughter and before being used.
- Storage times: beef up to 3 weeks; veal 1–3 weeks; lamb 10–15 days; pork 7–14 days.
- Hang and store meat between 3 and 4°C.

Full information on meat, including cattle, sheep and pigs, can be obtained at www.qmscotland.co.uk.

Offal and other edible parts of the carcass

Offal is the name given to the edible parts taken from the inside of a carcass of meat: liver, kidneys, heart and sweetbreads. Tripe, brains, tongue, head and oxtail are also sometimes included under this term.

Fresh offal (unfrozen) should be purchased as required and can be refrigerated under hygienic conditions at a temperature of 21°C, at a relative humidity of 90 per cent for up to seven days. Frozen offal must be kept in a deep freeze and defrosted in a refrigerator as required.

Liver

- **Calf's liver** is considered the best in terms of tenderness and flavour. It is also the most expensive.
- **Lamb's liver** is mild in flavour, light in colour and tender. Sheep's liver, being from an older animal, is firmer in substance, deeper in colour and has a stronger flavour.
- **Ox** or **beef liver** is the cheapest and, if taken

from an older animal, can be coarse in texture and strong in flavour. It is usually braised.

- **Pig's liver** has a strong, full flavour and is used mainly for pâté recipes.

Quality points
- Liver should look fresh, moist and smooth, with a pleasant colour and no unpleasant smell.
- Liver should not be dry or contain an excessive number of tubes.

Food value
Liver is a good source of protein and iron, and also contains vitamins A and D. It is low in fat.

Meat varies considerably in its fat content. This is found round the outside of meat, in marbling and inside the meat fibres. The visible fat (saturated) should be trimmed off as much as possible before cooking.

Kidneys

- **Lamb's kidneys** are light in colour, delicate in flavour and ideal for grilling and frying.
- **Sheep's kidneys** are darker in colour and stronger in flavour.
- **Calf's kidneys** are light in colour, delicate in flavour and used in a variety of dishes.
- **Ox kidney** is dark in colour, strong in flavour, and is either braised or used in pies and puddings (mixed with beef).
- **Pig's kidneys** are smooth, long and flat and have a strong flavour.

Quality points
- Suet – the saturated fat in which kidneys are encased – should be left on otherwise the kidneys will dry out. The suet should be removed when kidneys are being prepared for cooking.
- Both suet and kidneys should be moist and have no unpleasant smell.

Food value
This is similar to that of liver.

Hearts

- **Lamb's hearts** are small and light; they are normally served whole.

- **Sheep's hearts** are dark and solid; they can be dry and tough unless cooked carefully.
- **Ox** or **beef hearts** are dark coloured and solid, and tend to be dry and tough.
- **Calf's hearts**, coming from a younger animal, are lighter in colour and more tender.

Most hearts need slow braising to tenderise them.

Quality points
Hearts should not be too fatty and should not contain too many tubes. When cut they should be moist, not sticky, and with no unpleasant smell.

Food value
Hearts are a good source of protein, which is needed for growth and repair of the body.

Sweetbreads

These are the pancreas and thymus glands, known as heart breads and neck. The heart bread is round, plump and of better quality than the neck bread, which is long and uneven in shape. Calf's heart bread, considered the best, weighs up to 600 g, lamb's heart bread up to 100 g.

Quality points
- Heart and neck breads should be fleshy and of good size.
- They should be creamy white in colour and have no unpleasant smell.

Food value
Sweetbreads are an easily digested source of protein, which makes them valuable for use in invalid diets.

Tripe

Tripe is the stomach lining or white muscle of the ox, consisting of the rumen or paunch and the honeycomb tripe (considered the best); sheep tripe, darker in colour, is obtainable in some areas.

Quality points
Tripe should be fresh, with no signs of stickiness or unpleasant smell.

Food value
Tripe contains protein, is low in fat and high in calcium.

Brains

Calves' brains are those normally used. They must be fresh and have no unpleasant smell. They are a good source of protein with trace elements.

Tongues

Ox tongues, lamb and sheep tongues are those most used in cooking. Ox tongues are usually salted then soaked before being cooked. Lamb tongues are cooked fresh.

Quality points
- Tongues must be fresh and have no unpleasant smell.
- There should not be an excess of waste at the root end.

Head

Sheep's heads can be used for stock, pigs' head for brawn (a cold meat preparation) and calves' heads for speciality dishes (e.g. calf's head vinaigrette). Heads should be fresh, not sticky, well fleshed and free from any unpleasant smell.

Oxtail

Oxtails usually weigh 1½–2 kg; they should be lean with not too much fat. There should be no sign of stickiness and no unpleasant smell.

Suet

Beef suet should be creamy-white, brittle and dry. Other meat fat should be fresh, not sticky, and with no unpleasant smell.

Marrow

Marrow is obtained from the bones of the leg of beef. It should be of good size, firm, creamy-white and odourless. Sliced, poached marrow may be used as a garnish for some meat dishes and savouries.

Bones

Bones must be fresh, not sticky, with no unpleasant smell and preferably meaty as they are used for stock, the foundation for so many preparations.

Preservation of meat

Salting

Meat can be pickled in brine; this method of preservation may be applied to silverside, brisket and ox tongues. Salting is used in the production of bacon, before the sides of pork are smoked, and for hams.

Chilling

This means that meat is kept at a temperature just above freezing point in a controlled atmosphere. Chilled meat cannot be kept in the usual type of cold room for more than a few days, sufficient time for the meat to hang, enabling it to become tender.

Freezing

Small carcasses, such as lamb and mutton, can be frozen; their quality is not affected by freezing. They can be kept frozen until required and then thawed out before being used. Some beef is frozen, but it is inferior in quality to chilled beef.

Canning

Large quantities of meat are canned; corned beef is worth mentioning here since it has a very high protein content. Pork is used for tinned luncheon meat.

Meat substitutes

Textured vegetable protein (TVP)

This is a meat substitute manufactured from protein derived from wheat, oats, cottonseed, soybean and other sources. The main source of TVP is the soybean; this is due to its high protein content.

TVP is used chiefly as a meat extender, varying from 10 to 60 per cent replacement of fresh meat. Some caterers on very tight budgets make use of it, but its main use is in food manufacturing.

By partially replacing the meat in certain dishes – such as casseroles, stews, pies, pasties, sausage rolls, hamburgers, meat loaf and pâté – it is possible to reduce costs, meet nutritional targets and serve food that is acceptable in appearance.

Soya protein can also be useful in making vegetarian dishes.

Myco-protein

A meat substitute such as Quorn (see below) is produced from a plant that is a distant relative of the mushroom. This myco-protein contains protein and fibre, and is the result of a fermentation process similar to the way yoghurt is made. It may be used as an alternative to chicken or beef or in vegetarian dishes.

Quorn

Quorn is a low-fat food that can be used in a variety of dishes (e.g. oriental stir-fry). Quorn does not shrink during preparation and cooking. Quorn mince or pieces can be substituted for chicken or minced meats. Its mild savoury flavour means that it complements the herbs and spices in a recipe and it is able to absorb flavour. Frozen Quorn may be cooked straight from the freezer or may be defrosted overnight in the refrigerator. Once thawed, it must be stored in the refrigerator and used within 24 hours. Recipes using Quorn can be found in Chapter 11 (Vegetarian dishes). Quorn is a low-fat, high-protein food.

Health, safety and hygiene

For information on maintaining a safe and secure working environment, a professional and hygienic appearance, and clean food production areas, equipment and utensils, as well as food hygiene, please refer to Chapters 17 and 18. Additional health and safety points to reduce the risk of cross-contamination are as follows.

- When preparing uncooked meat or poultry, and then cooked food, or changing from one type of meat or poultry to another, equipment, working areas and utensils must be thoroughly cleaned, or changed.

- If colour-coded boards are used, it is essential to always use the correct colour-coded boards for the preparation of foods, and different ones for cooked foods.
- Store uncooked meat and poultry on trays to prevent dripping, in separate refrigerators at a temperature of 3–5°C – preferably at the lower temperature. If separate refrigerators are not available then store in separate areas within the one refrigerator.
- Wash all work surfaces with a bactericidal detergent to kill bacteria. This is particularly important when handling poultry and pork.
- When using boning knives a safety apron acts as a protection; if a great deal of boning is being done then protective gloves are also available.

To maintain the quality and safety of meat and poultry dishes it is advisable to check internal temperatures by means of a probe. The recommended temperatures are shown in Table 8.1.

Table 8.1   Recommended internal temperatures*

Beef	rare: 52°C; medium 57°C; well done 66°C
Lamb	pink: 57°C; well done 66°C
Pork	73°C
Veal	66°C
Turkey/chicken	77°C
Duck	pink 57°C; well done 62°C

* Environmental Health Officers may require higher temperatures for best practice

Origins

From the earliest times, man has been a carnivorous animal. Because meat provides so much protein and essential vitamins, early people could spend less of their time eating and could successfully turn their energies to activities that, in time, placed them above their peers. Meat was from the first equated with life and early hunting was designed to supply a plentiful amount of animals. Although today there has been a reappraisal of the importance of meat in the diet – whether its drawbacks, like cholesterol and high price, outweigh its value as a protein provider or, in the case of vegetarians, ethical considerations –

meat is still the most expensive item on the budget and a great deal of thought should be put into choosing and using it wisely.

Butcher's meat today is largely a product of selective breeding and feeding techniques, whereby animals are reared carefully to reach high standards and meet specific needs: the present-day demand is for lean and tender meat – modern cattle, sheep and pigs are well fleshed yet compact creatures compared to their forebears of a century ago.

Choosing and buying

Meat from specific parts of an animal may be cut and cooked according to local custom and, more strictly, by religious observance – especially in Jewish kosher and Mohammedan halal butchery, which stipulates the killing of the animal by an authorised person of the religion, total voiding of the blood by draining, soaking and salting, and the consumption of the meat within 72 hours. Kosher dietary laws further demand that only the forequarters of permitted animals – goats, sheep, deer and cattle – may be used.

Meat is a natural and therefore not a uniform product, varying in quality from carcass to carcass, while flavour, texture and appearance are determined by the type of animal and the way it has been fed. There is no reason to think that flavour is obtained only in meat that possessed a proportion of fat, although fat does give a characteristic flavour to meat and helps to keep it moist during roasting. Neither is the colour of meat any guide to quality. Consumers are inclined to choose light-coloured meat – bright red beef, for example – because they think that it will be fresher than an alternative dark-red piece. Freshly butchered beef is bright red because the pigment in the tissues, myoglobin, has been chemically affected by the oxygen in the air. After several hours, the colour changes to dark red or brown as the pigment is further oxidised to become metamyoglobin. The colour of fat can vary from almost pure white in lamb, to bright yellow in beef. Colour depends on the feed, on the breed and, to a certain extent, on the time of year.

The most useful guide to tenderness and quality is a knowledge of the cuts of meat and their location on the carcass. The various cuts are described under their respective headings (see below), but in principle the leanest and tenderest cuts – the 'prime' cuts – come from the hindquarters. The 'coarse' cuts, or meat from the neck, legs and forequarters, those parts of the animal that have had plenty of muscular exercise and where fibres have become hardened, provide meat for braising and stewing. Many consider these cuts to have more flavour, although they require slow cooking to make them tender. The meat from young animals is generally more tender and since tenderness is a prime factor, animals may be injected before slaughter with an enzyme, such as papin, which softens the fibres and muscles. This merely speeds up a natural and more satisfactory process: meat contains its own proteolytic enzymes, which gradually break down the protein cell walls as the carcass ages; that is why meat is hung for from 10 to 20 days in controlled conditions of temperature and humidity before being offered for sale. Meat that is aged longer becomes more expensive as the cost of refrigeration is high and the meat itself shrinks because of evaporation and the trimming of the outside hardened edges.

Cooking

Meat is an extremely versatile product that can be cooked in a multitude of ways, and matched with practically any vegetable, fruit and herb. The cut (shin, steak, brisket), the method of heating (roasting, braising, grilling), and the time and temperature all affect the way the meat will taste. Raw meat is difficult to chew because the muscle fibre contains an elastic protein (collagen), which is softened only by mincing – as in steak tartare – or by cooking. When you cook meat, the protein gradually coagulates as the internal temperature increases. At 77°C coagulation is complete, the protein begins to harden and further cooking makes the meat tougher.

Since tenderness combined with flavour is the aim in meat cookery, much depends on the ratio of time and temperature. In principle, slow cooking retains the juices and produces a more tender result than does fast cooking at high temperatures. There are, of course, occasions when high temperatures are essential: for instance, you need to grill a steak under a hot flame for a very limited time in order to obtain a crisp, brown surface and a pink, juicy interior – using a low temperature would not give you the desired result. But in potentially tough cuts such as breast or where there is a quantity of connective tissue (neck of lamb), a slow rate of cooking converts the tissues to gelatine and helps to make the meat more tender. Meat containing bone will take longer to cook because bone is a poor conductor of heat. Tough or coarse cuts of meat should be cooked by braising, pot roasting or stewing. Marinating in a suitable marinade, such as wine and wine vinegar, helps to tenderise the meat and imparts an additional flavour. Searing meat in hot fat or in a hot oven before roasting or stewing helps to produce a crisp exterior by coagulating the protein but does not, as is widely supposed, seal in the juices. However, if the external temperature is too high and cooking prolonged, rapid evaporation and contraction of the meat will cause considerable loss of juices and fat. Salt sprinkled on meat before cooking will also hasten loss of moisture since salt is hygroscopic and absorbs water.

Meat bones are useful for giving flavour to soups and stocks, especially beef ones with plenty of marrow. Veal bones are gelatinous and help to enrich and thicken soups and sauces. Fat can be rendered down for frying, or used as an ingredient when suet or lard is called for.

To take this one step further, when fibrous proteins are heated they contract and squeeze out the associated water. For example, when a steak is cooked the proteins contract, therefore squeezing out all the water/juices. If the heat is increased or continues, the steak will then become dry and, consequently, the eating quality will be impaired. Cuts of meat also contain elastin and collagen: elastin (the muscle group associated with tendons and arteries) is extremely stretchy and further cooking adds to its strength; collagen (the main muscle proteins, which amount to the highest proportion of mass in the muscle) is rather tough

and chewy. Meat that has a higher proportion of both, usually from the major and highly worked muscle groups, would not be suitable for prime cooking. However these cuts of meat may be cooked for longer at the correct temperature (braising), dissolving the collagen as it is water soluble, forming gelatine and offering a tasty joint of meat.

Prime cuts, such as beef fillets, have little collagen in their make-up (approximately 3 per cent) and do not require long cooking to tenderise the joint. Although most chefs would adopt a high temperature for a short period on the prime cuts, this does not always yield a perfect result. Due to the lack of fat and collagen in such cuts of meat, high heat will render the muscle fibres dry and, consequently, the eating quality is impaired. A lower temperature and longer in the oven will produce a gradual heat, therefore there is less extreme coagulation in the tissues and less fluid will have been squeezed out in the process.

To put this theory into simple terms – traditionally, when cooking meat, a fillet steak (for example) would be sealed in hot oil (180°C–200°C or even hotter) and then the heat would be reduced slightly to finish the cooking. The process that takes place is one of (to put it scientifically) 'thermal energy' or molecular conduction: the first layer of molecules heating the next, and so on, until the desired degree of cooking is achieved at the core (rare, medium, etc.). To achieve a core temperature of 55°C–60°C, 25 per cent of the meat would be overcooked. Therefore if the temperature was to be reduced to a constant 59°C (just before the protein collapses) and the meat cooked for longer, adopting the molecular conduction theory, more than 95 per cent of the meat would be perfectly cooked.

When cooking meats at low temperatures there is one obvious flaw: the meat will not be exposed to the high cooking temperatures that develop that beautiful roasted flavour. This chemical reaction of browning is called the Maillard reaction and is an extremely complicated chain of reactions that involves carbons, proteins, sulphurs, etc. One thing we do know about this reaction is that at 140°C and above, you will start to release the wonderful roasted meat flavours. Therefore, when slow-cooking meats they will need to be started very quickly on a hot pan on the stove to initiate this Maillard reaction in the meat and give the meat a roasted flavour. In some cases you will need to quickly return the meat to the pan to re-caramelise the outside; alternatively, if the joint is dense and large, remove from the low oven and increase the temperature to 190–200°C. When the oven is up to temperature, return the joint to it for a short while to crisp up the outside. The density of the meat and size of the joint will ensure that there will be very little secondary cooking or residual heat left to cook through to the core.

The collagen that makes up connective tissue requires long cooking at moderate temperature to render it supple in the mouth and to be converted into gelatine (a form of secondary/internal basting). When basting, care should be taken not to destroy the secondary basting properties of the collagen as at temperatures above 88°C the collagen will dissolve rapidly into the braising medium, impairing the eating quality. As cooking methods and understanding of meats develop, we now know more about the effect that heat has on the make-up of meat. Therefore, the traditional braising method of bringing the casserole to a simmer and placing it in the oven at 140°C could, in theory, render the structure of the meat dry due to the fact that at 88°C collagen rapidly dissolves into the cooking medium, yielding a beautifully gelatinous and well-flavoured sauce, and making the eating quality of the meat dry and tough.

To modernise the braising approach the cooking medium would need to be at between 80°C and 85°C; this is best controlled on the top of the stove. Alternatively, set your oven at 90°C (approximately) checking the cooking medium once in a while.

All the techniques above, which are used to slow-cook prime, secondary and highly worked muscle groups, are very controlled and accurate, and rely on constant attention to ensure that they are not rapidly cooking, and that they are in fact actually cooking, if cooking at low temperatures. The general rule of thumb is: the more collagen,

the higher the temperature needed to enable the collagen to dissolve, forming gelatine that will then in turn baste the meat and offer a perfectly braised and moist piece of meat.

When slow-cooking prime joints, the rule of thumb is to reduce the temperature of cooking as, in some cases, shrinkage can occur from 59°C ranging up to 65°C for sirloin of beef.

Sirloin of beef obviously has more collagen than fillet (it is essentially a worked muscle group) and is generally cooked on a high heat, either roasted or pan-fried. To adopt the above method, you can render the sirloin extremely tender, full of moisture, with a roasted outer and the flavoursome roasted meat taste that is craved. An average sirloin joint for roasting can weigh from 2–5 kg whole off the bone. The method is to seal the meat on the outside, as you would normally, place into a pre-heated oven at 180°C, cook at 180°C for 10 minutes, then reduce the temperature to 64°C (the oven door will need to be open at this stage). Once the oven has come down to 64°C, close the door and cook for a further 1 hour 50 minutes. This will give you an extremely tender piece of sirloin.

The effect of heat on meat cookery

The roasting and low-temperature cooking of meat is covered in detail in Chapter 2 (pages 23–8).

The Maillard reaction

When cooking meats, flavour is developed. This happens when the meat proteins are heated with sugars to temperatures above 140°C, and a series of chemical reactions occur, known as the Maillard reaction. During this process, sugars and amino acids react together. The sugars come from carbohydrates and the amino acids from the protein. In the first stage of the reaction the proteins and carbohydrates are degraded into smaller sugars and amino acids. Next, the sugar rings open and the resulting aldehydes and acids react with the amino acids to produce a wide range of chemicals. These new modules then react among themselves to produce the main flavour compounds.

Controlling the Maillard reaction is difficult. A chef must know how much heat to apply to a piece of meat to produce the right flavour. The Maillard reaction takes place quickly and only at temperatures above 140°C. These high temperatures will occur only at the surface of the meat. Inside there is water, which cannot be heated above 100°C without turning to steam. Flavour will be developed more quickly if you increase the surface area of the meat.

The combination of attempting not to heat above 40°C those muscles that contain little connective tissue, while heating those parts where there is lots of connective tissue to temperatures above 70°C, and at the same time ensuring that some parts are heated to above 130°C, makes the cooking of meats a complex process.

Always ensure that the outside of the meat is cooked at a high temperature (until it is a dark brown colour), in order to seal in and develop the flavour. Cook meats with little connective tissue for only a short time. Seal the outside so that it is browned and so that the inside does not become tough (e.g. by grilling, frying or roasting).

Meats with lots of connective tissue should be cooked for longer so that all the connective tissue denatures and the bundles of coagulated muscle proteins fall apart, rendering the meat tender (e.g. by stewing or braising) (Barham, 2000).

Lamb and mutton

Lamb is the meat from a sheep under a year old; above that age the animal is called a 'hogget' and its meat becomes mutton. The demand for lamb in preference to mutton is partly due to the fact that the lamb carcass provides smaller cuts of more tender meat. Mutton needs to be well ripened by long hanging before cooking and, as it is usually fatty, needs a good deal of trimming as well.

Good-quality lamb should have fine, white fat, with pink flesh where freshly cut; in mutton the flesh is a deeper colour. Lamb has a very thin, parchment-like covering on the carcass, known as the 'fell', which is usually left on roasts to help them maintain their shape during cooking. It should, however, be removed from chops. The flesh of a younger lamb is usually more tender. A good way to judge age is through weight – especially with legs of lamb: the highest quality weighs about 2.3 kg and never more than 4 kg. Smaller chops are also more tender and, therefore, more expensive. Mutton is rarely sold; when it is, it is much less expensive than lamb.

As a guide, when ordering allow approximately 100 g meat off the bone per portion, and 150 g on the bone per portion. It must be clearly understood, however, that the weights given can only be approximate. They must vary according to the quality of the meat and also according to the purpose for which the meat is being butchered. For example, a chef will often cut differently from a shop butcher (a chef frequently needs to consider the presentation of the particular joint, while the butcher is more often concerned with economical cutting). In the text that follows, simple orders of dissection are given for each carcass. In general, bones need to be removed only when preparing joints, so as to facilitate carving. The bones are used for stock and the excess fat can be rendered down for second-class dripping.

Joints, uses and weights

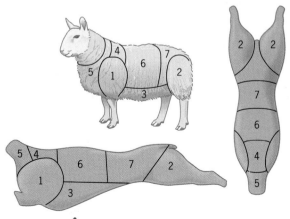

Figure 8.1   Joints of lamb

Table 8.2 ✒ Joints, uses and weights (numbers in left-hand column refer to Figure 8.1)

Joint	Uses	Approximate weight Lamb (kg)	Approximate weight Mutton (kg)
whole carcass		16	25
(1) shoulder (two)	roasting, stewing	3	4½
(2) leg (two)	roasting (mutton boiled)	3½	5½
(3) breast (two)	roasting, stewing	1½	2½
(4) middle neck	stewing	2	3
(5) scrag end	stewing, broth	½	1
(6) best end rack (two)	roasting, grilling, frying	2	3
(7) saddle	roasting, grilling, frying	3½	5½
kidneys	grilling, sauté		
heart	braising		
liver	frying		
sweetbreads	braising, frying		
tongue	braising, boiling		

Quality of lamb (sheep under 1 year old) and mutton

- A good-quality animal should be compact and evenly fleshed.
- The lean flesh should be firm, of a pleasing dull-red colour and of a fine texture or grain.
- There should be an even distribution of surface fat, which should be hard, brittle and flaky in structure and a clear white colour.
- In a young animal the bones should be pink and porous, so that when cut a degree of blood is shown in their structure. As age progresses the bones become hard, dense and white, and inclined to splinter when chopped.

Order of dissection of a carcass

1 Remove the shoulders.
2 Remove the breasts.
3 Remove the middle neck and scrag.
4 Remove the legs.
5 Divide the saddle from the best end.

Table 8.3 ✒ Common cooking methods

Saddle	roast, pot roast (poêlé)
Loin	roast
Fillet	grill, fry
Loin chop	grill, fry, stew, braise
Chump chop	grill, fry, stew, braise
Kidney	grill, sauté

Preparation of joints and cuts

Shoulder

- **Roasting:** clean and trim the knucklebone so as to leave approximately 3 cm of clean bone.
- **Boning:** remove the blade bone and upper arm bone (see Figure 8.2), tie with string; the

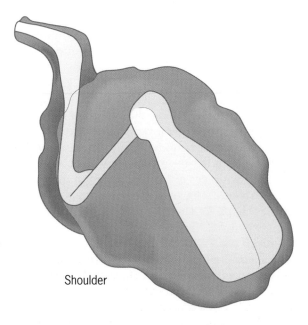

Shoulder

Figure 8.2 ✒ Shoulder of lamb, showing three bones

shoulder may be stuffed (see recipe 4) before tying.

- **Cutting for stews:** bone out, cut into even 25–50 g pieces.
- **Roasting:** remove the pelvic or aitchbone; trim the knuckle cleaning 3 cm of bone; trim off excess fat and tie with string if necessary.

Breasts

- Remove excess fat and skin.
- **Roasting:** bone, stuff and roll, tie with string.
- **Stewing:** cut into even 25–50 g pieces.

Middle neck

- **Stewing:** remove excess fat, excess bone and gristle; cut into even 50 g pieces; this joint, when correctly butchered, can give good uncovered second-class cutlets.

Scrag-end

- **Stewing:** this can be chopped down the centre, the excess bone, fat and gristle removed, and cut into even 50 g pieces, or boned out and cut into pieces.

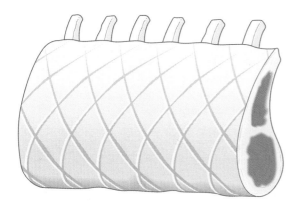

Figure 8.3 Best end (rack) of lamb

Saddle

The saddle may be divided as follows: remove the skin, starting from head to tail and from breast to back; split down the centre of the backbone to produce two loins; each loin can be roasted whole, boned and stuffed, or cut into loin and chump chops.

- A full saddle is illustrated in Figure 8.5.
- For large banquets it is sometimes found better to remove the chumps and use short saddles.
- Saddles may also be boned and stuffed.

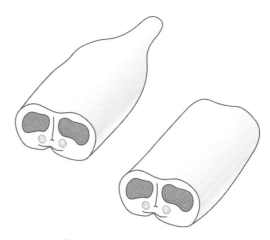

Figure 8.4 Saddle of lamb

Saddle for roasting

- Skin and remove the kidney.
- Trim the excess fat and sinew.
- Cut off the flaps leaving about 15 cm each side so as to meet in the middle under the saddle.
- Remove the aitch, or pelvic, bone.
- Score neatly and tie with string.
- For presentation the tail may be left on, protected with foil and tied back.
- The saddle can also be completely boned, stuffed and tied.

Loin for roasting

- Skin, remove excess fat and sinew, remove the pelvic bone, tie with string.

Loin, boned and stuffed

- Remove the skin, excess fat and sinew. Bone out, replace the fillet and tie with string. When stuffed, bone out, season, stuff and tie.

Chops

Loin chops

- Skin the loin, remove the excess fat and sinew, then cut into chops approximately 100–150 g in weight.

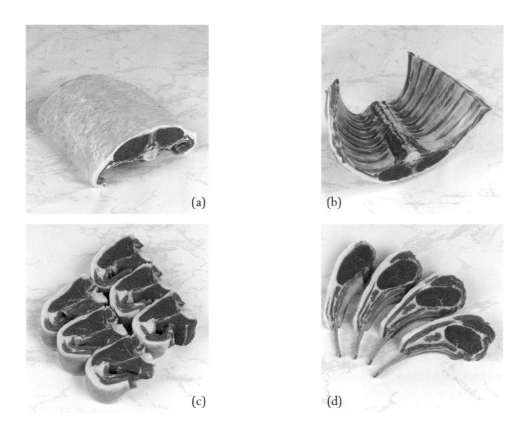

Figure 8.5 ✐ (a) Saddle of lamb; (b) pair of best ends of lamb; chump; (c) lamb loin chops; (d) lamb cutlets

- A first-class loin chop should have a piece of kidney skewered in the centre.

Double loin chop (also known as a Barnsley chop)

- These are cut approximately 2 cm across a saddle on the bone.
- When trimmed they are secured with a skewer and may include a piece of kidney in the centre of each chop.

Chump chops

- These are cut from the chump end of the loin.
- Cut into approximately 150 g chops, trim where necessary.

Noisette

- This is a cut from a boned-out loin.
- Cut slantwise into approximately 2 cm thick slices, bat out slightly, trim into a cutlet shape.

Rosette

- This is a cut from a boned-out loin approximately 2 cm thick. It is shaped round and tied with string.

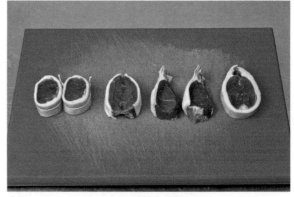

Figure 8.6 ✐ Left to right: rosette, valentine, noisette, Barnsley (double loin) chop

Best end (rack)

Best end preparation
- Remove the skin from head to tail and from breast to back.
- Remove the sinew and the tip of the blade bone.
- Complete the preparation of the rib bones as indicated in Figure 8.3.
- Clean the sinew from between the rib bones and trim the bones.
- Score the fat neatly to approximately 2 mm deep.
- Trim the overall length of the rib bones to two and a half times the length of the nut of meat.
- **Roasting:** prepare as above.
- **Cutlets:** prepare as for roasting, excluding the scoring, and divide evenly between the bones, or the cutlets can be cut from the best end and prepared separately. A double cutlet consists of two bones; therefore a six-bone best end yields six single or three double cutlets.

Preparation of offal

Kidney

- **Grilling:** skin and split three-quarters of the way through lengthwise; cut out and discard the gristle, and skewer.
- **Sauté:** skin and remove the gristle. Cut slantways into 6–8 pieces.

Hearts

- **Braising:** remove the tubes and excess fat.

Liver

- Remove skin, gristle and tubes and cut into thin slices on the slant.

Sweetbreads

- Wash well, blanch and trim.
- Soak in salted water for 2–3 hours to remove any traces of blood.

Tongue

- Remove the bone and gristle from the throat end.
- Soak in cold water for 2–4 hours. If salted, soak for 3–4 hours.

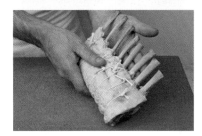

Figure 8.7 Preparation of best end: (a) remove bark/skin leaving as much fat as possible on the joint; (b) mark/score 2 cm from end of bone; (c) score down the middle of the back of the bone, scoring the cartilage; (d) pull skin fat and meat from the bone (to bring out the bone ends – an alternative to scraping them); (e) remove the elastin; (f) tie

Lamb recipes

Roast

1 Roasting of lamb and mutton

Cal 1262 KJ	Cal 301 kcal	Fat 20.2 g	Sat Fat 10.5 g	Carb 0.0 g	Sugar 0.0 g	Protein 29.5 g	Fibre 0.0 g	*

1 Season the joints lightly with salt and place on a trivet, or bones, in a roasting tray.
2 Place a little vegetable oil or dripping on top and cook in a hot oven at 175–185°C.
3 Baste frequently and reduce the heat gradually when necessary, as for example in the case of large joints.
4 Roast for approximately 20 minutes per ½ kilo, plus another 20 minutes.
5 To test if cooked, place on a tray and press firmly in order to see if the juices released contain any blood.
6 In general, all joints should be cooked through. If joints are required pink, reduce the cooking time by a quarter. For internal temperatures, see Table 8.1.
7 Allow to stand for approximately 10–15 minutes before carving; if this is not done the meat will tend to shrink and curl.

Note: Where applicable name the origin and breed of the lamb (e.g. Southdown, Shropshire). For further information visit www.qmscotland.co.uk.

Allow approximately 150 g meat on the bone per portion (legs, shoulders, saddle or loin rump, best end and breast).

HEALTHY EATING TIP
- Use an unsaturated vegetable oil (e.g. sunflower).
- Make sure the fat is hot so that less will be absorbed during the roasting.
- The lamb will produce additional fat as it roasts.

Variations
Variations include:
- several peeled cloves of garlic inserted into the flesh of joints before roasting
- a little rosemary sprinkled into boned joints before tying
- sprigs of rosemary placed on roasting joints halfway through cooking
- in small-scale cookery, vegetables (e.g. potatoes, parsnips, onions, carrots), left whole or cut into large pieces, can be roasted in with the meat
- slow cook – roast at 200°C for 20 minutes then reduce temperature to 130°C, basting frequently; if required the leg can be flavoured with slices of peeled garlic cloves inserted into slashes cut into the flesh before cooking.

* Using leg of lamb, 1 portion (113 g lamb)

2 Roast gravy

1 Place the roasting tray on the stove over a gentle heat to allow the sediment to settle.
2 Carefully strain off the fat, leaving the sediment in the tray.
3 Return to the stove and brown carefully, deglaze with brown stock.
4 Allow to simmer for a few minutes.
5 Correct the seasoning and colour, then strain and skim.

Note: This can be made at the end of roasting (see also recipe 29 in Chapter 3). In some establishments the gravy served with stuffed joints, lamb, pork and veal is slightly thickened with diluted cornflour, fecule or arrowroot.

Carving

Roast leg

Holding the bone, carve with a sharp knife at an angle of 45 degrees and take off each slice as it is cut. Continue in this manner along the joint, turning it from side to side as the slices get wider.

Shoulder

To obtain reasonable-sized slices of meat, carve the flesh side, not the skin side, of the joint. Having obtained the slices, carve round the bones. Due to the awkward shape of the bone structure, the shoulder may be boned out, rolled and tied before cooking to facilitate carving.

Roast saddle

- **Carving on the bone:** there are two usual ways of carving the saddle, one is by carving lengthways either side of the backbone, the other by making a deep cut lengthwise either side of the backbone and then slicing across each loin. It is usual to carve the saddle in thick slices.
- **Carving off the bone:** for economical kitchen carving it is often found best to bone the loins out whole, carve into slices, then re-form on the saddle bone.
- The fillets may be left on the saddle or removed; in either case they are carved and served with the rest of the meat.

Roast loin

- **On the bone:** proceed as for the saddle.
- **Boned-out:** cut in slices across the joint; when stuffed, the slices are cut slightly thicker.

Roast best end or racks of lamb

Divide into cutlets by cutting between bones.

Service

All roast joints are served garnished with watercress and a sauceboat of roast gravy separately. When carved, serve a little gravy over the slices as well as a sauceboat of gravy. Mint sauce should be served with roast lamb and redcurrant jelly should be available. For roast mutton, redcurrant jelly and/or onion sauce should be served, with mint sauce available.

3 Roast leg of lamb with mint, lemon and cumin

Cal 2192 KJ	Cal 524 kcal	Fat 39.1 g	Sat Fat 13.7 g	Carb 0.3 g	Sugar 0.3 g	Protein 39.7 g	Fibre 0.0 g	Salt 0.3 g	*

	4 portions	10 portions
mint	25 g	62.5 g
lemons, juice of	2	5
cumin	2 tsp	5 tsp
olive oil	4 tbsp	10 tbsp
leg of lamb	3.5 kg	2 x 3.5 kg

1 Place the mint, lemon juice, cumin and olive oil in a food processor.
2 Rub the mixture into the lamb in a suitable roasting tray.
3 Roast the lamb in the normal way.
4 Serve on a bed of boulangère or dauphinoise potatoes and a suitable green vegetable, e.g leaf spinach with toasted pine nuts, or with a couscous salad (see page 118).

*Using a 225 g portion of lamb

4 Stuffing for lamb

Cal	Cal	Fat	Sat Fat	Carb	Sugar	Protein	Fibre	*
824 KJ	198 kcal	14.1 g	7.7 g	15.6 g	1.9 g	3.1 g	0.0 g	

	For 1 joint
suet, chopped	50 g
onions, chopped and cooked in a	
little butter or margarine without colour	50 g
egg yolk or small egg	1
white breadcrumbs	100 g
pinch powdered thyme	
pinch chopped parsley	
salt, pepper	
grated zest of lemon	

1 Combine all the ingredients together.

Note: This can be used for stuffing joints (e.g. loin, shoulder, breast). Variations can be found in recipe 73. For mint sauce see Chapter 4, recipe 10.

HEALTHY EATING TIP

• Use the minimum amount of salt – the herbs, pepper and lemon provide plenty of flavour.

* Using egg yolk

5 Best end or rack of lamb with breadcrumbs and parsley

1 Roast the best end.
2 Ten minutes before cooking is completed cover the fat surface of the meat with a mixture of 25–50 g of fresh white breadcrumbs mixed with plenty of chopped parsley, an egg and 25–50 g melted butter or margarine.
3 Return to the oven to complete the cooking, browning carefully.

Variations
Variations include:
• mixed fresh herbs used in addition to parsley
• finely chopped garlic added
• chopped fresh herbs, shallots and mustard.

6 Roast loin of lamb with anchovies and red wine

Cal	Cal	Fat	Sat Fat	Carb	Sugar	Protein	Fibre	Salt
3598 KJ	860 kcal	73.1 g	30.2 g	0.3 g	0.3 g	39.7 g	0.0 g	1.3 g

	4 portions	10 portions
salt, pepper		
olive oil	50 ml	125 ml
loins (approx 1.5 kg each)	3	7–8
red wine	250 ml	625 ml
mustard	1 tsp	2½ tsp
anchovies	8 (25 g)	10 (60 g)

1 Season and oil, then roast the prepared loins in the oven.
2 When the lamb is cooked, allow to rest.
3 Deglaze the pan with the red wine.
4 Add the mustard and reduce to a sauce consistency.
5 Strain, then add the chopped anchovies.
6 Serve the lamb sliced. Mask with the sauce.
7 Serve on a bed of fresh leaf spinach.

7 Roast saddle of lamb with rosemary mash

	4 portions	10 portions
saddle of lamb, boned		
milk	250 ml	625 ml
rosemary	2 sprigs	5 sprigs
potato, mashed	1.3 kg	3.2 kg

1 Bone the saddle of lamb and roast in the normal way.
2 Bring the milk to the boil with the rosemary. Remove from the heat, cover and leave to infuse for 10–15 minutes.
3 To make the rosemary mash, prepare a potato purée using the milk infused with rosemary.

8 Slow-cooked shoulder of lamb with vegetables

	4 portions	10 portions
boned shoulder of lamb, rolled and tied	1	3
olive oil		
salt, pepper		
rosemary	6 sprigs	18 sprigs
thyme	6 sprigs	18 sprigs
garlic, crushed and chopped	4 cloves	10 cloves
red onions, quartered	2	5
carrots, turned	3	7½
celery batons	2 sticks	5 sticks
leeks, shredded	1	3
tomatoes, halved	6	18
bay leaves, chopped	2	5
canned plum tomatoes, chopped	375 g	950 g
red wine or dry cider	½ bottle	1½ bottles

1 Rub the lamb with oil, and season with salt and pepper. Place in a suitable roasting tray and cook in an oven at 200°C for 15 minutes.
2 Remove from the oven and reduce the temperature to 140°C.
3 Add the remaining ingredients to the roasting tray.
4 Cover with a lid or aluminium foil and cook for 2½ to 3 hours (removing the foil 40 minutes before the end) until the lamb is tender and sticky.
5 Remove the herbs, then remove the lamb and allow to rest.
6 Carve the lamb and serve on top of the vegetables.
7 To make the sauce, once the vegetables are removed, reduce the cooking liquor to the required consistency. Add a tablespoon of redcurrant jelly, mix well, correct seasoning, then strain.
8 Couscous makes a good accompaniment.

9 Best end of lamb boulanger (carré d'agneau boulanger)

1 Prepare a dish of savoury potatoes (see page 526).
2 Roast the joint.
3 Remove from the tray 15 minutes before completion of cooking.
4 Place on top of the cooked potatoes.
5 Return to the oven to complete the cooking.
6 Serve the joint whole or carved, as required, on the potatoes.
7 Garnish with watercress and serve with a sauceboat of gravy separately.

Note: Any roast lamb joint may be served in this manner.

Grill

10 Grilled cutlets (côtelettes d'agneau grillées)

1 Season the cutlets lightly with salt and mill pepper.
2 Brush with oil or fat.
3 When cooked on the bars of the grill, place the prepared cutlet on the preheated bars that have been greased.
4 Cook for approximately 5 minutes, turn and complete the cooking.
5 When cooked under the salamander, place on a greased tray, cook for approximately 5 minutes, turn and complete the cooking.
6 Serve dressed, garnished with a deep-fried potato and watercress. A compound butter (e.g. parsley, herb or garlic) may also be served (see page 65).
7 Each cutlet bone may be capped with a cutlet frill.

HEALTHY EATING TIP
• When served with boiled new potatoes and boiled or steamed vegetables, the plate of food becomes more 'balanced'.

11 Mixed grill

Cal 2050 KJ	Cal 488 kcal	Fat 40.8 g	Sat Fat 19.3 g	Carb 0.0 g	Sugar 0.0 g	Protein 30.4 g	Fibre 0.0 g	*

	4 portions	10 portions
sausages	4	10
cutlets	4	10
kidneys	4	10
tomatoes	4	10
mushrooms	4	10
rashers streaky bacon	4	10
deep-fried potato, to serve		
watercress, to serve		
parsley butter (see page 65), to serve		

HEALTHY EATING TIP
• Add only a small amount of compound butter and serve with plenty of potatoes and vegetables.

* 1 portion (2 cutlets). With deep-fried potatoes, parsley and watercress, 1 portion provides: 3050 kJ/726 kcal Energy; 59.2 g Fat; 26.6 g Sat Fat; 20.2 g Carb; 2.5 g Sugar; 29.5 g Protein; 4.9 g Fibre

1 Grill in the order listed above.
2 Dress neatly on an oval flat dish or plates.
3 Garnish with deep-fried potato, watercress and a slice of compound butter on each kidney or offered separately.

Note: These are the usually accepted items for a mixed grill, but it will be found that there are many variations to this list (e.g. steaks, liver, a Welsh rarebit and fried egg).

Figure 8.8 The ingredients for a mixed grill

12 Lamb kebabs (*shish kebab*)

Kebabs, a dish of Turkish origin, are pieces of food impaled and cooked on skewers over a grill or barbecue. There are many variations and different flavours can be added by marinating the kebabs in oil, wine, vinegar or lemon juice with spices and herbs for 1–2 hours before cooking. Kebabs can be made using tender cuts, or mince of lamb and beef, pork, liver, kidney, bacon, ham, sausage and chicken, using either the meats individually or combining two or three. Vegetables and fruit can also be added (e.g. onion, apple, pineapple, peppers, tomatoes, aubergine). Kebabs can be made using vegetables exclusively (e.g. peppers, onion, aubergine, tomatoes). Kebabs are usually served with a pilaff rice (see page 162).

The ideal cuts of lamb are the nut of the lean meat of the loin, best end or boned-out meat from a young shoulder of lamb.

1 Cut the meat into squares and place them on skewers with squares of green pepper, tomato, onion and bay leaves in between.
2 Sprinkle with powdered thyme and cook over a hot grill.
3 Serve with pilaff rice, or with chickpeas and finely sliced raw onion.

Variations
Variations include:
- miniature kebabs (one mouthful) can be made, impaled on cocktail sticks, grilled and served as a hot snack at receptions
- fish kebabs can be made using a firm fish, such as monkfish, and marinating in olive oil, lemon or lime juice, chopped fennel or dill, garlic and a dash of Tabasco or Worcester sauce.

13 Grilled loin or chump chops, or noisettes of lamb

1 Season the chops or noisettes lightly with salt and mill pepper.
2 Brush with fat and place on hot greased grill bars or place on a greased baking tray.
3 Cook quickly for the first 2–3 minutes on each side, in order to seal the pores of the meat.
4 Continue cooking steadily, allowing approximately 12–15 minutes in all.

Note: A compound butter may also be served, and deep-fried potatoes.

Variations
Variations include sprigs of rosemary or other herbs laid on the chops during the last few minutes of grilling to impart flavour.

Sauté

14 Fried cutlets

1 Season and carefully cook in a sauté pan.
2 Garnish as required (e.g. as noted in recipes 10 and 11).

HEALTHY EATING TIP

- Lightly oil the pan with an unsaturated oil to fry the cutlets. Drain off any excess fat after the frying is complete.
- Use the minimum amount of salt and serve with plenty of vegetables.

15 Breadcrumbed cutlets (côtelettes d'agneau panées)

1 Pass the prepared and flattened cutlets through seasoned flour, eggwash and fresh white bread-crumbs. Pat firmly, then shake off surplus crumbs.
2 Shallow-fry in hot clarified butter, margarine or oil for the first few minutes; then allow to cook gently.
3 Turn, and continue cooking until a golden-brown (approx. 5 minutes each side).
4 To test if cooked, press firmly – no signs of blood should appear.

Note: These may be served with a garnish of pasta, such as spaghetti with tomato sauce or noodles with butter or oil.

HEALTHY EATING TIP
• Lightly oil the pan with an unsaturated oil to fry the cutlets. Drain off any excess fat after the frying is complete.
• Serve with plenty of vegetables.

16 Noisettes of lamb or fillet of lamb sauté (noisettes d'agneau sautées)

1 Season and shallow-fry on both sides in a sauté pan.
2 Serve with the appropriate garnish (see below) and sauce. Unless specifically stated, a jus-lié or demi-glace should be served.

Suitable garnishes
• Tomatoes filled with jardinière of vegetables and château potatoes.
• Balls of cauliflower mornay and château potatoes.
• Artichoke bottoms filled with carrot balls and noisette potatoes.
• Artichoke bottoms filled with asparagus heads and noisette potatoes.
• Artichoke bottoms filled with peas and cocotte potatoes.

Note: Fillet of lamb should be trimmed of fat and sinew before cooking.

HEALTHY EATING TIP
• Trim off as much fat as possible before cooking.
• Grilling or braising is a healthier way of cooking.
• Add starchy carbohydrate and vegetables to proportionally reduce the amount of fat.

17 Lamb noisettes with thyme and blueberries

Cal	Cal	Fat	Sat Fat	Carb	Sugar	Protein	Fibre	Salt	*
3335 KJ	797 kcal	65.7 g	29.2 g	3.0 g	2.7 g	38.9 g	1.6 g	1.3 g	

	4 portions	10 portions
lamb noisettes	8	20
olive oil	2 tbsp	5 tbsp
red wine	250 ml	625 ml
fresh thyme	4 sprigs	10 sprigs
lamb stock	250 ml	625 ml
blueberries	200 g	500 g
salt, pepper		

1 Shallow-fry the noisettes in olive oil.
2 Deglaze the pan with wine, then add the thyme.
3 Add the lamb stock and reduce to a sauce consistency.
4 Add the blueberries, then season.
5 Serve the lamb with the blueberries and the sauce.

Using a 225 g portion of lamb, and blackberries in place of blueberries

18 Lamb fillets with beans and tomatoes

	4 portions	10 portions
olive oil	approx. 50 ml	approx. 125 ml
onions, finely chopped	50 g	125 g
garlic, crushed and chopped	2	5
dried cannellini beans, soaked	500 g	1¼ kg
lamb stock	1 litre	2½ litres
bay leaves	2	5
salt, pepper		
cherry tomatoes	750 g	1 kg
lamb fillets	900 g	2¼ kg

1 Heat the olive oil in a suitable pan, and gently fry the onion and garlic. Rinse the beans, drain and add to the pan.
2 Add the stock and bay leaves. Bring to the boil. Simmer for approximately 1 hour until the beans are tender. Season.
3 Cook the cherry tomatoes in a hot oven at 190°C with a drizzle of oil.
4 Rub a little olive oil into the lamb fillets. Leave for approximately 20 minutes at room temperature.
5 Season the lamb and shallow-fry. Serve with the tomatoes and the beans neatly arranged on a plate.

19 Valentine of lamb

1 Prepare a short saddle with all the bones, kidneys and internal fat removed.
2 Split into two loins.
3 Trim off excess fat and sinew.
4 Cut across the muscle grain into thick boneless chops.
5 Slice three parts through the lean meat and open to give a double-sized cut surface (butterfly cut).

Note: Valentines are cooked in the same way as noisettes and rosettes. They may also be grilled or braised. Best end may be used in place of the loin.

HEALTHY EATING TIP
- Grilling or braising is a healthier way of cooking.
- Add starchy carbohydrate and vegetables to proportionally reduce the amount of fat.
- Trim off as much fat as possible before cooking.

20 Lamb valentine steaks with fresh pea hummus

Cal	Cal	Fat	Sat Fat	Carb	Sugar	Protein	Fibre	Salt	*
4686 KJ	1121 kcal	95.1 g	33.5 g	17.6 g	3.6 g	50.5 g	7.9 g	0.4 g	

	4 portions	10 portions
lamb steaks (2 per portion)	8	20
olive oil	2 tbsp	5 tbsp
Hummus		
peas	600 g	1½ kg
garlic cloves, crushed and chopped	4	10
ground cumin	1 tsp	2½ tsp
lemon juice	½ tsp	1 tsp
mint leaves, chopped	1 tsp	2 tsp
extra virgin olive oil	10 tbsp	25 tbsp
tahini paste	2 tbsp	5 tbsp

1 To make the hummus, cook the peas and drain well. Purée them in a food processor with the garlic, cumin, lemon juice, mint, extra virgin olive oil and tahini paste.
2 Season the valentines, then grill them or shallow-fry in the olive oil.
3 Serve with the pea hummus

*Using a 225 g portion of lamb

Braise

21 Braised loin or chump chops (*chops d'agneau braisées*)

Cal	Cal	Fat	Sat Fat	Carb	Sugar	Protein	Fibre
1452 KJ	349 kcal	23.4 g	10.8 g	9.4 g	3.8 g	25.8 g	1.2 g

	4 portions	10 portions
chops	4	10
salt, pepper		
onion	100 g	250 g
carrot	100 g	250 g
flour (white or wholemeal)	25 g	60 g
tomato purée	1 level tsp	2½ level tsp
brown stock	500 ml	1¼ litre
bouquet garni		
clove garlic, optional	1	2
parsley, chopped		

1 Fry the seasoned chops in a sauté pan quickly on both sides in hot fat.
2 When turning the chops, add the mirepoix (onion and carrot).
3 Draw aside and drain off the surplus fat.
4 Add the flour and mix in, singe in the oven or on top of the stove. (Alternatively, use flour that has been browned in the oven.)
5 Add the tomato purée and the hot stock.
6 Stir until thoroughly mixed.
7 Add the bouquet garni and garlic, season, skim and allow to simmer; cover with a lid.
8 Cook (preferably in the oven), skimming off all fat and scum.
9 When cooked, transfer the chops to a clean pan.
10 Correct the seasoning and consistency of the sauce.
11 Skim off any fat and pass the sauce through a fine strainer over the chops.
12 Serve sprinkled with chopped parsley.

Note: Lamb steaks cut from the chump end of the leg can also be cooked in this way.

HEALTHY EATING TIP
• Trim fat from the chops before frying.
• Use the minimum amount of salt.
• Lightly oil the pan with an unsaturated oil to fry the cutlets. Drain off any excess fat after the frying is complete.
• Brush the potatoes with oil.
• Serve with a large portion of vegetables.

Variations
Variations include the following additions after the sauce has been strained:
• cooked pulse beans (e.g. haricot, butter, flageolet)
• cooked neatly cut vegetables (e.g. carrots, turnips, swede, green beans, peas).

22 Chops Champvallon (chops d'agneau Champvallon)

Cal	Cal	Fat	Sat Fat	Carb	Sugar	Protein	Fibre
1727 KJ	414 kcal	23.5 g	10.8 g	24.3 g	2.2 g	27.6 g	1.9 g

	4 portions	10 portions
chops, preferably chump	4	10
flour	25 g	60 g
salt, pepper		
onions	100 g	250 g
clove garlic (optional)	1	2
brown stock	250 ml	625 ml
potatoes, sliced	400 g	1¼ kg
parsley, chopped, to serve		

1 Pass the chops through seasoned flour.
2 Fry quickly on both sides in hot fat or oil.
3 Shred the onions finely and toss lightly in butter, with garlic if using, and place in a shallow earthenware dish.
4 Place the chops on top, cover with brown stock.

5 Add ½ cm sliced potatoes neatly arranged with a knob or two of good dripping on top, or brush with oil.
6 Cook in a hot oven at 230–250°C until the potatoes are cooked and a golden-brown colour (approx. 1½–2 hours).
7 Serve sprinkled with chopped parsley in the cleaned earthenware dish.

HEALTHY EATING TIP
- Trim off as much fat as possible before cooking.
- Grilling or braising is a healthier way of cooking.
- Add starchy carbohydrate and vegetables to proportionally reduce the amount of fat.

23 Braised lamb shanks with ratatouille

Cal	Cal	Fat	Sat Fat	Carb	Sugar	Protein	Fibre	*
2020 KJ	483 kcal	27.3 g	9.6 g	23.7 g	10.5 g	37.1 g	8.6 g	

	4 portions	10 portions
lamb shanks	4	10
olive oil	3 tbsp	7 tbsp
red onions, finely chopped	50 g	125 g
garlic cloves, crushed, finely chopped	2	5
aubergine large, diced 1 cm dice	1	2
courgettes, diced 1 cm dice	3	7
plum tomatoes (canned)	400 g	1 kg
lamb stock	250 ml	625 ml
flageolet beans (canned), rinsed and drained	400 g	1 kg
fresh oregano, chopped	1 tbsp	2½ tbsp
fresh rosemary, chopped	1 tbsp	2½ tbsp
clear honey	1 tbsp	2½ tbsp
salt, pepper		

1 Season the lamb shanks. Heat the oil in a suitable braising pan, fry the shanks on all sides until golden brown. Remove from pan and set aside.
2 Add the chopped onion and garlic, sweat until soft.
3 Add the diced aubergine and courgettes, cook for 5 minutes.

4 Stir in the chopped plum tomatoes and stock.
5 Place the lamb shank back with the vegetables. Bring to the boil, reduce heat, cover and braise in the oven for 1 hour.
6 Remove the lamb. Stir in the flageolet beans, add the herbs and honey. Simmer, check all the vegetables are soft.
7 Replace the lamb and allow the shanks to steep in the vegetables.
8 Correct the seasoning and consistency.
9 Serve with mashed potatoes or couscous.

HEALTHY EATING TIP
- Fry the shanks in a little olive oil and drain off any excess fat.
- Skim any fat from the cooked sauce before adding the beans.
- Serve with a large portion of potatoes or couscous and colourful seasonal vegetables.
- Add the minimum amount of salt.

* *Using edible portion of meat (90 g), with broad beans used to replace flageolet beans*

Stew

24 Brown lamb or mutton stew (navarin d'agneau)

Cal 1320 KJ	Cal 314 kcal	Fat 18.7 g	Sat Fat 6.2 g	Carb 9.4 g	Sugar 3.2 g	Protein 27.9 g	Fibre 1.3 g	*

	4 portions	10 portions
stewing lamb	500 g	1½ kg
oil	2 tbsp	5 tbsp
salt, pepper		
carrot	100 g	250 g
onion	100 g	250 g
clove of garlic (optional)	1	3
flour (white or wholemeal)	25 g	60 g
tomato purée	1 level tbsp	2¼ level tbsp
brown stock (mutton stock or water)	500 g	1¼ litre
bouquet garni		
parsley, chopped, to serve		

1 Trim the meat and cut into even pieces.
2 Partly fry off the seasoned meat in the oil, then add the carrot, onion and garlic, and continue frying.
3 Drain off the surplus fat, add the flour and mix.
4 Singe in the oven or brown on top of the stove for a few minutes, or add previously browned flour.
5 Add the tomato purée and stir with a wooden spoon.
6 Add the stock and season.
7 Add the bouquet garni, bring to the boil, skim and cover with a lid.
8 Simmer gently until cooked (preferably in the oven) for approx. 1–2 hours.
9 When cooked, place the meat in a clean pan.
10 Correct the sauce and pass it on to the meat.
11 Serve sprinkled with chopped parsley.

HEALTHY EATING TIP
- Trim off as much fat as possible before frying and drain all surplus fat after frying.
- Use the minimum amount of salt to season the meat.
- Serve with plenty of potatoes and vegetables.

Variations
A variation includes a garnish of vegetables (glazed carrots and turnips, glazed button onions, potatoes, peas and diamonds of French beans), which may be cooked separately or in the stew.

* *Using sunflower oil*

Figure 8.9 Modern presentation of navarin of lamb cutlets with grilled vegetables. Figure 1.2 on page 5 shows a traditional presentation

25 Curried lamb (kari d'agneau)

Cal 1699 KJ	Cal 405 kcal	Fat 26.6 g	Sat Fat 10.0 g	Carb 14.8 g	Sugar 11.6 g	Protein 27.7 g	Fibre 3.2 g	*

	4 portions	10 portions
stewing lamb	500 g	1½ kg
salt, pepper		
oil	3 tbsp	8 tbsp
onions	200 g	500 g
clove garlic	1	2½
curry powder	10 g	25 g
flour (white or wholemeal)	10 g	25 g
tomato purée	10 g	25 g
stock or water	½ litre	1½ litres
chutney, chopped	25 g	60 g
desiccated coconut	25 g	60 g
sultanas	25 g	60 g
apple, chopped	50 g	125 g
root ginger, grated		

1 Trim the meat and cut into even pieces.
2 Season and quickly colour in hot oil.
3 Add the chopped onion and chopped garlic, cover with a lid and allow to sweat for a few minutes. Drain off the surplus fat.
4 Add the curry powder and flour, mix in and cook out.
5 Mix in the tomato purée and gradually add the hot stock; stir thoroughly; bring to the boil and season with salt; skim.
6 Allow to simmer; add the rest of the ingredients.
7 Cover with a lid and simmer in the oven or on top of the stove until cooked.
8 Correct the seasoning and consistency; skim off all fat. At this stage a little cream or yoghurt may be added.
9 Serve accompanied with rice, which may be plain boiled, pilaff or pilaff with saffron (see page 162).

Note: This recipe is a European version. Authentic Asian recipes can be found in Chapter 10: International cookery.

HEALTHY EATING TIP

• Trim off as much fat as possible before frying and drain all surplus fat after frying.
• Use the minimum amount of salt to season the meat.
• Skim all fat from the finished dish and add low-fat yoghurt.
• Serve with plenty of rice, chapatis and dhal.

Variations
There are many other accompaniments to curry – for example, grilled Bombay duck (dried fish fillets) and poppadoms (thin vegetable wafers), which are grilled or deep-fried. Others include:

• chopped chutney
• chow-chow
• sultanas
• quarters of orange
• desiccated coconut
• sliced banana
• slices of lemon
• chopped onions
• chopped apple
• diced cucumber in natural yoghurt
• segments of lime
• mint in natural yoghurt
• raita (see page 402).

* *Using sunflower oil*

26 Irish stew

Cal	Cal	Fat	Sat Fat	Carb	Sugar	Protein	Fibre
1339 KJ	319 kcal	11.2 g	5.2 g	26.1 g	5.7 g	30.2 g	5.0 g

	4 portions	10 portions
stewing lamb	500 g	1½ kg
salt, pepper		
bouquet garni		
potatoes	400 g	1 kg
onions	100 g	250 g
celery	100 g	250 g
savoy cabbage	100 g	250 g
leeks	100 g	250 g
button onions	100 g	250 g
parsley, chopped		

1 Trim the meat and cut into even pieces. Blanch and refresh.
2 Place in a shallow saucepan, cover with water, bring to the boil, season with salt and skim. If tough meat is being used, allow ½–1 hour stewing time before adding any vegetables.
3 Add the bouquet garni. Turn the potatoes into barrel shapes.
4 Cut the potato trimmings, onions, celery, cabbage and leeks into small neat pieces and add to the meat; simmer for 30 minutes.

5 Add the button onions and simmer for a further 30 minutes.
6 Add the potatoes and simmer gently with a lid on the pan until cooked.
7 Correct the seasoning and skim off all fat.
8 Serve sprinkled with chopped parsley.

Note: Alternatively, a more modern approach is to cook the meat for 1½–2 hours until almost tender, then add the vegetables and cook until all are tender. Optional accompaniments include Worcester sauce and/or pickled red cabbage.

HEALTHY EATING TIP

• Trim as much fat as possible from the stewing lamb and skim all fat from the finished dish.
• Use the minimum amount of salt.
• Serve with colourful seasonal vegetables to create a 'healthy' dish.

27 White lamb stew (blanquette d'agneau)

Cal	Cal	Fat	Sat Fat	Carb	Sugar	Protein	Fibre	*
1181 KJ	283 kcal	15.5 g	7.8 g	9.2 g	3.9 g	27.3 g	0.0 g	

	4 portions	10 portions
stewing lamb	500 g	1½ kg
white stock	750 ml	1½ litres
onion, studded	50 g	125 g
carrot	50 g	125 g
bouquet garni		
salt, pepper		
butter, margarine or oil	25 g	60 g
flour	25 g	60 g
cream, yoghurt or quark	2–3 tbsp	5 tbsp
parsley, chopped		

1 Trim the meat and cut into even pieces. Blanch and refresh.
2 Place in a saucepan and cover with cold water.
3 Bring to the boil then place under running cold water until all the scum has been washed away.

4 Drain and place in a clean saucepan and cover with stock, bring to the boil and skim.
5 Add whole onion and carrot, and bouquet garni, season lightly with salt and simmer until tender, approximately 1–1½ hours.
6 Meanwhile prepare a blond roux with the butter and flour and make into a velouté with the cooking liquor. Cook out for approximately 20 minutes.
7 Correct the seasoning and consistency, and pass through a fine strainer on to the meat, which has been placed in a clean pan.
8 Reheat, mix in the cream and serve, finished with chopped parsley.
9 To enrich this dish a liaison of yolks and cream is sometimes added at the last moment to the boiling sauce, which must not be allowed to reboil, otherwise the eggs will scramble and the sauce will curdle.

HEALTHY EATING TIP

- Trim as much fat as possible from the lamb before cooking.
- Use the minimum amount of salt.
- Reduce the fat content by using low-fat yoghurt in place of the cream when reheating.
- Serve with mashed potato with spring onion and colourful vegetables.

* Using butter and 2½ tbsp low-fat yoghurt

28 Hot pot of lamb or mutton

Cal 1505 KJ	Cal 360 kcal	Fat 17.0 g	Sat Fat 6.4 g	Carb 22.0 g	Sugar 1.8 g	Protein 29.0 g	Fibre 2.5 g	*

	4 portions	10 portions
stewing lamb	500 g	1¼ kg
salt, pepper		
onions, shredded	100 g	250 g
potatoes	400 g	1¼ kg
brown stock	1 litre	2½ litres
oil (optional)	25 g	60 g
parsley, chopped		

1 Trim the meat and cut into even pieces.
2 Place in a deep earthenware dish. Season with salt and pepper.
3 Lightly sauté the onions in the oil, if desired. Mix the onion and approx. three-quarters of the potatoes (thinly sliced) together.
4 Season and place on top of the meat; cover three parts with stock.
5 Neatly arrange an overlapping layer of the remaining potatoes on top, sliced about 2 mm thick.
6 Thoroughly clean the edges of the dish and place to cook in a hot oven at 230–250°C until lightly coloured.
7 Reduce the heat and simmer gently until cooked, approximately 1½–2 hours.
8 Press the potatoes down occasionally during cooking.
9 Serve with the potatoes brushed with butter or margarine and sprinkle with the chopped parsley.

Note: Neck chops or neck fillet make a succulent dish.

Variations
Variations include:
- use leek in place of onion
- add 200 g lambs' kidneys
- quickly fry off the meat and sweat the onions before putting in the pot
- add 100–200 g sliced mushrooms
- add a small tin of baked beans, or a layer of thickly sliced tomatoes before adding the potatoes
- use sausages in place of lamb.

* Using sunflower oil

Miscellaneous

29 Shepherd's pie (cottage pie)

Cal 1744 KJ	Cal 415 kcal	Fat 25.3 g	Sat Fat 9.1 g	Carb 22.1 g	Sugar 2.5 g	Protein 26.3 g	Fibre 1.6 g	*

	4 portions	10 portions
onions, chopped	100 g	250 g
oil	35 g	100 g
lamb or mutton (minced), cooked	400 g	1¼ kg
salt, pepper		
Worcester sauce	2–3 drops	5 drops
potato, cooked	400 g	1¼ kg
butter or margarine	25 g	60 g
milk or eggwash		
jus-lié or demi-glace	125–250 ml	300–600 ml

1 Cook the onion in the fat or oil without colouring.
2 Add the cooked meat from which all fat and gristle has been removed.
3 Season and add Worcester sauce (sufficient to bind).
4 Bring to the boil; simmer for 10–15 minutes.
5 Place in an earthenware or pie dish.
6 Prepare the potatoes – mix with the butter or margarine, then mash and pipe, or arrange neatly on top.
7 Brush with the milk or eggwash.
8 Colour lightly under salamander or in a hot oven.
9 Serve accompanied with a sauceboat of jus-lié.

Note: This dish prepared with cooked beef is known as cottage pie. When using reheated meats, care must be taken to heat thoroughly and quickly.

Variations
Variations include:
- add 100–200 g sliced mushrooms
- add a layer of thickly sliced tomatoes, then sprinkle with rosemary
- mix a tin of baked beans in with the meat
- sprinkle with grated cheese and brown
- vary the flavour of the mince by adding herbs or spices
- the potato topping can also be varied by mixing in grated cheese, chopped spring onions or herbs, or by using duchess potato mixture
- serve lightly sprinkled with garam masala and with grilled pitta bread.

* Using sunflower oil, with hard margarine in topping

HEALTHY EATING TIP
- Use an oil rich in unsaturates (olive or sunflower) to lightly oil the pan.
- Drain off any excess fat after the lamb has been fried.
- Try replacing some of the meat with baked beans or lentils, and add tomatoes and/or mushrooms to the dish.
- When served with a large portion of green vegetables, a healthy balance is created.

30 Minced lamb or mutton *(hachis d'agneau ou de mouton)*

1 Prepare the meat as for shepherd's pie (recipe 29).
2 Place on a dish that has been pre-piped with a border of duchess potatoes, dried for a few minutes in the oven, eggwashed and lightly browned.

Variations

Variations include the addition of sliced mushrooms, sweetcorn or cooked small pasta, and other variations as listed in recipe 29.

31 Moussaka

Cal	Cal	Fat	Sat Fat	Carb	Sugar	Protein	Fibre	*
1909 KJ	455 kcal	33.3 g	11.1 g	10.5 g	5.1 g	28.9 g	2.8 g	

	4 portions	10 portions
onions	50 g	125 g
small clove garlic	1	2
butter, margarine or oil	25 g	60 g
tomato purée	25 g	60 g
cooked mutton/lamb, diced or minced	400–600 g	1–1½ kg
demi-glace or jus-lié	125 ml	300 ml
salt, pepper		
aubergine	200 g	500 g
flour (white or wholemeal)		
oil	60 ml	150 ml
tomatoes	200 g	500 g
breadcrumbs	25 g	60 g
Parmesan cheese, grated	25 g	60 g
melted butter, margarine or oil, as required		
parsley, chopped, to serve		

1 Finely chop the onions and garlic.
2 Cook in the butter, margarine or oil without colour.
3 Mix in the tomato purée and the cooked mutton or lamb.
4 Add the demi-glace and bring to the boil.
5 Correct the seasoning and allow to simmer for 10–15 minutes. The mixture should be fairly dry.
6 Peel the aubergines and cut into ½ cm slices.
7 Pass the slices of aubergine through the flour.
8 Fry the slices of aubergine in shallow hot oil on both sides and drain.
9 Peel the tomatoes and cut into ½ cm slices.
10 Place the mutton mixture into an earthenware dish.
11 Cover the mixture with the slices of tomato, and then neatly with the slices of aubergine.

12 Season with salt and pepper.
13 Sprinkle with breadcrumbs, cheese and melted butter.
14 Gratinate in a hot oven at 230–250°C.
15 Sprinkle with chopped parsley and serve.

Note: This is a dish of Greek origin.

HEALTHY EATING TIP

- Use an oil rich in unsaturates (olive or sunflower) to lightly oil the pan.
- Use the minimum amount of salt.
- Oven bake the aubergines to reduce the fat content, and omit the butter from the topping of breadcrumbs and cheese.
- Serve with a large mixed salad.

Variations
Variations include:
- minced beef may be used in place of mutton
- it may be seasoned with a little cinnamon and oregano
- it may be finished by masking the dish, when all the ingredients have been added, with 250 ml (600 ml for 10 portions) of thin béchamel sauce to which two beaten eggs have been added; if this method is being adopted, then the breadcrumbs, cheese and melted butter should be added after the béchamel
- a vegetarian recipe for moussaka can be found on page 463.

* *Using hard margarine and sunflower oil*

32 Chinese spice lamb casserole

	4 portions	10 portions
shoulder of lamb, diced	900 g	2¼ kg
ground cumin	1 tsp	2 tsp
Chinese five-spice powder	1 tsp	2 tsp
flour	1 tsp	2 tsp
oil	2 tbsp	5 tbsp
onion, finely chopped	100 g	250 g
leeks, finely shredded	100 g	250 g
salt, pepper		
rosemary	2 sprigs	5 sprigs
lamb stock	250 ml	625 ml

1 Season the lamb with cumin and five-spice powder. Mix well into the meat and refrigerate overnight.
2 Sprinkle the lamb with the flour and mix well.
3 Quickly fry the lamb in half the oil until a golden brown colour. Drain.
4 Gently fry the onion and leek to a light-brown colour.
5 Place the lamb, onion and leek into a suitable casserole or braising pan. Season. Add the rosemary and lamb stock. Stir and bring to the boil.
6 Cook in a moderate oven at 170–180°C for approximately 1 hour. Check seasoning.
7 Serve with mashed potatoes or noodles.

Offal

33 Grilled lambs' kidneys (rognons grillés)

Cal	Cal	Fat	Sat Fat	Carb	Sugar	Protein	Fibre
614 KJ	147 kcal	10.3 g	5.9 g	0.1 g	0.1 g	13.7 g	0.0 g

1 Season the prepared skewered kidneys (see recipe 12).
2 Brush with melted butter, margarine or oil.
3 Place on preheated greased grill bars or on a greased baking tray.
4 Grill fairly quickly on both sides (approx. 5–10 minutes depending on size).
5 Serve with parsley butter, picked watercress and straw potatoes.

HEALTHY EATING TIP
• Use the minimum amount of salt.
• Serve with plenty of starchy carbohydrate and vegetables.

34 Devilled lambs' kidneys

Cal	Cal	Fat	Sat Fat	Carb	Sugar	Protein	Fibre	Salt	*
1017 KJ	243 kcal	11.8 g	4.5 g	3.8 g	2.0 g	26.4 g	0.0 g	1.0 g	

	4 portions	10 portions
lambs' kidneys	8	20
olive oil	1 tbsp	2½ tbsp
salt, pepper		
amontillado sherry	62 ml	180 ml
white wine vinegar	1 tbsp	2½ tbsp
redcurrant jelly	1 tsp	2½ tsp
Worcester sauce	3 drops	7 drops
double cream	1 tbsp	2½ tbsp
English mustard	1 tsp	2½ tsp
fresh mixed herbs, chopped		

1 Prepare the kidneys, cut in half, remove the white ducts and cut into quarters.
2 Heat the oil in the pan, season the kidneys. When cooked, remove.
3 Add the sherry to the pan. Bring to the boil. Add the vinegar and redcurrant jelly.
4 Add the Worcester sauce. Season.
5 Add the cream and mustard. Simmer and reduce to a sauce consistency; do not allow to boil. Check seasoning.
6 Add the kidneys and warm through.
7 Serve on a bed of pilaff rice (see page 162), garnished with chopped herbs.

Using a 150 g portion of kidney

35 Lambs' kidneys sautéed with sherry vinegar

	4 portions	10 portions
lambs' kidneys	8	20
oil	50 ml	125 ml
butter	50 g	125 g
sherry vinegar	50 ml	125 ml
parsley, chopped	1 tsp	2 tsp

1 Prepare the kidneys and open from bulge side. Secure with cocktail sticks or cut in half lengthways.
2 Heat the oil in a shallow pan, add the kidneys, cook for 1–2 minutes, add the butter and baste.
3 Add the sherry vinegar and chopped parsley. Baste the kidneys in the liquor and serve.

36 Kidney sauté (rognons sautés)

Cal 1680 KJ	Cal 400 kcal	Fat 28.3 g	Sat Fat 4.3 g	Carb 15.5 g	Sugar 3.7 g	Protein 21.8 g	Fibre 1.8 g	*

	4 portions	10 portions
sheep's kidneys	8	20
butter, margarine or oil	50 g	125 g
demi-glace or jus-lié	250 ml	625 ml

1 Skin and halve the kidneys. Remove the sinews.
2 Cut each half into 3 or 5 pieces and season.
3 Fry quickly in a frying pan using the butter, margarine or oil for approximately 4–5 minutes.
4 Place in a colander to drain, then discard the drained liquid.
5 Deglaze pan with demi-glace, correct the seasoning and add the kidneys.
6 Do not reboil before serving as kidneys will toughen.

Variations
After draining the kidneys, the pan may be deglazed with white wine, sherry or port. As an alternative, a sauce suprême (see page 53) may be used in place of demi-glace.

A further variation includes kidney sauté Turbigo. Cook as for kidney sauté then add 100 g small button mushrooms cooked in a little butter, margarine or oil, and 8 small 2 cm long grilled or fried chipolatas. Serve with the kidneys in an entrée dish, garnished with heart-shaped croutons (double these amounts for 10 portions).

HEALTHY EATING TIP
- Lightly oil the pan using an unsaturated oil (olive or sunflower).
- Drain off any excess fat.
- Add the minimum amount of salt to the demi-glace.
- Serve with plenty of starchy carbohydrates and vegetables.

* Using sunflower oil

37 Braised lambs' hearts (coeurs d'agneau braisés)

Cal 1489 KJ	Cal 354 kcal	Fat 19.0 g	Sat Fat 5.6 g	Carb 5.0 g	Sugar 4.3 g	Protein 41.2 g	Fibre 1.7 g	*

	4 portions	10 portions
lambs' hearts	4	10
salt, pepper		
fat or oil	25 g	60 g
onions	100 g	250 g
carrots	100 g	250 g
brown stock	500 ml	1¼ litre
bouquet garni		
tomato purée	10 g	25 g
demi-glace or jus-lié	250 ml	625 ml

1 Remove tubes and excess fat from the hearts.
2 Season and colour quickly on all sides in hot fat to seal the pores.
3 Place into a small braising pan (any pan with a tight-fitting lid that may be placed in the oven) or in a casserole.
4 Place the hearts on the lightly fried sliced vegetables.
5 Add the stock, which should come two-thirds of the way up the meat; season lightly.
6 Add the bouquet garni and tomato purée and, if available, add a few mushroom trimmings.

7 Bring to the boil, skim, cover with a lid and cook in a moderate oven at 150–200°C.
8 After 1½ hours add the demi-glace or jus-lié, reboil, skim and strain.
9 Continue cooking until tender.
10 Remove the hearts and correct the seasoning, colour and consistency of the sauce.
11 Pass the sauce on to the sliced hearts and serve.

HEALTHY EATING TIP

- Lightly oil the pan using an unsaturated oil (olive or sunflower).
- Drain off any excess fat and skim all fat from the finished dish.
- Keep added salt to a minimum.

Variations
The hearts can be prepared and cooked as above and, prior to cooking, the tube cavities can be filled with a firm stuffing (see e.g. recipe 4).

* *Using sunflower oil*

38 Fried lambs' liver and bacon (foie d'agneau au lard)

Cal 1039 KJ	Cal 250 kcal	Fat 20.1 g	Sat Fat 3.8 g	Carb 0.1 g	Sugar 0.1 g	Protein 17.2 g	Fibre 0.0 g	*

	4 portions	10 portions
liver	300 g	1 kg
butter, margarine or oil, for frying	50 g	125 g
streaky bacon	50 g	125 g
	(approx. 4 rashers)	(approx. 10 rashers)
jus-lié	125 ml	300 ml

1 Skin the liver and remove the gristle. Cut into thin slices on the slant.
2 Pass the slices of liver through seasoned flour. Shake off the excess flour.
3 Fry quickly on both sides in hot fat.

4 Remove the rind and bone from the bacon and grill on both sides.
5 Serve the liver and bacon with a cordon of jus-lié and a sauceboat of jus-lié.

HEALTHY EATING TIP

- Keep added salt to a minimum.
- Use a small amount of an unsaturated oil to fry the liver.
- Serve with plenty of potatoes and vegetables.

* *Using oil, jus-lié and reduced stock*

39 Shallow-fried lambs' sweetbreads

	4 portions	10 portions
sweetbreads	8	20
oil	50 ml	125 ml
butter	50 g	125 g
lemon juice	1	3
parsley, chopped	½ tsp	1 tsp

1 Trim the sweetbreads, blanch for 30 seconds, then retrim if necessary. Pass through seasoned flour.
2 Shallow-fry in oil for 2 minutes, turning.
3 Add butter to pan (*beurre noisette*), then add the lemon juice and chopped parsley.
4 Drain and serve.

Note: A little sherry vinegar may be added in place of or as well as the lemon juice.

Beef

Butchery

Side of beef (approximate weight 180 kg)

A whole side is divided between the wing ribs and the fore ribs.

Hindquarter of beef

Dissection of the hindquarter
- Remove the rump suet and kidney.
- Remove the thin flank.
- Divide the loin and rump from the leg (topside, silverside, thick flank and shin).
- Remove the fillet.
- Divide the rump from the sirloin.
- Remove the wing ribs.
- Remove the shin.
- Bone out the aitchbone.
- Divide the leg into the three remaining joints (silverside, topside and thick flank).

Preparation of joints and cuts of hindquarter
- **Shin:** bone out, remove excess sinew; cut or chop as required.
- **Topside:** roasting – remove excess fat, cut into joints and tie with string; braising as for roasting; stewing – cut into dice or steaks as required.
- **Silverside:** remove the thigh bone; this joint is usually kept whole and pickled in brine prior to boning.
- **Thick flank:** as for topside.
- **Rump:** bone out; cut off the first outside slice for pies and puddings. Cut into approximately 1½ cm slices for steaks. The point steak – considered the tenderest – is cut from the pointed end of the slice.

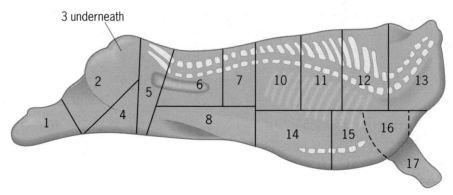

Figure 8.10 Side of beef

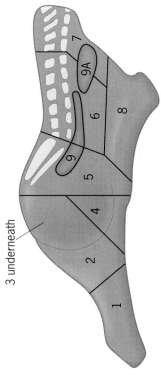

Figure 8.11 ✐ Hindquarter of beef

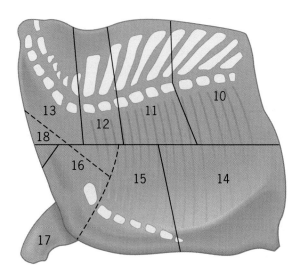

Figure 8.12 ✐ Forequarter of beef

Table 8.4 ✐ Joints, uses and weights of the hindquarter (numbers in left-hand column refer to Figure 8.11)

Joint	Uses	Approx. weight (kg)
(1) shin	consommé, beef tea, stewing, braising	7
(2) topside	braising, stewing, second-class roasting	10
(3) silverside	pickled in brine then boiled, braising, second-class roasting	14
(4) thick flank (knuckle)	braising and stewing, flash frying, second-class roasting	12
(5) rump	grilling and frying as steaks, braised in the piece	10
(6) sirloin	roasting, grilling and frying in steaks	9
(7) wing ribs	roasting, grilling and frying in steaks	5
(8) thin flank	stewing, boiling, sausages	10
(9) fillet	roasting, grilling and frying in steaks	3
(9A) fat and kidney		1

Note: The original catering joints are based on French cuts. Butchers refer to shin as leg of beef, and to shank as shin.

Forequarter of beef

Dissection of the forequarter
- Remove the shank.
- Divide in half down the centre.
- Take off the fore ribs.
- Divide into joints.

Alternative terms for joints:
- The back ribs from the leg of mutton cut are known as Jacob's ladder.
- A tied rib joint is nicknamed an oven buster.

Table 8.5 ✎ Joints, uses and weights of the forequarter (numbers in left-hand column refer to Figure 8.12)

Joint	Uses	Approx. weight (kg)
(10) fore rib	roasting and braising	8
(11) middle rib	roasting and braising	10
(12) chuck rib (feather blade and round blade)	stewing and braising	15
(13) sticking piece	stewing and sausages	9
(14) plate (flank)	stewing and sausages	10
(15) brisket	pickled in brine and boiled, pressed beef	19
(16) leg of mutton cut	braising and stewing	11
(17) shank	consommé, beef tea	6
(18) clod	braising, stewing, pies, sausages	5

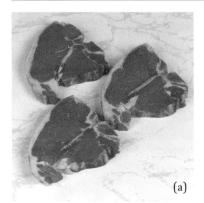

(a)

(b)

Figure 8.13 ✎ (a) T-bone steaks; (b) fillet and loin of beef

Beef offal

Table 8.6 ✎ Uses of beef offal

Offal	Uses
tongue	pickled in brine, boiling, braising
heart	braising
liver	braising, frying
kidney	stewing, soup
sweetbread	braising, frying
tripe	boiling, braising
tail	braising, soup
suet	suet paste and stuffing, or rendered down for first-class dripping
bones	beef stocks

Quality of beef

- The lean meat should be bright red, with small flecks of white fat (marbled).
- The fat should be firm, brittle in texture, creamy-white in colour and odourless. Older animals and dairy breeds have fat that is usually a deeper-yellow colour.

Salting

Salting, especially of meat, is an ancient preservation technique. The salt draws out moisture and creates an environment inhospitable to bacteria. If salted in cold weather (so that the meat does not spoil while the salt has time to take effect), salted meat can last for years.

Today, salting is still used with bacon and other pork and beef products – e.g. dried beef, corned beef (see below) and pastrami – which are made by soaking beef in a 10 per cent salt water brine for several weeks.

The history of 'corned beef'

'Corned' is a form of curing; it has nothing to do with corn. The name comes from Anglo-Saxon times, before refrigeration. In those days, the meat was dry-cured in coarse 'corns' of salt. Pellets of salt, some the size of kernels of corn, were rubbed into the beef to keep it from spoiling and to preserve it.

Today, brining – the use of salt water – has replaced the dry salt cure, but the name 'corned beef' is still used, rather than 'brined' or 'pickled' beef. Commonly used spices that give corned beef its distinctive flavour are peppercorns and bay leaf. (Of course, the spices used may vary regionally.)

40 Brine (saumure)

cold water	2½ litres	1	Boil all the ingredients together for 10 minutes, skimming frequently.
saltpetre	15 g	2	Strain into a china, wooden or earthenware container.
salt	½–1 kg		
bay leaf	1	3	When the brine is cold, add the meat.
juniper berries	6	4	Immerse the meat for up to 10 days under refrigeration.
brown sugar	50 g		
peppercorns	6		

Classifications and their respective joints

The cuts of beef vary considerably, from the very tender fillet steak to the tough brisket or the shin, and there is a greater variety of cuts in beef than for any other type of meat. While their names may vary, there are 14 primary cuts from a side of beef, each one composed of muscle, fat, bone and connective tissue. The least developed muscles, usually from the inner areas, can be roasted or grilled, while leaner and more sinewy meat is cut from the more highly developed external muscles. Exceptions are rib and loin cuts, which come from external but basically immobile muscles.

Knowing where the cuts come from helps to designate the cooking method.

Fillet

Taken from the back of the animal, this is the tenderest part, cut from the centre of the sirloin.

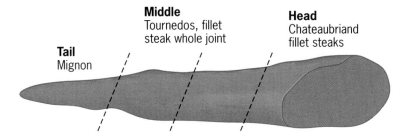

Middle
Tournedos, fillet steak whole joint

Head
Chateaubriand fillet steaks

Tail
Mignon

Figure 8.14 ✎ Cuts of fillet of beef

It is usually cut into steaks and can be fried or grilled.

Sirloin

A boneless steak, which is more tender than rump, but not as tender as fillet. It is suitable for grilling or frying.

Rump

A good-quality cut, though it is less tender than fillet or sirloin. It is suitable for grilling or frying.

Rib

Sold on the bone or unboned and rolled, it is suitable for roasting.

Topside

A lean, tender cut from the hindquarters, it is suitable for braising or pot roasting.

Silverside

Taken from the hindquarters, this is a cut from the round. It can be pot roasted or used for traditional boiled beef.

Flank

A boneless cut from the mid-to-hindquarters; suitable for braising or stewing.

Skirt

A boneless rather gristly cut. It is usually stewed or made into mince.

Brisket

A cut from the fore end of the animal, below the shoulder. Quite a fatty joint, it is sold on or off the bone or salted. It is suitable for slow roasting.

Preparation of joints and cuts

Sirloin

- **Roasting:** carefully cut back the covering fat in one piece for approximately 10 cm. Trim off the

sinew, replace the covering fat and tie with string if necessary.

Method 1: whole on the bone *Aloyau de boeuf*
Saw through the chine bone, lift back the covering fat in one piece for approx. 10 cm. Trim off the sinew and replace the covering fat. Tie with string if necessary. Ensure that the fillet has been removed.

Method 2: boned out
The fillet is removed and the sirloin boned out, and the sinew is removed as before. Remove the excess fat and sinew from the boned side. This joint may be roasted open, or rolled and tied with string.

- **Grilling and frying:** prepare as above and cut into steaks as required.
  - *Minute steaks:* cut into 1 cm slices, flatten with a cutlet bat dipped in water, making as thin as possible, then trim.
  - *Sirloin steaks (entrecôte):* cut into 1 cm slices and trim (approx. weight 150 g).
  - *Double sirloin steaks:* cut into 2 cm-thick slices and trim (approx. weight 250–300 g).
  - *Porterhouse and T-bone steak:* porterhouse steaks are cut including the bone from the rib end of the sirloin; T-bone steaks are cut from the rump end of the sirloin, including the bone and fillet.

Fillet

As a fillet of beef can vary from 2½ to 4½ kg it follows that there must be considerable variation in the number of steaks obtained from it. A typical breakdown of a 3 kg fillet would be as follows.

- **Chateaubriand:** double fillet steak 3–10 cm thick, 2–4 portions. Average weight 300 g–1 kg. Cut from the head of the fillet, trim off all the nerve and leave a little fat on the steak.
- **Fillet steaks:** approximately 4 steaks of 100–150 g each, 1½–2 cm thick. These are cut as shown in Figure 8.14 and trimmed as for chateaubriand.
- **Tournedos:** approximately 6–8 at 100 g each, 2–4 cm thick. Continue cutting down the fillet.

Remove all the nerve and all the fat, and tie each tournedos with string.

- **Tail of fillet:** approximately ½ kg. Remove all fat and sinew, and slice or mince as required.
- **Whole fillet:** preparation for roasting and pot roasting (poèlé) – remove the head and tail of the fillet, leaving an even centre piece from which all the nerve and fat is removed. This may be larded by inserting pieces of fat bacon cut into long strips, with a larding needle.

Wing rib (côte de boeuf)

This joint usually consists of the last three rib bones, which, because of their curved shape, act as a natural trivet and because of its prime quality make it a first-class roasting joint, for hot or cold, particularly when it is to be carved in front of the customer.

To prepare, cut seven-eighths of the way through the spine or chine bone, remove the nerve, saw through the rib bones on the underside 5–10 cm from the end. Tie firmly with string. When the joint is cooked the chine bone is removed to facilitate carving.

- **Thin flank:** trim off excessive fat and cut or roll as required.

Forequarter

- Fore ribs and middle ribs – prepare as for wing ribs.
- Chuck ribs, sticking piece, brisket, plate, leg of mutton cut, shank – bone out, remove excess fat and sinew, and use as required.

Beef offal

- **Tongue:** remove bone and gristle from the throat end.
- **Hearts:** remove arterial tubes and excess fat.
- **Liver:** skin, remove the gristle and cut into thin slices on the slant.
- **Kidney:** skin, remove the gristle and cut as required.
- **Sweetbreads:** soak in salted water for 2–3 hours to remove any traces of blood; wash well, trim, blanch and refresh.
- **Tripe:** wash well and soak in cold water, then cut into even pieces.
- **Tail:** cut between the natural joints, trim off excess fat. The large pieces may be split in two.

Beef recipes

Roasting

Testing whether a joint of beef is cooked

Using a temperature probe
When using a temperature probe, insert it into the part of the joint that was thickest before the food was placed in the oven. The internal temperature reached should be as follows:

- rare meat – 52–55°C
- medium done – 66–71°C
- just done – 78–80°C.

Without using a temperature probe
- Remove the joint from the oven and place on a plate or dish.
- Firmly press the surface of the meat so that some juice issues.
- Check the colour of the juice: *red* indicates the meat is underdone; *pink* indicates the meat is medium done; *clear* indicates that the meat is cooked through.

41 Roasting of beef (boeuf rôti)

Cal	Cal	Fat	Sat Fat	Carb	Sugar	Protein	Fibre
911 KJ	217 kcal	10.3 g	4.7 g	0.0 g	0.0 g	31.2 g	0.0 g

Suitable joints for roasting are: first class – sirloin, wing ribs, fore ribs, fillet; second class – topside, middle ribs.

1 Season joints with salt, place on a trivet or bones in a roasting tray.
2 Place a little dripping or oil on top and cook in a hot oven at 230–250°C.
3 Baste frequently and reduce the heat gradually when necessary, as for example in the case of large joints.
4 Roasting time is approximately 15 minutes per ½ kg, plus 15 minutes.
5 To test if cooked, place on a tray and press firmly in order to see if the juices released contain any blood.
6 Beef is normally cooked underdone and a little blood should show in the juice.
7 On removing the joint from the oven, rest for 15 minutes to allow the meat to set and facilitate carving, then carve against the grain.

Notes: Where applicable, name the origin and breed of the beef (e.g. Aberdeen Angus, Hereford). (For further information visit www.qmscotland.co.uk.)

Roast gravy can be made when the joint is cooked and removed from the roasting tray (see recipe 2). Serve the slices moistened with a little gravy

Serve with Yorkshire pudding (recipe 42) (allowing 25 g flour per portion) and garnish with watercress. Serve sauceboats of gravy and horseradish sauce separately.

HEALTHY EATING TIP
• Use an unsaturated vegetable oil (e.g. sunflower).
• Make sure the fat is hot so that less will be absorbed during roasting – the beef will produce additional fat as it roasts.

Variations
Some roughly chopped onion, carrot and celery can be added to the roasting tray approximately 30 minutes before the joint is cooked to give additional flavour to the gravy.

42 Yorkshire pudding

	4 portions	10 portions
flour	85 g	215 g
eggs	2	5
milk	85 ml	215 ml
water	40 ml	100 ml
dripping or oil	20 g	50 g

1 Place the flour and eggs into a mixing bowl and mix to a smooth paste.
2 Gradually add the milk and water, and place in the refrigerator for 1 hour. Pre-heat the oven to 190°C.
3 Heat the pudding trays in the oven with a little dripping or oil in each well.
4 Carefully ladle the mixture in, up to about two-thirds full.
5 Place in the oven and slowly close the door (if you have a glass-fronted door it will be easy to monitor progress; if not, after about 30 minutes check the puddings). The myth about opening the door during cooking has an element of truth in it – however, it is slamming and the speed at which the door is opened that have most effect, so have just a small, careful peek to check for doneness.
6 For the last 10 minutes of cooking, invert the puddings (take out and turn upside down in the tray) to dry out the base.
7 Serve immediately.

43 Horseradish sauce (sauce raifort)

	4 portions	10 portions
horseradish, grated	25–30 g	60–85 g
cream, lightly whipped	120 ml	300 ml
vinegar or lemon juice	1 tbsp	2½ tbsp
salt, pepper		

1 Wash, peel and rewash the horseradish.
2 Grate finely and mix all the ingredients together. Season to taste.

HEALTHY EATING TIP
• Add the minimum amount of salt.
• Use crème fraiche in place of cream.

44 Slow-roast beef with tarragon and caper sauce

Cal 2050 KJ	Cal 490 kcal	Fat 25.1 g	Sat Fat 7.1 g	Carb 5.2 g	Sugar 4.4 g	Protein 62.4 g	Fibre 0.3 g	Salt 2.2 g

	4 portions	10 portions
rump hearts, tafelspitz or topside	1 kg	2½ kg
olive oil		
salt, pepper		
Sauce		
tarragon	2 tbsp	5 tbsp
horseradish sauce	2 tsp	5 tsp
Dijon mustard	1 tbsp	5 tbsp
lemon	½	1½
Greek yoghurt	200 g	500 g
capers	2 tbsp	5 tbsp

1 Rub the beef with the olive oil and season.
2 Brown all over in a hot frying pan.
3 Place in a roasting try in an oven at 80°C for approximately 3½ hours.
4 For the sauce, combine all the ingredients together, mixing well.
5 Carve the beef and serve with the sauce.

Note: This is a very simple, quick sauce to make.

45 Five-bone rib of beef with mushroom sauce

	Serves up to 18
five-bone rib of beef	
salt, pepper	
Sauce	
mushrooms, sliced	500 g
butter	75 g
garlic cloves, crushed and chopped	3
flour	25 g
dry white wine	500 ml
double cream	200 ml
Parmesan, grated	1 tbsp

1 Place the beef in a suitable roasting tin, season, place in the oven and cook as required – approx. 15 minutes per 400 g at 250°C.
2 Remove, cover with aluminium foil and allow to rest.
3 Sauté the mushrooms in butter until soft. Add the garlic and cook for 1 minute.
4 Add the flour and cook for a further minute, mixing well.
5 Add the wine and bring slowly to the boil. Lower the heat and simmer for approximately 10 minutes, stirring occasionally.
6 Stir in the cream and Parmesan just prior to serving. Serve with the beef.

Variations
Alternatively use a chicken velouté, flavoured with white wine garnished with sliced mushrooms and finished with cream.

46 Chateaubriand with Roquefort butter

Cal	Cal	Fat	Sat Fat	Carb	Sugar	Protein	Fibre	Salt
2368 KJ	566 kcal	43.3 g	19.9 g	0.0 g	0.0 g	44.0 g	0.0 g	0.6 g

	2–3 portions
olive oil	
1 chateaubriand	500 g
salt, pepper	
Roquefort cheese	25 g
unsalted butter	40 g
ground black pepper	½ tsp

1 Heat the olive oil in a hot frying pan and brown the chateaubriand all over.

2 Season the chateaubriand and place in the oven at 190°C; the timing depends on the degree of cooking required.
3 Remove from oven, allow to rest, then carve into thick slices.
4 Mash together the Roquefort cheese, butter and black pepper. Form into a roll using aluminium foil or cling film. Refrigerate.
5 Place a slice of Roquefort and butter on each slice of chateaubriand. Serve with deep-fried potatoes and a tossed green salad.

47 Slow-cooked sirloin, lyonnaise onions, carrot purée

For the beef

	4 portions	10 portions
salt, pepper		
sirloin, denuded, with fat tied back on	1–1.2 kg	2½ kg
oil	50 ml	125 ml
clove garlic, sliced	1	2
sprig thyme	1	1
bay leaf	2	5
jus de viande	150 ml	375 ml

For the lyonnaise onions

	4 portions	10 portions
onions	2	5
pinch of salt		
knob of butter		

For the carrot purée

	4 portions	10 portions
medium carrots	10	30
star anise	1	2

For the beef

1 Pre-heat the oven to 180°C. Season the beef and heat the oil in the pan. Add the garlic, thyme, bay leaf and beef.
2 Place the beef in the oven for 15 minutes. Remove, then turn the oven down to 69°C. When this new temperature has been reached, return the beef to the oven for a further 1 hour 10 minutes, depending on the thickness. The core temperature should be 60°C; use a probe to check this.

For the lyonnaise onions

1 Finely slice the onions and put them into a large induction pan while cold.
2 Put on heat number 5 on induction.
3 Season.
4 When they are starting to colour, turn down to 15 and bring down for approximately 2 hours.
5 Finish the butter in a risotto pan on the stove.

For the carrot purée

1 Peel the carrots and juice three-quarters of them into a small pan.
2 Cut the remaining carrots into evenly sliced 1 cm pieces and place into the carrot juice.
3 Boil the carrots, making sure to scrape down the sides of the pan.
4 For the last 8 minutes of cooking, before all the liquid has completely evaporated, drop in the star anise.
5 Remove the pod and then blitz the purée for 7 minutes; pass through a chinois and chill.

To finish

1 While the beef is cooking make the carrot purée and the lyonnaise onions and keep warm.
2 When the beef is cooked, remove from the oven and carve equally. Place a portion of carrot purée and lyonnaise onions on each plate. Top with the beef and pour over the jus de viande; garnish with sprigs of chervil and serve.

Note: Although adopting the same slow-cooking method as in recipe 44, a slightly higher temperature is used here initially as the collagen content of the sirloin is a little higher.

Grilling

Figure 8.15 ✎ Grilling steak

Degrees of cooking grilled meats

- Very rare (or blue) – cooked over a fierce heat for a few seconds on each side.
- Rare – the cooked meat has a reddish tinge.
- Medium – the cooked meat is slightly pinkish.
- Well done – thoroughly cooked with no sign of pinkness.

Testing whether grilled meat is cooked

Using a temperature probe
When using a temperature probe, insert it into the part of the joint that was thickest before the food was placed in the oven. The internal temperature reached should be as follows:

- rare – 45–50°C
- medium – 55–60°C
- well done – 75–77°C.

Without a temperature probe
Test with finger pressure: the springiness, or resilience, of the meat, together with the amount of blood issuing from it, indicates the degree to which it is cooked. This calls for experience, but if the meat is placed on a plate and tested, then the more underdone the steak the greater the springiness and the more blood will be shown on the plate.

48 Grilled beef

Cal 706 KJ	Cal 168 kcal	Fat 6.0 g	Sat Fat 2.7 g	Carb 0.0 g	Sugar 0.0 g	Protein 28.6 g	Fibre 0.0 g	*

Approximate weight per portion: 100–150 g. (In many establishments these weights will be exceeded.)

* 1 portion (100 g cooked weight)

The following cuts may be cooked in this way:

- rump steak
- point steak
- double fillet steak (chateaubriand)
- fillet steak
- tournedos
- porterhouse or T-bone steak (see **page 266**)
- sirloin steak (entrecôte)
- double sirloin steak
- minute steak
- rib eye steak.

All steaks may be lightly seasoned with salt and pepper, and brushed on both sides with oil. Place on hot preheated greased grill bars. Turn halfway through the cooking and brush occasionally with oil. Cook to the degree ordered by the customer.

Serve garnished with watercress and deep-fried potato, and offer a suitable sauce, such as compound butter or sauce béarnaise.

To barbecue

1 **Choice of meat:** some fat is required for flavour, but not too much. Ensure size and thickness are uniform to allow even cooking. Suitable cuts include: T-bone steaks, rib steaks, double lamb chops and noisettes, well-trimmed pork cutlets and steaks.

2 **Seasoning:** add salt and pepper, brush lightly with oil before placing on the barbecue. Take care when using marinades, some may contain glucose, which burns easily. Try marinating with wine and herbs, avoid marinating oils, which may ignite and spoil the barbecue.

3 **Choice and preparation of barbecue:** gas is the preferred choice for temperature control. Allow time to preheat the barbecue: 30 minutes for gas, 1½ hours for charcoal. If cooking on charcoal always wait for the flames to go out and the embers to start glowing before commencing cooking.
   – Secure a layer of tinfoil over the barbecue.
   – Wait until the grill bars are hot or the charcoal embers glow.
   – Remove tin foil and brush the grill bars with a firm, long-handled wire brush to remove any unwanted debris.

4 **Cooking:** place the seasoned and lightly oiled meat at a 45° angle on the barbecue and seal one side. Rotate through another 45° angle, allow to cook, then turn the meat and repeat the process. Ensure the temperature is controlled and that the meat does not burn or blacken unnecessarily. Only cook as much meat as required at one time; if left for too long it will dry out and become tough. Use a meat probe to ensure the correct internal temperature is reached: 72°C for 2 minutes.

5 Serve with fresh crisp vegetables or salads and traditional barbecue dips and sauces.

Note: Burgers and sausages should be cut open, checked and cooked for longer if necessary. Barbecued food may look well cooked when it isn't. Further advice is available at www.qmsscotland.co.uk.

Sauté

49 Sirloin steak with mushroom, tomato, tarragon and white wine sauce (entrecôte chasseur)

Cal	Cal	Fat	Sat Fat	Carb	Sugar	Protein	Fibre	*
1878 KJ	449 kcal	24.5 g	13.7 g	1.5 g	1.3 g	55.7 g	0.5 g	

	4 portions	10 portions
butter or oil	50 g	125 g
sirloin steaks (approx. 150–200 g each)	4	10
salt, pepper		
dry white wine	60 ml	150 ml
chasseur sauce (see page 55)	¼ litre	625 ml
parsley, chopped		

1 Heat the butter or oil in a sauté pan.
2 Lightly season the steaks on both sides with salt and pepper.
3 Fry the steaks quickly on both sides, keeping them underdone.
4 Dress the steaks on a serving dish.
5 Pour off the fat from the pan.
6 Deglaze with the white wine. Reduce by half and strain.
7 Add the chasseur sauce, reboil, correct the seasoning.
8 Coat the steaks with the sauce.
9 Sprinkle with chopped parsley and serve.

HEALTHY EATING TIP
- Use little or no salt to season the steaks.
- Fry in a small amount of an unsaturated oil and drain off all excess fat after frying.
- Serve with plenty of boiled new potatoes or a jacket potato and a selection of vegetables.

* Using 175 kg steak

50 Sirloin steak with red wine sauce *(entrecôte bordelaise)*

Cal 3013 KJ	Cal 717 kcal	Fat 62.2 g	Sat Fat 21.6 g	Carb 6.0 g	Sugar 3.0 g	Protein 26.1 g	Fibre 1.4 g	*

	4 portions	10 portions
butter or oil	50 g	125 g
sirloin steaks (approx. 150–200 g each)	4	10
red wine	60 ml	150 ml
red wine sauce (see page 54)	½ litre	½ litre
parsley, chopped		

1 Heat the butter or oil in a sauté pan.
2 Lightly season the steaks on both sides with salt and pepper.
3 Fry the steaks quickly on both sides, keeping them underdone.
4 Dress the steaks on a serving dish.
5 Pour off the fat from the pan.
6 Deglaze with the red wine. Reduce by half and strain.
7 Add the red wine sauce, reboil and correct the seasoning.
8 Coat the steaks with the sauce.
9 Sprinkle with chopped parsley and serve.

Note: Traditionally, two slices of beef bone marrow, poached in stock for 2–3 minutes, would be placed on each steak.

HEALTHY EATING TIP
• Use little or no salt to season the steaks.
• Fry in a small amount of an unsaturated oil and drain off all excess fat after frying.
• Serve with plenty of boiled new potatoes or a jacket potato and a selection of vegetables.

* Using sunflower oil and 150 g raw steak per portion. Using sunflower oil and 200 g raw steak per portion provides: 3584 kJ/853 kcal Energy; 73.6 g Fat; 26.2 g Sat Fat; 6.0 g Carb; 3.0 g Sugar; 34.4 g Protein; 1.4 g Fibre

51 Tournedos

1 Lightly season and shallow-fry on both sides in a sauté pan.
2 Serve with an appropriate garnish or sauce (see Variations, below).

Note: Traditionally tournedos is cooked underdone and served on a round croûte of bread fried in butter.

Variations
Tournedos can be served with a variety of sauces, such as chasseur, red wine or mushroom, and numerous garnishes (e.g. diced cubed potatoes, wild or cultivated mushrooms).

HEALTHY EATING TIP
• Use little or no salt to season the steaks.
• Fry in a small amount of an unsaturated oil and drain off all excess fat after frying.
• Serve with plenty of boiled new potatoes or a jacket potato and a selection of vegetables.

52 Beef stroganoff (sauté de boeuf stroganoff)

Cal	Cal	Fat	Sat Fat	Carb	Sugar	Protein	Fibre	*
1364 KJ	325 kcal	23.7 g	7.9 g	1.7 g	1.7 g	21.2 g	0.3 g	

	4 portions	10 portions
fillet of beef (tail end)	400 g	1½ kg
butter, margarine or oil	50 g	125 g
salt, pepper		
shallots, finely chopped	25 g	60 g
dry white wine	125 ml	300 ml
cream	125 ml	300 ml
lemon, juice of	¼	½
parsley, chopped		

1 Cut the meat into strips approximately 1 × 5 cm.
2 Place the butter in a sauteuse over a fierce heat.
3 Add the beef strips, lightly season with salt and pepper, and allow to cook rapidly for a few seconds. The beef should be brown but underdone.
4 Drain the beef into a colander. Pour the butter back into the pan.

5 Add the shallots, cover with a lid and allow to cook gently until tender.
6 Drain off the fat, add the wine and reduce to one-third.
7 Add the cream and reduce by a quarter.
8 Add the lemon juice and the beef strips; do not reboil. Correct the seasoning.
9 Serve lightly sprinkled with chopped parsley. Accompany with pilaff rice (see page 162).

HEALTHY EATING TIP
• Use little or no salt to season the steaks.
• Fry in a small amount of an unsaturated oil and drain off all excess fat after frying.
• Serve with a large portion of rice and a salad.

* Using sunflower oil

53 Peppered fillet steaks with brandy cream sauce

	4 portions	10 portions
black peppercorns	2 tbsp	5 tbsp
fillet steaks	4	10
olive oil	2 tbsp	5 tbsp
brandy	3 tbsp	7 tbsp
double cream	150 ml	375 ml
Worcester sauce	1 tbsp	2½ tbsp
salt, pepper		

1 Crush the peppercorns well and press into the steaks.
2 Shallow-fry the steaks in the oil to the required degree of cooking. Remove and deglaze the pan with the brandy. Ignite and reduce slightly.
3 Add the cream and Worcester sauce. Bring to the boil.
4 Season. Serve the steaks masked with the sauce, accompanied by a suitable potato and vegetable or a tossed green salad.

Boil

54 Boiled silverside, carrots and dumplings

Cal	Cal	Fat	Sat Fat	Carb	Sugar	Protein	Fibre
1068 KJ	254 kcal	10.1 g	4.6 g	15.5 g	5.5 g	26.3 g	2.6 g

	4 portions	10 portions
silverside, pre-soaked in brine (recipe 40)	400 g	1¼ kg
onions	200 g	500 g
carrots	200 g	500 g
suet paste (see page 634)	100 g	250 g

1 Soak the meat in cold water for 1–2 hours to remove excess brine.
2 Place in a saucepan and cover with cold water, bring to the boil, skim and simmer for 45 minutes.
3 Add the whole prepared onions and carrots and simmer until cooked.
4 Divide the suet paste into even pieces and lightly mould into balls.
5 Add the dumplings and simmer for a further 15–20 minutes.
6 Serve by carving the meat across the grain, garnish with carrots, onions and dumplings, and moisten with a little of the cooking liquor.

Note: It is usual to cook a large joint of silverside (approximately 6 kg), in which case soak it overnight and allow 25 minutes per ½ kg plus 25 minutes.

HEALTHY EATING TIP
- Adding carrots, onions, boiled potatoes and a green vegetable will give a healthy balance.

Variations
- Herbs can be added to the dumplings.
- Boiled brisket and tongue can be served with the silverside.
- French-style boiled beef is prepared using unsalted thin flank or brisket with onions, carrots, leeks, celery, cabbage and a bouquet garni, all cooked and served together accompanied with pickled gherkins and coarse salt.

Stew

55 Sauté of beef (ragoût) (sauté de boeuf)

This term is often applied to a brown beef stew, and it will be found that the word 'sauté' in this case is used instead of the word 'ragoût'. Alternatively, a sauté may be made using first-class meat (e.g. fillet). The meat is then sautéed quickly and served in a finished sauce; this would be a typical à la carte dish.

56 Brown beef stew *(ragoût de boeuf)*

Cal 907 KJ	Cal 216 kcal	Fat 11.0 g	Sat Fat 2.9 g	Carb 7.7 g	Sugar 2.5 g	Protein 21.9 g	Fibre 1.0 g	*

	4 portions	10 portions
prepared stewing beef	400 g	1¼ kg
dripping or oil	25 g	60 g
onions	75 g	180 g
carrots	75 g	180 g
flour (white or wholemeal)	25 g	60 g
tomato purée	1 tbsp	2½ tbsp
brown stock	750 ml	2¼ litre
bouquet garni		
clove of garlic (optional)	1	2
salt, pepper		
parsley, chopped		

1 Remove excess sinew and fat from the beef.
2 Cut into 2 cm pieces.
3 Fry quickly in hot fat until lightly browned.
4 Add the roughly cut onion and carrot, and continue frying to a golden colour.
5 Add the flour and mix in; singe in the oven or brown on top of the stove for a few minutes, or use previously browned flour.
6 Add the tomato purée and stir in with a wooden spoon.
7 Mix in the stock, bring to the boil and skim.
8 Add the bouquet garni and garlic (if required), season and cover with a lid; simmer gently until cooked, preferably in the oven, for approximately 1½–2 hours.
9 When cooked place the meat into a clean pan.
10 Correct the seasoning of the sauce and pass on to the meat.
11 Serve with chopped parsley sprinkled on top of the meat.

HEALTHY EATING TIP

- Trim as much fat as possible from the raw beef and fry in a small amount of an unsaturated oil.
- Keep added salt to a minimum.
- Add a cooked pulse bean, a jacket potato and green vegetables to proportionally reduce the overall fat content.

Variations
Variations include:
- add a cooked pulse bean (e.g. butter, haricot, flageolet)
- add lightly sautéed mushrooms, wild or cultivated, once sauce is strained
- glazed vegetables can be added as a garnish.

* Using sunflower oil

57 Boeuf bourguignonne

	4 portions	10 portions
Beef		
beef shin pre-soaked in red wine (see below) for 12 hours	600 g	1½ kg
olive oil	50 ml	125 ml
bottle of inexpensive red Bordeaux wine	1	2
onion	100 g	250 g
carrot	100 g	250 g
celery sticks	75 g	180 g
leek	100 g	250 g
cloves of garlic	2	5
sprig fresh thyme	1	2
bay leaf	1	2
seasoning		
veal/brown stock to cover		
Garnish		
button onions, cooked	12 (150 g)	30 (300 g)
cooked bacon lardons	150 g	300 g
button mushrooms, cooked	12 (150 g)	30 (150 g)
parsley, chopped	2 tsp	5 tsp
To finish		
mashed potato	300 g	750 g
washed, picked spinach	300 g	750 g
cooked green beans	250 g	625 g

1 Pre-heat the oven to 180°C.
2 Trim the beef shin of all fat and sinew, and cut into 2½ cm-thick rondelles.
3 Heat a little oil in a thick-bottomed pan and seal/brown the shin. Place in a large ovenproof dish.
4 Meanwhile, reduce the red wine by half.
5 Peel and trim the vegetables as appropriate, then add them to the pan that the beef has just come out of and gently brown the edges. Then place this, along with the garlic and herbs, in the ovenproof dish with the meat.

6 Add the reduced red wine to the casserole, then pour in enough stock to cover the meat and vegetables. Bring to the boil, then cook in the oven pre-heated to 180°C for 40 minutes; after that, turn the oven down to 90–95°C and cook for a further 4 hours until tender.
7 Remove from the oven and allow the meat to cool in the liquor. When cold, remove any fat. Reheat gently at the same temperature to serve.
8 Heat the garnish elements separately and sprinkle over each portion. Serve with a mound of mashed potato, wilted spinach and buttered haricots verts. Finish the whole dish with chopped parsley.

Note: Another classic. Other joints of beef can be used here: beef or veal cheek can be used, reducing the time for the veal, or modernise the dish by using the slow-cooked fillet preparation and serving the same garnish.

Figure 5.16   Boeuf bourguignonne

58 Curried beef *(kari de boeuf)*

1 Proceed as for curried lamb (recipe 25), using 500 g stewing beef.
2 Adjust cooking times until meat is tender.

HEALTHY EATING TIP

- Trim off as much fat as possible before frying and drain all surplus fat after frying.
- Use a minimum amount of salt to season the meat.
- Skim all fat from the finished dish and add low-fat yoghurt.
- Serve with plenty of rice, chapatis and dhal.

59 Beef curry with coconut and ginger

Cal 1933 KJ	Cal 462 kcal	Fat 18.6 g	Sat Fat 4.3 g	Carb 22.4 g	Sugar 11.0 g	Protein 54.8 g	Fibre 3.0 g	Salt 2.2 g	*

	4 portions	10 portions
oil	4 tbsp	10 tbsp
onions, finely chopped	2	5
garlic, crushed and chopped	3	7
fresh ginger, grated	2 g	5 g
green chillies, chopped	2	5
curry powder, Madras	3 tsp	7 tsp
cumin	1 tsp	2½ tsp
cardamom pods	10	25
topside or chuck steak, diced	880 g	2.2 kg
flour	40 g	100 g
coconut milk	400 ml	1 litre
tomato purée	2 tbsp	5 tbsp
brown stock	300 ml	750 ml
salt, pepper		

1 Heat half the oil in a suitable pan.
2 Add the onions and fry gently until lightly brown.
3 Add the garlic, ginger and chilli, and cook for approximately 2 minutes, then add the curry powder, cumin and cardamom pods.
4 Heat the remaining oil in the pan. Pass the beef through the flour. Sear the beef in the oil. Add the cooked ingredients to the pan.
5 Add the coconut milk, tomato purée and stock. Season. Bring to the boil. Place in an ovenproof dish and cook in the oven for 2–3 hours at 150°C, stirring occasionally.
6 Serve with pilaff rice and naan bread.

60 Provençal-style stew

	4 portions	10 portions
trimmed beef rib	1½ kg	3¾ kg
red wine	500 ml	1¼ litres
parsley, coarsely chopped	1 tbsp	2½ tbsp
garlic cloves, crushed and chopped	5	12
thyme	4 sprigs	10 sprigs
orange peel, finely chopped	2 strips	5 strips
celery, chopped	50 g	125 g
olive oil	3 tbsp	7 tbsp
streaky bacon, finely diced	125 g	310 g
onions, finely chopped	100 g	250 g
beef stock	300 ml	750 ml
salt, pepper		
brandy	2 tbsp	5 tbsp
black olives, stoned	100 g	250 g

1 Marinade the beef with the wine, parsley, garlic, half the thyme, half the orange peel and one celery stick. Refrigerate overnight.
2 Remove the beef from the marinade, drain and dry. Strain the marinade, reserving the liquid. Discard the herbs and vegetables.
3 Heat 2 tbsp of olive oil in a suitable pan, and gently fry the lardons of bacon, onions, remaining garlic and celery until lightly coloured. Remove from the pan.
4 Add the remaining oil to the pan, quickly fry the beef on all sides until golden brown.
5 Return the vegetables to the pan with the beef, add the liquid and the stock. Season and bring to boil.
6 Add the brandy, the remaining thyme and orange peel and the olives. Cover with a lid. Cook in the oven for 3½–4 hours at 140°C.
7 Remove the beef and skim the fat from the cooking liquor. Correct seasoning
8 Portion the beef and serve with the cooking liquor.
9 Serve with mashed potatoes and olive oil separately.

61 Goulash (Hungarian) (goulash de boeuf)

Cal	Cal	Fat	Sat Fat	Carb	Sugar	Protein	Fibre
1625 KJ	389 kcal	20.4 g	6.0 g	26.1 g	3.9 g	26.9 g	1.7 g

	4 portions	10 portions
prepared stewing beef	400 g	1¼ kg
lard or oil	35 g	100 g
onions, chopped	100 g	250 g
flour	25 g	60 g
paprika	10–25 g	25–60 g
tomato purée	25 g	60 g
stock or water	750 ml approx.	2 litres approx.
turned potatoes or small new potatoes	8	20
choux paste (see recipe 62)	125 ml	300 ml

1 Remove excess fat from the beef. Cut into 2 cm square pieces.
2 Season and fry in the hot fat until slightly coloured. Add the chopped onion.
3 Cover with a lid and sweat gently for 3 or 4 minutes.
4 Add the flour and paprika, and mix in with a wooden spoon.
5 Cook out in the oven or on top of the stove. Add the tomato purée, mix in.
6 Gradually add the stock, stir to the boil, skim, season and cover.
7 Allow to simmer, preferably in the oven, for approximately 1½–2 hours until the meat is tender.

HEALTHY EATING TIP

- Trim off as much fat as possible before frying and drain all surplus fat after frying.
- Use the minimum amount of salt to season the meat.
- Skim all fat from the finished sauce.
- Serve with a large side salad.

8 Add the potatoes and check that they are covered with the sauce. (Add more stock if required.)
9 Re-cover with the lid and cook gently until the potatoes are cooked.
10 Skim, and correct the seasoning and consistency. A little cream or yoghurt may be added at the last moment.
11 Serve sprinkled with a few gnocchis made from choux paste (see recipe 62), reheated in hot salted water or lightly tossed in butter or margarine.

62 Choux paste for gnocchi (for use with stew)

Sufficient for 8 portions as a garnish

1 Prepare the choux paste following the recipe on page 635, omitting the sugar.
2 Place the mixture into a piping bag with a ½ cm or 1 cm plain tube.
3 Pipe into a shallow pan of gently simmering salted water, cutting the mixture into 2 cm lengths with a small knife, dipping the knife into the water frequently to prevent sticking.
4 Poach very gently for approximately 10 minutes. If not required at once lift out carefully into cold water and, when required, reheat in hot salted water.

63 Glazed vegetables (for use with stew)

1 To cook glazed carrots and turnips, turn or cut into even shapes.
2 Barely cover with water in separate thick-bottomed pans and add 25–50 g butter or margarine per ½ kg of vegetables.
3 Season very lightly and allow to cook fairly quickly so as to evaporate the water.
4 Check that the vegetables are cooked, if not add a little more water; then toss over a quick fire to give a glossy appearance and a little colour.
5 Care should be taken with turnips as they may break up easily.
6 Button mushrooms, if of good quality, need not be peeled, but a slice should be removed from the base of the stalk. Wash well, then use whole, halved, quartered or turned, depending on their size. They may be coloured first in the oil, butter or margarine, then cooked in a little stock and butter and seasoned lightly; cover with a lid and cook for a few minutes only.

Note: Glazed carrots, turnips, button onions, peas, diamonds of French beans and mushrooms may be used. The vegetables are cooked separately and they may be mixed in, arranged in groups or sprinkled on top of the stew.

HEALTHY EATING TIP
• Keep the amount of butter used to a minimum so that only a few grams per portion remain.
• Use little or no salt.

Bake

64 Steak pie

Cal 1442 KJ	Cal 346 kcal	Fat 22.2 g	Sat Fat 2.9 g	Carb 13.6 g	Sugar 1.8 g	Protein 24.3 g	Fibre 0.4 g	*

	4 portions	10 portions
prepared stewing beef (chuck steak)	400 g	1½ kg
oil or fat	50 ml	125 ml
onion, chopped (optional)	100 g	250 g
few drops Worcester sauce		
parsley, chopped	1 tsp	3 tsp
water, stock, red wine or dark beer	125 ml	300 ml
salt, pepper		
cornflour	10 g	25 g
short, puff or rough puff pastry (see pages 611–612 and 624–626)	100 g	250 g

1 Cut the meat into 2 cm strips then cut into squares.
2 Heat the oil in a frying pan until smoking, add the meat and quickly brown on all sides.
3 Drain the meat off in a colander.
4 Lightly fry the onion.
5 Place the meat, onion, Worcester sauce, parsley and the liquid in a pan, season lightly with salt and pepper.
6 Bring to the boil, skim, then allow to simmer gently until the meat is tender.
7 Dilute the cornflour with a little water, stir into the simmering mixture, reboil and correct seasoning.

8 Place the mixture into a pie dish and allow to cool.
9 Cover with the pastry, eggwash and bake at 200°C for approximately 30–45 minutes.

Note: 25–50 per cent wholemeal flour may be used in the pastry in place of plain flour.

HEALTHY EATING TIP

• Use little or no salt as the Worcester sauce contains salt.
• Fry in a small amount of an unsaturated oil and drain off all excess fat after frying.
• There will be less fat in the dish if short paste is used.
• Serve with boiled potatoes and plenty of vegetables.

Variations
Variations include:
• adding 50–100 g ox or sheep's kidneys with skin and gristle removed and cut into neat pieces
• adding 50–100 g sliced or quartered mushrooms
• adding 1 heaped tsp tomato purée and some mixed herbs
• in place of cornflour the meat can be tossed in flour before frying off.

* Using puff pastry (McCance data)

Steam

65 Steak pudding

Cal 1369 KJ	Cal 326 kcal	Fat 17.3 g	Sat Fat 7.8 g	Carb 20.6 g	Sugar 1.0 g	Protein 23.0 g	Fibre 1.1 g

	4 portions	10 portions
suet paste (see page 634)	200 g	500 g
prepared stewing beef (chuck steak)	400 g	1½ kg
Worcester sauce		
parsley, chopped	1 tsp	2½ tsp
salt, pepper		
onion, chopped (optional)	50–100 g	200 g
water	125 ml approx.	300 ml approx.

1 Line a greased ½ litre basin with three-quarters of the suet paste and retain one-quarter for the top.
2 Mix all the other ingredients, except the water, together.
3 Place in the basin with the water to within 1 cm of the top.
4 Moisten the edge of the suet paste, cover with the top and seal firmly.

5 Cover with greased greaseproof paper and also, if possible, foil or a pudding cloth tied securely with string.
6 Cook in a steamer for at least 3½ hours.
7 Serve with the paper and cloth removed, clean the basin, place on a round flat dish and fasten a napkin round the basin.

Note: Extra gravy should be served separately. If the gravy in the pudding is to be thickened, the meat can be lightly floured.

HEALTHY EATING TIP

• Use little or no salt as the Worcester sauce contains salt.
• Trim off as much fat as possible from the raw stewing beef.
• Serve with plenty of potatoes and vegetables.

Variations
Variations include:
• adding 50–100 g ox or sheep's kidneys cut in pieces with skin and gristle removed
• adding 50–100 g sliced or quartered mushrooms
• steak pudding can also be made with a cooked filling, in which case simmer the meat until cooked in brown stock with onions, parsley, Worcester sauce and seasoning; cool quickly and proceed as above, steaming for 1–1½ hours.

Braise

66 Shin of beef in stout, ale and honey

Cal	Cal	Fat	Sat Fat	Carb	Sugar	Protein	Fibre	Salt
2481 KJ	593 kcal	22.6 g	8.7 g	34.3 g	31.0 g	54.0 g	1.4 g	1.6 g

	4 portions	10 portions
shin of beef	900 g	2¼ kg
vegetable oil	1 tbsp	2½ tbsp
tomato purée	1 tbsp	2½ tbsp
pale ale	500 ml	1¼ litres
clear honey	100 g	250 g
Marinade		
onions, chopped	2	5
stout	440 ml	1100 ml
thyme	3 sprigs	7
rosemary	3 sprigs	7
parsley	3 sprigs	7
bay leaves	2	5
garlic cloves, crushed and chopped	6	15
fine sea salt	1 tsp	2½ tsp
English mustard	1 tsp	2½ tsp
black peppercorns	1 tsp	2½ tsp

1 Prepare the marinade. Mix all the ingredients together – onions, stout, thyme, rosemary, parsley, bay leaves, garlic, sea salt, English mustard, black peppercorns.
2 Place the shin of beef in the marinade and refrigerate for 8–12 hours.
3 Remove the shin from the marinade, dry and reserve the marinade.
4 Heat the oil in a suitable pan. Add the shin and brown all over on all sides. Pour the marinade over the shin. Add the tomato purée and the ale. Bring to the boil. Cover with a lid and cook in the oven at 140°C for 3–3½ hours.
5 Ten minutes before the finish of the cooking, drizzle the honey over the meat. Return uncovered to the oven to glaze.
6 Remove from the oven, carve the shin of beef and serve with the sauce.
7 Serve with mashed potatoes and glazed baby carrots.

67 Braised steaks

Cal 990 KJ	Cal 237 kcal	Fat 12.1 g	Sat Fat 3.2 g	Carb 9.3 g	Sugar 3.8 g	Protein 23.1 g	Fibre 1.1 g	*

	4 portions	10 portions
stewing beef	400 g	1¼ kg
dripping or oil	25 g	60 g
onions	75 g	180 g
carrots	75 g	180 g
flour, browned in the oven	25 g	60 g
tomato purée	25 g	60 g
brown stock	750 ml	2 litres
bouquet garni		
clove of garlic (optional)	1	2–3
salt, pepper		
parsley, chopped		

1 Remove excess sinew and fat from the beef.
2 Cut into ½–1 cm thick steaks.
3 Fry quickly in hot fat until lightly browned.
4 Add the roughly cut onion and carrot and continue frying to a golden colour. Mix in the flour.
5 Add the tomato purée and stir in with a wooden spoon.
6 Mix in the stock, bring to the boil and skim.

7 Add the bouquet garni and garlic (if desired), season and cover with a lid; simmer gently until cooked, preferably in the oven, for approximately 1½–2 hours.
8 When cooked place the meat into a clean pan.
9 Correct the sauce and pass on to the meat.
10 Serve lightly sprinkled with chopped parsley.

Note: Braised steaks may be garnished with vegetables (turned or cut in neat, even pieces) or a pasta (e.g. noodles).

HEALTHY EATING TIP

- Trim off as much fat as possible before frying and drain off all surplus fat after frying.
- Use a minimum amount of salt to season the meat.
- Skim all fat from the finished sauce.
- Serve with plenty of potatoes and vegetables.

* Using oil and white flour

68 Braised steak and dumplings

1 Prepare 100 g suet paste (see page 634) and make two small dumplings per portion.
2 Add the dumplings to the steak (recipe 67) after the sauce has been strained and simmer gently for 20 minutes.

69 Carbonnade of beef (Belgian) (*carbonnade de boeuf*)

Cal 1037 KJ	Cal 247 kcal	Fat 9.1 g	Sat Fat 1.8 g	Carb 14.0 g	Sugar 8.1 g	Protein 24.7 g	Fibre 1.1 g

	4 portions	10 portions
lean beef (topside)	400 g	1¼ kg
salt, pepper		
flour (white or wholemeal)	25 g	60 g
dripping or oil	25 g	60 g
onions, sliced	200 g	500 g
beer	250 ml	625 ml
caster sugar	10 g	25 g
tomato purée	25 g	60 g
brown stock		

1 Cut the meat into thin slices.
2 Season with salt and pepper and pass through the flour.
3 Quickly colour on both sides in hot fat and place in a casserole.
4 Fry the onions to a light brown colour. Add to the meat.

5 Add the beer, sugar and tomato purée and sufficient brown stock to cover the meat.
6 Cover with a tight-fitting lid and simmer gently in a moderate oven at 110–125°C until the meat is tender (approx. 2 hours).
7 Skim, correct the seasoning and serve.

HEALTHY EATING TIP
- Trim off as much fat as possible before frying and drain off all surplus fat after frying.
- Use the minimum amount of salt to season the meat.
- Skim all fat from the finished sauce.
- Serve with plenty of potatoes and vegetables.

70 Braised beef (*boeuf braisé*)

Cal 1380 KJ	Cal 329 kcal	Fat 14.3 g	Sat Fat 3.3 g	Carb 26.8 g	Sugar 4.7 g	Protein 24.7 g	Fibre 2.4 g	*

	4 portions	10 portions
lean beef (topside or thick flank)	400 g	1¼ kg
dripping or oil	25 g	60 g
onions	100 g	250 g
carrots	100 g	250 g
brown stock	500 ml	1¼ litre
salt, pepper		
bouquet garni		
tomato purée	25 g	60 g
demi-glace or jus-lié	250 ml	625 ml

Method 1
1 Trim and tie the joint securely.
2 Season and colour quickly on all sides in hot fat to seal the pores.
3 Place into a small braising pan (any pan with a tight-fitting lid that may be placed in the oven) or in a casserole.
4 Place the joint on the lightly fried, sliced vegetables.
5 Add the stock, which should come two-thirds of the way up the meat, and season lightly.

6 Add the bouquet garni and tomato purée and, if available, add a few mushroom trimmings.
7 Bring to the boil, skim and cover with a lid; cook in a moderate oven at 110–125°C.
8 After approximately 1½ hours' cooking, remove the meat.
9 Add the demi-glace or jus-lié, reboil, skim and strain.
10 Replace the meat; do not cover, but baste frequently and continue cooking for approximately 2–2½ hours in all. Braised beef should be well cooked (approximately 35 minutes per ½ kg plus 35 minutes). To test if cooked, pierce with a trussing needle, which should penetrate the meat easily and there should be no sign of blood.
11 Remove the joint and correct the colour, seasoning and consistency of the sauce.
12 To serve: remove the string and carve slices across the grain. Pour some of the sauce over the slices and serve the remainder of the sauce in a sauceboat.

Method 2

As for Method 1, but use for cooking liquor either:
- jus-lié
- half brown stock or red wine and half demi-glace.

Method 3

As for Method 1, but when the joint and vegetables are browned, sprinkle with 25 g (60 g for 10 portions) flour and singe in the oven; add the tomato purée, stock and bouquet garni; season and complete the recipe.

Note: Suitable garnishes include spring vegetables or pasta (e.g. noodles, page 149). Red wine may be used in place of stock.

HEALTHY EATING TIP
- Trim off as much fat as possible before frying and drain off all surplus fat after frying.
- Use the minimum amount of salt.
- Skim all fat from the finished sauce.
- Serve with plenty of potatoes and vegetables.

* Using sunflower oil

71 Brisket braised in its own marinade

	4 portions	10 portions
brisket	1 kg	2½ kg
red wine	300 ml	750 ml
cold water	300 ml	750 ml
bay leaves	2	5
fresh thyme	2 sprigs	5 sprigs
salt, pepper		
olive oil	2 tbsp	5 tbsp
lardons of bacon	100 g	250g
butter	50 g	125g
carrots, thinly sliced	4	10
parsnips, in batons	2	5
leeks, thinly sliced	2	5
celery, thinly sliced	2 sticks	5 sticks
fennel, thinly sliced	1	2½
clove of garlic, crushed and chopped	2	5
fresh thyme, chopped	1 tsp	2½ tsp
bay leaf	1	2
beef stock	600 ml	1½ litres

1 Marinate the brisket with the red wine, cold water, bay leaves and thyme. Chill and place in a refrigerator overnight.
2 Remove from the marinade. Season.
3 Quickly brown the brisket in the oil in a suitable pan. Remove.
4 Add the lardons of bacon. Quickly fry then drain.
5 Add the butter to the pan. Add the remaining ingredients, except the stock. Cook gently for a few minutes until lightly browned.
6 Place the brisket and bacon back in the pan. Add the marinade and stock.
7 Cover and place in an oven for approximately 3–3½ hours cooking at 140°C.
8 When cooked, remove the brisket. Wrap in foil and allow to rest for up to an hour.
9 Skim the excess fat from the cooking liquor and strain. Boil and slightly reduce. Check the seasoning.
10 Carve the brisket in thick slices. Serve with the vegetables and sauce.

72 Beef olives (paupiettes de boeuf)

Cal 1134 KJ	Cal 271 kcal	Fat 13.1 g	Sat Fat 2.6 g	Carb 13.6 g	Sugar 5.0 g	Protein 25.4 g	Fibre 1.5 g	*

	4 portions	10 portions
stuffing (see recipe 73)	50 g	125 g
lean beef (topside)	400 g	1¼ kg
salt, pepper		
dripping or oil	35 g	100 g
carrot	100 g	250 g
onion	100 g	250 g
flour, browned in the oven	25 g	60 g
tomato purée	25 g	60 g
brown stock	500–750 ml	1¼–1½ litres
bouquet garni		

1 Prepare the stuffing (recipe 73).
2 Cut the meat into thin slices across the grain and bat out.
3 Trim to approximately 10 x 8 cm, chop the trimmings finely and add to the stuffing.
4 Season the slices of meat lightly with salt and pepper, and spread a quarter of the stuffing down the centre of each slice.
5 Roll up neatly and secure with string.
6 Fry off the meat to a light-brown colour, add the vegetables and continue cooking to a golden colour.

7 Drain off the fat into a clean pan and make up to 25 g fat if there is not enough (increase the amount for 10 portions). Mix in the flour.
8 Mix in the tomato purée, cool and then mix in the boiling stock.
9 Bring to the boil, skim, season and pour on to the meat.
10 Add the bouquet garni.
11 Cover and simmer gently, preferably in the oven, for approximately 1½–2 hours.
12 Remove the string from the meat.
13 Skim, correct the sauce and pass on to the meat.

HEALTHY EATING TIP

Use little or no salt to season the steaks.
• Fry in a small amount of an unsaturated oil and drain off all excess fat after frying.
• Serve with a large portion of potatoes and vegetables

* Using 625 ml stock

73 Stuffing

	4 portions	10 portions
white or wholemeal breadcrumbs	50 g	125 g
parsley, chopped	1 tsp	3 tsp
pinch of thyme		
egg, to bind	approx. ½	1
prepared chopped suet	5 g	25 g
sweated onion, finely chopped	25 g	60 g
salt, pepper		

1 Mix all the ingredients together with the available chopped meat trimmings.

Variations
Other stuffings may be used – for example, sausage meat, various herbs, duxelle. Veal, pork or chicken olives can be prepared and cooked using this method.

HEALTHY EATING TIP
• Use the minimum amount of salt.

Offal

74 Tripe and onions

Cal 430 KJ	Cal 102 kcal	Fat 1.7 g	Sat Fat 0.9 g	Carb 12.6 g	Sugar 5.7 g	Protein 9.9 g	Fibre 0.7 g	*

	4 portions	10 portions
tripe	400 g	1½ kg
milk and water	500 ml	1½ litre
onions, sliced	200 g	500 g
salt, pepper		
flour or cornflour	25 g	60 g

1 Wash the tripe well. Cut into neat 5 cm squares.
2 Blanch and refresh.
3 Cook the tripe in the milk and water with the onions.
4 Season and simmer for 1½–2 hours.
5 Gradually add the diluted flour or cornflour, stir with a wooden spoon to the boil.
6 Simmer for 5–10 minutes, correct the seasoning and serve.

Note: An alternative thickening is 125 ml (310 ml for 10 portions) of béchamel in place of the cornflour and milk.

HEALTHY EATING TIP
- Keep the added salt to a minimum.
- Thicken with cornflour and semi-skimmed milk for a lower-fat dish.

* *Using semi-skimmed milk and water 50/50*

75 Ox tongue *(langue de boeuf)*

1 Ox tongues are usually pickled in brine, so wash and place in cold water, bring to the boil, skim and simmer for 3–4 hours.
2 Cool slightly, then peel off the skin and trim off the root.

3 Secure into a neat shape on a board, in a wooden frame, or in a mould if required for cold buffet display.

Note: Unsalted ox tongues may also be braised whole.

76 Braised ox tongue with Madeira sauce *(langue de boeuf braisé au Madère)*

1 Cut the cooked tongue in 3 mm thick slices and arrange neatly in an entrée dish.
2 Sauce over with Madeira sauce (see page 57) and heat through slowly and thoroughly without being allowed to boil.

77 Braised ox liver and onions (foie de boeuf lyonnaise)

Cal	Cal	Fat	Sat Fat	Carb	Sugar	Protein	Fibre
1141 KJ	275 kcal	18.5 g	3.6 g	10.1 g	4.0 g	17.4 g	1.1 g

	4 portions	10 portions
liver	300 g	1 kg
flour (white or wholemeal)	25 g	60 g
salt, pepper		
dripping or oil	50 g	125 g
onions, sliced	200 g	500 g
brown stock	500 ml	1½ litres
tomato purée	25 g	60 g
bouquet garni		
clove garlic	1	2

1 Prepare the liver by removing the skin and tubes, then cut into slices.
2 Pass the sliced liver through seasoned flour.
3 Fry on both sides in hot fat. Place in a braising pan or casserole.

4 Fry the onion to a golden brown, drain and add to the liver.
5 Just cover with the stock and add the tomato purée, bouquet garni and garlic.
6 Season lightly and cover with a lid.
7 Simmer gently in the oven until tender (approx. 1½–2 hours).
8 Correct the sauce and serve.

HEALTHY EATING TIP
• Use little or no salt to season the liver.
• Fry in a small amount of an unsaturated oil and drain off all excess fat after frying.
• Serve with boiled new potatoes and plenty of vegetables.

78 Braised oxtail (ragoût de queue de boeuf)

Cal	Cal	Fat	Sat Fat	Carb	Sugar	Protein	Fibre
2481 KJ	595 kcal	38.0 g	12.0 g	12.3 g	4.7 g	51.6 g	1.4 g

	4 portions	10 portions
oxtail	1 kg	2½ kg
dripping or oil	50 g	125 g
onion	100 g	250 g
carrot	100 g	250 g
flour, browned in the oven	35 g	100 g
tomato purée	25 g	60 g
brown stock	1 litre	2½ litre
bouquet garni		
clove garlic	1	2
salt, pepper		
parsley, chopped		

1 Cut the oxtail into sections. Remove the excess fat.
2 Fry on all sides in hot fat.
3 Place in a braising pan or casserole.
4 Add the fried roughly cut onion and carrot.
5 Mix in the flour.
6 Add tomato purée, brown stock, bouquet garni and garlic, and season lightly.
7 Bring to the boil, then skim.
8 Cover with a lid and simmer in the oven until tender (approx. 3 hours).

9 Remove the cooked oxtail from the sauce, place in a clean pan.
10 Correct the sauce, pass on to the meat and reboil.
11 Serve sprinkled with chopped parsley.

Note: This is usually garnished with glazed turned or neatly cut carrots and turnips, button onions, peas and diamonds of beans. Oxtail must be very well cooked so that the meat comes away from the bone easily.

HEALTHY EATING TIP
• Keep added salt to a minimum.
• Fry in a small amount of an unsaturated oil and drain off all excess fat after frying.
• Serve with mashed potato and additional green vegetables.

Variations
Haricot oxtail can be made using the same recipe with the addition of 100 g (250 g for 10 portions) cooked haricot beans, added approximately ½ hour before the oxtail has completed cooking.

79 Oxtail with Guinness

	4 portions	10 portions
oxtail	1.2 kg	4 kg
flour, to coat		
olive oil	3 tbsp	7 tbsp
celery, cut into batons	4 sticks	10 sticks
onions, finely chopped	2	5
carrots, thinly sliced	2	5
Guinness	440 ml	1 litre
tinned tomatoes	750 g	1875 g
bay leaves	2	5
garlic cloves	6	15
salt, pepper		

1 Place the oxtail pieces through the flour.
2 Heat the oil in a suitable pan. Fry the oxtail on both sides until golden brown. Remove.
3 Heat the remaining oil in the pan. Cook the celery, onion and carrots until they begin to soften.
4 Pour on the Guinness and bring to the boil.
5 In a clean pan, layer the oxtail with the vegetable and beer mixture, tomatoes (chopped), bay leaves and garlic. Season. Top up with water or brown stock to cover the oxtail.
6 Bring to the boil. Place in an oven at 140°C and cook for 3–3½ hours.
7 When cooked, serve with potato and celeriac mash and roasted root vegetables.

Miscellaneous

80 Hamburg or Vienna steak (bitok)

Cal 681 KJ	Cal 162 kcal	Fat 6.7 g	Sat Fat 1.9 g	Carb 12.7 g	Sugar 1.0 g	Protein 13.8 g	Fibre 1.0 g

	4 portions	10 portions
onion, finely chopped	25 g	60 g
butter, margarine or oil	10 g	25 g
lean minced beef	200 g	500 g
small egg	1	2–3
breadcrumbs	100 g	250 g
cold water or milk	2 tbsp approx.	60 ml approx.

1 Cook the onion in the fat without colour, then allow to cool.
2 Add to the rest of the ingredients and mix in well.
3 Divide into even pieces and, using a little flour, make into balls, flatten and shape round.
4 Shallow-fry in hot fat on both sides, reducing the heat after the first few minutes, making certain they are cooked right through.
5 Serve with a light sauce, such as sauce piquante (page 57).

Note: The 'steaks' may be garnished with French-fried onions (page 496) and sometimes with a fried egg.

HEALTHY EATING TIP

• Use a small amount of an unsaturated oil to cook the onion and to shallow-fry the meat.
• The minced beef will produce more fat, which should be drained off.
• Serve with plenty of starchy carbohydrate and vegetables.

81 Hamburger, American style

Hamburgers – now more commonly known as burgers – were originally made using 200 g of minced beef per portion. The meat used should be pure beef with 20–25 per cent beef fat by weight. Less fat than this will result in a tough, dry hamburger. If more fat is used the hamburgers will be unpalatable, nutritionally undesirable and will shrink considerably during cooking.

The meat should be passed twice through a mincer, which helps to make for a more tender product. The minced meat should be lightly mixed and moulded into patties. Over-mixing the beef can cause toughness.

Hamburgers should not be pricked while cooking as the juices will seep out leaving a dry product.

Note: Mini burgers (one mouthful) can be served as hot snacks at receptions.

Variations

Variations in seasonings and ingredients can be added to the minced beef, but traditionally the sauces and garnishes offered are sufficient. These can include: ketchup, mustard, mayonnaise, chilli sauce, horseradish, cheese, raw onion rings, lettuce, avocado slices, bacon and various pickles and relishes; freshly fried chips and/or cut pieces of raw vegetables (e.g. carrot, celery, spring onions) can be added. The bun may be plain or seeded (sesame seeds).

Alternative fillings can include:
* *cheese* – either on its own, or added to the beef
* *egg* – a freshly fried egg, or added to the beef
* *chicken* – a freshly grilled portion of chicken, either minced or in the piece
* *fish* – a freshly grilled portion of a whole fish (cod or haddock)
* *vegetables* – a selection of freshly grilled, or fried vegetables (e.g. onions, peppers, aubergines, mushrooms).

82 Cornish pasties

Cal 1217 KJ	Cal 290 kcal	Fat 16.2 g	Sat Fat 6.0 g	Carb 29.3 g	Sugar 1.2 g	Protein 8.7 g	Fibre 1.8 g

	4 portions	10 portions
short paste (see **page 611**)	200 g	500 g
potato (raw), finely diced	100 g	250 g
raw beef, chuck or skirt, cut in thin pieces	100 g	250 g
onion or leeks, chopped	50 g	125 g
swede (raw), finely diced (optional)	50 g	125 g
eggwash		

1 Roll out the short paste to 3 mm thick and cut into rounds 12 cm in diameter.
2 Mix the remaining ingredients together, moisten with a little water and place in the rounds in piles. Eggwash the edges.
3 Fold in half and seal; flute the edge and brush with eggwash.
4 Cook in a moderate oven at 150–200°C for ½–1 hour.

5 Serve with a suitable sauce (see pages 52–64), or hot or cold as a snack.

Note: Cooked meat can be used in place of raw.

HEALTHY EATING TIP
* Use the minimum amount of salt.
* Brush a little oil over the potatoes.
* Adding baked beans, tomatoes and/or mushrooms will 'dilute' the fat from the meat.
* Serve with a large portion of vegetables.

Variations

Variations include:
* potato, onion or leek, and turnip or swede, fresh herbs
* bacon, hard-boiled eggs and leeks
* lamb, carrot and potato
* apples, cinnamon, cloves, brown sugar, cider.

Veal

Veal is obtained from good-quality carcasses weighing around 100 kg. This quality of veal is required for first-class cookery and is produced from calves slaughtered at between 12 and 24 weeks.

The ethical debate

The use of veal crates rocked the UK in a major campaign in the 1980s. Peter Roberts, founder of leading anti-factory farming group Compassion in World Farming, took a test case against the veal crate-farming monks of Storrington Priory. Veal literally became a dirty word. Consumers avoided the product en masse. Veal farms were forced to switch to more humane methods or go out of business. The campaign was finally won when the UK Government declared that the veal crate would be banned from 1990. Then, in 1994, protests against the export of live calves to veal crates on the continent resulted in the European Union agreeing to ban the veal crate and, from 2007, calves will no longer legally be kept in narrow crates.

Despite this change in the law, some people are still wary of consuming veal. However, banning veal from our shopping lists for ever could be condemning dairy calves to a worse fate – being shot at birth.

In order to keep them productive, dairy cows must take a break from milk producing and have a new calf every year. As the number of calves born to all the dairy cows in the country is so huge, there are many that are not used to replace dairy cows, as well as all the male calves that can't be used for dairy farming. Thus, ethically rearing calves for four to six months then selling them as veal allows a far more humane solution to the over-abundance of calves. The age of the animal at slaughter really shouldn't be an issue for meat-eaters either: veal calves are generally slaughtered at five or six months – precisely the same age range as pigs for pork and sheep for lamb.

There is a system of veal calf rearing that is far more extensive and humane than the Dutch crate.

The resulting product, from free-range calves that have lived unconfined, used to be known as 'bobby veal' but is now being marketed as rosé veal, in acknowledgement of the pink tinge of its meat – an indication that, as well as enjoying freedom of movement, the calf is also able to ruminate on a diet that includes some roughage.

Calves for rosé veal are now being reared under both conventional and organic systems. In the former, calves are weaned from their mother shortly after birth (like all dairy calves) but are then reared in loose stalls, in large barns open at either end to let in daylight. They live in small groups, with straw bedding and an 'ad lib' diet (accessible at all times) of both milk and cereal-based feed. They can also graze freely on their bedding. It's an indoor system, with the obvious and desirable benefits of grass underfoot and sunlight overhead. The standard of welfare depends, in the end, on the conscientiousness of the practitioner, but well-maintained indoor housing with plenty of space is at least an environment in which a group of calves can thrive and grow, and should not suffer unduly.

This alternative to crate farming not only provides tasty meat but offers one of the most constructive and humane solutions to the particularly challenging ethical problem of redundant dairy calves and, with the help of wider consumer awareness, could be the answer to putting veal back on the map.

Butchery

The average weight of English or Dutch milk-fed veal calves is 18 kg. The joints of veal are as follows (the numbers refer to those used in Figure 8.17).

1 Knuckle	4 Best end	7 Scrag
2 Leg	5 Shoulder	8 Breast
3 Loin	6 Neck end	

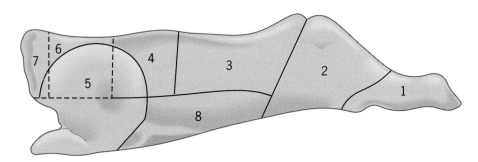

Figure 8.17 🖋 Side of veal

Table 8.7 🖋 Joints, uses and weights of veal (numbers in left-hand column refer to Figure 8.17)

Joint	Uses	Approximate weight (kg)
(1) knuckle	osso buco, sauté, stock	2
(2) leg	roasting, braising, escalopes, sauté	5
(3) loin	roasting, frying, grilling	3½
(4) best end	roasting, frying, grilling	3
(5) shoulder	braising, stewing	5
(6) neck end	stewing, sauté	2½
(7) scrag	stewing stock	1½
(8) breast	stewing, roasting	2½
kidneys	stewing (pies and puddings), sauté	–
liver	frying	–
sweetbreads	braising, frying	–
head	boiling, soup	4
brains	boiling, frying	–
bones	stock	–

Figure 8.18 🖋 Veal kidneys

Figure 8.19 🖋 Veal escalopes

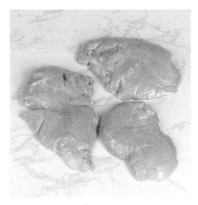

Figure 8.20 🖋 Veal sweetbreads

Order of dissection

- Remove the shoulders.
- Remove the breast.
- Take off the leg.
- Divide the loin and best end from the scrag and neck end.
- Divide the loin from the best end.

Table 8.8 ✐ Joints of the leg (see Figure 8.21)

Cuts	Weight	Proportion	Uses
cushion or nut	2¾ kg	15%	escalopes, roasting, braising, sauté
under cushion or under nut	3 kg	17%	escalopes, roasting, braising, sauté
thick flank	2½ kg	14%	escalopes, roasting, braising, sauté
knuckle (whole)	2½ kg	14%	osso buco, sauté
bones (thigh and aitch)	2½ kg	14%	stock, jus-lié, sauces
usable trimmings	2 kg	11%	pies, stewing

A haunch of veal will generally have the rump attached: the rump weighs about 2½ kg. The thick flank may also be known as a knuckle.

Corresponding joints in beef

- Cushion = topside.
- Under cushion = silverside.
- Thick flank = thick flank.

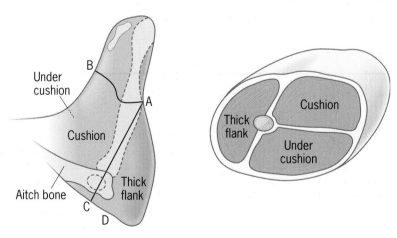

Figure 8.21 ✐ Dissection of a leg of veal

Dissecting a leg of veal

1 Remove the knuckle by dividing the knee joint (Figure 8.21: A) and cut through the meat away from the cushion line (Figure 8.21: A–B).
2 Remove the aitch bone (Figure 8.21: C) at thick end of the leg, separating it at the ball and socket joint.
3 Remove all the outside skin and fat, thus exposing the natural seams. It will now be seen that the thigh bone divides the meat into two-thirds and one-third (thick flank).
4 Stand the leg on the thick flank with point D (Figure 8.21) uppermost. Divide the cushion from the under cushion, following the natural seam, using the hand and the point of a knife. Having reached the thigh bone, remove it completely.
5 When the boned leg falls open, the three joints can easily be seen joined only by membrane. Separate and trim the cushion, removing the loose flap of meat.
6 Trim the under cushion, removing the layer of thick gristle. Separate into three small joints through the natural seams. It will be seen that one of these will correspond with the round in silverside of beef.
7 Trim the thick flank by laying it on its round side and making a cut along the length about 2½ cm deep. A seam is reached and the two trimmings can be removed.

The anticipated yield of escalopes from this size of leg would be 62½ kg – that is, 55 kg × 100 g or 73 kg × 80 g.

Preparation of the joints and cuts of veal

Shin
- **Stewing (on the bone) (osso buco):** cut and saw into 2–4 cm thick slices through the knuckle.
- **Sauté:** bone out and trim, then cut into even 25 g pieces.

Leg
- **Braising or roasting whole:** remove the aitch bone, clean and trim 4 cm off the knuckle bone. Trim off the excess sinew.

- **Braising or roasting the nut:** remove all the sinew; if there is insufficient fat on the joint then bard thinly and secure with string.
- **Escalopes:** remove all the sinew, cut into large 50–75 g slices against the grain and bat out thinly.
- **Sauté:** remove all the sinew and cut into 25 g pieces.

Loin and best end
- **Roasting:** bone out and trim the flap, roll out and secure with string. This joint may be stuffed before rolling.
- **Frying:** trim and cut into cutlets.

Shoulder
- **Braising:** bone out as for lamb; usually stuffed.
- **Stewing:** bone out, remove all the sinew and cut into 25 g pieces.

Neck end and scrag
- **Stewing and sauté:** bone out and remove all the sinew; cut into approximately 25 g pieces.

Breast
- **Stewing:** as for neck end.
- **Roasting:** bone out, season, stuff and roll up, then tie with string.

Kidneys
- Remove the fat and skin and cut down the middle lengthwise.
- Remove the sinew and cut into thin slices or neat dice.

Liver
- Skin if possible, remove the gristle and cut into thin slices on the slant.

Sweetbreads
- Soak in several changes of cold salted water to remove blood, which would darken the sweetbreads during cooking.
- Blanch and refresh, then peel off the membrane and connective tissues. The sweetbreads can then be pressed between two trays with a weight on top, and refrigerated.

Head
- Bone out by making a deep incision down the middle of the head to the nostrils.

- Follow the bone carefully and remove all the flesh in one piece.
- Lastly, remove the tongue.
- Wash the flesh well and keep covered in acidulated water.
- Wash off, blanch and refresh.
- Cut into 2–5 cm squares.
- Cut off the ears and trim the inside of the cheek.

Brains
- Using a chopper or saw, remove the top of the skull, making certain that the opening is large enough to remove the brain undamaged.
- Soak the brain in running cold water, then remove the membrane, or skin, and wash well to remove all blood.
- Keep in cold salted water until required.

Quality of veal

- Veal is available all year round.
- The flesh should be pale pink in colour and firm in structure – not soft or flabby.
- Cut surfaces should be slightly moist, not dry.
- Bones, in young animals, should be pinkish white, porous and with a degree of blood in their structure.
- The fat should be firm and pinkish white.
- The kidney should be firm and well covered with fat.

Veal recipes

Where applicable, give the origin and breed of the veal. (For further information visit www.qmscotland.co.uk.)

Stew

83 Brown veal stew *(ragoût de veau)*

Proceed as for brown beef stew (recipe 56), using veal in place of beef and allowing 1–1½ hours' cooking time.

84 Fricassée of veal *(fricassée de veau)*

Cal	Cal	Fat	Sat Fat	Carb	Sugar	Protein	Fibre	*
992 KJ	236 kcal	13.6 g	7.5 g	5.3 g	0.4 g	23.3 g	0.2 g	

	4 portions	10 portions
boned stewing veal (shoulder or breast)	400 g	1¼ kg
margarine, butter or oil	35 g	100 g
flour	25 g	60 g
white veal stock	500 ml	1¼ litres
salt, pepper		
egg yolk	1	2–3
cream (dairy or vegetable)	2–3 tbsp	5–7 tbsp
squeeze of lemon juice		
parsley, chopped, to finish		
heart-shaped croutons, to finish		

1 Trim the meat. Cut into even 25 g pieces.
2 Sweat the meat gently in the butter without colour in a sauté pan.
3 Mix in the flour and cook out without colour.
4 Allow to cool.
5 Gradually add boiling stock just to cover the meat, stir until smooth.
6 Season, bring to the boil, skim.
7 Cover and simmer gently on the stove until tender (approx. 1½–2 hours).
8 Pick out the meat into a clean pan. Correct the sauce.
9 Pass on to the meat and reboil. Mix the yolk and cream in a basin.
10 Add a little of the boiling sauce, mix in and pour back on to the meat, shaking the pan until thoroughly mixed; do not reboil. Add the lemon juice.
11 Serve, finished with chopped parsley and heart-shaped croutons fried in butter or oil.

HEALTHY EATING TIP
• Add the minimum amount of salt.
• Serve with oven-baked croutons brushed with olive oil or sippets.
• A large serving of starchy carbohydrates and vegetables will help to proportionally reduce the fat content.

Variations
A variation is to add mushrooms and button onions. Proceed as for this recipe but, after 1 hour's cooking, pick out the meat, strain the sauce back on to the meat and add 8 small button onions. Simmer for 15 minutes, add 8 small white button mushrooms, washed and peeled if necessary, then complete the cooking. Finish and serve as in this recipe. This is known as *fricasée de veau à l'ancienne*.

* Using butter

85 White stew or blanquette of veal *(blanquette de veau)*

Proceed as for white lamb stew recipe (recipe 27),
using 400 g of prepared stewing veal.

HEALTHY EATING TIP

- Use the minimum amount of salt.
- Reduce the fat content by using low-fat yoghurt
  in place of the cream when reheating.
- Serve with mashed potato with spring onion and
  colourful vegetables.

Roast

86 Roast stuffed breast of veal *(poitrine de veau farcie)*

Cal 1154 KJ	Cal 276 kcal	Fat 14.0 g	Sat Fat 7.2 g	Carb 14.8 g	Sugar 1.4 g	Protein 23.4 g	Fibre 0.6 g	*

1 Bone, trim, season and stuff.
2 Tie with string, then cook and serve as for a roast.

* *Using 100 g meat*

87 Veal stuffing

	4 portions	10 portions
breadcrumbs (white or wholemeal)	100 g	250 g
onion, cooked in oil, butter or margarine without colour	50 g	125 g
pinch of chopped parsley		
suet, chopped	50 g	125 g
good pinch of powdered thyme or rosemary		
lemon, grated zest and juice of	½	1
salt, pepper		

1 Combine all the ingredients.
2 This mixture may be used for stuffing joints or may
  be cooked separately in buttered paper or in a
  basin in the steamer for approximately 1 hour.

Variations
The stuffing for veal joints may be varied by using:
- orange in place of lemon
- the addition of duxelle
- leeks in place of onion
- various herbs
- adding a little spice (e.g. ginger, nutmeg, allspice).

HEALTHY EATING TIP

- Use the minimum amount of salt; rely on the herbs
  and lemon for flavour.
- Use a little unsaturated oil to cook the onion.

88 Roast veal four-bone rib

Cal	Cal	Fat	Sat Fat	Carb	Sugar	Protein	Fibre	Salt
494 KJ	118 kcal	3.1 g	1.0 g	1.0 g	0.3 g	21.6 g	0.1 g	0.8 g

6–8 portions

veal	4-bone rib (approx 800 g)
salt, pepper	
Dijon mustard	2 tsp
garlic cloves, cut into slivers	2
cold water	
fresh thyme	2 sprigs

1 Place the joint in a roasting tray and season. Score the joint, rub the mustard into the joint and insert garlic into the incisions.

2 Pour sufficient cold water into the tray to cover the base. Add the thyme to the water and place in the oven at 200°C for 10–15 minutes. Then cover with foil and reduce the temperature to 190°C. Cook for a further 20 minutes per 450 g.

3 Add more water as necessary to keep liquid in the bottom of the pan, and baste occasionally.

4 After cooking allow the joint to rest in a warm place for 15–20 minutes before carving.

5 Use the pan juices to make the gravy or sauce, or serve with a suprême sauce with mushrooms.

Grill

89 Grilled veal cutlet (côte de veau grille)

Cal	Cal	Fat	Sat Fat	Carb	Sugar	Protein	Fibre	*
990 KJ	236 kcal	9.7 g	2.6 g	0.0 g	0.0 g	36.9 g	0.0 g	

1 Lightly season the prepared chop with salt and mill pepper.

2 Brush with oil. Place on previously heated grill bars.

3 Cook on both sides for 8–10 minutes in all.

4 Brush occasionally to prevent the meat from drying.

5 Serve with watercress, a deep-fried potato and a suitable sauce or butter, such as béarnaise or compound butter, or on a bed of plain or flavoured mashed potato (see page 521).

Note: Sprigs of rosemary may be added to the chop before or halfway through cooking.

HEALTHY EATING TIP
- Use the minimum amount of salt to season the meat.
- Serve with a small amount of sauce or butter and a large portion of mixed vegetables.

* Using sunflower oil

90 Grilled veal sweetbreads

1 Blanch, braise, cool and press the sweetbreads.

2 Cut in halves crosswise, pass through melted butter and grill gently on both sides.

3 Serve with a sauce and garnish as indicated.

Note: In some recipes the sweetbreads may be passed through butter and crumbs before being grilled, and garnished with noisette potatoes, buttered carrots, purée of peas and béarnaise sauce.

Boil

91 Calf's tongue with a pomegranate sauce

Cal	Cal	Fat	Sat Fat	Carb	Sugar	Protein	Fibre	Salt
118 KJ	494 kcal	3.1 g	1.0 g	1.0 g	0.3 g	21.6 g	0.1 g	4.2 g

	4 portions	10 portions
calf's tongues (approx 200 g each)	2	5
olive oil	4 tbsp	10 tbsp
onion, finely chopped	1	2
pomegranates, quartered with seeds removed	4	10
chicken stock	500 ml	1¼ litres
dry sherry	180 ml	400 ml
seasoning		

1 Soak the tongues in salted water for 1 hour then drain.
2 Put the tongues in a large saucepan and cover with cold water. Bring to the boil. Reduce and simmer gently with the lid on for about 30 minutes.
3 Drain the water and let the tongues cool. Peel off the skin.
4 Heat the oil in a suitable pan. Add the onion and sauté for 2 minutes until lightly brown. Add the tongues and gently sear for another 2 minutes.
5 Add the pomegranate seeds, stock and sherry, and simmer very gently for 1 hour. The tongues should be tender and the sauce reduced. Season.
6 Serve the tongues slices with the sauce (note that the sauce may be strained).

Note: Creamed mash potatoes are an ideal accompaniment to this dish.

Braise

92 Braised veal (noix de veau braise)

Cal	Cal	Fat	Sat Fat	Carb	Sugar	Protein	Fibre
792 KJ	190 kcal	90.0 g	1.7 g	5.3 g	4.5 g	21.9 g	1.1 g

	4 portions	10 portions
carrots	100 g	250 g
onions	100 g	250 g
butter, margarine or oil	25 g	60 g
cushion or nut of veal	400 g	1¼ kg
tomato purée	25 g	60 g
bouquet garni		
brown veal stock	250 ml	625 ml
jus-lié	250 ml	625 ml

1 Slice the carrots and onions thickly. Fry lightly and place in a braising pan.
2 Trim and tie the joint with string and fry quickly on all sides.
3 Place on the bed of roots.
4 Add the tomato purée, bouquet garni, stock, jus-lié and some mushroom trimmings if available. Season lightly.
5 Bring to the boil, skim, cover with a lid and cook gently in a moderate oven at 150–200°C for 1 hour.
6 Remove the lid and continue cooking with the lid off for a further 30 minutes, basting frequently.
7 Remove the joint from the sauce, take off the strings.
8 Correct the colour, consistency and seasoning of the sauce.
9 Pass through a fine conical strainer. Carve in slices against the grain.
10 Pour some of the sauce over the slices and serve a sauceboat of sauce separately.

Note: For larger joints allow 30–35 minutes per ½ kg plus 35 minutes (approx.) cooking time; 125 ml red wine may replace the same amount of jus-lié. Noodles are often served with this dish.

HEALTHY EATING TIP

• Lightly oil the pan with an unsaturated oil to fry the carrots and onions. Skim any fat from the finished sauce.
• Use the minimum amount of salt.
• Serve with plenty of noodles and green vegetables.

93 Braised stuffed shoulder of veal

Cal	Cal	Fat	Sat Fat	Carb	Sugar	Protein	Fibre	*
824 KJ	196 kcal	9.0 g	1.9 g	5.0 g	4.1 g	24.0 g	1.1 g	

	4 portions	10 portions
shoulder of veal, boned	400 g	1¼ kg
onion	100 g	250 g
carrot	100 g	250 g
dripping or oil	25 g	60 g
tomato purée	50 g	125 g
brown veal stock	250 ml	625 ml
bouquet garni		
jus-lié or demi-glace	250 ml	625 ml
clove garlic, crushed	1	2

1 Bone out the shoulder, season, stuff (recipe 87) and secure with string. Cook and serve as for braised veal (recipe 92).
2 For larger joints allow 30–35 minutes per ½ kg plus 35 minutes (approx.) cooking time.

* Using sunflower oil

94 Braised shin of veal (osso buco)

Cal	Cal	Fat	Sat Fat	Carb	Sugar	Protein	Fibre	*
1748 KJ	416 kcal	28.6 g	7.8 g	9.3 g	4.1 g	28.5 g	1.9 g	

	4 portions	10 portions
meaty knuckle of veal	1½ kg	3¾ kg
salt, pepper		
flour	25 g	60 g
butter or margarine	50 g	125 g
oil	60 ml	150 ml
onion	50 g	125 g
small clove garlic	1	2–3
carrot	50 g	125 g
leek	25 g	60 g
celery	25 g	60 g
dry white wine	60 ml	150 ml
white stock	60 ml	150 ml
tomato purée	25 g	60 g
bouquet garni		
tomatoes, concassée	200 g	500 g
parsley and basil, chopped		
lemon or orange, grated zest and juice of	½	1

1 Prepare the veal knuckle by cutting and sawing through the bone in 5 cm thick pieces.
2 Season the veal pieces with salt and pepper, and pass through flour on both sides.
3 Melt the butter and oil in a sauté pan.
4 Add the veal slices and cook on both sides, colouring slightly.
5 Add the finely chopped onion and garlic, cover with a lid and allow to sweat gently for 2–3 minutes.

6 Add the carrot, leek and celery cut in brunoise, cover with a lid and allow to sweat for 3–4 minutes. Pour off the fat.
7 Deglaze with the white wine and stock. Add the tomato purée.
8 Add the bouquet garni, replace the lid and allow the dish to simmer gently, preferably in an oven, for 1 hour.
9 Add the tomato concassée, correct the seasoning.
10 Replace the lid, return to the oven and allow to continue simmering until the meat is so tender that it can be pulled away from the bone easily with a fork.
11 Remove the bouquet garni, add the lemon juice, correct the seasoning and serve sprinkled with a mixture of chopped fresh basil, parsley, and grated orange and lemon zest (known as gremolata).

Note: A risotto with saffron may be served separately. Osso buco is an Italian regional dish that has many variations.

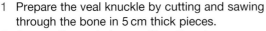

HEALTHY EATING TIP
• Use the minimum amount of salt to season the meat and in the finished sauce.
• Lightly oil the pan with an unsaturated oil and drain off any excess after the frying is complete.
• Serve with a large portion of risotto.

* Using hard margarine and sunflower oil

95 Braised calf's cheeks with vegetables

	4 portions	10 portions
salt, pepper		
calf's cheeks	800 g	2 kg
olive oil	2 tbsp	5 tbsp
ground cumin	½ tsp	1¼ tsp
white peppercorns	½ tsp	1¼ tsp
cloves	4	10
celery, 5 mm dice	1 stick	2 sticks
bay leaves	2	5
garlic cloves	8	20
leeks, finely shredded	1	2½
onions, chopped	1	2½
shallots, quartered	2	5
savoy cabbage	400 g	1 kg
dry white wine	500 ml	1¼ litres
cider	350 ml	875 ml
chopped chives	½ tsp	1 tsp

1 Season the cheeks.
2 Heat the oil in a suitable pan. Sear the cheeks on all sides. Remove and keep warm. Add to the pan the cumin, peppercorns, cloves, celery, bay leaves, garlic, leeks, onions, shallots. Cook until the vegetables start to brown.
3 Add the cabbage and cook until wilted and slightly brown.
4 Add half the white wine and three-quarters of the cider.
5 Return the cheeks to the pan. Cover and braise in the oven for approximately 2½ hours until the meat is tender.
6 Remove the cheeks and vegetables from the juices. Set aside and keep warm.
7 Strain the juices and return to the pan. Then add the remaining wine and cider. Bring to the boil. Reduce to a sauce consistency.
8 Return the cheeks to the pan and simmer, basting with the sauce until it is syrupy and the meat is glazed.
9 To serve, place the vegetables on plates with the cheeks on top. Mask with the sauce and sprinkle with chopped chives.
10 Serve with polenta or couscous

Bake

96 Hot veal and ham pie

Cal 1394 KJ	Cal 332 kcal	Fat 20.7 g	Sat Fat 8.1 g	Carb 8.9 g	Sugar 0.8 g	Protein 27.9 g	Fibre 0.7 g

	4 portions	10 portions
bacon rashers	100 g	250 g
stewing veal without bone	400 g	1¼ kg
hardboiled egg, chopped or quartered	1	2
parsley, chopped	1 tsp	2 tsp
onion, chopped	50 g	125 g
salt, pepper		
stock (white)	250 ml	625 ml
rough puff or puff paste (see pages 624–626)	100 g	250 g

1 Bat out the bacon thinly and use it to line the bottom and sides of a ½ litre pie dish, reserving two or three pieces for the top.
2 Trim the veal, cut it into small pieces and mix with the egg, parsley and onion. Season and place in the pie dish.
3 Just cover with stock. Add the rest of the bacon.
4 Roll out the pastry, eggwash the rim of the pie dish and line with a strip of pastry 1 cm wide. Press this down firmly and eggwash.
5 Without stretching the pastry, cover the pie and seal firmly.
6 Trim off any excess pastry with a sharp knife, notch the edge neatly, eggwash and decorate.
7 Allow to rest in the refrigerator or a cool place.
8 Place on a baking sheet in a hot oven at 200°C for 10–15 minutes until the paste has set and is lightly coloured.
9 Remove the pie from oven, cover with foil and return to the oven, reducing the heat to 190°C for 15 minutes, to 160°C for a further 15 minutes, then to 140°C.

10 Complete the cooking at this temperature ensuring that the liquid is gently simmering.

Note: Variations include rabbit, pork, chicken or guinea fowl in place of veal.

HEALTHY EATING TIP
- Little or no salt is needed – there is plenty in the bacon.
- Serve with plenty of starchy carbohydrate and vegetables to proportionally reduce the fat.

Sauté/fry

97 Fried veal cutlet (côte de veau sautée)

1 Season and cook in a sauté pan, in clarified butter or oil and butter, on both sides for 8–10 minutes in all. (Chops must be started in hot fat and the heat reduced in order to allow the meat to cook through.)
2 Serve with a suitable garnish (e.g. jardinière of vegetables or braised celery) or noodles, and finish with a cordon of jus-lié.

98 Escalope of veal

Cal	Cal	Fat	Sat Fat	Carb	Sugar	Protein	Fibre	*
2079 KJ	495 kcal	39.8 g	11.4 g	10.3 g	0.5 g	24.7 g	1.0 g	

	4 portions	10 portions
nut or cushion of veal	400 g	1¼ kg
seasoned flour	25 g	60 g
egg	1	2
breadcrumbs	50 g	125 g
oil		
for frying	50 g	125 g
butter	50 g	125 g
beurre noisette (optional)	50 g	125 g
jus-lié (page 59)	60 ml	150 ml

1 Trim and remove all sinew from the veal.
2 Cut into four even slices and bat out thinly using a little water.

3 Flour, egg and crumb. Shake off surplus crumbs. Mark with a palette knife.
4 Place the escalopes into shallow hot fat and cook quickly for a few minutes on each side.
5 Dress on a serving dish or plate.
6 An optional finish is to pour over 50 g *beurre noisette* (nut brown butter), and finish with a cordon of jus-lié (see page 59).

Figure 8.22 Veal escalope Holstein

HEALTHY EATING TIP

- Use an unsaturated oil to fry the veal.
- Make sure the fat is hot so that less will be absorbed into the crumb.
- Drain the cooked escalope on kitchen paper.
- Use the minimum amount of salt.
- Serve with plenty of starchy carbohydrate and vegetables.

- *Escalope of veal with spaghetti and tomato sauce:* prepare escalopes as for this recipe, then garnish with spaghetti with tomato sauce (page 147), allowing 10 g spaghetti per portion.

* Fried in sunflower oil, using butter to finish

Variations

Variations include the following.

- *Escalope of veal Viennoise:* as for this recipe, but garnish the dish with chopped yolk and white of egg and chopped parsley; on top of each escalope place a slice of peeled lemon decorated with chopped egg yolk, egg white and parsley, an anchovy fillet and a stoned olive; finish with a little lemon juice and nut brown butter.
- *Veal escalope Holstein (Figure 8.22):* prepare and cook the escalopes as for this recipe; add an egg fried in butter or oil, and place two neat fillets of anchovy criss-crossed on each egg; serve.

Figure 8.23 Escalope of veal Viennoise

99 Breadcrumbed veal escalope with ham and cheese (*escalope de veau cordon bleu*)

Cal 2632 KJ	Cal 627 kcal	Fat 48.1 g	Sat Fat 16.3 g	Carb 12.0 g	Sugar 1.3 g	Protein 37.1 g	Fibre 0.7 g	*

	4 portions	10 portions
nut or cushion of veal	400 g	1¼ kg
slices of cooked ham	4	10
slices of Gruyère cheese	4	10
seasoned flour	25 g	60 g
egg	1	2
breadcrumbs	50 g	125 g
oil	50 g	125 g
butter (optional)	100 g	250 g
beurre noisette (optional)	50 g	125 g
jus-lié (page 59)	60 ml	150 ml

1 Trim and remove all sinew from the veal.
2 Cut into 8 even slices (20 for 10 portions) and bat out thinly using a little water.
3 Place a slice of ham and a slice of cheese on to 4 (10 for 10 portions) of the veal slices, cover with the remaining slices and press together firmly.
4 Flour, egg and crumb. Shake off all surplus crumbs. Mark on one side with a palette knife.

Figure 8.24 Veal cordon bleu

5 Place the escalopes marked side down into the hot oil (with butter if desired) and cook quickly for a few minutes on each side, until golden brown.
6 An optional finish is to serve coated with 50 g (125 g for 10 portions) nut brown butter (*beurre noisette*) and a cordon of jus-lié.

Note: Veal escalopes may be cooked plain (not crumbed), in which case they are only slightly batted out.

HEALTHY EATING TIP
• No added salt is needed as there is plenty in the ham and cheese.
• This is a high-fat dish, so serve with plenty of starchy carbohydrate and vegetables to 'dilute' the fat.

* Fried in sunflower oil, using butter to finish

100 Veal escalope with Madeira (*escalope de veau au Madère*)

Cal	Cal	Fat	Sat Fat	Carb	Sugar	Protein	Fibre	*
967 KJ	231 kcal	12.1 g	7.1 g	5.6 g	0.8 g	23.4 g	0.2 g	

	4 portions	10 portions
butter or margarine	50 g	125 g
seasoned flour	25 g	60 g
veal escalopes, slightly batted	4	10
Madeira	30 ml	75 ml
demi-glace or jus-lié	125 ml	300 ml

1 Heat the butter in a sauté pan.
2 Lightly flour the escalopes. Fry to a light-brown colour on both sides.
3 Drain off the fat from the pan. Deglaze with the Madeira.
4 Add the demi-glace and bring to the boil.
5 Correct the seasoning and consistency.
6 Pass through a fine strainer onto the escalopes and serve.

Note: In place of Madeira, sherry or Marsala may be used.

HEALTHY EATING TIP
• Use a small amount of oil to fry the escalopes, and drain the cooked escalopes on kitchen paper.
• Serve with plenty of potatoes and vegetables.

* Using 100 g escalopes

101 Veal escalope with cream and mushrooms (*escalope de veau à la crème et champignons*)

Cal	Cal	Fat	Sat Fat	Carb	Sugar	Protein	Fibre	*
1574 KJ	379 kcal	29.0 g	17.6 g	5.6 g	0.8 g	24.3 g	0.5 g	

	4 portions	10 portions
butter, margarine or oil	50 g	125 g
seasoned flour	25 g	60 g
veal escalopes, slightly batted	4	10
button mushrooms	100 g	250 g
sherry or white wine	30 ml	125 ml
double cream	125 ml	300 ml
salt, cayenne		

1 Heat the butter in a sauté pan. Lightly flour the escalopes.
2 Cook the escalopes on both sides with the minimum of colour. They should be a delicate light brown.
3 Place the escalopes in a serving dish, cover and keep warm.
4 Peel, wash and slice the mushrooms.
5 Gently sauté the mushrooms in the same butter and pan as the escalopes and then add them to the escalopes.

6 Drain off all the fat from the pan. Deglaze the pan with the sherry or wine.
7 Add the cream, bring to the boil and season.
8 Reduce to a lightly thickened consistency. Correct the seasoning.
9 Pass through a fine strainer over the escalopes and mushrooms.

Note: An alternative method of preparing the sauce is to use half the amount of cream and an equal amount of chicken velouté (page 53). This dish may be served with pasta.

HEALTHY EATING TIP
• Use a small amount of oil to fry the escalopes, and drain the cooked escalopes on kitchen paper.
• Serve with plenty of boiled potatoes and vegetables to proportionally reduce the fat.

* Using 100 g escalopes

Figure 8.25 Veal escalope with cream and mushrooms on a bed of tagliatelle

102 Veal escalopes with Parma ham and mozzarella cheese (involtini di vitello)

Cal	Cal	Fat	Sat Fat	Carb	Sugar	Protein	Fibre
1642 KJ	394 kcal	26.1 g	15.5 g	0.1 g	0.1 g	39.8 g	0.0 g

	4 portions	10 portions
small, thin veal escalopes	400 g (8 in total)	1¼ kg (20 in total)
flour		
Parma ham, thinly sliced	100 g	250 g
mozzarella cheese, thinly sliced	200 g	500 g
fresh leaves of sage	8	20
or		
dried sage	1 tsp	2½ tsp
salt, pepper		
butter, margarine or oil	50 g	125 g
Parmesan cheese, grated		

1 Sprinkle each slice of veal lightly with flour and flatten.
2 Place a slice of Parma ham on each escalope.
3 Add several slices of mozzarella cheese to each.
4 Add a sage leaf or a light sprinkling of dried sage.
5 Season, roll up each escalope, and secure with a toothpick or cocktail stick.
6 Melt the butter in a sauté pan, add the escalopes and brown on all sides.
7 Transfer the escalopes and butter to a suitably sized ovenproof dish.
8 Sprinkle generously with grated Parmesan cheese and bake in a moderately hot oven at 190°C for 10 minutes.
9 Clean the edges of the dish and serve.

HEALTHY EATING TIP
• Use a small amount of oil to fry the escalopes, and drain the cooked escalopes on kitchen paper.
• No added salt is necessary as there is plenty of salt in the cheese.
• Serve with plenty of vegetables.

103 Veal stroganoff

Cal	Cal	Fat	Sat Fat	Carb	Sugar	Protein	Fibre	Salt	*
2000 KJ	478 kcal	35.0 g	17.7 g	10.4 g	8.2 g	27.0 g	2.2 g	2.2 g	

	4 portions	10 portions
butter	50 g	125 g
olive oil	2 tbsp	5 tbsp
lean veal, cut from the nut or loin	400 g	2¼ kg
onion, finely chopped	1	2
button mushrooms, sliced	400 g	1 kg
brandy	4 tbsp	10 tbsp
veal stock	200 ml	500 ml
soured cream	300 ml	750 ml
Dijon mustard	2 tbsp	5 tbsp
salt, pepper		

1 Heat the butter and olive oil in a frying pan over a high heat. Quickly fry the veal cut into strips. Remove and keep warm.
2 Sauté the chopped onion for approximately 3 minutes. Add the mushrooms and sauté together until cooked.
3 Add the brandy, reduce well, add the stock and soured cream. Stir well.
4 Finish with the mustard, then season. Add the meat. Serve immediately with noodles, braised rice or tagliatelle.

*Using sherry in place of brandy

Offal

104 Calf's liver and bacon (foie de veau au lard)

Cal	Cal	Fat	Sat Fat	Carb	Sugar	Protein	Fibre
998 KJ	238 kcal	13.4 g	5.0 g	2.8 g	2.7 g	26.9 g	1.1 g

	4 portions	10 portions
calf's liver	300 g	1 kg
flour		
oil, for frying	50 g	125 g
streaky bacon	50 g	125 g
jus-lié (page 59)	125 ml	300 ml

1 Skin the liver and remove the gristle.
2 Cut in slices on the slant.
3 Pass the slices of liver through flour. Shake off the excess flour.
4 Quickly fry on both sides in hot oil.
5 Remove the rind and bone from the bacon and grill on both sides.
6 Serve the liver and bacon with a cordon of jus-lié and a sauceboat of jus-lié separately.

Variations

Variations include the following.
- Fry in butter and sprinkle with powdered sage.
- Fry in butter, remove the liver, deglaze the pan with raspberry vinegar and powdered thyme.
- When cooked, sprinkle with chopped parsley and a few drops of lemon juice.
- Flour, egg and breadcrumb the liver before cooking.
- The liver may be lightly brushed with oil and grilled.

HEALTHY EATING TIP

- Bacon is salty, so no added salt is needed.
- Use a little unsaturated oil to fry the liver, and drain off any excess fat.
- Serve with boiled new potatoes and a variety of vegetables.

105 Calf's liver with onions and Madeira wine

	4 portions	10 portions
oil	50 ml	125 ml
calf's liver, trimmed	400 g	1 kg
butter	50 g	125 g
onions, sautéed and softened in butter	50 g	125 g
Madeira	60 ml	150 ml

1 Heat the oil in a shallow pan and flavour the liver; cook quickly on both sides, add butter.
2 Add the softened onions, then the Madeira, cook for 30 seconds. Serve.

106 Braised veal sweetbreads (white) *(ris de veau braisé – à blanc)*

Cal	Cal	Fat	Sat Fat	Carb	Sugar	Protein	Fibre	*
1103 KJ	263 kcal	20.7 g	4.4 g	1.7 g	0.0 g	17.6 g	0.0 g	

	4 portions	10 portions
heart-shaped sweetbreads	8	20
salt, pepper		
onion	100 g	250 g
carrot	100 g	250 g
oil, margarine or butter	50 g	125 g
bouquet garni		
veal stock	250 ml	625 ml

1 Wash, blanch, refresh and trim the sweetbreads (see page 295).
2 Season and place in a casserole or sauté pan on a bed of roots smeared with the oil, margarine or butter.
3 Add the bouquet garni and stock.
4 Cover with buttered greaseproof paper and a lid.
5 Cook in a moderate oven at 150–200°C for approximately 45 minutes.
6 Remove the lid and baste occasionally with cooking liquor to glaze.
7 Serve with some of the cooking liquor, thickened with diluted arrowroot if necessary, and passed on to the sweetbreads.

Note: Sweetbreads are glands, and two types are used for cooking. The thymus glands (throat) are usually long in shape and are of inferior quality. The pancreatic glands (stomach) are heart-shaped and of superior quality.

Variations

Variations include the following.

- *Braised veal sweetbreads (brown):* prepare as in this recipe, but place on a lightly browned bed of roots. Barely cover with brown veal stock, or half-brown veal stock and half jus-lié. Cook in a moderate oven at 150–160°C without a lid (for approx. 1 hour), basting frequently. Cover with the corrected, strained sauce to serve. (If veal stock is used, thicken with arrowroot.)
- *Braised veal sweetbreads with vegetables:* braise white with a julienne of vegetables in place of the bed of roots, the julienne served in the sauce.

* *Using hard margarine and sunflower oil*

107 Sweetbread escalope *(escalope de ris de veau)*

1 Braise the sweetbreads white, press slightly between two trays and allow to cool.
2 Cut into slices ½–1 cm thick, dust with flour and shallow-fry.
3 Serve with suitable garnish and sauce (e.g. on a bed of leaf spinach; coat with mornay sauce and glaze).

108 Sweetbread escalope (crumbed) *(escalope de ris de veau)*

1 Braise the sweetbreads white, press slightly and allow to cool.
2 Cut into thick slices; flour, egg and crumb, then shallow-fry.
3 Serve with a suitable garnish (e.g. asparagus tips) and a cordon of jus-lié. Finish with nut brown butter (optional).

Pork and bacon

The keeping quality of pork is less than that of other meat; therefore it must be handled, prepared and cooked with great care. Pork should always be well cooked.

Butchery

The cuts of pork are shown in Figure 8.26.

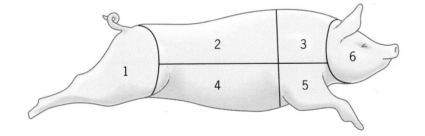

1 Leg
2 Loin
3 Spare rib of neck
4 Belly
5 Shoulder
6 Head

Figure 8.26   Pig carcass dissection

Table 8.9 ✎ Cuts, uses and weights of pork (numbers in left-hand column refer to Figure 8.26)

Joint	Uses	Approximate weight (kg)
(1) leg	roasting and boiling	5
(2) loin	roasting, frying, grilling	6
(3) spare rib	roasting, pies	5½
(4) belly	pickling, boiling, stuffed, rolled and roasted	2
(5) shoulder (hand)	roasting, sausages, pies	3
(6) head (whole)	brawn	4
trotters	grilling, boiling	
kidneys	sauté, grilling	
liver	frying, pâté	

When 5–6 weeks old a piglet is known as a sucking or suckling pig. Its weight is then between 5 and 10 kg.

Order of dissection

- Remove the head.
- Remove the trotters.
- Remove the leg.
- Remove the shoulder.
- Remove the spare ribs.
- Divide the loin from the belly.

Preparation of the joints and cuts of pork

Leg
- **Roasting:** remove the pelvic or aitch bone, trim and score the rind neatly – that is, with a sharp-pointed knife, make a series of 3 mm deep incisions approximately 2 cm apart all over the skin of the joint; trim and clean the knuckle bone.
- **Boiling:** it is usual to pickle the joint either by rubbing dry salt and saltpetre into the meat or by soaking in a brine solution (recipe 40); then remove the pelvic bone, trim and secure with string if necessary.

Loin
- **Roasting (on the bone):** saw down the chine bone in order to facilitate carving; trim the excess fat and sinew and score the rind in the direction that the joint will be carved; season and secure with string.
- **Roasting (boned out):** remove the fillets and bone out carefully; trim off the excess fat and sinew, score the rind and neaten the flap, season, replace the filet mignon, roll up and secure the string; this joint is sometimes stuffed.
- **Grilling or frying chops:** remove the skin, excess fat and sinew, then cut and saw or chop through the loin in approximately 1 cm slices; remove the excess bone and trim neatly.

Spare rib
- **Roasting:** remove the excess fat, bone and sinew, and trim neatly.
- **Pies:** remove the excess fat and sinew, bone out and cut as required.

Belly
- Remove all the small rib bones, season with salt, pepper and chopped sage, roll and secure with string. This joint may be stuffed.

Shoulder
- **Roasting:** the shoulder is usually boned out, the excess fat and sinew removed, seasoned, scored and rolled with string; it may be stuffed and can also be divided into two smaller joints.
- **Sausages and pies:** skin, bone out and remove the excess fat and sinew; cut into even pieces or mince.

Head
- These are usually boned and pressed by specialist pork butchers to make a cold meat called brawn.

Trotters
- Boil in water for a few minutes, scrape with the back of a knife to remove the hairs, wash off in cold water and split in half.

Kidneys
- Remove the fat and skin, cut down the middle lengthwise. Remove the sinew and cut into slices or neat dice.

Liver
- Skin if possible, remove the gristle and cut into thin slices on the slant.

Figure 8.27 ✎ Leg of pork, boned and rolled

Figure 8.28 ✎ Boned leg of pork

Figure 8.29 ✎ Loin of pork

Figure 8.30 ✎ Pork chops

Figure 8.31 ✎ Gammon

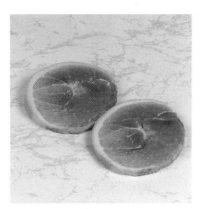

Figure 8.32 ✎ Gammon steaks

Signs of quality

- Lean flesh should be pale pink, firm and of a fine texture.
- The fat should be white, firm, smooth and not excessive.

- Bones should be small, fine and pinkish.
- The skin or rind should be smooth.

Pork recipes

Where applicable name the origin and breed of the pork (e.g. Gloucester Old Spot, Tamworth). For further information visit www.qmscotland.co.uk.

Roast

108 Roast leg of pork

Cal	Cal	Fat	Sat Fat	Carb	Sugar	Protein	Fibre	*
1357 KJ	323 kcal	22.4 g	8.9 g	0.0 g	0.0 g	30.4 g	0.0 g	

1 Prepare leg for roasting (see page 23).
2 Moisten with water, oil, cider, wine or butter and lard then sprinkle with salt, rubbing it well into the cracks of the skin. This will make the crackling crisp.
3 Place on a trivet in a roasting tin with a little oil or dripping on top.
4 Start to cook in a hot oven at 230–250°C, basting frequently.
5 Gradually reduce the heat to 180–185°C, allowing approximately 25 minutes per ½ kg plus another 25 minutes. Pork must always be well cooked. If using a probe, the minimum temperature should be 72°C for 2 minutes.

6 When cooked, remove from the pan and prepare a roast gravy from the sediment (see page 243).
7 Remove the crackling and cut into even pieces for serving.
8 Serve the joint garnished with picked watercress and accompanied by roast gravy, sage and onion dressing (recipe 109) and apple sauce (recipe 110). If to be carved, proceed as for roast lamb (page 244).

Note: Other joints can also be used for roasting (e.g. loin, shoulder and spare rib).

* *113 g portion*

109 Sage and onion dressing for pork

	4 portions	10 portions
onion, chopped	50 g	125 g
pork dripping	50 g	125 g
white breadcrumbs	100 g	250 g
pinch chopped parsley		
good pinch powdered sage		
salt, pepper		

1 Cook the onion in the dripping without colour.
2 Combine all the ingredients. Dressing is usually served separately.

HEALTHY EATING TIP
• Use a small amount of unsaturated oil to cook the onion.
• Add the minimum amount of salt.

Note: Modern practice is to refer to this as a dressing if served separately to the meat, but as stuffing if used to stuff the meat.

110 Apple sauce

cooking apples	400 g
sugar	50 g
margarine or butter	25 g

1 Peel, core and wash the apples.
2 Place with other ingredients in a covered pan and cook to a purée.
3 Pass through a sieve or liquidise.

111 Roast loin of pork with apple and onion sauce

	4 portions	10 portions
cooking apple, peeled and quartered	2	5
onion, quartered	1	2
salt, pepper		
cider	60 ml	180 ml
loin of pork	950 g	2.375 kg

1 Place the apples and onion in a roasting tin.
2 Season, add cider, place the pork on top, score the skin and rub salt over the skin.

3 Place in the oven at 200°C for 25 minutes then reduce the temperature to 170°C and continue to cook for 45 minutes until done.
4 Remove from the tray to rest; cover loosely with foil.
5 Mash the apples and onions in a processor, reheat and adjust the consistency with cider.
6 Slice the pork. Serve with the sauce and roast gravy.

112 Roast pork belly with shallots and champ potatoes

Cal	Cal	Fat	Sat Fat	Carb	Sugar	Protein	Fibre	Salt
5439 KJ	1300 kcal	95.0 g	41.5 g	50.0 g	7.9 g	65.0 g	5.3 g	1.1 g

	4 portions	10 portions
boned pork belly, rind removed	1.2 kg	2½ kg
salt, pepper		
olive oil	1 tbsp	3 tbsp
shallots	20	50
butter	70 g	175 g
potatoes, peeled and chopped	1 kg	25 kg
spring onions, chopped	8	20
double cream	4 tbsp	10 tbsp

1 Place the pork on a rack in a roasting tray; season and oil. Roast in the oven for 3–3½ hours at 150°C.
2 Peel the shallots, fry gently in half the butter until caramelised. Keep warm.
3 Purée the potatoes.
4 Melt the remaining butter in a pan and sauté the spring onions until soft. Add the spring onion and the butter to the potato purée.
5 Add the cream and mix well.
6 Serve the pork with the caramelised shallots and potato.
7 Serve with a reduced brown stock flavoured with cider; alternatively, a red wine sauce may be served. Accompany with a suitable green vegetable.

113 Slow roast pork belly

	4 portions	10 portions
boned pork belly, with rind	1.2 kg	3 kg

1 Pre-heat oven to 145°C.
2 Season the pork with salt and pepper.
3 Place on a rack in a large roasting tray, skin side up.

4 Roast for 4½–5 hours, then remove from the tray.
5 Pour off excess fat and make a gravy.
6 Carve into thick slices and serve with apple sauce, sage and onion dressing and a suitable potato and vegetable.

114 Spare ribs of pork in barbecue sauce

Cal	Cal	Fat	Sat Fat	Carb	Sugar	Protein	Fibre	*
6151 KJ	1465 kcal	12.6 g	37.3 g	20.3 g	17.1 g	63.5 g	0.3 g	

	4 portions	10 portions
onion, finely chopped	100 g	250 g
clove of garlic, chopped	1	2
oil	60 ml	150 ml
vinegar	60 ml	150 ml
tomato purée	150 g	375 g
honey	60 ml	150 ml
brown stock	250 ml	625 ml
Worcester sauce	4 tbsp	10 tbsp
dry mustard	1 tsp	2 tsp
pinch thyme		
salt		
spare ribs of pork	2 kg	5 kg

1 Sweat the onion and garlic in the oil without colour.
2 Mix in the vinegar, tomato purée, honey, stock, Worcester sauce, mustard and thyme, and season with salt.
3 Allow the barbecue sauce to simmer for 10–15 minutes.
4 Place the prepared spare ribs fat side up on a trivet in a roasting tin.

5 Brush the spare ribs liberally with the barbecue sauce.
6 Place in a moderately hot oven: 180–200°C.
7 Cook for ¾–1 hour.
8 Baste generously with the barbecue sauce every 10–15 minutes.
9 The cooked spare ribs should be brown and crisp.
10 Cut the spare ribs into individual portions and serve.

HEALTHY EATING TIP
• Sweat the onion and garlic in a little unsaturated oil.
• No added salt is necessary as the Worcester sauce is salty.

* *Using sunflower oil*

Grill

115 Grilled pork chop (côte de porc grillé)

Cal	Cal	Fat	Sat Fat	Carb	Sugar	Protein	Fibre	*
816 KJ	194 kcal	7.4 g	2.7 g	7.3 g	6.8 g	24.4 g	0.2 g	

1 Season the chop on both sides with salt and mill pepper.
2 Brush with melted fat and either grill on both sides with moderate heat for approximately 10 minutes or cook in a little fat in a plat à sauté or other suitable pan.
3 Serve accompanied by a sharp sauce (e.g. of charcutière – page 58).

HEALTHY EATING TIP
• Pork is a fatty meat. Grilling will reduce the overall fat content.

Using lean meat only

116 Pork loin steaks with pesto and mozzarella

Cal	Cal	Fat	Sat Fat	Carb	Sugar	Protein	Fibre	Salt	*
3531 KJ	844 kcal	66.3 g	25.6 g	0.5 g	0.4 g	61.2 g	0.0 g	1.4 g	

	4 portions	10 portions
salt, pepper		
loin steaks	4	10
olive oil (if frying)	2 tbsp	5 tbsp
pesto	4 tsp	10 tsp
mozzarella	4 slices	10 slices

1 Season, then shallow-fry or grill the steaks until almost cooked.
2 Spread the pesto on top of each steak and top each with a slice of mozzarella.
3 Finish under the grill for approximately 1 minute until the cheese is golden and just cooked through.
4 Serve with a suitable pasta, e.g. buttered noodles, and a green vegetable or tossed salad.

Using a 225 g portion of pork and 60 g of mozzarella

Bake

117 Baked pork chop with apple (côte de porc à la flamande)

Cal	Cal	Fat	Sat Fat	Carb	Sugar	Protein	Fibre	*
730 KJ	173 kcal	4.9 g	1.7 g	8.9 g	8.9 g	24.0 g	1.4 g	

	4 portions	10 portions
pork chops	4	10
salt, pepper		
oil		
dessert apples	300 g	750 g

1 Season the chops with salt and mill pepper.
2 Half cook on both sides in a little oil in a sauté pan.
3 Peel, core and slice the apples and place in an earthenware dish.
4 Put the chops on the apples. Sprinkle with a little fat.
5 Complete the cooking in a moderate oven at 180–200°C for approximately 10–15 minutes. Clean the dish and serve.

HEALTHY EATING TIP
• Lightly oil the pan with a little unsaturated oil to half-cook the chops. It should not be necessary to add more fat in the oven.
• Use the minimum amount of salt.

Variations
- Pineapple rings may be used in place of apple.
- The chops may be grilled and garnished with slices of peeled, cooked apples sprinkled with caster or demerara sugar.
- The chops may be brushed with honey and grilled.

- The chops may be grilled and served with braised red cabbage and a slice of onion and sage tart (made with short pastry, covered with lightly fried onions, sprinkled with sage and baked).

* Using lean meat only

Sauté

118 Pork escalopes

Pork escalopes are usually cut from the prime cuts of meat in the leg or loin, and can be dealt with in the same way as a leg of veal. They may be cut into 75–100 g slices, flattened with a meat bat, and used plain or crumbed and served with vegetables or a pasta (noodles) with a suitable sauce (e.g. Madeira, or as for pork medallions (recipe 119), or as with veal escalope recipes (page 303).

Figure 8.33 ✎ Breadcrumbed pork escalope with noodles in tomato sauce

119 Pork medallions

Pork fillet can be cut into 2 cm pieces, sautéed on both sides and finished with a variety of sauces and garnishes (e.g. a coarse-grain mustard and red onion sauce, or a sauce made from four parts apple purée and one part cream or natural yoghurt, with a smooth consistency).

120 Pork escalopes with Calvados sauce

Cal 1856 KJ	Cal 447 kcal	Fat 34.2 g	Sat Fat 20.3 g	Carb 12.7 g	Sugar 12.5 g	Protein 22.8 g	Fibre 1.1 g	*

	4 portions	10 portions
crisp eating apples (e.g. russet)	2	5
cinnamon	¼ tsp	¾ tsp
lemon juice	1	2
brown sugar	2 tsp	5 tsp
butter, melted	25 g	70 g
4 pork escalopes (see recipe 118)	4 × 100 g	10 × 100 g
butter, margarine or oil	50 g	125 g
shallots or onions, finely chopped	50 g	125 g
Calvados	30 ml	75 ml
double cream or natural yoghurt	125 ml	300 ml
salt, cayenne pepper basil, sage or rosemary, chopped		

1 Core and peel the apples.
2 Cut into ½ cm thick rings and sprinkle with a little cinnamon and a few drops of lemon juice.
3 Place on a baking sheet, sprinkle with brown sugar and a little melted butter, and caramelise under the salamander or in the top of a hot oven.
4 Lightly sauté the escalopes on both sides in the butter.
5 Remove from the pan and keep warm.

6 Add the chopped shallots to the same pan, cover with a lid and cook gently without colouring (use a little more butter if necessary).
7 Strain off the fat, leaving the shallots in the pan, and deglaze with the Calvados.
8 Reduce by a half, add the cream or yoghurt, seasoning and herbs.
9 Reboil, correct the seasoning and consistency, and pass through a fine strainer onto the meat.
10 Garnish with slices of caramelised apple.

Note: Calvados can be replaced with twice the amount of cider and reduced by three-quarters as an alternative. Add a crushed clove of garlic and 1 tablespoon of continental mustard (2–3 cloves and 2½ tablespoons for 10 portions). Special care must be taken if using yoghurt not to overheat, otherwise the sauce will curdle.

HEALTHY EATING TIP
• Use a little unsaturated oil to sauté the chops.
• Add the minimum amount of salt.
• Try using yoghurt stabilised with a little cornflour, or half cream and half yoghurt.

* *Using lean meat only, and double cream*

Deep-fry

121 Sweet and sour pork

Cal 3067 KJ	Cal 730 kcal	Fat 43.9 g	Sat Fat 9.2 g	Carb 69.7 g	Sugar 54.7 g	Protein 13.4 g	Fibre 1.6 g	*

	4 portions	10 portions
loin of pork, boned	250 g	600 g
sugar	12 g	30 g
dry sherry	70 ml	180 ml
soy sauce	70 ml	180 ml
cornflour	50 g	125 g
vegetable oil, for frying	70 ml	180 ml
oil	2 tbsp	5 tbsp
clove garlic	1	2
fresh root ginger	50 g	125 g
onion, chopped	75 g	180 g
green pepper, in 1 cm dice	1	2½
chillies, chopped	2	5
sweet and sour sauce (recipe 122)	210 ml	500 ml
pineapple rings (fresh or canned)	2	5
spring onions	2	5

1 Cut the boned loin of pork into 2 cm pieces.
2 Marinate the pork for 30 minutes in the sugar, sherry and soy sauce.
3 Pass the pork through cornflour, pressing the cornflour in well.
4 Deep-fry the pork pieces in oil at 190°C until golden brown, then drain. Add the tablespoons of oil to a sauté pan.

5 Add the garlic and ginger, and fry until fragrant.
6 Add the onion, pepper and chillies, sauté for a few minutes.
7 Stir in the sweet and sour sauce (recipe 122), bring to the boil.
8 Add the pineapple cut into small chunks, thicken slightly with diluted cornflour. Simmer for 2 minutes.
9 Deep-fry the pork again until crisp. Drain, mix into the vegetables and sauce or serve separately.
10 Serve garnished with rings of spring onions or button onions.

HEALTHY EATING TIP

- Use hot sunflower oil to fry the pork and a small amount of an unsaturated oil to fry the vegetables.
- No added salt is needed, as the soy sauce is high in sodium.
- Serve with plenty of rice or noodles, and additional vegetables.

Using sunflower oil

122 Sweet and sour sauce

Cal 877 KJ	Cal 207 kcal	Fat 0.0 g	Sat Fat 0.0 g	Carb 49.3 g	Sugar 48.9 g	Protein 1.1 g	Fibre 0.3 g

	4 portions	10 portions
white vinegar	375 ml	1 litre
brown sugar	150 g	375 g
tomato ketchup	125 ml	300 ml
Worcester sauce	1 tbsp	2½ tbsp
seasoning		

1 Boil the vinegar and sugar in a suitable pan.
2 Add the tomato ketchup, Worcester sauce and seasoning.
3 Simmer for a few minutes then use as required (e.g. in recipe 121). This sauce may also be lightly thickened with cornflour.

Stir-fry

123 Stir-fried pork fillet

Cal	Cal	Fat	Sat Fat	Carb	Sugar	Protein	Fibre
831 KJ	199 kcal	9.8 g	2.2 g	5.1 g	4.2 g	22.9 g	0.8 g

	4 portions	10 portions
shallots, finely chopped	2	6
garlic (optional), chopped	1 clove	2 cloves
button mushrooms	200 g	400 g
olive oil		
pork fillet	400 g	2 kg
Chinese five-spice powder	1 pinch	2 pinches
soy sauce	1 tbsp	2 tbsp
clear honey	2 tsp	3 tsp
dry white wine	2 tbsp	5 tbsp
salt, pepper		

1 Gently fry the shallots, garlic and sliced mushrooms in a little oil in a frying pan or wok.

2 Add the pork cut into strips, stir well, increase the heat, season and add the Chinese five-spice powder; cook for 3–4 minutes then reduce the heat.

3 Add the soy sauce, honey and wine, and reduce for 2–3 minutes.

4 Correct the seasoning and serve.

HEALTHY EATING TIP

- Use a small amount of an unsaturated oil to fry the vegetables and the pork.
- No extra salt is needed, as soy sauce is added.
- Adding more vegetables and a large portion of rice or noodles can reduce the overall fat content.

Braise

124 Braised honey-glazed blade of pork with sage and onion pesto, served in a garlic-flavoured risotto

Cal	Cal	Fat	Sat Fat	Carb	Sugar	Protein	Fibre	*
2317 KJ	554 kcal	31.3 g	7.7 g	23.2 g	20.7 g	46.0 g	0.9 g	

	4 portions	10 portions
pork blade cut from forequarter of pork	4 × 250 g	10 × 250 g
well-reduced brown stock	125 ml	375 ml
Marinade		
honey	250 ml	625 ml
soft brown sugar	75 g	180 g
star anise	4	10
cider vinegar	2 tbsp	5 tbsp
Pesto		
sage leaves	50 g	125 g
flat parsley	25 g	62 g
Parmesan	25 g	62 g
toasted pinenuts	25 g	62 g
shallots, chopped	12 g	30 g
clove garlic, crushed and chopped	3 tbsp	8 tbsp
olive oil		
salt, pepper		

1 For the pesto, chop all the ingredients together finely in a processor to form a sauce-like consistency.

2 Marinate the pork for 24 hours in the honey marinade (made by mixing together all the marinade ingredients).

3 Pack into single portions and steam. Cook at 89°C for 5 hours.

4 Reheat the well-reduced stock mix with a little of the marinade; place the pork on a suitable dish, mask with the stock and marinade, then glaze in the oven.

5 Serve on a bed of garlic-flavoured risotto (see page 163). Mask with the glaze, place a little pesto around the plate.

Note: It is advisable to vacuum-pack the blades for steaming at 89°C for 5 hours. Once cooked these can be rapidly chilled in a water bath and kept in the refrigerator at 3°C. They can then be reheated and glazed for service. For service, the blade may be boned before glazing. Blade is a modern cut of pork that is popular in gastropubs and bistros; loin chops may be used instead.

HEALTHY EATING TIP

• Use the minimum amount of salt in the pesto and risotto.

* Based on edible portion of meat (135 g)

125 Pork casserole with black pudding crust

	4 portions	10 portions
loin of pork, diced	750 g	2 kg
seasoned flour	25 g	60 g
oil	3 tbsp	7 tbsp
butter	25 g	60 g
onion, finely chopped	1	3
leek, finely shredded	1	3
garlic, crushed and chopped	2 cloves	5
white wine or cider	150 ml	375 ml
brown stock	150 ml	375 ml
black pudding	200 g	500 g

1 Pass the pork through the seasoned flour.
2 Heat half the oil in a suitable casserole with the butter.
3 Quickly fry off the pork in batches, drain well and remove the meat.
4 Add the remaining oil to the pan, add the onion, leek and garlic. Sweat until slightly coloured.
5 Return the meat to the casserole, add the wine and stock. Bring to the boil. Place in the oven for approximately 1 hour at 150°C.
6 Slice the black pudding and place the slices on top of the casserole, overlapping slightly. Brush with oil and place back in the oven for approximately 20 minutes.
7 Serve with creamed potato and a suitable vegetable.

Offal

126 Faggots with onion sauce

Cal	Cal	Fat	Sat Fat	Carb	Sugar	Protein	Fibre	Salt
2310 KJ	552 kcal	34.6 g	10.5 g	22.5 g	2.8 g	40.6 g	1.1 g	0.9 g

	4 portions	10 portions
vegetable oil	25 ml	60 ml
onion, finely chopped	1	2
belly of pork	450 g	1.125 kg
lamb and pig's heart	100 g	250 g
pigs liver, finely chopped	175 g	430 g
mace	½ tsp	1 tsp
chives, chopped	4 tbsp	10 tbsp
sage, chopped	1 tsp	2 tsp
egg	1	2
salt, pepper		
white breadcrumbs	100 g	250 g

1 Place the oil in a suitable pan, heat and cook the onions until coloured.
2 Mince the belly of pork and the lamb's heart finely.
3 In a bowl mix the minced belly of pork, lamb's heart and pig's liver.
4 Add the cooled, chopped onions, mace, chives, sage, beaten egg and seasoning. Bind with the breadcrumbs.
5 Form the mixture into balls – two per person. Chill for approximately 1 hour.
6 Shallow-fry the faggots in vegetable oil until cooked and golden brown.

7 Serve with onion sauce (see page 56).

8 Faggots may also be served with a purée of yellow split peas (pease pudding).

Note: A faggot is a kind of meatball, a traditional dish in the UK, especially the south-west of England, Wales and the Black Country. It is made from meat offcuts and offal, especially pork. A faggot is traditionally made from pig heart, liver and fatty belly meat or bacon minced together, with herbs added for flavouring and sometimes breadcrumbs. The mixture is shaped in the hand into balls, wrapped round with 'caul' (a membrane from the pig's abdomen) and baked. A similar dish, *almondega*, is traditional in Portugal.

Miscellaneous

127 Sausage toad in the hole

	4 portions	10 portions
sausages	8	20
oil or dripping		
Yorkshire pudding (recipe 42)		

1 Place the sausages in a roasting tray or ovenproof dish with a little oil or dripping.

2 Place in a hot oven at 200–210°C for 5–10 minutes.

3 Remove, add the Yorkshire pudding and return to the hot oven until the sausages and Yorkshire pudding are cooked (approx. 15–20 minutes).

4 Cut into portions and serve with a lightly thickened gravy or sauce.

Note: Other meats may be cooked and served this way: for example, chops, steak, corned beef, vegetarian sausages.

HEALTHY EATING TIP

- Drain off some of the fat after cooking the sausages.
- Use semi-skimmed milk to make the batter.
- Serve with boiled, mashed or jacket potatoes, and plenty of seasonal vegetables.

128 Forcemeat

This is a term given to numerous mixtures of meats (usually veal and pork); meat and poultry; poultry; game; fish; vegetables and bread.

Forcemeats range from a simple sausage meat to the finer mixtures used in the making of hot mousses (ham, chicken, fish) and soufflés. Also included are mixtures of bread, vegetables and herbs, which alternatively are referred to as stuffings.

Forcemeats are used for galantines, raised pies, terrines, meatballs and a wide variety of other dishes.

129 Crepinettes

These are small sausages, usually made from a forcemeat of veal, lamb, pork or chicken encased either in caul or paper-thin slices of salt pork. Other ingredients are sometimes added (e.g. chopped mushrooms or truffle). Crepinettes are usually covered with melted butter or good-quality oil, coated with fresh white breadcrumbs and grilled, sautéed or cooked in the oven. Traditionally they are served with potato purée and a well-flavoured demi-glace-type sauce.

Bacon

Bacon is the cured flesh of a bacon-weight pig that is specifically reared for bacon – because its shape and size yield economic bacon joints. Bacon is cured either by dry salting and then smoking or by soaking in brine followed by smoking. Green bacon is brine-cured but not smoked; it has a milder flavour but does not keep for as long as smoked bacon.

Depending on the degree of salting during the curing process bacon joints may or may not require soaking in cold water for a few hours before being cooked.

Butchery

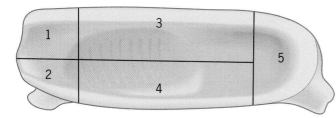

1. Collar
2. Hock
3. Back
4. Streaky
5. Gammon

Grilling cuts

Gammon

Figure 8.34 Cuts of bacon

Preparation of joints and cuts

Collar
- **Boiling:** remove bone (if any) and tie with string.
- **Grilling:** remove the rind, trim off the outside surface and cut into thin slices (rashers), across the joint.

Hock
- **Boiling:** leave whole or bone out and secure with string.

Back and streaky
- **Grilling:** remove all bones and rind, and cut into thin rashers.
- **Frying:** remove the rind, trim off the outside surface, and cut into rashers or chops of the required thickness.

Gammon
- **Grilling:** fairly thick slices are cut from the middle of the gammon; they are then trimmed and the rind removed.
- **Frying:** as for grilling.

Table 8.10 ✒ Cuts, uses and weights of bacon (numbers in left-hand column refer to Figure 8.34)

Joint	Uses	Approximate weight (kg)
(1) collar	boiling, grilling	4½
(2) hock	boiling, grilling	4½
(3) back	grilling, frying	9
(4) streaky	grilling, frying	4½
(5) gammon	boiling, grilling, frying	7½

Quality

- There should be no sign of stickiness.
- There should be a pleasant smell.
- The rind should be thin, smooth and free from wrinkles.
- The fat should be white, smooth and not excessive in proportion to the lean.
- The lean should be a deep-pink colour and firm.

Note: Do not confuse ham with gammon.

Bacon recipes

Boil

130 Boiled bacon (hock, collar or gammon)

Cal	Cal	Fat	Sat Fat	Carb	Sugar	Protein	Fibre	*
1543 KJ	367 kcal	30.5 g	12.2 g	0.0 g	0.0 g	23.1 g	0.0 g	

1 Soak the bacon in cold water for 24 hours before cooking. Change the water (see note, page 323).
2 Bring to the boil, skim and simmer gently (approx. 25 minutes per ½ kg, plus another 25 minutes). Allow to cool in the liquid.
3 Remove the rind and brown skin; carve.
4 Serve with a little of the cooking liquor.

Note: Boiled bacon may be served with pease pudding (page 509) and a suitable sauce such as parsley (page 52).

* Using 113 g per portion

Grill

131 Grilled back or streaky rashers

1 Arrange on a baking tray.
2 Grill on both sides under the salamander.

132 Bacon chops with honey and orange sauce

Cal	Cal	Fat	Sat Fat	Carb	Sugar	Protein	Fibre
1233 KJ	296 kcal	17.9 g	9.0 g	15.1 g	13.9 g	19.4 g	2.7 g

	4 portions	10 portions
4 bacon chops		
(trimmed weight)	4 × 100 g	10 × 100 g
butter, margarine or oil	50 g	125 g
oranges	2	5
lemon, juice of	½	1½
honey	1 dsp	2½ dsp
arrowroot	½ tsp	1 tsp

1 Ensure that the chops are well trimmed of fat.
2 Lightly fry the chops on both sides in the butter, margarine or oil without colouring.
3 Remove from the pan and keep warm.
4 Thinly remove the zest from one orange so that no white pith remains; cut into very fine julienne; blanch and refresh.
5 Peel and segment both oranges, ensuring that all the white pith and pips are removed. Retain all the juice.

6 Boil the orange and lemon juice and honey; lightly thicken with diluted arrowroot.
7 Strain the sauce, add the julienne of orange and pour over the chops.
8 Garnish with the segments of orange.

HEALTHY EATING TIP
• Grill or dry-fry the chops.
• Serve with plenty of potatoes and vegetables.

Variations
Variations include:
• using 1 orange and 1 pink grapefruit instead of 2 oranges
• using a small tin of peaches, or apricots or pineapple in place of the oranges.

133 Grilled gammon rashers

Cal	Cal	Fat	Sat Fat	Carb	Sugar	Protein	Fibre	
958 KJ	228 kcal	12.2 g	4.8 g	0.0 g	0.0 g	29.5 g	0.0 g	*

1 Brush the rashers with fat on both sides and cook on greased, preheated grill bars on both sides for approximately 5–10 minutes in all.
2 Serve with watercress and any other food as indicated (such as tomatoes, mushrooms, eggs). If a sauce is required, serve any sharp demi-glace sauce.

* *Using 100 g per portion*

134 Griddled gammon with apricot salsa

Cal	Cal	Fat	Sat Fat	Carb	Sugar	Protein	Fibre
1112 KJ	266 kcal	14.2 g	4.2 g	8.1 g	7.4 g	26.9 g	1,0 g

	4 portions	10 portions
gammon steaks	4 × 150 g	10 × 150 g
oil		
Apricot salsa		
fresh apricots or dried, reconstituted, stoned and chopped	200 g	500 g
lime, grated rind and juice	1	3
fresh root ginger, grated	2 tsp	5 tsp
clear honey	2 tsp	5 tsp
olive oil	1 tbsp	2½ tsp
sage, chopped, fresh	1 tbsp	2½ tbsp
spring onions, chopped	4	10
salt, pepper		

1 Heat the griddle pan, lightly oil it then cook the gammon steaks.
2 Make the salsa: mix together in a processor the apricots, lime rind and juice, ginger, honey, olive oil and sage.
3 Add the finely chopped spring onions, correct the seasoning then mix well.

Note: The texture should be the consistency of thick cream but coarse. A little extra olive oil may be required or some apricot juice.

HEALTHY EATING TIP
- Use more juice and less oil in the salsa to reduce the fat.
- Gammon is a salty meat, so no extra salt is needed.
- Serve with a large portion of potatoes and vegetables or salad.

Roast

135 Roasted joint of bacon

Cal	Cal	Fat	Sat Fat	Carb	Sugar	Protein	Fibre
1021 KJ	245 kcal	14.8 g	4.9 g	0.0 g	0.0 g	28.0 g	0.0 g

1 Soak the joint in cold water for 24 hours (see note, page 323).
2 Remove from the water. Dry well.
3 Place on a roasting tray and roast for approximately 25 minutes per ½ kilo, plus another 25 minutes.
4 Remove from the oven and allow to stand for 5 minutes before carving.
5 Use the sediment to make roast gravy (see recipe 2), having checked for saltiness.
6 The joint may be cooked in foil and, for the last 25–30 minutes, cooked out of the foil.

Bake

136 Baked bacon and pineapple

Cal	Cal	Fat	Sat Fat	Carb	Sugar	Protein	Fibre	*
1101 KJ	264 kcal	14.8 g	4.9 g	4.9 g	4.9 g	28.1 g	0.2 g	

1 Hock, collar or gammon may be used.
2 Soak the bacon joint in cold water for approximately 24 hours (if necessary – see note on page 323).
3 Change the water.
4 Cover with fresh water, bring to the boil and skim; simmer gently for half the required cooking time (30 minutes per ½ kg, plus another 30 minutes).
5 Allow to cool. Remove the rind and brown skin.
6 Cover the fat surface of the joint with demerara sugar – press well into the surface. Stud with 12–24 cloves.
7 Arrange a layer of tinned pineapple rings down the centre of the joint (secure with cocktail sticks if necessary).
8 Place the joint in a baking tin for the second half of the cooking time.
9 Bake in a moderate oven at 200°C, basting frequently with pineapple juice until well cooked.
10 Remove the cloves and pineapple.
11 Carve in thickish slices and serve garnished with the pineapple.

Variations

Variations include the following.
• Replace pineapple with tinned peaches or apricots.
• Use clear honey in place of demerara sugar and, according to requirements, omit or use the fruit.

HEALTHY EATING TIP
• Remove some of the outer fat after boiling.
• Serve with plenty of potatoes and vegetables.

* *Using 1 ring of pineapple*

Braise

137 Sauerkraut with frankfurters and garlic sausage (*choucroûte garni*)

Cal	Cal	Fat	Sat Fat	Carb	Sugar	Protein	Fibre	*
2832 KJ	682 kcal	50.2 g	19.1 g	28.8 g	7.4 g	30.4 g	5.3 g	

	4 portions	10 portions
lard or margarine	50 g	125 g
sauerkraut	400 g	1¼ kg
streaky bacon	300 g	1 kg
whole peeled carrots	2	5
onion, studded	1	3
bouquet garni	1	2
juniper berries	10	25
peppercorns	5	12
salt, pepper		
white wine	125 ml	300 ml
bacon rind	100 g	250 g
garlic sausage	200 g	500 g
frankfurter sausages	8	20
boiled potatoes	8	20

1 Grease a braising pan well with the lard or margarine.
2 Place a layer of sauerkraut in the bottom of the pan.
3 Place the piece of streaky bacon on top with the carrots, onion and bouquet garni; add the juniper berries and peppercorns tied in a muslin bag.
4 Cover with the remainder of the sauerkraut, season and add the white wine.
5 Cover with bacon rind and a tight-fitting lid.
6 Place in a moderate oven at 180°C and braise gently for 1 hour.
7 Remove the streaky bacon and replace with the garlic sausage. Continue braising for another hour until the sauerkraut is tender.

8 Reheat the frankfurters if canned, or poach in water or stock if fresh.

9 Remove the sauerkraut from the oven and discard the bacon rind.

10 Slice the streaky bacon, garlic sausage, carrots and frankfurters.

11 Dress the sauerkraut in an earthenware dish with the sliced items.

12 Serve plain boiled potatoes separately.

Note: Sauerkraut is pickled white cabbage and is a traditional German dish.

HEALTHY EATING TIP

• Lightly oil the braising pan and drain off as much fat as possible after the bacon and sausage are cooked.

• Serve with plenty of boiled potatoes and colourful vegetables.

* Using margarine

Fry

138 Fried bacon

Cal	Cal	Fat	Sat Fat	Carb	Sugar	Protein	Fibre	*
977 KJ	233 kcal	20.3 g	7.2 g	0.0 g	0.0 g	12.5 g	0.0 g	

Fry on both sides in a frying pan in very little fat.

* Using sunflower oil, 1 portion (50 g)

References

Barham, P. (2000) *The Science of Cooking.* Springer-Verlag.

Suprême of chicken (page 336) with asparagus and truffle

Chicken chasseur (recipe 9)

...rgrilled chicken (recipe 11)
...vegetables

chapter 9

POULTRY AND GAME

Unit 210   **Prepare and cook poultry**

NVQ

Unit 623 (2FP4)   **Prepare poultry for basic dishes**
Unit 624 (2FP5)   **Prepare game for basic dishes**
Unit 630 (2FC4)   **Cook and finish basic poultry dishes**
Unit 631 (2FC5)   **Cook and finish basic game dishes**

Prepare poultry and game

Practical skills
The candidate will be able to:
1 Demonstrate the correct use of tools and equipment to prepare poultry
2 Demonstrate preparation skills for poultry according to dish specification
3 Demonstrate portion control with cuts of poultry and game
4 Apply flavourings to cuts of poultry and game
5 Apply coatings to cuts of poultry and game
6 Demonstrate safe and hygienic practices
7 Undertake correct storage procedures for poultry and game

Underpinning knowledge
The candidate will be able to:
1 Identify different types of poultry and game
2 Explain the quality points of poultry and game
3 State the most commonly used cuts for poultry and game
4 Describe methods used for the preservation of poultry and game
5 Describe the advantages/disadvantages of preservation methods for poultry and game
6 Explain portion sizes/weights of poultry and game

7 State the correct temperature for storing poultry and game

Cook poultry

Practical skills

The candidate will be able to:

1 Demonstrate correct use of tools and equipment to cook poultry and game
2 Apply appropriate cooking methods and principles to poultry and game
3 Make sauces, coulis, gravies and jus for poultry and game dishes
4 Prepare dressings for poultry and game dishes
5 Make appropriately flavoured butters/oils for poultry dishes
6 Prepare garnishes for poultry and game dishes

7 Apply finishing skills to poultry and game dishes
8 Assemble dish according to dish specifications
9 Demonstrate safe and hygienic practices
10 Evaluate the finished dish

Underpinning knowledge

The candidate will be able to:

1 Identify tools and equipment used to cook different types of poultry and game
2 Identify suitable cooking methods for poultry and game
3 Explain reasons for applying cooking principles to poultry and game
4 Explain how to determine when poultry and game is cooked
5 Describe the skills needed to check and finish the dish to specification

Poultry

The term 'poultry' in its general sense is applied to all domestic fowl bred for food, and includes turkeys, geese, ducks, fowls and pigeons.

Originally fowl were classified according to size and feeding by specific names as shown in Table 9.1.

Table 9.1 ✎ Traditional classification of fowl

	Weight (kg)	Number of portions
single baby chicken (poussin)	3/10½	1
double baby chicken (poussin)	½–¾	2
small roasting chicken	¾–1	3–4
medium roasting chicken	1–2	4–6
large roasting or boiling chicken	2–3	6–8
capon	3–4½	8–12
old boiling fowl	2½–4	

There is approximately 15–20 per cent bone in poultry.

Types

- **Spring chickens:** poussin 4–6 weeks old, used for roasting and grilling.
- **Broiler chickens:** 3–4 months old, used for roasting, grilling, casserole.
- **Medium roasting chickens:** fully grown, tender prime birds, used for roasting, grilling, sauté, casserole, suprêmes and pies.
- **Large roasting or boiling chickens:** used for roasting, boiling, casserole, galantine.
- **Capons:** specially bred, fattened cock birds used for roasting.
- **Old hens:** used for stocks and soups.

Food value

The flesh of poultry is more easily digested than that of butchers' meat. It contains protein and is therefore useful for building and repairing body tissues and providing heat and energy. The fat content is low and contains a high percentage of unsaturated acids.

Storage

Chilled birds should be stored between 3°C and 5°C. Oven-ready birds are eviscerated and should be stored in a refrigerator. Frozen birds must be kept in a deep freeze until required, but must be completely thawed, preferably in a refrigerator, before being cooked. This procedure is essential to reduce the risk of food poisoning: chickens are potential carriers of salmonella and if birds are cooked from the frozen state there is the risk of the required degree of heat to kill off salmonella not reaching the centre of the birds.

When using frozen poultry, check that:

- the packaging is undamaged
- there are no signs of freezer burns, which are indicated by white patches on the skin.

Frozen birds should be defrosted by moving them from the freezer to a refrigerator.

Quality points

- Plump breast, pliable breast bone and firm flesh.
- Skin white and unbroken. Broiler chickens have a faint bluish tint.
- Corn-fed are yellow. Free range have more colour, a firmer texture and more flavour.
- Bresse chickens are specially bred in France and are highly regarded.

Old birds have coarse scales, large spurs on the legs and long hairs on the skin.

Trussing

Roasting

- Clean the legs by dipping in boiling water for a few seconds, then remove the scales with a cloth.
- Cut off the outside claws leaving the centre ones, trim these to half their length.

- To facilitate carving remove the wishbone.
- Place the bird on its back.
- Hold the legs back firmly.
- Insert a trussing needle through the bird, midway between the leg joints.
- Turn on to its side.
- Pierce the winglet, the skin of the neck, the skin of the carcass and the other winglet.
- Tie the ends of the string securely.
- Secure the legs by inserting the needle through the carcass and over the legs, take care not to pierce the breast.

Figure 9.2   Trussing chicken for roasting

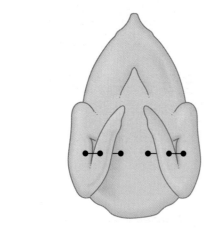

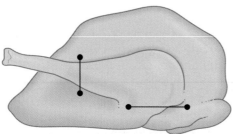

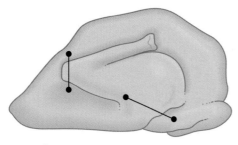

Figure 9.1   Trussing a chicken for roasting and boiling

Boiling and pot roasting

- Proceed as for roasting.
- Cut the leg sinew just below the joint.
- Bend back the legs so that they lie parallel to the breast and secure when trussing, *or* insert the legs through incisions made in the skin at the rear end of the bird, and secure when trussing.

Cutting for sauté, fricassée, pies, etc.

- Remove the feet at the first joint.
- Remove the legs from the carcass.
- Cut each leg in two at the joint.
- Remove the wishbone. Remove the winglets and trim.
- Remove the wings carefully, leaving two equal portions on the breast.
- Remove the breast and cut in two.
- Trim the carcass and cut into three pieces.

Cuts of chicken

The pieces of cut chicken are as follows (the numbers refer to Figure 9.3).

Leg {
4 drumstick
3 thigh
1 wing
2 breast
5 winglet
6 carcass

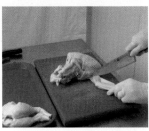

Figure 9.4   Preparing chicken for sauté

Preparation for grilling

- Remove the wishbone.
- Cut off the claws at the first joint.
- Place the bird on its back.
- Insert a large knife through the neck end and out of the vent.
- Cut through the backbone and open out.
- Remove back and rib bones.

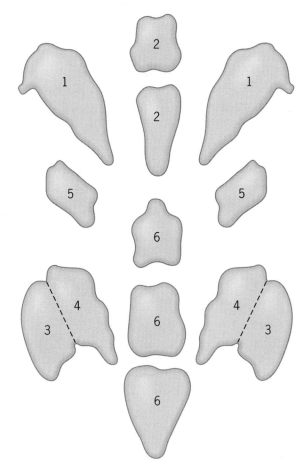

Figure 9.3   Cuts of chicken

Figure 9.5   Preparation of chicken for spatchcock and grilling

Preparation for suprêmes

A suprême is the wing and half the breast of a chicken with the trimmed wing bone attached; the white meat of one chicken yields two suprêmes.

- Use a chicken weighing 1¼–1½ kg.
- Cut off both the legs.
- Remove the skin from the breasts.
- Remove the wishbone.
- Scrape the wing bone bare adjoining the breasts.
- Cut off the winglets near the joints leaving 1½–2 cm of bare bone attached to the breasts.

- Cut the breasts close to the breastbone and follow the bone down to the wing joint.
- Cut through the joint.
- Lay the chicken on its side and pull the suprêmes off, using the knife to assist.
- Lift the fillets from the suprêmes and remove the sinew from each.
- Make an incision lengthways, along the thick side of the suprêmes; open and place the fillets inside.
- Close, lightly flatten with a bat moistened with water, and trim if necessary.

Figure 9.6   Preparation of chicken for suprêmes

Preparation for ballotines

A ballotine is a boned, stuffed leg of bird.

- Using a small, sharp knife remove the thigh bone.
- Scrape the flesh off the bone of the drumstick towards the claw joint.

- Sever the drumstick bone leaving approximately 2–3 cm at the claw joint end.
- Fill the cavities in both the drumstick and thigh with a savoury stuffing.
- Neaten the shape and secure with string using a trussing needle.

Ballotines of chicken may be cooked and served using any of the recipes for chicken sauté presented in this chapter.

Figure 9.7 Preparation of chicken for ballotines

Cutting of cooked chicken (roasted or boiled)

* Remove the legs and cut in two (drumstick and thigh) (see page 335).
* Remove the wings.
* Separate the breast from the carcass and divide in two.
* Serve a drumstick with a wing and the thigh with the breast.

Turkey

Turkeys can vary in weight from 3½ to 20 kg. They are trussed in the same way as chicken. The wishbone should always be removed before trussing in order to facilitate carving. The sinews should be drawn out of the legs. Allow 200 g per portion raw weight.

When cooking a large turkey the legs may be removed, boned, rolled, tied and roasted separately from the remainder of the bird. This will reduce the cooking time, and enable the legs and breast to cook more evenly (see below).

Stuffings may be rolled in foil, steamed or baked and thickly sliced. If a firmer stuffing is required, mix in one or two raw eggs before cooking.

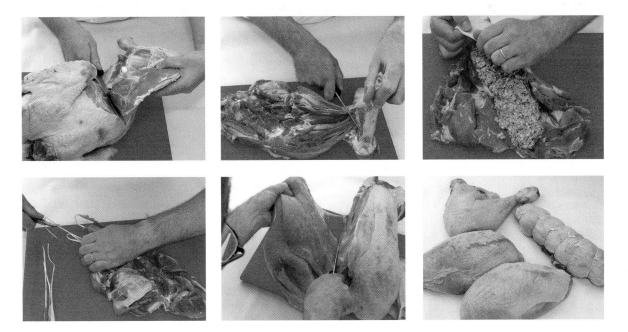

Figure 9.8 Boning, stuffing, rolling and tying turkey in six steps

Quality points

- Large full breast with undamaged skin and no signs of stickiness.

- Legs smooth with supple feet and a short spur.

As birds age the legs turn scaly and the feet harden.

Duck, duckling, goose, gosling

Approximate sizes are as follows.

- **Duck:** 3–4 kg
- **Goose:** 6 kg
- **Duckling:** 1½–2 kg
- **Gosling:** 3 kg

Quality points

- Plump breasts.
- Webbed feet tear easily.

- Lower back bends easily.
- Feet and bill should be yellow.

Preparation for roasting

This is the same as for chicken (page 333). The gizzard is not split but trimmed off with a knife. Roast goose is cooked and served as for roast duck.

Game

For recipes and information on game, please refer to the second part of this chapter (starting on page 360).

Poultry recipes

Turkey

1 Roast turkey (dinde rôti)

Cal	Cal	Fat	Sat Fat	Carb	Sugar	Protein	Fibre	*
836 KJ	200 kcal	11.75 g	4.0 g	0.0 g	0.0 g	29.0 g	0.0 g	

	4 portions	10 portions
Chestnut stuffing		
chestnuts	200 g	500 g
sausage meat	600 g	1½ kg
chopped onion	50 g	125 g
Parsley and thyme stuffing		
chopped onion	50 g	125 g
oil, butter or margarine	100 g	250 g
salt, pepper		
breadcrumbs		
(white or wholemeal)	100 g	250 g
pinch powdered thyme		

	4 portions	10 portions
pinch chopped parsley		
turkey liver (raw), chopped		
turkey	5 kg	12 kg
fat bacon	100 g	250 g
brown stock	375 ml	1 litre
bread sauce, to serve **(page 60)**		

1. Slit the chestnuts on both sides using a small knife.
2. Boil the chestnuts in water for 5–10 minutes.
3. Drain and remove the outer and inner skins while warm.

338

4 Cook the chestnuts in a little stock for 5 minutes.
5 When cold, dice and mix into the sausage meat and cooked onion.
6 For the parsley and thyme stuffing, cook the onion in oil, butter or margarine without colour.
7 Remove from the heat, and add the seasoning, crumbs and herbs.
8 Mix in the raw chopped liver (optional) from the bird.
9 Truss the bird firmly (removing the wishbone first).
10 Season with salt and pepper.
11 Cover the breast with fat bacon.
12 Place the bird in a roasting tray on its side and coat with 200 g dripping or oil.
13 Roast in a moderate oven at 180–185°C.
14 Allow to cook on both legs; complete the cooking with the breast upright for the last 30 minutes.
15 Baste frequently and allow 15–20 minutes per ½ kg. If using a temperature probe, insert in the thickest part of the leg for a reading of 77°C.
16 Bake the two stuffings separately in greased trays until well cooked.

17 Prepare the gravy from the sediment and the brown stock. Correct the seasoning and remove the fat.
18 Remove the string and serve with the stuffings, roast gravy, bread sauce and/or hot cranberry sauce.
19 The turkey may be garnished with chipolata sausages and bacon rolls.

Note: When the turkey is cooked, to facilitate carving, remove and de-bone the legs. For ease of carving, before cooking turkeys may be completely boned and each leg must have the tough sinew removed. The breasts and the legs can both be stuffed, rolled and tied prior to roasting.

* No accompaniments, 200 g raw with skin and bone. With stuffing, roast gravy and bread sauce, 1 portion (200 g raw, with skin and bone) provides: 1589 kJ/380 kcal Energy; 24.0 g Fat; 8.4 g Sat Fat; 8.6 g Carb; 1.6 g Sugar; 34.0 g Protein; 0.9 g Fibre

2 Turkey escalopes

1 100 g slices cut from boned out turkey breast can be: lightly floured and gently cooked on both sides in butter, oil or margarine with a minimum of colour; or floured, egged and crumbed, and shallow-fried.

2 Serve with a suitable sauce and/or garnish (e.g. pan-fried turkey escalope cooked with oyster mushrooms and finished with white wine and cream).

3 Cranberry sauce

cranberries	400 g
water	100 ml
sugar	50 g

1 Simmer all ingredients together in a covered pan (not iron or aluminium) until soft.
2 The sauce may be sieved or liquidised if required.

Variation
For a variation half orange juice and half water, plus some grated orange zest may be used.

Chicken

4 Roast chicken (poulet rôti)

Cal	Cal	Fat	Sat Fat	Carb	Sugar	Protein	Fibre	*
1134 KJ	270 kcal	16.0 g	5.3 g	0.0 g	0.0 g	28.3 g	0.0 g	

	4 portions	10 portions
chicken, 1¼–1½ kg	1	2½
salt, pepper		
oil, butter or margarine	50 g	125 g
brown stock	125 ml	300 ml
game chips	25 g	60 g
bread sauce, to serve		
(page 60)	125 ml	300 ml

1 Lightly season the chicken inside and out with salt.
2 Place on its side in a roasting tin.
3 Cover with the oil, butter or margarine.
4 Place in hot oven for approximately 20–25 minutes. Turn on to the other leg.
5 Cook for a further 20–25 minutes approximately. Baste frequently.
6 To test if cooked, pierce with a fork between the drumstick and thigh and hold over a plate. The juice issuing from the chicken should not show any sign of blood. If using a temperature probe, proceed as for turkey (recipe 1). Place breast side down to retain all cooking juices.
7 Make roast gravy with the stock and sediment in the roasting tray.
8 Serve with game chips.

HEALTHY EATING TIP
• Use only a little salt to season the chicken and an unsaturated oil to cover it.
• Drain all fat from the roasting tray before making the roast gravy.
• Serve with plenty of potatoes and vegetables.

Note: Roast gravy and bread sauce are served separately. Always remove the trussing string from the bird before serving.

Variations
• Roast chicken and bacon: serve with four grilled rashers of streaky bacon, which may be rolled (after cooking).
• Spring chickens can be cooked and served as above with a reduced cooking time according to the weight of the birds. They can also be served with a savoury sauce (e.g. chasseur, Italienne, pepper, piquante or Madeira).

* Without accompaniments 200 g raw, with skin and bone. With game chips and bread sauce, 1 portion (200 g raw, with skin and bone) provides: 2513 kJ/598 kcal Energy; 46.8 g Fat; 17.3 g Sat Fat; 6.9 g Carb; 2.4 g Sugar; 37.8 g Protein; 1.1 g Fibre

5 Roast chicken with lemon and mustard

Cal	Cal	Fat	Sat Fat	Carb	Sugar	Protein	Fibre	Salt
2092 KJ	500 kcal	38.0 g	10.2 g	0.7 g	0.6 g	38.5 g	0.0 g	0.9 g

	4 portions
chicken	1 × 1½ kg chicken
lemon	2
olive oil	2 tbsp
Dijon mustard	2 tsp
salt, pepper	

1 Place the chicken in a roasting tray. Pierce one of the lemons with a fork and place inside the chicken.
2 Grate the zest of the other lemon and squeeze the juice into a bowl.

3 Mix the zest and juice with the olive oil and mustard. Season well with salt and pepper. Spread the lemon dressing all over the chicken, massaging in gently.
4 Roast in the oven for 15 minutes at 200°C then reduce to 180°C and cook for a further 20 minutes per 400 g.
5 When cooked, remove from roasting tray, remove the lemon, carve into portions and serve on a bed of rösti potatoes (recipe 60) and watercress.

6 Roast chicken with dressing (poulet rôti à l'anglaise)

Cal 1363 KJ	Cal 327 kcal	Fat 20.4 g	Sat Fat 3.7 g	Carb 6.7 g	Sugar 0.7 g	Protein 29.5 g	Fibre 0.3 g	*

onion, chopped	25 g
oil, butter or margarine	50 g
salt, pepper	
pinch chopped parsley	
pinch powdered thyme	
breadcrumbs (white or wholemeal)	50 g
the chopped chicken liver (raw) (optional)	

1 This recipe is as for roast chicken (recipe 4), but served with dressing, so proceed as for recipe 4 then make the dressing as follows.
2 Gently cook the onion in the oil, butter or margarine without colour.
3 Add the seasoning, herbs and breadcrumbs.
4 Mix in the liver.
5 Correct the seasoning and bake or steam separately, approximately 20 minutes.

HEALTHY EATING TIP
• Use a little unsaturated oil to cook the onion.
• Keep the added salt to a minimum.
• Serve with plenty of potatoes and vegetables.

* Based on average edible portion of roasted meat (100 g)

7 Sauté of chicken (poulet sauté)

Cal 1329 KJ	Cal 320 kcal	Fat 22.3 g	Sat Fat 8.1 g	Carb 0.3 g	Sugar 0.3 g	Protein 29.3 g	Fibre 0.0 g	*

	4 portions	10 portions
chicken, 1¼–1½ kg	1	2½
butter, margarine or oil	50 g	125 g
salt, pepper		
jus-lié or demi-glace	250 ml	625 ml
parsley, chopped		

1 Prepare the chicken for sauté (see page 334).
2 Place the butter, margarine or oil in a sauté pan on a fairly hot stove.
3 Season the pieces of chicken and place in the pan in the following order: drumsticks, thighs, carcass, wings, winglets and breast (tougher pieces first, as they take longer to cook).
4 Cook to a golden brown on both sides.
5 Cover with a lid and cook on the stove or in the oven until tender.
6 Remove the chicken pieces and dress neatly in an entrée dish.
7 Drain off all fat from the sauté pan.
8 Return to the heat, add the jus-lié or demi-glace and simmer for 3–4 minutes.

9 Correct the seasoning and skim.
10 Pass through a fine strainer on to the chicken.
11 Sprinkle with chopped parsley and serve.

Note: The cleaned chicken giblets may be used in the making of the sauce.

HEALTHY EATING TIP
• Use a minimum amount of salt to season the chicken.
• The fat content can be reduced if the skin is removed from the chicken.
• Use a little unsaturated oil to cook the chicken, and drain off all excess fat from the cooked chicken.
• Serve with a large portion of new potatoes and seasonal vegetables.

* Based on average edible portion of roasted meat (100 g)

8 Chicken sauté with mushrooms *(poulet sauté aux champignons)*

Cal 947 KJ	Cal 227 kcal	Fat 12.6 g	Sat Fat 5.4 g	Carb 0.8 g	Sugar 0.7 g	Protein 27.4 g	Fibre 0.0 g	*

	4 portions	10 portions
butter, margarine or oil	50 g	125 g
chicken, 1¼–1½ kg	1	2½
shallot, chopped	10 g	25 g
button mushrooms	100 g	250 g
dry white wine	60 ml	150 ml
demi-glace or jus-lié	250 ml	625 ml
salt, pepper		
parsley, chopped		

1 Prepare the chicken as for recipe 7, up to step 5.
2 Remove the chicken pieces and dress neatly in an entrée dish.
3 Add the shallots and mushrooms to the pan; cook gently for 3–4 minutes without colour. Drain off the fat, add the white wine, return to the heat and reduce by half.
4 Add the demi-glace or jus-lié, simmer for 5 minutes and correct the seasoning.
5 Pour over the pieces of chicken, sprinkle with chopped parsley.

* Based on average edible portion of roasted meat (100 g)

9 Chicken sauté chasseur *(poulet sauté chasseur)*

Cal 2430 KJ	Cal 579 kcal	Fat 45.8 g	Sat Fat 20.7 g	Carb 2.1 g	Sugar 1.6 g	Protein 37.6 g	Fibre 1.5 g	*

	4 portions	10 portions
butter, margarine or oil	50 g	125 g
salt, pepper		
chicken, 1¼–1½ kg, cut for sauté	1	2½
shallots, chopped	10 g	25 g
button mushrooms	100 g	250 g
dry white wine	3 tbsp	8 tbsp
jus-lié, demi-glace or reduced brown stock	250 ml	625 ml
tomatoes concassée	200 g	500 g
parsley and tarragon, chopped		

Figure 9.9 Ballotines of chicken chasseur

1 Place the butter, margarine or oil in a sauté pan on a fairly hot stove.
2 Season the pieces of chicken and place in the pan in the following order: drumsticks, thighs, carcass, wings, winglets and breast.
3 Cook to a golden brown on both sides.
4 Cover with a lid and cook on the stove or in the oven until tender. Dress neatly in a suitable dish.
5 Add the shallots to the sauté pan, cover with a lid, cook on a gentle heat for 1–2 minutes without colour.
6 Add the washed, sliced mushrooms and cover

HEALTHY EATING TIP
- Use a minimum amount of salt to season the chicken.
- The fat content can be reduced if the skin is removed from the chicken.
- Use a little unsaturated oil to cook the chicken, and drain off all excess fat from the cooked chicken.
- Serve with a large portion of new potatoes and seasonal vegetables.

with a lid; cook gently for 3–4 minutes without colour. Drain off the fat.

7 Add the white wine and reduce by half. Add the jus-lié, demi-glace or reduced brown stock.

8 Add the tomatoes concassée; simmer for 5 minutes.

9 Correct the seasoning and pour over the chicken.

10 Sprinkle with chopped parsley and tarragon; serve.

Note: Ballotines of chicken chasseur can be prepared as above or lightly braised (as shown in Figure 9.9).

* *Using butter*

10 Chicken spatchcock (poulet grillé à la crapaudine)

Cal	Cal	Fat	Sat Fat	Carb	Sugar	Protein	Fibre
1560 KJ	372 kcal	24.1 g	8.0 g	0.0 g	0.0 g	38.9 g	0.0 g

	4 portions	10 portions
chicken, 1¼–1½ kg	1	2½

1 Cut horizontally from below the point of the breast over the top of the legs down to the wing joints, without removing the breasts. Fold back the breasts.

2 Snap and reverse the backbone into the opposite direction so that the point of the breast now extends forward.

3 Flatten slightly. Remove any small bones.

4 Skewer the wings and legs in position.

5 Season with salt and mill pepper.

6 Brush with oil or melted butter.

7 Place on preheated grill bars or on a flat tray under a salamander.

8 Brush frequently with melted fat or oil during cooking and allow approximately 15–20 minutes on each side.

9 Test if cooked by piercing the drumstick with a needle or skewer – there should be no sign of blood.

10 Serve garnished with picked watercress and offer a suitable sauce separately (e.g. devilled sauce or a compound butter).

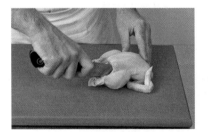  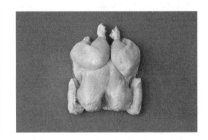

Figure 9.10 Spatchcock chicken: (a) cut either side of the backbone; (b) remove the backbone; (c) prepared for cooking

HEALTHY EATING TIP

- Use a minimum amount of salt to season the chicken.
- The fat content can be reduced if the skin is removed from the chicken.
- Use a small amount of an unsaturated oil to brush the chicken.
- Serve with a large portion of potatoes and vegetables.

11 Grilled chicken (poulet grillé)

Cal	Cal	Fat	Sat Fat	Carb	Sugar	Protein	Fibre	*
975 KJ	234 kcal	15.7 g	4.3 g	0.0 g	0.0 g	23.3 g	0.0 g	

1 Season the chicken with salt and mill pepper, and prepare as for grilling (see page 335).
2 Brush with oil or melted butter or margarine, and place on preheated greased grill bars or on a barbecue or a flat baking tray under a salamander.
3 Brush frequently with melted fat during cooking; allow approximately 15–20 minutes each side.
4 Test if cooked by piercing the drumstick with a skewer or trussing needle; there should be no sign of blood issuing from the leg.
5 Serve garnished with picked watercress and offer a suitable sauce separately.

Note: Grilled chicken is frequently served garnished with streaky bacon, tomatoes and mushrooms. The chicken may be marinated for 2–3 hours before grilling, in a mixture of oil, lemon juice, spices, herbs, freshly grated ginger, finely chopped garlic, salt and pepper. Chicken or turkey portions can also be grilled and marinated beforehand if wished (breasts or boned-out lightly battered thighs of chicken).

HEALTHY EATING TIP
- Use a minimum amount of salt and an unsaturated oil.
- Garnish with grilled tomatoes and mushrooms.
- Serve with Delmonico potatoes and green vegetables.

* Based on chicken with bone, wing and leg quarters

12 Suprêmes of chicken with spinach and tomato sauce

Cal	Cal	Fat	Sat Fat	Carb	Sugar	Protein	Fibre	Salt
1766 KJ	422 kcal	24.0 g	7.1 g	8.6 g	5.5 g	44.0 g	3.7 g	2.9 g

	4 portions	10 portions
chicken suprêmes (approx. 150 g each)	4	10
olive oil		
spinach	500 g	1¼ kg
salt, pepper		
fresh tomato sauce (page 60)	500 ml	1¼ litres
mozzarella	4 slices	10 slices
	(approx. 75 g)	(approx. 187 g)

1 Shallow-fry the chicken in olive oil until almost cooked.
2 Cook the spinach in a large pan until just wilted. Season.
3 Place the spinach in a suitable dish with the suprêmes on top. Cover with fresh tomato sauce.
4 On each suprême place a slice of mozzarella.
5 Finish in the oven until the chicken is fully cooked and the cheese has melted.
6 Serve immediately, neatly dressed on plates.

13 Suprême of chicken in cream sauce (suprême de volailles à la crème)

Cal	Cal	Fat	Sat Fat	Carb	Sugar	Protein	Fibre
1627 KJ	402 kcal	28.2 g	17.3 g	5.5 g	0.7 g	31.2 g	0.2 g

	4 portions	10 portions
butter, margarine or oil	50 g	125 g
flour	25 g	60 g
suprêmes of chicken (page 336)	4	10
dry sherry or white wine	30 ml	125 ml
double cream or non-dairy cream	125 ml	300 ml
salt, cayenne		

1 Heat the butter or oil in a sauté pan. Lightly flour the suprêmes.
2 Cook the suprêmes gently on both sides (7–9 minutes) with the minimum of colour.
3 Place the suprêmes in an earthenware serving dish; cover to keep warm.
4 Drain off the fat from the pan.
5 Deglaze the pan with the sherry or white wine.
6 Add the cream, bring to the boil and season.
7 Allow to reduce to a lightly thickened consistency. Correct the seasoning.
8 Pass through a fine strainer on to the suprêmes and serve.

Note: An alternative method of preparing the sauce is to use half the amount of cream (fresh or non-dairy) and an equal amount of chicken velouté (page 53).

HEALTHY EATING TIP

- The fat content can be reduced if the skin is removed from the chicken.
- Use a small amount of an unsaturated oil to cook the chicken, and drain off all the fat from the pan.
- The fat content will be less if half cream and half velouté is used.
- Serve with boiled potatoes and vegetables.

14 Fried chicken (deep-fried)

Cal	Cal	Fat	Sat Fat	Carb	Sugar	Protein	Fibre
1754 KJ	421 kcal	28.6 g	6.1 g	14.5 g	0.4 g	27.2 g	0.5 g

1 Cut the chicken as for sauté and: coat with either flour, egg and crumbs (pané); or pass through a light batter (page 187) to which herbs can be added.
2 For suprêmes, make an incision, stuff with a compound butter (page 65), flour, egg and crumb, and deep-fry as in Chicken Kiev (recipe 16).

HEALTHY EATING TIP

- The fat content can be reduced if the skin is removed from the chicken.

15 Crumbed breast of chicken with asparagus (suprême de volaille aux pointes d'asperges)

Cal 1831 KJ	Cal 439 kcal	Fat 26.4 g	Sat Fat 8.9 g	Carb 15.7 g	Sugar 1.5 g	Protein 35.5 g	Fibre 1.3 g

	4 portions	10 portions
suprêmes of chicken (page 336)	4 × 125 g	10 × 125 g
egg	1	2
breadcrumbs (white or wholemeal)	50 g	125 g
oil	50 g	125 g
butter or margarine	50 g	125 g
butter	50 g	125 g
jus-lié	60 ml	150 ml
asparagus	200 g	500 g

1 Pané the chicken suprêmes. Shake off all surplus crumbs.
2 Neaten and mark on one side with a palette knife.
3 Heat the oil and fat in a sauté pan.
4 Gently fry the suprêmes to a golden brown on both sides (6–8 minutes).
5 Dress the suprêmes on a flat dish and keep warm.
6 Mask the suprêmes with the remaining butter cooked to the nut brown stage.
7 Surround the suprêmes with a cordon of jus-lié.
8 Garnish each suprême with a neat bundle of asparagus points (previously cooked, refreshed and reheated with a little butter).

HEALTHY EATING TIP

- Use a minimum amount of salt.
- Remove the skin from the suprêmes and fry in a little unsaturated vegetable oil. Drain on kitchen paper.
- Try omitting the additional cooked butter.
- Serve with plenty of boiled new potatoes and vegetables.

16 Chicken Kiev (traditional)

	4 portions	10 portions
suprêmes of chicken	4 × 150 g	10 × 150 g
butter	100 g	250 g
seasoned flour	25 g	65 g
eggs	2	5
breadcrumbs	100 g	250 g

1 Make an incision along the thick sides of the suprêmes. Insert 25 g cold butter into each. Season.
2 Pass through seasoned flour, eggwash and crumbs, ensuring complete coverage. Eggwash and crumb twice if necessary.
3 Deep-fry, drain and serve.

Note: Chopped garlic and parsley can be added to the butter before insertion to add a variation, or other fine herbs can be used – for example, tarragon or chives.

17 Coronation chicken

Cal	Cal	Fat	Sat Fat	Carb	Sugar	Protein	Fibre	*
1435 KJ	346 kcal	27.7 g	4.8 g	2.0 g	1.7 g	22.3 g	0.2 g	

boiled chicken, cut into slices or 2 cm dice	800 g
curry paste or curry powder	1 tbsp
mayonnaise	250 ml
onion, finely chopped	50 g
olive oil	2 tbsp
fresh pineapple, 1 cm dice	100 g

HEALTHY EATING TIP

• The fat content will be reduced if low-fat Greek yoghurt or fromage frais is used in place of the mayonnaise, again lightly flavoured with curry.

1 Either mix the curry paste in the mayonnaise or sweat the onion in olive oil. Add the curry powder, sweat for further 2–3 minutes. Allow to cool, add to the mayonnaise.

2 Add the pineapple to the chicken, bind with the curried mayonnaise. Serve on fresh lettuce leaves. Garnish with strips of fresh red pimento.

Note: This is a popular dish usually served on buffets and as a sandwich filler. It consists of pieces of cooked chicken bound with curry-flavoured mayonnaise. The recipe presented here is a typical one.

Variations
There are a number of variations:
• dice of fresh pineapple and sultanas may be added to the chicken
• the curried mayonnaise may be finished with lightly whipped cream or fromage frais, or a Greek yoghurt
• alternatively, decorate with flakes of fresh coconut.

* Based on an 125 g serving

18 Confit chicken leg with leeks and artichokes

	4 portions	10 portions
confit oil*	1 litre	2½ litres
garlic cloves	4	10
bay leaf	1	3
sprig of thyme		
chicken legs	4 × 200 g	10 × 200 g
vegetable oil	50 ml	125 ml
globe artichokes, prepared, cooked and cut into quarters	4	10
whole leeks, blanched	2	5
brown chicken stock	250 ml	625 ml
butter	50 g	125 g
chives, chopped	1 tbsp	3 tbsp
seasoning		

* Confit oil is 50/50 olive oil and vegetable oil infused with herbs, garlic, whole spice or any specific flavour you wish to impart into the oil; then, through slow cooking in the oil, the foodstuff picks up the flavour.

1 Gently heat the confit oil, add the garlic, bay and thyme.

2 Put the chicken legs in the oil and place on a medium to low heat, ensuring the legs are covered.

3 Cook gently for 3–3½ hours.

4 To test if the legs are cooked, squeeze the flesh on the thigh bone and it should just fall away.

5 When cooked, remove the legs carefully and place on a draining tray.

6 Heat the vegetable oil in a medium sauté pan, add the artichokes and leeks, colour slightly and then add the brown chicken stock.

7 Reduce the heat to a simmer and cook for 4–5 minutes; meanwhile place the confit leg on a baking tray and place in a pre-heated oven at 210°C; remove when the skin is golden brown (approx. 5 minutes), taking care as the meat is delicate.

8 Place the chicken in a serving dish or on a plate, check the leeks and artichokes are cooked through, and bring the stock to a rapid boil, working in the butter to form an emulsion.

9 Add the chopped chives to the sauce and nap over the chicken leg.

Note: This is a great dish to utilise the by-product of the chicken crown; it is not only very cost-effective but has great depth of flavour due to the work the muscle group involved has done.

19 Boiled or poached chicken with rice and suprême sauce (poulet poché au riz, sauce suprême)

Cal	Cal	Fat	Sat Fat	Carb	Sugar	Protein	Fibre	*
5259 KJ	1252 kcal	86.0 g	35.7 g	59.6 g	1.5 g	63.3 g	1.9 g	

	4 portions	10 portions
boiling fowl, 2–2½ kg	1	2–3
studded onion	50 g	125 g
carrot	50 g	125 g
celery	50 g	125 g
bouquet garni		
peppercorns	6	12
salt		
Pilaff		
onion, chopped	50 g	125 g
butter, margarine or oil	50 g	125 g
rice (long grain)	200 g	500 g
chicken stock	500 ml	1¼ litres
Sauce		
butter, margarine or oil	75 g	180 g
flour	75 g	180 g
chicken stock	1 litre	2½ litres
cream (or non-dairy cream)	4 tbsp	10 tbsp
lemon juice, a few drops		

1 Place the chicken in cold water. Bring to the boil and skim.
2 Add the peeled, whole vegetables, bouquet garni, peppercorns and salt.

3 Simmer until cooked. To test, remove the chicken from the stock and hold over a plate to catch the juices from the inside of the bird. There should be no sign of blood. Also test the drumstick with a trussing needle, which should penetrate easily to the bone.
4 For the sauce, prepare ½ litre (1½ litres for 10 portions) of velouté from the cooking liquor and the ingredients listed above, cook out, correct the seasoning and pass through a fine strainer.
5 Finish with cream. Prepare a pilaff of rice (see page 162).
6 To serve, cut into portions. Dress the rice neatly in an entrée dish, arrange the portions of chicken on top and coat with the sauce.

HEALTHY EATING TIP
- Use the minimum amount of salt.
- Remove the skin from the cooked chicken.
- Try reducing or omitting the cream used to finish the sauce.
- Serve with plenty of rice and vegetables or salad.

* Using hard margarine

20 Chicken à la king (emincé de volaille à la king)

Cal	Cal	Fat	Sat Fat	Carb	Sugar	Protein	Fibre	*
1226 KJ	292 kcal	16.7 g	7.8 g	3.2 g	0.8 g	30.4 g	0.9 g	

	4 portions	10 portions
button mushrooms	100 g	250 g
butter, margarine or oil	25 g	60 g
red pimento, skinned	50 g	125 g
cooked boiled chicken	400 g	1¼ kg
sherry	30 ml	75 ml
chicken velouté	125 ml	150 ml
cream or non-dairy cream	30 ml	75 ml

1 Wash, peel and slice the mushrooms.
2 Cook them without colour in the butter or margarine.
3 If using raw pimento, discard the seeds, cut the pimento into dice and cook with the mushrooms.

4 Cut the chicken into small, neat slices.
5 Add the chicken to the mushrooms and pimento.
6 Drain off the fat. Add the sherry.
7 Add the velouté and bring to the boil.
8 Finish with the cream and correct the seasoning.
9 Place in a serving dish and decorate with small strips of cooked pimento.

Note: 1 or 2 egg yolks may be used to form a liaison with the cream mixed into the boiling mixture at the last possible moment and immediately removed from the heat. Chicken à la king may be served in a border of golden brown duchesse potato, or a pilaff of rice may be offered as an accompaniment. It is suitable for a hot buffet dish.

HEALTHY EATING TIP

• Use the minimum amount of salt.
• Remove the skin from the cooked chicken.
• Try reducing or omitting the cream used to finish the sauce.
• Serve with plenty of rice and vegetables or salad.

* Using butter or hard margarine

Figure 9.11 Chicken à la king

21 Chicken vol-au-vent (vol-au-vent de volaille)

Cal	Cal	Fat	Sat Fat	Carb	Sugar	Protein	Fibre	*
2754 KJ	656 kcal	50.7 g	21.2 g	20.0 g	0.6 g	31.0 g	0.9 g	

	8 portions
puff pastry (page 624)	400 g
oil	
eggwash	
boiling chicken, 2 kg	1
chicken velouté	½ litre
cream	4 tbsp

1 Prepare the puff pastry using ½ kg flour, ½ kg margarine and ¼ litre water.
2 Roll out sufficient to cut eight rounds of 8 cm diameter.
3 Turn upside-down on a lightly greased, damped baking sheet.
4 Using a smaller plain cutter dipped in hot oil, make incisions halfway through each, leaving a border of approximately ½ cm.
5 Eggwash, rest for 20 minutes then bake in a hot oven at 220–230°C for approximately 20–25 minutes.
6 When cool, remove the lids carefully with a small knife.
7 Empty out the raw pastry from the centre.
8 Cook the chicken as for boiled chicken (recipe 19).

9 Make a velouté and cook out; correct the seasoning and pass through a fine strainer; finish with cream.
10 Remove all skin and bone from the chicken.
11 Cut into neat pieces, mix with the sauce.
12 Fill the warm vol-au-vents to overflowing.
13 Add the lids, garnish with picked parsley and serve.

Note: Chicken and mushroom vol-au-vents can be made with the addition of 100 g of washed button mushrooms cut into quarters and cooked in a little stock with a few drops of lemon juice and 5 g butter.

HEALTHY EATING TIP

• Use the minimum amount of salt.
• Try leaving out the added cream from the velouté.
• The addition of mushrooms will slightly dilute the overall fat content.

* Using hard margarine

22 Chicken pancakes (crêpes de volaille)

Cal	Cal	Fat	Sat Fat	Carb	Sugar	Protein	Fibre
1423 KJ	339 kcal	18.9 g	6.3 g	24.7 g	3.4 g	19.0 g	1.1 g

	4 portions	10 portions
Pancake		
flour	100 g	250 g
egg	1	2–3
salt, pepper		
parsley, chopped		
milk (whole or skimmed)	¼ litre	600 ml
butter or margarine, melted	10 g	25 g
lard or oil	5 g	12½ g
Filling		
thick béchamel or		
chicken velouté	125 ml	300 ml
cooked chicken, free		
from bone and skin	200 g	500 g
salt, pepper		

1 Sieve the flour into a bowl and make a well in the centre.
2 Add the egg, salt, pepper, parsley and milk.
3 Gradually incorporate the flour from the sides of the bowl and whisk to a smooth batter.
4 Mix in the melted butter.
5 Heat the pancake pan; clean thoroughly.
6 Add the lard or oil; heat until smoking.
7 Add sufficient mixture to thinly cover the bottom of the pan.
8 Cook for a few seconds until light brown.
9 Turn and cook on the other side. Turn out onto a plate.
10 Wipe the pan clean and make a total of 8 small or 4 large pancakes (20 or 10 for 10 portions).
11 Meanwhile, prepare the filling by boiling the sauce.
12 Cut the chicken into neat small pieces and add to the sauce.
13 Mix in and correct the seasoning.
14 Divide the mixture between the pancakes, roll up each one and place in an earthenware dish.
15 Reheat in a hot oven and serve.

Note: Additions to the pancake filling can include mushrooms, ham, sweetcorn, etc., and the pancakes can be finished with a sauce such as mornay or chasseur.

HEALTHY EATING TIP
• Use semi-skimmed milk and the minimum of salt to make the pancakes.
• Lightly oil a well-seasoned pan with an unsaturated oil to fry the pancakes.
• Season the chicken with the minimum amount of salt.

23 Fricassée of chicken (fricassée de volaille)

Cal	Cal	Fat	Sat Fat	Carb	Sugar	Protein	Fibre	
2699 KJ	643 kcal	51.3 g	23.3 g	7.4 g	0.6 g	38.2 g	0.4 g	*

	4 portions	10 portions
chicken, 1¼–1½ kg	1	2–3
salt, pepper		
butter, margarine or oil	50 g	125 g
flour	35 g	100 g
chicken stock	½ litre	1¼ litres
egg yolks	1–2	5
cream or non-dairy cream	4 tbsp	10 tbsp
parsley, chopped		

1 Cut the chicken as for sauté (page 334); season with salt and pepper.
2 Place the butter in a sauté pan. Heat gently.
3 Add the pieces of chicken. Cover with a lid.
4 Cook gently on both sides without colouring. Mix in the flour.
5 Cook out carefully without colouring. Gradually mix in the stock.
6 Bring to the boil and skim. Allow to simmer gently until cooked.
7 Mix the yolks and cream in a basin (liaison).
8 Pick out the chicken into a clean pan.
9 Pour a little boiling sauce on to the yolks and cream and mix well.
10 Pour all back into the sauce, combine thoroughly but do not reboil.
11 Correct the seasoning and pass through a fine strainer.

12 Pour over the chicken, reheat without boiling.
13 Serve sprinkled with chopped parsley.
14 Garnish with heart-shaped croutons, fried in butter, if desired.

Note: A fricassée of chicken with button onions and mushrooms can be made in a similar way, with the addition of 50–100 g button onions and 50–100 g button mushrooms. They are peeled and the mushrooms left whole, turned or quartered depending on size and quality. The onions are added to the chicken as soon as it comes to the boil and the mushrooms 15 minutes later. Heart-shaped croutons may be used to garnish. This is a classic dish known as *fricassée de volaille à l'ancienne*.

HEALTHY EATING TIP

• Keep added salt to a minimum throughout the cooking.
• Use a little unsaturated oil to cook the chicken, and drain off all excess fat after cooking.
• Try oven-baking the croutons brushed with olive oil.
• The sauce is high in fat, so serve with plenty of starchy carbohydrate and vegetables.

* *Using butter*

Figure 9.12 ✎ Fricassée of chicken

24 Chicken pie

Cal	Cal	Fat	Sat Fat	Carb	Sugar	Protein	Fibre	*
3357 KJ	7.99 kcal	62.6 g	25.1 g	16.4 g	1.9 g	43.3 g	1.8 g	

	4 portions	10 portions
chicken, 1¼–1½ kg	1	2–3
salt, pepper		
streaky bacon	100 g	250 g
button mushrooms	100 g	250 g
onion, chopped	1	2½
chicken stock	½ litre	625 ml
pinch of chopped parsley		
hardboiled egg, chopped	1	2
puff pastry (page 624)	200 g	500 g

1 Cut the chicken as for sauté (page 334) or bone out completely and cut into pieces 4x1 cm.
2 Season lightly with salt and pepper.
3 Wrap each piece in very thin streaky bacon. Place in a pie dish.
4 Add the washed, sliced mushrooms and remainder of the ingredients, except the pastry.
5 Add sufficient cold stock to barely cover the chicken.

6 Cover with puff pastry and allow to rest in a refrigerator.
7 Eggwash and bake at 200°C for approximately 30 minutes, until the paste has set and the juice is simmering.
8 Reduce heat to 160–180°C and continue cooking for 45 minutes.

Note: If the pie is to be served cold, a soaked leaf of gelatine can be laid on the chicken before covering with pastry.

HEALTHY EATING TIP

• Add little or no salt – the bacon is salty.
• Remove the skin from the chicken.
• Serve with plenty of starchy carbohydrate and a large mixed salad.

* *Using hard margarine in the pastry*

25 Curried chicken (kari de poulet)

Cal	Cal	Fat	Sat Fat	Carb	Sugar	Protein	Fibre	*
2755 KJ	656 kcal	49.9 g	17.1 g	15.1 g	11.8 g	37.4 g	2.3 g	

	4 portions	10 portions
chicken, 1¼–1½ kg	1	2–3
salt		
oil	50 g	125 g
onion, chopped	200 g	500 g
clove garlic, chopped	1	2
flour	10 g	25 g
curry powder	10 g	25 g
tomato purée	25 g	60 g
chicken stock	½ litre	1¼ litre
sultanas	25 g	60 g
chutney, chopped	25 g	60 g
desiccated coconut	10 g	25 g
apple, chopped	50 g	125 g
root ginger or ground ginger, grated	10 g or 5 g	25 g or 12 g

1 Cut the chicken as for sauté (page 334), season lightly with salt.
2 Heat the oil in a sauté pan, add the chicken.
3 Lightly brown on both sides.
4 Add the onion and garlic.
5 Cover with lid; cook gently for 3–4 minutes.
6 Mix in the flour and curry powder.
7 Mix in the tomato purée. Moisten with stock.
8 Bring to the boil, skim.

9 Add the remainder of the ingredients. Simmer until cooked.
10 The sauce may be finished with 2 tablespoons cream or yoghurt.

Note: Accompany with 100 g plain boiled rice and/or grilled poppadom(s); see page 254 for extra accompaniments.

HEALTHY EATING TIP
• Use the minimum amount of salt.
• Remove the skin from the chicken.
• Use a small amount of an unsaturated vegetable oil to brown the chicken.
• Skim all the fat from the finished dish.
• Use low-fat yoghurt to finish the sauce.
• Serve with plenty of rice and a vegetable dish.

Variations
This is a European recipe in use today. For a traditional Asian recipe the curry powder would be replaced by either curry paste or a mixture of freshly ground spices (e.g. turmeric, cumin, allspice, fresh ginger, chilli, clove). See also Chapter 10: International cooking.

* *Using sunflower oil*

26 Braised rice with chicken livers (pilaff aux foies de volailles)

Cal	Cal	Fat	Sat Fat	Carb	Sugar	Protein	Fibre	*
1115 KJ	265 kcal	17.0 g	7.2 g	22.4 g	0.3 g	7.0 g	0.6 g	

	4 portions	10 portions
chicken livers	100 g	250 g
salt, mill pepper		
butter, margarine or oil	25 g	60 g
demi-glace or jus-lié	60 ml	150 ml
braised rice (**page 162**)	200 g	500 g

1 Trim the livers; cut into 1 cm pieces.
2 Season lightly with salt and pepper.
3 Fry quickly in the butter in a frying pan. Drain well.
4 Mix with the demi-glace or jus-lié; do not reboil.
5 Correct the seasoning.
6 Make a well in the rice on the dish.
7 Serve the livers in the centre of the rice.

* *Using hard margarine*

27 Chicken in red wine (coq au vin)

Cal 4794 KJ	Cal 1141 kcal	Fat 95.7 g	Sat Fat 32.9 g	Carb 16.6 g	Sugar 2.3 g	Protein 49.0 g	Fibre 1.7 g	*

	4 portions	10 portions
roasting chicken, 1½ kg	1	2–3
lardons	50 g	125 g
small chipolatas	4	10
button mushrooms	50 g	125 g
butter or margarine	50 g	125 g
sunflower oil	3 tbsp	7 tbsp
small button onions	12	30
red wine	125 ml	300 ml
brown stock *or* red wine	500 ml	900 ml
butter or margarine	25 g	60 g
flour	25 g	60 g
heart-shaped croutons	4	10
parsley, chopped		

1 Cut the chicken as for sauté (page 334). Blanch the lardons.
2 If the chipolatas are large divide into two.
3 Wash and cut the mushrooms into quarters.
4 Sauté the lardons, mushrooms and chipolatas in a mixture of butter/margarine and oil. Remove when cooked.
5 Lightly season the pieces of chicken and place in the pan in the correct order (see recipe 7) with button onions. Sauté until almost cooked. Drain off the fat.
6 Just cover with red wine and brown stock; cover with a lid and finish cooking.
7 Remove the chicken and onions, place into a clean pan.
8 Lightly thicken the liquor with a *beurre manié* from the 25 g (or 60 g) butter/margarine and 25 g (or 60 g) flour.
9 Pass the sauce over the chicken and onions, add the mushrooms, chipolatas and lardons. Correct the seasoning and reheat.
10 Serve garnished with heart-shaped croutons with the points dipped in chopped parsley.

HEALTHY EATING TIP
- Use a well-seasoned pan to dry-fry the lardons and chipolatas, then add the mushrooms.
- Use the minimum amount of added salt.
- Drain all the fat from the cooked chicken.
- Garnish with ovenbaked croutons.
- Serve with plenty of starchy carbohydrate and vegetables.

* *Using sunflower oil and hard margarine*

Duck

28 Duck breast steaks with berries

	4 portions	10 portions
duck breasts, skinned and scored	4	10
extra virgin olive oil	2 tbsp	5 tbsp
blackberries or blueberries	300 g	750 g
raspberry vinegar	4 tbsp	10 tbsp
bramble jelly or redcurrant jelly	4 tbsp	10 tbsp

1 Season and shallow-fry the duck breasts in the olive oil, skin side down, and finish in the oven at 200°C if required.
2 Meanwhile, place the berries, vinegar and jelly in a pan and heat gently until the jelly has melted. Simmer and remove from the heat.
3 Stir in 2 tbsp of the extra virgin olive oil for 4 portions and 5 tbsp for 10 portions.
4 Carve the breasts into slices and serve on top of the sauce with a garnish of spring vegetables.

29 Poached duck legs in white wine sauce

Cal	Cal	Fat	Sat Fat	Carb	Sugar	Protein	Fibre	Salt
1343 KJ	321 kcal	15.5 g	9.0 g	11.8 g	10.2 g	7.0 g	1.8 g	0.2 g

	4 portions	10 portions
duck legs (approx. 90 g each)	4	10
onion, finely chopped	1	2
rosemary	2 sprigs	5
parsley stalks	5	12
thyme	4 sprigs	10
carrots, cut into macedoine	2	5
leeks, finely shredded	1	2
courgettes macedoine	1	2
white wine	700 ml	1¾ litres
cold water or chicken stock		
double cream	100 ml	250 ml
salt, pepper		
butter, to finish		

1 Season the duck legs, quickly fry in a dry frying pan to colour both sides.
2 Place the onion, rosemary, parsley and thyme in a suitable casserole pan.
3 Add half the carrot, leek and courgettes to the pan.
4 Add the duck legs.
5 Add the white wine and stock or water to cover the duck legs. Bring to the boil, cover with a lid. Cook in the oven at 180°C for approximately 45 minutes.
6 Remove from the oven; remove the duck legs from the pan and keep warm.
7 Place the casserole on high heat and reduce the liquid by half. Strain and return the liquid to the casserole.
8 Add the remaining carrots, leek and courgettes to the liquid and boil for a few minutes.
9 Add the cream and reduce to the consistency of a sauce. Correct the seasoning and finish with butter.
10 Serve the duck legs with the sauce, creamed potatoes and vegetables.

30 Roast duck or duckling (canard ou caneton rôti)

Cal	Cal	Fat	Sat Fat	Carb	Sugar	Protein	Fibre	*
3083 KJ	734 kcal	60.5 g	16.9 g	8.2 g	7.8 g	40.0 g	1.4 g	

	4 portions	10 portions
duck	1	2–3
salt		
oil		
brown stock	¼ litre	600 ml
salt, pepper		
bunch watercress	1	2
apple sauce (page 314)	125 ml	300 ml

1 Lightly season the duck inside and out with salt.
2 Truss and brush lightly with oil.
3 Place on its side in a roasting tin, with a few drops of water.
4 Place in a hot oven for 20–25 minutes.
5 Turn on to the other side.
6 Cook for a further 20–25 minutes. Baste frequently.
7 To test if cooked, pierce with a fork between the drumstick and thigh and hold over a plate. The juice issuing from the duck should not show any signs of blood. If using a probe, the temperature should be 62°C.
8 Prepare the roast gravy with the stock and the sediment in the roasting tray. Correct the seasoning, remove the surface fat.
9 Serve garnished with picked watercress.
10 Accompany with a sauceboat of hot apple sauce, a sauceboat of gravy, and game chips. Also serve a sauceboat of sage and onion dressing as described in recipe 31.

Note: If the duck is required pink, the temperature should be 57°C.

HEALTHY EATING TIP

- Use the minimum amount of salt to season the duck and the roast gravy.
- Take care to remove all the fat from the roasting tray before making the gravy.
- This dish is high in fat and should be served with plenty of boiled new potatoes and a variety of vegetables.

* With apple sauce and watercress

Figure 9.13   Duck with orange (whole), with braised red cabbage, chateau potatoes and jug of orange jus

31 Dressing for duck

	4 portions	10 portions
onion, chopped	100 g	250 g
duck fat or butter	100 g	250 g
powdered sage	¼ tsp	½ tsp
parsley, chopped	¼ tsp	½ tsp
salt, pepper		
white or wholemeal breadcrumbs	100 g	250 g
duck liver (optional), chopped	50 g	125 g

1 Gently cook the onion in the fat without colour.
2 Add the herbs and seasoning. Mix in the crumbs and liver.
3 Cook the stuffing separately.
4 Cook and serve as for roast duck.

32 Duckling with orange sauce (caneton bigarade)

Cal	Cal	Fat	Sat Fat	Carb	Sugar	Protein	Fibre	*
3125 KJ	744 kcal	60.1 g	17.1 g	11.8 g	9.3 g	39.9 g	0.1 g	

	4 portions	10 portions
duckling, 2 kg	1	2–3
butter	50 g	125 g
carrots	50 g	125 g
onions	50 g	125 g
celery	25 g	60 g
bay leaf	1	2–3
small sprig thyme	1	2–3
salt, pepper		
brown stock	250 ml	625 ml
arrowroot	10 g	25 g
oranges	2	5
lemon	1	2
vinegar	2 tbsp	5 tbsp
sugar	25 g	60 g

1 Clean and truss the duck. Use a fifth of the butter to grease a deep pan. Add the mirepoix (vegetables and herbs).
2 Season the duck. Place the duck on the mirepoix.
3 Coat the duck with the remaining butter.
4 Cover the pan with a tight-fitting lid.
5 Place the pan in the oven at 200–230°C.
6 Baste occasionally; cook for approximately 1 hour.

7 Remove the lid and continue cooking the duck, basting frequently until tender (about a further 30 minutes).

8 Remove the duck, cut out the string and keep the duck in a warm place. Drain off all the fat from the pan.

9 Deglaze with the stock, bring to the boil and allow to simmer for a few minutes.

10 Thicken by adding the arrowroot diluted in a little cold water.

11 Reboil, correct the seasoning, degrease and pass through a fine strainer.

12 Thinly remove the zest from half the oranges and the lemon(s), and cut into fine julienne.

13 Blanch the julienne of zest for 3–4 minutes, then refresh.

14 Place the vinegar and sugar in a small sauteuse and cook to a light caramel stage.

15 Add the juice of the oranges and lemon(s).

16 Add the sauce and bring to the boil.

17 Correct the seasoning and pass through a fine strainer.

18 Add the julienne to the sauce; keep warm.

19 Remove the legs from the duck, bone out and cut into thin slices.

20 Carve the duck breasts into thin slices and dress neatly.

21 Coat with the sauce and serve.

Note: An alternative method of service is to cut the duck into eight pieces, which may then be either left on the bone or the bones removed.

* *Using butter*

HEALTHY EATING TIP

• Use the minimum amount of salt to season the duck and the final sauce.
• Take care to remove all the fat from the roasting tray before deglazing with the stock.
• Reduce the fat by removing the skin from the duck, and 'balance' this fatty dish with a large portion of boiled potatoes and vegetables.

Figure 9.14　Duck with orange (portion), with chateau potatoes and orange jus, and red cabbage underneath

33 Confit duck leg with red cabbage and green beans

	4 portions	10 portions
confit oil*	1 litre	2½ litres
garlic cloves	4	10
bay leaf	1	3
sprig of thyme	1	2
duck legs	4 × 200 g	10 × 200 g
butter	50 g	125 g
green beans, cooked and trimmed	300 g	750 g
braised red cabbage (see page 484)	250 g	625 g
seasoning		

* Confit oil is 50/50 olive oil and vegetable oil infused with herbs, garlic, whole spice or any specific flavour you wish to impart into the oil; then, through slow cooking in the oil, the foodstuff picks up the flavour.

1 Gently heat the confit oil, add the garlic, bay leaf and thyme.
2 Put the duck legs in the oil and place on a medium to low heat, ensuring the legs are covered.
3 Cook gently for 4–4½ hours (if using goose, 5–6½ hours may be needed).
4 To test if the legs are cooked, squeeze the flesh on the thigh bone and it should just fall away.
5 When cooked, remove the legs carefully and place on a draining tray.
6 When drained, put the confit leg on a baking tray and place in a pre-heated oven at 210°C; remove when the skin is golden brown (approx. 9–10 minutes), taking care as the meat is delicate.
7 Heat the butter in a medium sauté pan and reheat the green beans.
8 Place the braised cabbage in a small pan and reheat slowly.
9 Place the duck leg in a serving dish or plate along with the red cabbage and green beans.

Note: Confit duck legs can be prepared up to three or four days in advance. Remove them carefully from the fat they are stored in, clean off any excess fat and place directly into the oven. This is a great time-saver in a busy service.

34 Cranberry and orange dressing for duck

Cal	Cal	Fat	Sat Fat	Carb	Sugar	Protein	Fibre	*
398 KJ	93 kcal	0.2 g	0.0 g	22.7 g	22.7 g	1.3 g	4.2 g	

	4 portions	10 portions
cranberries	400 g	1 kg
granulated sugar	50 g	125 g
red wine	125 ml	250 ml
red wine vinegar	2 tbsp	5 tbsp
orange zest and juice	2	4

1 Place the cranberries in a suitable saucepan with the rest of the ingredients.
2 Bring to the boil and simmer gently for approximately 1 hour, stirring from time to time.
3 Remove from the heat and leave to cool. Use as required.

Note: The dressing may also be liquidised if a smooth texture is required.

* Using margarine reduced to half

35 Haricot bean stew with duck confit

Cal 2777 KJ	Cal 666 kcal	Fat 45.3 g	Sat Fat 16.0 g	Carb 29.6 g	Sugar 5.4 g	Protein 36.9 g	Fibre 9.4 g	*

	4 portions	10 portions
haricot beans, dried	200 g	500 g
carrot	1	2
onion, studded with cloves	1	2
pork rind, cut into 5 mm dice	200 g	500 g
belly of pork	200 g	500 g
thyme	1 sprig	2 sprigs
chicken stock	1 litre	2¼ litres
onions, finely chopped	50 g	125 g
crushed chopped garlic	2	5
duck fat	2 tbsp	4½ tbsp
tomato purée	2 tbsp	4½ tbsp
plum tomatoes, skinned, deseeded and diced	300 g	750 g
white wine	125 ml	250 ml
belly of pork (salted)	200 g	500 g
duck confit	2 legs	10 legs
ground white pepper, to taste		

1 Place the haricot beans in a suitable saucepan, cover with water, bring to the boil and simmer for 15 minutes.
2 Drain, place in another saucepan with the carrot, onion, pork rind, belly of pork and thyme.
3 Cover with chicken stock. Bring to the boil and simmer for 1 hour.

4 Remove the carrot, onion and thyme.
5 Lightly sauté the chopped onion and garlic in the duck fat until golden brown.
6 Add the tomato purée, the tomatoes and the white wine.
7 Cook for 10 minutes, then add the beans.
8 Purée the salted pork in a food processor (remove any bones first). Fold this into the beans. Continue to cook for approximately 1 hour.
9 Take special care during the cooking, making sure that the beans do not become too dry. If necessary, moisten with white wine, stock or water.
10 During the last ten minutes of cooking add the duck confit.
11 Correct the seasoning.
12 Serve immediately in a suitable dish garnished with flat parsley sprigs.

HEALTHY EATING TIP
• No added salt is needed as salted pork is added.
• Try using a larger amount of bean stew and less pork and duck fat to reduce the fat content.

* Based on 100 g raw meat and 10 g pork fat per person

Goose

36 Traditional roast goose

1 Roast in oven, allowing 15 minutes per 450 g plus another 15 minutes.
2 Serve with roast gravy, hot apple sauce, and sage and onion dressing (recipe 31).

37 Roast goose with citrus fruits

	4 portions	10 portions
oven-ready goose, crowned	1 × 4 kg	2 × 5 kg
orange	1	3
lemon	1	3
lime	1	3
salt and pepper		
chicken stock	400 ml	1 litre
confit fat	1 litre	2½ litre
confit goose legs (see duck confit, recipe 33)	2	4

1 Pre-heat the oven to 210°C. Take the goose and crown (see page 362), remove all pens and down.
2 Lightly score the fat in a harlequin style 3 mm apart, being careful not to penetrate the meat into both breasts.
3 Zest and juice the citrus fruits and mix together, season, place the shells of the fruit inside the goose carcass and ensure it is tightly packed.
4 Place a cooking wire over a drip tray and place the goose on top, pour the zest and the juice mix over the breasts and rub into the fat incisions.

5 Place the tray with the goose into a hot pre-heated oven and leave for 10 minutes.
6 Meanwhile bring the stock the boil; after the first 10 minutes of cooking carefully open the oven door and pour the hot stock over the goose – this will supercharge the oven and goose, releasing more fat from the breasts. Close the oven door and drop the temperature to 150°C.
7 Leave for 50–60 minutes, basting at 20–minute intervals with the fat and stock in the roasting tray.
8 For the last 30 minutes add the confit legs to the oven. Remove the legs and crown from the oven, placing the crown breast-side down to ensure maximum moisture retention.
9 Remove the breasts and carve into portions, giving each serving both leg and breast meat.
10 Serve with traditional accompaniments such as sage and onion dressing and apple sauce, or in a modern style.

Note: A great recipe to utilise all the goose, with both muscle groups afforded different methods of cookery to maximise their respective flavour and texture.

38 Roast goose with two dressings

	4–6 portions
free-range goose	1
salt, pepper	
chicken stock	250 ml
port	250 ml
Dressing 1	
dried apricots	100 g
port	60 ml
onion, finely chopped	1
back bacon, diced	50 g
butter	50 g
garlic, crushed and chopped	2 cloves
sausage meat	450 g
fresh breadcrumbs	85 g
fresh parsley, chopped	2 tbsp
fresh chopped thyme	½ tsp
chestnuts, peeled cooked and roughly chopped	150 g
egg	1
salt, pepper	
Dressing 2	
shallots, finely diced	350 g
butter	50 g
caster sugar	15 g
orange grated, zest and juice only	1
fresh sage, chopped	4 tbsp
hazelnuts, roasted, skinned and roughly chopped	100 g
fresh white breadcrumbs	150 g
egg	1
salt, pepper	

1 Trim off excess fat from the goose. Prick the skin of the goose. Season. Roast in the oven at 190°C, allowing 30 minutes per kg.
2 To test whether the goose is cooked, pierce the fattest part of the thigh with a skewer. If the juices run clear the goose is cooked. Rest for approximately 30 minutes and keep warm.
3 Drain the fat from the roasting tray. Deglaze the pan with good chicken stock and the port. Reduce and make the roast gravy, strain, skim off excess fat.

Dressing 1
1 Soak the dried apricots in the port for 1 hour.
2 Fry the onion and bacon gently in the butter until the onion is slightly brown and the bacon cooked.
3 Add the garlic, fry for 1 minute and allow to cool.
4 Mix into the sausage meat. Add the breadcrumbs, parsley, thyme and chestnuts. Bind with the egg. Place in a baking dish and cook in the oven at 180°C for approximately 20 minutes.

Dressing 2
1 Fry the shallots gently in butter until golden brown.
2 Add the caster sugar, orange zest and juice. Cook to a syrup.
3 Allow to cool. Add the sage to the shallots with the hazelnuts, breadcrumbs and egg. Season.

Note: Put aside the excess goose fat for roast potatoes and roast vegetables.

Guineafowl

39 Suprêmes of guineafowl with a pepper and basil coulis

Cal	Cal	Fat	Sat Fat	Carb	Sugar	Protein	Fibre	Salt	*
904 KJ	216 kcal	4.7 g	1.3 g	7.8 g	7.3 g	35.8 g	1.9 g	0.5 g	

	4 portions	10 portions
red peppers	3	7
olive oil	150 ml	375 ml
fresh basil, chopped	2 tbsp	5 tbsp
salt, pepper		
guineafowl suprêmes (approx. 150 g each)	4	10

1 Skin the peppers by brushing with oil and gently scorching in the oven or under the grill. Alternatively, use a blowtorch with great care. Once scorched, peel the skin from the peppers, cut in half and deseed.

2 Place the skinned and deseeded peppers in a food processor, blend with the olive oil and pass through a strainer.
3 Add the chopped basil and season.
4 Season the guineafowl and either shallow-fry or grill.
5 Pour the coulis on to individual plates. Place the guineafowl on top and serve immediately.

*Using chicken in place of guineafowl

Game

Game is the name given to certain wild birds and animals that are eaten. There are two types of game:

1 feathered
2 furred.

Origins

The word game is used, for culinary purposes, to describe animals or birds that are hunted for food, although many types of categorised game are now being bred domestically (e.g. squab (pigeon), duck, venison). Wild animals, because of their diet and general lifestyle, have select enzymes in their tissues, which are more abundant in game than in poultry. These tissues break down or metabolise meat proteins; they become active about 24 hours after the animal has been killed, softening the meat, and making it gelatinous and more palatable, as well as giving the characteristic 'gamey' flavour. They also contain micro-organisms (anaerobes), which also help to break down the proteins.

Choosing and buying

The most important factor when buying game is to know its 'life age' and its 'hanging age', since this will determine the method of cookery to be used. Indications of age are by no means infallible, but there are some general guidelines when buying young birds – soft-textured feet, pliable breastbones – and young partridges have pointed flight feathers (the first large feather of the wing), while in older birds these feathers are more rounded. There are many other distinctive guidelines you can use when selecting game, however the grading of game is a specialised subject and best left to the experts.

Hanging of game

Game bought from a main dealer will probably have been hung correctly. If, however, you require your game (or any other meat that benefits from hanging) to be hung specifically for you, speak to your butcher or game dealer. The general rules are to hang in a cool, dry, airy place, protected from flies to prevent maggot infestation. However, there is no real need to hang game, due to the metabolic enzymes present, so if you object to the strong flavour hanging promotes, a short hanging period, or no hanging at all, may be preferable. As a general rule you should hang the carcass until you detect the first whiff of tainting. In Britain, birds are usually hung from their heads, feet down, and rabbits and other game hung with their heads down.

Cooking of game

Game meat responds best to roasting. Young game birds in particular should be roasted and it is traditional to leave them unstuffed. Due to the

Table 9.2 Seasonality of game

	JAN	FEB	MAR	APR	MAY	JUN	JUL	AUG	SEP	OCT	NOV	DEC
Furred												
Hare												
Rabbit												
Venison												
Feathered												
Goose (wild)												
Goose (farmed)												
Grouse								12th				
Mallard												
Moorhen												
Partridge (English grey leg)												
Partridge (French red leg)												
Pheasant												
Pigeon (farmed)												
Pigeon (English wood)												
Quail												
Snipe								12th				
Teal												
Woodcock												

Code: .
Available
At best

361

low fat content of game, especially wild non-domestic varieties, added fat in the form of sliced streaky bacon, lardons and the like can be wrapped around the bird to help baste while cooking, thus retaining moisture. Older, tougher game or high-worked muscle groups, such as a haunch of venison, should be casseroled or made into pies or terrines. Marinating in oil, vinegar or wine with herbs and spices helps make tough meat more tender; it may also enhance the taste and it speeds up the action of the metabolic enzyme that breaks the game down.

Storage of game

It would be wise to allow game to be hung at specific game dealers as current legislation does not allow a normal kitchen environment to hang or pluck game. Game should be wrapped well and careful consideration given to its age; strict labelling is essential because, when in prime condition, the meat may have a slightly tainted smell, which may be difficult to discern from the smell that denotes the meat is past its best.

Preparation

Drawing and washing

This is the process that is carried out when the bird is sold with all its entrails still inside. To remove, make a small lateral incision into the backside of the bird, then insert your forefinger and index finger, and roll them around the inner cavity of the bird, thus loosening the membrane that holds in the innards. When loose, remove from the wider backside and discard. Ensure that all the innards are removed, wash and dry well.

Tunnel boning, leg removal and crowning

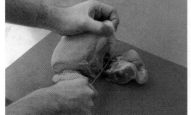

Figure 9.15 ✏ Leg removal and preparing the crown

Figure 9.16 ✏ Tunnel boning, demonstrated on a leg of lamb

Preparation of ballotines

  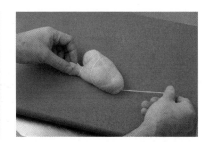

Figure 9.17 ✎ Preparation of ballotines

Some notes on cooking with game

When game birds (e.g. pheasant, partridge, grouse) are roasted they should always be served on a croûte of fried bread, garnished with thick round pieces of toasted French bread spread with game farce (recipe 40), game chips and picked watercress.

As game birds are deficient in fat, a thin slice of fat bacon (bard) should be tied over the breast during cooking to prevent it from drying; this is also placed on the breast when serving. Roast gravy, bread sauce and browned breadcrumbs (toasted or fried) are served separately.

Information on the nutritional value of the main types of game is provided in Table 9.3.

Pigeon

As pigeons do not have gall bladders it is not necessary to remove the livers when they are drawn and cleaned.

Tender young pigeons less than 12 months old can be roasted, pot roasted, or split open and

grilled and served (for example, with a Robert, charcutière or devilled sauce).

Young pigeons can be cut in half, flattened slightly, seasoned, shallow-fried in butter, and cooked and finished as for sautés of chicken (e.g. chasseur, bordelaise).

Quail

Only plump birds with firm white fat should be selected. When prepared the entrails are drawn, but the heart and liver are retained inside the birds. They may be roasted, spit roasted, cooked 'en casserole' or poached in a rich, well-flavoured chicken or veal stock (or a combination of both).

Quails may also be boned out from the back and stuffed with a forcemeat.

Hare and rabbits

The ears of hare and rabbits should tear easily. With old hare, the lip is more pronounced than in young animals. The rabbit is distinguished from the hare by its shorter ears, feet and body.

Table 9.3 ✎ Nutritional information for venison in comparison with other meats

	Fat g/100 g	Protein g/100 g	Iron mg/100 g	Cholesterol mg/100 g
venison	1.6	22.2	3.3	29
chicken	2.1	22.3	0.7	90
beef	12.9	20.4	1.3	48
lamb	12.3	19.0	¼	78
pork	2.2	21.7	0.8	64

Venison

Venison is the meat of the red deer, fallow deer and roebuck. Of these three, the meat of the roebuck is considered to have the best and most delicate eating quality. The prime cuts are the legs, loins and best ends. The shoulder of young animals can be boned, rolled and roasted, but if in any doubt as to its tenderness, it should be cut up and used for stewed or braised dishes.

The main types available are:

- roe deer
- fallow deer
- red deer
- sika deer.

Venison is available from most catering butchers. It is a good meat to use when planning healthier menus as it contains little fat. The fat in venison is mainly polyunsaturated and therefore lower in cholesterol.

Venison is a good source of protein as 100 g of venison supplies 68.5 per cent of the daily value for protein for only 179 calories and 1.4 g of saturated fat. Venison is also a good source of iron, providing 28.2 per cent of the daily value of iron in a 100 g serving. It is also a very good source of vitamin B12, providing 60 per cent of the recommended daily amount of this vitamin, as well as a significant amount of several other B vitamins, including riboflavin (it offers 40 per cent of riboflavin's daily value, 38 per cent of niacin's daily value and 21.5 per cent of the daily value for vitamin B6).

Vitamins B12 and B5 are both needed to prevent the build-up of a potentially dangerous molecule called 'homocysteine' in the body. High levels of homocysteine can cause damage to the blood vessels and contribute to the development of diabetic heart disease.

Quality points

- The flesh should be dark red in colour.
- The flesh should be dry and firm.
- The carcass should have a good amount of flesh and a close grain texture.
- The flesh should be lean, with little fat.
- There should be no unpleasant smell.

Cuts and joints of venison

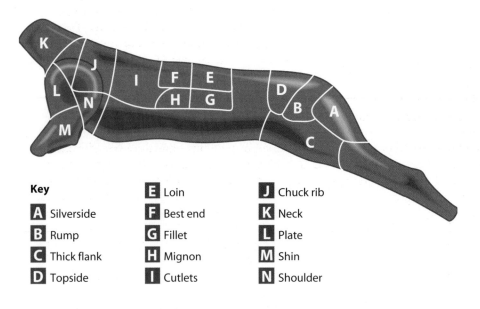

Key

A	Silverside	E	Loin	J	Chuck rib
B	Rump	F	Best end	K	Neck
C	Thick flank	G	Fillet	L	Plate
D	Topside	H	Mignon	M	Shin
		I	Cutlets	N	Shoulder

Figure 9.18 ✐ Cuts and joints of venison

Table 9.4 ✎ Examples of cuts and joints of venison

Cut	Joints	Approximate weights	Uses
Haunch	Silverside	2 kg	Stewing, braising
	Topside	2 kg	Roasting, braising
	Thick flank	1.5 kg	Stewing
	Rump dice, escalopes	1.5 kg	Roasting, braising, frying
Saddle	Saddle	8 kg	
	Loin	1.4 kg	
	Noisettes	1 kg	
	Chops	1 kg	
	Filet mignon	0.5 kg	Roasting, braising, frying
Best end	Best end cutlets	1.5 kg	Frying, roasting, braising
Fillet	Fillet	1 kg	Escalopes, medallions, steaks
Shin	Shin	0.5 kg	Dice, mince, stewing
Neck	Neck	2 kg	Grilling, dice mince, stewing
Shoulder	Shoulder	4 kg	
	Chuck rib	2 kg	mince, burgers, sausages

Note: Weights will vary according to breed of venison and time of year.

Storage
After slaughter, carcasses should be hung well in a cool place for several days and, when cut into joints, are usually marinated before being cooked. Joints of venison should be well fleshed and a dark brownish-red colour.

Cutlets, chops and steaks
1 Venison cutlets (cut from the best end) and chops (cut from the loin) are usually well trimmed and cooked by shallow-frying, provided that the meat is tender. If in doubt, they should be braised.
2 After they are cooked they should be removed from the pan, the fat poured off and the pan deglazed with stock, red wine, brandy, Madeira, or sherry, which is then added to the accompanying sauce.
3 A spicy, peppery sauce is usually offered, which can be varied by the addition of any one or more extra ingredients (e.g. cream, yoghurt, redcurrant jelly, choice of cooked beetroot, sliced button or wild mushrooms, cooked pieces of chestnut, and so on).
4 Accompaniments can include, for example, a purée of a root vegetable (e.g. celeriac, turnip,

swede, carrot, parsnip or any combination of these).
5 Venison steaks, or escalopes, are cut from the boned-out nuts of meat from the loins, trimmed well and thinned slightly with a meat bat.
6 The escalopes can be quickly shallow-fried and finished as for cutlets and chops, and served with a variety of accompanying sauces and garnishes.
7 Roast haunch of venison, which may also be braised, is popular served hot or cold.

Wild boar

For good quality, buy animals obtained from suppliers using as near as possible 100 per cent pure breeding stock wild boars that are free to roam and forage for food, rather than those that have been penned and fed.

Animals between 12 and 18 months old, weight 60–75 kg on the hoof, are best slaughtered in the late summer when their fat content is lower. The meat should be hung for 7 to 10 days before being used.

Young boar up to the age of six months are sufficiently tender for cooking in noisettes and cutlets, and joints for roasting. The prime cuts of older animals (e.g. leg, loin, best end) can be marinated and braised. Boar's head is prepared by boning the head and stuffing it with a forcemeat to which strips of ox tongue, *foie gras*, truffles and pistachio nuts can be added. The head is tied securely in a cloth and simmered gently. When cooled it is completely coated and the tusks are re-inserted. Boar's head is a traditional Christmas cold buffet dish served with a spicy sauce (e.g. Cumberland).

Game recipes

General

40 Game farce

	4 portions	10 portions
butter or margarine	50 g	125 g
salt, pepper		
game livers	100 g	250 g
onion, chopped	25 g	60 g
sprigs of thyme		
bay leaf		

1 Heat half the fat in a frying pan.
2 Quickly toss the seasoned livers, onion and herbs, browning well but keeping underdone. Pass through a sieve or mincer.
3 Mix in the remaining butter.
4 Correct the seasoning.

Pigeon

41 Roast pigeon with red chard, celeriac and treacle

	4 portions	10 portions
celeriac, peeled and cut into 2½ cm dice	1	2
milk and water, to cook the celeriac		
squab pigeon crowns (350–400 g each)	4	10
butter, to place in the squab cavity	50 g	125 g
parsnip batons	12	30
butter, to cook the parsnips	75 g	185 g
vegetable stock	200 ml	500 ml
reduced brown stock	100 ml	250 ml
red chard, picked and washed	200 g	500 g
black treacle	5 g	15 g

1 In a saucepan, cook the chopped celeriac until soft in a mixture of half milk and half water.
2 Drain off all the liquid, then purée the celeriac in a food processor.
3 When smooth, place in a clean pan and return to the stove. Cook until thick, letting as much moisture evaporate as possible.

4 Pre-heat the oven to 180°C. Adjust the seasoning to taste.
5 Roast the squab on the bone for 3 minutes on its back and 3 minutes on its breast.
6 Remove and rest with the butter evenly placed in the cavity to add extra moisture to the bird.
7 Cook the parsnips in butter and vegetable stock, place to one side and keep warm.
8 Wilt the chard, season and drain.
9 Warm the celeriac purée and place on the plate with the chard and the parsnip batons.
10 Carefully remove the two breasts from the bone, place on the chard and liberally drizzle the sauce over the breasts and the plate.
11 If red chard is unavailable you can substitute with spinach or pak choi.
12 Reduce brown stock by half again, add treacle sauce and plate.

Note: All elements of this dish can be used elsewhere – for example, the celeriac purée is a suitable component for most poultry dishes.

42 Pot au feu of pigeon

	4 portions	10 portions
squabs, legs removed	6 (approx. 2 kg)	10 (approx. 3½ kg)
carrot, peeled and cut into 4 laterally	1	3
celery stick, cut into 4	1	3
baby turnips	8	20
medium turnips, peeled and blanched	2	4
leek, washed, cut in rounds	1	3
small shallots, peeled and left whole	8	20
smoked streaky bacon, rind removed	100 g	250 g
chicken/game stock	400 ml	1 litre
bouquet garni with 4 black peppercorns and 1 clove garlic	1	3
salt		

1 Place the squab legs in a large casserole and arrange the vegetables tightly in one layer with the legs, add the bacon, then cover with the stock to about 4 cm above the ingredients (you may need to top this up with water).
2 Add the muslin-wrapped bouquet garni. Season with salt and bring to a gentle boil.
3 Skim off any impurities, cover with a lid (leaving a small gap), and simmer gently for 50 minutes.
4 Skim off any fat or impurities, then add the squab breasts and cook for a further 12 minutes.

5 Taste the broth, correct the seasoning and serve with rich mashed potato or minted new potatoes, depending on the season.

Note: This is a family or social dish, designed to be placed in the middle of the table and served with warm, crusty bread, mashed potato or buttered new potatoes.

43 Sauté of pigeon salad with rocket, Parmesan and beetroot

	4 portions	10 portions
squab crowns (350–400 g each) (see page 362)	4	10
oil	50 ml	125 ml
pigeon/game glaze (reduced stock from pigeon bones)	50 ml	125 ml
salad dressing	50 ml	125 ml
salt and pepper		
cooked beetroot batons	100 g	250 g
mixed salad leaves	200 g	500 g
rocket, washed and picked	250 g	600 g
shaved Parmesan	50 g	125 ml

1 Remove the breasts from the crowns (see page 362) and cut each breast into three.

2 Heat the oil in a pan, place in the squab and sauté for 2–3 minutes with a little colour, leaving the meat pink.
3 Remove from the pan and place on a draining wire in a warm place. Add the squab glaze and dressing to the pan, removing all sediment.
4 Season the squab before presenting on the plate.
5 Pour into a small dish and allow to cool slightly. Arrange the squab and beetroot in the centre of a plate, dress the mixed leaves, rocket and Parmesan and place carefully on the squab. Finish the dish with the remaining jus/dressing.

Note: This is a great summer dish as the squabs could even be chargrilled or cooked on a barbecue for greater depth of flavour. Alternatively, this preparation would be just as effective with partridge.

Pheasant

44 Poached pheasant crown with chestnuts and cabbage

	4 portions	10 portions
chicken stock	2 litres	5 litres
pheasant crowns (see page 362)	2	5
butter	50 g	125 g
savoy cabbages, cored, shredded and blanched	2	5
cooked bacon lardons	75 g	187.5 g
reduced chicken stock	250 g	625 g
cooked chestnuts	175 g	437.5 g
double cream	50 ml	125 ml
parsley, chopped	5 g	12.5 g
salt and pepper		
lemons, juice of	1	2½

1 Bring the stock up to a simmer and place the crowns in it; simmer for 11 minutes.
2 Meanwhile, place the butter in a medium pan on a

moderate heat and melt. Add the cabbage and bacon lardons and 100 ml of reduced chicken stock.
3 When the cabbage and bacon have formed an emulsion with the butter and stock, put to one side and retain.
4 Remove the pheasant crowns and rest for 2–3 minutes breast-side down.
5 Remove the breasts from the crown and check if cooked; if not quite cooked place back in the cooking liquor for 1–2 minutes. Then place the cooked breasts in a serving dish and keep warm.
6 Add the cooked chestnuts to the remaining reduced chicken stock and bring to the boil, adding the cream. At this point add the chopped parsley and check the seasoning – if the sauce appears to be rich this can be modified with a little lemon juice. You should not be able to taste the lemon but using it allows the deep flavours of the sauce to come through.
7 Place the cabbage mix in the centre of the plate

and top this with the pheasant; finish with the sauce over and around, ensuring an even distribution of chestnuts.

Note: With the legs from the crowns, why not make a pheasant leg garbure and serve as a secondary part of the preparation, taking the dish from four portions to eight.

45 Roast breast of pheasant with vanilla and pear

	4 portions	10 portions
cold water	250 ml	625 ml
caster sugar	90 g	225 g
salt (for curing the breasts*)	90 g	225 g
large pheasant breasts, removed from the bone with skin and wing tip attached	4	10
unsalted butter	70 g	175 g
shallots, diced	4	9
large vanilla beans, scraped to gather the seeds	1	3
dry white wine, preferably Chardonnay	150 ml	375 ml
pear/apple cider	300 ml	750 ml
whipping cream	300 ml	750 ml
preserved ginger, finely chopped	15 g	35 g
freshly ground black pepper		
salt		
dry red wine	250 ml	625 ml
honey	75 g	185 g
coriander seeds, toasted and finely crushed	10 g	25 g
pears (preferably red), halved, cored and sliced into 1 cm-thick slices	2	5
sprigs of chervil		

* 'Cure' is used in the same way here as for curing bacon, using the salt and the sugar in the recipe.

To cure the pheasant
1 In a large bowl combine the water, 25 g/62.5 g each of sugar and salt, mixing to dissolve.
2 Add the pheasant breasts, cover with plastic wrap and refrigerate overnight.

To make the sauces
1 In a large sauté pan, heat 1 tbsp/2½ tbsp of the butter over medium to medium-high heat. Add the shallots, cooking until tender (about 3 minutes). Add the vanilla bean and seeds, white wine, cider and cream. Bring to a simmer, cooking until the liquids are reduced and thickened to sauce consistency (about 10 minutes). Add the ginger, season with salt and pepper, keep warm.
2 In another saucepan, combine the red wine and the honey. Bring to a simmer over high heat, cooking until reduced to coat the back of a spoon (about 15 minutes). Reserve.

To cook the pheasants
1 Pre-heat the oven to 190°C.
2 In a large sauté pan, add 2 tbsp/5 tbsp butter and melt over a high heat. Season the pheasant with salt, pepper and coriander. Add the pheasant skin-side down, cooking until browned and well seared (about 5 minutes). Turn over and transfer the pan to the lower rack of the oven. Cook until just about medium (about 6 to 8 minutes, depending on the size of the pheasant breast). Carefully remove the hot pan from the oven. Allow to rest a couple for of minutes before cutting.
3 In another large pan, heat 1 tbsp/2½ tbsp of the butter over high heat. Add the pears, cooking until they just begin to soften slightly (about 2 minutes). Add 2 tbsp/5 tbsp of the sugar, cooking and stirring occasionally until browned on the edges (about 4 minutes). Remove the pears and keep warm.

To serve
1 Position the pear slices in the centre of the plate. Slice the pheasant on a bias to yield 4 or 6 thin broad slices. Spoon the vanilla-ginger and red wine sauce over and around the pheasant and on the plate. Garnish with the vanilla bean and sprigs of chervil over the pheasant. Serve immediately.

Note: This dish will work equally well with corn-fed chicken or guineafowl. Vanilla extract can be used instead of vanilla pods.

Partridge

46 Roast partridge

	4 portions	10 portions
grey-legged partridges (approx. 400 g each), oven-ready, with livers	4	10
unsalted butter	20 g	50 g
groundnut oil	20 g	50 g
salt		
freshly ground pepper		
roasting juices from veal, pork or beef	70 ml	175 ml
water	50 ml	125 ml

1 Shorten the wings and sear the partridges under a flame to remove the feather stubs. Remove any trace of gall from the liver. Wash briefly, pat dry and reserve.
2 In a roasting tray sear the wing bones and the partridges in butter and oil for 2 minutes on each side and 2 minutes on the breast (6 minutes in total) until they are brown.
3 Season with salt and pepper, and roast in the pre-heated oven for 5–6 minutes, according to the size of the partridges.
4 Remove from the oven and place the partridges on a cooling wire breast-side down, cover loosely with aluminium foil and allow to rest.
5 In the same roasting tray, fry the livers in the remaining butter and oil for 1 minute, and reserve. Spoon out the excess fat and add the roasting juices and water to the winglets, bring to the boil then simmer for 5 minutes.
6 Taste and season with salt and pepper, then strain through a fine sieve.
7 Serve with roasted seasonal vegetables (e.g. roast parsnips, carrots and braised cabbage). Suggested accompaniments: bread sauce, roast gravy, watercress and game chips.

Note: Simply roasted partridge is a great autumnal and winter base for most accompaniments: braised cabbage, roast carrots, parsnips, and so on.

47 Braised partridge with cabbage

Cal	Cal	Fat	Sat Fat	Carb	Sugar	Protein	Fibre	*
750 KJ	337 kcal	57.6 g	14 g	11.5 g	6.2 g	17.8 g	0.0 g	

	4 portions	10 portions
old partridges	2	5
lard, butter, margarine or oil	100 g	250 g
cabbage	400 g	1¼ kg
belly of pork or bacon, in the piece	100 g	250 g
carrot, peeled and grooved	1	2–3
studded onion	1	2–3
bouquet garni		
white stock	1 litre	2½ litres
frankfurter sausages or pork chipolatas	8	20

1 Season the partridges, rub with fat, brown quickly in a hot oven and remove.
2 Trim the cabbage, remove the core, separate the leaves and wash thoroughly.
3 Blanch the cabbage leaves and the belly of pork for 5 minutes. Refresh and drain well to remove all water. Remove the rind from the pork.
4 Place half the cabbage in a deep ovenproof dish; add the pork rind, the partridges, carrot, onion, bouquet garni, stock and the remaining fat; season lightly.
5 Add the remaining cabbage and bring to the boil, cover with greased greaseproof paper or foil, put on a lid and braise slowly until tender (approx. 1½–2 hours).
6 Add the sausages halfway through the cooking time, placing them under the cabbage.
7 Remove the bouquet garni and the onion and serve everything else, the pork and carrot being sliced.

Note: Older or red-legged partridges are suitable for this dish.

* Based on 100 g cooked meat and oil

Grouse

	4 portions	10 portions
Grouse		
young grouse (approx. 750 g each), wings removed	4	10
hearts and livers from the grouse		
sage leaves	4	10
butter	20 g	50 g
salt and pepper		
Stock		
Oil	30 ml	80 ml
grouse wings		
giblets		
large onion	1	2
celery stick	1	3
carrot	1	3
red wine	250 ml	625 ml
water		
sprig of thyme		
bay leaf	1	3
Toast		
small slices of bread	16	40
duck fat		
To serve		
bread sauce		
bunches watercress	1	2
game chips		

1 Trim the wings from the young grouse, draw and reserve the livers, hearts and giblets. Season birds liberally inside and out, and put the livers and hearts back in with a sage leaf and a knob of butter. Pre-heat the oven to its maximum (approx. 240°C).
2 Brown the wings and the remaining giblets with the diced onion, celery and carrot. Deglaze pan with red wine, cover with water and simmer for 30 minutes with the thyme and bay leaf. Strain and reserve.
3 Meanwhile, fry the bread in duck fat. Make bread sauce and pick through watercress.
4 To cook, place birds at top of oven and leave for 6 minutes, by which time the legs should be starting to brown.
5 Put bird back in oven for another 7 minutes until, when inserted into the deepest point above the wing, a temperature probe reads 57–60°C.
6 Remove from the pan and leave the birds to rest for 10 minutes in a warm place, on top of the toast, so that the blood drips into it.
7 Put the roasting tray over a flame, add a splash of brandy and the stock, and allow to bubble down to a thin gravy.
8 To serve, scoop out the liver, heart and *foie gras*, mash these up and serve on the toast. Stick a bunch of the watercress into the grouse's cavity and put the bird and toast onto a plate with some bread sauce and game chips. Pour a little of the gravy over each bird and serve remaining gravy separately.

Note: Good-quality grouse is essential for this dish – birds that have not been over-hung. The meat will already have a strong pungent flavour embedded in it from the birds' diet of heather.

Quail

49 Quail with pomegranate and blood orange

	4 portions	10 portions
oil	10 ml	25 ml
butter	50 g	125 g
salt and pepper		
oven-ready quails		
(approx. 75 g each)	8	20
blood oranges	2	5
pomegranate	1	2
mixed leaves	200 g	650 g
split cooked green beans	100 g	250 g
vinaigrette		

1 Pre-heat the oven to 180°C.
2 Heat a medium saucepan and add the oil and butter.
3 Season the quails and place in the pan, backs down, colour evenly all over, place in a roasting tray and cook for 6 minutes.
4 Meanwhile, segment the oranges and set aside.
5 Remove the seeds from the pomegranate and also set aside.
6 When cooked, remove the quails from the oven and rest for 2–3 minutes.
7 Remove the quail breasts from the bone and slice into 4 pieces.
8 On the centre of the plate combine the dressed leaves, beans and oranges with a dessertspoon of vinaigrette.
9 Place the quail around the leaves, finish with the pomegranate seeds and serve immediately.

Note: This recipe can also be applied to partridge and squab by adjusting the cooking times. Alternatively you can substitute the mixed leaves for a sauerkraut preparation, and removing the pomegranate will give you a hot starter to serve in the autumn/winter months.

50 Pot-roasted quail with roast carrots and mashed potato

	4 portions	10 portions
quails (approx. 75 g each)	12	30
pancetta, thinly sliced	12 (approx. 250 g)	30 (approx. 625 g)
fresh sage leaves	12	30
vegetable oil	15 ml	50 ml
salt and freshly ground pepper		
carrots, peeled and cut into quarters	3 (100 g)	8 (250 g)
dry white wine	125 ml	310 ml
red wine	125 ml	310 ml
brown stock	250 ml	625 ml
unsalted butter	50 g	125 g
portions of mashed potato	4 (200 g)	10 (500 g)

1 Wash the quails thoroughly inside and out, then place them in a large colander to drain for at least 20 minutes; pat the quail dry.
2 Stuff the cavity of each bird with 1 slice of pancetta and 1 sage leaf.
3 Put the oil in a large thick-bottomed roasting pan on high heat. When the fat is hot, add all the quails in a single layer and cook until browned on one side, gradually turning them, and continue cooking until they are evenly browned all over.
4 Lightly sprinkle the quails with salt and pepper, then add the carrots and cook for a couple of minutes until a slight colour appears.
5 Add the wine and brown stock then turn the birds once, let the wine bubble for about 1 minute, then lower the heat to moderate and partially cover the pan. Cook the quails until the meat feels very tender when poked with a fork and comes away from the bone (approx. 35 minutes).
6 Check from time to time that there are sufficient juices in the pan to keep the birds from sticking; if this does occur, add 1 to 2 tbsp of water at a time. When the quail are done, transfer them to a warmed tray and reserve.
7 Turn up the heat and reduce the cooking juices to a glaze – enough to coat all the birds, scraping the bottom of the pan with a wooden spoon to loosen any cooking residues.

8 Add the butter and whisk in to form an emulsion; at this point if the sauce splits or is too thick add a little water and re-boil.
9 Remove the carrots from the pan and place neatly on the plate with the potato purée.
10 Pour the juices over the quail and serve immediately.

Rabbit

51 Rabbit saddle stuffed with its own livers

	4 portions	10 portions
Saddle		
long saddles rabbit (approx. 400 g each), livers retained	3	5
spinach leaves	100 g	250 g
thin slices Parma ham	9	23
Lentil sauce		
brown chicken stock	300 ml	750 ml
cold butter, diced	40 g	100 g
plum tomatoes, cut into concassée	3	8
cooked umbri or puy lentils	30 g	75 g
chives, chopped	1 tsp	4 tsp
sherry vinegar, to taste		
To serve		
spinach, picked, washed and wilted	300 g	750 g

For the rabbit

1 Split the two natural halves of the rabbit liver with a sharp knife.
2 Keeping them as whole as possible, remove any sinew. Wrap the livers in the spinach leaves.
3 Trim off any excess fat from the belly flaps of the rabbit.
4 Lay the spinach-wrapped livers in the cavity of the rabbit.
5 Lay 2 pieces of the Parma ham on a 30 cm-square sheet of kitchen foil and place the rabbit saddle with the livers facing upwards on the ham.
6 Roll into a sausage shape, twisting the ends of the foil to ensure a tight parcel.
7 Repeat with the remaining rabbits and place in the fridge overnight to rest.

For the lentil sauce

1 Place the chicken stock in a saucepan, bring to the boil and simmer until the volume has reduced to 150 ml.
2 Add the butter to the reduced stock and whisk to an emulsion, add the tomatoes, lentils and chives, and adjust the seasoning to taste. Finish with the sherry vinegar so you can just taste the acid in the background.

To complete

1 Pre-heat the oven to 180°C. Place the rabbit saddles on a baking tray and roast for 17 minutes, turning after 10 minutes.
2 Remove the rabbit from the oven and rest for 3–4 minutes in the foil.
3 Remove the foil from the rabbit and slice each saddle into 4 equal pieces.
4 Lay the sliced rabbit on wilted spinach and garnish the dish with the lentil sauce. Serve immediately

Note: If thinking ahead, the best approach for this dish is to prepare the rabbit saddle the day before or at least 8 hours before cooking, to allow the meat to rest and form an even cylinder – otherwise, when sliced, it will tend to spring open.

52 Braised baron of rabbit with olives and tomatoes

	4 portions	10 portions
farm-raised rabbit barons (approx. 750–800 g each), including bones and trim for gravy	2	5
carrot	1	3
onion	1	3
celery stick	1	3
olive oil	90 ml	225 ml
balsamic vinegar	15 ml	40 ml
caster sugar	10 g	25 g
bottle (750 ml) dry white wine	1	2½
butter, to brown the meat		
basil leaves ⎫	12	30
black olives ⎬ Mediterranean	32	80
pieces home- ⎪ influence		
dried tomato ⎭	8	20
salt and pepper		

1 Well ahead of time, prepare the sauce; cut the rabbits across at the point where the ribs end and chop the forequarters into small pieces.
2 Cut the vegetables into a mirepoix.
3 In a large saucepan, brown the bones and mirepoix in 2 tbsp/5 tbsp of the olive oil.

4 Add the vinegar and sugar, and toss to coat. Cook until light brown.
5 Pour over almost all the white wine, reserving about 1 glass/2½ glasses (150 ml/375 ml) for deglazing the roasting pan later. Boil hard to reduce until almost all the liquid has gone and it is syrupy.
6 Just cover with cold water, return to the boil and skim.
7 Turn down and simmer for 1½ hours.
8 Sieve the resulting stock into a bowl, wash out the saucepan and return the stock to it.
9 Bring back to the boil, skim again and, once more, return to a slow simmer until reduced by half. Reserve.
10 Cut the rabbit legs into two (thigh and drumstick), and the rack into two.
11 In a large saucepan, brown the meat cuts in foaming butter; when golden brown add the finished stock and cook for a further 1½ hours.
12 When cooked, pass the sauce through a fine strainer, bring to the boil and reduce by half.
13 While reducing, put the rabbit into a casserole/serving dish, julienne the basil and remove the stones from the olives.
14 When the sauce is reduced by half, add the tomatoes, olives and basil. Correct the seasoning, pour over the rabbit and serve.

Note: This is a great braised rabbit dish base. The 'Mediterranean influence' can be omitted, substituted with a British theme – woodland mushrooms, parsnips – and served with braised cabbage.

53 Casserole of tame rabbit forestiere

	4 portions	10 portions
farmed rabbits (approx. 750 g each), including bones and trim for the sauce	2	5
mirepoix	300 g	750 g
oil	70 ml	175 ml
red wine	500 ml	1¼ litres
reduced brown stock	500 ml	1¼ litres
white wine	250 ml	625 ml
button onions	16	40
ceps	250 g	625 g
cream	250 ml	625 g
chives, chopped	20 g	50 g
pre-blanched bacon lardons	500 g	1½ litres
salt and pepper		

1 Remove the legs front and back; cut the saddle into four and the hind legs into two.
2 Take the rest of the carcass (the rib, belly flank, neck and shoulder blades) and brown with the mirepoix in half the oil.
3 Add the red wine and 300 ml/750 ml of the stock, bring to the boil and turn down to a simmer.
4 Cover and simmer for 1½ hours.
5 Meanwhile, put the remaining oil in a thick-bottomed pan or casserole and brown the pieces of rabbit.
6 Place in a clean earthenware dish and then in a pre-heated oven for 15 minutes, turning after 10 minutes.
7 Add a small ladle of the cooking stock to the roasting pan and cook for a further 10–15 minutes, basting through the cooking process.
8 While it is cooking, heat a little oil in a pan, brown the onions and ceps, and add the rest of the stock. Cook through and reserve.
9 Remove the rabbit from the oven and place in a serving dish, retain and keep warm.
10 Meanwhile, add the white wine and deglaze the roasting dish. Pass the cooked stock into the reduced wine and reduce rapidly to 200 ml.
11 Add the onions, ceps, cream, chives and cooked bacon. Adjust the seasoning and pour over the rabbit.
12 This can be served with mashed potato, gratin dauphinoise, or anything autumnal or with a winter influence (e.g. a selection of root vegetables).

Note: This a great winter casserole and can be made a day in advance if needed. It uses a classic sauce forestiere, which can be adapted to use button mushrooms (instead of ceps), different herbs, etc. – the choice is yours.

Hare

54 Jugged hare

	4 portions	10 portions
Hare		
hare (approx. 2½ kg each), skinned and cut into pieces	1	3
rendered duck fat/lard	25 g	65 g
plain flour	20 g	50 g
cold water	400 ml	1 litre
redcurrant jelly	2 tsp	5 tsp
salt and pepper		
Marinade		
red wine	750 ml	1875 ml
mirepoix	250 g	625 g
black peppercorns	10	25
bay leaves	2	5
juniper berries, crushed	3	8

For the hare

1 Remove as much blood as possible from the cavity (the game supplier should have retained the blood once the hare had been killed and butchered). Reserve the blood in the fridge well covered.

2 Remove the legs front and back, trim off the rib cage and cut the long saddle into 4 pieces.

3 Mix all the marinade ingredients together and boil for 5 minutes. Allow to cool to room temperature.

4 Once room temperature is achieved, pour the marinade over the hare pieces and place in the fridge for 24 hours.

5 Pre-heat the oven to 125°C, drain the hare pieces out of the marinade and separate from the mirepoix.

6 Place a little of the rendered duck fat or lard in a thick-bottomed pan and brown the hare pieces well. Place in a casserole along with the vegetable mirepoix from the marinade and the flour and cook for 2 minutes.

7 Add the marinating liquid and the rest of the ingredients (redcurrant jelly, seasoning), mix well and bring to the boil. Place in the oven with a tight-fitting lid for 3 hours until tender.

8 When cooked remove from the oven and strain the cooking liquor, placing the cooked hare in a serving dish. Discard the vegetables and bring the liquor up to the boil, simmer and skim if necessary.

9 Take the retained blood and mix with a little red wine vinegar and water so that it is less solidified. Add to the sauce but *do not boil* as this will split the mix.

10 Pour over the hare pieces and serve with mashed potato and seasonal winter vegetables.

Note: Traditionally, fried heart-shaped croutons, with the points dipped in the sauce, and chopped parsley are used as a garnish. Once the *liaison au sang* (blood thickening) is added to the sauce, it must not be boiled as this will coagulate the blood and the sauce will appear to be split.

Venison

55 Pot roast rack of venison with buttered greens and Merlot sauce

	4 portions	10 portions
Venison		
venison rack, bones cleaned and trimmed	2 kg	5 kg
vegetable oil	50 ml	125 ml
small mirepoix	250 g	625 g
clarified butter	100 g	250 g
garlic cloves	2	5
sprig of thyme	1	3
salt and pepper		
Merlot sauce		
oil	100 g	200 g
venison trimmings and bones	450 g	1 kg
cracked pepper	½ tsp	1½ tsp
bay leaf	1	3
sprig thyme	1	2
carrot, peeled and roughly chopped	1	3
onion, peeled and roughly chopped	½	2
garlic cloves, split	2	5
Merlot wine	330 ml	800 ml
chicken stock	1½ litres	2½ litres
Greens		
Butter	50 g	125 g
spinach leaves	250 g	500 g
spring cabbage, cut into 1½ cm strips (blanched for 2 minutes and refreshed in an ice bath)	1	2
escarole, stalks removed	1	3

For the Merlot sauce

1 In a large saucepan, heat the oil over a medium heat. Working in batches to prevent steaming and give a good colour, cook the venison trimmings until brown, add the cracked pepper, bay leaf and thyme. Remove from the pan and set aside in a bowl.

2 Reduce the heat and, in the same pan, cook the carrots, onion and garlic for about 10 minutes or until brown. Return the meat to the pan and stir well.

3 Raise the heat and, when the pan is quite hot, add the wine. Bring to the boil.

4 Boil rapidly until the volume of liquid has reduced by half. Add the chicken stock, return to the boil, then lower the heat right down and cook the sauce for about 1 hour.

5 Stir every 10 minutes to prevent sticking and skim off any sediment that rises to the surface.

6 When the sauce has reduced to approx. 400 ml, pour it through a fine strainer into a clean pan.

7 Bring to the boil and simmer until the volume of liquid has reduced to 200 ml/500 ml, giving a rich plum-coloured sauce.

For the venison

1 Pre-heat the oven to 180°C. Trim the venison so that the bones rise 5 cm above the meat. Tie the venison with kitchen string at intervals along the joint, tying 3 pieces of string between each bone.

2 Place a large pan with a tight-fitting lid over a high heat, add the oil and seal the venison, turning until it is a light golden colour all over.

3 Transfer the meat to a tray and cook the mirepoix in the same way.

4 Add the venison back to the pan, placing it on top of the mirepoix, and cover in the clarified butter. Add the garlic, thyme and seasoning. Place in the oven for 20–25 minutes until medium rare (the residual heat will cook it further).

5 Remove from the oven and set aside to rest for 10 minutes.

To complete

1 Add the butter to a pan, place in the greens and heat through, warm the sauce and then slice the venison.

2 Lay the buttered greens in the centre of the plate with the venison on top and finish with the Merlot sauce.

Note: The rich Merlot sauce can be use for other rich meat dishes; it can be made two or three days ahead and stored in an airtight container in the refrigerator.

56 Medallions of venison with red wine, walnuts and chocolate

	4 portions	10 portions
vegetable oil	50 ml	125 ml
trimmed venison loin	750 g	1800 g
salt and pepper		
Merlot sauce		
(see page 377)	200 ml	500 ml
broken walnut pieces	40 g	100 g
70 per cent bitter		
chocolate in small		
broken pieces	50 g	125 g

1 Pre-heat the oven to 190°C. Heat the oil in a heavy frying pan and seal the venison loin, add salt and pepper, place on a baking tray and then in the oven, and cook for 6–8 minutes medium rare or according to taste.
2 Meanwhile, warm the sauce and add the broken walnuts.
3 Slice the venison loin equally, nap over the sauce and sprinkle liberally with chocolate pieces.

Note: This method of sprinkling the chocolate on afterwards allows you to taste the sauce and the chocolate separately.

Wild boar

57 Marinade for wild boar

	4 portions	10 portions
red wine	½ litre	1¼ litres
red wine vinegar	3 tbsp	7½ tbsp
bay leaf	1	2½
onion, sliced	½	1¼
gin	1 measure	2½ measures
crushed juniper berries	1 tbsp	2½ tbsp

1 Combine all the ingredients and use as required.

Note: This marinade is used in recipes 58 and 59.

58 Ragout of wild boar with wild rice

	4 portions	10 portions
wild boar meat, diced	400 g	1¼ kg
marinade (recipe 57)	½ litre	1¼ litres
butter	50 g	125 g
walnut oil	1 tbsp	2½ tbsp
matignon (carrot, onion,		
celery, cut into small dice)	400 g	1½ kg
flour (for roux)	100 g	250 g
wild boar brown stock	1 litre	2½ litres
tomato purée	50 g	125 g
smoked bacon strips	100 g	250 g
button onions	100 g	250 g
wild mushrooms	300 g	1 kg
brandy	1 measure	2½ measures
salt, pepper		
wild rice, to serve		
chives, chopped, to serve		
heart-shaped fried-		
bread croutons	4	10

1 Place the diced wild boar in the marinade, to cover, for 24 hours.
2 Remove the wild boar from marinade and drain.
3 Seal the meat in butter and walnut oil and sweat off.
4 Add the matignon and flour to a pan with a little butter and cook the roux out.
5 Add the stock, tomato purée and sieved marinade; cook for 1 hour.
6 Add the meat and cook for a further hour.
7 Add the bacon, button onions and mushrooms; simmer for 15–20 minutes.
8 Add the brandy and remove from the heat.
9 Correct the seasoning.
10 Serve with wild rice, chopped chives and heart-shaped fried-bread croutons.

59 Wild boar medallions with morels and lentils

Cal 1887 KJ	Cal 451 kcal	Fat 24.0 g	Sat Fat 4.5 g	Carb 12.4 g	Sugar 5.6 g	Protein 22.4 g	Fibre 2.1 g	Salt 4.0 g	*

	4 portions	10 portions
medallions wild boar	8 × 50–75 g	20 × 50–75 g
marinade (recipe 57)	2 tbsp	5 tbsp
lentils	100 g	250 g
ham stock	½ litre	1¼ litres
onion, chopped	1	2–3
rashers smoked bacon, chopped	3	7–8
butter	10 g	25 g
walnut oil	60 ml	150 ml
shallots, chopped	2	5
morels, washed	100 g	250 g
brandy	30 ml	75 ml
brown wild boar stock	¼ litre	600 ml
chives, chopped	5 g	12 g
salt, pepper		

1 Place the wild boar medallions in the marinade (recipe 57) and leave overnight. Soak the lentils overnight.
2 When thoroughly soaked, drain the lentils and add to the ham stock with the onion and smoked bacon; bake in the oven for approximately 45 minutes.
3 Sauté the medallions of wild boar in the butter and walnut oil; remove from the pan, place on the cooked lentils and keep hot.
4 Add a little butter to the pan, then add the chopped shallots, morels, measure(s) of brandy, stock and marinade; reduce to a sauce.
5 Correct the seasoning and serve sprinkled with chopped chives.

Using venison, mushrooms, sherry and blackberries

60 Wild boar medallions with juniper berries and rösti

	4 portions	10 portions
Medallions		
loin of wild boar	400 g	1 kg
red wine	250 ml	625 ml
juniper berries, crushed	6	15
bay leaves	1	3
sprigs of fresh thyme	1	3
garlic cloves	2	5
vegetable oil		
jus-lié flavoured with red wine	125 ml	300 ml
salt, pepper		
Rösti		
potatoes	400 g	1 kg
oil, sufficient to fry		
salt, pepper		

For the medallions
1 Cut the loin of boar into slices, 2 per portion. Flatten lightly until the medallions are ½ cm thick.
2 Marinade the medallions in the red wine, juniper berries, herbs and garlic. Leave to marinade overnight.
3 Remove from the marinade, then drain and season lightly.

4 Quickly fry in hot oil until both sides are golden brown. Remove and keep warm.
5 Remove the oil from pan. Add the marinade.
6 Bring to the boil and simmer for 10 minutes. Allow to reduce by half.
7 Add the red wine jus-lié. Bring back to the boil. Correct the seasoning and consistency. Strain.
8 Place the medallions on plates. Mask with sauce and serve with rösti (see below).

For the rösti
1 Wash and steam the potatoes with their skins on. (Do not overcook the potatoes.) Peel and grate into large strips.
2 Heat some oil in a suitable frying pan. Add the potatoes, then season and stir until they start to colour.
3 Press the potatoes down in the pan. Allow to brown, then turn the 'cake' to brown the other side.
4 Turn out and serve.

Variations
You may add to the rösti some lardons of crispy bacon, finely chopped sweated onion, and sweated red and green peppers.

379

Paella (recipe 65)

Cae
(rec

Pecan pie (recipe 81)
with chocolate sauce

chapter 10

INTERNATIONAL DISHES

Contributes to the units listed below

VRQ

Unit 208 Prepare and cook fruit
and vegetables

NVQ

Unit 633 (2FC7) Cook and finish basic
vegetable dishes

See page 466 for learning outcomes

VRQ

Unit 209 Prepare and cook meat
and offal

NVQ

Unit 629 (2FC3) Cook and finish basic
meat dishes

See page 229 for learning outcomes

VRQ

Unit 210 Prepare and cook poultry

NVQ

Unit 630 (2FC4) Cook and finish basic
poultry dishes

See page 331 for learning outcomes

International cookery

The word 'ethnic' refers to the common national or cultural traditions of groups of people. Many ethnic groups move from country to country and settle; as our multi-ethnic society continues to grow, it is increasingly important to have a basic understanding of the commodities available, the styles of cooking and some of the more popular dishes. Many countries – such as China, Japan, India and those in the Middle East – have long-established cookery traditions, using a wide range of foods and dating back two or three thousand years.

In many groups, religious influences affect what people eat. Muslims are traditionally forbidden alcohol and pork, and only meat that has been prepared by a halal butcher is permitted. Most Hindus do not eat meat and none eats beef as the cow is a sacred animal to them (strict Hindus are vegetarians). Many Sikhs are also vegetarians, as are strict Buddhists. The Jewish religion has strict dietary laws: shellfish, pork and birds of prey are forbidden. Strict Jews eat only meat that has been slaughtered in a particular way, known as kosher meat. Milk and meat must neither be used together in cooking nor served at the same meal, and three hours should elapse between eating food containing milk and food containing meat.

'Ethnic' cookery also varies within specific countries: the UK subdivides into England, Scotland, Wales and Northern Ireland; the once subcontinent of India subsequently became India, Pakistan and Bangladesh. In terms of cookery styles and dishes there are often further divisions within these and most other countries according to area or region.

Asian, Middle Eastern and Far Eastern cookery makes considerable use of a range of spices and herbs. Ideally, spices are freshly ground (in some dishes up to five or six spices may be used) and then carefully fried at the beginning of recipes to extract the maximum flavour. Inevitably, to save time and labour, a variety of different strengths and blends of ready-prepared mixes of spices are available (curry powder or paste), which may be hot, medium or mild, or may be named after the area of the country in which they are traditionally used. Garam masala and five-spice powder are two other mixes in common use. Many ready-prepared sauces are also available.

It would be impossible within a chapter, and even within a book, to present a comprehensive study of international cookery; the recipes that follow are examples from a number of countries.

International recipes

Caribbean

The history of the West Indies reveals the many cultural influences brought to the islands over the centuries, which makes it difficult to generalise or to standardise the various types of cuisine that still exist. The Dutch, English, French and Spanish have left their individual traditions, and African, Chinese and Creole immigrants have added their own styles to the culture and gastronomy.

In the Caribbean there is an abundance of exotic fruits and vegetables, fresh fish and shellfish, pork as the main source of meat, plenty of poultry, and dried pulses and cereals, all cooked in interesting combinations, with simplicity but with an emphasis on the intense aroma of spices to make it more significant.

1 Metagee (saltfish with coconut and plantains)

Cal	Cal	Fat	Sat Fat	Carb	Sugar	Protein	Fibre	*
1675 KJ	399 kcal	16.5 g	13.5 g	46.4 g	11.3 g	18.3 g	6.5 g	

	4 portions	10 portions
saltfish pieces	200 g	500 g
green plantains	400 g	1 kg
yam	100 g	250 g
sweet potato	100 g	250 g
onion, shredded	100 g	250 g
tomato, skinned deseeded, diced	100 g	250 g
sprig of thyme		
desiccated coconut	100 g	250 g
white stock	250 ml	600 ml
okra	4	10

1 Soak the saltfish in cold water for 30 minutes.
2 Dice the plantain, yam and sweet potato into 1 cm cubes and place in a pan with the onion and tomato.
3 Sprinkle with thyme. Arrange pieces of saltfish on top. Sprinkle with desiccated coconut. Cover with white stock.

4 Top and tail the okra. Do not cut, otherwise the starchy substance will be released. Place the okra in with the fish and vegetables.
5 Bring to the boil and simmer gently until the vegetables and fish are cooked.
6 Serve hot in a suitable dish, decorated with the okra on top.

Note: When possible it is preferable to use coconut milk in place of white stock and desiccated coconut.

HEALTHY EATING TIP
• This is a salty dish. Serve with extra okra and a large portion of rice.

* Using salt cod

China

The People's Republic of China has 28 provinces, five major religions, eight dialects, with Mandarin as the common tongue, and more than one thousand million inhabitants. There are, however, only four main styles of cookery, these being the Canton, Peking, Shanghai and Szechwan styles, which correspond to the southern, northern, eastern and western regions respectively.

The gastronomy of China is recognised as one of the world's greatest. A certain depth of knowledge is necessary to understand the fundamentals of Chinese cookery and service, which are, however, based on traditional peasant diets and long traditions which ensured that everything was used, no food thrown away and a few ingredients stretched inventively with an accent on taste, flavour and aroma. The repertoire is extensive even though the staple ingredient is rice, and almost everything is cooked in a wok or a steamer. Chinese meals do not follow the western pattern of a sequence of courses, as several dishes are laid on the table at once, although there is a movement from light to heavy and then back to light. The use of chopsticks means that everything is cut into small pieces before it is cooked, and the chefs use only a chopper for all work – even for the very realistic carvings in vegetables and fruit for which they are famous.

Of the four aforementioned regions, Cantonese cookery is perhaps preferred internationally; here, rice is most widely used, sweet and sour dishes are favoured, duck and other foods are given a glossy finish, and many of the dishes are cooked by steaming. Peking cookery features noodles rather than rice, and there are other farinaceous items such as steamed dumplings and pancake dishes;

the dishes are more substantial and the cookery more cosmopolitan than elsewhere in the country; more foods are deep-fried and generally there is greater crispness of texture. Shanghai cookery is more robust, with greater use of flour and oil, greater emphasis on garlic, ginger and other spices, and a more peppery result; here also it is the tradition to serve noodles instead of rice. The cookery of the western region of Szechwan, bordering on India and Myanmar, is noted for its hot spiciness, including the use of chillies.

Figure 10.1 Preparation for stir-fry vegetables

2 Almond chicken

Cal 2380 KJ	Cal 572 kcal	Fat 41.0 g	Sat Fat 11.1 g	Carb 12.9 g	Sugar 7.4 g	Protein 38.8 g	Fibre 3.6 g	*

	4 portions	10 portions
peanut oil	60 ml	150 ml
suprêmes of chicken, thinly sliced	4	10
onions, finely chopped	100 g	250 g
chives, chopped	25 g	60 g
cucumber	100 g	250 g
carrot	100 g	250 g
water chestnuts, sliced	200 g	500 g
bamboo shoots, sliced	50 g	125 g
mushrooms, finely sliced	100 g	250 g
soy sauce	60 ml	150 ml
whole blanched almonds	100 g	250 g
butter, margarine or oil	50 g	125 g

1 Heat the peanut oil in a sauté pan or wok, season and stir-fry the chicken over a fierce heat for 2–3 minutes.
2 Add the onion, chives, cucumber, carrot, water chestnuts, bamboo shoots and mushrooms, and season.
3 Continue to stir-fry over a fierce heat for 5 minutes.
4 Add the soy sauce and cook for 1 minute.
5 Meanwhile sauté the almonds in a little butter, margarine or oil until golden brown.
6 Place the chicken and vegetables into a suitable dish for serving and garnish with the almonds.
7 Serve with a braised or pilaff rice (page 162).

HEALTHY EATING TIP
- The fat content can be significantly reduced by using half the amount of oil, skinning the chicken and dry-frying the almonds.
- Serve with plenty of rice and a vegetable dish.

* Using butter and canned bamboo shoots

3 Fried noodles with shredded pork

Cal	Cal	Fat	Sat Fat	Carb	Sugar	Protein	Fibre
1471 KJ	352 kcal	20.3 g	3.3 g	32.8 g	2.7 g	11.5 g	1.7 g

	4 portions	10 portions
pork fillet, cut into batons	100 g	250 g
dark soy sauce	1½ tsp	4–5 tsp
granulated sugar	1 tsp	2–3 tsp
cornflour	10 g	25 g
water	60 ml	150 ml
vegetable oil	60 ml	150 ml
Chinese egg noodles	150 g	375 g
beansprouts	150 g	375 g
Chinese dried mushrooms	2	5
dry sherry	1 tsp	2–3 tsp
chicken stock	125 ml	300 ml
light soy sauce	1 tsp	2–3 tsp
sesame oil	½ tsp	1 tsp
spring onions for garnish	2 tsp	5 tsp

1 Marinate the pork in half the dark soy sauce, add half the sugar and cornflour, seasoning, half the water and half the oil. Allow to stand for 15 minutes.
2 Blanch the noodles in boiling salted water for 1 minute, refresh and drain.

3 In a suitable pan, heat sufficient oil to deep-fry the noodles. Drain on kitchen paper or in a cloth.
4 Heat the remainder of the oil in a wok. Add the beansprouts. Cook quickly and remove.
5 Add the pork and cook until lightly browned.
6 Add the beansprouts to the pork and add the mushrooms.
7 Blend the remaining cornflour with the rest of the water and add all the remaining ingredients. Stir this into the pork and simmer until thickened.
8 Place the noodles in a suitable serving dish, place the pork in the centre and garnish with chopped spring onions.

HEALTHY EATING TIP

- Rely on the soy sauce for flavour, no added salt is needed.
- Use a little unsaturated oil to fry the beansprouts and pork.
- Serve with plenty of noodles and extra vegetables or salad.

4 Sole with mushrooms and bamboo shoots

Cal	Cal	Fat	Sat Fat	Carb	Sugar	Protein	Fibre	*
284 KJ	68 kcal	1.0 g	0.0 g	3.8 g	0.6 g	11.0 g	0.4 g	

	4 portions	10 portions
fillet of lemon or Dover sole, cut into goujons	200 g	500 g
sherry	2 tbsp	5 tbsp
soy sauce	2 tbsp	5 tbsp
salt, pepper		
cornflour	10 g	25 g
egg white, lightly beaten	1	2
fresh ginger, grated	10 g	25 g
onion, finely chopped	25 g	60 g
mushrooms, sliced	50 g	125 g
bamboo shoots, sliced	50 g	125 g
pinch of monosodium glutamate (MSG) (optional)		
white stock	30 ml	75 ml

1 Place the goujons of fish into a small basin, add half the sherry and half the soy sauce.
2 Season, mix in half the cornflour and stir in the egg white.
3 Carefully take out the goujons and deep-fry until golden brown. Drain.
4 Heat a little oil in a frying pan or wok, add the grated ginger and chopped onion; fry for 1 minute.

HEALTHY EATING TIP

- Use an unsaturated oil to fry the goujons, and drain on kitchen paper.
- Omit the MSG – flavour is provided by the soy sauce, sherry and ginger.
- Serve with a large portion of rice or noodles and extra vegetables.

5 Add the mushrooms and bamboo shoots; fry for 1 minute.

6 Blend the remaining sherry and cornflour together, add the monosodium glutamate and stock. Pour into a wok and cook, stirring, for 1–2 minutes.

7 Place the sole into a suitable serving dish, mask with the mushroom and bamboo shoot sauce and serve.

* Using canned bamboo shoots

Note: Monosodium glutamate (MSG) is traditionally used to season Chinese dishes, but it has a high sodium content so it is advisable to leave it out.

5 Chinese vegetables and noodles

Cal 2332 KJ	Cal 554 kcal	Fat 21.6 g	Sat Fat 1.8 g	Carb 80.6 g	Sugar 5.7 g	Protein 14.3 g	Fibre 1.9 g	*

	4 portions	10 portions
Chinese noodles	400 g	1¼ kg
oil	60 ml	150 ml
celery	100 g	250 g
carrot, cut in paysanne	100 g	250 g
bamboo shoots	50 g	125 g
mushrooms, finely sliced	75 g	180 g
Chinese cabbage, shredded	75 g	180 g
beansprouts	100 g	250 g
soy sauce	30 ml	75 ml
garnish (spring onions, sliced lengthways and quickly stir-fried)	4	10

1 Cook the noodles in boiling salted water for about 5–6 minutes until *al dente*. Refresh and drain.

2 Heat the oil in a wok and stir-fry all the vegetables, except the beansprouts, for 1 minute. Then add the beansprouts and cook for a further minute.

3 Add the drained noodles, stirring well; allow to reheat through.

4 Correct the seasoning.

5 Serve in a suitable dish, garnished with the spring onions.

HEALTHY EATING TIP
- Keep added salt to a minimum.
- Use an unsaturated oil (olive or sunflower) and reduce the quantity used.

* Using canned bamboo shoots

Dim sum

Dim sum are tasty little snacks of over 1500 varieties, which are steamed, fried or baked. A selection should be offered, traditionally served with Chinese tea. They are suitable for snack meals and can be offered as cocktail appetisers. Two examples, recipes 6 and 7, follow.

6 Har gau wontons

Cal	Cal	Fat	Sat Fat	Carb	Sugar	Protein	Fibre	*
140 KJ	33 kcal	0.7 g	0.2 g	4.5 g	0.3 g	2.6 g	0.1 g	

Makes 25–30

Dough

wheat starch	75 g
fecule	40 g
boiling water	125 ml
extra fecule for kneading	

Filling

shoulder of pork or chicken, minced	125 g
raw prawns, chopped	125 g
water chestnuts, diced	30 g
bamboo shoots, diced	30 g
salt	
sugar	1 tsp
sesame oil	½ tsp
cornflour	1 tbsp
small egg, beaten	
oil	

1 Sieve the wheat starch and fecule into a bowl. Gradually add the boiling water and beat to form a softish dough.
2 Sprinkle fecule over the work surface, place dough on to work surface and knead well for approximately 10 minutes until a smooth dough is obtained. Cover until needed.

3 Mix the pork, prawns and vegetables together.
4 Add salt, sugar and sesame oil, cornflour and egg.
5 Mix thoroughly.
6 Divide dough into two pieces and roll out to form four thin sausages, roughly 2 cm in diameter.
7 Cut off a piece 2 cm long and roughly flatten. Using a suitable implement, such as a small Chinese cleaver, flatten to form a round. (The cleaver should be lightly oiled.) These should be wafer thin, known as a wrapper.
8 Spoon about 1 tsp of filling into the middle of each wrapper. Hold the dumpling in one hand and shape it around the filling. Seal it by making a series of pleats across the top.
9 Place in a lightly oiled steamer basket and steam for 10 minutes.

HEALTHY EATING TIP

- Season with the minimum amount of salt.
- If chicken (rather than pork) is used, this provides a healthy balanced dish.

* Cornflour analysis used for fecule; minced pork used

7 Sui mai

Cal	Cal	Fat	Sat Fat	Carb	Sugar	Protein	Fibre	*
138 KJ	33 kcal	0.8 g	0.2 g	4.6 g	0.2 g	2.1 g	0.1 g	

Makes 25–30

Dough

as for recipe 6

Filling

minced pork or chicken	175 g
raw prawns, chopped	60 g
spring onion	40 g
water chestnuts, diced	30 g
bamboo shoots, chopped	30 g
salt	1 tsp
sugar	1 tsp
light soy sauce	1 tsp
sesame oil	1 tsp
cornflour	1 tsp
small egg, beaten	

crab coral for garnish, diced
oil

1 Prepare the dough as in recipe 6.
2 Mix the meat, prawns and vegetables together.
3 Add salt, sugar, soy, sesame oil, cornflour and egg.
4 Mix well to combine all ingredients.
5 Chill mixture well.
6 Place a wonton wrapper in the palm of the hand. Spoon approximately 10–15 g of filling into the middle.
7 Using the fingers to shape and the palm of the hand to press, shape the wrapper around the stuffing. The top stays open but the wonton wrapper fits the filling like a tight coat.

8 Dot the filling with crab coral garnish.
9 Place into a lightly oiled steamer. Steam for 15–20 minutes and serve at once.

* *Cornflour analysis used for fecule; minced pork used*

HEALTHY EATING TIP
• Rely on the soy sauce for flavour, no added salt is needed.
• If chicken (rather than pork) is used, this provides a healthy balanced dish.

Greece

Greek cooking offers very fresh ingredients, well flavoured with herbs and a hint of spiciness, and cooked as simply as possible – that is, stewed, grilled or roasted, with an emphasis on the use of olive oil, olives, yoghurt and lemon juice to enhance the products. Fish is used in great variety, including salt cod, baby squid, octopus, sea urchins and fresh sardines. Lamb is very popular, as is veal and poultry.

8 Taramasalata (paste of smoked cod's roe)

Cal	Cal	Fat	Sat Fat	Carb	Sugar	Protein	Fibre
2933 KJ	709 kcal	64.0 g	9.6 g	21.1 g	3.2 g	12.6 g	0.8 g

	4 portions	10 portions
white bread, without crusts	150 g	375 g
milk	125 ml	300 ml
smoked cod's roe, skinned	150 g	375 g
onion, finely chopped (optional)	50 g	125 g
clove garlic, optional	1	2–3
salt, pepper		
olive or vegetable oil	250 ml	625 ml
stoned olives, to serve		
lemon wedges, to serve		

1 Soak the bread in the milk for 2–3 minutes. Squeeze dry.

2 Place all the ingredients except the oil in a food processor and liquidise. Gradually add the oil to make a smooth paste.
3 Place into individual ramekin dishes, decorate with stoned olives and garnish with lemon wedges. Serve with hot toast or hot pitta bread.

Note: Serve as an hors d'oeuvre or appetiser. *Tarama* is the salted roe of the grey mullet, tuna fish or smoked cod's roe.

HEALTHY EATING TIP
• Season with minimum amount of salt.
• Serve with crudités and plenty of hot pitta bread.

9 Avgolemono soup (egg and lemon soup)

Cal	Cal	Fat	Sat Fat	Carb	Sugar	Protein	Fibre
278 KJ	66 kcal	3.1 g	0.9 g	8.0 g	0.5 g	2.1 g	0.0 g

	4 portions	10 portions
chicken stock	750 ml	2 litres
patna rice	35 g	100 g
seasoning		
yolks plus egg (the egg is optional)	2 plus 1	5 plus 2
lemon, juice of	½	1

1 Bring the stock to the boil, add the rice and stir well.

2 Season and cook for 12–15 minutes, then remove from the heat.
3 In a basin thoroughly mix the yolks, egg and lemon juice.
4 Add 1 tbsp of the stock a little at a time to the egg and lemon mixture, beating continuously.
5 Add a further 6 tbsp, mixing continuously. If added too quickly the mixture will curdle.
6 Return the mixture to the stock and heat gently, mixing all the time to cook the egg and to thicken before serving.

10 Kalamarakia yemista (stuffed squid)

Cal 1984 KJ	Cal 474 kcal	Fat 26.2 g	Sat Fat 3.0 g	Carb 42.2 g	Sugar 20.5 g	Protein 19.9 g	Fibre 1.9 g	*

	4 portions	10 portions
medium-sized squid	4	10
onion, finely chopped	50 g	125 g
clove garlic, crushed and chopped	1	2–3
oil	60 ml	150 ml
wholegrain rice	100 g	250 g
fish stock	250 ml	725 ml
pine kernels	50 g	125 g
raisins	100 g	250 g
parsley, chopped		
salt, pepper		
dry white wine	125 ml	250 ml
tomatoes, skinned, deseeded, diced	200 g	500 g

1 Prepare the squid: pull the body and head apart, remove the transparent pen from the bag and any soft remaining part. Rinse under cold water. Pull off the thin purple membrane on the outside.
2 Remove the tentacles and cut into pieces. Remove the ink sac. Reserve the ink to finish the sauce.
3 Sweat the onion and garlic in the oil.
4 Add the rice and moisten with half the fish stock. Stir and add the chopped tentacles, pine kernels, raisins and chopped parsley. Season. Stir well

and allow to simmer for 5–8 minutes so that the rice is partly cooked.
5 Stuff the squid loosely with this mixture. Seal the end by covering with aluminium foil.
6 Lay the squid in a sauté pan with the remaining fish stock, white wine and tomatoes.
7 Cover with a lid and cook in a moderate oven at 180°C for 30–40 minutes, turning the squid gently during cooking. Cook very gently or the squid will burst.
8 When cooked, remove the squid and place in a suitable serving dish.
9 Reboil the cooking liquor and reduce by one-third. Strain the ink into the sauce, boil and reduce for 5 minutes. Check the seasoning.
10 Mask the squid with the sauce and finish with chopped parsley to serve.

HEALTHY EATING TIP
• Season with the minimum amount of salt.
• Use an unsaturated oil (olive or sunflower) and reduce the quantity used.
• Serve with a large mixed salad.

* Using approx 400 g raw squid

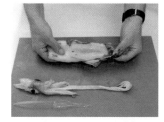

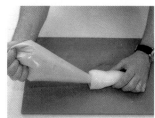

Figure 10.2 ✎ Preparation in four steps and stuffing of a squid; parts of a squid

11 Dolmades (stuffed vine leaves)

Cal	Cal	Fat	Sat Fat	Carb	Sugar	Protein	Fibre
1457 KJ	350 kcal	25.6 g	3.4 g	28.1 g	7.6 g	3.7 g	1.1 g

	4 portions	10 portions
vine leaves	8	20
Filling		
onion, finely chopped	50 g	125 g
clove garlic, crushed		
and chopped	1	2–3
olive oil	60 ml	150 ml
brown rice	100 g	250 g
tomato purée	25 g	50 g
white stock	60 ml approx.	150 ml approx.
salt, pepper		
pine kernels	25 g	50 g
fresh mint, chopped		
fresh dillweed, chopped		
currants	25 g	50 g
clove garlic, crushed		
and chopped	1	2–3
lemon, juice of	½	1
pinch of sugar		
olive oil		

1 Blanch the fresh vine leaves in boiling salted water for 1 minute, refresh and drain.
2 To make the filling: sweat the onion and garlic in the oil without colour.
3 Add the brown rice and tomato purée, and moisten with the stock. Stir in the pine kernels, herbs and currants. Simmer on top of the stove, or cover with a lid and place in the oven, until half cooked.

4 Correct the seasoning. Stuff each vine leaf with the rice mixture and roll up, making sure that the ends are closed.
5 In a sauté pan add the other clove of garlic and the lemon juice and sprinkle with sugar and oil.
6 Lay the stuffed vine leaves in the sauté pan and sprinkle with more lemon juice.
7 Add water or white stock to almost cover the leaves and season. Cover with aluminium foil.
8 Bring to the boil, draw to the side of the stove, cook gently until tender. Alternatively, place in a moderate oven at 180°C covered with a lid for about 30 minutes until tender.
9 When cooked, serve in a suitable earthenware dish in the cooking liquor, which has been thickened with egg yolks and finished with lemon juice. This is avgolemono sauce (see recipe 12).

Note: The word *dolmades* comes from a Turkish verb meaning 'to stuff'. Dolmades may also be eaten cold, served with a lemon vinaigrette dressing, and as part of an hors d'oeuvre assortment.

HEALTHY EATING TIP

• Use less olive oil to sweat the onion and garlic.
• Serve with a small amount of avgolemono sauce (recipe 12), or lightly dress with vinaigrette.
• Season with the minimum amount of salt.

12 Avgolemono sauce

Cal	Cal	Fat	Sat Fat	Carb	Sugar	Protein	Fibre
131 KJ	32 kcal	2.7 g	0.8 g	0.3 g	0.2 g	1.5 g	0.0 g

	4 portions	10 portions
egg yolks	2	5
lemon, juice of	½	1
stock (cooking liquor)	250 ml	625 ml

1 Beat egg yolks and lemon juice over a bain-marie until light.
2 Add the stock gradually and return to the saucepan.
3 Cook over a low heat until the sauce thickens but does not boil.

13 Baklavas (filo pastry with nuts and sugar)

Cal	Cal	Fat	Sat Fat	Carb	Sugar	Protein	Fibre	*
5488 KJ	1314 kcal	83.5 g	35.8 g	132.6 g	85.2 g	16.6 g	6.1 g	

	4 portions	10 portions
filo pastry (recipe 14), sheets of	12 (200 g)	30 (500 g)
clarified butter or ghee	200 g	500 g
hazelnuts, flaked	100 g	250 g
almonds, nibbed	100 g	250 g
caster sugar	100 g	250 g
cinnamon	10 g	25 g
grated nutmeg		
Syrup		
unrefined sugar or caster sugar	200 g	500 g
lemons, grated zest and juice of	2	5
water	60 ml	150 ml
orange, grated zest and juice of	1	2
cinnamon stick	1	2
rose water		

1 Prepare a shallow tray slightly smaller than the sheets of filo pastry by brushing with melted clarified butter or ghee.
2 Place the sheets of filo pastry on the tray, brushing each with the fat.

3 Prepare the filling by mixing the nuts, sugar and spices together; place into the prepared tray, layered alternately with the filo pastry. Brush each layer with the clarified fat so that there are at least 2–3 layers of filling separated by filo pastry.
4 Cover completely with filo pastry and brush with the clarified fat.
5 Mark the pastry into diamonds, sprinkle with water and bake in a moderately hot oven at 190°C for approximately 40 minutes.
6 Meanwhile make the syrup: place all the ingredients, except the rose water, in a saucepan and bring to the boil. Simmer for 5 minutes, pass through a fine strainer and finish with 2–3 drops of rose water.
7 When the baklavas are baked, cut into diamonds, place on a suitable serving dish and mask with the syrup.

HEALTHY EATING TIP
• Use oil to brush the sheets of filo pastry.
• Less sugar can be used in the filling as it should be sweet enough with the syrup used for masking.

* *Using ½ recipe of filo pastry, and ghee*

14 Filo pastry

	4 portions	10 portions
strong flour	1 kg	2½ kg
water	250–375 ml	¾ litre
vinegar	1 tbsp	2–3 tbsp
salt	2 tsp	5 tsp
olive oil	4 tbsp	10 tbsp

1 Sift the flour in a bowl.
2 Add the water, vinegar and salt to the bowl; mix ingredients to a thick paste.
3 Add the oil, very slowly, while working the mixture.
4 Mix until the dough becomes smooth and elastic. Cover for 30 minutes.

5 Split the paste into suitable pieces.
6 First roll out with an ordinary rolling pin, then use a very thin rolling pin, or pasta machine, to make the paste wafer thin.
7 The pastry is now ready for use. It must be covered with a damp or oiled cloth when not being rolled out or before use.

Note: Always cover filo pastry with a damp cloth or polythene when not using, otherwise it dries quickly and is difficult to handle. Filo pastry can be purchased ready made.

India

There are 28 states in this subcontinent, each with its own capital. India is the second most populous country in the world, with the majority of its people being Hindus. Religion plays an important part in choice of food and method of cookery.

The northern part of India and Pakistan use what is called the Mogul style of cooking, the Mogul dynasty of the Shahs having installed itself as long ago as 1526 at the capital, Delhi. They were hearty meat-eaters and used wheat more than rice. Tandoori cooking is done here and there is greater emphasis on presentation than elsewhere in the subcontinent. Apart from this it does not differ very much cuisine-wise from the other countries of this region.

15 Chemmeen kari

Cal	Cal	Fat	Sat Fat	Carb	Sugar	Protein	Fibre
1205 KJ	290 kcal	22.1 g	14.1 g	4.8 g	3.7 g	20.5 g	3.9 g

	4 portions	10 portions
king-size prawns, raw (preferably) or cooked	400 g	1 kg
salt		
malt vinegar	4 tsp	10 tsp
onion, finely chopped	50 g	125 g
vegetable oil	4 tsp	10 tsp
red chillies	4	10
desiccated coconut	100 g	250 g
mustard seeds	1 tsp	2½ tsp
curry leaves	10	25
fresh ginger, finely chopped	25 g	62 g
cloves garlic, crushed and chopped	2	5
ground turmeric	1 tsp	2½ tsp
ground coriander	12 g	30 g
chilli powder	½ tsp	1¼ tsp
garam masala	½ tsp	1¼ tsp
tomato flesh, deseeded and chopped	100 g	250 g
hot water	125 ml	312 ml

1 Shell the prawns and de-vein them by slitting the back.
2 Rub the prawns with salt and half the vinegar and keep aside.
3 Sweat the onions in a little of the oil until very slightly golden brown in colour. Remove from the heat, add the chillies, coconut and mustard seeds.

Place in the oven, stirring occasionally, for approximately 8 minutes, or continue to sweat on top of the stove to extract the flavours. Remove from the heat, place in a food processor and blend to a fine paste. This is the masala.

4 Heat the oil in a wok or other suitable pan and fry the curry leaves for 1 minute. Add the ginger and garlic and fry for a further minute. Add the turmeric, ground coriander, chilli powder and garam masala. Stir-fry for 1–2 minutes.
5 Add the tomatoes, hot water and salt, to taste. Bring to the boil, simmer for 5 minutes.
6 Drain the prawns. Add them to the pan. Mix well, continue to cook until the prawns are tender (if you are using raw prawns this usually takes 8–10 minutes). They will curl and turn a pinky-orange colour. Add the remaining vinegar. Do not overcook the prawns otherwise they will become hard and dry.
7 Serve immediately, garnished with coriander leaves.

Note: This is a prawn curry from the south of India.

HEALTHY EATING TIP
- No added salt is needed – there are plenty of other flavours.
- Use a little unsaturated oil to sweat the onions.
- Serve with a large portion of rice and a vegetable dish.

16 Tandoori prawns (grilled spiced prawns)

Cal 869 KJ	Cal 207 kcal	Fat 21.1 g	Sat Fat 13.5 g	Carb 0.5 g	Sugar 0.3 g	Protein 4.7 g	Fibre 0.0 g

	4 portions	10 portions
king-size prawns	12	30
unsalted butter	100 g	250 g
fresh ginger, grated	1 tsp	2½ tsp
clove garlic, crushed and chopped	1	2–3
chilli powder	1 tsp	2½ tsp
ground cumin	1 tsp	2½ tsp
ground coriander	1 tsp	2½ tsp
fresh coriander leaves		
salt, pepper		
Garnish		
lettuce leaves		
onion rings		
chillies, chopped	2	5
lemon, cut into wedges	1	2

1 Shell and wash the prawns, leaving the heads attached. Place in a shallow tray.

2 Melt the butter and add all the spices, including the coriander leaves and seasoning.
3 Pour this melted butter mixture over the prawns.
4 Gently grill on both sides under the salamander for 5–6 minutes.
5 Serve on a bed of lettuce, garnished with onion rings, chillies and lemon.

Note: This dish should be prepared using fresh prawns, but, if unobtainable, cooked prawns may be used, in which case the prawns should be reheated for 2–3 minutes. Tandoori prawns may be served as a first or fish course.

HEALTHY EATING TIP
- Use the minimum amount of salt and less butter.
- Serve with a large portion of Indian flat bread, salad and cucumber raita.

17 Palak lamb

Cal 1669 KJ	Cal 403 kcal	Fat 32.0 g	Sat Fat 8.8 g	Carb 5.9 g	Sugar 5.0 g	Protein 23.5 g	Fibre 1.4 g	*

	4 portions	10 portions
vegetable ghee or oil	62 ml	155 ml
cumin seeds	1 tsp	2½ tsp
onion, finely chopped	50 g	125 g
fresh ginger, finely chopped	12 g	30 g
clove garlic, crushed and chopped	1	3
shoulder, loin or leg of lamb	400 g	1 kg
hot curry paste	2 tsp	5 tsp
natural yoghurt	125 ml	312 ml
salt, to taste		
tomato purée	25 g	625 g
spinach, chopped	200 g	500 g
coriander and lemon, to garnish		

1 Heat the ghee or oil in a frying pan.
2 Add the cumin seeds; fry for 1 minute.
3 Add the onion; fry until golden brown.
4 Add the ginger and garlic; stir-fry until all is brown.

5 Add the lamb cut into 2 cm dice; simmer for 15–20 minutes.
6 Add the curry paste, yoghurt and salt.
7 Cook for 5 minutes; add water if necessary to prevent sticking.
8 Stir in the tomato purée and spinach. Cover and simmer for 10–15 minutes until lamb is tender.
9 Serve garnished with lemon quarters and coriander leaves.

Note: This is a medium-spiced dish from the Punjab.

HEALTHY EATING TIP
- Use a smaller amount of unsaturated oil. Drain off the excess fat after cooking the lamb, and before adding the curry paste and yoghurt.
- Add the minimum amount of salt; there is plenty of flavour from the spices.
- Serve with a large portion of rice and a vegetable dish.

* Using lean meat and vegetable oil

18 Lamb pasanda

Cal 1686 KJ	Cal 405 kcal	Fat 31.5 g	Sat Fat 15.4 g	Carb 7.4 g	Sugar 5.6 g	Protein 24.6 g	Fibre 1.0 g	*

	4 portions	10 portions
ghee or unsalted butter	32 g	80 g
onion, finely chopped	150 g	375 g
shoulder, leg or loin of lamb, diced	400 g	1 kg
clove of garlic, crushed and chopped	2	4
fresh ginger, finely chopped	12 g	30 g
natural yoghurt	125 ml	312 ml
ground turmeric	2½ g (½ tsp)	5½ g (1½ tsp)
ground coriander	10 g (2 tsp)	25 g (5 tsp)
ground cumin	5 g (1 tsp)	12½ g (2½ tsp)
ground nutmeg	2½ g (½ tsp)	5½ g (1¼ tsp)
pinch of cayenne pepper		
single cream	125 ml	312 ml
ground almonds	25 g	62½ g
salt	2½ g (½ tsp)	5½ g (1½ tsp)
garam masala	5 g (1 tsp)	12½ g (2½ tsp)
toasted almonds, to serve		

1 Melt the butter in a frying pan. Sweat the onions until just lightly brown.
2 Add the lamb and cook until sealed.
3 Add the garlic, ginger, yoghurt, turmeric, coriander, cumin, nutmeg and cayenne pepper. Just cover with water and bring to the boil.
4 Cover with a suitable lid; simmer for 30–45 minutes or until the meat is tender.
5 Stir in the cream, ground almonds, salt and garam masala.
6 Bring back to the boil. Simmer for a further 5 minutes.
7 Serve garnished with toasted almonds.

HEALTHY EATING TIP
• Use a smaller amount of unsaturated oil.
• Drain off the excess fat before adding the water.
• Add the minimum amount of salt and try adding natural yoghurt in place of the cream.
• Serve with a large portion of rice and a vegetable dish.

* Using lean meat and unsalted butter

19 Kashmira lamb

Cal 1812 KJ	Cal 437 kcal	Fat 36.0 g	Sat Fat 8.8 g	Carb 6.5 g	Sugar 4.5 g	Protein 23.0 g	Fibre 0.4 g	*

	4 portions	10 portions
tikka paste	100 g	250 g
natural yoghurt	125 ml	312 ml
shoulder, loin or leg of lamb	400 g	1 kg
ghee or oil	62 ml	155 ml
cumin seeds	1 tsp	2½ tsp
cardamom pods	4	10
cloves	4	10
cinnamon sticks	4	10
onions, finely chopped	100 g	250 g
clove garlic, crushed and chopped	1	1½
fresh ginger, finely chopped	12 g	30 g
salt, to taste		
ground chilli	½ tsp	1¼ tsp
fresh coriander/roasted almonds, to garnish		

1 Mix together the tikka paste and yoghurt in a suitable bowl.
2 Dice the lamb into 2 cm cubes and marinate in the yoghurt mixture for a minimum of 1 hour.
3 Heat the ghee or oil in a suitable frying pan.
4 Add the cumin seeds, cardamom, cloves and cinnamon; fry for 1 minute.
5 Add the onion, garlic and ginger. Fry for 5 minutes or until golden brown.

HEALTHY EATING TIP
• Use a smaller amount of unsaturated oil.
• Drain off the excess fat after frying the lamb.
• Add the minimum amount of salt.
• Serve with rice, dhal and a vegetable dish.

6 Add the lamb; fry together for 10–15 minutes. Add a little water if necessary to prevent sticking.
7 Add salt and chilli. Cover and simmer for a further 15 minutes or until the lamb is tender.
8 Serve garnished with coriander leaves and roasted almonds.

Note: This is a medium-spiced dish from northern India.

* *Using lean meat and vegetable oil*

20 Beef do-piazza

Cal	Cal	Fat	Sat Fat	Carb	Sugar	Protein	Fibre	*
329 KJ	320 kcal	22.8 g	5.1 g	5.4 g	4.0 g	23.6 g	0.8 g	

	4 portions	10 portions
topside or chuck steak, cubed	400 g	1 kg
vegetable ghee or oil	62 ml	155 ml
onion, finely chopped	100 g	250 g
fresh ginger, finely chopped	12 g	30 g
clove garlic, crushed and chopped	1	3
medium curry powder	3 tsp	7½ tsp
natural yoghurt	125 ml	312 ml
lemon, juice of	½	1½
large onion, cut into rings	1	2
salt, to taste		
julienne of lemon rind		

1 Fry the beef in the oil until brown.
2 Add the onions and continue to fry until brown. Drain off the excess oil.
3 Add the ginger, garlic and curry powder; fry for a further 5 minutes.
4 Remove from the heat; add the yoghurt and lemon juice.
5 Simmer for 1–1½ hours, adding small amounts of water or stock during the cooking to prevent sticking.
6 Fry the onion rings in oil until golden brown. Keep some for the garnish, add the remainder to the beef. Season with the salt.
7 Serve garnished with the onion rings and the julienne of lemon rind.

Note: This is a medium-spiced dish from the Punjab.

HEALTHY EATING TIP

- Use a smaller amount of unsaturated oil to fry the beef and the onion rings.
- Drain off the excess fat after frying the meat and onions. Drain the onion rings on kitchen paper.
- Use the minimum amount of salt.
- Serve with rice or flat bread and a vegetable dish.

* *Using lean meat and vegetable oil*

21 Beef Madras

Cal 1417 KJ	Cal 340 kcal	Fat 22.8 g	Sat Fat 3.7 g	Carb 10.8 g	Sugar 9.3 g	Protein 23.5 g	Fibre 0.8 g	*

	4 portions	10 portions
topside or chuck steak, cubed	400 g	1 kg
vegetable ghee or oil	68 ml	155 ml
onion, finely chopped	100 g	250 g
clove garlic, crushed and chopped	2	5
hot Madras curry paste	3 tsp	7½ tsp
tomato purée	50 g	125 g
mango chutney, chopped	5 g	125 g
lemon, juice of	½	1½
brown beef stock	500 ml	1¼ litres
seasoning, to taste		

1 Fry the beef in the oil until sealed and brown; add the onion and garlic, and continue to fry for a further 5 minutes.
2 Add the curry paste and mix well; cook for a further 2 minutes.
3 Add the remaining ingredients, cover with brown stock and bring to the boil. Simmer for 1–1½ hours, or until tender.
4 Correct the seasoning and consistency.
5 Garnish with coriander leaves and serve with pilaff rice.

Note: This is a hot curry from southern India.

HEALTHY EATING TIP
• Use a smaller amount of unsaturated oil to fry the beef, and drain off the excess fat before adding the curry paste.
• Use the minimum amount of salt.
• Serve with pilaff rice and a vegetable dish.

* *Using lean meat and vegetable oil*

22 Keema matar (medium-spiced mince and peas)

Cal 1726 KJ	Cal 417 kcal	Fat 34.1 g	Sat Fat 8.8 g	Carb 5.6 g	Sugar 2.6 g	Protein 22.0 g	Fibre 1.7 g	*

	4 portions	10 portions
minced beef	400 g	1 kg
vegetable ghee or oil	62 ml	155 ml
onion, finely chopped	100 g	250 g
clove garlic, crushed and chopped	1	3
fresh ginger, finely chopped	12 g	30 g
medium curry paste	4 tsp	10 tsp
brown stock or water	250 ml	625 ml
frozen peas	100 g	250 g
fresh coriander, chopped	4 tsp	10 tsp
lemon, juice of	½	1¼

1 Fry the beef in the oil until brown.
2 Add the onions and garlic. Fry for a further 5 minutes.
3 Add the ginger and curry paste; cook for a further 8 minutes, adding spoonfuls of water or stock to prevent burning.
4 Add the rest of the water or stock, peas, chopped coriander and lemon juice.
5 Simmer for 20 minutes or until cooked. Serve.

Note: This recipe is suitable for low-cost catering.

HEALTHY EATING TIP
• Lightly oil the pan to fry the beef and onion, and drain off any excess fat.
• Skim any fat from the surface of the finished dish.
• Use the minimum amount of salt.
• Serve with pilaff rice and a vegetable dish.

* *Using lean meat and vegetable oil*

23 Tandoori chicken

Cal	Cal	Fat	Sat Fat	Carb	Sugar	Protein	Fibre	*
1436 KJ	342 kcal	14.1 g	4.6 g	10.1 g	8.6 g	44.6 g	0.3 g	

	4 portions
chicken, cut as for sauté (page 334)	1¼–1½ kg
salt	1 tsp
lemon, juice of	1
plain yoghurt	300 ml
small onion, chopped	1
clove garlic, peeled	1
ginger, piece of, peeled and quartered	5 cm
fresh hot green chilli, sliced	½
garam masala	2 tsp
ground cumin	1 tsp
few drops each red and yellow colouring	

1 Cut slits bone-deep in the chicken pieces.
2 Sprinkle the salt and lemon juice on both sides of the pieces, lightly rubbing into the slits; leave for 20 minutes.
3 Combine the remaining ingredients in a blender or food processor.
4 Brush the chicken pieces on both sides, ensuring the marinade goes into the slits. Cover and refrigerate for 6–24 hours.
5 Preheat the oven to the maximum temperature.
6 Shake off as much of the marinade as possible from the chicken pieces; place on skewers and bake for 15–20 minutes or until cooked.

7 Serve with red onion rings and lime or lemon wedges.

HEALTHY EATING TIP
• Skin the chicken and reduce the salt by half.
• Serve with rice and vegetables.

* *Estimated edible meat used; vegetable oil used*

Figure 10.3 ✎ Tandoori chicken

24 Chicken palak (chicken fried with spinach and spices)

Cal	Cal	Fat	Sat Fat	Carb	Sugar	Protein	Fibre	*
1575 KJ	378 kcal	21.9 g	9.5 g	4.4 g	3.5 g	41.3 g	1.9 g	

	4 portions	10 portions
chicken, cut for sauté	1 × 1½ kg	2 × 1½ kg
ghee or butter, margarine or oil	50 g	125 g
onion, finely chopped	50 g	125 g
clove garlic, crushed and chopped	1	2–3
fresh ginger	25 g	60 g
green chilli	1	2
ground cumin	1 tsp	2½ tsp
ground coriander	1 tsp	2½ tsp
spinach, washed and finely chopped	250 g	625 g
tomatoes, skinned, deseeded, diced	200 g	500 g
chicken stock	250 ml	625 ml

1 Gently fry the chicken in the fat until golden brown.
2 Remove the chicken; fry the onion and garlic until lightly browned. Add the spices and sweat for 3 minutes.
3 Stir in the spinach, add the tomatoes and season. Add the chicken pieces.
4 Add the chicken stock, bring to the boil.
5 Cover with a lid and cook in a moderate oven at 180°C for 30 minutes or until the chicken is tender. Stir occasionally, adding more stock if necessary.

6 Serve in a suitable dish with rice, chapatis (see page 409) and dhal (see page 401).

HEALTHY EATING TIP
- Skin the chicken and fry in a small amount of unsaturated oil.
- Skim excess fat from the finished dish.
- Serve with plenty of rice, dhal, chapatis and a vegetable dish.

Estimated edible meat used; butter used

Figure 10.4 Chicken palak

25 Chicken tikka

Cal	Cal	Fat	Sat Fat	Carb	Sugar	Protein	Fibre	*
1780 KJ	427 kcal	27.1 g	5.2 g	5.5 g	5.1 g	41.3	0.6 g	

	4 portions	10 portions
chicken, cut for sauté	1 × 1½ kg	2½ × 1½ kg
natural yoghurt	125 ml	250 ml
grated ginger	1 tsp	2½ tsp
ground coriander	1 tsp	2½ tsp
ground cumin	1 tsp	2½ tsp
chilli powder	1 tsp	2½ tsp
clove garlic, crushed and chopped	1	2–3
lemon, juice of	½	1
tomato purée	50 g	125 g
onion, finely chopped	50 g	125 g
oil	60 ml	150 ml
lemon, wedges of	4	10
seasoning		

1 Place the chicken pieces into a suitable dish.
2 Mix together the yoghurt, seasoning, spices, garlic, lemon juice and tomato purée.
3 Pour this over the chicken, mix well and leave to marinate for at least 3 hours.

4 In a suitable shallow tray, add the chopped onion and half the oil.
5 Lay the chicken pieces on top and grill under the salamander, turning the pieces over once or gently cook in a moderate oven at 180°C for 20–30 minutes.
6 Baste with the remaining oil.
7 Serve on a bed of lettuce garnished with wedges of lemon.

HEALTHY EATING TIP
- Skin the chicken and keep the added salt to a minimum.
- Use half the amount of unsaturated oil.
- Serve with rice and a vegetable dish.

Estimated edible meat used

26 Kori cassi (Mangalorean chicken)

Cal	Cal	Fat	Sat Fat	Carb	Sugar	Protein	Fibre	*
3827 KJ	924 kcal	78.3 g	48.3 g	16.2 g	13.6 g	46.3 g	10.4 g	

	4 portions	10 portions
oil	50 ml	125 ml
red chillies	60 g	150 g
coriander seeds	40 g	100 g
black malabar peppercorns	2½ tsp	6 tsp
cumin seeds	2½ tsp	6¼ tsp
fenugreek seeds	1 tsp	2¼ tsp
coconut, freshly grated	500 g	1¼ kg
cloves of garlic	8	20
chicken cut for sauté (page 334)	1	2½
salt		
turmeric	2 tsp	5 tsp
onion, finely chopped	250 g	625 g
water	250 ml	625 ml
tamarind pulp	25 g	62 g
Tarka		
ghee	30 g	75 g
ground fenugreek	½ tsp	1¼ tsp
ground cumin	1 tsp	2½ tsp
onion, finely chopped	50 g	125 g

1 In a little oil, roast the chillies, coriander, peppercorns, cumin and fenugreek, separately.

2 Grind these spices with the coconut and garlic to a fine paste in a processor, adding a little water.
3 Marinate the chicken with salt and turmeric.
4 Heat the oil in a suitable pan and sauté the chopped onions until light brown. Remove from the heat and add the coconut spice mixture.
5 Return to heat and simmer for approximately 20 minutes. Add the water, bring to the boil, add the chicken. Simmer for approximately 15 minutes.
6 Add the tamarind pulp and continue to simmer until the chicken is cooked through.
7 Prepare the tarka: heat the ghee, fry the spices, add the onion and sauté until lightly coloured.
8 Pour over the chicken and serve.

HEALTHY EATING TIP

- Lightly oil the pan using an unsaturated oil to roast the spices.
- Reduce the amount of oil used to sauté the onions and skim fat from the cooked chicken.
- Little or no salt is needed.
- Serve with plenty of rice and vegetables.

* Estimated edible meat used

27 Dhal

Cal	Cal	Fat	Sat Fat	Carb	Sugar	Protein	Fibre	*
1083 KJ	258 kcal	11.1 g	6.6 g	29.6 g	2.0 g	12.4 g	2.7 g	

	4 portions	10 portions
lentils	200 g	500 g
turmeric	1 tsp	2½ tsp
ghee, butter or oil	50 g	125 g
onion, finely chopped	50 g	125 g
garlic clove, crushed and chopped	1	2–3
green chilli, finely chopped (optional)	1	2–3
cumin seeds	1 tsp	2½ tsp

1 Place the lentils in a saucepan and cover with water. Add the turmeric, bring to the boil and gently simmer until cooked. Stir occasionally.
2 In a suitable pan, heat the fat and sweat the onion, garlic, chilli (if using) and cumin seeds. Stir into the lentils and season.

3 Serve hot to accompany other dishes. The consistency should be fairly thick but spoonable.

Note: Dhal is made from lentils and is an important part of the basic diet for many Indian people. It can also be made using yellow split peas.

HEALTHY EATING TIP

- Lightly oil a pan to sweat the onion.
- This dish is high in protein and starchy carbohydrate, and low in fat. It is a very useful accompaniment for many higher-fat dishes and will help to dilute the overall fat content.

* Using butter

28 Alu-chole (vegetarian curry)

Cal	Cal	Fat	Sat Fat	Carb	Sugar	Protein	Fibre	*
1214 KJ	290 kcal	17.5 g	1.6 g	26.6 g	5.3 g	10.6 g	5.5 g	

	4 portions	10 portions
vegetable ghee or oil	45 ml (3 tsp)	112 ml (7½ tsp)
small cinnamon sticks	4	10
bay leaves	4	10
cumin seeds	5 g (1 tsp)	12½ g (2½ tsp)
onion, finely chopped	100 g	250 g
cloves garlic, finely chopped and crushed	2	5
plum tomatoes, canned, chopped	400 g	1 kg
hot curry paste	45 ml (3 tsp)	112 g (7½ tsp)
salt, to taste		
potatoes in 1 cm dice	100 g	250 g
water	125 ml	312 ml
chickpeas, canned, drained	400 g	1 kg
coriander leaves, chopped	50 g	125 g
tamarind sauce or lemon juice	30 g (2 tsp)	75 g (5 tsp)

1 Heat the ghee in a suitable pan.
2 Add the cinnamon, bay leaves and cumin seeds; fry for 1 minute.
3 Add the onion and garlic. Fry until golden brown.
4 Add the chopped tomatoes, curry paste and salt, and fry for a further 2–3 minutes.
5 Stir in the potatoes and water. Bring to the boil. Cover and simmer until the potatoes are cooked.
6 Add the chickpeas; allow to heat through.
7 Stir in the coriander leaves and tamarind sauce or lemon juice; serve.

Note: This is a dish from northern India.

HEALTHY EATING TIP

- Use a small amount of unsaturated oil to fry the spices and onion.
- Skim the fat from the finished dish.
- No added salt is necessary.
- This can be served as a vegetarian dish with rice, or to accompany meat and chicken dishes.

* *Using lemon juice and vegetable oil*

Figure 10.5 An accompaniment to curry: naan bread (recipe 43)

Raita

Raita is a south Asian condiment based on yoghurt (*dahi*) and used as a sauce or dip. The yoghurt is seasoned with cilantro, cumin, mint, cayenne pepper, garlic, and other herbs and spices. Vegetables such as cucumber and onion are mixed in. The mixture is served chilled. Raita has a cooling effect on the palate, which makes it a good foil for spicy Indian dishes.

Southern Indian cuisine, such as that found in the Bangalore region, often uses finely chopped or diced carrots mixed with *dahi* yoghurt.

29 Yoghurt with cucumber raita

	4 portions
cucumbers	2
salt	
chopped spring onions	2 tbsp
yoghurt	500 ml
cumin seeds	1½ tsp
lemon juice	1
fresh coriander or mint, chopped	

1 Peel the cucumbers, halve them lengthways and remove the seeds. Cut into small dice.

2 Sprinkle the dice with salt and leave for 15 minutes then drain away the liquid and rinse the cucumbers quickly in cold water. Drain well.
3 Combine the onion, yoghurt and lemon juice; taste to see if more salt is required.
4 Roast the cumin seeds in a dry pan, shaking the pan or stirring constantly until brown.
5 Bruise or crush the seeds and sprinkle over the yoghurt mixture.
6 Serve chilled, garnished with mint and coriander.

Note: This is a dish from Punjab, northern India.

30 Palak pachchadi (raita)

		4 portions
fresh spinach		200 g
ghee or vegetable oil		2 tsp
black mustard seeds		1 tsp
cumin seeds		1 tsp
ground cumin		1 tsp
fenugreek seeds		½ tsp
chilli powder	(optional)	⅛ tsp
salt		
yoghurt		500 ml

1 Wash the spinach thoroughly in several changes of water. Remove any tough stems and put the leaves into a saucepan with very little water. Cover and steam over a low heat until the spinach is tender. Drain and chop finely.
2 In a small pan heat the ghee or oil, and fry the mustard seeds until they pop. Add the cumin seeds, ground cumin and fenugreek seeds; cook until golden brown, but do not allow to burn. Remove from the heat, stir in the chilli power, if desired, add salt and allow to cool. Mix in the yoghurt, then stir this mixture into the spinach.
3 Serve cold or at room temperature as a side dish with rice and curry or with one of the Indian breads.

31 Yoghurt with bananas (kela raita)

	4 portions
large ripe bananas	4
lemon juice	
cumin seeds	1 tsp
yoghurt	250 ml
freshly grated or desiccated coconut	3 tbsp
salt	½ tsp
sugar	2 tsp

1 Slice the bananas and sprinkle with lemon juice
2 Roast the cumin seeds in a dry pan, shaking or stirring constantly until brown.
3 Combine the yoghurt with all the ingredients except the banana. If desiccated coconut is used, moisten it first by sprinkling with about 2 tbsp of water and tossing it with the fingers until it is no longer dry.
4 Fold the banana into the yoghurt mixture.
5 Chill and serve.

32 Garlic or lasun raita 1

	4 portions
plain yoghurt	500 ml
cloves garlic, peeled and minced	6
green chillies, chopped	2
bunch of cilantro leaves, chopped	
salt, to taste	
mint, chopped	½ tsp

1 Combine all the ingredients.
2 Transfer to a serving bowl.

33 Garlic or lasun raita 2

	4 portions
plain yoghurt or *dahi*	500 ml
fresh mint leaves, washed and finely chopped	2 tbsp
small red onion, peeled and finely chopped	1
salt and sugar, to taste	
black pepper	¼ tsp

1 Combine all the ingredients.
2 Transfer to a serving bowl.

34 Yoghurt and onion salad – dahi kachumber (Maharashtra)

	4 portions
onions	3
salt	
yoghurt	250 ml
fresh ginger, finely grated	1 tsp
medium tomatoes, peeled and chopped	2
fresh green chillies, seeded and chopped	3
chopped fresh cilantro or coriander	3 tbsp
seasoning	

1 Cut the onions into thin slices, sprinkle with salt and set aside for 20 minutes.
2 Squeeze out as much liquid as possible.
3 Mix together the yoghurt and ginger then fold in the onions and the rest of the ingredients.
4 Cover and chill thoroughly before serving.

35 Beetroot raita or chukander ka raita

	4 portions
plain yoghurt	800 ml
grated coconut	125 g
salt	
beetroot, boiled, peeled and diced	1 small
ghee	1 tsp
mustard seeds	½ tsp
curry leaves (*meetha neem*)	5–6
black gram or *urad/urd/urid* dal	1 tsp
red chillies, broken into small pieces	2 whole

1 Mix the yoghurt, coconut, salt and beetroot. Place in a serving bowl.
2 Heat the fat in a small pan; add the mustard seeds, curry leaves and gram dal.
3 When the seeds splutter, add the red chillies. Stir for a few seconds.
4 Pour over the yoghurt mixture.
5 Serve chilled.

36 Pepper bhajee

Cal	Cal	Fat	Sat Fat	Carb	Sugar	Protein	Fibre	*
852 KJ	204 kcal	13.1 g	1.5 g	20.0 g	8.8 g	4.0 g	5.3 g	

	4 portions	10 portions
oil	45 ml (3 tsp)	112 ml (7½ tsp)
black mustard seeds	5 g (1 tsp)	12½ g (2½ tsp)
onion, finely chopped	100 g	250 g
hot curry powder	30 ml (2 tsp)	75 ml (5 tsp)
plum tomatoes, canned, chopped	100 g	250 g
potatoes cut into 1 cm cubes	200 g	500 g
mixed red and green peppers, cut in half, deseeded and finely shredded	600 g	1½ kg
seasoning		

1 Heat the oil in a suitable pan. Fry the mustard seeds for 1 minute.
2 Add the onions and fry until golden brown in colour.
3 Stir in the curry powder. Cook for 1 minute. Add the tomatoes.
4 Add the potatoes and peppers. Mix well.
5 Add a little water to prevent sticking. Cover the pan and cook for 15 minutes. Season and serve.

HEALTHY EATING TIP
• Use a small amount of unsaturated oil to fry the spices and onion.
• Skim the fat from the finished dish.
• No added salt is necessary.
• Use to accompany meat dishes.

Reduced to half using margarine

37 Onion bhajias

Cal	Cal	Fat	Sat Fat	Carb	Sugar	Protein	Fibre	*
630 KJ	152 kcal	12.1 g	1.3 g	8.5 g	1.7 g	2.9 g	2.4 g	

	4 portions	10 portions
bessan or gram flour	45 g (3 tsp)	112 g (7½ tsp)
hot curry powder	5 g (1 tsp)	12½ g (2½ tsp)
salt		
water	75 ml (5 tsp)	187 ml (12½ tsp)
onion, finely shredded	100 g	250 g

1 Mix together the flour, curry powder and salt.
2 Blend in the water carefully to form a smooth, thick batter.
3 Stir in the onion, stir well.
4 Drop the mixture off a tablespoon into deep oil at 200°C. Fry for 5–10 minutes until golden brown.
5 Drain well and serve as a snack with mango chutney as a dip.

HEALTHY EATING TIP
• Use the minimum amount of salt.
• Make sure the oil is hot so that less is absorbed into the surface. Drain on kitchen paper.

* Reduced to half using margarine

38 Pakora (batter-fried vegetables and shrimps)

Cal	Cal	Fat	Sat Fat	Carb	Sugar	Protein	Fibre	*
1040 KJ	249 kcal	13.9 g	1.7 g	18.4 g	3.3 g	14.0 g	5.0 g	

	4 portions	10 portions
bessan (chickpea flour)	125 g	250 g
water	375 ml	750 ml
turmeric	¼ tsp	½ tsp
ground coriander	1 tsp	2 tsp
cayenne	¼ tsp	½ tsp
salt		

1 Sieve the flour and slowly add the water, whisking continuously.
2 Pass through a strainer.
3 Add the turmeric, coriander and cayenne pepper, season with salt. Allow to stand for 15 minutes.
4 Dip the chosen vegetables and shrimps or prawns into the batter (see 'Variations', below), coating well.
5 Deep-fry in hot oil at 190°C until a light saffron colour.
6 Drain well and serve with chutney.

Note: This can be served as a reception or bar snack or as a main course. Unlike plain wheat flour, batter made with bessan produces a non-porous surface and no fat will penetrate to the food inside.

Variations
Vegetables such as batons of carrot, florets of cauliflower, florets of broccoli, sliced aubergines, batons of celery, slices of par-boiled peeled or unpeeled potato, batons of parsnip, and large cooked shrimps or prawns (peeled and seasoned with salt and curry powder) can be used.

HEALTHY EATING TIP
• Use the minimum amount of salt.
• Make sure the oil is hot so that less is absorbed into the surface. Drain on kitchen paper.

* Using vegetable oil, and a mixture of vegetables and shrimp

39 Samosas

	40–60 pasties	100–150 pasties
short pastry made from ghee fat and fairly strong flour as the dough (should be fairly elastic)	400 g	1 kg

1 Take a small piece of dough, roll into a ball 2 cm in diameter. Keep the rest of the dough covered with either a wet cloth, clingfilm or plastic, otherwise a skin will form on the dough.
2 Roll the ball into a circle about 9 cm round on a lightly floured surface. Cut the circle in half.
3 Moisten the straight edge with eggwash or water.

4 Shape the semicircle into a cone. Fill the cone with approximately 1½ tsp of filling (e.g. recipes 40 and 41), moisten the top edges and press together well.
5 The samosas may be made in advance, covered with clingfilm or plastic, and refrigerated before being deep-fried.
6 Deep-fry at 180°C until golden brown; remove from fryer and drain well.
7 Serve on a suitable dish garnished with coriander leaves. Serve a suitable chutney separately.

Variations
Suggested samosa fillings are given in recipes 40 and 41.

Figure 10.6 Preparation of samosas in six steps

40 Samosa filling: potato

Cal 257 KJ	Cal 86 kcal	Fat 7.4 g	Sat Fat 1.3 g	Carb 4.6 g	Sugar 0.1 g	Protein 0.7 g	Fibre 0.3 g

	4 portions	10 portions
potatoes, peeled	200 g	500 g
vegetable oil	1½ tsp	3¾ tsp
black mustard seeds	½ tsp	1¼ tsp
onions, finely chopped	50 g	125 g
fresh ginger, finely chopped	12 g	30 g
fennel seeds	1 tsp	2½ tsp
cumin seeds	¼ tsp	1 tsp
turmeric	¼ tsp	1 tsp
frozen peas	75 g	187 g
salt, to taste		
water	2½ tsp	6¼ tsp
fresh coriander, finely chopped	1 tsp	2½ tsp
garam masala	½ tsp	2½ tsp
pinch of cayenne pepper		

1 Cut the potatoes into ½ cm dice; cook in water until only just cooked.
2 Heat the oil in a suitable pan, add the mustard seeds and cook until they pop.
3 Add the onions and ginger. Fry for 7–8 minutes, stirring continuously until golden brown.
4 Stir in the fennel, cumin and turmeric, add the potatoes, peas, salt and water.
5 Reduce to a low heat, cover the pan and cook for 5 minutes.
6 Stir in the coriander; cook for a further 5 minutes.
7 Remove from the heat, stir in the garam masala and the cayenne seasoning.
8 Remove from the pan, place into a suitable bowl to cool before using.

HEALTHY EATING TIP
- Use the minimum amount of salt.
- Use a small amount of unsaturated oil to fry the mustard seeds and the onion.
- Skim any fat from the finished dish.

41 Samosa filling: lamb

Cal 516 KJ	Cal 125 kcal	Fat 11.6 g	Sat Fat 3.4 g	Carb 3.9 g	Sugar 0.1 g	Protein 1.6 g	Fibre 0.2 g

	4 portions	10 portions
saffron	½ tsp	1¼ tsp
boiling water	2½ tsp	6¼ tsp
vegetable oil	3 tsp	7½ tsp
fresh ginger, finely chopped	12 g	30 g
cloves garlic, crushed and chopped	2	5
onions, finely chopped	50 g	125 g
salt, to taste		
lean lamb, minced	400 g	1 kg
pinch of cayenne pepper		
garam masala	1 tsp	2½ tsp

1 Infuse the saffron in the boiling water; allow to stand for 10 minutes.
2 Heat the vegetable oil in a suitable pan. Add the ginger, garlic, onions and salt, stirring continuously.

Fry for 7–8 minutes, until the onions are soft and golden brown.
3 Stir in the lamb, add the saffron with the water. Cook, stirring the lamb until it is cooked.
4 Add the cayenne and garam masala, reduce the heat and allow to cook gently for a further 10 minutes.
5 The mixture should be fairly tight with very little moisture.
6 Transfer to a bowl and allow to cool before using.

HEALTHY EATING TIP
- No added salt is necessary.
- Use a small amount of unsaturated oil to fry the onions and lamb.
- Drain off the excess fat before adding the water.

42 Chapatis

Cal	Cal	Fat	Sat Fat	Carb	Sugar	Protein	Fibre
1066 KJ	254 kcal	12.1 g	1.4 g	32.0 g	1.1 g	6.4 g	4.5 g

	4 portions	10 portions
wholewheat flour	200 g	500 g
pinch of salt		
water	125 ml	213 ml
vegetable oil		

1 Sieve the flour and salt, add the water and knead to a firm dough.
2 Knead on a floured table until smooth and elastic.
3 Cover with a damp cloth or polythene and allow to relax for 30–40 minutes.
4 Divide into 8 pieces (20 pieces for 10 portions), flatten each and roll into a circle 12–15 cm in diameter.
5 Lightly grease a frying pan with the oil, add the chapatti and cook as for a pancake. Traditionally chapatis are allowed to puff by placing them over an open flame.
6 Just before serving reheat the chapatis under the salamander.

Note: Chapatis are cooked on a *tawa* or frying pan. They are made fresh for each meal, and are dipped into sauces and used to scoop up food.

HEALTHY EATING TIP
• Use the minimum amount of salt.
• Lightly oil a well-seasoned pan to cook the chapati, or dry-fry.
• Chapatis are a useful accompaniment for fattier meat dishes.

43 Naan bread

Cal	Cal	Fat	Sat Fat	Carb	Sugar	Protein	Fibre	*
1619 KJ	386 kcal	20.5 g	12.0 g	48.3 g	5.0 g	10.1 g	1.8 g	

	6 portions
strong flour	350 g
caster sugar	1½ tsp
salt	1 tsp
baking powder	½ tsp
fresh yeast	15 g
warm milk (38°C)	150 ml
unsweetened plain yoghurt	150 ml
butter	100 g
poppy seeds	2 tbsp

1 Sift the flour into a suitable bowl and add the sugar, salt and baking powder.
2 Dissolve the yeast in the milk and stir in the yoghurt. Mix thoroughly with the flour to form a dough.
3 Knead the dough until it is smooth. Cover with a clean cloth and leave to rise in a warm place for about 4 hours.
4 Divide the risen dough into 12 equal portions and roll into balls, on a lightly floured surface.
5 Flatten the balls into oblong shapes, using both hands and slapping the naan from one hand to the other.
6 Cook the naan bread on the sides of the tandoori oven or on a lightly greased griddle or heavy-bottomed frying pan.
7 Cook the naan on one side only. Brush the raw side with clarified butter and poppy seeds, turn over, cook the other side or brown under a salamander.

Note: This recipe comes from Punjab and goes well with tandoori meat dishes as well as vindaloos. Traditionally, naans are baked in clay ovens. They must be eaten fresh and hot, and served immediately.

HEALTHY EATING TIP
• Cook the bread without added fat.
• Naan bread is a useful accompaniment for fattier meat dishes.

* With clarified butter – using ghee

Indonesia

Indonesia includes Bali, Borneo, Java and Sumatra, and was previously known as the East Indies; it is an agricultural economy that produces rice as its staple food and many kinds of spice, mainly for export. The first two cultural and religious influences were the arrival of Buddhists and Hindus from India, who were followed by Portuguese settlers, then a century later by the Dutch. Immigrants came in large numbers from China and had a great deal of influence on the islands' cookery.

44 Gado-gado (vegetable salad with peanut dressing)

Cal	Cal	Fat	Sat Fat	Carb	Sugar	Protein	Fibre
1329 KJ	320 kcal	24.8 g	3.8 g	16.0 g	6.6 g	9.0 g	3.1 g

	4 portions	10 portions
white cabbage, finely shredded and washed	200 g	500 g
beansprouts, washed	100 g	250 g
cooked potato, cut into 1 cm dice	200 g	500 g
tomato, skinned, deseeded, diced	50 g	125 g
seasoning		
eggs, hardboiled	2	5
Dressing		
vegetable oil	60 ml	150 ml
onion, finely chopped	50 g	125 g
clove garlic, crushed and chopped	1	2–3
green chilli, finely chopped	1	2–3
crunchy peanut butter	50 g	125 g
malt vinegar	2 tsp	5 tsp
coconut milk	125 ml	250 ml

1 Drain the cabbage and beansprouts and mix together.
2 Add the potato and tomato; season lightly.
3 Arrange neatly into individual dishes just prior to service and decorate with quarters of hardboiled egg.
4 Prepare the dressing: heat the oil in a sauteuse and stir-fry the onion, garlic and chilli for 2 minutes.
5 Stir in the peanut butter, vinegar and coconut milk; simmer for a further 2–3 minutes.
6 Pour the hot sauce over the salad or serve separately.

Note: This dish is popular throughout Indonesia. It may be served as a starter or with a main meal and rice.

HEALTHY EATING TIP
- Lightly oil a pan using an unsaturated oil to fry the onion.
- The peanut butter and coconut milk are high in fat, so use less sauce and more vegetables.

45 Rendang (Indonesian beef curry)

Cal 2090 KJ	Cal 504 kcal	Fat 40.8 g	Sat Fat 24.1 g	Carb 7.5 g	Sugar 4.6 g	Protein 27.1 g	Fibre 5.6 g

	4 portions	10 portions
cooking oil	45 ml (3 tsp)	112 ml (7½ tsp)
onion, finely chopped	100 g	250 g
cloves garlic, crushed and chopped	2	5
fresh ginger, finely chopped	12 g	30 g
hot Thai curry blend	30 g (2 tsp)	75 g (5 tsp)
ground lemon grass	5 g (1 tsp)	12½ g (2½ tsp)
desiccated coconut	100 g	250 g
rump or sirloin, cut into thin strips	400 g	1 kg
salt, to taste		
creamed coconut	100 g	250 g
hot water	250 ml	625 ml

1 Heat the oil in a suitable pan. Fry the onions, garlic and ginger until lightly coloured.
2 Add the curry blend and lemon grass; continue to fry for a further 2 minutes.
3 Add the desiccated coconut; fry for a further minute.
4 In a separate pan, quickly fry the beef, to seal. Drain off the excess oil and place the beef in a clean saucepan. Season.
5 Blend the coconut and hot water to make coconut milk and add to the beef.
6 Add the other ingredients that have been prepared.
7 Bring to boil, simmer until the beef is tender and the liquid has evaporated; stir occasionally. The curry should be quite dry.
8 Serve with prawn crackers.

HEALTHY EATING TIP
- Lightly oil a pan using an unsaturated oil to fry the onion.
- Skim any fat from the finished dish.
- Little or no salt is required.
- Serve with rice or noodles and additional vegetables.

46 Nasi goreng (rice with bacon, chicken and soy sauce)

Cal 2334 KJ	Cal 562 kcal	Fat 42.6 g	Sat Fat 13.9 g	Carb 25.2 g	Sugar 2.2 g	Protein 21.0 g	Fibre 0.6 g

	4 portions	10 portions
vegetable oil	60 ml	150 ml
onion, finely chopped	100 g	250 g
clove garlic, crushed and chopped	1	2–3
red chilli, finely chopped	1	2–3
small lardons of bacon	200 g	500 g
cooked chicken, cut into 2 cm slices	100 g	250 g
soy sauce	2 tbsp	5 tbsp
rice cooked as pilaff, dry and fluffy	250 g	625 g
Garnish		
eggs, beaten and seasoned	2	5
cucumber, finely sliced	50 g	125 g

1 Heat a little oil in a wok, add the onion, garlic and chilli, and stir-fry. Add the lardons of bacon and cook quickly.
2 Add the cooked chicken and cook for a further 2–3 minutes.
3 Add the soy sauce and cooked rice. Reheat the rice thoroughly. Stir occasionally.
4 For the garnish, heat a little oil in a small frying pan. Beat the egg well with seasoning. Pour this into the frying pan, cook one side, turn over and cook the other. Turn out onto a board. Cut into thin strips.
5 Serve in a suitable dish, garnished with strips of the cooked egg and slices of cucumber.

Note: Prawns are sometimes added to this dish.

HEALTHY EATING TIP
- Use a small amount of an unsaturated vegetable oil to fry the onion and bacon.
- Drain off any excess fat before adding the cooked chicken.
- This dish will be high in salt from the bacon and soy sauce, so no additional salt is needed.

Japan

Japanese cuisine is a reflection of the traditional Japanese art and culture that draws inspiration from the beauty of seasonal changes, and attempts to achieve harmony with the natural surroundings.

The underlying philosophy of Japanese cuisine is to capture the essence of the seasonal changes by using vegetables, fruits and fish associated with the particular time of year, and by retaining the natural flavour of the ingredients. Aesthetic and artistic presentation of the food is paramount. Ingredients are often used raw or with minimum cooking, with the preparation focused on the enhancement of the natural flavour and texture of the ingredients. As a result, the freshness and quality of the ingredients becomes essential. It is these Japanese presentation skills and cooking approaches that gave inspiration to nouvelle cuisine.

Key components of a traditional Japanese diet are rice, noodles, vegetables, seaweeds, fish, shellfish, soybean products (tofu, miso and age) and fruits. The Japanese did not eat meat until late 1800 because of the Buddhist principles that forbade eating four-legged animal meat. However, today meat – mainly beef, pork and chicken – is very much a part of the general Japanese diet, though the amount consumed is small by European standards.

Japanese cookery is widely recognised as being beneficial to health because no saturated fat or dairy products – other than eggs – are generally used.

Traditional Japanese cooking methods are boiling, simmering, steaming, grilling and frying (deep, shallow and stir). No oven is required.

The main Japanese seasoning ingredients are as follows.

- **Dashi stock:** stock made with dried bonito flakes (*hana-gatsuo*) and dried kelp seaweed (*konbu*) or dried shiitake mushrooms.
- **Japanese soy sauces (dark and light):** made from fermented soybeans, wheat and salt. Japanese soy sauces have a different flavour from the Chinese varieties. They are less salty and lighter in colour. It is important to use the correct kind.
- **Sake:** rice wine, of the same kind as that served as a drink.
- **Mirin:** light golden syrupy wine, which has approximately 14 per cent alcohol content, and is used only in cooking, either to add sweetness or to glaze grilled food.
- **Miso:** fermented soybean paste. It comes in a wide variety, each having a distinct aroma, degree of saltiness, fermentation and colour. It is used primarily for soups and dressings in a wide variety of dishes.
- **Sesame oil:** generally used in small amounts for flavouring.

One type of Japanese cooking that has really gone global is **sushi**. Sushi refers to dishes that use vinegared rice. Sushi can be made with numerous kinds of cooked or raw ingredients. There is sushi unique to each region of Japan, using cooked or raw fish, shellfish, braised or raw vegetables, or thin, miniature omelettes, or a combination of these. A Japanese set meal (*tei-shoku*) usually has five components: two bowl dishes and three plate dishes. The two bowls are hot steamed rice and hot soup. The three plates comprise a meat or fish dish, and a vegetable or soybean dish, or a plate combining the two. All dishes are served at the same time.

The following are some of the authentic Japanese recipes that go well with European dishes.

47 Sushi rice

	4 portions
Japanese short-grain rice	400 ml (2 cups)
water	340 ml
Sushi vinegar	
Japanese rice vinegar	60 ml (4 tbsp)
caster sugar	1½ tbsp
salt	½ tsp

1 Put the rice into a bowl and rinse with water until the water runs clear.
2 Drain the washed rice in a sieve and leave it for 5 minutes or until the water drains off completely.
3 Prepare the sushi vinegar by dissolving the sugar and salt in the vinegar.
4 Place the rice in a heavy-bottomed medium-sized pan or rice cooker and add 340 ml of water.
5 Cover tightly and bring the pan slowly to the boil over a medium heat. Continue to boil for 2 minutes, then reduce the heat to a simmer and cook for a further 5–8 minutes or until all the water has been absorbed and you can hear a crackling noise. It is crucial not to take off the lid during this cooking process in order to achieve the right firm texture.
6 Turn the heat off and allow the pan to sit on the stove undisturbed for 1–2 minutes.
7 Take the cover off the pan and turn the rice out into a large bowl. Sprinkle the vinegar mixture over the hot rice and mix it carefully with a wooden spatula without crushing the grains. To keep the grains separate, toss the rice with horizontal cutting movements. Remember, unless the rice is just cooked, the vinegar will not be absorbed.
8 Spread the rice onto a large chopping board or wooden sushi tub. Cool the rice down to room temperature by fanning. This prevents the rice going soggy and produces a sheen.
9 Once the rice has cooled down to room temperature, it is ready for use.
10 To keep sushi rice from drying out, place in a container and cover with a damp tea towel. Sushi rice should be eaten the same day it is prepared. It does not keep for more than a day. It should not be refrigerated as the rice will harden and become unpleasant to the palate.

Note: Sushi rice is called *shari* in Japanese. *Shari* makes sushi, so it is very important to get proper Japanese rice. In order to make the correct texture of sushi rice the ratio 1 (rice): 1 (liquid) is critical. The total liquid quantity includes the amount of rice vinegar in sushi vinegar mixture that will be added to the hot cooked rice later. Sushi rice can be made in advance, stored in a container, then covered with a damp tea towel.

48 Steamed rice

	4 portions
Japanese short-grain rice	400 ml (2 cups)
water	400 ml

1 Put the rice into a bowl and rinse with water until the water runs clear.
2 Place the rice in a heavy-bottomed medium-sized pan or rice cooker and add 400 ml of water.
3 Cover tightly and bring the pan slowly to the boil over a medium heat. Continue to boil over high heat for 2 minutes. Cook, then turn the heat down to a simmer and cook for a further 5–8 minutes or until all water has been absorbed and you can hear a crackling noise. To achieve the right texture, it is crucial not to take off the lid during the cooking process.
4 Turn off the heat and let it steam for 5 minutes, then the rice is ready to serve.

Note: To cook Japanese rice, the water to rice ratio is 1 (rice): 1 (water). Steamed rice can be made in advance and wrapped in clingfilm; it freezes very well. Reheat in a microwave oven for approximately 1 or 2 minutes.

49 Teri-yaki chicken (pan-fried chicken coated with soya mirin sauce)

Cal	Cal	Fat	Sat Fat	Carb	Sugar	Protein	Fibre
596 KJ	143 kcal	9.8 g	2.6 g	0.5 g	0.0 g	13.4 g	0.0 g

	4 portions
large boned chicken thighs with skin	4
Sauce	
mirin (syrupy Japanese rice wine)	4 tsp
sake (Japanese rice wine)	1 tsp
Japanese soy sauce	1½ tsp
Garnish	
spring onion, thinly sliced	1 tbsp

1 Heat a non-stick frying pan over a moderate heat until hot.
2 Add the chicken pieces skin side down. In order to squeeze the fat and excess moisture out of the skin, cook skin side until the skin becomes crispy and golden brown. If the skin is browning too quickly, take the pan off the heat occasionally to slow down the process and prevent burning.
3 When the skins are all crisp and golden brown, take the pieces out of the frying pan then place onto a piece of kitchen towel and drain the fat.
4 Wipe the remaining chicken fat clean from the frying pan using a kitchen towel.

5 Return the chicken pieces to the cleansed frying pan, then cook the flesh side for 1 minute.
6 Reverse the chicken pieces yet again to skin side and add mirin, sake and soy sauce to the pan.
7 Increase the heat slightly to bring the sauces to the boil. When the sauce is syrupy and starts to bubble, turn the chicken pieces frequently to coat with the sauce without burning. A pair of tongs is ideal for this operation.
8 When all the chicken pieces are cooked through, add grated ginger to the sauce. The chicken should look glossy and well coated with the sauce. Serve immediately with the remaining thickened sauce. Sprinkle with spring onion slices and sesame seeds for garnish.

HEALTHY EATING TIP
- No added salt is needed.
- Serve with a large portion of rice and additional vegetables.

Mexico

The food of this Spanish-speaking nation has become very popular in many countries. Mexico has an old-established cuisine that stems from the Native Americans to the Aztecs, and then from the Spanish who arrived there in 1519, along with some French influence, which came with the installation of Emperor Maximilian. It is based on an abundance of native ingredients made extremely hot by the use of chillies, cooked simply without roasting or baking, supported by accompaniments made of maize, which plays a much larger part in the diet than wheat.

50 Tortillas

Cal	Cal	Fat	Sat Fat	Carb	Sugar	Protein	Fibre
1064 KJ	254 kcal	10.3 g	1.1 g	35.4 g	0.4 g	5.5 g	2.2 g

	4 portions	10 portions
wholemeal flour	100 g	250 g
cornmeal flour	100 g	250 g
water	250 ml	625 ml

1 Sieve the flours together into a bowl, add a pinch of salt and enough water to make a smooth dough.
2 Knead well until elastic. Divide into 12 or 16 pieces (30 or 40 for 10 portions), depending on the size of the tortilla required.
3 Place a ball of dough between two pieces of well-oiled greaseproof paper (or use silicone paper). Roll the dough into a circle (diameter 10–15 cm).
4 Lightly oil a frying pan. Peel off the top layer of paper and place the tortilla in the pan. Cook for 2 minutes. Remove the top paper, turn over and cook the other side for 2 minutes. Both sides should be quite pale and dry.
5 Keep the tortillas warm for service, stacking between pieces of dry greaseproof paper.

Note: Tortillas are served with all Mexican meals. Although in Mexico a special flour is used, tortillas may be produced using cornmeal and wholemeal flour. The tortilla can be served in different ways: when crisp and golden it is called a tostada; these are served with red kidney beans, cheese and a chilli sauce.

Chilli sauce is usually purchased as a commercial product, but it can be made by mixing together tomato ketchup and Tabasco sauce, or by making a fresh tomato coulis (page 51), strengthened with tomato purée and finished with Tabasco.

HEALTHY EATING TIP
- Use a very little unsaturated vegetable oil to cook the tortillas.
- Tortillas may be made lighter by adding 1 tsp (2½ tsp for 10 portions) baking powder.

Variations
- A filling of kidney beans with a little grated cheese and chilli sauce can be used to make enchiladas. Serve with a mixed salad.
- Tacos are tortillas curled into a shell shape and fried, usually filled with picadillo (see recipe 51) and served with salad and chilli sauce.
- Tortillas that are rolled and filled, then served with a sauce, are called enchiladas.

51 Picadillo

Cal	Cal	Fat	Sat Fat	Carb	Sugar	Protein	Fibre	*
1945 KJ	467 kcal	32.6 g	6.6 g	18.6 g	13.4 g	26.2 g	2.4 g	

	4 portions	10 portions
oil	60 ml	150 ml
minced lean beef	400 g	1 kg
onion, finely chopped	100 g	250 g
clove garlic, crushed and chopped	1	2–3
chilli, finely chopped	1	2–3
tomatoes, skinned, deseeded and diced	100 g	250 g
tomato purée	50 g	125 g
cumin seed	¼ tsp	½ tsp
raisins	50 g	125 g
brown stock or water	250 ml	625 ml
cornflour	18 g	36 g
green olives, chopped	25 g	60 g
capers, chopped	25 g	60 g
seasoning		
flaked almonds, roasted	50 g	125 g

1 Heat the oil in a frying pan, add the minced beef and brown quickly.
2 Add the onion, garlic and chopped chilli pepper. Season and cook for a further 3 minutes.
3 Pour off the excess oil and place the meat into a suitable saucepan.
4 Add to the saucepan the tomatoes, tomato purée, cumin seed and raisins.

5 Barely cover with brown stock or water and simmer gently for 30 minutes.
6 Lightly thicken with a little diluted cornflour, and stir in the olives and capers.
7 Correct the seasoning and consistency. Finish by adding the roasted flaked almonds.

Note: Picadillo is also used as a filling for tacos.

HEALTHY EATING TIP
- Dry-fry the minced beef in a well-seasoned pan and drain off all excess fat.
- Use the minimum amount of salt.
- Use to fill tortillas (recipe 50) and serve with a green salad.

* Using gherkins to replace capers

52 Burritos (Mexican pancakes)

Cal	Cal	Fat	Sat Fat	Carb	Sugar	Protein	Fibre
3481 KJ	832 kcal	47.6 g	13.0 g	60.2 g	9.8 g	45.2 g	10.3 g

	4 portions	10 portions
pancake batter (recipe 53)	250 ml	625 ml
portions chilli con carne (recipe 77)	4	10
mornay sauce, flavoured with Dijon-type mustard	500 ml	1¼ litres
grated cheese (Parmesan or Cheddar)		

1 Make the pancakes in the usual way (see recipe 53).
2 Fill the pancakes with chilli con carne (recipe 77). Place in a suitable earthenware dish.
3 Mask with the mornay sauce and sprinkle with grated cheese.
4 Glaze under the salamander or in a hot oven and serve.

HEALTHY EATING TIP
- No added salt is needed; there is plenty of salt in the cheese.
- Serve with a large mixed salad.

53 Pancake batter

Cal	Cal	Fat	Sat Fat	Carb	Sugar	Protein	Fibre	*
1034 KJ	248 kcal	15.4 g	3.4 g	22.2 g	3.2 g	6.3 g	0.8 g	

	4 portions	10 portions
flour (white or wholemeal)	100 g	250 g
pinch of salt		
egg	1	2
milk, whole or skimmed	250 ml	625 ml
melted butter, margarine or oil	10 g	25 g
oil, for frying		

1 Sieve the flour and salt into a bowl; make a well in the centre.
2 Add the egg and milk, gradually incorporating the flour from the sides; whisk to a smooth batter.
3 Mix in the melted butter. Heat the pancake pan, clean thoroughly.
4 Add a little oil; heat until smoking.
5 Add enough mixture to just cover the bottom of the pan thinly.
6 Cook for a few seconds until brown.
7 Turn and cook on the other side. Turn on to a plate.
8 Repeat until all the batter is used up.

* Using whole milk and vegetable oil

The Middle East

The spread of Islam has played a significant role in the development of traditional Middle Eastern cuisine. The death of the prophet Muhammad in the year AD 632 was followed by victorious wars waged by the followers of his faith. The establishment of an Islamic empire, stretching across Asia, North Africa, Spain and Sicily, brought together cooking styles and refinements in eating habits. Great value is attached to food as a means of offering hospitality. Regional differences do not have much to do with national boundaries but depend more on geography, history and local produce.

54 Hummus (chickpea and sesame seed paste)

Cal	Cal	Fat	Sat Fat	Carb	Sugar	Protein	Fibre
1546 KJ	367 kcal	15.3 g	2.0 g	39.2 g	3.0 g	20.9 g	1.7 g

	4 portions	10 portions
chickpeas, soaked	300 g	750 g
seasoning		
sesame seed paste (tahini)	75 g	187 g
clove garlic, crushed and chopped	1	2–3
onion, finely chopped	50 g	125 g
lemon, juice of	1	2
paprika	5 g	10 g

1 Cook the chickpeas in simmering water for 2 hours. Drain well.
2 Purée the chickpeas in a food processor, add seasoning, sesame seed paste, garlic and onion. Finish with lemon juice.
3 Place into a suitable serving dish decorated with a line of paprika.

Note: Serve with pitta bread as a starter or as an accompaniment to main dishes.

HEALTHY EATING TIP
- Use the minimum amount of salt.
- Serve with plenty of hot pitta bread and crudités to make a healthy starter.

55 Tabbouleh (cracked wheat salad)

Cal	Cal	Fat	Sat Fat	Carb	Sugar	Protein	Fibre
582 KJ	140 kcal	7.9 g	0.9 g	15.5 g	1.0 g	2.1 g	0.3 g

	4 portions	10 portions
cracked wheat (bulgar)	75 g	187 g
onion, finely chopped	25 g	60 g
cucumber, diced	50 g	125 g
tomato, peeled, deseeded, diced	50 g	125 g
salt, pepper		
vegetable oil	30 ml	75 ml
lemon, juice of	½	1
fresh parsley and mint, chopped		

1 Cover the cracked wheat with cold water and leave to soak for 10 minutes. Drain well, place into a suitable basin.
2 Add the onion, cucumber and tomato; season with salt and pepper.
3 Mix in the oil and lemon juice, stir in the chopped parsley and chopped mint.
4 Serve on individual side plates, dressed in lettuce leaves.

Note: Serve with hummus or kebabs.

HEALTHY EATING TIP
- Use the minimum amount of salt.
- Use half the amount of an unsaturated oil.

56 Kibbeh bil sanieh (spiced lamb with cracked wheat)

Cal 3338 KJ	Cal 803 kcal	Fat 51.6 g	Sat Fat 16.7 g	Carb 49.5 g	Sugar 10.6 g	Protein 36.7 g	Fibre 0.9 g	*

	4 portions	10 portions
bulgar (cracked wheat)	200 g	500 g
leg or shoulder of lamb, boned and diced	400 g	1 kg
onion, finely chopped	50 g	125 g
cinnamon	1 tsp	2½ tsp
seasoning		
cold water	2 tbsp	5 tbsp
Filling		
onion, finely chopped	50 g	125 g
clove garlic, crushed and chopped	1	2
oil	60 ml	150 ml
lamb, minced	200 g	500 g
allspice	½ tsp	1 tsp
pine kernels	50 g	125 g
chopped raisins	50 g	125 g
butter or margarine, melted	50 g	125 g

1 Cover the cracked wheat with cold water and allow to stand for 5 minutes. Drain well.
2 Place the lamb in a food processor with the finely chopped onion, cinnamon and seasoning; blend to a smooth paste. Add the tablespoons of cold water and mix well.
3 Add the well-drained cracked wheat. Blend in a food processor until a smooth paste is formed.

4 For the filling: first, sweat the onion and garlic together in the oil. Add the minced lamb, allow to brown quickly.
5 Mix in the allspice, pine kernels and raisins.
6 In a suitable dish, spread half of the lamb and wheat mixture on the bottom (the kibbeh). Cover with the filling. Finish by topping with the rest of the kibbeh.
7 Cut diagonal lines over the top to make diamond shapes and brush the melted butter or margarine over the top.
8 Bake in a moderately hot oven, 190°C for approximately 45 minutes. The surface should be brown and crisp. Baste occasionally with a few tablespoons of stock, so that the interior is moist.

Note: This is eaten with salad, pitta bread, hummus and yoghurt, served hot or cold.

HEALTHY EATING TIP
• Use a small amount of an unsaturated oil to sweat the onion and brown the lamb.
• Drain off any excess fat from the filling.
• Serve with plenty of pitta bread, salad, yoghurt and hummus.

* Using butter

Couscous

This is the national dish of the Maghreb: the North African countries of Morocco, Tunisia and Algeria, of Berber origin. A type of couscous has been adopted by other Arab countries, which call it Maghebia; it is different from the North African dish. Couscous itself is a type of fine semolina.

The basic process for the preparation of couscous is the steaming of the grain over a stew or broth. This is generally made with lamb or chicken and a variety of vegetables. Chickpeas are usually added and sometimes raisins. The broth is often coloured red with tomato purée or yellow with saffron.

The actual process of cooking the couscous is very simple, but calls for careful handling of the grain. The aim is to make it swell and become extremely light, each grain soft, delicate and separate. The grain must never cook in the broth or sauce, but only in the steam. The couscousier, the pot traditionally used, is in two parts: the bottom part is the round pan in which the stew is cooked; the top consists of a sieve, which holds the couscous.

The treatment of the grain is always the same, whatever the sauce. Recipe 57 is for a basic Moroccan couscous.

57 Couscous

Cal 2146 KJ	Cal 515 kcal	Fat 28.5 g	Sat Fat 12.6 g	Carb 42.2 g	Sugar 14.7 g	Protein 25.3 g	Fibre 2.8 g	*

	4 portions	10 portions
couscous	200 g	500 g
lean stewing lamb *or*	400 g *or*	1 kg *or*
stewing lamb	200 g	500 g
stewing beef *or*		
chicken, cut for	200 g *or*	500 g *or*
sauté	1½ kg	3¾ kg
olive oil	2 tbsp	5 tbsp
onion, finely chopped	50 g	125 g
clove garlic, crushed		
and chopped	1	2–3
celery	100 g	250 g
leek	100 g	250 g
carrot	100 g	250 g
chickpeas	25 g	60 g
seasoning		
ground ginger (optional)	¼ tsp	½ tsp
saffron (optional)	¼ tsp	½ tsp
raisins	50 g	125 g
courgettes	100 g	250 g
tomatoes, skinned,		
deseeded, diced	50 g	125 g
parsley, chopped		
tomato purée	50 g	125 g
cayenne pepper		
paprika	½ tsp	1 tsp
butter or margarine	50 g	125 g

1 Soak the couscous in warm water for 10 minutes.
2 Fry the meat in the oil until browned and sealed. Remove quickly, fry the onions and garlic.
3 Drain, place the meat, onions and garlic into a saucepan.
4 Add the celery, leeks and carrots cut into 1½cm dice. Add the chickpeas, cover with water, season.
5 Add the ginger and saffron. Bring to the boil and simmer for about 1 hour.
6 Drain the couscous, place in the top part of the couscousier and steam for 30 minutes. Alternatively, place the couscous in a metal colander lined with muslin. Fit into the top of the saucepan, making sure that the liquid from the stew does not touch the steamer as the couscous will become lumpy. Stir occasionally.

7 Add to the stew the raisins and courgettes, the tomato, chopped parsley and tomato purée. Cook for a further 30 minutes.
8 Remove approximately 250 ml (625 ml) sauce from the stew and stir in the cayenne pepper, enough to make it strong and fiery. Finish with paprika.
9 To serve, pile the couscous into a suitable serving dish, preferably earthenware, add knobs of butter or margarine and work into the grains with a fork.
10 Carefully arrange the meat and vegetables over the couscous and pour the broth over. Serve the hot peppery sauce separately.
11 Alternatively, the couscous, meat and vegetables, the broth and the peppery sauce can be served in separate bowls.

Note: A pre-cooked couscous is also available.

HEALTHY EATING TIP

- No additional salt is needed.
- Add only a small amount of fat to the couscous before adding the meat and vegetables.
- The fat content will be reduced if skinned chicken is used or less lamb/beef and more vegetables.

* *Using lamb and butter*

Figure 10.7 Couscous (with peas, chives, tomato concassée and mint)

58 Couscous with chorizo sausage and chicken

Cal	Cal	Fat	Sat Fat	Carb	Sugar	Protein	Fibre
1590 KJ	380 kcal	13.1 g	4.3 g	34.1 g	1.7 g	33.1 g	0.3 g

	4 portions	10 portions
couscous	250 g	625 g
olive oil	1 tbsp	1½ tbsp
garlic cloves, finely chopped	2	3
chorizo sausage	150 g	400 g
suprêmes of chicken, skinned	3	7
sunblush tomatoes	75 g	200 g
fresh parsley	¼ tsp	½ tsp

1 Prepare the couscous in a suitable bowl and gently pour over 300 ml (750 ml for 10 portions) of boiling water.
2 Stir well, cover and leave to stand for 5 minutes.
3 Heat the olive oil in a suitable frying pan, add the chopped garlic, then sauté for 1 minute.
4 Add the chorizo sausage, (sliced 1 cm thick) and the chicken cut into fine strips. Cook for 5–6 minutes.
5 Add the couscous, sunblush tomatoes (skinned or diced) and parsley, mix thoroughly and heat for a further 2–3 minutes.
6 Drizzle with olive oil, serve as a warm salad.
7 Garnish with mixed leaves and flat parsley.

HEALTHY EATING TIP

- Using an unsaturated oil (sunflower or olive), lightly oil the pan to sauté the garlic.
- Drain off any excess fat after cooking the sausage and chicken.
- Serve with mixed leaves.

59 Khoshaf (dried fruit with nuts, perfumed with rose and orange water)

Cal	Cal	Fat	Sat Fat	Carb	Sugar	Protein	Fibre
1554 KJ	370 kcal	16.3 g	1.1 g	51.3 g	50.9 g	7.6 g	6.9 g

	4 portions	10 portions
dried apricots	100 g	250 g
prunes	100 g	250 g
dried figs	100 g	250 g
raisins	100 g	250 g
rose water	1 tbsp	2½ tbsp
orange blossom water	1 tbsp	2½ tbsp
blanched almonds, halved	50 g	125 g
pine kernels	50 g	125 g

1 Wash the fruit if necessary, soak overnight.
2 Drain, place fruit in a large saucepan, cover with water and bring to boil. Simmer for 10 minutes.
3 Add the rose water and the orange blossom water.
4 Place into a serving dish sprinkled with the almonds and pine kernels.

Figure 10.8 Khoshaf

Note: During Ramadan, Muslims fast all day and eat only after sunset. This is one of the dishes enjoyed during Ramadan. It can be served hot or cold.

Israeli kosher cooking

Israel is populated by a total of some 4 million Jewish and Arab people. The Jewish people in Israel are mainly immigrants from Europe who have come from Germany, Poland and Russia; there are also immigrants from Spain and Portugal; more recently, Jewish minorities from North African countries including Ethiopia, Syria and Iran have made their homes in Israel. No matter where they originated, Jewish people still carry on the cooking traditions of the time when Israel was their God-given homeland and in accordance with the food laws as written in the Torah, which comprises the first five books of the Old Testament.

'Kosher' is a Jewish word meaning 'pure' or 'clean'. It governs the fish, birds and animals that orthodox Jews are allowed to eat, how they must be slaughtered, and how the meat must be 'koshered'; milk and meat may not be cooked together nor eaten at the same meal, and separate cooking and serving utensils must be kept specifically for each. After eating any form of meat it is not permitted to consume any milk foods, including cheese, for three hours. Products bearing the seal of the Beth Din – the authority appointed and approved by the Chief Rabbi – should be used. Shellfish, game birds and pork products are forbidden.

The laws also govern the way certain foods are stored, the kitchen and its equipment, and the cook's personal knives. Knives in use for general catering may not be used for kosher catering.

Many interesting dishes are made for the many Jewish festivals in the calendar, and only unleavened bread, called *matzos*, may be eaten during the Feast of the Passover, which commemorates the night when a destroying angel smote the first-born of the Egyptians but spared those in the houses where the doorposts and lintels had been daubed with blood.

60 Potato latkes

Cal	Cal	Fat	Sat Fat	Carb	Sugar	Protein	Fibre
909 KJ	218 kcal	12.9 g	1.8 g	22.1 g	1.4 g	4.7 g	1.6 g

	4 portions	10 portions
potatoes, washed, peeled and grated	400 g	1 kg
onion, finely chopped	50 g	125 g
salt, pepper		
egg	1	2
plain flour or breadcrumbs	1 tbsp	2½ tbsp

1 Wash the grated potatoes, drain well and mix in a basin with the finely chopped onion.
2 Season with salt and pepper and add the beaten egg, flour or breadcrumbs and season.
3 Heat a little oil in a shallow pan and place potato mixture in 50 g pieces into it.
4 Cook on both sides for 3–4 minutes until golden brown; serve immediately.

Note: A little grated carrot or courgette may be added to the potato.

HEALTHY EATING TIP
- Use the minimum amount of salt.
- Use a little unsaturated oil to fry the potato mixture, then drain on kitchen paper.

61 Koenigsberger klops (meatballs)

Cal 849 KJ	Cal 201 kcal	Fat 6.0 g	Sat Fat 2.4 g	Carb 14.3 g	Sugar 2.8 g	Protein 23.3 g	Fibre 0.7 g	*

	4 portions	10 portions
bread (white or wholemeal)	75 g	187 g
egg	1	2
minced beef	200 g	500 g
minced veal	200 g	500 g
onion, chopped	50 g	125 g
salt, pepper		
parsley, chopped		
paprika	¼ tsp	½ tsp
lemon rind, grated	½ tsp	1 tsp
lemon, juice of	½	1
Worcester sauce	1 tsp	2½ tsp
brown vegetable stock	1 litre	2½ litre
cornflour or arrowroot		
tomato purée		
capers	25 g	60 g
gherkins	25 g	60 g

1 Remove the crusts from the bread and soak the bread in water.
2 Mix together the beaten egg and meat.
3 Sweat the chopped onion in a little oil until soft, then allow to cool and add to the meat.
4 Season with salt and pepper; add the chopped parsley.
5 Squeeze out excess water from the bread; add the bread to the meat.

6 Add the paprika, lemon rind and juice, and Worcester sauce; mix well.
7 Form into 18 g balls for a reception snack or 75 g balls for a main course (serve 2 per portion).
8 Cook in boiling vegetable stock, cover and simmer until cooked. Remove when cooked and keep warm.
9 Boil the remaining stock, lightly thicken with arrowroot or cornflour, and colour slightly by adding a little tomato purée.
10 Season with salt and pepper; add the chopped capers and gherkins.
11 Reheat the meatballs in the gravy. Serve the small balls with cocktail sticks.

Note: This may be served as a reception snack or main course.

HEALTHY EATING TIP
- Add little or no salt, rely on the Worcester sauce for flavour.
- Skim any fat from the stock after cooking the meatballs.
- Serve with pasta or noodles and a green salad.

Using white flour; gherkin analysis used for capers

62 Cholla bread

	Makes 2 loaves
butter or margarine	56 g
strong flour	500 g
caster sugar	18 g
salt	1 tsp
egg	63 g
yeast	25 g

1 Rub the butter or margarine into the sieved flour in a suitable basin.
2 Mix the sugar, salt and egg together.
3 Disperse the yeast in the water.

4 Add all these ingredients to the sieved flour and mix well to develop the dough. Cover with a damp cloth or plastic and allow to ferment for about 45 minutes.
5 Divide into 125–150 g strands and begin to plait as follows:

4–strand plait	5–strand plait
2 over 3	2 over 3
4 over 2	5 over 2
1 over 3	1 over 3

6 After moulding place on a lightly greased baking sheet and eggwash lightly.
7 Prove in a little steam until double in size. Eggwash

again lightly and decorate with maw seeds (poppy seeds).

8 Bake in a hot oven, at 220°C for 25–30 minutes.

Figure 10.9 Cholla bread

63 Matzo fritters

Cal	Cal	Fat	Sat Fat	Carb	Sugar	Protein	Fibre	*
2079 KJ	494 kcal	21.2 g	3.7 g	68.2 g	31.1 g	12.0 g	1.4 g	

	4 portions	10 portions
matzos (wafers of unleavened bread)	3	7
milk	250 ml	625 ml
eggs, separated	2	5
matzo meal	150 g	375 g
brown sugar	100 g	250 g
salt		
cinnamon	¼ tsp	1 tsp
vegetable oil	60 ml	150 ml

1 Sprinkle warm water over the matzos. Place on a baking sheet and dry in a hot oven for 1 minute.
2 In a suitable basin beat the milk and egg yolks together, add the matzo meal, sugar, salt and cinnamon.

3 Fold in the stiffly beaten egg whites.
4 Spread this mixture on one side of each matzo. Fry in hot oil on the batter side until brown.
5 Spread batter on other side and fry again until brown.
6 Serve hot, sprinkled with sugar.

HEALTHY EATING TIP
• Use the minimum amount of salt.
• Fry in a small amount of an unsaturated oil and drain on kitchen paper.

* *Using semi-skimmed milk, matzo biscuits used as matzo flour*

64 Blitz kuchen (baked fluffy batter with nuts and cinnamon)

Cal 2971 KJ	Cal 710 kcal	Fat 41.5 g	Sat Fat 17.3 g	Carb 68.9 g	Sugar 28.9 g	Protein 19.7 g	Fibre 3.1 g	*

	4 portions	10 portions
cake flour	200 g	500 g
baking powder	10 g	25 g
butter or margarine	100 g	250 g
caster sugar	100 g	250 g
eggs, separated	4	10
lemon, grated rind of	½	1
milk	60 ml	150 ml
egg white	1	2–3
water	1 tbsp	2–3 tbsp
cinnamon	¼ tsp	1 tsp
mixed nuts, chopped	100 g	250 g

1 Sieve the flour and baking powder into a suitable bowl.
2 Cream the fat and sugar together until light and white.
3 Gradually add the egg yolks to the butter and sugar, beating continuously. Add the lemon rind.
4 Gradually add the flour, beating well, then add the milk. Cream well. (Add a little more milk if necessary.)
5 Beat the egg whites until full peak.
6 Gently fold the egg whites into the batter.
7 Heat a lightly oiled 20 cm frying pan, suitable for placing in the oven. Pour in sufficient batter to cover the surface and spread with diluted egg white.
8 Sprinkle liberally with caster sugar, cinnamon and chopped mixed nuts.
9 Bake in a moderate oven at 190°C for about 20 minutes. Serve hot or cold.

* Using semi-skimmed milk, plain flour used

Figure 10.10 Blitz kuchen

Spain

The flavours of Spain, like much else of its culture, are influenced by the Moors who, for seven centuries, ruled a large part of the country. The country's closeness to North Africa and the almost tropical culture of its southern and eastern coastal strip, have done much to preserve a culinary tradition reliant on almonds, saffron, chickpeas, egg yolk, honey and quince, as well as the onion, garlic, olive oil, tomato and lamb common to Mediterranean countries. The cooking can be rich and distinctive. Many of its popular dishes are mixtures of fish, shellfish, meat, poultry and game, with an assortment of vegetables and cereals.

65 Paella (savoury rice with chicken, fish, vegetables and spices)

Cal 3383 KJ	Cal 804 kcal	Fat 31.0 g	Sat Fat 6.2 g	Carb 48.8 g	Sugar 3.8 g	Protein 85.7 g	Fibre 1.3 g	*

	4 portions	10 portions
cooked lobster	400 g	1 kg
squid	200 g	500 g
gambas (Mediterranean prawns), cooked	400 g	1 kg
mussels	400 g	1 kg
white stock	1 litre	2½ litres
pinch of saffron		
onion, finely chopped	50 g	125 g
clove garlic, finely chopped	1	2–3
red pepper, diced	50 g	125 g
green pepper, diced	50 g	125 g
roasting chicken, cut for sauté	1½ kg	3¾ kg
olive oil	60 ml	150 ml
short-grain rice	200 g	500 g
thyme		
bay leaf		
seasoning		
tomatoes, skinned, deseeded, diced	200 g	500 g
lemon wedges, to finish		

1. Prepare the lobster: cut it in half, remove the claws and legs, discard the sac and trail. Remove the meat from the claws and cut the tail into 3–4 pieces, leaving the meat in the shell.
2. Clean the squid, pull the body and head apart. Extract the transparent 'pen' from the body. Rinse well, pulling off the thin purple membrane on the outside. Remove the ink sac. Cut the body into rings and the tentacles into 1 cm lengths.
3. Prepare the gambas by shelling the body.
4. Shell the mussels and retain the cooking liquid.
5. Boil the white stock and mussel liquor together, infused with saffron. Simmer for 5–10 minutes.
6. Sweat the finely chopped onion in a suitable pan, without colour. Add the garlic and the peppers.
7. Sauté the chicken in olive oil until cooked and golden brown, then drain.
8. Add the rice to the onions and garlic and sweat for 2 minutes.
9. Add about 200 ml white stock and mussel liquor.
10. Add the thyme, bay leaf and seasoning. Bring to the boil, then cover with a lightly oiled

greaseproof paper and lid. Cook for 5–8 minutes, in a moderately hot oven at 180°C.
11. Add the squid and cook for another 5 minutes.
12. Add the tomatoes, chicken and lobster pieces, mussels and gambas. Stir gently, cover with a lid and reheat the rice in the oven.
13. Correct the consistency of the rice if necessary by adding more stock, so that it looks sufficiently moist without being too wet. Correct the seasoning.
14. When all is reheated and cooked, place in a suitable serving dish, decorate with 4 (10) gambas and 4 (10) mussels halved and shelled. Finish with wedges of lemon.

Note: For a traditional paella a raw lobster may be used, which should be prepared as follows. Remove the legs and claws and crack the claws. Cut the lobster in half crosswise, between the tail and the carapace. Cut the carapace in two lengthwise. Discard the sac. Cut across the tail in thick slices through the shell. Remove the trail, wash the lobster pieces and cook with the rice.

HEALTHY EATING TIP
- To reduce the fat, skin the chicken and use a little unsaturated oil to sweat the onions and fry the chicken.
- No added salt is necessary.
- Serve with a large green salad.

* *Using edible chicken meat*

Figure 10.11   Paella

66 Cocido madrileno (pork with chickpeas)

Cal	Cal	Fat	Sat Fat	Carb	Sugar	Protein	Fibre	*
1424 KJ	339 kcal	13.3 g	4.7 g	21.5 g	4.8 g	34.6 g	1.3 g	

	4 portions	10 portions
garlic sausage or Spanish chorizo	100 g	250 g
loin of pork, boned	400 g	1 kg
smoked bacon	50 g	125 g
chickpeas, dried	100 g	250 g
potato	100 g	250 g
carrot	100 g	250 g
onion, finely chopped	100 g	250 g
seasoning		

1 Cut the sausage and the pork into 1 cm dice, and the bacon into lardons.
2 Place the sausage, bacon and pork into a large saucepan, cover with water or white stock, and add the chickpeas. Bring to the boil and skim.
3 Simmer gently for 30 minutes, then add the vegetables. Add more water or white stock if necessary, season well and simmer for another hour until the meat is very tender.
4 Traditionally the broth is served first, then the vegetables and meat.

HEALTHY EATING TIP
• Skim all the fat from the surface of the liquid after cooking the meat.
• No added salt is needed.

* Using chorizo

Thailand

Among the Southeast Asian cuisines Thai owes the least to any European influences and could be described as a cross between Chinese and Indian, sharing similarities with Malaysian and Indonesian. Rice is the staple food, as in other Asian countries, and is eaten at all meals.

Presentation of carved fruit and vegetables is important. The four predominant elements are hot, salty, sweet and sour. These are supplied by chillies, garlic, ginger, galangal (a relation of ginger), soy sauce, coconut, basil and lemon grass. *Hampla* (a sauce of fermented figs) and coriander also play a major part in the flavouring components.

67 Thai fish cakes

Cal	Cal	Fat	Sat Fat	Carb	Sugar	Protein	Fibre
395 KJ	95 kcal	5.8 g	0.9 g	0.7 g	0.2 g	10.0 g	0.1 g

	4 portions	10 portions
salmon, filleted and skinned	100 g	250 g
cod, filleted and skinned	100 g	250 g
sesame oil	½ tsp	1¼ tsp
garlic cloves	2	5
root ginger, grated	1 tbsp	2¼ tbsp
red chillies (small)	½	1
soy sauce	1 tsp	1½ tsp
lemon grass	12 g	30 g
salt	2 g	5 g
pepper	2 g	5 g
lime juice	10 ml (2 tsp)	25 ml (5 tsp)
sunflower oil for cooking	10 ml (2 tsp)	25 ml (5 tsp)

1 Pass all ingredients, except the oil for cooking, in a food processor, blend until bound together and smooth.
2 Turn out and divide into 12 small cakes for 4 portions, 30 for 10 portions. The cakes should be at least 2 cm thick.
3 Heat the oil in a suitable pan, place the fish cakes in, allowing approximately 3 minutes each side.
4 Serve immediately garnished with flat leaf parsley and Thai cucumber salad.

HEALTHY EATING TIP
- No added salt is needed.
- Use a little unsaturated oil to fry the fish cakes, and drain on kitchen paper.
- Serve with plenty of fragrant Thai rice and extra vegetables.

Figure 10.12 ✐ Thai fish cakes with sweet chilli sauce

68 Thai cucumber salad

Cal	Cal	Fat	Sat Fat	Carb	Sugar	Protein	Fibre
234 KJ	56 kcal	0.1 g	0.0 g	12.7 g	12.2 g	0.8 g	0.6 g

	4 portions	10 portions
rice or white wine vinegar	125 ml	300 ml
brown sugar	40 g (2 tbsp)	100 g (5 tbsp)
salt, pepper		
cucumbers	200 g	500 g
shallots	4	10
chilli pepper flakes	¼ tsp	¾ tsp
cilantro or parsley, chopped	1 tsp	2½ tsp

1 In a suitable bowl, whisk together the vinegar, sugar, salt and pepper.
2 Cut the cucumber into fine slices and finely shred the shallots. Place these in a bowl with the pepper flakes, cilantro or parsley.
3 Pour over the vinegar/sugar mixture, toss together, marinate for 30 minutes before serving.

Note: Cilantro is another name for fresh coriander.

69 Chicken dumplings (*kha nom jeeb sai gai*)

Cal	Cal	Fat	Sat Fat	Carb	Sugar	Protein	Fibre	
3243 KJ	775 kcal	27.8 g	3.6 g	100.6 g	16.5 g	30.6 g	1.9 g	*

	Makes approx. 50 dumplings
glutinous rice flour	3 tbsp
rice flour	250 g (12 tbsp)
arrowroot	3 tbsp
water	350 ml
vegetable oil	2½ tbsp
banana leaves for steaming	
Filling	
vegetable oil	4 tbsp
garlic mixture (recipe 70)	2 tbsp
minced chicken	450 g
onion finely chopped	50 g
nam pla (fish sauce)	3 tbsp
sugar	3 tbsp
To serve	
garlic oil	1–2 tbsp
lettuce leaves	
cucumber slices	
spring onion	
vinaigrette	

1 Prepare the dough. Place the glutinous rice flour in a suitable pan with 250 g of rice flour and 1 tbsp of the arrowroot. Stir in the water and oil.
2 Place over a gentle heat and cook, stirring constantly, until the mixture forms a ball, leaving the sides of the pan clean.

3   Transfer the mixture to a bowl and allow to cool slightly. When the dough is just warm, add a further 2 tbsp of rice flour and rest of the arrowroot, knead until smooth and shiny. Cover with a damp cloth.

4   Heat 2 tbsp of oil in a frying pan, add the garlic mixture (recipe 70) and stir-fry for one minute.

5   Add the chicken and stir-fry for 3–5 minutes until cooked.

6   Add the onion, nam pla and sugar, cook, stirring until all the liquid has been absorbed. Place the mixture into a bowl, set aside until cold.

7   Roll the dough into small balls, about 1 cm in diameter, flatten each ball into a round.

8   Place approximately 1 tsp of filling into the centre of each round.

9   Draw up the sides to enclose the filling in an onion shape. Alternatively, place the filling on one half of each dough round and fold the remaining halves over to form semi-circles. Crimp the edges.

10 Place a layer of torn banana leaves in the top of a bamboo steamer. Brush the leaves with oil and prick them all over with a fork.

11 Arrange the dumplings on top of the leaves. Steam for 10–15 minutes until cooked.

12 To serve, brush the dumplings generously with garlic oil. Serve with lettuce, cucumber and onion salad.

HEALTHY EATING TIP

• Reduce the fat by skinning the chicken and using a little unsaturated oil to fry the garlic mixture and chicken.
• Brush the cooked dumplings lightly with garlic oil before serving.

* *Using stock for nam pla, vegetable oil for garlic oil*

70 Garlic mixture *(kru tium prig tai)*

garlic, crushed	2 tbsp
coriander root or stem, chopped	2 tbsp
ground black pepper	½ tbsp

1   Pound all ingredients together to form a smooth paste.

2   This mixture may be made in advance and stored in the refrigerator.

Note: This is an essential ingredient in many Thai dishes.

71 Fish sauce *(nam pla)*

This is a commercially prepared bottle sauce made from anchovies, similar to anchovy essence. It is widely used in Thai cooking to accentuate the flavours of other ingredients, rather than impart its own 'fishy' flavour.

72 Thai pork spare ribs (seeh krong mhoo)

Cal	Cal	Fat	Sat Fat	Carb	Sugar	Protein	Fibre	*
913 KJ	218 kcal	9.8 g	3.5 g	18.1 g	16.7 g	15.7 g	0.2 g	

	4 portions	10 portions
pork spare ribs	400 g	1 kg
garlic mixture (recipe 70)	2 tbsp	5 tbsp
salt		
dark soy sauce	2 tbsp	5 tbsp
ground ginger	1 tsp	2½ tsp
brown sugar	1 tbsp	2½ tbsp
honey	2 tbsp	5 tbsp

1 Mix all the ingredients, except the spare ribs, together.
2 Place the spare ribs in a suitable dish, pour over the other ingredients, mix well so that the ribs are well coated. Allow to marinate for at least 2 hours.

3 Bake the spare ribs with the marinade in a moderate oven, 180°C, until well cooked (approx. 1 hour).
4 Serve immediately.

HEALTHY EATING TIP
• No added salt is needed.
• Drain off the fat from the cooked spare ribs.
• Serve with plenty of rice and vegetables.

* Using stock sauce for nam pla, and canned bamboo shoots

73 Thai spicy fried rice (khow bhud khie mau)

Cal	Cal	Fat	Sat Fat	Carb	Sugar	Protein	Fibre	*
1697 KJ	401 kcal	9.3 g	1.7 g	69.8 g	6.8 g	13.9 g	2.8 g	

	4 portions	10 portions
minced beef	100 g	250 g
red kidney beans, cooked	100 g	250 g
nam pla	1½ tbsp	3 tbsp
dark soy sauce	1 tbsp	2½ tbsp
red chillies, seeded and finely chopped	4	10
cloves of garlic, crushed and chopped	3	7
salt	½ tsp	1¼ tsp
vegetable oil	2 tbsp	5 tbsp
green beans, cut into 1 cm lengths	10	25
cooked Thai rice	750 g	1.875 kg
sugar	1 tbsp	2½ tbsp
fresh basil or mint leaves		

1 Combine the minced beef and kidney beans in a shallow dish. Stir in the nam pla and soy sauce. Cover and set aside for 30 minutes to allow flavours to blend.

2 In a small basin, mix the chillies, garlic and salt together.
3 Heat the oil in a wok, add the chilli mixture and stir-fry for 1 minute.
4 Add the beef mixture, cook, stirring continuously for 3 minutes. Add the green beans and stir-fry for 3 minutes more.
5 Stir in the rice and sugar, stir until the rice is well heated through. Check core temperature 72°C. Make sure all the ingredients are thoroughly mixed. Correct seasoning.
6 Serve in a suitable dish, garnish with basil or mint leaves.

HEALTHY EATING TIP
• No added salt is needed.
• Use a small amount of unsaturated oil to fry the beef and drain off any excess fat.

* Using stock for nam pla

74 Thai pork with chilli and basil (bhud prig noh mai)

Cal 493 KJ	Cal 119 kcal	Fat 8.1 g	Sat Fat 1.5 g	Carb 2.7 g	Sugar 2.1 g	Protein 8.9 g	Fibre 0.7 g	*

	4 portions	10 portions
vegetable oil	2 tbsp	5 tbsp
clove garlic, crushed and chopped	1	3
chillies, finely chopped	2	5
pork fillet, thinly sliced	150 g	375 g
ground black pepper		
nam pla	1 tbsp	2½ tbsp
sugar	½ tsp	1¼ tsp
bamboo shoots, shredded	50 g	125 g
onion, finely chopped	50 g	125 g
green pepper, deseeded and finely shredded	½	1
chicken stock or water	4 tbsp	10 tbsp
fresh basil leaves, chopped	4 tbsp	10 tbsp

1 Heat the oil in a wok. Add the garlic and chilli and stir-fry until the garlic is golden.
2 Add the pork, pepper, nam pla and sugar, stirring constantly.

3 Stir in the bamboo shoots with the onion, green pepper and stock.
4 Cook for approximately 5 minutes. Stir in the basil leaves and cook for a further minute. Season with black pepper.
5 Serve immediately with steamed Thai rice.

HEALTHY EATING TIP

- Use less unsaturated vegetable oil to fry the pork.
- Serve with plenty of steamed Thai rice and vegetables.

Variations

In place of pork, use fillet or rump steak, chicken breast, ostrich or shelled prawns. If bamboo shoots are omitted, the dish is called *Bhud kra prau*.

* *Using stock for nam pla*

75 Thai mussaman curry

Cal 1977 KJ	Cal 475 kcal	Fat 33.2 g	Sat Fat 18.1 g	Carb 19.4 g	Sugar 9.7 g	Protein 26.9 g	Fibre 1.8 g	*

	4 portions	10 portions
shoulder or loin of lamb, diced	400 g	1 kg
hot water	500 ml	1½ litre
creamed coconut	175 g	400 g
fish glaze	1 tbsp	2 tbsp
whole green cardamoms	8	20
cinnamon stick	½	1¼
tamarind liquid	5 tsp	12 tsp
lemon, juice of	½	1
caster sugar	12 g	30 g
roasted peanuts	50 g	125 g
Curry paste		
cayenne pepper	¾ tsp	2 tsp
ground coriander	1 tbsp	2½ tbsp
ground cumin	½ tsp	1½ tsp
ground cinnamon	½ tsp	1½ tsp
whole green cardamoms	2	4½
lemon rind, grated	½	1½
onion, finely chopped	75 g	187 g
cloves garlic, crushed and chopped	3	7
vegetable oil	1 tbsp	2½ tbsp
dried shrimp paste	½ tsp	¾ tsp

1 Fry the lamb quickly in vegetable oil to a golden-brown colour.
2 Place the lamb in a saucepan of hot water with the potatoes, coconut milk, fish glaze, cardamoms and cinnamon, and bring slowly to the boil, stirring continuously.
3 Allow to simmer for 1 hour.
4 Stir in the curry paste (see below), tamarind liquid, lemon juice and sugar. Simmer for a further 5 minutes.
5 Serve garnished with roasted peanuts.

Curry paste
1 Place all the spices and lemon rind together in a suitable bowl.

2 Lightly fry the onion and garlic in the oil until cooked but not coloured.
3 Add the shrimp paste and stir well.
4 Place in a liquidiser with the spices and 3 tbsp cold water. Blend until smooth.

HEALTHY EATING TIP
- Use very little unsaturated oil to fry the onion for the curry paste.
- Drain any fat from the fried lamb and skim all fat from the cooked sauce.
- Serve with plenty of rice and vegetables to dilute the fat.

* Using oyster sauce for shrimp paste, glaze = stock reduced, tamarind pulp diluted for liquid

USA

It is not easy to encompass all that can be classed as American cuisine, as it is an amalgam of the cooking traditions of the waves of immigrants who went there seeking a better way of life than that offered by their mother country. These people had to adopt their styles of cooking to the conditions that prevailed where they settled, but they kept to the basics, which means it is still possible to find communities with what are now regarded as regional specialities but that had their origins outside the USA.

The major influences may have been Dutch, French, English and Native American, but almost every other nationality in the world is now represented in the USA and, in addition to Creole and Cajun in the deep south, there are Spanish, Mexican, Jewish, German, Swiss, Scandinavian, Chinese, Japanese and many other forms of cookery included in the basic American mode of living (and which are even more noticeable in the places where such people live).

America is one of the world's most prolific producer of foods, thus allowing a very interesting and widely varied menu, and many good dishes are accepted as international favourites.

Indigenous cooking has grown up, in which dishes developed from forgotten cultures, simply inspired by local ingredients, have developed. The style of cooking sometimes referred to as Tex Mex – using beans, chilli pepper and corn pancakes, and corn chips with avocado pear as basic ingredients – is typical of this development.

76 Caesar salad

Cal	Cal	Fat	Sat Fat	Carb	Sugar	Protein	Fibre	*
1494 KJ	361 kcal	32.2 g	7.9 g	5.1 g	2.0 g	12.9 g	1.2 g	

	4 portions	10 portions
cos lettuce (medium size)	2	4
croutons, 2 cm square	16	40
eggs, fresh	2	4
Dressing		
garlic, finely chopped	1 tsp	2 tsp
anchovy fillets, mashed	4	8
lemon juice	1	2
virgin olive oil	6 tbsp	15 tbsp
white wine vinegar	1 tbsp	2 tbsp
salt, black mill pepper		
To serve		
Parmesan, freshly grated	75 g	150 g

1 Separate the lettuce leaves, wash, dry thoroughly and refrigerate.
2 Lightly grill or fry (in good fresh oil) the croutons on all sides.
3 Plunge the eggs into boiling water for 1 minute, remove and set aside.
4 Break the lettuce into serving-sized pieces and place into a salad bowl.
5 Mix the dressing, break the eggs, spoon out the contents, mix with a fork, add to the dressing and mix into the salad.
6 Mix in the cheese, scatter the croutons on top and serve.

431

Note: Because of the lightly cooked eggs they must be perfectly fresh, and the salad must be prepared and served immediately. In the interests of food safety, the eggs are sometimes hardboiled. Alternatively the salad may be garnished with hardboiled gull's eggs.

HEALTHY EATING TIP

- No added salt is needed; anchovies and cheese are high in salt.
- Oven bake the croutons.
- Serve with fresh bread or rolls.

* *Using toast for croutons*

Figure 10.13 ✎ Preparation of Caesar salad

Figure 10.14 ✎ Caesar salad

77 Chilli con carne (beef with beans in chilli sauce)

Cal	Cal	Fat	Sat Fat	Carb	Sugar	Protein	Fibre	*
1741 KJ	414 kcal	18.9 g	3.1 g	28.0 g	6.2 g	35.7 g	9.1 g	

	4 portions	10 portions
dried kidney beans or pinto beans	200 g	500 g
lean topside of beef	400 g	1 kg
sunflower oil	60 ml	150 ml
onions, finely chopped	100 g	250 g
cloves garlic, crushed and chopped	2	5
chilli powder	2 tsp	5 tsp
oregano	1 tsp	2–3 tsp
ground cumin	½ tsp	1 tsp
tomato purée	50 g	125 g
tomatoes, skinned, deseeded, diced	200 g	500 g
white or brown stock	500 ml	1¼ litre

1 Soak the beans in cold water for 24 hours. Drain, cover with cold water and bring to the boil. Boil for 10 minutes then simmer gently until tender.

2 Prepare the beef by removing all the excess fat and cutting into batons 5 cm long × ½ cm wide, or mincing.
3 Heat a little of the oil in a frying pan and quickly fry the beef until golden brown.
4 Drain the beef, place in a suitable saucepan.
5 Add a little more oil to the frying pan, add the onions and garlic, and fry quickly until a light golden colour.
6 Stir in the chilli powder, oregano and cumin and cook for a further 3 minutes. Add to the beef.
7 Stir in the tomato purée, tomatoes and seasoning, and cover with white or brown stock.
8 Gently cook by simmering on the stove, or cover and cook in a moderate oven at 180°C for 1½–2 hours.
9 Check constantly to make sure that the meat does not become too dry. Add a little more stock or water if necessary.
10 Drain the cooked beans and add to the cooked beef.
11 Serve in an earthenware dish sprinkled with chopped parsley.

Note: Originally from Texas and Mexico, chilli con carne is now eaten throughout the United States. This dish must be quite moist – the consistency of a stew. Chilli powders and chilli seasonings vary in strength, therefore the amount used may be varied.

HEALTHY EATING TIP
- Lightly oil the pan using an unsaturated oil.
- Drain all fat from the cooked beef.
- Adding more beans and serving with rice and extra vegetables will dilute the fat.

78 Hash brown potatoes

Cal	Cal	Fat	Sat Fat	Carb	Sugar	Protein	Fibre
954 KJ	228 kcal	11.3 g	5.3 g	25.8 g	0.9 g	7.1 g	2.0 g

	4 portions	10 portions
potatoes	600 g	2 kg
butter or margarine	25 g	60 g
lardons of bacon	100 g	250 g
seasoning		

1 Wash, peel and rewash the potatoes.
2 Coarsely grate the potatoes, rewash quickly and then drain well.
3 Melt the fat in a suitable frying pan. Add the lardons of bacon, fry until crisp and brown, remove from the pan and drain.
4 Pour the fat back into the frying pan, add the grated potato and season.
5 Press down well, allow 2 cm thickness, and cook over a heat for 10–15 minutes or in a moderate oven at 190°C until a brown crust forms on the bottom.
6 Turn out into a suitable serving dish and sprinkle with the lardons of bacon and chopped parsley.

HEALTHY EATING TIP
- Dry-fry the lardons in a well-seasoned pan.
- Brush a little oil over the potatoes and cook in a hot oven. Use the minimum amount of salt.

79 Clam chowder

There is a recipe for clam chowder in Chapter 3: Stocks, soups and sauces (page 84).

Note: A chowder is usually an unpassed shellfish soup. It originated in the USA, where there are many regional variations. Clams, oysters, scallops and fresh or frozen crabs may be used.

80 Succotash (butter beans, sweetcorn and bacon in cream sauce)

Cal	Cal	Fat	Sat Fat	Carb	Sugar	Protein	Fibre
1157 KJ	277 kcal	15.3 g	7.9 g	25.6 g	2.8 g	10.7 g	5.4 g

	4 portions	10 portions
lardons of bacon	50 g	125 g
butter or margarine	25 g	60 g
butter beans, cooked	350 g	1 kg
sweetcorn, cooked	150 g	375 g
cream sauce	125 ml	300 ml
seasoning		

HEALTHY EATING TIP
- Dry-fry the lardons in a well-seasoned pan and drain off the excess fat.
- Add the minimum amount of salt.
- Serve with starchy carbohydrate to dilute the fat.

1 Quickly fry the lardons of bacon in the fat.
2 Add the drained butter beans and sweetcorn.
3 Bind with cream sauce, correct the seasoning and finish with cream.
4 Serve in a suitable dish, sprinkled with chopped parsley.

81 Pecan pie

Cal	Cal	Fat	Sat Fat	Carb	Sugar	Protein	Fibre
4178 KJ	1001 kcal	65.0 g	19.8 g	97.2 g	93.3 g	13.0 g	2.9 g

	4 portions	10 portions
sweet pastry (page 614)	150 g	375 g
eggs	3	7–8
soft brown sugar	200 g	500 g
vanilla essence		
pinch of salt		
melted butter or margarine	75 g	180 g
treacle syrup	6 tbsp	15 tbsp
pecan nuts, coarsely chopped	200 g	500 g

1 Line an 18–20 cm flan ring with the sweet pastry and partly bake blind. Prepare the filling from the remaining ingredients, as follows.
2 Lightly heat the eggs and sugar together with the vanilla essence and salt.
3 Stir in the melted butter or margarine and syrup, and add the chopped pecan nuts.
4 Pour this mixture into the flan case and decorate with pecan halves.
5 Bake in a moderately hot oven at 180°C for 30–35 minutes until the filling is set. Cover with aluminium foil if the pastry starts to get too dark.
6 Serve with cream, ice cream or yoghurt.

Figure 10.15 Pecan pie

Squash and spinach
ravioli (recipe 11)

Bean goulash
(recipe 33)

Crisp polenta and
roasted Mediterranean
vegetables (recipe 12)

chapter 11

VEGETARIAN DISHES

Contributes to the units listed below

VRQ
Unit 208   **Prepare and cook fruit and
                              vegetables**

NVQ
Unit 626 (2FP7)   **Prepare vegetables for basic
                              dishes**

Unit 633 (2FC7)   **Cook and finish basic
                              vegetable dishes**

See page 467 for learning outcomes

VRQ
Unit 212   **Prepare and cook rice,
                              pasta, grains and egg dishes**

NVQ
Unit 639 (2FPC4)   **Prepare, cook and finish
                              basic rice dishes**

Unit 640 (2FPC5)   **Prepare, cook and finish
                              basic pasta dishes**

Unit 641 (2FPC6)   **Prepare, cook and finish
                              basic pulse dishes**

Unit 643 (2FPC8)   **Prepare, cook and finish
                              basic egg dishes**

Unit 647 (2FPC12)   **Prepare, cook and finish
                              basic grain dishes**

See pages 131, 141 and 468 for learning outcomes

The vegetarian diet

According to the Vegetarian Society, vegetarians who eat milk products and eggs enjoy excellent health. Vegetarian diets are consistent with dietary guidelines and can meet recommended dietary allowances for nutrients. You can get enough protein from a vegetarian diet as long as the variety of foods and the amounts consumed are adequate. Meat, fish and poultry are major contributors of iron, zinc and B vitamins in most diets, and vegetarians need to pay special attention to getting sufficient amounts of these nutrients.

What vegetarians need to eat every day

Here's a quick summary from the Vegetarian Society of what vegetarians need to eat every day:

- 4 or 5 servings of fruit and vegetables
- 3 or 4 servings of cereals/grains or potatoes
- 2 or 3 servings of pulses, nuts and seeds
- 2 servings of milk, cheese, eggs or soya products (e.g. tofu)
- a small amount of vegetable oil, margarine or butter
- some yeast extract that has been fortified with vitamin B12.

A guide to vegetarian proteins

Here's a quick rundown of vegetarian foods that are high in protein, as well as a few suggestions on how to make the most of them.

Dairy products

Milk

- **Buttermilk:** buttermilk is excellent in baked goods, and also as a soup and salad dressing base. It lends a rich, hearty flavour with fewer calories than milk or cream. The tangy flavour of buttermilk goes well with sweet fruits such as peaches, cherries and pears, particularly as crème fraiche. The acidic properties of buttermilk make it an effective and flavourful marinade, particularly with poultry. It is used as an acidic ingredient in baked goods to combat the dingy greyish discolouring often caused by the chemical reaction of blueberries, walnuts and other foods that give off a blue cast. It also promotes the browning of baked goods and improves texture.
- **Condensed milk:** condensed milk is a generic term for milk that has had 60 per cent of its water removed by evaporation. With sweetened condensed milk, great quantities of sugar were added first, accounting for 40–45 per cent of the total volume before evaporation. Once all the water is removed, it is a very sticky and sweet mixture. Unsweetened condensed milk, however, is simply called evaporated milk.
- **Evaporated milk.**
- **Goats' milk.**

Cream

- **Crème fraiche:** soured cream with a higher fat content.
- **Soured cream:** has 18 per cent fat content and is soured by the addition of a starter.

Yoghurt

- Yoghurt is a cultured milk product made from cows', ewes', goats' or buffalo milk. It is available plain or in a variety of fruit flavours.

Butter

- **Ghee:** ghee is clarified butter without any solid particles or water. It is used in India and throughout South Asia in daily cooking. A good-quality ghee adds a great aroma, flavour and taste to food. Ghee can be a great asset for people who are on low-fat diet since even a modest quantity of ghee can add a lot of flavour to food compared to other oil or fat products. According to the ancient Ayurveda, a moderate amount of ghee is the best cooking oil. Ghee can generally be found in the 'ethnic' section of any big grocery store or in any Indian/South Asian store. Be sure to buy ghee that comes from an animal such as a cow; do not buy an artificial ghee made by hydrogenating vegetable oil. Ghee is produced 'properly' when water is completely evaporated from butter. To find out if the water has been evaporated properly, pour some heated butter into small piece of paper. Set the paper on fire. If you hear a crackling noise, this indicates the presence of water. Heat the butter some more. With experience you will be able to tell if ghee is 'done', by examining its smell and colour.

Cheese

Dairy products are an important source of calcium as well as protein, but be careful not to overdo it on cheese by making sure you eat plenty of pulses too.

- **Vegetarian cheese:** cheese made using non-animal rennet is now widely available, so look out for the words 'suitable for vegetarians' on the packet, or if buying from a cheese-monger ask if it is suitable.

A note on Parmesan

Unfortunately, there is no such thing as vegetarian Parmesan, so the recipes in this chapter that use it are not, strictly speaking, truly vegetarian. Although dishes including Parmesan may be acceptable to, say, demi-vegetarians and those who prefer to avoid meat, they are not suitable for strict vegetarians. Use vegetarian Cheddar as a substitute ingredient where possible. If Parmesan is being used to garnish a finished dish, offer it separately if you can so that diners can choose for themselves whether or not they wish to add it.

Eggs
- Hens' eggs
- Quails' eggs
- Ducks' eggs
- Goose eggs
- Turkey eggs
- Gulls' eggs

Grains, rice and cereals
- Wheat (whole, cracked, bulgar, flakes, bran, germ, semolina, couscous)
- Buckwheat
- Barley
- Corn (or maize – sweetcorn, popcorn, polenta)
- Millet
- Oats
- Rye
- Quinoa
- Wild rice

Rice
- White
- Brown
- White and black sticky rice
- White and brown long-grain rice
- Basmati rice
- White short-grain rice (also known as pudding rice)

- Thai fragrant (or jasmine) rice
- Red rice
- Italian risotto rice (Arborio, Carnaroli, Vialone Nano)
- Valencia (paella) rice

Nuts
- Almonds
- Brazil nuts
- Cashew nuts
- Coconuts
- Hazelnuts
- Macadamia nuts
- Peanuts
- Pecans
- Pine nuts
- Pistachios
- Sweet chestnuts
- Walnuts

Seeds
- Poppy
- Pumpkin
- Sesame
- Sunflower
- Linseeds

Vegetarian recipes

Stocks

There are more stock recipes in Chapter 3: Stocks, soups and sauces.

1 White vegetable stock

Cal 4 KJ	Cal 1 kcal	Fat 0.0 g	Sat Fat 0.0 g	Carb 0.2 g	Sugar 0.2 g	Protein 0.0 g	Fibre 0.0 g

	4 portions	10 portions
onions	100 g	250 g
carrots	100 g	250 g
celery	100 g	250 g
leeks	100 g	250 g
water	3¾ litres	1½ litres

1 Roughly chop all the vegetables.
2 Place all the ingredients into a saucepan, add the water, bring to the boil.
3 Allow to simmer for approximately 1 hour.
4 Skim if necessary. Strain and use.

2 Brown vegetable stock

Cal 4 KJ	Cal 1 kcal	Fat 0.0 g	Sat Fat 0.0 g	Carb 0.2 g	Sugar 0.2 g	Protein 0.0 g	Fibre 0.0 g

	4 portions	10 portions
onions	100 g	250 g
carrots	100 g	250 g
celery	100 g	250 g
leeks	100 g	250 g
sunflower oil	60 ml	150 ml
tomatoes	50 g	125 g
mushroom trimmings	50 g	125 g
peppercorns	6	15
water	1½ litres	3¾ litres
yeast extract	5 g	10 g

1 Roughly chop all the vegetables.
2 Fry the onions, carrots, celery and leeks in the sunflower oil until golden brown.
3 Drain the vegetables, place into a suitable saucepan.

4 Add all the other ingredients except the yeast extract.
5 Cover with the water, bring to the boil.
6 Add the yeast extract, simmer gently for approximately 1 hour.
7 Skim if necessary. Strain and use.

HEALTHY EATING TIP

• Lightly oil the pan and drain off any excess after the frying is complete.
• Skim the fat from the finished dish.
• The yeast extract contains salt, so very little or no additional salt should be required when this stock is used for sauces.

Soups

There are more soup recipes in Chapter 3: Stocks, soups and sauces.

3 Cream of spinach and celery soup

	4 portions	10 portions
shallots, peeled and chopped (small mirepoix)	2	5
leeks, washed and chopped (small mirepoix)	1	2
cloves of garlic, peeled and chopped	5	7
corn oil	2 tbsp	5 tbsp
celery sticks, washed and chopped (small mirepoix)	4	10
flour	15 g	35 g
fresh spinach, well washed	500 g	1¼ kg
soya milk	600 ml	1½ litres
vegetable stock (see recipes 1 & 2)	600 ml	
salt, to taste		

1 Cook the shallots, leeks and garlic in the oil for a few minutes, without colour.
2 Add the celery and cook for another few minutes until starting to soften.
3 Add the flour and mix well, then throw in the spinach and mix around. Add the soya milk and vegetable stock slowly, ensuring there are no lumps.
4 Stir continuously, bring to a simmer, then switch off and remove from heat. Cover and leave for a few minutes.
5 Blend until smooth in a food processor. Check seasoning and serve.

4 Carrot and butterbean soup

Cal	Cal	Fat	Sat Fat	Carb	Sugar	Protein	Fibre	Salt
891 KJ	213 kcal	5.9 g	0.7 g	33.4 g	19.3 g	8.5 g	8.1 g	3.6 g

	4 portions	10 portions
onions, peeled and chopped	1	2
cloves of garlic, chopped	2	5
sunflower oil	15 ml	35 ml
large to medium carrots, brunoise	6	15
carrot juice	500 ml	1¼ litres
vegetable stock	500 ml	1¼ litres
cooked butter beans	400 g	1 kg
seasoning		

1 Cook the onion and garlic in the oil for a few minutes, without colour, then add the carrots and stir well.
2 Add the carrot juice and vegetable stock. Bring to the boil, turn down to a simmer and cook for about 15 minutes until the carrot is cooked through.
3 Add the beans and cook for a further 5 minutes or so until they are heated through.
4 Liquidise in a food processor until smooth; check seasoning.

5 Vegetable and barley soup

	4 portions	10 portions
corn oil	50 ml	125 ml
onions, finely diced	1	2
leeks, cut into rounds	1	2
carrots, peeled and roughly chopped	2	3
celery sticks, cut into ½ cm dice	2	3
cloves of garlic, crushed	2	4
large potatoes, peeled and cut into ½ cm dice	3	7
dried pearl barley	150 g	375 g
vegetable stock	1½ litres	3¾ litres
head of Swiss chard, washed and shredded (including stalks)	1	2
seasoning		

1 Heat the oil in a pan large enough to hold all the ingredients.
2 Place the onions, leeks, carrots and celery in the oil and cook until slightly golden.
3 Add the garlic and cook for a further 2 minutes. Add the potato and cook for a further 2 minutes.
4 Add the barley and vegetable stock. Bring to the boil then simmer for 15 minutes, until the potatoes are just soft.
5 Stir in the Swiss chard and cook for a further 2 minutes.
6 Check the seasoning, correct if necessary then serve.

6 Leek, potato and pea soup

	4 portions	10 portions
medium leeks, cut into thin round slices	2	5
onion, peeled and finely sliced	2	2
cloves of garlic	2	4
corn oil	50 ml	125 ml
large potatoes, peeled and cut in to 1½ cm dice	3	7
vegetable stock	400 ml	1 litre
peas, fresh or frozen	200 g	500 g
seasoning		
fresh mint leaves, finely shredded	4	10

1 Cook the leeks, onions and garlic in the oil for a few minutes without colour.
2 Add the potatoes and cook for a further 2 minutes, again without colour.
3 Add the vegetable stock, bring to the boil, stirring occasionally to prevent sticking, then turn down to a simmer until the potatoes are just about cooked.
4 Add the peas and cook for a further 2 minutes until tender.
5 Allow to stand for a minute or two before blending in the food processor.
6 Blend until smooth, correct the seasoning, stir in the mint and serve.

7 Fresh tomato and tofu soup

	4 portions	10 portions
onion, large, finely chopped	1	2
vegetable oil	25 ml	60 ml
cloves of garlic, crushed and chopped	2	5
tomato juice	500 ml	1¼ litres
soft tofu	300 g	750 g
seasoning		
Tabasco		
tomatoes, skinned, deseeded, cut into concassée	100 g	250 g
parsley, chopped		
basil, chopped		

1 Sweat the chopped onion in the oil without colour. Add the garlic. Mix well.
2 Allow to cool.
3 Add the tomato juice and tofu; season well.
4 Add a dash of Tabasco to taste.
5 Liquidise, pass through a fine strainer.
6 Correct the seasoning and consistency.
7 Serve well chilled, garnished with tomato concassée. Sprinkle with chopped basil and parsley.

Note: This is a summer soup – serve cold.

Sauces

There are more sauce recipes in Chapter 3: Stocks, soups and sauces.

8 Broccoli sauce

Cal 344 KJ	Cal 83 kcal	Fat 5.9 g	Sat Fat 0.6 g	Carb 2.6 g	Sugar 0.8 g	Protein 4.9 g	Fibre 1.8 g

	4 portions	10 portions
cooked broccoli	200 g	500 g
sunflower seeds	40 g	100 g
water	500 ml	1¼ litres
smetana or silken tofu (page 450)	125 ml	300 ml
lemon, juice of	½	1–1½
seasoning		

1 Place the broccoli, sunflower seeds and water into a liquidiser with the smetana and lemon juice. Liquidise until smooth.

2 Strain through a coarse strainer into a small saucepan. Correct the seasoning and consistency.
3 Heat very gently before serving. *Do not boil.*

Note: Balsamic vinegar (15 ml for 4; 50 ml for 10) walnut oil (10 ml; 25 ml) and chopped basil may be added to boost the flavour.

HEALTHY EATING TIP
• Use the minimum amount of salt.

Pasta, rice and polenta

9 Vegetarian lasagne

Cal 2993 KJ	Cal 713 kcal	Fat 46.2 g	Sat Fat 8.5 g	Carb 54.6 g	Sugar 16.5 g	Protein 22.9 g	Fibre 11.8 g

	4 portions	10 portions
sheets of lasagne	10	30
sunflower oil	125 ml	300 ml
onions, finely chopped	100 g	250 g
garlic cloves, chopped	2	5
mushrooms, sliced	200 g	500 g
seasoning		
medium-sized courgettes	2	5
oregano	3 g	9 g
tomato skinned, deseeded and diced	200 g	500 g
tomato purée	50 g	125 g
broccoli (small florets)	300 g	750 g
carrots	100 g	250 g
pine kernels	25 g	60 g
béchamel	250 ml	625 ml
Parmesan cheese, grated	50 g	125 g
natural yoghurt	250 ml	625 ml

1 Cook the lasagne sheets in boiling salted water until al dente; refresh and drain.
2 Heat half the oil and sweat the onion and garlic.
3 Add the mushrooms and continue to cook without colour. Season.
4 Heat the remaining oil in a sauteuse, add the courgettes, cut into 1 cm dice and lightly fry; sprinkle with the oregano. Cook until crisp, add the tomato concassée and tomato purée.
5 Add the broccoli florets and carrots (cut into ½ cm dice), previously blanched and refreshed. Mix together with the pine kernels.
6 Make a cheese sauce using the béchamel and half the grated cheese; finish with the natural yoghurt.

HEALTHY EATING TIP
• Try using a mixture of white and green lasagne.
• Use a little unsaturated oil to sweat the onion.
• Make the béchamel with semi-skimmed milk.
• No added salt is needed.

7 Grease a suitable ovenproof dish well with the sunflower oil and place a layer of lasagne in the bottom.
8 Cover with a layer of mushrooms, then a layer of lasagne, then the broccoli and tomato mixture, then lasagne, then cheese sauce. Continue to do this, finishing with a layer of cheese sauce on the top.

9 Sprinkle with remaining grated Parmesan.
10 Bake in a preheated oven at 180°C for 20–25 minutes.

Note: To prevent dryness, add a little tomato juice with the broccoli and tomato mixture, or use tinned plum tomatoes for a better result.

10 Parmesan gnocchi and tomato sauce

Cal	Cal	Fat	Sat Fat	Carb	Sugar	Protein	Fibre	Salt
1402 KJ	335 kcal	12.3 g	6.0 g	43.8 g	5.0 g	15.1 g	3.0 g	2.5 g

	4 portions	10 portions
Parmesan gnocchi		
Desiree potatoes	350 g	875 g
Parmesan	75 g	185 g
egg yolks	2	5
butter	10 g	25 g
seasoning		
pasta flour	125 g	300 g
Tomato sauce		
carrot	75 g	185 g
celery	20 g	50 g
butter	25 g	60 g
vegetable oil	25 g	60 g
clove of garlic	½	1
sprig of thyme	1	2
juniper berries	1	2
bay leaf	1	2
plum tomato	200 g	500 g
tomato purée	10 g	25 g
vegetable stock	500 ml	1¼ litres
cream	25 g	60 g
sherry vinegar, to taste		

1 Place 4 large Desiree potatoes in an oven at 180°C for 1 hour.
2 Grate the Parmesan using a fine grater.
3 Pass the cooked potato through a drum sieve while still warm.
4 Add the Parmesan, egg yolks, butter and seasoning.
5 Mix until smooth, but do not over-work.
6 Incorporate the flour until all absorbed.
7 Wrap the dough in clingfilm and allow to rest for 30 minutes.
8 Roll and shape into 1 cm pieces.

9 Blanch the gnocchi in simmering water until they float.
10 Refresh the gnocchi and reserve until required.

Tomato sauce
1 Cut the carrot and celery into small pieces.
2 Heat the butter and oil in a pan, sweat down the carrot and celery with the garlic, thyme, juniper berries and bay leaf for 10 minutes.
3 Roughly chop the tomatoes and add to the pan with the tomato purée. Cook for 15 minutes.
4 Add the vegetable stock and reduce by half.
5 Add the cream and reduce by half.
6 Remove the bay leaf and thyme, add the sherry vinegar, then blitz until smooth.
7 Reserve until required.

To finish
1 Gently sauté the gnocchi in a little oil, and warm the sauce gently.
2 Combine the two together and finish with fresh herbs and shaved Parmesan.

Figure 11.1 Parmesan gnocchi and tomato sauce

11 Ravioli of squash and spinach with wild mushroom sauce

	4 portions	10 portions
Squash ravioli		
butternut squash, diced	500 g	1¼ kg
butter	100 g	250 g
salt	10 g	25 g
spinach	250 g	625 g
pasta dough		
(see **page 146**)	400 g	1 kg
Wild mushroom sauce		
onions, finely sliced	50 g	125 g
button mushrooms,		
finely sliced	75 g	185 g
wild mushrooms, sliced	60 g	150 g
clove of garlic	½	1
bay leaf	1	2
sprig of thyme	1	2
butter	10 g	25 g
dried cep	5 g	12 g
Noilly Prat (dry vermouth)	75 g	185 g
vegetable stock	200 g	500 g
cream	100 g	250 g
seasoning		

Ravioli

1 Peel the butternut squash, remove the seeds and chop the flesh roughly.
2 Cook the squash in the butter with the salt over a medium heat until soft.
3 Add the spinach and cook for a further minute.
4 Drain off the butter and chill the mixture until firm.
5 Once the mixture is firm, roll out and cut into 40 pieces.
6 Roll the pasta dough and make the ravioli to the required shape.
7 Place on a floured tray and reserve until required.

Sauce

1 Sweat down the onions, fresh mushrooms, garlic and aromats in the butter for 10 minutes.
2 Add the dried cep and sweat for a further 5 minutes.
3 Add the Noilly Prat and reduce completely.
4 Add the vegetable stock and reduce by three-quarters.
5 Add the cream and bring to the boil. Remove the thyme and bay leaf.
6 Blitz the sauce until smooth, season and reserve until required.

To serve

1 To serve the dish, blanch the ravioli in simmering, salted water for 3 minutes.
2 Heat the sauce gently in a pan. Drain the ravioli and add to the sauce.
3 Finish with chopped chives and serve as required.

Figure 11.2 ✦ Ravioli of squash and spinach

12 Crisp polenta and roasted Mediterranean vegetables

	4 portions	10 portions
Polenta		
water	200 ml	500 ml
butter	30 g	75 g
polenta flour	65 g	160 g
Parmesan, grated	25 g	60 g
egg yolks	1	2
crème fraiche	110 g	275 g
seasoning		
Roasted vegetables		
red peppers	2	5
yellow peppers	2	5
courgettes	2	5
red onions	2	5
vegetable oil	200 ml	500 ml
seasoning		
clove of garlic	1	3
sprigs of thyme	2	5

Polenta

1 Bring the water and the butter to the boil.
2 Season the water well and whisk in the polenta flour.
3 Continue to whisk until very thick.
4 Remove from the heat and add the Parmesan, egg yolk and crème fraiche.
5 Whisk until all incorporated; check the seasoning.
6 Set in a lined tray.
7 Once set, cut using a round cutter or cut into squares.
8 Reserve until required.

Roasted vegetables

1 Roughly chop the vegetables into large chunks. Ensure the seeds are removed from the peppers.
2 Toss the cut vegetables in the oil and season well.
3 Place the vegetables in an oven with the aromats for 30 minutes at 180°C.
4 Remove from the oven and drain. Reserve until required.

To serve

1 To serve the dish, shallow-fry the polenta in a non-stick pan until golden on both sides.
2 Warm the roasted vegetables and place them in the middle of the plate. Place the polenta on top.
3 Finish with rocket salad and balsamic dressing.

Figure 11.3 ✎ Crisp polenta and roasted Mediterranean vegetables

13 Polenta and vegetable terrine

Cal 2106 KJ	Cal 508 kcal	Fat 32.7 g	Sat Fat 15.6 g	Carb 45.1 g	Sugar 5.0 g	Protein 8.2 g	Fibre 3.8 g	*

	6 portions
water	1½ litres
butter	150 g
grated nutmeg	
white mill pepper	
salt	
polenta	325 g
cream cheese *or*	25 g
Parmesan, freshly grated	
extra virgin olive oil	45 ml (3 tbsp)

1 Bring the water to the boil, with the butter, nutmeg and seasoning.
2 Rain in the polenta and mix thoroughly for about 5–10 minutes.
3 Mix in the cream cheese or Parmesan (some fresh chopped herbs may also be added at this stage if desired).
4 Lightly oil a suitable terrine or loaf tin, line with clingfilm (this will make it easier to turn out the terrine).
5 Pour a thin layer of warm polenta mix into the bottom of the tin. Arrange a layer of vegetables (see below for suggestions) on top, cover this layer with more polenta; repeat the process until the terrine is full.
6 Cover with clingfilm and chill for several hours until firm to the touch.
7 Turn out, slice and serve on a suitable plate on a mirror of fresh tomato sauce or another suitable vegetable sauce; garnish with coriander.

Vegetables for the terrine

A variety of vegetables may be used. For example, cooked broccoli, button onions, courgettes, carrots, green beans, baby sweetcorn, red, green or yellow peppers (blanched). For a 170 g terrine allow approximately 2 courgettes, 2 peppers (one each of red, green or yellow), 6 florets of broccoli, 2 baby sweetcorn, and 50 g green beans.

Note: This terrine makes a very suitable vegetarian starter; it may be made using roasted vegetables (page 503).

HEALTHY EATING TIP
• Use little or no salt; there is plenty in the cheese.
• Try to add less butter to the polenta.

* *Using cream cheese*

14 Polenta and lentil cakes with roasted vegetables served with cucumber and yoghurt sauce

Cal 1898 KJ	Cal 452 kcal	Fat 15.2 g	Sat Fat 4.1 g	Carb 55.6 g	Sugar 7.9 g	Protein 25.2 g	Fibre 4.3 g

	4 portions	10 portions
puy lentils	250 g	625 g
vegetable stock	250 ml	625 ml
fine polenta	75 g	187 g
Parmesan cheese, grated	25 g	62 g
egg, beaten	1	3
leeks, finely chopped and blanched	75 g	187 g
crushed garlic, finely chopped	1	3
seasoning		
olive oil	3 tbsp	8 tbsp

Sauce

cucumber	250 g	625 g
natural yoghurt	250 ml	625 ml
mint, chopped	¼ tsp	1¼ tsp
chives, chopped	1 tsp	2½ tsp

1 Wash the lentils and cook in salted water for about 25 minutes until tender but still firm. Drain well, refresh and drain again. Dry on a suitable cloth.
2 Bring the vegetable stock to the boil, rain in the polenta and cook gently, stirring until thickened.
3 Add the Parmesan and beaten egg; season.
4 Mix in the lentils, polenta, leeks and garlic.

5 Correct seasoning; cool and shape into four (or ten) round cakes.
6 Place in the fridge and chill well for at least 1 hour.
7 Heat the olive oil in a suitable pan, gently fry the cakes for about 3–4 minutes on each side until heated through and well browned.
8 To make the sauce, liquidise the peeled cucumber with the yoghurt, finish with chopped mint and chives.
9 To serve, place a small amount of the sauce onto a plate and place the cakes on top. Garnish the plate with freshly roasted vegetables.

HEALTHY EATING TIP
- No additional salt is needed.
- Use less olive oil to fry the cakes, and drain on kitchen paper.
- Brush the vegetables with a little unsaturated oil when roasting.

Figure 11.4 Polenta and lentil cakes with roasted vegetables, served with cucumber and yoghurt sauce

15 Risotto of Jerusalem artichoke and truffle

	4 portions	10 portions
shallots, diced	50 g	125 g
vegetable oil	10 g	25 g
risotto rice (Carnaroli)	150 g	375 g
white wine	75 ml	180 ml
vegetable stock	1 litre	2½ litres
artichoke purée	10 g	25 g
butter	50 g	125 g
seasoning		
Parmesan Reggiano, grated		
truffle oil		
chives, chopped	5 g	12 g
chervil, freshly picked		
truffle, chopped (optional)	25 g	62 g

1 Sweat the shallots in the oil, without colour, for 5 minutes.
2 Add the rice and sweat for a further minute.
3 Add the wine and cook out until completely reduced.
4 Add the stock ladle by ladle until the rice is 95 per cent cooked. (You may not need all the stock.)
5 Add the purée and butter and reduce until emulsified.
6 Season the risotto then add the Parmesan, truffle and chives.
7 To serve, place the risotto in a bowl and garnish with some picked chervil and freshly sliced truffle (optional).

Tofu

Tofu is a product of the soya bean and is generally available in two forms: silken tofu, made from lightly pressed soya bean curd; firm tofu, which is more heavily pressed. Soft or regular tofu has a texture somewhere between the two.

16 Tofu steak

Cal 602 KJ	Cal 144 kcal	Fat 7.6 g	Sat Fat 0.9 g	Carb 9.2 g	Sugar 1.4 g	Protein 10.2 g	Fibre 0.1 g

	4 portions
Japanese bean curd	2 blocks
Or	*or*
Chinese bean curd	1 block 5 cm square
cornflour, seasoned with	
salt and pepper	1 tbsp
vegetable oil	1 tbsp
Sauce	
fresh ginger, grated	1 tbsp
spring onion, finely sliced	2 tbsp
shiitake mushrooms, sliced	4
Japanese soy sauce	2 tbsp
sake (Japanese rice wine)	2 tbsp
mirin (Japanese sweet wine)	1 tbsp
sugar	½ tsp
water	2 tbsp
cornflour (diluted with 1 tbsp water)	1 tsp
Garnish	
spring onion, finely sliced	2 tbsp
lettuce leaves	4
tomato, thinly sliced	1

1 Drain off any liquid from the package of bean curd.
2 To refresh the bean curd, rinse the blocks with cold water, then steep them in warm or hot water for 10 minutes. Pat the blocks dry with paper towels. Wrap the blocks with tea towels and weigh them down with the chopping board for 10 minutes to drain off excess water.
3 Cut the blocks in half (quarter if using a 5 cm square block) and dust with seasoned cornflour.

4 Put half the vegetable oil in a frying pan or skillet and heat until sizzling. Sear the block of bean curd in one row over high heat. Turn the blocks over to sear them golden brown on both sides. Set aside these blocks and keep them warm.
5 Add the remaining vegetable oil to a small saucepan over medium heat and sauté the ginger and spring onion for half a minute. Add the sliced mushroom and continue to sauté for a further half minute. Add the soy sauce, sake and mirin, sugar, reserved mushroom liquid or water (if fresh mushrooms are used) and then stir, bring to the boil. Then add the diluted cornflour to thicken; keep stirring, bring quickly to the boil and adjust the seasoning with salt and pepper if required.
6 Place the bean curd blocks on a warm individual plate arranged with lettuce and tomato, and pour the sauce over each block. Garnish the centre of each bean curd block with spring onion. Serve hot.

Note: This is an excellent alternative to steak for non-meat eaters.

HEALTHY EATING TIP
- Use a little sunflower or olive oil to fry the bean curd, or dry-fry.
- The soy sauce is high in sodium, so no added salt is needed.

17 Barbecued tofu

Cal	Cal	Fat	Sat Fat	Carb	Sugar	Protein	Fibre	*
821 KJ	198 kcal	13.5 g	1.9 g	7.8 g	5.2 g	10.5 g	0.5 g	

	4 portions	10 portions
spring onions, chopped	3	7
garlic cloves, crushed and chopped	4	10
maple syrup or honey	30 ml (2 tbsp)	75 ml (5 tbsp)
black pepper	2 g	5 g
soy sauce	60 ml (4 tbsp)	90 ml (10 tbsp)
sesame oil	30 ml (2 tbsp)	75 ml (5 tbsp)
rice wine or sake	30 ml (2 tbsp)	75 ml (5 tbsp)
toasted ground sesame seeds	1 tbsp	2½ tbsp
solid tofu, cubes	400 g	1 kg
broccoli florets	10	25

1 Mix together the chopped onions, garlic, maple syrup, pepper, soy sauce, sesame oil, rice wine or sake and the sesame seeds until thoroughly mixed.
2 Marinate the tofu in this mixture for several hours.
3 Remove from the marinade, grill or fry the tofu.
4 Boil the marinade and serve with the tofu in individual bowls with cooked broccoli florets.
5 Serve separately on a bed of plain boiled or steamed fragrant Thai rice.

HEALTHY EATING TIP
• Grill the marinated tofu and serve with fragrant Thai rice and vegetables to make an interesting vegetarian dish.

* Using maple syrup

18 Warm tofu and asparagus salad

Cal	Cal	Fat	Sat Fat	Carb	Sugar	Protein	Fibre	*
723 KJ	173 kcal	11.7 g	2.0 g	8.5 g	6.2 g	9.1 g	2.6 g	

	4 portions	10 portions
olive oil	1 tbsp	2½ tbsp
clove garlic, crushed and chopped	1	2
red onion, finely chopped	1 small	2
sundried tomatoes, cut in julienne	100 g	250 g
lemon	½	1½
seasoning		
ground black pepper		
firm tofu	200 g	500 g
vegetable stock	2 tbsp	5 tbsp
mixed leaves for garnish (e.g. radicchio, lamb's lettuce, frisée, endive)		
asparagus, cooked	200 g	500 g
toasted cashews	50 g	125 g

Figure 11.5 Warm tofu and asparagus salad

1 Heat the olive oil in a suitable pan. Add the garlic and the onion, and fry quickly until lightly coloured.
2 Add the sundried tomatoes and sauté for a further minute.
3 Add the lemon juice and grated lemon zest.
4 Season and add the tofu and the vegetable stock.

5 Cover and simmer gently for approximately 10 minutes.
6 Place the tofu mixture on suitable plates; garnish with mixed leaves.
7 Finish by placing the warmed asparagus on top. Sprinkle with toasted cashew nuts.

HEALTHY EATING TIP
- Use a little olive oil in a well-seasoned pan to fry the onions and garlic.
- Add the minimum amount of salt.
- Serve with warm bread rolls to increase the starchy carbohydrate.

* Using an increased quantity of fresh tomatoes

19 Tofu dressings and dips

Blend the following ingredients in a food processor until smooth: 800 g tofu; 3 tbsp lemon juice or vinegar. Add the following, as required.

Garlic and dill
- 2 cloves crushed and chopped garlic
- 2 tsp of chopped dill

Curry
- 1 finely chopped onion sweated in 1 tbsp of olive oil; add 2 tsp of curry powder; sweat for a further 2 minutes; add to the tofu and mix well.

Cheese and garlic
- Add 50 g freshly grated Parmesan and 2 cloves of crushed and chopped garlic.

Ginger
- Add 2 tsp of freshly grated ginger, a dash of Tabasco and 1 tsp freshly chopped parsley.

Avocado
- Add the purée of two avocado pears, 50 g of finely chopped onion and a dash of Tabasco

Herb
- Add 3 tsp of freshly chopped herbs (e.g. basil, oregano, tarragon, chives, parsley).

20 Crispy deep-fried tofu

Cal	Cal	Fat	Sat Fat	Carb	Sugar	Protein	Fibre	*
543 KJ	131 kcal	8.9 g	0.0 g	1.0 g	0.5 g	11.8 g	0.0 g	

	4 portions	10 portions
firm tofu, cut into cubes	200g	500g

1 Coat the tofu cubes with any of the following: flour, egg and breadcrumbs; milk and flour; cornstarch; arrowroot.
2 Deep-fry the tofu at 180°C, until golden brown. Drain.
3 Serve garnished with freshly grated ginger and julienne of herbs.
4 Serve with a tomato sauce flavoured with coriander.

HEALTHY EATING TIP
- Use an unsaturated oil to fry the tofu.
- Make sure the oil is hot so that less is absorbed.
- Alternatively, try dry-frying the tofu.

* 50 g

Vegetable dishes

21 Spiced aubergine purée

	4–6 portions
diced aubergine	1 kg
salt	20 g
cumin	5 g
tomato purée	45 g
water	200 ml
rose harissa	15 g
vegetable nage	200 ml

1 Dice the aubergine and mix with the salt and cumin in a suitable bowl.
2 Allow to stand for 30 minutes.
3 Dry in a cloth and deep-fry for 10 minutes.
4 Purée with the rest of the ingredients and pass.

Note: This purée can be added to rice or couscous, or used as a filling for stuffed vegetables. It can also be used as a garnish for meat dishes.

22 Chicory flamande

Cal	Cal	Fat	Sat Fat	Carb	Sugar	Protein	Fibre	Salt	*
561 KJ	134 kcal	13.4 g	8.1 g	5.0 g	2.2 g	1.1 g	1.3 g	1.8 g	

	4 portions	10 portions
heads chicory, cleaned	4	10
butter	60 g	150 g
lemon juice	1	3
chicken stock	150 ml	375 ml
salt	1 tsp	2½ tsp
freshly ground white pepper	1 g	2½ g
sugar	1 tsp	2½ tsp
paprika or chopped parsley to garnish	¼ tsp	¾ tsp

1 Arrange the chicory in a buttered ovenproof dish.
2 Melt the butter with the lemon juice, stock, salt and pepper, sugar and pepper, then pour over the chicory.
3 Cover with a lid or a piece of buttered greaseproof (waxed) paper and cook in preheated moderate oven (180°C) for 35–40 minutes.
4 Remove the lid and brown top under a preheated grill.
5 Sprinkle with paprika or chopped parsley.

Note: This is a version of braised chicory served as a first course or as a vegetable accompaniment.

23 Vegetable pie

Cal 1406 KJ	Cal 336 kcal	Fat 20.6 g	Sat Fat 11.7 g	Carb 25.9 g	Sugar 13.0 g	Protein 14.5 g	Fibre 4.5 g	Salt 0.8 g	*

	4 portions	10 portions
milk	500 ml	1.25 litres
onion, finely chopped	1	2
bouquet garni	1	2
pinch of nutmeg		
butter	60 g	150 g
flour	45 g	110 g
mild cheese, grated	30 g	75 g
large pinch dry mustard		
small pinch cayenne		
salt and freshly		
ground black pepper		
diced or sliced		
cooked vegetables		
(e.g. beans, peas,		
carrots, corn, fennel,		
broccoli, cauliflower,		
peppers, mushrooms,		
celery)	550 g	1375 g
rough puff or		
flaky pastry	1 × 375 g	2 × 375 g
beaten egg, to glaze		

1 Heat the milk in a saucepan with the onion, bouquet garni and nutmeg until bubbles form around the edge.

2 Remove from heat and leave to stand for 5 minutes, then remove the bouquet garni.
3 Melt the butter in a heavy saucepan, stir in the flour and cook on a low heat for 1 minute.
4 Remove from the heat, cool a little and add the milk, stirring until smoothly blended.
5 Return to a medium heat and stir until boiling.
6 Remove from the heat, stir in the cheese, mustard and cayenne; season with salt and pepper.
7 Fold the cooked vegetables into the sauce and cool completely.
8 Spoon the mixture into a pie dish just large enough to hold it.
9 Cover with the pastry (dough) and chill for 20 minutes.
10 Cut a few small slits in the top and brush with beaten egg.
11 Bake in a pre-heated hot oven at 230°C for 10–15 minutes or until the crust is well risen and beginning to brown, then reduce the heat to moderate (180°C) and continue baking until the crust is golden brown and the filling heated through (a further 25–30 minutes).
12 Cover the top loosely with foil if the crust is browning too much.
13 Serve very hot.

Using semi-skimmed milk

24 Cauliflower and lentil curry

	4 portions	10 portions
red or brown lentils	125 g	300 g
onions, finely chopped	2	5
butter or ghee	60 g	150 g
chilli powder, or to taste	½ tsp	1 tsp
turmeric	½ tsp	1 tsp
curry powder	½ tsp	1 tsp
desiccated coconut	½ tsp	1 tsp
cauliflower, cut into florets	1	2½
salt	250 ml	625 ml
lemon juice	1	2

1 Place the lentils in a saucepan, cover with fresh cold water and simmer gently for about 20 minutes or until almost tender. Drain.
2 Fry the onions in butter or ghee until soft.
3 Add spices and coconut and cook gently, stirring, for 3 minutes.
4 Add the cauliflower, salt, lentils and water.
5 Cover tightly and cook on a low heat for 15–20 minutes or until the cauliflower and lentils are soft.
6 Stir in the lemon juice.
7 Taste and correct the seasoning.
8 Serve as a main course with rice, poppadoms and 1 or 2 side dishes of chutneys.

25 Chinese-style stir-fry vegetables

Cal	Cal	Fat	Sat Fat	Carb	Sugar	Protein	Fibre
1429 KJ	340 kcal	31.9 g	4.2 g	9.1 g	4.2 g	4.7 g	4.5 g

	4 portions	10 portions
beansprouts	100 g	250 g
button mushrooms	100 g	250 g
carrots	100 g	250 g
celery	100 g	250 g
cauliflower	100 g	250 g
broccoli	100 g	250 g
French beans	50 g	125 g
red peppers	50 g	125 g
green peppers	50 g	125 g
baby sweetcorn	50 g	125 g
sunflower oil	125 ml	300 ml
grated root ginger	5 g	12 g
soy sauce	60 ml	150 ml
ground white or mill pepper, to season		

1 Wash the beansprouts; wash and slice the mushrooms. Peel the carrots and cut into large batons. Trim the celery and cut into large batons. Wash the cauliflower and broccoli, and cut into florets. Top and tail the French beans and cut in halves. Wash and slice the peppers. Trim the baby sweetcorn as necessary. The green vegetables may be quickly blanched and refreshed to retain their colour.

2 Heat the sunflower oil in a wok or frying pan and add all the vegetables. Fry and continuously stir for approximately 3 minutes.

3 Add the grated ginger, cook for 1 minute. Add the soy sauce, stir well.

4 Correct the seasoning, serve immediately.

HEALTHY EATING TIP

- No additional salt is needed; there is plenty of flavour from the soy sauce, ginger and pepper.
- Use a smaller amount of sunflower oil.
- Serve with a large portion of rice or noodles.

Figure 11.6 Cooking Chinese-style stir-fry vegetables

26 Courgette and potato cakes with mint and feta cheese

Cal	Cal	Fat	Sat Fat	Carb	Sugar	Protein	Fibre
910 KJ	219 kcal	13.6 g	7.4 g	15.4 g	2.4 g	9.5 g	1.6 g

	6 portions
courgettes	3 large
potatoes	350 g
fresh mint, chopped	2 tbsp
spring onions, finely chopped	2
feta cheese	200 g
eggs	1
plain flour	25 g
butter	25 g
olive oil	1 tbsp
salt, pepper	

1 Lightly scrape the courgettes to remove the outside skin. Place in a food processor to purée. Remove, sprinkle with salt to remove the excess moisture, leave for 1 hour. Rinse under cold water, squeeze out all excess moisture, dry on a clean cloth.

2 Steam or par boil the potatoes for 8–10 minutes. Cool and peel.

3 Carefully grate the potatoes, place in a bowl, then season.

4 Add the courgettes, mint, spring onion, chopped feta cheese and the beaten egg. Mix well.

5 Divide the mixture into 6 and shape into cakes approximately 1 cm thick.

6 Dust with flour.

7 Brush the cakes with melted butter and oil, place on a baking sheet, cook in an oven at 200°C for 15 minutes; turn over and continue to cook for a further 15 minutes.
8 Serve on suitable plates garnished with fresh blanched mint leaves and a salsa verde.

HEALTHY EATING TIP
- Make sure the puréed courgettes are rinsed well to remove the added salt.
- Use a little sunflower oil to brush the cakes before cooking.

27 Fettuccini of courgette with chopped basil and balsamic vinegar

	4 portions	10 portions
courgettes	2 large	5 large
olive oil	50 ml	125 ml
olive oil, to finish	20 ml	125 ml
balsamic vinegar, to finish	20 ml	50 ml
basil leaves, shredded	2	5

1 Slice the courgettes finely lengthwise, using a mandolin (Japanese slicer).
2 Heat the olive oil in a suitable pan. Sauté the courgette slices quickly without colour for 35 seconds.
3 Place on suitable plates. Drizzle with olive oil and balsamic vinegar, and top with shredded basil leaves.

Note: This may be served as a vegetarian starter or as a garnish for fish and meat dishes.

28 Asparagus wrapped in puff pastry with Gruyère

Cal 2017 KJ	Cal 485 kcal	Fat 37.7 g	Sat Fat 15.0 g	Carb 23.4 g	Sugar 2.5 g	Protein 15.9 g	Fibre 0.8 g

	4 portions	10 portions
Gruyère cheese	175 g	400 g
Parmesan, freshly grated	3 tbsp	7 tbsp
crème fraiche	250 ml	625 ml
puff pastry (page 624)	350 g	875 g
eggwash or milk, for brushing		
asparagus, freshly cooked	350 g	875 g
salt, pepper		
watercress, for garnish		

1 Cut the Gruyère cheese into 1 cm dice. In a suitable bowl, mix the Parmesan cheese and crème fraiche; season.
2 Roll out the puff pastry to approximately ¼ cm thick and cut into squares approximately 18 × 18 cm.
3 Brush the edges with eggwash or milk.
4 Divide the crème fraiche, putting equal amounts

Figure 11.7 Asparagus wrapped in puff pastry with Gruyère cheese

onto the centre of each square. Lay the asparagus on top. Place the diced Gruyère cheese firmly between the asparagus.

5 Fold the opposite corners of each square to meet in the centre, like an envelope. Firmly pinch the seams together to seal them. Make a small hole in the centre of each one to allow the steam to escape. Place on a lightly greased baking sheet.

6 Allow to relax for 20 minutes in the refrigerator. Brush with eggwash or milk, sprinkle with Parmesan.

7 Bake in a hot oven at 200°C for approximately 20–25 minutes until golden brown.

8 Serve garnished with watercress.

HEALTHY EATING TIP

• The puff pastry and cheese make this dish high in fat. Serve with plenty of starchy carbohydrate to dilute it.

29 Ratatouille pancakes with a cheese sauce

Cal	Cal	Fat	Sat Fat	Carb	Sugar	Protein	Fibre
2398 KJ	571 kcal	35.8 g	6.5 g	46.1 g	19.0 g	19.6 g	6.5 g

	4 portions	10 portions
Pancake batter		
(see page 568)		
flour	100 g	250 g
skimmed milk	250 ml	625 ml
egg	1	2–3
pinch of salt		
sunflower margarine,		
melted	10 g	25 g
Ratatouille (see page 479)		
courgettes	200 g	500 g
aubergines	200 g	500 g
red pepper	1	2–3
green pepper	1	2–3
tomatoes	100 g	250 g
yellow pepper	1	2–3
onion, chopped	50 g	125 g
clove garlic, chopped	1	2
sunflower oil	4 tbsp	10 tbsp
tin plum tomatoes	400 g	1¼ kg
tomato purée	50 g	125 g
Cheese sauce (page 52)		
skimmed milk	500 ml	1¼ litres
sunflower oil	50 g	125 g
flour	50 g	125 g
onion, studded with clove	1	2–3
Parmesan, grated	25 g	60 g
egg yolk	1	2–3
seasoning		

1 Prepare and make the pancakes.

2 Prepare the ratatouille and cheese sauce.

3 Season with salt and cayenne pepper.

4 Fill the pancakes with the ratatouille, roll up and serve on individual plates or on a service dish, coated with cheese sauce and sprinkled with grated Parmesan. Finish by gratinating under the salamander.

HEALTHY EATING TIP

• Less oil is needed to prepare the ratatouille.
• No added salt is needed as the cheese is salty.
• Serve with a large mixed salad.

30 Vegetable curry with rice pilaff

Cal	Cal	Fat	Sat Fat	Carb	Sugar	Protein	Fibre
1814 KJ	432 kcal	35.5 g	7.4 g	23.5 g	16.3 g	6.4 g	6.7 g

	4 portions	10 portions
mixed vegetables (e.g. cauliflower, broccoli, peppers, carrots, courgettes, mushrooms, aubergines)	600 g	1½ kg
sunflower margarine	100 g	250 g
onions, chopped finely	150 g	375 g
garam masala	25 g	60 g
creamed coconut (or 50 g/125 g desiccated coconut)	25 g	60 g
curry sauce made using vegetable stock (pages 440 and 441)	500 ml	1¼ litre

1 Prepare the vegetables: cut the cauliflower and broccoli into small florets, blanch and refresh; cut the peppers in half, remove the seeds, cut into 1 cm dice; cut the carrots into large dice, blanch and refresh; cut the courgettes into 1 cm dice; leave the mushrooms whole; cut the aubergines into 1 cm dice.
2 Heat the margarine and sweat the onion.
3 Add the garam masala; sweat for approximately 2 minutes and add the coconut.
4 Add all the vegetables; sweat together for approximately 5 minutes.
5 Add the curry sauce, bring to the boil and gently simmer until all the vegetables are cooked but crunchy in texture.
6 Serve in a suitable dish with a rice pilaff garnished with flaked almonds, poppadoms and a curry tray with mango chutney.

Note: To the basic recipe of rice pilaff (page 162) using 100 g rice, add 50 g roasted flaked almonds after cooking (increase the quantities by 2½ for 10 portions). A recipe for alu-chole, a vegetarian curry from northern India, can be found on page 402.

HEALTHY EATING TIP

- Use a small amount of an unsaturated oil to sweat the onions.
- No added salt is necessary if the stock used contains yeast extract.

31 Vegetable biryani

Cal	Cal	Fat	Sat Fat	Carb	Sugar	Protein	Fibre
2014 KJ	482 kcal	7.3 g	0.9 g	91.3 g	9.9 g	12.2 g	4.6 g

	4 portions	10 portions
basmati rice	400 g	1¼ kg
oil	2 tbsp	5 tbsp
cinnamon stick	½	1
cardamom pods	4	10
cloves	4	10
onions, sliced	100 g	250 g
clove garlic	1	2–3
green chilli, finely chopped	1	2–3
root ginger, grated	1 tbsp	2–3 tbsp
mixed vegetables (e.g. carrots, celery, broccoli, cauliflower, French beans)	600 g	1½ kg
tomatoes, blanched, deseeded and chopped, or canned plum tomatoes	400 g	1¼ kg
tomato purée	25 g	60 g
salt, pepper		
coriander leaves, chopped		

1 Wash, soak and drain the rice.
2 Partly cook the rice in boiling salted water for 3 minutes. Refresh and drain well.
3 Heat the oil in a suitably sized pan. Add the crushed cinnamon, cardamom and cloves, and sweat for 2 minutes.
4 Add the sliced onions, garlic, chilli and ginger. Continue to sweat until soft.

5 Prepare the vegetables: cut the carrots and celery into batons, the cauliflower and broccoli into florets and the French beans into 2½ cm lengths.
6 Add the vegetables to the pan, and fry for 2–3 minutes.
7 Add the tomatoes and tomato purée. Season.
8 Make sure there is sufficient moisture in the pan to cook the vegetables; usually a little water needs to be added. Ideally, though, the vegetables should cook in their own juices, combined with the tomatoes.
9 When the vegetables are partly cooked, layer them in a casserole or suitable pan with the rice. (Make sure that there is sufficient liquid to cook the rice.)

10 Cover the casserole, finish cooking in a moderate oven at 180°C for about 20 minutes, or until the rice is tender.
11 Sprinkle with chopped coriander leaves and serve.

HEALTHY EATING TIP
- Keep added salt to a minimum.
- Use a little unsaturated oil to sweat the spices, onions and vegetables.

32 Vegetable and nut stroganoff

Cal 2098 KJ	Cal 500 kcal	Fat 41.5 g	Sat Fat 7.0 g	Carb 12.0 g	Sugar 7.0 g	Protein 15.7 g	Fibre 6.4 g

	4 portions	10 portions
sunflower oil	4 tbsp	10 tbsp
onions, finely chopped	50 g	125 g
Chinese leaves, shredded	300 g	1 kg
celery, in paysanne	6 sticks	15 sticks
button mushrooms, sliced	300 g	1 kg
mixed nuts (e.g. peanuts, cashews, hazelnuts)	200 g	500 g
paprika	1 tsp	2–3 tsp
English or continental mustard	1 tsp	2–3 tsp
white wine	125 ml	300 ml
unsweetened vegetable creamer or smetana	125 ml	300 ml
seasoning		

1 Heat the oil and sweat the onions for 2–3 minutes.
2 Add the Chinese leaves, celery and mushrooms. Cook for 5 minutes.
3 Add the nuts whole. Stir in the paprika and diluted mustard.
4 Add the white wine, bring to the boil and simmer for 5 minutes.
5 Season. Cool slightly, add heat-stable unsweetened vegetable creamer or smetana. Serve with a dish of plain-boiled wholewheat noodles tossed in sunflower margarine or wholegrain pilaff rice.

Pulse dishes

33 Bean goulash

Cal	Cal	Fat	Sat Fat	Carb	Sugar	Protein	Fibre
1728 KJ	411 kcal	17.9 g	2.7 g	50.0 g	7.3 g	17.3 g	18.5 g

	4 portions	10 portions
red kidney or haricot beans, dried	200 g	500 g
sunflower oil	60 ml	150 ml
onion, finely chopped	50 g	125 g
clove garlic, crushed	1	2–3
paprika	25 g	60 g
red peppers	2	5
green pepper	1	2–3
yellow pepper	1	2–3
button mushrooms, sliced	200 g	500 g
tomato purée	50 g	125 g
vegetable stock	750 ml	2 litre
bouquet garni		
seasoning		
small turned potatoes, cooked	8	20
parsley, chopped, to serve		

1 Soak the beans for 24 hours in cold water. Drain, place into a saucepan. Cover with cold water, bring to the boil and simmer until tender.
2 Heat the oil in a sauté pan, sweat the onion and garlic without colour for 2–3 minutes and add the paprika; sweat for a further 2–3 minutes.
3 Add the peppers, cut in halves, remove the seeds and cut into 1 cm dice. Add the button mushrooms; sweat for a further 2 minutes.
4 Add the tomato purée, vegetable stock and bouquet garni. Bring to the boil and simmer until the pepper and mushrooms are cooked.

5 Remove the bouquet garni. Add the drained cooked beans, correct the seasoning and stir.
6 Garnish with potatoes (or gnocchi) and chopped parsley.
7 Serve wholegrain pilaff or wholemeal noodles separately.

HEALTHY EATING TIP
- Use less sunflower oil to sweat the onions.
- Add a pinch of salt.
- Serve with rice or noodles and a green salad or mixed vegetables.

Figure 11.8 Bean goulash

34 Mexican bean pot

Cal	Cal	Fat	Sat Fat	Carb	Sugar	Protein	Fibre
672 KJ	161 kcal	1.2 g	0.2 g	27.0 g	4.6 g	12.3 g	14.0 g

	4 portions	10 portions
red kidney or haricot beans, dried	300 g	1 kg
onions, finely chopped	100 g	250 g
carrots, sliced	100 g	250 g
tomato, skinned, deseeded and diced	200 g	500 g
cloves garlic, crushed and chopped	2	5
paprika	10 g	25 g
dried marjoram	3 g	9 g
small fresh chilli, finely chopped	1	2–3
small red pepper, finely diced	1	2–3
yeast extract	5 g	12 g
chives, chopped		
seasoning		

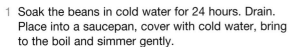

HEALTHY EATING TIP
- No added salt is needed; there is plenty in the yeast extract.
- Serve with a selection of colourful vegetables.

1 Soak the beans in cold water for 24 hours. Drain. Place into a saucepan, cover with cold water, bring to the boil and simmer gently.
2 When three-quarters cooked, add all the other ingredients except the chopped chives.
3 Continue to simmer until all is completely cooked.
4 Serve sprinkled with chopped chives.

Figure 11.9 Mexican bean pot

Miscellaneous

35 Oriental stir-fry Quorn

Cal	Cal	Fat	Sat Fat	Carb	Sugar	Protein	Fibre
836 KJ	200 kcal	11.8 g	1.3 g	11.6 g	7.3 g	12.7 g	5.6 g

	4 portions	10 portions
soy sauce	62 ml	156 ml
ginger, freshly grated	12 g	30 g
black pepper, to taste		
Quorn pieces, defrosted	200 g	500 g
vegetable oil	1 tbsp	3 tbsp
spring onions	8	20
red pepper, halved, deseeded and finely sliced	1	3
yellow pepper, halved, deseeded and finely sliced	1	3
green pepper, halved, deseeded and finely sliced	1	3
dry sherry	1 tbsp	3 tbsp
vegetable stock	62 ml	156 ml
sugar	¼ tsp	1 tsp
cornflour	6 g	15 g
blanched almonds or cashews	50 g	100 g

1 Prepare a marinade by mixing the soy sauce with the ginger, and season with black pepper.

2 Add the Quorn pieces, mix well and chill for 1 hour.
3 Strain the Quorn from the marinade. In a wok, add half the vegetable oil and stir-fry the Quorn quickly for approximately 4 minutes. Remove from the wok.
4 Add the remaining oil, and fry the spring onion and peppers for another 1–2 minutes.
5 Return the Quorn to the wok.
6 Add the strained marinade, sherry, stock and sugar. Bring to the boil.
7 Thicken lightly with the cornflour. Add the blanched almonds or cashews and stir gently to enable the ingredients to be covered with the sauce.
8 Serve with noodles or rice.

HEALTHY EATING TIP
- Use a little unsaturated oil to fry the Quorn, onions and peppers.
- No added salt is needed; there is plenty of flavour from the soy sauce, ginger and stock.

Note: Quorn may be used in stews, pies and casseroles in place of meat. See page 233 or www.quorn.com for information on Quorn.

36 Vegetarian strudel

Cal 2117 KJ	Cal 504 kcal	Fat 27.6 g	Sat Fat 4.0 g	Carb 54.1 g	Sugar 10.5 g	Protein 14.3 g	Fibre 9.7 g	Salt 0.0 g

	4 portions	10 portions
Strudel dough		
strong flour	200 g	500 g
pinch of salt		
sunflower oil	25 g	60 g
egg	1	2–3
water at 37°C	83 ml	125 ml
Filling		
large cabbage leaves	200 g	500 g
sunflower oil	4 tbsp	10 tbsp
onion, finely chopped	50 g	125 g
cloves garlic, chopped	2	5
courgettes	400 g	1 kg
carrots	200 g	500 g
turnips	100 g	250 g
tomato, skinned, deseeded and diced	300 g	750 g
tomato purée	25 g	60 g
toasted sesame seeds	25 g	60 g
wholemeal breadcrumbs	50 g	125 g
fresh chopped basil	3 g	9 g
seasoning		
eggwash		

1 To make the strudel dough, sieve the flour with the salt and make a well.
2 Add the oil, egg and water, and gradually incorporate the flour to make a smooth dough; knead well.
3 Place in a basin, cover with a damp cloth; allow to relax for 3 minutes.
4 Meanwhile, prepare the filling: take the large cabbage leaves, wash and discard the tough centre stalks, blanch in boiling salted water for 2

minutes, until limp. Refresh and drain well in a clean cloth.
5 Heat the oil in a sauté pan, gently fry the onion and garlic until soft.
6 Peel and chop the courgettes into ½ cm dice, blanch and refresh. Peel and dice the carrots and turnips, blanch and refresh.
7 Place the well-drained courgettes, carrots and turnips into a basin, add the tomato concassée, tomato purée, sesame seeds, breadcrumbs and chopped basil, and mix well. Season.
8 Roll out the strudel dough to a thin rectangle, place on a clean cloth and stretch until extremely thin.
9 Lay the drained cabbage leaves on the stretched strudel dough, leaving approximately a 1 cm gap from the edge.
10 Place the filling in the centre. Eggwash the edges.
11 Fold in the longer side edges to meet in the middle. Roll up.
12 Transfer to a lightly oiled baking sheet. Brush with the sunflower oil.
13 Bake for 40 minutes in a preheated oven at 180–200°C.
14 When cooked, serve hot, sliced on individual plates with a cordon of tomato sauce made with vegetable stock, or tomato coulis.

HEALTHY EATING TIP
- Use the minimum amount of salt.
- Use a little unsaturated oil to cook the onion and garlic.

37 Vegetarian moussaka

Cal 2249 KJ	Cal 536 kcal	Fat 29.1 g	Sat Fat 7.0 g	Carb 46.2 g	Sugar 11.4 g	Protein 25.5 g	Fibre 6.4 g

	4 portions	10 portions
TVP mince (natural flavour)	100 g	250 g
onion, finely chopped	50 g	125 g
clove garlic, chopped	1	2–3
sunflower oil	4 tbsp	10 tbsp
tomato, skinned, deseeded and diced	200 g	500 g
tomato purée	50 g	125 g
pinch oregano		
seasoning		
vegetable stock	500 ml	1¼ litre
yeast extract	5 g	12 g
arrowroot	10 g	25 g
potatoes	400 g	1¼ kg
large aubergines	2	5
wholemeal flour	25 g	60 g
sunflower oil		
cheese sauce (**page 52**)	25 g	60 g
Parmesan cheese, grated	25 g	60 g

1 Pre-soak the TVP mince in cold water for 2–3 hours. Cook the onion and garlic in the sunflower oil until lightly coloured.
2 Add the drained TVP.
3 Add the tomato concassée, tomato purée, oregano and seasoning.

4 Add the vegetable stock to cover. Bring to the boil; simmer for 5 minutes.
5 Add the yeast extract, stir well.
6 Dilute the arrowroot with a little water and gradually stir into the TVP.
7 Bring back to the boil. Simmer for 2 minutes.
8 Cook the potatoes with the skins on, by steaming or boiling. Peel and slice into ½ cm slices.
9 Slice the aubergines into ½ cm slices, pass through the wholemeal flour, shallow-fry in the sunflower oil on both sides, until golden brown. Drain on kitchen paper.
10 In a suitable ovenproof dish arrange layers of TVP mixture and overlapping slices of potato and aubergines.
11 Make the cheese sauce (page 52) and pour on top, sprinkle with the grated Parmesan cheese.
12 Bake in a preheated oven at 190°C for approximately 30 minutes.

HEALTHY EATING TIP
- Use a little unsaturated oil to cook the onion and garlic.
- No added salt is needed.
- Try ovenbaking the aubergines brushed with a little oil.

38 Goats' cheese and beetroot tarts, with salad of watercress

Cal 2377 KJ	Cal 568 kcal	Fat 37.7 g	Sat Fat 9.0 g	Carb 43.6 g	Sugar 7.5 g	Protein 18.6 g	Fibre 1.8 g	Salt 1.7 g

	4 portions	10 portions
puff pastry	400 g	1 kg
shallots	150 g	375 g
cooked beetroot	200 g	500 g
goats' cheese	200 g	500 g
bunch watercress	1	2

1 Roll the puff pastry to a thickness of 3 mm.
2 Chill the rolled puff pastry for 10 minutes.
3 Finely slice the shallots and sweat down without colour.
4 Cut the puff pastry into four discs approximately 150 mm in diameter.

Figure 11.10   Goats' cheese and beetroot tarts, with salad of watercress

5 Chill the pastry discs for 10 minutes.
6 Dice the cooked beetroot into pieces 10 x 10 mm.
7 To make the tarts, place the shallots on the pastry discs.
8 Cook at 180°C for 12 minutes.

9 Once cooked, remove from the oven and top with the diced beetroot and crumbled goats' cheese.
10 To finish the dish, place the tarts on plates and finish with picked watercress and vinaigrette.

39 Caribbean fruit curry

Cal 1729 KJ	Cal 412 kcal	Fat 19.6 g	Sat Fat 6.1 g	Carb 57.2 g	Sugar 51.6	Protein 5.4 g	Fibre 8.3 g	*

	4 portions	10 portions
pineapple	1 small	1 large
dessert apples	2	5
small dessert pears	2	5
mangoes	2	5
bananas	2	5
guava	1	2–3
pawpaw	1	2–3
rind and juice of lime, grated	1	2–3
onion, chopped	50 g	125 g
sunflower margarine	25 g	60 g
sunflower oil	60 ml	150 ml
Madras curry powder	50 g	125 g
wholemeal flour	25 g	60 g
ginger, freshly grated	10 g	25 g
desiccated coconut	50 g	125 g
tomato, skinned, deseeded and diced	100 g	250 g
tomato purée	25 g	60 g
yeast extract	5 g	12 g
sultanas	50 g	125 g
fruit juice	½ litre	1¼ litres
cashew nuts	50 g	125 g
single cream or smetana	60 ml	150 ml

1 Skin and cut the pineapple in half, remove the tough centre. Cut into 1 cm chunks. Peel the apples and pears, remove the cores, cut into 1 cm pieces. Peel and slice the mangoes. Skin and cut the bananas into 1 cm pieces. Cut the guavas and pawpaws in half, remove the seeds, peel, dice into 1 cm pieces. Marinate the fruit in the lime juice.
2 Fry the onion in the sunflower margarine and oil until lightly brown, add the curry powder, sweat together, add the wholemeal flour and cook for 2 minutes.
3 Add the ginger, coconut, tomato concassée, tomato purée and sultanas.
4 Gradually add sufficient boiling fruit juice to make a light sauce.
5 Add yeast extract, stir well. Simmer for 10 minutes.
6 Add the sultanas, fruit juice and cashew nuts, stir carefully, allow to heat through.
7 Finish with cream or smetana.
8 Serve in a suitable dish; separately serve poppadoms, wholegrain pilaff rice and a green salad.

HEALTHY EATING TIP
- Lightly oil a well-seasoned pan with the sunflower oil to fry the onion.
- No added salt is needed.
- Try finishing the dish with low-fat yoghurt in place of the cream.
- Serve with plenty of starchy carbohydrate and salad.

* Using single cream

40 Samosas

A basic recipe for samosas (which may be made using vegetarian alternatives) can be found in Chapter 10: International dishes.

41 Tempura

Cal 3397 KJ	Cal 815 kcal	Fat 55.9 g	Sat Fat 7.4 g	Carb 67.4 g	Sugar 5.3 g	Protein 14.8 g	Fibre 5 g

4 portions

vegetable oil	500 ml
courgettes, sliced	2
sweet potato, scrubbed and sliced	1
green pepper, seeds removed and cut into strips	1
shiitake mushroom, stalks removed and halved if large	4
onion, sliced as half moons	1
parsley sprigs, to garnish	4
Batter (NB: all ingredients must be stored in the fridge until just before mixing)	
egg yolk	
ice-cold water	200 ml
plain flour, sifted	100 g
Tentsuyu dipping sauce (optional)	
dashi stock	200 ml
mirin	3 tbsp
soy sauce	3 tbsp
grated ginger	½ tsp

1 To prevent splattering during the frying, make sure to dry all deep-fry ingredients thoroughly first with a kitchen towel.
2 For the batter, beat the egg yolk lightly and mix with the ice-cold water.
3 Add ½ the flour to the egg and water mixture. Give the mixture a few strokes. Add the rest of the flour all at once. Stroke the mixture a few times with chopsticks or a fork until the ingredients are loosely combined. The batter should be very lumpy. If over-mixed, tempura will be oily and heavy.
4 To prepare the vegetables, heat the oil to 160°C.
5 Dip the vegetables into the batter, a few pieces at a time. Fry until just crisp and golden (about 1½ minutes).
6 Drain the cooked vegetables on a kitchen towel.

7 Serve immediately with a pinch of salt, garnished with parsley sprigs and lemon wedges, dry-roasted salt or with Tentsuyu dipping sauce in a small bowl with grated ginger. If you prefer to have the tempura with the Tentsuyu sauce, combine the ingredients in a small saucepan before sifting the flour; heat it through and leave to one side. This dish can also be served with an accompaniment of grated white radish.

Note: To make a success of Tempura, it is essential that all ingredients are ice cold. The batter should not be lumpy and you should fry only a few pieces at once. Any vegetable with a firm texture can be used.

HEALTHY EATING TIP
- Use sunflower or groundnut oil for frying.
- Drain excess oil on kitchen paper.

Figure 11.11 ✎ Tempura

Cauliflower

Celery

Asparagus

Parsnips

Garlic

Fennel

roccoli

Plum
tomatoes

Carrots

chapter 12

VEGETABLES, PULSES AND GRAINS

VRQ

Unit 208   **Prepare and cook fruit and vegetables**

NVQ

Unit 626 (2FP7)   **Prepare vegetables for basic dishes**

Unit 633 (2FPC7)   Cook and finish basic vegetable dishes

Prepare fruit and vegetables

Practical skills
The candidate will be able to:
1 Check that fruit, vegetables and accompanying ingredients are of the correct type, quantity and quality
2 Demonstrate the correct use of tools and equipment to prepare fruit and vegetables
3 Peel, wash or trim fruit and vegetables, and prepare according to dish specifications
4 Store prepared fruit and vegetables appropriately prior to cooking if required
5 Assemble vegetables prior to cooking
6 Demonstrate safe and hygienic practices

Underpinning knowledge
The candidate will be able to:
1 Identify commonly used fruit and vegetables
2 Identify the seasons for commonly used fruit and vegetables
3 Group fruit and vegetables into classifications
4 Identify the quality points for fruit and vegetables
5 Identify correct storage procedures for fruit and vegetables to maintain quality, nutrients and the reduction of waste
6 State the most commonly used preparation methods for fruit and vegetables

7 Identify additions and coatings used when preparing vegetables for cooking

8 State the preservation methods for fruit and vegetables

Cook fruit and vegetables

Practical skills
The candidate will be able to:

1 Demonstrate the correct use of tools and prepare equipment to cook fruit and vegetables
2 Cook and assemble fruit and vegetables to dish specifications using appropriate skills
3 Hold and serve cooked fruit and vegetables
4 Store vegetables safely after cooking, if appropriate
5 Demonstrate safe and hygienic practices

Underpinning knowledge
The candidate will be able to:

1 Identify suitable tools and equipment to cook fruit and vegetables
2 Identify cooking methods for fruit and vegetables
3 Identify cooking liquids and sauces
4 Explain the cooking principles for fruit and vegetables
5 Explain the actions to be carried out to check the quality of fruit and vegetable dishes
6 Describe finishing and garnishing requirements for fruit and vegetable dishes
7 Explain how cooked fruit and vegetables should be held correctly for service
8 Explain how cooked fruit and vegetables should be stored correctly after cooking

Unit 647 (2FPC12) Prepare, cook and finish basic grain dishes

Prepare and cook grains

Practical skills
The candidate will be able to:

1 Use the correct type and amount of grain for the dish specification
2 Demonstrate the correct use of tools and equipment to prepare grain dishes
3 Prepare and cook grain or products according to dish specifications
4 Demonstrate control of the cooking process to obtain the required quality
5 Assemble and finish the dish in line with dish/customer requirements
6 Evaluate finished grain dishes
7 Demonstrate safe and hygienic practices

Underpinning knowledge
The candidate will be able to:

1 Identify commonly used types of grain and their use
2 Identify sauces and additions
3 Identify the appropriate tools and equipment to prepare grain dishes
4 Identify preparation and cooking methods for grains
5 Describe the cooking process and adjustments necessary for grain dishes
6 Describe the skills needed to check and finish to specification
7 State the correct holding and storage procedures for grain dishes

Unit 641 (2FPC6) Prepare, cook and finish basic pulse dishes

Prepare and cook pulses

Practical skills

The candidate will be able to:

1. Demonstrate the correct type and amount of pulses for the dish specification
2. Choose the quality of pulse required for the dish
3. Demonstrate the correct use of tools and equipment to prepare the pulse dishes
4. Prepare and cook the pulses according to the dish specification
5. Demonstrate the appropriate skills and controls required during the cooking process to obtain the required quality
6. Assemble and finish the dish according to the specification and customer requirements
7. Evaluate the finished pulse dishes
8. Demonstrate safe and hygienic practices

Underpinning knowledge

The candidate will be able to:

1. Identify the various types of pulses
2. Identify suitable equipment to prepare the pulse dishes
3. Describe the various preparation and cooking methods suitable for pulses
4. Describe any adjustments that need to be made to pulse recipes
5. Describe the various skills required to cook and finish the dish to specification
6. State the correct holding and storage procedures for pulses and pulse dishes

Vegetables

Vegetable classification

Vegetable is a culinary term that generally refers to the edible part of a plant. The definition is traditional rather than scientific and is somewhat arbitrary and subjective. All parts of herbaceous plants eaten as food by humans, whole or in part, are normally considered vegetables. Mushrooms, though belonging to the biological kingdom fungi, are also commonly considered vegetables. In general, vegetables are thought of as being savoury, not sweet, although there are many exceptions; in most countries, they are associated with poultry, meat or fish as part of a meal or as an ingredient. Nuts, grains, herbs, spices and culinary fruits are not normally considered vegetables. Some vegetables are botanically classed as fruits: tomatoes are berries, and avocados are drupes, but both are commonly used as vegetables because they are not sweet.

Since 'vegetable' is not a botanical term, there is no contradiction in referring to a plant part as a fruit while also being considered a vegetable. Given this general rule of thumb, vegetables can also include leaves (lettuce), stems (asparagus), roots (carrots), flowers (broccoli), bulbs (garlic), seeds (peas and beans) and botanical fruits such as cucumbers, squash, pumpkins and capsicums. Botanically, fruits are reproductive organs (ripened ovaries containing one or many seeds), while vegetables are vegetative organs that sustain the plant.

Nutritional value

Vegetables are eaten in a variety of ways as part of main meals and as snacks. The nutrient content of different types varies considerably. With the exception of pulses, vegetables provide little protein or fat. Vegetables contain water-soluble vitamins like vitamin B and vitamin C, fat-soluble vitamins including vitamin A and vitamin D, as well as carbohydrates and minerals. Root vegetables contain starch or sugar for energy, a small but valuable amount of protein, some mineral salts and vitamins. They are also useful sources of cellulose and water. Green vegetables are rich in mineral salts and vitamins, particularly vitamin C and carotene. The greener the leaf, the larger the quantity of vitamins present. The chief mineral salts are calcium and iron.

Purchasing and selection

The purchasing of vegetables is affected by:

- the perishable nature of the products
- varying availability owing to seasonal fluctuations, and supply and demand
- the effects of preservation (e.g. freezing, drying, canning vegetables).

The high perishability of vegetables causes problems not encountered in other markets. Fresh vegetables are living organisms and will lose quality quickly if not properly stored and handled. Automation in harvesting and packaging speeds the handling process and helps retain quality.

The EU vegetable quality grading system is:

- **Extra class:** produce of the highest quality
- **Class 1:** produce of good quality
- **Class 2:** produce of reasonably good quality
- **Class 3:** produce of low market quality.

Quality and purchasing points

Root vegetables must be:

- clean, free from soil
- firm, not soft or spongy
- sound
- free from blemishes
- of an even size
- of an even shape.

Green vegetables must be absolutely fresh and have leaves that are bright in colour, crisp and not wilted. In addition:

- cabbage and Brussels sprouts should be compact and firm
- cauliflowers should have closely grown flowers, a firm white head and not too much stalk or too many outer leaves
- peas and beans should be crisp and of medium size; pea pods should be full and beans not stringy
- blanched stems must be firm, white, crisp and free from soil.

Storage

Many root and non-root vegetables that grow underground can be stored over winter in a root cellar or other similarly cool, dark and dry place, to prevent the growth of mould, greening and sprouting. Care should be taken in understanding the properties and vulnerabilities of the particular roots to be stored. These vegetables can last through to early spring and be almost as nutritious as when fresh.

During storage, leafy vegetables lose moisture and vitamin C degrades rapidly. They should be stored for as short a time as possible in a cool place in a container, such as a plastic bag or a sealed plastic container.

Storage points

- Store all vegetables in a cool, dry, well ventilated room at an even temperature of 4–8°C, which will help to minimise spoilage. Check vegetables daily and discard any that are unsound.
- Remove root vegetables from their sacks and store in bins or racks.
- Store green vegetables on well-ventilated racks.
- Store salad vegetables in a cool place and leave in their containers.
- Store frozen vegetables at −18°C or below. Keep a check on use-by dates, damaged packages and any signs of freezer burn.
- The fresher the vegetables the better the flavour, so ideally they should not be stored at all. However, as in many cases storage is necessary, then it should be for the shortest time possible.

- Green vegetables lose vitamin C quickly if they are bruised, damaged, stored for too long or overcooked.

Health, safety and hygiene

For information on maintaining a safe and secure working environment, a professional and hygienic appearance, and clean food production areas, equipment and utensils, as well as food hygiene, please refer to Chapters 17 and 18. Additional health and safety points are as follows.

- If vegetables are stored at the incorrect temperature micro-organisms may develop.
- If vegetables are stored in damp conditions moulds may develop.
- To prevent bacteria from raw vegetables passing on to cooked vegetables, store them in separate areas.

- Thaw out frozen vegetables correctly and *never* refreeze them once they have thawed out.

Preparing and cooking vegetable dishes

Approximate times only are given in the recipes in this chapter for the cooking of vegetables, as quality, age, freshness and size all affect the length of cooking time required. Young, freshly picked vegetables will need to be cooked for a shorter time than vegetables that have been allowed to grow older and that may have been stored after picking.

As a general rule, all root vegetables (with the exception of new potatoes) are started off by cooking in cold salted water. Those vegetables that grow above the ground are started in boiling salted water; this is so that they may be cooked as quickly as possible for the minimum period of

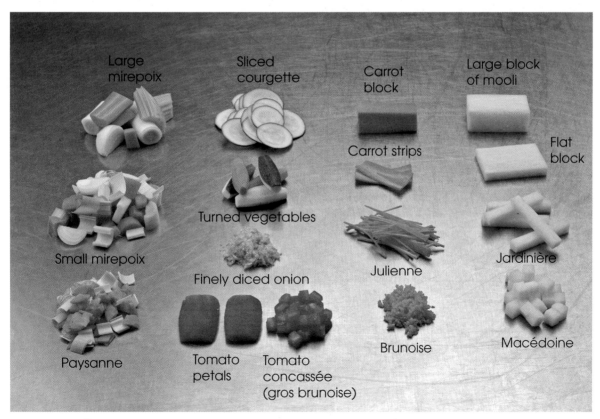

Figure 12.1 ✎ Cuts of vegetables

473

time so that maximum flavour, food value and colour are retained. (See also 'Blanching', below.)

All vegetables cooked by boiling may also be cooked by steaming. The vegetables are prepared in exactly the same way as for boiling, placed into steamer trays, lightly seasoned with salt and steamed under pressure for the minimum period of time in order to conserve maximum food value and retain colour. High-speed steam cookers are ideal for this purpose and also because of the speed of cooking they offer; batch cooking (cooking in small quantities throughout the service) can be practised instead of cooking large quantities prior to service, refreshing and reheating.

Many vegetables are cooked from raw by the stir-fry method, a quick and nutritious method of cooking.

Fresh vegetables are important foods both from an economic and nutritional point of view. Vegetables are an important part of our diet, therefore it is essential to pay attention to quality, purchasing, storage and efficient preparation and cooking if the nutritional content of vegetables is to be conserved. (Potatoes are discussed separately in Chapter 13.)

Blanching

Delicate vegetables – particularly green vegetables – must be blanched in salted boiling water and then refreshed in ice-cold water to arrest the cooking process. The main reason for this is because, between the temperatures of 66°C and 77°C, chlorophyll is unstable. Chlorophyll is the green pigment in any plant that photosynthesises. For this reason it is important to get through this temperature zone as quickly as possible.

When preparing pulses and lentils, cook them in sparkling bottled water. The sparkling motion helps ensure even cooking through momentum; the reason for using bottled water over tap water is the reduced calcium. Especially in hard-water areas there is a lot of calcium. Calcium actually blocks the pores of pulses, causing beans to 'boil in their jackets', then the jacket bursts and the pulses are undesirable. Bottled water allows the fluid to pass through the tiny pores and cook evenly, perfectly.

Cuts of vegetables

The size to which the vegetables are cut may vary according to their use; however, the shape does not change.

Julienne (strips)

- Cut the vegetables into 2 cm lengths (short julienne).
- Cut the lengths into thin slices.
- Cut the slices into thin strips.
- Double the length gives a long julienne, used for garnishing (e.g. salads, meats, fish, poultry dishes).

Brunoise (small dice)

- Cut the vegetables into convenient-sized lengths.
- Cut the lengths into 2 mm slices.
- Cut the slices into 2 mm strips.
- Cut the strips into 2 mm squares.

Macédoine (½ cm dice)

- Cut the vegetables into convenient lengths.
- Cut the lengths into ½ cm slices.
- Cut the slices into ½ cm strips.
- Cut the strips into ½ cm squares.

Jardinière (batons)

- Cut the vegetables into 1½ cm lengths.
- Cut the lengths into 3 mm slices.
- Cut the slices into batons (3 × 3 × 15 mm).

Paysanne

There are at least four accepted methods of cutting paysanne. In order to cut economically, the shape of the vegetables should dictate which method to choose. All are cut thinly.

- 1 cm sided triangles.
- 1 cm sided squares.
- 1 cm diameter rounds.
- 1 cm diameter rough-sided rounds.

Concassée

Roughly chopped (e.g. skinned and deseeded tomatoes are roughly chopped for many food preparations) (see page 500).

Vegetable recipes

Artichoke

1 Globe artichokes, traditional *(artichauts en branche)*

Cal	Cal	Fat	Sat Fat	Carb	Sugar	Protein	Fibre	*
32 KJ	8 kcal	0.0 g	0.0 g	1.4 g	1.4 g	0.6 g	0.0 g	

1 Allow 1 artichoke per portion.
2 Cut off the stems close to the leaves.
3 Cut off about 2 cm across the tops of the leaves.
4 Trim the remainder of the leaves with scissors or a small knife.
5 Place a slice of lemon at the bottom of each artichoke.
6 Secure with string.
7 Simmer in gently boiling, lightly salted water (to which a little ascorbic acid – one vitamin C tablet – may be added) until the bottom is tender (20–30 minutes).
8 Refresh under running water until cold.
9 Remove the centre of the artichoke carefully.
10 Scrape away all the furry inside (the choke) and leave clean.
11 Replace the centre, upside down.
12 Reheat by placing in a pan of boiling salted water for 3–4 minutes.
13 Drain and serve accompanied by a suitable sauce.

Note: Artichokes may also be served cold with vinaigrette sauce. Do not cook artichokes in an iron or aluminium pan because these metals cause a chemical reaction that will discolour them.

* Not including sauce

2 Artichoke bottoms *(fonds d'artichauts)*

1 Cut off the stalk and pull out all the underneath leaves.
2 With a large knife, cut through the artichoke leaving only 1½ cm at the bottom of the vegetable.
3 With a small, sharp knife, while holding the artichoke upside down, peel carefully, removing all the leaf and any green part, keeping the bottom as smooth as possible. If necessary smooth with a peeler.
4 Rub immediately with lemon and keep in lemon water or ascorbic acid solution.
5 Using a spoon or the thumb, remove the centre furry part, which is called the choke. The choke is sometimes removed after cooking.
6 Artichoke bottoms should always be cooked in a blanc (see recipe 3).

Note: Artichoke bases may be served as a vegetable; they are sometimes filled with another vegetable (e.g. peas, spinach). When they are served ungarnished they are usually cut into quarters.

3 Blanc

	4 portions	10 portions
flour	10 g	20 g
cold water	½ litre	1 litre
salt, to taste		
lemon, juice of	½	1

1 Mix the flour and water together.
2 Add the salt and lemon juice. Pass through a strainer.
3 Place in a pan, bring to the boil, stirring continuously.

Note: Alternatively, artichokes may be cooked in ½ litre water, 2 vitamin C tablets (ascorbic acid), 30 ml oil and salt (multiply the quantities by 2½ for 10 portions).

HEALTHY EATING TIP
• Use the minimum amount of salt.

4 Purée of Jerusalem artichokes *(topinambours en purée)*

	4 portions	10 portions
Jerusalem artichokes	600 g	1½ kg
salt, pepper		
butter	25 g	60 g

1 Wash, peel and rewash the artichokes.
2 Cut in pieces if necessary. Barely cover with water; add a little salt.
3 Simmer gently until tender. Drain well.
4 Pass through a sieve, mouli or liquidise.
5 Return to the pan, reheat and mix in the butter; correct the seasoning and serve.

Note: 125 ml (300 ml for 10 portions) cream or natural yoghurt may be mixed in before serving.

HEALTHY EATING TIP
• Use the minimum amount of salt.

5 Jerusalem artichokes in cream sauce *(topinambours à la crème)*

1 Wash and peel the artichokes, then rewash. Cut to an even size.
2 Barely cover with water, add a little salt and simmer until tender; do not overcook.
3 Drain well and add 250 ml (600 ml for 10 portions) cream sauce (page 52).

Note: Cream sauce may be made using skimmed milk and natural yoghurt.

HEALTHY EATING TIP
• Use the minimum amount of salt.
• Try using half the amount of cream sauce and half natural yoghurt.

Asparagus

6 Asparagus (asperges)

Cal	Cal	Fat	Sat Fat	Carb	Sugar	Protein	Fibre
580 KJ	138 kcal	12.3 g	7.8 g	1.7 g	1.7 g	5.2 g	2.3 g

1 Using the back of a small knife, carefully remove the tips of the leaves.
2 Scrape the stem, either with the blade of a small knife or a peeler.
3 Wash well. Tie into bundles of about 12 heads.
4 Cut off the excess stem.
5 Cook in lightly salted boiling water for approximately 5–8 minutes.
6 Test if cooked by gently pressing the green part of the stem, which should be tender; do not overcook.
7 Lift carefully out of the water. Remove the string, drain well and serve.

Note: Allow 6–8 good-sized pieces per portion; an average bundle will yield 3–4 portions. Serve a suitable sauce separately (hollandaise or melted butter). Asparagus is usually served as a separate course. It may also be served cold, in which case it should be refreshed immediately when cooked in order to retain the green colour. Serve with vinaigrette or mayonnaise.

The fresher the asparagus, the faster it will cook. When cooked, asparagus should be slightly firm, not soft and mushy.

7 Asparagus points or tips (pointes d'asperges)

Note: Young thin asparagus, 50 pieces to the bundle, is known as sprew or sprue. It is prepared in the same way as asparagus except that, when it is very thin, the removal of the leaf tips is dispensed with. It may be served as a vegetable. Asparagus tips are also used in numerous garnishes for soups, egg dishes, fish, meat and poultry dishes, cold dishes, salad, and so on.

Microwaved asparagus

As the flavour of asparagus is mild and can be leached out very easily through the cooking medium, a method of cookery that ensures that no flavour is lost in the cooking process is microwaving.

To microwave, place a piece of clingfilm over a plate that will fit in the microwave and, more importantly, is microwave safe. Spread the clingfilm with a little oil and salt, evenly place the asparagus on the plate in a single layer. Cover the plate and asparagus with another piece of clingfilm, place in the microwave for 30 second stints until the asparagus is tender; serve immediately.

The benefit of this method is that it retains flavour and colour, and it can be cooked in minutes, as opposed to batch cooking, which will, invariably, over time cause the asparagus to lose flavour and colour the longer it is stored.

If larger-scale cooking is required the more traditional method should be used: cooking, say, 100 portions of asparagus in the microwave should be avoided for obvious reasons!

Aubergine

8 Fried aubergine (aubergine frite)

Cal	Cal	Fat	Sat Fat	Carb	Sugar	Protein	Fibre
994 KJ	225 kcal	3.8 g	3.8 g	10.1 g	5.9 g	1.9 g	5.2 g

1 Allow ½ an aubergine per portion.
2 Remove alternate strips with a peeler.
3 Cut into ½ cm slices on the slant.
4 Pass through seasoned flour or milk and flour.
5 Shake off all surplus flour.

6 Deep-fry in hot fat at 185°C. Drain well and serve.

Note: Aubergines may also be shallow-fried, grilled or griddled.

9 Griddled aubergines with lemon pesto

Cal	Cal	Fat	Sat Fat	Carb	Sugar	Protein	Fibre
1297 KJ	313 kcal	27.5 g	5.9 g	5.7 g	5.1 g	11.3 g	4.4 g

	4 portions	10 portions
aubergines, sliced into rounds	4	10
baby aubergine, sliced lengthways	4	10
Lemon pesto		
basil, chopped	1 tbsp	3 tbsp
roasted pine nuts	75 g	175 g
garlic clove, crushed and chopped	1	3
Parmesan cheese, grated	75 g	175 g
lemons, grated rind of	2	5
lemon juice	3 tbsp	7 tbsp
olive oil	3 tbsp	7 tbsp
seasoning		

1 Heat the griddle pan, place the aubergines on the pan and cook for 3 minutes on each side. Remove and arrange on serving dish.
2 Make the pesto, place the basil, pine nuts, garlic, Parmesan, lemon rind and juice, olive oil and seasoning in a food processor, then blend until smooth.
3 Drizzle the lemon pesto over the aubergines and serve.

HEALTHY EATING TIP
• No added salt is needed; there is plenty in the cheese.

Variations
Other vegetables may also be used – for example, courgettes.

10 Aubergine purée

The aubergines may be peeled or left with the skin on.

1 Dice the aubergines, sprinkle with cumin and salt, leave for 20 minutes.
2 Deep fry until golden brown and soft.
3 Purée and use as required.

11 Ratatouille

Cal	Cal	Fat	Sat Fat	Carb	Sugar	Protein	Fibre
579 KJ	138 kcal	12.6 g	1.7 g	5.2 g	4.6 g	1.3 g	2.4 g

	4 portions	10 portions
baby marrow (courgette)	200 g	500 g
aubergines	200 g	500 g
tomatoes	200 g	500 g
oil	50 ml	125 ml
onions, finely sliced	50 g	125 g
garlic clove, peeled and chopped	1	2
red peppers, diced	50 g	125 g
green peppers, diced	50 g	125 g
salt, pepper		
parsley, chopped	1 tsp	2–3 tsp

1 Trim off both ends of the marrow and aubergines.
2 Remove the skin using a peeler.
3 Cut into 3 mm slices or dice.
4 Concassée the tomatoes (peel, remove seeds, roughly chop).
5 Place the oil in a thick-bottomed pan and add the onions.
6 Cover with a lid and allow to cook gently for 5–7 minutes without colour.
7 Add the garlic, marrow and aubergine slices, and the peppers.
8 Season lightly with salt and mill pepper.
9 Allow to cook gently for 4–5 minutes, toss occasionally and keep covered.
10 Add the tomato and continue cooking for 20–30 minutes or until tender.
11 Mix in the parsley, correct the seasoning and serve.

Note: Tinned plum tomatoes with their juice may be used in place of fresh. This gives a more moist dish.

HEALTHY EATING TIP
- Use a little unsaturated oil to cook the onions.
- Use the minimum amount of salt.

Figure 12.2 Ingredients of ratatouille

12 Stuffed aubergine (aubergine farcie)

	4 portions	10 portions
aubergines	2	5
shallots, chopped	10 g	25 g
oil or fat, to fry		
mushrooms	100 g	250 g
parsley, chopped		
tomato concassée	100 g	250 g
salt, pepper		
demi-glace or jus-lié	125 ml	300 ml

Figure 12.3 Clockwise from top left: avocado, Italian aubergine, red pepper, yellow pepper, plum tomatoes

1 Cut the aubergines in two lengthwise.
2 With the point of a small knife make a cut round the halves approximately ½ cm from the edge, then make several cuts ½ cm deep in the centre.
3 Deep-fry in hot fat at 185°C for 2–3 minutes; drain well.
4 Scoop out the centre pulp and chop it finely.
5 Cook the shallots in a little oil or fat without colouring.

6 Add the well-washed mushrooms. Cook gently for a few minutes.
7 Mix in the pulp, parsley and tomato; season. Replace in the aubergine skins.
8 Sprinkle with breadcrumbs and melted butter. Brown under the salamander.
9 Serve with a cordon of demi-glace or jus-lié.

Carrot

13 Buttered carrots (carottes au beurre)

Cal	Cal	Fat	Sat Fat	Carb	Sugar	Protein	Fibre
297 KJ	71 kcal	5.1 g	3.3 g	5.8 g	5.8 g	0.7 g	2.8 g

	4 portions	10 portions
carrots	400 g	1 kg
salt, pepper		
sugar		
butter	25 g	60 g
parsley, chopped		

1 Peel and wash the carrots.
2 Cut into neat even pieces or turned barrel shapes.
3 Place in a pan with a little salt, a pinch of sugar and butter. Barely cover with water.
4 Cover with a buttered paper and allow to boil steadily in order to evaporate all the water.

5 When the water has completely evaporated check that the carrots are cooked; if not, add a little more water and continue cooking. Do not overcook.
6 Toss the carrots over a fierce heat for 1–2 minutes in order to give them a glaze.
7 Serve sprinkled with chopped parsley.

HEALTHY EATING TIP
• Use the minimum amount of salt.

14 Purée of carrots (purée de carottes)

Cal	Cal	Fat	Sat Fat	Carb	Sugar	Protein	Fibre
410 KJ	99 kcal	5.6 g	3.4 g	11.9 g	11.1 g	0.9 g	3.6 g

	4 portions	10 portions
carrots	600 g	1½ kg
salt, pepper		
butter or margarine	25 g	60 g

1 Wash, peel and rewash the carrots. Cut into pieces.
2 Barely cover with water, add a little salt. Simmer gently or steam until tender.
3 Drain well. Pass through a sieve or mouli.
4 Return to the pan, reheat and mix in the fat, correct the seasoning, and serve.

HEALTHY EATING TIP
• Use the minimum amount of salt.

15 Vichy carrots (carottes Vichy)

Cal	Cal	Fat	Sat Fat	Carb	Sugar	Protein	Fibre
338 KJ	82 kcal	5.4 g	3.4 g	8.0 g	7.5 g	0.7 g	2.4 g

1 Use the same ingredients as for buttered carrots (recipe 12), but substitute Vichy water for the liquid.
2 Peel and wash the carrots (which should not be larger than 2 cm in diameter).
3 Cut into 2 mm-thin slices on the mandolin.
4 Cook and serve as for buttered carrots.

HEALTHY EATING TIP
• Use the minimum amount of salt.

* Using water only

16 Carrots in cream sauce (carottes à la crème)

Cal	Cal	Fat	Sat Fat	Carb	Sugar	Protein	Fibre	*
511 KJ	123 kcal	8.2 g	4.6 g	11.5 g	7.8 g	1.4 g	2.5 g	

	4 portions	10 portions
carrots	400 g	1 kg
salt, pepper		
butter	25 g	60 g
parsley, chopped		
cream sauce	100 ml	250 ml

1 Prepare and cook carrots as for buttered carrots (recipe 12).
2 Mix with the sauce, correct the seasoning and serve.

Note: The cream sauce may be made with wholemeal flour, skimmed milk and natural yoghurt, or see page 52.

HEALTHY EATING TIP
• Use the minimum amount of salt.
• Try using half the amount of cream sauce and half natural yoghurt.

* Using a cream sauce based on béchamel with single cream added 40 : 10

Mushroom

17 Stuffed mushrooms (champignons farcis)

Cal	Cal	Fat	Sat Fat	Carb	Sugar	Protein	Fibre	*
577 KJ	137 kcal	13.1 g	1.8 g	3.2 g	0.3 g	1.9 g	2.1 g	

	4 portions	10 portions
grilling mushrooms	300 g	1 kg
shallots, chopped	10 g	25 g
butter, margarine or oil	50 g	125 g
breadcrumbs	25 g	60 g

1 Peel the mushrooms, remove stalks and wash well.
2 Retain 8 or 12 of the best mushrooms. Finely chop the remainder with the well-washed peelings and stalks.
3 Cook the shallots, without colour, in a little fat.
4 Add the chopped mushrooms and cook for 3–4 minutes (duxelle).

5 Grill the mushrooms as in recipe 17.
6 Place the duxelle in the centre of each mushroom.
7 Sprinkle with a few breadcrumbs and some melted butter.
8 Reheat in the oven or under the salamander; serve.

HEALTHY EATING TIP
• Use a little unsaturated oil to cook the shallots.

* Using sunflower oil

18 Grilled mushrooms (champignons grillés)

Cal	Cal	Fat	Sat Fat	Carb	Sugar	Protein	Fibre	*
499 KJ	119 kcal	12.8 g	1.7 g	0.0 g	0.0 g	0.9 g	1.3 g	

	4 portions	10 portions
grilling mushrooms	200 g	500 g
salt, pepper		
butter, margarine or oil	50 g	125 g

1 Peel the mushrooms, remove the stalks; wash and drain well.
2 Place on a tray and season lightly with salt and pepper.
3 Brush with melted fat or oil and grill on both sides for 3–4 minutes. Serve with picked parsley.

HEALTHY EATING TIP
• Use the minimum amount of salt.

* Using sunflower oil

Cabbage

19 Cabbage (chou vert)

Cal	Cal	Fat	Sat Fat	Carb	Sugar	Protein	Fibre
38 KJ	9 kcal	0.0 g	0.0 g	1.1 g	1.1 g	1.3 g	2.5 g

½ kg will serve 3–4 portions; 1¼ kg will serve 8–10 portions

1 Cut the cabbage in quarters.
2 Remove the centre stalk and outside leaves.
3 Shred and wash well.
4 Place into boiling lightly salted water.
5 Boil steadily or steam until cooked (approx. 5–10 minutes, according to age and type). Do not overcook.
6 Drain immediately in a colander and serve.

Note: Overcooking will lessen the vitamin content and also spoil the colour. This applies to cooking any green vegetable.

20 Spring greens (choux de printemps)

½ kg will serve 3–4 portions; 1¼ kg will serve 8–10 portions

Prepare and cook as for cabbage (recipe 18), for 10–15 minutes according to age and type. Do not overcook.

21 Stir-fry cabbage with mushrooms and beansprouts

Cal	Cal	Fat	Sat Fat	Carb	Sugar	Protein	Fibre
393 KJ	94 kcal	6.3 g	0.8 g	5.9 g	4.7 g	4.0 g	3.3 g

	4 portions	10 portions
sunflower oil	2 tbsp	5 tbsp
spring cabbage, shredded	400 g	1 kg
soy sauce	2 tbsp	5 tbsp
mushrooms	200 g	500 g
beansprouts	100 g	250 g
freshly ground pepper		

1 Heat the oil in a suitable pan (e.g. a wok).
2 Add the cabbage and stir for 2 minutes.
3 Add the soy sauce, stir well. Cook for a further minute.
4 Add the mushrooms, cut into slices, and cook for a further 2 minutes.
5 Stir in the beansprouts and cook for 1–2 minutes.
6 Stir well. Season with freshly ground pepper and serve.

Note: This recipe can be prepared without the mushrooms and/or beansprouts if desired.
Pak choi, a small Chinese cabbage, is ideal for this dish.

HEALTHY EATING TIP
• Reduce the oil by half when cooking the cabbage.
• No added salt is needed as soy sauce is used.

Figure 12.4 Vegetables from the cabbage family (clockwise from top left): kale, broccoli, cauliflower, Brussels sprouts, kohlrabi

22 Braised cabbage *(choux braisés)*

Cal	Cal	Fat	Sat Fat	Carb	Sugar	Protein	Fibre
215 KJ	52 kcal	0.6 g	0.2 g	9.4 g	8.5 g	2.6 g	4.0 g

	4 portions	10 portions
cabbage	½ kg	1¼ kg
salt, pepper		
carrots, sliced	100 g	250 g
onions, sliced	100 g	250 g
white stock	250 ml	625 ml
bouquet garni		
jus-lié	125 ml	300 ml

1 Quarter the cabbage, remove the centre stalk and wash.
2 Retain four (or ten) light green leaves, shred the remainder.
3 Blanch the leaves and shredded cabbage for 2–3 minutes; refresh.
4 Lay the blanched leaves flat on the table.
5 Place the remainder of the cabbage on the centre of each and season.
6 Wrap each portion of cabbage in a clean tea towel and shape into a fairly firm ball.
7 Remove from the tea towel. Place on a bed of sliced carrots and onions.
8 Add the stock halfway up cabbage, season and add the bouquet garni.
9 Bring to the boil, cover with a lid and cook in the oven for 1 hour.
10 Dress the cabbage in a serving dish.
11 Add the cooking liquor to the jus-lié, correct the seasoning and consistency; strain.
12 Pour over the cabbage and serve.

Note: Braised stuffed cabbage can be made with the addition of 25–50 g (60–125 g for 10 portions) sausage meat placed in the centre before shaping into a ball. This recipe can also be prepared using Chinese leaves.

HEALTHY EATING TIP
• Use the minimum amount of salt; rely on the stock for flavour.

23 Sauerkraut (pickled white cabbage) (choucroûte)

Cal	Cal	Fat	Sat Fat	Carb	Sugar	Protein	Fibre
75.5 KJ	19 kcal	0.1 g	0.0 g	3.2 g	2.8 g	1.3 g	2.7 g

	4 portions	10 portions
salt, pepper		
sauerkraut	400 g	1¼ kg
studded onion	50 g	125 g
carrot	50 g	125 g
bouquet garni		
peppercorns	6	15
juniper berries	6	15
white stock	250 ml	625 ml

1 Season the sauerkraut and place in a casserole or pan suitable for use in the oven.
2 Add the whole onion and carrot, the bouquet garni, peppercorns and berries.
3 Barely cover with good white stock. Cook with a buttered paper and lid.
4 Cook slowly in a moderate oven for 3–4 hours.
5 Remove the bouquet garni and onion. Cut the onion into slices.
6 Serve the sauerkraut garnished with slices of carrot.

Note: Garnished sauerkraut can be served as a main course (see page 327).

24 Braised red cabbage (choux à la flamande)

Cal	Cal	Fat	Sat Fat	Carb	Sugar	Protein	Fibre
754 KJ	180 kcal	15.2 g	8.4 g	7.8 g	7.7 g	3.4 g	3.2 g

	4 portions	10 portions
red cabbage	300 g	1 kg
salt, pepper		
butter	50 g	125 g
cooking apples	100 g	250 g
caster sugar	10 g	25 g
vinegar or red wine	125 ml	300 ml
bacon trimmings (optional)	50 g	125 g

Note: Other optional flavourings include 50 g sultanas, grated zest of one orange, pinch of ground cinnamon.

HEALTHY EATING TIP
• The fat and salt content will be reduced by omitting the bacon.

1 Quarter, trim and shred the cabbage. Wash well and drain.
2 Season lightly with salt and pepper.
3 Place in a well-buttered casserole or pan suitable for placing in the oven (not aluminium or iron because these metals will cause a chemical reaction that will discolour the cabbage).
4 Add the peeled and cored apples. Cut into 1 cm dice and sugar.
5 Add the vinegar and bacon (if using), cover with a buttered paper and lid.
6 Cook in a moderate oven at 150–200°C for 1½ hours.
7 Remove the bacon (if used) and serve.

Figure 12.5 Braised red cabbage

484

Brussels sprouts

25 Brussels sprouts *(choux de bruxelles)*

Cal	Cal	Fat	Sat Fat	Carb	Sugar	Protein	Fibre
82 KJ	20 kcal	0.0 g	0.0 g	1.9 g	1.8 g	3.1 g	3.2 g

½ kg will serve 3–4 portions; 1¼ kg will serve 8–10 portions

1 Using a small knife trim the stems and cut a cross 2 mm deep; remove any discoloured leaves. Wash well.
2 Cook in boiling lightly salted water, or steam, for 5–10 minutes according to size. Do not overcook.
3 Drain well in a colander and serve.

Note: Brussels sprouts with butter are cooked and served as outlined here, but brushed with 25–50 g melted butter (60–125 g for 10 portions). For Brussels sprouts with chestnuts, to every 400 g sprouts add 100 g cooked peeled chestnuts.

Cauliflower

26 Cauliflower *(chou-fleur nature)*

Cal	Cal	Fat	Sat Fat	Carb	Sugar	Protein	Fibre	*
142 KJ	34 kcal	0.9 g	0.2 g	3.0 g	2.5 g	3.6 g	1.8 g	

1 Allow 1 medium-sized cauliflower for 4 portions. Trim the stem and remove the outer leaves.
2 Hollow out the stem with a peeler or cut into florets. Wash.
3 Cook in lightly salted boiling water, or steam, for approximately 10–15 minutes. Do not overcook (if cut into florets, cook for only 3–5 minutes).
4 Drain well and serve cut into 4 even portions.

Note: Buttered cauliflower is brushed with 25–50 g melted butter before serving and can be sprinkled with chopped parsley.
Variations
Other variations include the following.

● Cauliflower fried in butter
1 Cut the cooked cauliflower into 4 portions.
2 Lightly colour on all sides in 25–50 g butter.

● Cauliflower, cream sauce
1 Cook and serve as for cauliflower.
2 Accompany with ½ litre cream sauce in a sauceboat.

● Cauliflower, melted butter
As for cauliflower, with a sauceboat of 100 g melted butter (see page 65).

● Cauliflower, hollandaise sauce
As for cauliflower, accompanied by a sauceboat of 1/8 litre hollandaise sauce (see page 63).

Note: Multiply the above quantities by 2½ for 10 portions.

* *Using no additions*

27 Cauliflower and garlic mash

1 Blend one cooked cauliflower with four roasted and peeled garlic cloves and 1 tbsp of virgin olive oil.
2 Season and finish with chopped parsley.
3 Suitable for serving with roast or baked cod.

28 Cauliflower au gratin, or cauliflower mornay (chou-fleur mornay)

Cal	Cal	Fat	Sat Fat	Carb	Sugar	Protein	Fibre	*
632 KJ	150 kcal	10.4 g	3.9 g	8.6 g	3.8 g	6.3 g	2.0 g	

1 Cut the cooked cauliflower into four.
2 Reheat in a pan of hot salted water (chauffant), or reheat in butter in a suitable pan.
3 Place in vegetable dish or on a greased tray.
4 Coat with ¼ litre mornay sauce (see page 52).
5 Sprinkle with grated cheese.
6 Brown under the salamander and serve.

HEALTHY EATING TIP
• No additional salt is needed as cheese is added.

* au gratin

29 Cauliflower polonaise (chou-fleur polonaise)

Cal	Cal	Fat	Sat Fat	Carb	Sugar	Protein	Fibre
575 KJ	139 kcal	11.9 g	6.9 g	4.1 g	1.9 g	4.0 g	1.7 g

1 Cut the cooked cauliflower into four. Reheat in a chauffant or in butter in a suitable pan.
2 Heat 50 g butter, add 10 g fresh breadcrumbs in a frying pan and lightly brown. Pour over the cauliflower, sprinkle with sieved hardboiled egg and chopped parsley.

Broccoli

30 Broccoli

Cal	Cal	Fat	Sat Fat	Carb	Sugar	Protein	Fibre
76 KJ	18 kcal	0.0 g	0.0 g	1.6 g	1.5 g	3.1 g	4.1 g

Cook and serve as for any of the cauliflower recipes (recipes 25–28). Green and purple broccoli, because of their size, need less cooking time than cauliflower. Broccoli is usually broken down into florets and, as such, requires very little cooking: once brought to the boil, 1–2 minutes should be sufficient. This leaves the broccoli slightly crisp.

Kale

31 Sea kale (chou de mer)

Cal	Cal	Fat	Sat Fat	Carb	Sugar	Protein	Fibre
33 KJ	8 kcal	0.0 g	0.0 g	0.6 g	0.6 g	1.4 g	0.0 g

½ kg will yield about 3 portions

1 Trim the roots and remove any discoloured leaves.
2 Wash well and tie into a neat bundle.
3 Cook in boiling lightly salted water for 15–20 minutes. Do not overcook.
4 Drain well, serve accompanied with a suitable sauce (e.g. melted butter, hollandaise).

32 Sea kale mornay or sea kale au gratin (chou de mer mornay)

Cal	Cal	Fat	Sat Fat	Carb	Sugar	Protein	Fibre
678 KJ	157 kcal	10.4 g	3.9 g	8.4 g	3.6 g	6.1 g	1.4 g

1 Trim the roots. Remove any discoloured leaves. Wash well and tie into a neat bundle. Cook in boiling salted water for 15–20 minutes. Do not overcook.
2 Reheat and cut into 5 cm lengths; place in a vegetable dish.

3 Coat with ½ litre mornay sauce (page 52) and sprinkle with grated cheese.
4 Brown under the salamander and serve.

Kohlrabi

33 Kohlrabi

Information about this vegetable can be found in *Advanced Practical Cookery*, listed in the References at the end of this chapter.

Spinach

34 Leaf spinach (epinards en branches)

Cal	Cal	Fat	Sat Fat	Carb	Sugar	Protein	Fibre	*
512 KJ	123 kcal	10.8 g	6.6 g	1.4 g	1.2 g	5.2 g	6.3 g	

½ kg will yield 2 portions

1 Remove the stems and discard them.
2 Wash the leaves very carefully in plenty of water, several times if necessary.
3 Wilt for 2–3 minutes, taking care not to overcook.
4 Place on a tray and allow to cool.

5 When required for service, either reheat and serve plain or place into a pan containing 25–50 g butter, loosen with a fork and reheat quickly without colouring.

* Using 25 g butter per ½ kg

35 Spinach purée (epinards en purée)

Cal	Cal	Fat	Sat Fat	Carb	Sugar	Protein	Fibre	*
588 KJ	143 kcal	11.9 g	6.7 g	3.3 g	3.1 g	5.7 g	4.2 g	

1 Cook, refresh and drain the spinach as above.
2 Pass through a sieve or mouli, or use a food processor.
3 Reheat in 25–50 g butter, mix with a wooden spoon, correct the seasoning and serve.

Note: Creamed spinach purée can be made by mixing in 30 ml cream and 60 ml béchamel or natural yoghurt before serving. Serve with a border of cream. An addition would be 1 cm triangle-shaped croutons fried in butter. Spinach may also be served with toasted pine kernels or finely chopped garlic.

* Using 25 g butter per ½ kg

Celery

36 Braised celery (céleri braisé)

Cal	Cal	Fat	Sat Fat	Carb	Sugar	Protein	Fibre	*
505 KJ	120 kcal	10.2 g	4.1 g	4.8 g	4.5 g	2.8 g	3.8 g	

	4 portions	10 portions
heads of celery	2	5
carrots, sliced	100 g	250 g
onion, sliced	100 g	250 g
bouquet garni		
white stock	¼ litre	625 ml
salt, pepper		
fat bacon or suet	50 g	125 g
crusts of bread	2	5
jus-lié or demi-glace		

1 Trim the celery heads and the root, cut off the outside discoloured stalks and cut the heads to approximately 15 cm lengths.
2 Wash well under running cold water.
3 Place in a pan of boiling water. Simmer for about 20 minutes until limp. Refresh and rewash.
4 Place the sliced vegetables in a sauté pan, sauteuse or casserole.
5 Add the celery heads whole or cut them in half lengthwise, fold over and place on the bed of roots.
6 Add the bouquet garni, barely cover with stock and season lightly.
7 Add the fat bacon or suet and the crusts of bread, cover with a buttered greaseproof paper and a tight lid, and cook gently in a moderate oven at 150–200°C for 2 hours or until tender.
8 Remove the celery from the pan, drain well and dress neatly.
9 Add the cooking liquor to an equal amount of jus-lié or demi-glace, reduce and correct the seasoning and consistency.
10 Mask the celery, finish with chopped parsley, and serve.

HEALTHY EATING TIP
- Use the minimum amount of salt.
- Use little or no bacon or suet.

Marrow and courgette

37 Marrow (courge)

Cal	Cal	Fat	Sat Fat	Carb	Sugar	Protein	Fibre
44 KJ	11 kcal	0.0 g	0.0 g	2.1 g	2.0 g	0.6 g	0.9 g

1 Peel the marrow with a peeler or small knife.
2 Cut in half lengthwise.
3 Remove the seeds with a spoon.
4 Cut into even pieces, approximately 5 cm square.
5 Cook in lightly salted boiling water, or steam, for 10–15 minutes. Do not overcook.
6 Drain well and serve.

Note: All the variations for cauliflower (recipes 25–28) may be used with marrow.

38 Stuffed marrow (courge farcie)

Cal	Cal	Fat	Sat Fat	Carb	Sugar	Protein	Fibre	*
805 KJ	194 kcal	17.4 g	7.9 g	6.0 g	2.9 g	3.6 g	0.8 g	

1 Peel the marrow and cut in half lengthwise.
2 Remove the seeds with a spoon.
3 Season and add the stuffing. Replace the two halves.
4 Cook as for braised celery (recipe 35) allowing about 1 hour.
5 To serve, cut into thick slices and dress neatly in a vegetable dish. Baby marrows are ideal for this.

HEALTHY EATING TIP
- Use the minimum amount of salt.
- Use little or no bacon or suet to cook the marrow.
- Use less fatty meat and more rice in the stuffing.

Note: Various stuffings may be used: 100 g sausage meat or 100 g rice for 4 portions; cooked rice with chopped cooked meat, seasoned with salt, pepper and herbs; well-seasoned cooked rice with sliced mushroom, tomatoes, etc; ratatoille.

* With sausage stuffing

Figure 12.6   Stuffed aubergine, courgette and tomato

39 Marrow provençale (courge provençale)

Cal	Cal	Fat	Sat Fat	Carb	Sugar	Protein	Fibre
524 KJ	126 kcal	10.6 g	6.5 g	6.4	5.7 g	1.8 g	1.4 g

	4 portions	10 portions
marrow	400 g	1 kg
onion, chopped	50 g	125 g
clove garlic, chopped	1	2–3
oil or butter	50 g	125 g
salt, pepper		
tomatoes, skinned, deseeded and diced	400 g	1 kg
parsley, chopped		

1 Peel the marrow, remove the seeds and cut into 2 cm dice.
2 Cook the onion and garlic in the oil in a pan for 2–3 minutes without colour.
3 Add the marrow, season lightly with salt and pepper.
4 Add the tomato concassée.
5 Cover with a lid, cook gently in the oven or on the side of the stove for 1 hour or until tender.
6 Sprinkle with chopped parsley and serve.

Note: Baby marrows may be served similarly, but reduce the cooking time to 5–10 minutes.

HEALTHY EATING TIP
- Use a little unsaturated oil to cook the onion.
- Use the minimum amount of salt.

40 Baby marrow (courgette) *(courgette)*

Cal	Cal	Fat	Sat Fat	Carb	Sugar	Protein	Fibre
113 KJ	27 kcal	0.1 g	0.0 g	5.9 g	0.4 g	1.0 g	0.8 g

¾ kg yields about 4 portions; 2 kg yields about 10 portions)

1 Wash. Top and tail, and cut into round slices 3–6 cm thick.
2 Gently boil in lightly salted water, or steam, for 2 or 3 minutes. Do not overcook.

3 Drain well and serve either plain or brushed with melted butter or margarine and/or sprinkled with chopped parsley.

Note: Because they are tender, courgettes are not peeled or deseeded.

41 Courgettes and peppers griddled with penne and Brie

Cal	Cal	Fat	Sat Fat	Carb	Sugar	Protein	Fibre
2498 KJ	593 kcal	21.0 g	8.9 g	82.3 g	10.4 g	23.8 g	6.0 g

	4 portions	10 portions
courgettes, finely sliced	4	10
red peppers cored, deseeded, sliced	1	3
green peppers	1	3
yellow peppers	1	3
penne	400 g	1 kg
olive oil	2 tbsp	3 tbsp
Brie	175 g	400 g
dill chopped	1 tbsp	2½ tbsp
seasoning		

HEALTHY EATING TIP

• No added salt is needed; there is plenty in the cheese.

Note: Gorgonzola, Camembert or other suitable cheeses may be used.

1 Heat a griddle pan, lightly oil, place the courgettes and peppers on the pan, cook for 5 minutes, turning occasionally.
2 Cook the penne al dente, refresh, drain, reheat in olive oil.
3 Add the griddled vegetables, diced Brie and dill. Season and serve.

42 Shallow-fried courgettes *(courgettes sautées)*

Cal	Cal	Fat	Sat Fat	Carb	Sugar	Protein	Fibre	*
456 KJ	111 kcal	10.7 g	6.6 g	1.9 g	1.8 g	1.9 g	0.9 g	

1 Prepare as for recipe 39.
2 Gently fry in hot oil or butter for 2 or 3 minutes, drain and serve.

* Using butter

43 Deep-fried courgettes (courgettes frites)

Cal	Cal	Fat	Sat Fat	Carb	Sugar	Protein	Fibre	*
481 KJ	111 kcal	11.4 g	1.4 g	1.8 g	1.7 g	1.8 g	0.9 g	

1 Prepare as for recipe 39.
2 Pass through flour, or milk and flour, or batter, and deep-fry in hot fat at 185°C. Drain well and serve.

* Using vegetable oil

Squash

Squash is a vegetable of many varieties, which may be used as for any of the recipes for marrow and courgettes (recipes 36–42). Squash can also be used for ratatouille (recipe 10).

Chicory

44 Braised chicory (endive au jus)

Cal	Cal	Fat	Sat Fat	Carb	Sugar	Protein	Fibre	*
304 KJ	73 kcal	6.8 g	4.3 g	1.8 g	0.0 g	1.0 g	1.0 g	

½ kg will yield 3 portions

1 Trim the stem, remove any discoloured leaves, wash.
2 Place in a well-buttered casserole or pan suitable to place in the oven.
3 Season lightly with salt and a little sugar if desired (to counteract the bitterness).
4 Add the juice of half a lemon to prevent discoloration.
5 Add 25–50 g butter per ½ kg and a few drops of water.
6 Cover with a buttered paper and lid.
7 Cook gently in a moderate oven at 150–200°C for 1 hour.
8 Dress and serve.

* Using 25 g butter per ½ kg

45 Shallow-fried chicory (endive meunière)

Cal	Cal	Fat	Sat Fat	Carb	Sugar	Protein	Fibre	*
484 KJ	118 kcal	12.0 g	7.3 g	4.8 g	1.3 g	0.9 g	1.5 g	

1 Cook the chicory as for recipe 43.
2 Drain, shallow-fry in a little butter and colour lightly on both sides.
3 Serve with 10 g per portion nut brown butter, lemon juice and chopped parsley.

* Using 37.5 g butter

Beans

46 Broad beans (fèves)

Cal	Cal	Fat	Sat Fat	Carb	Sugar	Protein	Fibre	*
344 KJ	81 kcal	0.6 g	0.1 g	5.0 g	0.4 g	7.9 g	6.5 g	

½ kg will yield about 2 portions

1 Shell the beans and cook in boiling salted water for 10–15 minutes until tender. Do not overcook.
2 If the inner shells are tough, remove before serving.

Variations
Variations include:
● brushing with butter
● brushing with butter then sprinkling with chopped parsley
● binding with ½ litre cream sauce or fresh cream.

* 100g portion

47 French beans (haricots verts)

Cal	Cal	Fat	Sat Fat	Carb	Sugar	Protein	Fibre
646 KJ	154 kcal	2.9 g	0.5 g	28.5 g	2.1 g	5.1 g	5.9 g

½ kg will yield 3–4 portions

1 Top and tail the beans, carefully and economically.
2 Using a large sharp knife cut the beans into strips 5 cm × 3 mm.
3 Wash.
4 Cook in lightly salted boiling water, or steam, for 5–10 minutes, until tender.
5 Do not overcook. Drain well and serve.

Variations
Variations include:
● brushing the beans with butter
● gently tossing the cooked beans in butter over heat without colour
● adding to 400 g cooked French beans, 50 g shallow-fried onions
● combining 400 g cooked French beans with 100 g cooked flageolet beans.

48 Runner beans

Cal	Cal	Fat	Sat Fat	Carb	Sugar	Protein	Fibre
80 KJ	19 kcal	0.2 g	0.0 g	2.7 g	00.0 1.3	1.9 g	3.4 g

1 Wash and string the beans with a small knife, then cut them into thin strips approximately 4–6 cm long.
2 Cook in boiling lightly salted water, or steam, for approximately 10 minutes.
3 Drain well and serve. Do not overcook.

Sweetcorn

49 Corn on the cob (maïs)

Cal	Cal	Fat	Sat Fat	Carb	Sugar	Protein	Fibre
646 KJ	154 kcal	2.9 g	0.5 g	28.5 g	2.1 g	5.1 g	5.9 g

Allow 1 cob per portion

1 Trim the stem.
2 Cook in lightly salted boiling water for 10–20 minutes or until the corn is tender. Do not overcook.
3 Remove the outer leaves and fibres.
4 Serve with a sauceboat of melted butter.

Note: Creamed sweetcorn can be made by removing the corn from the cooked cobs, draining well and binding lightly with cream (fresh or non-dairy), béchamel or yoghurt.

Celeriac

50 Celeriac

Cal	Cal	Fat	Sat Fat	Carb	Sugar	Protein	Fibre	
264 KJ	65 kcal	5.5 g	3.3 g	2.3 g	3.3 g	1.2 g	3.7 g	*

Celeriac, or celery root, makes an excellent soup and is a versatile vegetable that can be prepared and served raw as an hors d'oeuvre or as a hot vegetable using any of the carrot recipes (recipes 12–15).

* Using butter

51 Buttered celeriac, turnips or swedes

Cal	Cal	Fat	Sat Fat	Carb	Sugar	Protein	Fibre
253 KJ	60 kcal	5.4 g	3.3	2.5 g	2.5 g	0.7 g	1.9 g

	4 portions	10 portions
celeriac, turnips or swedes	400 g	1 kg
salt, sugar		
butter	25 g	60 g
parsley, chopped		

1 Peel and wash the vegetables.
2 Cut into neat pieces or turn barrel shaped.
3 Place in a pan with a little salt, a pinch of sugar and the butter. Barely cover with water.
4 Cover with a buttered paper and allow to boil steadily in order to evaporate all the water.
5 When the water has completely evaporated check that the vegetables are cooked; if not, add a little more water and continue cooking. Do not overcook.
6 Toss the vegetables over a fierce heat for 1–2 minutes to glaze.
7 Drain well, and serve sprinkled with chopped parsley.

52 Purée of celeriac, turnips, swedes or parsnips

Cal	Cal	Fat	Sat Fat	Carb	Sugar	Protein	Fibre	*
395 KJ	95 kcal	5.9 g	3.3 g	9.2 g	6.4 g	1.8 g	4.7 g	

	4 portions	10 portions
celeriac, turnips, swedes or parsnips	600 g	1½ kg
salt, pepper		
butter	25 g	60 g

1 Wash, peel and rewash the vegetables. Cut into pieces if necessary.
2 Barely cover with water; add a little salt.
3 Simmer gently until tender, or steam. Drain well.
4 Pass through a sieve or mouli, or use a food processor.
5 Return to the pan, reheat and mix in the butter, correct the seasoning and serve.

Variations
Combination vegetable purée can include, for example, swede and carrot, parsnip and potato.

* *Using mixed vegetables and 25 g butter*

Figure 12.7 Root vegetables (left to right): parsnip, carrots, celeriac, horseradish, radishes, mooli

Parsnip

53 Parsnips (panais)

Cal	Cal	Fat	Sat Fat	Carb	Sugar	Protein	Fibre
235 KJ	56 kcal	0.0 g	0.0 g	13.5 g	2.7 g	1.3 g	2.5 g

1 Wash well. Peel the parsnips and re-wash well.
2 Cut into quarters lengthwise, remove the centre root if tough.
3 Cut into neat pieces and cook in lightly salted water until tender, or steam.
4 Drain and serve with melted butter or in a cream sauce.

Note: Parsnips may be roasted in the oven in a little fat or in with a joint, and can be cooked and prepared as a purée.

Salsify

54 Salsify (salsifi)

Cal	Cal	Fat	Sat Fat	Carb	Sugar	Protein	Fibre
76 KJ	18 kcal	0.0 g	0.0 g	2.8 g	2.8 g	1.9 g	0.0 g

½ kg will yield 2–3 portions

1 Wash, peel and rewash the salsify.
2 Cut into 5 cm lengths.
3 Cook in a blanc as for artichokes (recipe 3). Do not overcook.

4 Salsify may then be served as for any of the cauliflower recipes (recipes 25–28). It may also be passed through batter and deep-fried.

Note: Alternatively, salsify may be cooked in boiling water acidulated with ascorbic acid.

The thicker part of the root cooks more quickly than the thin part due to the density variance of this vegetable.

Beetroot

55 Beetroot *(betterave)*

Cal	Cal	Fat	Sat Fat	Carb	Sugar	Protein	Fibre
92 KJ	22 kcal	0.0 g	0.0 g	5.0 g	5.0 g	0.9 g	1.3 g

1 Select medium-sized or small beetroots, carefully twist off the green leaves (do not cut).
2 Wash well in cold water, cover with water and simmer gently until the skin is easily removed by rubbing between the fingers.

Note: Do not cut or prick with a knife as the beetroots will 'bleed' and turn pale.

Variations
Beetroot may also be cooked in a steamer, and can also be served hot:
● in cream sauce
● coated in herb-flavoured oil (see page 68)
● coated in butter and marmalade.

56 Golden beetroot with Parmesan

	4 portions	10 portions
golden beetroot	400 g	1 kg
Parmesan, freshly grated	50 g	125 g
seasoning		

1 Peel the golden beetroot and cut into 5 mm slices. Either steam or plain boil until tender.
2 Drain well and place in a suitable serving dish. Sprinkle with Parmesan and grill under the salamander or in the oven.

Onion

57 Fried onions (oignons sautées ou oignons lyonnaise)

Cal	Cal	Fat	Sat Fat	Carb	Sugar	Protein	Fibre	*
681 KJ	162 kcal	12.9 g	2.4 g	10.4 g	00.0	1.8 g	2.6 g	
					10.4			

½ kg will yield approximately 2 portions

1 Peel and wash the onions, cut in halves, slice finely.
2 Cook slowly in 25–50 g oil in a frying pan, turning frequently until tender and nicely browned; season lightly with salt.

HEALTHY EATING TIP
• Use a little unsaturated oil to cook the onion.
• Use the minimum amount of salt.

* *Using peanut oil*

58 French-fried onions (oignons frites à la française)

Cal 661 KJ	Cal 159 kcal	Fat 11.7 g	Sat Fat 1.6 g	Carb 12.3 g	Sugar 3.5 g	Protein 2.0 g	Fibre 1.0 g	*

1 Peel and wash the onions.
2 Cut into 2 mm slices, against the grain. Separate into rings.
3 Pass through milk and seasoned flour.
4 Shake off the surplus. Deep-fry in hot fat at 185°C.
5 Drain well on kitchen paper, season lightly with salt and serve.

HEALTHY EATING TIP
• Make sure the oil is hot so that less is absorbed into the onions.
• Drain on kitchen paper.
• Use the minimum amount of salt.

* Using 50 g onions, to give 83.5 g finished weight

Figure 12.8 ✒ Preparation and cooking of French-fried onions

59 Braised onions (oignons braisés)

Cal 245 KJ	Cal 58 kcal	Fat 0.4 g	Sat Fat 0.1 g	Carb 10.9 g	Sugar 10.4 g	Protein 3.4 g	Fibre 2.8 g

1 Select medium even-sized onions, allow ½ kg per 2–3 portions.
2 Peel, wash and cook in lightly salted boiling water for 30 minutes, or steam.
3 Drain and place in a pan or casserole suitable for use in the oven.
4 Add bouquet garni, half cover with stock; put on the lid and braise gently at 180–200°C in the oven until tender.

5 Drain well and dress neatly in a vegetable dish.
6 Reduce the cooking liquor with an equal amount of jus-lié or demi-glace. Correct the seasoning and consistency and pass. Mask the onions and sprinkle with chopped parsley.

Note: A more modern approach is to use balsamic vinegar to deglaze; demi-glace is rarely used.

Leek

60 Braised leeks (poireaux braisés)

Cal	Cal	Fat	Sat Fat	Carb	Sugar	Protein	Fibre
130 KJ	31 kcal	0.0 g	0.0 g	5.6 g	5.4 g	2.3 g	2.8 g

½ kg of leeks will yield 2 portions

1 Cut the roots from the leeks, remove any discoloured outside leaves and trim the green.
2 Cut through lengthwise and wash well under running water.
3 Tie into a neat bundle.
4 Place in boiling lightly salted water for 5 minutes, or steam.
5 Place on a bed of root vegetables.
6 Barely cover with stock, add the bouquet garni and season lightly.
7 Cover with a lid and cook for ½–1 hour or until tender.
8 Remove the leeks from the pan and fold neatly; arrange in a vegetable dish.
9 Meanwhile add jus-lié to the cooking liquor; correct the seasoning and consistency.
10 Pour the sauce over the leeks.

Note: Boiled leeks are prepared as above, cooking for 10–15 minutes. Drain well, cut the string and serve plain or brushed with melted butter. Leeks may also be served coated with cream or parsley sauce.

Peas

61 Peas

Cal	Cal	Fat	Sat Fat	Carb	Sugar	Protein	Fibre
62 KJ	260 kcal	0.4 g	0.1 g	9.8 g	3.7 g	5.4 g	4.8 g

1 kg of fresh peas and ¼ kg of frozen peas will yield about 4 portions; ½ kg of mangetout will yield 4–6 portions

Fresh peas
1 Shell and wash the peas.
2 Cook in lightly salted boiling water or steam with a sprig of mint until tender. Do not overcook. Drain in a colander.
3 Add 25 g butter and ½ tsp caster sugar, toss gently.
4 Serve with blanched, refreshed mint leaves.

Frozen peas
1 Cook in lightly salted boiling water for approximately 1 minute or until tender. Drain in a colander.
2 Add 25 g butter and ½ tsp caster sugar; toss gently (optional).
3 Serve with blanched refreshed mint leaves.

Mangetout
1 Top and tail, wash and drain.
2 Cook in boiling salted water for 2–3 minutes, until slightly crisp.
3 Serve whole, brushed with butter.

Sugar snap peas
1 Proceed as for mangetout.

62 Peas French-style (petit pois à la française)

Cal	Cal	Fat	Sat Fat	Carb	Sugar	Protein	Fibre
515 KJ	123 kcal	5.6 g	3.4 g	12.9 g	5.8 g	5.9 g	5.7 g

	4 portions	10 portions
peas (in the pod)	1 kg	2½ kg
spring or button onions	12	40
small lettuce	1	2–3
butter	25 g	60 g
salt		
caster sugar	½ tsp	1 tsp
flour	5 g	12 g

1 Shell and wash the peas and place in a sauteuse.
2 Peel and wash the onions, shred the lettuce and add to the peas with half the butter, a little salt and the sugar.
3 Barely cover with water. Cover with a lid and cook steadily, preferably in the oven, until tender.
4 Correct the seasoning.
5 Mix the remaining butter with the flour and shake into the boiling peas until thoroughly mixed; serve.

Note: When using frozen peas, allow the onions to almost cook before adding the peas.

Pimento

63 Stuffed pimento (piment farci)

Cal	Cal	Fat	Sat Fat	Carb	Sugar	Protein	Fibre
1291 KJ	308 kcal	11.4 g	6.7 g	48.8 g	5.3 g	5.4 g	3.1 g

	4 portions	10 portions
medium-sized red pimentos	4	10
carrots, sliced	50 g	125 g
onions, sliced	50 g	125 g
bouquet garni		
white stock	½ litre	1¼ litres
salt, pepper		
Pilaff		
rice (long grain)	200 g	500 g
salt, pepper		
onion, chopped	50 g	125 g
butter	50 g	125 g

1 Place the pimentos on a tray in the oven or under the salamander for a few minutes, or deep-fry in hot oil at 180°C, until the skin blisters, or use a blow torch to remove the skin.
2 Remove the skin and stalk carefully, and empty out all the seeds.
3 Stuff with a well-seasoned pilaff of rice (ingredients as listed above), which may be varied by the addition of mushrooms, tomatoes, ham, etc.

4 Replace the stem.
5 Place the pimentos on the sliced carrot and onion in a pan suitable for the oven; add the bouquet garni, stock and seasoning. Cover with a buttered paper and lid.
6 Cook in a moderate oven at 180–200°C for 1 hour or until tender.
7 Serve garnished with picked parsley.

HEALTHY EATING TIP

- This dish is low in fat if the pimentos are placed in the oven or under the salamander and the butter/oil kept to a minimum.
- Add little or no salt.
- If extra vegetables are added to the rice, and a vegetable stock used, this dish can be a useful vegetarian starter.

Tomato

64 Grilled tomatoes (tomates grillées)

Cal 121 KJ	Cal 29 kcal	Fat 1.3 g	Sat Fat 0.3 g	Carb 3.5 g	Sugar 3.5 g	Protein 1.1 g	Fibre 1.9 g	*

Allow 1 or 2 per portion according to size; ½ kg will yield 3–4 portions.

1 Wash the tomatoes, and remove the eyes with a small knife.
2 Place on a greased, seasoned baking tray.
3 Make an incision 2 mm cross-shape on the opposite side to the eye and peel back the four corners.
4 Brush with oil and season lightly with salt and pepper.
5 Grill under a moderately hot salamander. Serve garnished with picked parsley or fresh basil leaves.

HEALTHY EATING TIP
• Use a little unsaturated oil to brush over the tomatoes.
• Add a minimum amount of salt.

* Using sunflower oil

65 Stuffed tomatoes (tomates farcies)

Cal 430 KJ	Cal 102 kcal	Fat 5.9 g	Sat Fat 3.5 g	Carb 10.6 g	Sugar 5.7 g	Protein 2.5 g	Fibre 2.2 g

	4 portions	10 portions
medium-sized tomatoes	8	20
Duxelle		
shallots, chopped	10 g	25 g
butter, oil or margarine	25 g	60 g
mushrooms	150 g	375 g
salt, pepper		
clove garlic, crushed (optional)	1	2–3
breadcrumbs (white or wholemeal)	25 g	60 g
parsley, chopped		

1 Wash the tomatoes, remove the eyes.
2 Remove ¼ of the tomato with a sharp knife.
3 Carefully empty out the seeds without damaging the flesh.
4 Place on a greased baking tray.
5 Cook the shallots in a little oil, butter or margarine without colour.
6 Add the washed chopped mushrooms, season with salt and pepper; add the garlic if using and cook for 2–3 minutes.
7 Add a little of the strained tomato juice, the breadcrumbs and the parsley; mix to a piping consistency. Correct the seasoning. At this stage several additions may be made (e.g. chopped ham, cooked rice).
8 Place the mixture in a piping bag with a large star tube and pipe into the tomato shells. Replace the tops.
9 Brush with oil, season lightly with salt and pepper.
10 Cook in a moderate oven at 180–200°C for 4–5 minutes.
11 Serve garnished with picked parsley or fresh basil or rosemary.

HEALTHY EATING TIP
• Use a small amount of an unsaturated oil to cook the shallots and brush over the stuffed tomatoes.
• Add the minimum amount of salt.
• Adding cooked rice to the stuffing will increase the amount of starchy carbohydrate.

66 Basic tomato preparation (tomate concassée)

	4 portions	10 portions
tomatoes	400 g	1¼ kg
shallots or onions, chopped	25 g	60 g
butter, margarine or oil	25 g	60 g
salt, pepper		

1 Plunge the tomatoes into boiling water for 5–10 seconds – the riper the tomatoes the less time is required. Refresh immediately.
2 Remove the skins, cut in halves across the tomato and remove all the seeds.
3 Roughly chop the flesh of the tomatoes.
4 Meanwhile, cook the chopped onion or shallot without colour in the oil, butter or margarine.
5 Add the tomatoes and season lightly.
6 Simmer gently on the side of the stove until the moisture is evaporated.

Note: This is a cooked preparation that is usually included in the normal *mise-en-place* of a kitchen as it is used in a great number of dishes.

Fennel

67 Fennel (fenouil)

Cal	Cal	Fat	Sat Fat	Carb	Sugar	Protein	Fibre
21 KJ	5 kcal	0.0 g	0.0 g	0.7 g	0.7 g	0.6 g	2.2 g

1 Trim the bulb, remove the stalks and leaves and wash well.
2 Cook in lightly salted boiling water for 15–20 minutes. Do not overcook.
3 Drain well, cut into portions and serve as for any of the cauliflower recipes (recipes 25–28).

Note: The foliage of this plant is a herb of distinctive flavour used in fish cookery and salads. One good-sized bulb will serve 2–4 portions. Fennel may also be braised as for celery (recipe 35).

Okra

68 Ladies' fingers (okra) in cream sauce (okra à la crème)

Cal	Cal	Fat	Sat Fat	Carb	Sugar	Protein	Fibre	*
928 KJ	221 kcal	20.2 g	9.8 g	5.7 g	5.7 g	4.4 g	3.2 g	

	4 portions	10 portions
ladies' fingers (okra)	400 g	1½ kg
butter or margarine	50 g	125 g
cream sauce	¼ litre	625 ml

1 Top and tail the ladies' fingers.
2 Blanch in lightly salted boiling water, or steam; drain.
3 Sweat in the margarine or butter for 5–10 minutes, or until tender.
4 Carefully add the cream sauce.
5 Bring to the boil, correct the seasoning and serve in a suitable dish.

Note: Okra may also be served brushed with butter or sprinkled with chopped parsley.

HEALTHY EATING TIP
- Use a little unsaturated oil to sweat the okra.
- Try using half cream sauce and half yoghurt, adding very little salt.

* *Using hard margarine*

Figure 12.9 ✏ Clockwise from top left: okra, sweetcorn, French beans, mangetout, peas, beansprouts

Miscellaneous

69 Mixed vegetables (macédoine de légumes, Jardinière de légumes)

Cal	Cal	Fat	Sat Fat	Carb	Sugar	Protein	Fibre
58 KJ	14 kcal	0.1 g	0.0 g	2.5 g	1.7 g	1.0 g	2.1 g

	4 portions	10 portions
carrots	100 g	250 g
turnips	50 g	125 g
salt		
French beans	50 g	125 g
peas	50 g	125 g

1 Peel and wash the carrots and turnips; cut into ½ cm dice (macédoine) or batons (jardinière); cook separately in lightly salted water, do not overcook. Refresh.
2 Top and tail the beans; cut into ½ cm dice, cook and refresh, do not overcook.
3 Cook the peas and refresh.
4 Mix the vegetables and, when required, reheat in hot salted water.
5 Drain well, serve brushed with melted butter.

70 Mixed fried vegetables in batter (légumes en fritot)

Cal	Cal	Fat	Sat Fat	Carb	Sugar	Protein	Fibre	*
1062 KJ	253 kcal	16.5 g	3.6 g	22.7 g	2.7 g	4.9 g	3.1 g	

The following vegetables are prepared in small pieces and may also be served individually: cauliflower, fennel, broccoli, parsnips, celery, salsify, French beans, courgettes.

1 Boil or steam the vegetables (except the courgettes) keeping them slightly firm.
2 Marinate in oil, lemon juice and chopped parsley.
3 Dip in batter (see page 187).
4 Deep-fry in hot fat 180°C until golden brown.
5 Drain on kitchen paper and serve.

HEALTHY EATING TIP
- Use semi-skimmed milk and a pinch of salt to make the batter.
- Make sure the fat is hot so that less will be absorbed into the batter.
- Drain on kitchen paper.

* Fried in peanut oil

71 Grilled vegetables (or griddled vegetables)

Cal 1386 KJ	Cal 336 kcal	Fat 32.1 g	Sat Fat 4.7 g	Carb 9.0 g	Sugar 8.2 g	Protein 2.9 g	Fibre 3.8 g

	4 portions	10 portions
courgettes	2	5
aubergine	1	3
red pepper	1	3
yellow pepper	1	3
tomatoes	2	5
seasoning		
balsamic vinegar	2 tbsp	5 tbsp
Marinade		
extra virgin olive oil	2 tbsp	5 tbsp
cloves of garlic, crushed and chopped	2	5
fresh thyme, chopped	1 tsp	2½ tsp
fresh basil leaves, chopped	1 tsp	2½ tsp
fresh rosemary, chopped	1 tsp	2½ tsp

HEALTHY EATING TIP
- Use less oil in the marinade and lightly brush the vegetables with the marinade before grilling.
- Add little or no salt to the marinade.

1 Cut the courgettes lengthways into 3 mm and aubergines into 5 mm rounds. Cut each pepper in half, deseed and cut each half into two. Skin the tomatoes, halve and deseed. Marinate the vegetables with the prepared marinade, making sure that all the vegetables are coated. Cover and leave for 8–12 hours.
2 Brush a suitable grill tray with oil and place the vegetables from the marinade on to it.
3 Grill the courgettes and tomatoes for approximately 2 minutes, and the aubergines and peppers for approximately 4 minutes.
4 Season lightly. Place on suitable serving dishes, sprinkle with balsamic vinegar.

Note: Other vegetables that may be included are celery, fennel and chicory. It is advisable to blanch these in boiling water for 30–60 seconds, refresh and drain before marinating and grilling.

Figure 12.10 Grilled vegetables

72 Roasted vegetables

Cal	Cal	Fat	Sat Fat	Carb	Sugar	Protein	Fibre
343 KJ	82 kcal	3.6 g	0.6 g	10.0 g	8.6 g	3.0 g	3.8 g

	4 portions	10 portions
red onions, small	1	3
red peppers	1	3
yellow peppers	1	3
courgettes	2	5
aubergines	1	3
garlic, coarsely chopped	1–2 cloves	2–4 cloves
olive oil	1 tbsp	2½ tbsp
balsamic vinegar	1 tbsp	2½ tbsp
sea salt		
black mill pepper		
fresh rosemary		
fresh basil, roughly chopped		

1 Peel the vegetables. Cut the onion into 8 pieces. Cut the peppers into halves, deseed and cut each into approximately 4–6 even pieces. Cut the courgettes into 2 cm × 1 cm batons. Cut the aubergine into 2 cm × 1 cm batons.
2 Place all the vegetables (and the garlic) into a suitable roasting dish, sprinkle with the olive oil and balsamic vinegar.
3 Season lightly with sea salt and pepper.
4 Sprinkle with rosemary and basil.

5 Place in a pre-heated oven at 180°C for approximately 15 minutes.
6 Serve immediately.

Note: These vegetables may also be chilled and served with a salad as a starter.

HEALTHY EATING TIP
• Lightly brush the vegetables with the olive oil and add the minimum amount of salt.

Figure 12.11 Roasted vegetables

73 Straw vegetables

	4 portions	10 portions
carrots	50 g	125 g
leeks	50 g	125 g
celery	50 g	125 g
potatoes	100 g	250 g
fennel	50 g	125 g
parsnip	100 g	250 g

1 Wash and prepare all the vegetables.
2 Cut each vegetable into fine julienne.
3 Wash well, drain on a cloth, then dry well.
4 Fry the vegetables in hot oil (185°C) until golden brown and crisp. Drain.
5 Use as garnish.

74 Vegetable crisps

Vegetable crisps may be made from the following vegetables: parsnips, beetroot (golden is ideal), carrots, mooli, root ginger, potato, courgette, aubergine, sweet potato.

1 Peel and slice the vegetables very thinly (wash and dry the potatoes) using a mandolin.
2 Deep-fry in deep hot oil at 185°C until crisp.
3 Drain well on kitchen paper and use as a garnish.

HEALTHY EATING TIP
• Make sure the fat is hot so that less of it will be absorbed.
• Drain on kitchen paper.
• Limit the amount of these fatty vegetables when used as a garnish.

75 Vegetable moulds (mousse)

Cal	Cal	Fat	Sat Fat	Carb	Sugar	Protein	Fibre	*
839 KJ	203 kcal	17.4 g	9.0 g	5.3 g	5.0 g	6.8 g	2.5 g	

Many vegetables are suitable for making into moulds (usually dariole or small timbale moulds): for example, asparagus, broccoli, carrot, cauliflower, aubergine, fennel, spinach.

	4 portions	10 portions
eggs	3–4	7–10
seasoned vegetable purée	400 g	1 kg
double cream	2 tbsp	5 tbsp

1 Thoroughly mix the eggs without over-beating.
2 Pass them through a fine strainer on to the cold vegetable purée; add the cream and combine thoroughly.
3 Three-quarters fill the buttered moulds (this allows for expansion during cooking).
4 Place the moulds in a bain-marie of hot water and bake at 190°C until set.
5 Remove from the oven and allow to stand for 10 minutes before turning out.

Variations
Variations include the following:
• Béchamel sauce can be used in place of cream.
• Extra ingredients, spices or herbs may be added to the various moulds (e.g. chopped garlic with aubergine; toasted pine nuts in spinach; chopped coriander in carrot; grated Parmesan cheese with broccoli).
• Vegetable moulds can be served as vegetables, as a garnish or as a light course, in which case they would be served with a suitable sauce (e.g. asparagus mousse; mushroom sauce – page 53).

Vegetable soufflé uses the same basic recipe; keep the purée stiff. Separate the eggs, mix the yolks into the purée then fold in the stiffly beaten whites. Place the mixture into buttered and floured soufflé moulds; bake in a hot oven 220°C (425°F) until set.

* Using carrots

Figure 12.12 Carrot, broccoli and cauliflower mousse

Figure 12.13 Vegetable soufflé

Seaweed

Seaweed as a food

The influence of mankind on the family of plants known as seaweeds has been limited so they have not changed substantially over the last ten thousand years. However, parts of the sea are polluted so the location where seaweed is harvested is of paramount importance.

For centuries seaweed has also been used as a herb and to treat a number of ailments, including constipation, arthritis and colds. It improves the digestion and permits a better assimilation of sugars and fats.

76 Japanese sea vegetable stock

1½ litres

Known in Japan as 'dashi', this stock is ideal as a base for clear soups and noodle broths. The broth is fragrant and the glutamic acid that occurs naturally in the sea vegetable rounds out the flavour of the other ingredients in the dish.

If the stock is to be used in a dish flavoured with shoyu, the sea salt can be omitted.

Japanese kombu	10 cm stick
water	1½ litres
sea salt	1½ level tsp

1 Clean the kombu with a damp cloth.
2 Place it in the cold water and leave for 5 minutes.
3 Cover and bring to the boil.
4 Simmer for 5 minutes.
5 Strain and add salt to taste. The kombu can be used again in another dish.

77 Japanese dried mushroom stock

This stock is ideal for clear soups and noodle dishes, and can be used instead of fish stock for vegetarians. If the stock is to be used in a dish flavoured with shoyu, the sea salt can be omitted.

kombu	10 cm stick
dried shiitake mushrooms	3
water	1½ litres
sea salt	1½ level tsp

1 Clean the kombu with a damp cloth.
2 Place the mushrooms and kombu in the cold water and leave to soften for 5 minutes.
3 Take out the mushrooms, discard the fibrous lower part of the stem and slice the rest finely.
4 Return the mushrooms to the water, cover, bring to the boil slowly.
5 Simmer for 5 minutes.
6 The mushrooms can be left in or strained out and saved for use in another dish.
7 The kombu can be used again in another dish.
8 Add the salt.

78 Potato pancakes with dulse

	4 portions
cooked mashed potato	450 g
plain flour	25 g
dulse, finely chopped	7 g
egg	2
breadcrumbs	200 g

1 Mix the potato, flour and dulse well.
2 Divide into four.
3 Flour, dip in egg and coat with breadcrumbs
4 Shallow-fry.

79 Irish dulse soda scones

	4 portions
dried dulse	12 g
plain flour	450 g
bicarbonate of soda	1 tsp
salt	1 tsp
buttermilk or sour cream	340 ml
egg	1

1 Soak the dulse in water for 5 minutes.
2 Drain and chop the dulse finely.
3 Sieve the flour, bicarbonate of soda and salt into a suitable bowl, mixing thoroughly.
4 Add the chopped dulse.
5 Make a well in the centre. Add most of the buttermilk and work to a firm dough. Add the remainder of the buttermilk if necessary.
6 Turn out and knead lightly on a floured surface.
7 Using the palm of the hand, shape the dough into a round approximately 2 cm thick.
8 Score the surface into 4 or 6.
9 Brush with beaten egg.
10 Place on a lightly greased baking tray and bake in a preheated oven for 20–25 minutes at 200°C.

Pulses and grains

Pulses

Pulses are defined as annual leguminous crops, yielding from 1 to 12 grains or seeds of variable size, shape and colour within a pod.

The term 'pulse' is reserved for crops harvested solely for the dry grain. This therefore excludes green beans and green peas, which are considered vegetable crops. Also excluded are crops that are grown mainly for oil extraction (oilseeds like soybeans and peanuts), and crops that are used exclusively for sowing (e.g. clovers, alfalfa).

Pulses are important food crops due to their high protein and essential amino acid content. They contain 20–25 per cent of proteins, which is double that found in wheat and three times that found in rice.

Pulses are sometimes called 'poor man's meat'. Pulse protein is equivalent in quality to soy protein, which has been shown by the World Health Organization to be the equal of meat, milk and egg proteins.

All pulses, except for soya beans, are very similar in nutritional content. They are rich in protein, carbohydrate and fibre, and low in fat, which is mostly of the unsaturated kind. They are also important sources of some B vitamins. Fresh pulses contain vitamin C, but this declines after harvesting and virtually all is lost from dried pulses. Canned pulses, however, retain about half their vitamin C. (Frozen peas will have also lost about a quarter of their vitamin C content.) With the exception of canned, processed peas (which have been dried before canning), canning doesn't affect protein content, eliminates the need for soaking and considerably reduces cooking time compared to dried pulses.

One advantage of dried pulses is that they store very well for long periods if kept in a dry, airtight container away from the light. However, it is best to eat them as fresh as possible. Pulses toughen on storage and older ones will take longer to cook. Allow about 55 g dry weight per person, once soaked and cooked they will at least double in weight. Most dried pulses need soaking for several hours before they can be cooked; exceptions are all lentils, green and yellow split peas, black-eyed and mung beans.

Soaking times vary from 4–12 hours. It is usually most convenient to soak pulses overnight. Always discard the soaking water, rinse and cook in fresh water without any salt, which toughens the skins and makes for longer cooking. Changing the water will also help to reduce the flatulence some people suffer when eating pulses; also reputed to help is the addition of a pinch of aniseed, caraway, dill or fennel seeds.

Consumers should be aware that it is not safe to eat raw or undercooked kidney and soya beans. Soya beans should be soaked for at least 12 hours, drained and rinsed then covered with fresh water and brought to the boil. Soya beans should be boiled for the first hour of cooking. They can then be simmered for the remaining 2–3 hours that it takes to cook them.

Food value

Pulses are a good source of protein and carbohydrate, and therefore help to provide the body with energy. They also contain iron and vitamin B, are high in fibre and, with the exception of the soybean, contain no fat.

Storage

Chapter 17 (CD-ROM text) contains details of stock rotation procedures. In addition:

- store fresh pulses in a refrigerator at a temperature below 5°C
- store frozen pulses in a freezer at a temperature below −18°C
- store dried pulses in clean airtight containers off the floor in the dry store
- unpack tinned pulses and check that the tins are sound and undamaged.

Health, safety and hygiene

For information on health and safety and food hygiene, please refer to Chapters 17 and 18. Additional health and safety points for pulses are as follows.

- Always check pulses for food pests (e.g. flour moths) and any foreign matter (stones, etc.).
- When storing cooked pulses, keep them covered and in a refrigerator at a temperature below 5°C.
- To prevent risk of cross-contamination, store cooked pulses away from any raw foods.

Types of pulses

Beans
- **Aduki:** small, round, deep red, shiny, nutty and sweet (the flavour used in oriental confectionery).
- **Black:** glistening black skins, creamy flesh.

- **Black-eyed:** small white beans with a savoury, creamy flavour, and with a black 'scar' where they were joined to the pod. Used a lot in American and African cooking, they are the essential ingredient in the traditional southern-style dish 'Hoppin John' – a mixture of black-eyed beans, bacon and white rice traditionally eaten on New Year's Day.
- **Broad:** also known as fava beans, strongly flavoured.
- **Borlotti:** Italian beans with a mild bittersweet flavour; they're used in regional stews and often mixed with rice, and are particularly good in soups such as minestrone and *pasta e fagioli*.
- **Butter:** also known as lima beans, available large or small.
- **Cannellini:** Italian haricot, slightly larger than the English.
- **Dutch brown:** light brown in colour.
- **Flageolet:** pale green, kidney-shaped with a delicate flavour.
- **Ful mesdames:** also known as Egyptian brown beans; small, brown and knobbly, known as the field bean in the UK.
- **Haricot:** white, smooth and oval; used for baked beans.
- **Mung beans:** small, olive green in colour, good flavour, available split, whole and skinless. Widely used sprouted for their shoots.
- **Pinto beans:** the original ingredient of Mexican refried beans; an orange-pink bean with rust-coloured specks that grows freely across Latin America and throughout the American south-west; the bean is creamy-white in colour with a fluffy texture when cooked, and is good in soups, salads and rich stews.
- **Red kidney beans:** normally dark red-brown, this kidney-shaped bean holds its shape and colour and is therefore great in mixed bean salads and stews, including the traditional chilli con carne. Dried kidney beans need to be cooked carefully – soak for at least eight hours; after soaking, drain and rinse them, discarding the soaking water; put them into a pan with cold water to cover and bring to the boil – the beans must be boiled for 10 minutes to destroy

toxins; after this, simmer until cooked (approximately 45–60 minutes). The beans should have an even, creamy texture throughout – if the centre is still hard and white, they require longer cooking.
- **Soissons:** finest haricot beans.
- **Soy:** soybeans are very high in nutrients, especially protein, and they contain all the essential amino acids. They are processed into many forms: soy flour, TVP (meat substitute), tofu (curd), oils, margarine, soy milk and soy sauce.

Peas
- **Blue:** also known as marrowfat peas; pleasant flavour, floury texture, retain shape when cooked.
- **Chickpeas:** shaped like hazelnuts, they have a tasty nutty flavour when cooked. Chickpeas are used all over the world in dishes such as the Indian kabli chana or Spanish caldo gallego. Chickpeas are a key ingredient of hummus – a traditional Greek dip of cooked chickpeas, tahini, oil and garlic. They can be bought and soaked from dried, but canned chickpeas do just as well for most recipes.
- **Split green:** a sweeter variety than the blue pea; cook to a purée easily.
- **Split yellow:** cook to a purée easily.

Both yellow and green split peas are used for vegetable purées and soups.

Lentils
Lentils, varying in size and colour, can form a nutritious basis for a meal. Larger brown or green lentils retain their shape during cooking and are particularly good in soups. Red and yellow lentils cook down well, can be puréed and are used a great deal in Indian cooking, such as in a spicy dhal. Tiny green puy lentils have a distinctive flavour and also keep their shape and colour when cooked.

- **Orange:** several types, which vary in size and shade and may be sold whole or split.

- **Green or continental:** retain shape after cooking, available in small or large varieties.
- **Yellow:** of Asian origin, often used as a dhal accompaniment to curry dishes.
- **Red:** purée easily, used for soups and stews etc.
- **Indian brown:** red lentils from which the seed coat has not been removed; they purée easily.
- **Puy:** dark French lentils, varied in size, retain their shape when cooked and are considered the best of their type.
- **Dhal:** the Hindi word for dried peas and beans.

The use of pulses

Pulses are one of the most versatile commodities. They can be used extensively in a wide range of dishes. Imaginative and experimental use of different herbs, spices, flavourings and vegetables can give individual variation to the pulse recipes.

Several pulse recipes are presented in this book:

- Haricot bean and three bean salads (page 117)
- Pulse soups (page 73)
- Pease pudding (page 509)
- Bean goulash (page 460)
- Mexican bean pot (page 461)
- Moussaka (TVP) (page 463).

Cooking

Some pulses require pre-soaking in cold water before cooking; the soaking time will vary according the type and quality and the length of time they have been stored.

For soaking, pulses should be amply covered with cold water (they will expand gradually) and kept in a cold place. In some cases this may be for a few hours; in others it may be overnight, in which case they should be stored in the refrigerator at a temperature below 5°C. After soaking, salt should *not* be added before or during the cooking as this causes the pulses to toughen. Salt, however, may be added if required towards the end of the cookery process.

80 Dried beans (pulses)

Cal	Cal	Fat	Sat Fat	Carb	Sugar	Protein	Fibre
29 KJ	000 kcal7	0.0 g	0.0 g	1.1 g	0.8 g	0.8 g	3.2 g

½ kg will yield 8 portions

1 If necessary soak in cold water overnight in a cool place.
2 Change the water, refresh.
3 Cover with cold water. Do not add salt (as salt toughens the skin and lengthens the cooking time). Bring to the boil.
4 Skim as necessary.
5 Add 50 g carrot, 50 g studded onion, 50 g bacon bone or trimmings (optional) and bouquet garni.
6 Simmer until tender. Season lightly with salt.
7 Drain and serve.

Note: Black-eyed, borlotti, butter, haricot, kidney and flageolet beans require soaking only if they have been stored for a long time. Pulse beans can be served sprinkled with chopped parsley, mixed fresh herbs or chives. They can also be lightly dressed with a good-quality oil (natural or flavoured) and/or a suitably flavoured warm vinaigrette.

Puy lentils are a popular, green-coloured lentil that do not require soaking and hold their shape when cooked. They require only about 30 minutes' cooking and they can be braised in a little stock, vegetables, herbs, wine, etc. Usually cooked al dente, they are a suitable accompaniment for many meat, game and poultry dishes, and can be used as a garnish for roast and baked fish.

81 Pease pudding

Cal	Cal	Fat	Sat Fat	Carb	Sugar	Protein	Fibre	*
1277 KJ	304 kcal	15.6 g	6.5 g	29.6 g	2.3 g	13.1 g	6.5 g	

	4 portions	10 portions
yellow split peas, soaked	200 g	500 g
water	½ litre	1¼ litres
studded onion	50 g	125 g
carrot	50 g	125 g
bacon trimmings	50 g	125 g
butter or margarine	50 g	125 g
salt, pepper		

1 Place all the ingredients, except the butter or margarine and seasoning, in a saucepan with a tight-fitting lid.
2 Bring to the boil; cook in a moderate oven at 180–200°C for 2 hours.
3 Remove the onion, carrot and bacon and pass the peas through a sieve or use a food processor.
4 Return to a clean pan, mix in the butter or margarine, correct the seasoning and consistency (this should be firm).

HEALTHY EATING TIP
• No added salt is needed.
• Reduce the amount of butter or margarine added to the puréed peas.

* Using hard margarine

Grains

Cereal crops, or grains, are mostly grasses cultivated for their edible grains or seeds. Cereal grains are grown in greater quantities and provide more energy worldwide than any other type of crop; they are therefore known as 'staple crops'.

Food value

Grains are a rich source of carbohydrate. They supply most of their food energy as starch. They are also a significant source of protein. Whole grains are good sources of dietary fibre, essential fatty acids and other important nutrients. Rice, for example, is eaten as cooked entire grains (although rice flour is also produced). Oats are rolled, ground or cut into bits (steel-cut oats) and cooked into porridge (see below). Most other cereal grains are ground into flour or meal. During this process the outer layers of bran and germ are removed, reducing their nutritional value.

Storage

Cereals are best stored in airtight containers in a cool, dark, dry place. Whole grains can be stored for up to two years; flaked or cracked grains and flours should be used within two to three months of purchase.

Types of grain

Barley

Barley grows in a wider variety of climatic conditions than any other cereal. Usually found in the shops as **whole** or **pot barley** (or **polished pearl barley**) you can also buy **barley flakes** or **kernels**. It can be cooked on its own (one part grain to three parts water for 45–60 minutes) as an alternative to rice, pasta or potatoes, or added to stews. Malt extract is made from sprouted barley grains.

Barley must have its fibrous hull removed before it is eaten (hulled barley). Hulled barley still has its bran and germ and is considered a whole grain, making it a popular health food. Pearl barley is hulled barley that has been processed further to remove the bran.

Buckwheat

When roasted, the seeds of buckwheat are dark reddish-brown. It can be cooked (one part grain to two parts water for 6 minutes, leave to stand for 6 minutes) and served like rice, or it can be added to stews and casseroles. **Buckwheat flour** can be added to cakes, muffins and pancakes, where it imparts a distinctive flavour. Soba noodles, made from buckwheat, are an essential ingredient in Japanese cooking. Buckwheat is gluten free.

Corn/maize

Fresh corn – available in the form of sweetcorn and corn on the cob – is eaten as a vegetable. The dried grain is most often eaten as cornflakes or popcorn. The flour made from corn (**cornmeal**) is used to make Italian polenta, and can be added to

soup, pancakes and muffins. Cook polenta (one part grain to three parts water, for 15–20 minutes), stirring carefully to avoid lumps. Use it like mashed potato: it's quite bland, so try stirring in tasty ingredients like Gorgonzola, Parmesan and fresh herbs, or press it when cold, cut into slices, brush with garlicky olive oil, and grill. You can also get ready-made polenta. Tortillas are made from maize meal, as are quite a lot of snack foods. Don't confuse cornmeal with refined **corn starch/flour**, used for thickening. Corn is gluten free.

Millet

The millets are a group of small-seeded species of cereal crops or grains widely grown around the world for food and fodder.

The main millet varieties are:

- pearl millet
- foxtail millet
- proso millet, also known as common millet, broom corn millet, hog millet or white millet
- finger millet.

Coeliac patients can replace certain cereal grains in their diets by consuming millets in various forms, including breakfast cereals.

In western India, millet flour (called 'bajari' in Marathi) has been commonly used with 'jowar' (sorghum) flour for hundreds of years to make the local staple flat bread, 'bhakri'.

Millet can often be used in place of buckwheat, rice or quinoa.

The protein content in millet is very close to that of wheat; both provide about 11 per cent protein by weight. Millets are rich in B vitamins, especially niacin, B6 and folacin, calcium, iron, potassium, magnesium and zinc. Millets contain no gluten, so they cannot rise for bread. When combined with wheat or xanthan gum (for those who have coeliac disease), though, they can be used to make raised bread. Alone, they are suited to flatbread.

As none of the millets is closely related to wheat, they are appropriate foods for those with coeliac disease, as mentioned above, or other forms of allergies/intolerances of wheat.

Millet is an alternative to rice but the tiny grains need to be cracked before they will absorb water easily. Before boiling, sauté them with a little vegetable oil for 2–3 minutes until some are seen to crack, then add water carefully (one part grain to three parts water). Bring to the boil and simmer for 15–20 minutes until fluffy. **Millet flakes** can be made into porridge or added to muesli. **Millet flour** is available, sometimes also made into pasta.

Oats

There are various grades of **oatmeal, rolled oats** or **jumbo oat flakes**. All forms can be used to make porridge, combined with ground nuts to make a nut roast, or added to stews. Oatmeal is low in gluten so can't be used to make a loaf, but can be mixed with wheat flour to add flavour and texture to bread, muffins and pancakes. Oatmeal contains some oils and can become rancid, so watch the best-before date.

Oatmeal is created by grinding oats into a coarse powder; various grades are available depending on the thoroughness of the grinding (including coarse, pinhead and fine). The main uses of oats are:

- as an ingredient in baking
- in the manufacture of bannocks or oatcakes
- as a stuffing for poultry
- as a coating for some cheeses
- as an ingredient of black pudding
- for making traditional porridge (or 'porage').

Rice

Rice is one of the world's most important crops. There are three basic kinds in culinary terms: **long, medium** and **short grain**. Long grain is traditionally used in savoury dishes and **short grain** in dessert cooking, although this varies across the globe. **Wholegrain rice** has a nuttier taste and contains more fibre and nutrients, but takes longer to cook (use one part grain to two parts water for 35–40 minutes). **Arborio rice** is a medium- to long-grain rice and is used in risottos because it can absorb a good deal of cooking liquid without becoming too soft. **Rice flour** is available but, because it's gluten free, it can't be used to make a yeasted loaf. **Rice flakes** (brown and white) can be added to muesli or made into a milk pudding or porridge.

Wild rice

Not, in fact, a rice, but an aquatic grass! Difficulty in harvesting makes it expensive, but the colour (a purplish black) and its subtly nutty flavour make it a good base for a special dish or rice salad, and it can be economically mixed with other rices (but may need pre-cooking as it takes 45–50 minutes to cook, using one part grain to three parts water).

Red rice

An unmilled short-grain rice from the Camargue in France, with a brownish-red colour and a nutty flavour. It's slightly sticky when cooked, and particularly good in salads.

Rye

Rye is the only cereal (apart from wheat and barley) that has enough gluten to make a yeasted loaf. However, with less gluten than wheat, **rye flour** makes a denser, richer-flavoured bread. It's more usual to mix rye flour with wheat flour. **Rye grains** should be cooked using one part grain to three parts water for 45–60 minutes. **Kibbled rye** is often added to granary-type loaves. Rye grains can be added to stews, and **rye flakes** are good in muesli.

Spelt

Originating in the Middle East, Spelt is closely related to common wheat and has been popular for decades in eastern Europe. It has an intense nutty, wheaty flavour. The flour is excellent for breadmaking and spelt pasta is becoming more widely available.

Wheat

This is the most familiar cereal in Britain today, used for bread, cakes, biscuits, pastry, breakfast cereals and pasta. **Wheat grains** can be eaten whole (cook one part grain to three parts water for 40–60 minutes) and have a satisfying, chewy texture. **Cracked** or **kibbled wheat** is the dried whole grains cut by steel blades. **Bulgar wheat** is parboiled before cracking, has a light texture and only needs rehydrating by soaking in boiling water or stock. **Semolina** is a grainy yellow flour ground from durum or hard wheat, and is the main ingredient of dried Italian pasta. **Couscous** is made from semolina grains that have been rolled, dampened and coated with finer wheat flour. Soak in two parts of water/stock to rehydrate; traditionally, it is steamed after soaking. **Strong wheat flour** (with a high gluten content) is required for yeasted breadmaking. **Plain flour** is used for general cooking including cakes and shortcrust pastry. **Wheat flakes** are used for porridge, muesli and flapjacks.

Quinoa

Quinoa is an ancient crop that fed the South American Aztec Indians for thousands of years, and has recently been cultivated in Britain. It's a seed that is high in protein, making it useful for vegetarians.

The small, round grains look similar to millet, but are pale brown in colour. The taste is mild, and the texture firm and slightly chewy. It can be cooked like millet and absorbs twice its volume in liquid. Cook for 15 minutes (one part grain to three parts water); it's ready when all the grains have turned from white to transparent, and the spiral-like germ has separated). Use in place of more common cereals or pasta, or in risottos, pilaff and vegetable stuffings. It may be used in place of rice and is served in salads and some stuffings.

Ebly

A whole-grain durum wheat grown in France, this yields 2.5–3 times dry weight. Rich in dietary fibre and low in sodium, it is used as an alternative to rice, potatoes and pasta.

Sources: The Vegetarian Society (www.vegsoc.org) and www.wikipedia.org.

82 Quinoa stuffed avocado with sautéed mushrooms

Cal 1502 KJ	Cal 359 kcal	Fat 23.7 g	Sat Fat 4.0 g	Carb 24.1 g	Sugar 4.1 g	Protein 13.7 g	Fibre 3.4 g	Salt 0.4 g

	4 portions	10 portions
avocados	2	5
quinoa	150 g	375 g
sliced closed cup mushrooms	150 g	375 g
olive oil	15 ml	37 ml
plum tomatoes skinned, deseeded and finely chopped	2	5
orange segmented	1	3
fresh basil leaves chopped	25 g	62 g
lime, juice of	½	1¼
seasoning		

1 Halve the avocado pears and remove the stones.
2 Cook the quinoa in approximately 375 ml of water (4 portions) or 1 litre (10 portions) until all the liquid has been absorbed. This takes approximately 15 minutes. It may be necessary to add more water.
3 Sauté the mushrooms in a little oil.
4 Drain the quinoa and place in a suitable bowl. Add the remaining ingredients (except the sautéed mushrooms) and mix.
5 Stuff the avocados with this mixture.
6 Sprinkle the sautéed mushrooms on top of the avocados, decorate with a petal of tomato flesh.

83 Toasted quinoa salad

	4 portions	10 portions
uncooked quinoa	180 g	460 g
carrots, diced 6 mm	250 g	625 g
red peppers, finely chopped	125 g	300 g
parsley, chopped	1 tsp	2 tsp
onions, finely chopped	100 g	250 g
lemon, juice of	½	1
lime, juice of	½	1
soy sauce or tamari	1½ tbsp	3 tbsp
garlic clove, crushed and chopped	1	2
Tabasco	1 tsp	2 tsp

1 Rinse the quinoa and drain.
2 Place into a suitable pot over a moderate heat and dry toast until a few grains begin to pop.
3 Add approximately 375 ml of water (4 portions) or 1 litre (10 portions). Bring to the boil. Cover and simmer for approximately 15 minutes or until the quinoa has absorbed all the liquid.

4 Mix the carrot, red pepper, parsley and onion in a suitable bowl.

5 Add the cooled quinoa and toss to combine.

6 Whisk together the lemon and lime juices, soy or tamari, garlic and Tabasco.

7 Pour over the salad and combine well.

8 Chill until ready to serve.

84 Quinoa, cashew and grape salad

	4 portions	10 portions
quinoa	300 g	750 g
raw cashew nuts	120 g	300 g
raspberry or apple cider vinegar	4 tbsp	10 tbsp
mirin (Japanese wine)	2 tbsp	5 tbsp
salt, pepper		
fresh herbs such as rocket, mint, marjoram or dill, chopped	4 tsp	10 tsp
celery, finely sliced	2 sticks	5 sticks
seedless grapes, halved	200 g	500 g

1 Bring a large pan of lightly salted water to the boil. Add the quinoa and simmer for 12–15 minutes or until the grains are tender and the equatorial threads detached. Drain, rinse and drain again thoroughly. Spread out on a baking tray to dry.

2 In a dry, heavy frying pan, toast the cashews over a moderate to low heat, stirring frequently until they are golden brown. Remove to a bowl to cook then chop them roughly.

3 In a large bowl, combine the vinegar, mirin and ½ tsp salt. Toss in the herbs, then the celery, grapes, cooked quinoa and cashews. Adjust the seasoning to taste and leave the salad to stand for at least 1 hour before serving.

85 Mushroom ragout with barley

Cal	Cal	Fat	Sat Fat	Carb	Sugar	Protein	Fibre	Salt	*
695 KJ	166 kcal	10.3 g	5.2 g	12.2 g	3.5 g	7.1 g	2.5 g	4.1 g	

	4 portions	10 portions
dried morels	15	40
dried porcini	40 g	40 g
chicken or vegetable stock	700 ml	1¾ litres
butter	25 g	60 g
onion, finely chopped	1	2
celery, finely diced	1 stick	3 sticks
semi-pearled or pot barley	100 g	250 g
bay leaf	1	2
salt	½ tsp	1 tsp
fresh mixed selection of exotic and wild mushrooms, preferably including chanterelles	300 g	750 g
soured cream or crème fraiche	60 ml	150 ml
fresh parsley, roughly chopped	5 g	12 g

1 Pick over and clean the dried morels and porcini as necessary. Place the stock in a large saucepan and bring to the boil. Turn off the heat and add the dried mushrooms. Set aside to infuse for 30 minutes.

2 Melt half the butter in a frying pan and add the chopped onion and celery. Sauté for 2 minutes then lower the heat right down. Cover and cook for about 20 minutes until soft and sweet, stirring occasionally.

3 Using a slotted spoon, scoop the soaked mushrooms out of the stock and squeeze the excess liquid back into the saucepan. Roughly chop the rehydrated mushrooms and return them to the stock.

4 Add the sautéed onion and celery to the stock along with the barley, bay leaf and salt. Bring to the boil, cover and simmer over a very low heat for 45–50 minutes or until the barley is just tender and hardly any liquid remains in the saucepan. If the pan boils dry too quickly, top it up with a little hot water.

5 Meanwhile, clean and trim the fresh mushrooms as necessary and, if large, cut into generous bite-sized pieces. Melt the remaining butter in a frying pan and sauté the mushrooms for five minutes until just cooked.

6 When the barley is ready, stir the sautéed mushrooms into it, then the soured cream or crème fraiche. Serve sprinkled with chopped parsley.

Using oyster mushrooms, and mushrooms in place of morels

86 Herrings in oatmeal

Cal 1222 KJ	Cal 292 kcal	Fat 18.2 g	Sat Fat 6.4 g	Carb 18.4 g	Sugar 0.2 g	Protein 14.7 g	Fibre 1.7 g	Salt 4.3 g

	4 portions	10 portions
medium or pinhead oatmeal	100 g	250 g
salt, pepper		
rashers fatty bacon	8	20
small herrings, part-boned if desired	80 g	20 g
vegetable oil or butter, as needed	25 g	60 g
mustard, to serve		

1 Spread the oatmeal on a plate and season it with salt and pepper. Press the fish into the oatmeal turning them to coat evenly on both sides.

2 Press the bacon in a large, heavy frying pan and set over a low heat. Slowly cook so that the fat from the bacon melts a little into the pan to prove the cooking medium for the fish. Cook until the bacon is a little browned, then remove from the pan and keep warm.

3 Place the coated fish in the pan and add a little oil or butter if there doesn't seem to be enough fat to fry the fish. Cook over a moderate heat for 3 minutes on each side or until the fish is cooked through. Serve with the bacon and a dab of mustard.

Reference

Campbell, J., Foskett, D. and Ceserani, V. (2006) Advanced Practical Cookery: A Textbook For Education and Industry (4th edn). London: Hodder.

Red

sey
val

Mid

Estima

Bintje

chapter 13

POTATOES

What are potatoes?

Potatoes are tubers. A tuber is a fleshy, food-storing swelling at the tip of an underground stem, also called a stolon. Potatoes have white, brown, purple or red skin, and white or golden flesh.

Indigenous to Central and South America, potatoes were probably first domesticated in Chile. They were discovered by Europeans when Pizarro destroyed the Incan empire in Peru, and were brought back to Europe around 1570. From Spain they moved to England and Ireland – it's said that Sir Walter Raleigh introduced them in 1586, and they were popular by 1610.

Some, however, resisted them as a food for a long time. Until 1780, they were rigorously excluded from prudent French tables, as they were thought to cause leprosy. Devout Scottish Presbyterians refused to eat them because they weren't mentioned in the Bible. In Prussia, King Frederick William I threatened to cut off the noses and ears of all peasants who refused to plant them. Russian peasants considered them unclean and un-Christian, calling them devil's apples.

In colonial Massachusetts, USA, they were considered the spoor of witches. Ireland adopted the potato first, and even made it the foundation of its national diet – a fact that was to have terrible repercussions in 1845 when a late blight attacked the potato crop and caused the 'potato famine' that was to send Irish émigrés all over the world seeking a better life.

Potato varieties

Several named varieties of potato are grown in Britain and these will be available according to the season. The different varieties have differing characteristics and some are more suitable for certain methods of cooking than others (see Table 13.1 and Figure 13.1).

Table 13.1   Potato varieties and recommended cooking methods

Cara	boil, bake, chip, wedge
Charlotte	boil, salad use
Desiree	boil, roast, bake, chip, mash, wedge
Golden Wonder	boil, roast, crisps
King Edward	boil, bake, roast, mash, chip
Maris Piper	boil, roast, bake, chip
Pink Fir Apple	boil, salad use
Premiere	boil
Record	crisps
Romano	boil, bake, roast, mash
Saxon	boil, bake, chip
Wilja	boil, bake, chip, mash

Common potato cooking styles

This section describes what happens to the potato while cooking in three common styles.

Baked

For the best baked potatoes, long slow cooking is best. The skin becomes very crisp and turns darker because the starch just below the skin converts to sugar, which browns in heat. Make sure you cut a slit in the potato as soon as it comes out of the oven so the interior doesn't steam, which makes for a heavier consistency.

Mashed

Mashed potatoes can be made from Maris Bintje (season dependent). The starch in the potatoes, once again, absorbs water and swells during the cooking process. Then, when the potato is mashed or riced, the cells break open, releasing more starch, which makes the potatoes creamy and smooth. If you boil potatoes for mashing, return them to the hot pan after draining and shake over a medium heat for 2–3 minutes to dry the potatoes. Whatever the cooking method, add butter when you begin mashing.

The butter coats the cells and the starch so they absorb less liquid, making the potatoes less gluey and fluffier. The slower the mash is cooked the better for the starch as it has more structure in the final mixing process, allowing the potato to hold in more fat/liquid than if cooked by the more traditional quicker method.

A quick tip on the cooking of mash
Bring the potatoes up to the boil from cold as normal and boil for 2–3 minutes, remove and rinse in cold water, then repeat the process of boiling from cold and turn the heat down, not

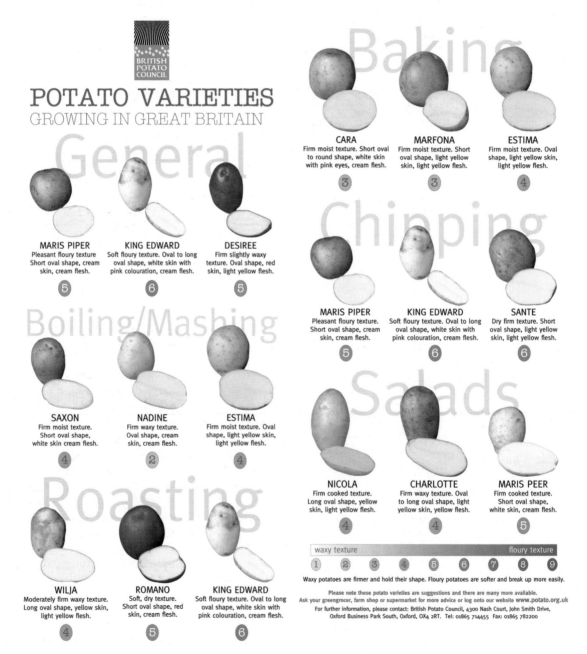

BRITISH POTATO COUNCIL

POTATO VARIETIES
GROWING IN GREAT BRITAIN

General

MARIS PIPER
Pleasant floury texture. Short oval shape, cream skin, cream flesh.
5

KING EDWARD
Soft floury texture. Oval to long oval shape, white skin with pink colouration, cream flesh.
6

DESIREE
Firm slightly waxy texture. Oval shape, red skin, light yellow flesh.
5

Boiling/Mashing

SAXON
Firm moist texture. Short oval shape, white skin cream flesh.
4

NADINE
Firm waxy texture. Oval shape, cream skin, cream flesh.
2

ESTIMA
Firm moist texture. Oval shape, light yellow skin, light yellow flesh.
4

Roasting

WILJA
Moderately firm waxy texture. Long oval shape, yellow skin, light yellow flesh.
4

ROMANO
Soft, dry texture. Short oval shape, red skin, cream flesh.
5

KING EDWARD
Soft floury texture. Oval to long oval shape, white skin with pink colouration, cream flesh.
6

Baking

CARA
Firm moist texture. Short oval to round shape, white skin with pink eyes, cream flesh.
3

MARFONA
Firm moist texture. Short oval shape, light yellow skin, light yellow flesh.
3

ESTIMA
Firm moist texture. Oval shape, light yellow skin, light yellow flesh.
4

Chipping

MARIS PIPER
Pleasant floury texture. Short oval shape, cream skin, cream flesh.
5

KING EDWARD
Soft floury texture. Oval to long oval shape, white skin with pink colouration, cream flesh.
6

SANTE
Dry firm texture. Short oval shape, light yellow skin, light yellow flesh.
6

Salads

NICOLA
Firm cooked texture. Long oval shape, yellow skin, light yellow flesh.
4

CHARLOTTE
Firm waxy texture. Oval to long oval shape, light yellow skin, yellow flesh.
4

MARIS PEER
Firm cooked texture. Short oval shape, white skin, cream flesh.
5

| waxy texture | | | | | | | | floury texture |
| 1 | 2 | 3 | 4 | 5 | 6 | 7 | 8 | 9 |

Waxy potatoes are firmer and hold their shape. Floury potatoes are softer and break up more easily.

Please note these potato varieties are suggestions and there are many more available.
Ask your greengrocer, farm shop or supermarket for more advice or log onto our website www.potato.org.uk
For further information, please contact: British Potato Council, 4300 Nash Court, John Smith Drive,
Oxford Business Park South, Oxford, OX4 2RT. Tel: 01865 714455 Fax: 01865 782200

Figure 13.1 ✎ Varieties of potatoes (British Potato Council)

even to a simmer. This will obviously take longer but will reduce the water absorption rate dramatically due to the starch wall created by the first process.

Roast

Roast potatoes are simply cut into chunks and parboiled slowly until just cooked on the inside. Drain and toss in a liberal amount of olive oil and seasoning, then roast at a high temperature (220°C) for 15 minutes. Remove, turn the temperature down to 180°C and baste every 5 minutes to ensure a crisp coat all over. Once cooked serve immediately, as prolonged holding will inevitably cause the inside to steam, making the outside soft and leathery.

Purchasing, selection and storage

Purchasing

Inspect and select your potatoes before buying or on delivery. Choose firm, smooth ones. Avoid excessively wrinkled, withered, cracked potatoes, and do not to buy those that have a lot of sprouts or green areas.

Selection

The careful selection of potatoes to suit the job in hand is essential as the variety chosen (see Figure 13.1) will be reflected in the end product. Potatoes come in two main specific categories: floury and waxy, as described below.

Cooked potatoes may have different textures, depending on whether they are 'waxy' or 'floury' varieties. This is due to changes that happen to the potato cells during cooking. 'Waxy' potatoes are translucent and may have a moist and pasty feel. 'Floury' potatoes are brighter and granular in appearance, leaving a drier feel. These differences influence the performance of the potato when cooked in different ways (*e.g.* boiling, versus roasting).

During cooking, as noted above, the starch in the potato starts to absorb water and swell in size. Potatoes need to be cooked for sufficient time to gelatinise the starch, or they will look and taste undercooked.

Floury potatoes

A type rather than a variety, floury potatoes are especially popular in the UK. They are suitable for baking, mashing and chipping as they have a soft, dry texture when cooked. They are not suitable for boiling, however, because they tend to disintegrate. Popular varieties of floury potato include King Edward and Maris Piper.

Figure 13.2   Floury potato

Waxy potatoes

These are more solid than floury potatoes and hold their shape when boiled, but do not mash well. They are particularly suitable for baked and layered potato dishes such as boulangère potatoes. Popular varieties include Cara and Charlotte.

Figure 13.3   Waxy potato

Storage

You can store potatoes for several months without affecting their quality; they should be stored at a constant temperature (3°C). If it is not possible to store them in this way, buying fresh potatoes regularly is best practice. There are three essential rules to bear in mind when storing potatoes: 'dry, dark and cool'. You should avoid light as this will cause sprouting and eventually the greening effect that contains mild toxins; if you have inadvertently purchased potatoes with this green tinge, remove the green bits and the rest of the potato is then fine to use.

The storage of the potato is perhaps the most important aspect of its life – the closer the temperature is to freezing point, the quicker the potato starch coverts to sugar, producing a sweet flesh, but a loss of structure and, often, discoloration.

Food value

Potatoes are a good source of vitamin C; they also contain iron, calcium, thiamin, nicotine acid, protein and fibre.

Yield

- ½ kg of old potatoes will yield approximately 3 portions.
- ½ kg of new potatoes will yield approximately 4 portions.
- 1½ kg of old potatoes will yield approximately 10 portions.
- 1¼ kg of new potatoes will yield approximately 10 portions.

Ready-prepared potatoes

Potatoes are obtainable in many convenience forms: peeled, turned, cut into various shapes for frying, or scooped into balls (Parisienne) or olive shape.

Chips are available fresh, frozen, chilled or vacuum packed.

Frozen potatoes are available as croquettes, hash browns, sauté and roast.

Mashed potato powder is also available.

Potato recipes

1 Plain boiled potatoes (pommes nature)

Cal	Cal	Fat	Sat Fat	Carb	Sugar	Protein	Fibre	*
487 KJ	116 kcal	0.1 g	0.0 g	28.6 g	0.6 g	2.0 g	1.5 g	

1 Wash, peel and rewash the potatoes.
2 Cut or turn into even-sized pieces allowing 2–3 pieces per portion.
3 Cook carefully in lightly salted water for approximately 20 minutes.
4 Drain well and serve.

* Using old potatoes

2 Parsley potatoes (pommes persillées)

Cal	Cal	Fat	Sat Fat	Carb	Sugar	Protein	Fibre	*
798 KJ	190 kcal	8.3 g	5.2 g	28.6 g	0.6 g	2.1 g	1.5 g	

1 Prepare and cook the potatoes as for plain boiled (recipe 1).
2 Brush with melted butter and sprinkle with chopped parsley.

* Using 10 g butter per portion, old potatoes

3 Mashed potatoes (pommes purée)

Cal 763 KJ	Cal 182 kcal	Fat 7.1 g	Sat Fat 4.4 g	Carb 29.0 g	Sugar 1.1 g	Protein 2.4 g	Fibre 1.5 g	*

1 Wash, peel and rewash the potatoes. Cut to an even size.
2 Cook in lightly salted water, or steam.
3 Drain off the water, cover and return to a low heat to dry out the potatoes.
4 Pass through a medium sieve or a special potato masher.
5 Return the potatoes to a clean pan.
6 Add 25 g butter per ½ kg and mix in with a wooden spoon.
7 Gradually add warm milk (30 ml), stirring continuously until a smooth creamy consistency is reached.
8 Correct the seasoning and serve.

HEALTHY EATING TIP
• Add a minimum amount of salt.
• Add a little olive oil in place of butter and semi-skimmed milk.

Variations
Variations of mashed potatoes can be achieved by:
• dressing in a serving dish and surrounding with a cordon of fresh cream
• placing in a serving dish, sprinkling with grated cheese and melted butter, and browning under a salamander

• adding 50 g diced cooked lean ham, 25 g diced red pepper and chopped parsley
• adding lightly sweated chopped spring onions
• adding a good-quality olive oil in place of butter
• adding a little garlic juice (use a garlic press)
• adding a little fresh chopped rosemary or chives
• mixing with equal quantities of parsnip
• adding a little freshly grated horseradish or horseradish cream.

* *Using old potatoes, butter and whole milk*

Figure 13.4 Mashed potatoes with spring onion

4 Duchess potatoes (basic recipe) (pommes duchesse)

Cal 819 KJ	Cal 195 kcal	Fat 8.2 g	Sat Fat 3.3 g	Carb 28.6 g	Sugar 0.6 g	Protein 3.5 g	Fibre 1.5 g	*

1 Wash, peel and rewash the potatoes. Cut to an even size.
2 Cook in lightly salted water.
3 Drain off the water, cover and return to a low heat to dry out the potatoes.
4 Pass through a medium sieve or a special potato masher or mouli.
5 Place the potatoes in a clean pan.
6 Add 1 egg yolk per ½ kg and stir in vigorously with a wooden spoon.
7 Mix in 25 g butter or margarine per ½ kg. Correct the seasoning.

8 Place in a piping bag with a large star tube and pipe out into neat spirals, about 2 cm in diameter and 5 cm tall, on to a lightly greased baking sheet.
9 Place in a hot oven at 230°C for 2–3 minutes in order to firm the edges slightly.
10 Remove from the oven and brush with eggwash.
11 Brown lightly in a hot oven or under the salamander.

* *Using old potatoes, whole milk, hard margarine*

5 Croquette potatoes (pommes croquettes)

Cal	Cal	Fat	Sat Fat	Carb	Sugar	Protein	Fibre	*
1699 KJ	405 kcal	25.4 g	6.6 g	40.8 g	1.1 g	6.0 g	2.2 g	

1 Use a duchess mixture moulded into cylinder
  shapes 5 × 2 cm.
2 Pass through flour, eggwash and breadcrumbs.
3 Reshape with a palette knife and deep-fry in hot
  deep oil (185°C) in a frying basket.
4 When the potatoes are a golden colour, drain well
  and serve.

HEALTHY EATING TIP
- Add the minimum amount of salt.
- Use peanut or sunflower oil to fry the croquettes,
  and drain on kitchen paper.

* Using hard margarine and frying in peanut oil

6 Potato cakes

Cal	Cal	Fat	Sat Fat	Carb	Sugar	Protein	Fibre
1058 KJ	254 kcal	4.9 g	4.9 g	21.5 g	0.8 g	3.4 g	1.6 g

1 Use a duchess mixture moulded into flat cakes,
  3 cm diameter, 1 cm thick.
2 Shallow-fry as for Macaire potatoes (recipe 16).

7 Baked jacket potatoes (pommes au four)

Cal	Cal	Fat	Sat Fat	Carb	Sugar	Protein	Fibre	*
401 KJ	94 kcal	0.2 g	0.0 g	21.8 g	0.9 g	2.7 g	1.6 g	

1 Select good-sized potatoes; allow one potato per
  portion.
2 Scrub well, make a 2 mm deep incision round the
  potato.
3 Place the potato, on a small mound of ground (sea)
  salt to help keep the base dry, on a tray in a hot
  oven at 230–250°C for about 1 hour. Turn the
  potatoes over after 30 minutes.
4 Test by holding the potato in a cloth and squeezing
  gently; if cooked it should feel soft.

Note: If the potatoes are being cooked by microwave,
prick the skins first.

Variations
Variations include the following.
- Split and filled with any of the following: grated
  cheese, minced beef or chicken, baked beans,
  chilli con carne, cream cheese and chives,
  mushrooms, bacon, ratatouille, prawns in
  mayonnaise, coleslaw, and so on.
- The cooked potatoes can also be cut in halves
  lengthwise, the potato spooned out from the skins,
  seasoned, mashed with butter, returned to the
  skins, sprinkled with grated cheese and reheated
  in an oven or under the grill.

** Using medium potato, 180 g analysis given per
potato*

HEALTHY EATING TIP
- Oven bake without sea salt.
- Fillings based on vegetables with little or no
  cheese or meat make a healthy snack meal.

8 Steamed potatoes (pommes vapeur)

Cal	Cal	Fat	Sat Fat	Carb	Sugar	Protein	Fibre	*
487 KJ	116 kcal	0.1 g	0.0 g	28.6 g	0.6 g	2.0 g	2.9 g	

1 Prepare the potatoes as for plain boiled (recipe 1); season lightly with salt.
2 Cook in a steamer and serve.

* *Using old potatoes*

9 Sauté potatoes (pommes sautées)

Cal	Cal	Fat	Sat Fat	Carb	Sugar	Protein	Fibre	*
1249 KJ	297 kcal	11.4 g	1.3 g	46.8 g	0.4 g	4.9 g	1.7 g	

1 Select medium even-sized potatoes. Scrub well.
2 Plain boil or cook in the steamer. Cool slightly and peel.
3 Cut into 3 mm slices.
4 Toss in hot shallow oil in a frying pan until lightly coloured; season lightly with salt.
5 Serve sprinkled with chopped parsley.

HEALTHY EATING TIP
• Use a little hot sunflower oil to fry the potatoes.
• Add little or no salt; the customer can add more if required.

* *Using old potatoes and sunflower oil*

10 Sauté potatoes with onions (pommes lyonnaise)

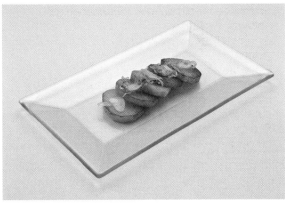

Figure 13.5 ✐ Preparation and service of sauté potatoes with onions

1 Allow ¼ kg onion to ½ kg potatoes.
2 Cook the onions as for fried onions (page 495).
3 Prepare sauté potatoes as for the recipe 9.
4 Combine the two and toss together.
5 Serve as for sauté potatoes.

HEALTHY EATING TIP
• Use a little hot sunflower oil to fry the potatoes.
• Add little or no salt; the customer can add more if required.

11 Crisps (game chips) (*pommes chips*)

Cal	Cal	Fat	Sat Fat	Carb	Sugar	Protein	Fibre	*
424 KJ	101 kcal	9.0 g	1.7 g	4.9 g	0.1 g	0.4 g	0.3 g	

1 Wash, peel and rewash the potatoes.
2 Cut in thin slices using a mandolin.
3 Wash well and dry in a cloth.
4 Cook in hot, deep fat (185°C) until golden brown and crisp.
5 Drain well and season lightly with salt.

Note: The selection of potato variety is crucial here as those that have a high simple sugar content will burn very quickly – Record or Golden Wonder are good varieties. Crisps are not usually served as a potato by themselves, but are used as a garnish and are also served with drinks and for snacks.

HEALTHY EATING TIP

• Use hot sunflower oil to fry the potatoes, and drain on kitchen paper.
• Add the minimum amount of salt; the customer can add more if required.

Variations
• Crisps can also be made from other root vegetables (e.g. parsnips, carrots, beetroot, turnips, swedes).

• Vegetable straw can be made by the same method, using any root vegetable or combination of vegetables.
• Vegetable crisps and straw can be used to garnish meat and poultry dishes, and with salads, sandwiches and snacks.

* Using old potatoes and peanut oil

Figure 13.6 Deep-fried potatoes in various shapes (clockwise from top left): straw potatoes, game chips, chips, French fries (matchsticks)

12 Wafer potatoes (pommes gaufrettes)

1 Wash, peel and rewash the potatoes.
2 Using a corrugated mandolin blade, cut in slices, giving a half turn in between each cut in order to obtain a wafer or trellis pattern.
3 Cook and serve as for crisps.

Figure 13.7 A mandolin and a truffle mandolin

13 Matchstick potatoes (pommes allumettes)

1 Select medium even-sized potatoes.
2 Wash, peel and rewash.
3 Trim on all sides to give straight edges.
4 Cut into slices 5 cm × 3 mm.
5 Cut the slices into 5 cm × 3 mm × 3 mm strips.
6 Wash well and dry in a cloth.

7 Fry in hot, deep fat (185°C) until golden brown and crisp. Drain.
8 Season lightly with salt and serve.

Note: These may also be blanched as for fried potatoes (recipe 14).

14 Fried or chipped potatoes (pommes frites)

Cal	Cal	Fat	Sat Fat	Carb	Sugar	Protein	Fibre	*
1541 KJ	367 kcal	15.8 g	2.8 g	54.1 g	0.0 g	5.5 g	1.5 g	

1 Prepare and wash the potatoes.
2 Cut into slices 1 cm thick and 5 cm long.
3 Cut the slices into strips 5 × 1 × 1 cm.
4 Wash well and dry in a cloth.
5 Cook in a frying basket without colour in moderately hot fat (165°C).
6 Drain and place on kitchen paper on trays until required.
7 When required, place in a frying pan and cook in hot fat (185°C) until crisp and golden.
8 Drain well, season lightly with salt and serve.

Note: Because chips are so popular, the following advice from the Potato Marketing Board is useful.

- Cook chips in small quantities; this will allow the oil to regain its temperature more quickly; chips will then cook faster and absorb less fat.

- Do not let the temperature of the oil exceed 199°C as this will accelerate the fat breakdown.

- Use oils high in polyunsaturates for a healthier chip.

- Ideally use a separate fryer for chips and ensure that it has the capacity to raise the fat temperature rapidly to the correct degree when frying chilled or frozen chips.

- Although the majority of chipped potatoes are purchased frozen, the Potato Marketing Board recommends the following potatoes for those who prefer to make their own chips:Maris Piper, Cara, Désirée.

HEALTHY EATING TIP

- Chipped potatoes may be blanched twice, first at 140°C, followed by a re-blanch at 160°C until lightly coloured.
- For healthy eating, blanch in a steamer until just cooked, drain and dry well – final temperature 165°C.

* Using old potatoes and peanut oil

15 Savoury potatoes *(pommes boulangère)*

Cal 595 KJ	Cal 142 kcal	Fat 5.3 g	Sat Fat 2.2 g	Carb 22.3 g	Sugar 1.8 g	Protein 2.8 g	Fibre 2.4 g	*

	4 portions	10 portions
potatoes	400 g	1¼ kg
onions	100 g	250 g
salt, pepper		
white stock	125 ml	350 ml
butter, margarine *or* oil	25–50 g	60–100 g
parsley, chopped		

1. Cut the potatoes into 2 mm slices on a mandolin. Keep the best slices for the top.
2. Peel, halve and finely slice the onions.
3. Mix the onions and potatoes together and season lightly with pepper and salt.
4. Place in a well-buttered shallow earthenware dish or roasting tin.
5. Barely cover with stock.
6. Neatly arrange overlapping slices of potato on top.
7. Brush lightly with oil.
8. Place in a hot oven at 230–250°C for 20 minutes until lightly coloured.
9. Reduce the heat and allow to cook steadily, pressing down firmly from time to time with a flat-bottomed pan.
10. When ready all the stock should be cooked into the potato. Allow 1½ hours cooking time in all.

11. Serve sprinkled with chopped parsley. If cooked in an earthenware dish, clean the edges of the dish with a cloth dipped in salt, and serve in the dish.

Note: Leeks can be used in place of onions for variety. This potato can be cooked under a joint of lamb, shoulder or leg. Place an oven rack with the meat on above the potatoes for the final 1½ hours of cooking. The juices from the meat will baste the potatoes as it cooks, then serve the lamb on top of the potato if the style of the restaurant dictates.

HEALTHY EATING TIP

- Use a little unsaturated oil to brush over the potatoes before placing in the oven.
- Add the minimum amount of salt; the stock provides flavour.
- This dish can be used to accompany fattier meat dishes and will help to dilute the fat.

* Using 25 g hard margarine. Using 50 g hard margarine: 787 kJ/187 kcal Energy; 10.3 g Fat; 4.4 g Sat Fat; 22.3 g Carb; 1.8 g Sugar; 2.8 g Protein; 2.4 g Fibre

16 Macaire potatoes (pommes Macaire)

Cal	Cal	Fat	Sat Fat	Carb	Sugar	Protein	Fibre	*
4392 KJ	1047 kcal	65.7 g	14.7 g	109.8 g	2.7 g	11.4 g	10.8 g	

½ kg will yield 2–3 portions

1 Prepare and cook as for baked jacket potatoes (recipe 7).
2 Cut in halves, remove the centre with a spoon, and place in a basin.
3 Add 25 g butter per ½ kg, a little salt and milled pepper.
4 Mash and mix as lightly as possible with a fork.
5 Using a little flour, mould into a roll, then divide into pieces, allowing one or two per portion.
6 Mould into 2 cm round cakes, flour lightly.
7 Shallow-fry on both sides in very hot oil and serve.

Note: Additions to potato cakes can include:

- chopped parsley or fresh herbs or chives or duxelle
- cooked chopped onion
- grated cheese.

* Using hard margarine and sunflower oil

17 Byron potatoes (classical variation of Macaire) (pommes Byron)

Cal	Cal	Fat	Sat Fat	Carb	Sugar	Protein	Fibre	*
2099 KJ	505 kcal	39.0 g	18.7 g	33.4 g	1.8 g	7.1 g	2.4 g	

1 Prepare and cook as for Macaire potatoes (recipe 16).
2 Using the back of a dessertspoon make a shallow impression on each potato.
3 Carefully sprinkle the centres with grated cheese. Make sure no cheese is on the edge of the potato.
4 Cover the cheese with cream.
5 Brown lightly under the salamander and serve.

* Using 1 tbsp each of cheese and double cream per person, analysis given per potato

18 Fondant potatoes (pommes fondantes)

Cal	Cal	Fat	Sat Fat	Carb	Sugar	Protein	Fibre	*
956 KJ	228 kcal	7.0 g	2.1 g	39.6 g	0.9 g	4.1 g	1.5 g	

1 Select small or even-sized medium potatoes.
2 Wash, peel and rewash.
3 Turn into eight-sided barrel shapes, allowing 2–3 per portion, about 5 cm long, end diameter 1½ cm, centre diameter 2½ cm.
4 Brush with melted butter, margarine or oil.
5 Place in a pan suitable for the oven.
6 Half cover with white stock, season lightly with salt and pepper.
7 Cook in a hot oven at 230–250°C, brushing the potatoes frequently with melted butter, margarine or oil.
8 When cooked the stock should be completely absorbed by the potatoes.
9 Brush with melted butter, margarine or oil and serve.

Figure 13.8 Fondant potatoes in various shapes

Note: Fondant potatoes can be lightly sprinkled with:

- thyme, rosemary or oregano (or this can be added to the stock)
- grated cheese (Gruyère and Parmesan or Cheddar)
- Chicken stock in place of white stock.

HEALTHY EATING TIP

- Use a little unsaturated oil to brush over the potatoes before and after cooking.
- No added salt is needed; rely on the stock for flavour.

* Using old potatoes and hard margarine for 1 portion (125 g raw potato)

19 Roast potatoes (pommes rôties) 1

Cal	Cal	Fat	Sat Fat	Carb	Sugar	Protein	Fibre	*
956 KJ	228 kcal	7.0 g	1.1 g	39.6 g	0.9 g	4.1 g	1.5 g	

1 Wash, peel and rewash the potatoes.
2 Cut into even-sized pieces (allow 3–4 pieces per portion).
3 Heat a good measure of oil or dripping in a roasting tray.
4 Add the well-dried potatoes and lightly brown on all sides.
5 Season lightly with salt and cook for about 1 hour in a hot oven at 230–250°C.
6 Turn the potatoes over after 30 minutes.
7 Cook to a golden brown. Drain and serve.

Note: Roast potatoes can be part-boiled for 10 minutes, refreshed and well dried before roasting. This will cut down on the cooking time and can also give a crisper potato.

HEALTHY EATING TIP

- Brush the potatoes with peanut or sunflower oil, with only a little in the roasting tray.
- Drain off all fat when cooked.

* Using old potatoes and peanut oil for 1 portion (125 g raw potato)

20 Roast potatoes (pommes rôties) 2

	4 portions
large roasting potatoes	6
dripping or 2nd-press olive oil	250 ml
seasoning	

1 Wash and peel the potatoes and cut into approx. 5 cm chunks.
2 Place in a pan of cold water, bring to the boil and cook slowly until just cooked; pre-heat the oven to 220°C.
3 Drain well. Meanwhile heat the dripping or oil in a pan, place the potatoes carefully in the roasting tray (with enough room to allow for roasting – too close together and they will steam).
4 Pour the hot oil or fat over the potatoes and place in the oven for 15 minutes.
5 After 15 minutes, reduce the heat to 180°C and baste every 5 minutes until the potatoes are golden and crisp.
6 Once cooked, serve immediately as prolonged holding will inevitably cause the inside to steam, making the outside soft and leathery

21 Château potatoes (pommes château)

1 Select small, even-sized potatoes and wash.
2 If they are of a fairly even size, they need not be peeled, but can be turned into barrel-shaped pieces approximately the size of fondant potatoes.
3 Place in a saucepan of boiling water for 2–3 minutes, refresh immediately. Drain in a colander.
4 Finish as for roast potatoes (recipe 20).

22 Cocotte potatoes (pommes cocotte)

1 Proceed as for château potatoes (recipe 21), but with the potatoes a quarter the size.
2 Cook in a sauté pan or frying pan.

23 Noisette potatoes (pommes noisette)

½ kg will yield 2 portions

1 Wash, peel and rewash the potatoes.
2 Scoop out balls with a noisette spoon.
3 Cook in a little oil in a sauté pan or frying pan. Colour on top of the stove and finish cooking in the oven at 230–250°C.

24 Potatoes with bacon and onions (pommes au lard)

Cal 836 KJ	Cal 199 kcal	Fat 10.1 g	Sat Fat 3.8 g	Carb 22.2 g	Sugar 1.8 g	Protein 6.4 g	Fibre 2.5 g	*

	4 portions	10 portions
peeled potatoes	400 g	1¼ kg
streaky bacon (lardons)	100 g	250 g
button onions	100 g	250 g
white stock	¼ litre	600 ml
salt, pepper		
chopped parsley		

HEALTHY EATING TIP
• Dry-fry the bacon in a well-seasoned pan and drain off any excess fat.
• Add little or no salt.

* Using old potatoes

1 Cut the potatoes into 1 cm dice.
2 Cut the bacon into ½ cm lardons; lightly fry in a little fat together with the onions and brown lightly.
3 Add the potatoes, half cover with stock, season lightly with salt and pepper. Cover with a lid and cook steadily in the oven at 230–250°C for approximately 30 minutes.
4 Correct the seasoning, serve in a vegetable dish, sprinkled with chopped parsley.

25 Potatoes cooked in milk with cheese *(gratin dauphinoise)* 1

Cal	Cal	Fat	Sat Fat	Carb	Sugar	Protein	Fibre
747 KJ	178 kcal	5.4 g	3.4 g	5.4 g	4.0 g	8.0 g	1.8 g

	4 portions	10 portions
potatoes	500 g	1¼ kg
milk	250 ml	600 ml
salt, pepper		
grated cheese, preferably		
Gruyère	50 g	125 g

1 Slice the peeled potatoes ½ cm thick.
2 Place in an ovenproof dish and cover with milk.
3 Season, sprinkle with grated cheese and cook in a moderate oven, 190°C, until the potatoes are cooked and golden brown.

26 Potatoes cooked in milk with cheese *(gratin dauphinoise)* 2

	4 portions
double cream	200 ml
milk	200 ml
cloves of garlic, crushed	1–2
large floury potatoes (750 g approx.)	2
salt, pepper	
butter	25 g
grated cheese (preferably Gruyère)	100 g

1 Pre heat the oven to 180°C.
2 Place the cream, milk and garlic in a saucepan and slowly bring to the boil. Remove and allow to cool.
3 Peel and thinly slice the potatoes (about 2 mm thick). Butter a small baking tray or earthenware, ovenproof dish and season lightly with salt and

pepper. Arrange slices of potato over the bottom of the dish overlapping as you go, lightly seasoning each layer with salt and pepper until all the potato is used.
4 Pour over the cream and milk mixture until the potatoes are just covered. Press down the potatoes with a fish slice or something flat so that the cream covers all the potatoes.
5 Bake in a moderate oven for 35 minutes.
6 Turn the oven down to 150°C and sprinkle the potatoes with grated cheese.
7 Cook until tender for a further 15 minutes (approx).
8 If the potatoes start to get too brown on top, cover with silver foil.

27 Delmonico potatoes *(pommes Delmonico)*

Cal	Cal	Fat	Sat Fat	Carb	Sugar	Protein	Fibre	*
900 KJ	214 kcal	6.3 g	3.7 g	37.5 g	2.7 g	4.4 g	2.0 g	

1 Wash, peel and rewash the potatoes.
2 Cut into 6 mm dice.
3 Barely cover with milk, season lightly with salt and pepper and allow to cook for 30–40 minutes.
4 Place in an earthenware dish, sprinkle with breadcrumbs and melted butter, brown in the oven or under the salamander and serve.

* Using old potatoes and whole milk

Figure 13.9 Delmonico potatoes

28 New potatoes (pommes nouvelles)

Cal	Cal	Fat	Sat Fat	Carb	Sugar	Protein	Fibre
383 KJ	91 kcal	0.1 g	0.0 g	22.0 g	0.8 g	1.9 g	2.4 g

Method 1

1 Wash the potatoes, and boil or steam in their jackets until cooked.
2 Cool slightly, peel while warm and place in a pan of cold water.
3 When required for service add a little salt and a bunch of mint to the potatoes; heat through slowly.
4 Drain well, serve brushed with melted butter and sprinkled with chopped mint, or decorate with blanched, refreshed mint leaves.

Method 2

1 Scrape the potatoes and wash well.
2 Place in a pan of lightly salted boiling water with a bunch of mint and boil gently until cooked (about 20 minutes). Serve as above.

Note: The starch cells of new potatoes are immature; to help break down these cells new potatoes are cooked in water that is already boiling.

Figure 13.10 Turned, cooked new potatoes (pink fir variety)

29 New rissolée potatoes (pommes nouvelles rissolées)

Cal	Cal	Fat	Sat Fat	Carb	Sugar	Protein	Fibre
610 KJ	145 kcal	6.1 g	1.1 g	22.0 g	0.8 g	1.9 g	2.4 g

1 New potatoes are cooked, drained and fried to a golden brown in oil or butter, or a combination of both.

30 Parmentier potatoes (pommes parmentier)

Cal	Cal	Fat	Sat Fat	Carb	Sugar	Protein	Fibre	*
1819 KJ	433 kcal	33.5 g	6.3 g	32.8 g	0.7 g	2.3 g	1.7 g	

½ kg will yield 2–3 portions

1 Select medium to large potatoes.
2 Wash, peel and rewash.
3 Trim on three sides and cut into 1 cm slices.
4 Cut the slices into 1 cm strips.
5 Cut the strips into 1 cm dice.
6 Wash well and dry in a cloth.
7 Cook in hot shallow oil in a frying pan until golden brown.
8 Drain, season lightly and serve sprinkled with chopped parsley.

* Using peanut oil

31 Swiss potato cakes (rösti)

Cal 700 KJ	Cal 168 kcal	Fat 10.5 g	Sat Fat 6.5 g	Carb 17.3 g	Sugar 0.7 g	Protein 2.2 g	Fibre 1.3 g	*

1 Allow 100 g unpeeled potato per portion.
2 Parboil in salted water (or steam) for approximately 5 minutes.
3 Cool, then shred into large flakes on a grater.
4 For 4 portions heat 50 g oil, butter or margarine in a frying pan.
5 Add the potatoes, and season lightly with salt and pepper.
6 Press the potato together and cook on both sides until brown and crisp.

Note: The potato can be made in a four-portion cake or in individual rounds.

Rösti may also be made from raw potatoes.

HEALTHY EATING TIP
• Lightly oil a well-seasoned pan with sunflower oil to fry the rösti.
• Use the minimum amount of salt.

Variations
• Add sweated chopped onion.
• Add sweated lardons of bacon.
• Use 2 parts of grated potato to 1 part grated apple.

* Using butter

Figure 13.11 Rösti

Rye bread
(recipe 96)

Multi-seed
bread

Fruit cake
(recipe 176)

Chocol
cookies

Potato and yoghurt bread

hortbread
ecipe 186)

Banana bread

chapter 14

PASTRY

Prepare hot and cold desserts and puddings

Practical skills
The candidate will be able to:
1 Prepare hot and cold desserts and puddings for cooking
2 Demonstrate the correct use of equipment to prepare hot and cold desserts and puddings
3 Demonstrate safe and hygienic practices

Underpinning knowledge
The candidate will be able to:
1 Identify different types of hot desserts and puddings
2 Identify different types of cold desserts
3 Explain the quality points of the main ingredients
4 Describe the most commonly used preparation methods for the production of hot and cold desserts and puddings
5 State how to adjust the quantity of ingredients to give the correct portion yield for hot and cold desserts and puddings
6 Identify correct storage procedures for hot and cold desserts and puddings

Cook and finish hot and cold desserts and puddings

Practical skills
The candidate will be able to:
1 Demonstrate the correct use of equipment to cook and finish hot and cold desserts and puddings

2 Produce different types of hot and cold desserts and puddings
3 Demonstrate finishing and presentation methods
4 Apply quality points to each stage of the process
5 Demonstrate safe and hygienic practices
6 Evaluate the finished product

Underpinning knowledge
The candidate will be able to:
1 Explain the cooking principles for hot and cold desserts and puddings
2 Identify sauces that may be served with hot and cold desserts and puddings
3 Describe finishing and decorating techniques
4 Explain the quality points when cooking and finishing hot and cold desserts and puddings
5 Identify correct holding and storage procedures for finished products

VRQ
Unit 214   Prepare and cook bakery products

NVQ
Unit 526 (1FPC8)   Cook and finish simple bread and dough products

Unit 644 (2FPC9)   Prepare, cook and finish basic bread and dough products

Unit 646 (2FPC11) Prepare, cook and finish basic cakes, sponges and scones

Prepare paste, biscuit, cake and sponge products

Practical skills
The candidate will be able to:
1 Prepare paste products for cooking
2 Prepare biscuit products for baking
3 Prepare cake and sponge mixtures for baking
4 Demonstrate the use of the correct tools and equipment to prepare paste, biscuit, cake and sponge products
5 Demonstrate safe and hygienic practices
6 Undertake correct storage procedures for paste, biscuit, cake and sponge products

Underpinning knowledge
The candidate will be able to:
1 Identify different types of paste products
2 State the uses for paste products
3 Identify different types of biscuit, cake and sponge products
4 State the uses for biscuit, cake and sponge products
5 Explain the quality points of the main ingredients
6 Describe the most commonly used preparation methods for the production of paste, biscuit, cake and sponge products
7 State how to adjust the quantity of ingredients to give the correct portion yield from paste, biscuit, cake and sponge products
8 Identify correct storage procedures for raw pastes

Cook and finish pastry, biscuit, cake and sponge products

Practical skills
The candidate will be able to:
1 Demonstrate correct use of tools and equipment used in the cooking and finishing of paste, biscuit, cakes and sponge products
2 Cook and finish paste products
3 Bake and finish biscuit, cake and sponge products
4 Demonstrate safe and hygienic practices
5 Evaluate the finished dish

Underpinning knowledge
The candidate will be able to:
1 Identify cooking principles for pastes, biscuits, cakes, sponges and fillings
2 Describe finishing and decorating techniques
3 Explain the quality points when checking finished paste, biscuit, cake and sponge products
4 State the storage procedures for finished products

Prepare fermented dough products

Practical skills
The candidate will be able to:
1 Prepare fermented dough products
2 Demonstrate the use of the correct tools and equipment to prepare dough products
3 Demonstrate safe and hygienic practices

Underpinning knowledge

The candidate will be able to:

1 Explain the purpose of the main ingredients for dough
2 Identify different types of dough
3 State the use for each dough type
4 Explain the quality points of the main ingredients
5 State the most commonly used preparation methods for the production of dough
6 State how to adjust the quantity of ingredients to give the correct portion yield from dough products
7 Identify the correct storage procedures for raw dough

Cook and finish fermented dough products

Practical skills

The candidate will be able to:

1 Demonstrate the use of correct tools and equipment to cook dough products
2 Cook dough products
3 Finish and present dough products
4 Demonstrate safe and hygienic practices
5 Evaluate the finished product

Underpinning knowledge

The candidate will be able to:

1 Identify cooking principles for dough products
2 Explain the quality points when checking finished dough products
3 Describe finishing requirements
4 State the storage procedures for finished products

Unit 645   **Prepare, cook and finish basic pastry products**

Baking, patisserie, confectionery and healthy eating

Today bakery goods, pastry and confectionery remain popular with the consumer, however there is now a demand for products that have reduced fat and sugar content as many people are keen to pursue a healthy lifestyle. Chefs will continue to respond to this demand by modifying recipes to reduce the fat and sugar content; they may also use alternative ingredients, such as low-calorie sweeteners where possible and unsaturated fats.

Egg custard-based desserts

Egg custard mixture provides the chef with a versatile basic set of ingredients that covers a wide range of sweets. Often the mixture is referred to as crème renversée. Some examples of sweets produced using this mixture are:

- crème caramel
- bread and butter pudding
- diplomat pudding
- cabinet pudding
- queen of puddings
- baked egg custard.

Savoury egg custard is used to make:

- quiches
- tartlets
- flans.

When a starch such as flour is added to the ingredients for an egg custard mix, this changes the characteristic of the end product.

Pastry cream (also known as confectioner's custard) is a filling used for many sweets, gâteaux, flans and tartlets, and as a basis for soufflé mixes. **Sauce anglaise** is used as a base for some ice creams. It is also used in its own right as a sauce to accompany a range of sweets.

Basic egg custard sets by coagulation of the egg protein. The first phase of this coagulation is the 'tender solid' when the temperature reaches 65°C. This only represents 12 per cent of the potential coagulation: the rest is caused by the ovoalbumin and occurs later in the heating, at 80°C, at which point the tender white becomes much firmer. The egg yolk proteins start to set at 70°C. The

Figure 14.1 Chocolate éclair, bread and butter pudding, rum and raisin ice cream on a crisped (baked) slice of apple

combination of both affords a setting temperature of 73°C. If the egg protein is overheated or overcooked, it will shrink and water will be lost from the mixture, causing undesirable bubbles in the custard. This loss of water is called syneresis.

Ingredients for egg custards

Eggs
Egg yolk is high in saturated fat. The yolk is a good source of protein and also contains vitamins and iron. The egg white is made up of protein (albumen) and water. The egg yolk also contains lecithin, which acts as an emulsifier in dishes such as mayonnaise.

Milk
Full-cream, skimmed or semi-skimmed can be used for these desserts.

Milk is a basic and fundamental element of our diets throughout our lives. It is composed of water, sugar and has a minimum of 3.5 per cent fat. It is essential in an infinite number of preparations, from creams, ice creams, yeast doughs, mousses and custards to certain ganaches, cookies, tuiles and muffins. A yeast dough will change considerably in texture, taste and colour if made with milk instead of water.

Milk has a lightly sweet taste and little odour. Two distinct processes are used to conserve it:

1 **pasteurisation** – the milk is heated to between 73°C and 85°C for a few seconds, then cooled quickly to 4°C
2 **sterilisation (UHT)** – the milk is heated to 140–150°C for 2 seconds, then cooled quickly.

Milk is homogenised to evenly disperse the fat, since the fat has a tendency to rise to the surface (see 'Cream', below).

Here are some useful facts about milk.

- Pasteurised milk has better taste and aroma than UHT milk.
- Milk is a useful agent in the development of flavour in sauces and creams, due to its lactic fermentation.
- Milk is an agent of colour, texture and aroma in doughs.
- Because of its lactic ferments, it facilitates the maturation of doughs and creams.
- There are other types of milk, such as sheep's, that are very interesting to use in many restaurant desserts.
- Milk is much more fragile than cream. In recipes, adding it in certain proportions is advisable for a much more subtle and fragile final product.

Cream

Cream is often added to egg custard desserts to enrich them and to improve the feel in the mouth (mouth-feel) of the final product. Indeed, it is used in many recipes because of its high fat content and great versatility.

Cream is the concentrated milk fat that is skimmed off the top of the milk when it has been left to sit. A film forms on the surface because of the difference in density between fat and liquid. This process is accelerated mechanically in large industries through heat and centrifuge.

Cream should contain at least 18 per cent butter fat. Cream for whipping must contain more than 30 per cent butter fat. Commercially frozen cream is available in 2 and 10 kg slabs. Types, packaging, storage and uses of cream are listed in Table 14.1.

All cream products must be kept in the refrigerator for health and safety reasons. Whipping and double cream may be whipped to make them lighter and to increase volume. Cream will whip more easily if it is kept at refrigeration temperature. Indeed, all dairy products must be kept in the refrigerator as they present the perfect medium for the growth of micro-organisms. Handle these products with care and remember that they will also absorb odour. Never store near onions or other strong-smelling foods.

There are two main methods for conserving cream:

1 **pasteurisation** – the cream is heated to 85–90°C for a few seconds and then cooled quickly; this cream retains all its flavour properties
2 **sterilisation (UHT)** – this consists of heating the cream to 140–150°C for 2 seconds; cream treated this way loses some of its flavour properties, but it keeps longer.

Always use pasteurised cream when possible – for example, in the restaurant when specialities are made for immediate consumption. Here we have the advantage and possibility of making 'ephemeral' patisserie (dessert cuisine) – for example, a chocolate bonbon that will be consumed immediately.

Here are some useful facts about cream.

- Cream whips with the addition of air, thanks to its fat content. This retains air bubbles formed during beating.

Figure 14.2   Chocolate mousse, lemon sorbet on a chocolate cup, chocolate clafoutis

Table 14.1 Types of cream

Type of cream	Legal minimum fat (%)	Processing and packaging	Storage	Characteristics and uses
half cream	12	homogenised and may be pasteurised or ultra-heat treated	2–3 days	does not whip; used for pouring; suitable for low-fat diets
cream or single cream	18	homogenised and pasteurised by heating to about 79.5°C for 15 seconds then cooled to 4.5°C. Automatically filled into bottles and cartons after processing. Sealed with foil caps. Bulk quantities according to local suppliers	2–3 days in summer; 3–4 days in winter under refrigeration	a pouring cream suitable for coffee, cereals, soup or fruit. A valuable addition to cooked dishes. Makes delicious sauces. Does not whip
whipping cream	35	not homogenised, but pasteurised and packaged as above	2–3 days in summer; 3–4 days in winter under refrigeration	the ideal whipping cream. Suitable for piping, cake and dessert decoration, ice-cream, cake and pastry fillings
double cream	48	slightly homogenised, and pasteurised and packaged as above	2–3 days in summer; 3–4 days in winter under refrigeration	a rich pouring cream which will also whip. The cream will float on coffee or soup
double cream 'thick'	48	heavily homogenised, then pasteurised and packaged. Usually only available in domestic quantities	2–3 days in summer; 3–4 days in winter under refrigeration	a rich spoonable cream that will not whip
clotted cream	55	heated to 82°C and cooled for about 4½ hours. The cream crust is then skimmed off. Usually packed in cartons by hand. Bulk quantities according to local suppliers	2–3 days in summer; 3–4 days in winter under refrigeration	a very thick cream with its own special flavour and colour. Delicious with scones, fruit and fruit pies
ultra-heat treated (UHT) cream	12 18 35	half (12%), single (18%) or whipping cream (35%) is homogenised and heated to 132°C for one second and cooled immediately. Aseptically packed in polythene and foil-lined containers. Available in bigger packs for catering purposes	6 weeks if unopened. Needs no refrigeration. Usually date stamped	a pouring cream

- Cream is an agent that adds texture.
- All cream, once boiled and cooled, can be whipped again with no problem.
- Also, once it is boiled and mixed or infused, with whatever we want (maintaining certain norms), it will whip again with no problem if first left to cool for 24 hours.
- To whip cream well, it must be cold (around 4°C). The warmer it is, the harder and slower it will be to whip. If it reaches 21°C, the disperse phase (what holds the air) will no longer be stable and hold aeration.
- Infusions with cream can be hot or cold. If cold, this requires an infusion time of at least 12 hours.

Traditional custard made from custard powder
Custard powder is used to make custard sauce. It is made from vanilla-flavoured cornflour with yellow colouring added, and is a substitute for eggs. The fat content is reduced when made using semi-skimmed milk as opposed to full-fat milk.

Figure 14.3 ✏ Cream caramel, fruit crumble, strawberry mousse

Points to remember

Egg custard-based desserts
- Always work in a clean and tidy way, complying with food hygiene regulations.
- Prevent cross-contamination occurring by not allowing any foreign substances to come into contact with the mixture.
- Always heat the egg yolks or eggs to 70°C, otherwise use pasteurised egg yolks or eggs.
- Follow the recipe carefully.

- Ensure that all heating and cooling temperatures are followed.
- Always store the end-product carefully at the right temperature.
- Check all weighing scales.
- Check all raw materials for correct use-by dates.
- Always wash your hands when handling fresh eggs or dairy products and other pastry ingredients.
- Never use cream to decorate a product that is still warm.
- Always remember to follow the Food Hygiene (Amendments) Regulations 1993/95.
- Check the temperature of the refrigerators and freezers, to see that they comply with the current regulations.

Fresh cream
- The piping of fresh cream is a skill; like all other skills it takes practice to become proficient. The finished item should look attractive, the piping being neat, simple, clean and tidy.
- All piping bags should be sterilised after each use as these may well be a source of contamination; alternatively use a disposable piping bag.
- Make sure that all the equipment you need for piping is hygienically cleaned before and after use to avoid cross-contamination.

Salt

Where salt is found

Salt (chemical name 'sodium chloride') is one of the most important ingredients. It is well known that salt is a necessary part of the human diet, present in small or large proportions in many natural foods. We generally associate it with seasoning of foods to improve their flavour, but it is also necessary in the making of many sweet dishes.

Characteristics and advantages of using salt in yeast dough

Salted dough is much more manageable than unsalted. Salt is usually added a few moments before the end of the kneading, since its function is to help expand the dough's volume.

Salt considerably enhances all preparations, whether they be sweet or salty.

It is a good idea to add a pinch of salt to all sweet preparations, nougats, chocolate bonbons and cakes to intensify flavours.

Salt softens sugar and butter, activates the taste buds and enhances all aromas.

What you need to know about salt

- Salt gives us the possibility of many combinations. At times, these may seem normal (like a terrine of *foie gras* and coarse salt), others surprising (like praline with coarse salt).
- The addition of salt enhances the flavour of foods when its quantity is well adjusted; but if we add it in greater quantity than we are used to, it produces a very interesting, completely unknown result. It certainly is not adequate in all of our preparations, so we should be careful and check the results of our combinations.

Eggs

The egg is one of the principal ingredients of the gastronomy world. Its great versatility and extraordinary properties as a thickener, emulsifier and stabiliser make its presence important in various creations in patisserie: sauces, creams, sponge cakes, custards and ice creams. Although it is not often the main ingredient, it plays specific and determining roles in terms of texture, taste and aroma, among other things. The egg is fundamental in preparation such as brioches, crèmes anglaises, sponge cakes and crèmes patissieres. The extent to which eggs are used (or not) makes an enormous difference to the quality of the product.

A good custard cannot be made without eggs, for they cause the required coagulation and give it the desired consistency and finesse.

Eggs are also an important ingredient in ice cream, where their yolks act as an emulsifier thanks to the lecithin they contain, which aids the emulsion of fats.

What you need to know about eggs

- Eggs act as a texture agent in, for example, patisseries and ice creams.
- They intensify the aroma of pastries like brioche.
- They enhance flavours.
- They give volume to whisked sponges and batters.
- They strengthen the structure of preparations such as sponge cakes.
- They act as a thickening agent – in crème anglaise, for example.
- They act as an emulsifier in preparations such as mayonnaise and ice cream.
- They act as a stabiliser – in ice cream, for example.
- A fresh egg should have a small, shallow air pocket inside it.
- The yolk of fresh egg should be bulbous, firm and bright.
- The fresher the egg, the more viscous the egg white.
- Eggs should be stored far from strong odours as, despite their shells, these are easily absorbed.
- In a whole 60 g egg, the yolk weighs about 20 g, the white 30 g and the shell 10 g.

Egg whites
- To avert danger of salmonella, if the egg white is not going to be cooked or will not reach a temperature of 70°C, use pasteurised egg whites. Egg white is available chilled, frozen or dried.
- Equipment must be scrupulously clean and free from any traces of fat, as this prevents the whites from whipping; fat or grease prevents the albumen strands from bonding and trapping the air bubbles.
- Take care that there are no traces of yolk in the white, as yolk contains fat.
- A little acid (cream of tartar or lemon juice) strengthens the egg white, extends the foam and produces more meringue. The acid also has the effect of stabilising the meringue.
- If the foam is over-whipped, the albumen strands, which hold the water molecules with the sugar suspended on the outside of the bubble, are overstretched. The water and sugar make contact and the sugar dissolves, making

the meringue heavy and wet. This can sometimes be rescued by further whisking until it foams up but very often you will find that you may have to discard the mixture and start again.

Meringues
Egg white forms a foam that is used for aerating sweets and many other desserts (see recipe 48).

Egg custard-based recipes

1 Baked egg custard

Cal	Cal	Fat	Sat Fat	Carb	Sugar	Protein	Fibre	*
780 KJ	186 kcal	8.4 g	0.0 g	19.0 g	19.0 g	8.7 g	0.0 g	

	4 portions	10 portions
medium eggs	3	7
sugar, caster or unrefined	50 g	125 g
vanilla essence	2–3 drops	5 drops
milk, whole or skimmed	½ litre	1¼ litres
grated nutmeg		

1 Whisk the eggs, sugar and essence.
2 Pour on the warmed milk, whisking continuously.
3 Pass through a fine strainer into a pie dish or individual dishes.

4 Add a little grated nutmeg. Wipe the edge of the pie dish or individual dishes clean.
5 Stand in a roasting tray half full of water and cook slowly in a moderate oven at 160°C for 45 minutes to 1 hour.
6 Clean the edges of the pie dish and serve.

Note: May be served with stewed fruit (e.g. rhubarb, apple).

* *Using whole milk*

2 Queen of puddings

Cal	Cal	Fat	Sat Fat	Carb	Sugar	Protein	Fibre
1522 KJ	362 kcal	14.7 g	6.8 g	50.0 g	41.2 g	10.9 g	0.9 g

	4 portions	10 portions
milk, whole or skimmed	½ litre	1¼ litres
eggs	3	7
caster or unrefined sugar	50 g	125 g
vanilla essence		
cake crumbs	75 g	180 g
butter or margarine	25 g	60 g
caster sugar for meringue	50 g	125 g
jam	50 g	125 g

1 Boil the milk.
2 Pour on to 2 yolks, 1 egg (5 yolks, 2 eggs for 10 portions), sugar and vanilla essence, whisk well.
3 Place the crumbs in a buttered pie dish or individual dishes.
4 Strain the custard on to the crumbs.
5 Bake in a moderate oven in a bain-marie for 30 minutes or until set.
6 Allow to cool.
7 For the meringue, stiffly beat the egg whites and fold in the caster sugar.
8 Spread the warmed jam over the baked mixture.
9 Using a large star tube, pipe the meringue to cover the jam.
10 Brown in a hot oven at 220°C and serve.

3 Bread and butter pudding

Cal 1093 KJ	Cal 260 kcal	Fat 11.6 g	Sat Fat 5.9 g	Carb 30.4 g	Sugar 23.4 g	Protein 10.6 g	Fibre 1.0 g	*

	4 portions	10 portions
sultanas	50 g	100 g
slices of white or wholemeal bread, spread with butter or margarine	2	5
eggs (medium)	3	7
sugar, caster or unrefined	50 g	125 g
vanilla essence or a vanilla pod	2–3 drops	5 drops
milk, whole or skimmed	½ litre	1¼ litres

1 Wash the sultanas and place in a pie dish or individual dishes.
2 Remove the crusts from the bread and cut each slice into four triangles; neatly arrange overlapping in the pie dish.
3 Prepare an egg custard as in recipe 1.
4 Strain on to the bread, dust lightly with sugar.
5 Cook and serve as for baked egg custard.

Note: For a crisp crust finish, sprinkle with icing sugar and brown well under the salamander.

Traditional bread and butter pudding is made in a pie dish and is of a soft consistency. To prepare individual plated portions in the contemporary fashion requires either more egg or bread which gives a firmer consistency.

Variations
- Before cooking, add either freshly grated nutmeg or orange zest, or a combination of both
- Fruit loaf, brioche or panettone in place of bread
- Chocolate bread and butter pudding – add 25 g chocolate powder to the egg custard mix
- Add soft, well-drained poached fruit (or tinned) (e.g. peaches, pears) to the bottom of the dish

* *Using white bread and butter*

Figure 14.4 Bread and butter pudding (modern)

HEALTHY EATING TIP
- Try using half wholemeal and half white bread.
- The fat content will be reduced by using semi-skimmed milk in the custard.
- Adding more dried fruit would reduce the need for so much sugar.

4 Cabinet pudding (pouding cabinet)

Cal	Cal	Fat	Sat Fat	Carb	Sugar	Protein	Fibre	*
1427 KJ	340 kcal	15.8 g	7.2 g	40.9 g	35.5 g	11.0 g	0.7 g	

	4 portions	10 portions
plain sponge cake	100 g	250 g
glacé cherries	25 g	60 g
currants and sultanas	25 g	60 g
angelica	10 g	25 g
milk, whole or skimmed	½ litre	1¼ litres
eggs (medium)	3–4	8–10
caster or unrefined sugar	50 g	125 g
vanilla essence or a		
vanilla pod	2–3 drops (1 pod)	7 drops (2 pods)

1 Cut the cake into ½ cm dice.
2 Mix with the chopped cherries and fruits (which can be soaked in rum).
3 Place in a greased, sugared charlotte mould or four dariole moulds. Do not fill more than halfway.
4 Warm the milk and whisk on to the eggs, sugar and essence (or vanilla pod).
5 Strain on to the mould.
6 Place in a roasting tin, half full of water; allow to stand for 5–10 minutes.
7 Cook in a moderate oven at 150–160°C for 30–45 minutes.
8 Leave to set for a few minutes before turning out.
9 Serve a fresh egg custard (recipe 1) or hot apricot sauce (recipe 62) separately.

Note: Diplomat pudding is made as for cabinet pudding, but served cold with either redcurrant, raspberry, apricot or vanilla sauce.

* Using whole milk and 3 eggs. Using whole milk and 4 eggs: 1512 kJ/360 kcal; 17.3 g Fat; 7.7 g Sat Fat; 40.9 g Carb; 35.5 g Sugar; 12.7 g Protein; 0.7 g Fibre

5 Cream caramel (crème caramel)

Cal	Cal	Fat	Sat Fat	Carb	Sugar	Protein	Fibre	*
868 KJ	207 kcal	7.2 g	3.3 g	30.2 g	30.2 g	7.3 g	0.0 g	

	4–6 portions	10–12 portions
Caramel		
sugar, granulated		
or cube	100 g	200 g
water	125 ml	250 ml
Cream		
milk, whole or skimmed	½ litre	1 litre
eggs (medium)	4	8
sugar, caster or unrefined	50 g	100 g
vanilla essence or a		
vanilla pod	3–4 drops	6–8 drops

1 Prepare the caramel by placing three-quarters of the water in a thick-based pan, adding the sugar and allowing to boil gently, without shaking or stirring the pan.
2 When the sugar has cooked to a golden-brown caramel colour, add the remaining quarter of the water, reboil until the sugar and water mix, then pour into the bottom of dariole moulds.
3 Prepare the cream by warming the milk and whisking on to the beaten eggs, sugar and essence (or vanilla pod).
4 Strain and pour into the prepared moulds.
5 Place in a roasting tin half full of water.
6 Cook in a moderate oven at approximately 160°C for about 40 minutes.
7 When thoroughly cold, loosen the edges of the cream caramel with the fingers, shake firmly to loosen and turn out on to a flat dish or plates.
8 Pour any caramel remaining in the mould around the creams.

Note: Cream caramels may be served with whipped cream or a fruit sauce such as passionfruit, and accompanied by a sweet biscuit (e.g. shortbread, palmiers).

Adding a squeeze of lemon juice to the caramel will invert the sugar, thus preventing recrystallisation.

* Using whole milk

6 Burned, caramelised or browned cream (crème brûlée)

Cal 1154 KJ	Cal 278 kcal	Fat 21.9 g	Sat Fat 12.1 g	Carb 14.8 g	Sugar 14.8 g	Protein 6.2 g	Fibre 0.0 g

	4 portions	10 portions
milk	125 ml	300 ml
double cream	125 ml	300 ml
natural vanilla essence or pod	3–4 drops	7–10 drops
eggs (medium)	2	5
egg yolk	1	2–3
caster sugar	25 g	60 g
demerara sugar		

1 Warm the milk, cream and vanilla essence in a pan.
2 Mix the eggs, egg yolk and caster sugar in a basin and add the warm milk. Stir well and pass through a fine strainer.
3 Pour the cream into individual dishes and place them into a tray half-filled with warm water.
4 Place in the oven at approximately 160°C for about 30–40 minutes, until set.
5 Sprinkle the tops with demerara sugar and glaze under the salamander or by blowtorch to a golden brown.
6 Clean the dishes and serve.

Variations
Sliced strawberries, raspberries or other fruits (e.g. peaches, apricots) may be placed in the bottom of the dish before adding the cream mixture, or placed on top after the creams are caramelised.

Figure 14.5 Cream caramels

Figure 14.6 A blowtorch, which may be used in this recipe: extreme care must be taken when using a blowtorch; the manufacturer's instructions must be followed explicitly because there is the danger of a gas explosion from the canister if used incorrectly

Egg-based sauces and creams

7 Sabayon sauce (sauce sabayon)

Cal	Cal	Fat	Sat Fat	Carb	Sugar	Protein	Fibre	*
454 KJ	108 kcal	3.4 g	1.0 g	13.3 g	13.3 g	1.8 g	0.0 g	

	8 portions
egg yolks	4–6
caster or unrefined sugar	100 g
dry white wine	¼ litre

1 Whisk the egg yolks and sugar in a 1 litre pan or basin (not aluminium) until white.
2 Dilute with the wine.
3 Place the pan or basin in a bain-marie of warm water.
4 Whisk the mixture continuously until it increases to four times its bulk and is firm and frothy.

Note: Sauce sabayon may be offered as an accompaniment to any suitable hot sweet (e.g. pudding soufflé or soufflés).

Variations
A sauce sabayon may also be made using milk in place of wine, which can be flavoured according to taste (e.g. vanilla, nutmeg, cinnamon).

* *Using 5 egg yolks*

8 Sabayon with Marsala (zabaglione)

Cal	Cal	Fat	Sat Fat	Carb	Sugar	Protein	Fibre
746 KJ	177 kcal	5.5 g	1.6 g	27.4 g	27.4 g	2.9 g	0.0 g

	4 portions	10 portions
egg yolks	8	20
caster or unrefined sugar	200 g	500 g
Marsala	150 ml	375 ml

1 Whisk the egg yolks and sugar in a bowl until almost white.
2 Mix in the Marsala.
3 Place the bowl and contents in a bain-marie of warm water.
4 Whisk the mixture continuously until it increases to four times its bulk and is firm and frothy.
5 Pour the mixture into glass goblets.
6 Accompany with a suitable biscuit (e.g. sponge fingers).

Note: This is a traditional Italian dessert, which is sometimes prepared in the restaurant in a special zabaglione pan.

Variations
Use sherry, whisky or brandy in place of the Marsala.

9 Fresh egg custard sauce (sauce à l'anglaise)

Cal	Cal	Fat	Sat Fat	Carb	Sugar	Protein	Fibre	*
1666 KJ	397 kcal	21.7 g	9.9 g	38.0 g	38.0 g	14.7 g	0.0 g	

	4 portions	10 portions
egg yolks	2	5
caster or unrefined sugar	25 g	60 g
vanilla essence or vanilla pod	2–3 drops	5–7 drops
milk, whole or skimmed	250 ml	625 ml

1 Mix the yolks, sugar and essence in a basin.
2 Whisk on the boiled milk and return to a thick-bottomed pan.
3 Place on a low heat and stir with a wooden spoon until it coats the back of the spoon. Do not allow to boil or the eggs will scramble.
4 Pour through a fine sieve into a bowl. Set on ice to arrest the cooking.

Variations
Other flavours may be used in place of vanilla. For example:
● coffee
● curaçao
● chocolate

- Cointreau
- rum
- Tia Maria
- brandy
- whisky
- ground cinnamon

- kirsch
- orange flower water.

Note: If using skimmed milk, double the number of egg yolks in order to achieve the right consistency.

* Using whole milk; four portions

10 Pastry cream (crème pâtissière)

Cal 4564 KJ	Cal 1087 kcal	Fat 31.7 g	Sat Fat 16.0 g	Carb 176.6 g	Sugar 129.3 g	Protein 34.8 g	Fibre 2.1 g	*

medium eggs	2
caster or unrefined sugar	100 g
flour, white or wholemeal	50 g
custard powder	10 g
milk, whole or skimmed	½ litre
vanilla pod or essence	

1 Whisk the eggs and sugar in a bowl until almost white.
2 Mix in the flour and custard powder.
3 Boil the milk in a thick-based pan.
4 Whisk on to the eggs, sugar and flour and mix well.
5 Return to the cleaned pan, stir to the boil.
6 Add a few drops of vanilla essence or a vanilla pod.
7 Remove from the heat and pour into a basin.
8 Place a piece of clingfilm over the top and press down to prevent a skin forming.

Variations
Pastry cream may be varied with other flavours. For example:
- rum
- lemon
- brandy

- praline
- Tia Maria
- strawberry
- lime
- passion fruit
- whisky
- almond
- orange
- Calvados.

Other variations include the following.
- *Chocolate pastry cream:* dissolve 100 g of couverture or 50 g cocoa powder in the milk and proceed as above.
- *Coffee pastry cream:* add coffee essence to taste and proceed as above.
- *Pastry cream* is a basic preparation used in many pastry dishes, e.g. as a base for soufflés and for some fruit flans or tartlets, as well as in many other pastries. Traditionally chocolate éclairs are filled with chocolate pastry cream and coffee éclairs with coffee pastry cream.

* Using white flour and whole milk

Basic mousses and variations

11 Basic fruit mousse

Makes 690 g, 9 portions

fruit purée	225 g
egg whites	115 g
caster sugar	100 g
gelatine sheets (bronze)	4
semi-whipped cream	225 g
desired liquor	25 g

1 Bring the fruit purée to just under boiling point.
2 Whip the egg whites to a snow, add the sugar and combine (this offers a softer, less dense meringue finish and homogenises into a mousse).
3 Slowly add the softened gelatine to the warmed purée.
4 Add all the ingredients and pour into the desired moulds.
5 To serve, unmould onto suitable plates, garnish with fresh fruit and a suitable coulis.

12 Mango mousse

Cal	Cal	Fat	Sat Fat	Carb	Sugar	Protein	Fibre	Salt
590 KJ	141 kcal	9.2 g	5.7 g	13.6 g	13.5 g	1.9 g	0.7 g	0.1 g

Makes 900 g, 15 portions

mango purée	400 g
egg whites	100 g
caster sugar	132 g
leaves gelatine (soaked)	8
cream	260 g
fresh mango to garnish	

1 Bring the mango purée to just under boiling point.
2 Whip the egg whites to a snow, add the sugar and combine (this offers a softer, less dense meringue finish and homogenises into a mousse).
3 Add the softened gelatine to the warmed purée, slowly add all the ingredients, pour into the desired moulds and allow to set.
4 To serve, unmould onto suitable plates, garnish with fresh mango.

13 Pear mousse

Makes 760 g, 12 portions

The recipe uses powdered egg whites instead of fresh. The principle reason for this – other than hygiene, as the powdered egg white would be pasteurised – is that the less water that is added to a preparation, the more the principle ingredient can be tasted because it is not being diluted by flavourless liquid. The addition of powdered egg whites will still offer the same properties as fresh egg whites, but using the liquid in the pear purée as a re-hydrating medium. The use of powdered egg whites lends itself better to low–medium flavours like that of pear.

leaves of gelatine (soaked)	8
pear purée	500 g
powdered egg whites	25 g
double cream	200 g
Poire William	20 ml

1 Soak the gelatine in cold water.
2 Whip the purée and powdered egg white until triple in volume; semi-whip the double cream.
3 Melt the gelatine in the Poire William and incorporate with the pear meringue.
4 Fold in the whipped cream and pipe into desired moulds. Allow to set.
5 To serve, unmould on to suitable plates, and garnish with suitable fruit and a fresh fruit coulis.

14 Caramel mousse

Cal	Cal	Fat	Sat Fat	Carb	Sugar	Protein	Fibre	Salt
2741 KJ	655 kcal	57.1 g	35.6 g	34.4 g	34.4 g	3.1 g	0.0 g	0.1 g

Makes 1560 g, 17 portions

leaves gelatine (soaked)	8
sugar	300 g
cream	500 ml
half-whipped cream	750 ml

1 Soften the gelatine in water.
2 Make a direct caramel with the sugar, being careful not to burn.
3 Carefully pour the cream over the caramel and simmer until the caramel has dissolved. Allow to cool, but not get completely cold.
4 Add the gelatine and then carefully fold in the whipped cream and pour into the appropriate moulds.
5 To serve, unmould on to suitable plates and garnish with fresh fruit.

15 White chocolate mousse

Cal 2208 KJ	Cal 532 kcal	Fat 41.3 g	Sat Fat 24.4 g	Carb 31.5 g	Sugar 31.5 g	Protein 10.4 g	Fibre 0.0 g	*

	4 portions	10 portions
milk, whole or skimmed	125 ml	300 ml
orange, grated zest	1	2–3
white chocolate	150 g	375 g
medium eggs	2	5
caster sugar	25 g	60 g
leaf gelatine	6 g	12 g
whipping cream, fromage frais or natural yoghurt	250 ml	625 ml

1 Heat the milk to boiling point with the grated zest of the orange.
2 Add the white chocolate and melt. Stir well, away from the heat.
3 Whisk the eggs and sugar together, add the hot milk and return to the saucepan.
4 Stir on the side of the stove until the mixture coats the back of a spoon, but do not boil. Remove from the heat.
5 Add the soaked and squeezed gelatine and bring down to setting point.
6 Fold in the whipping cream or alternative. Carefully and immediately pour into the mould.
7 Turn out and use as required.

Note: The mousse can be prepared in individual moulds, turned out onto plates, topped with poached fruit (e.g. pears, peaches, apricots) or fresh berries (e.g. loganberries, raspberries, strawberries). It can be coated with a suitable sauce (e.g. lemon, orange, lime, strawberry, Grand Marnier, grenadine).

* Using whole milk and whipped cream. Using whole milk and yoghurt: 1436 kJ/343 kcal Energy; 17.9 g Fat; 9.7 g Sat Fat; 34.7 g Carb; 34.7 g Sugar; 12.7 g Protein; 0.0 g Fibre

16 Avocado mousse with poached pear and strawberry sauce

Cal 1449 KJ	Cal 347 kcal	Fat 24.8 g	Sat Fat 10.4 g	Carb 28.4 g	Sugar 27.4 g	Protein 4.5 g	Fibre 2.9 g	*

	4 portions	10 portions
lemon, juice of	½	1
avocado purée	250 ml	625 ml
icing sugar	50 g	125 g
leaf gelatine	12 g	25 g
whipped cream, fromage frais or natural yoghurt	125 ml	300 ml

1 Add the lemon juice to the avocado purée.
2 Mix in the icing sugar.
3 Place the soaked and lightly squeezed gelatine into a small pan. Heat gently until it starts to boil.
4 Carefully add the gelatine to the purée, stirring well.
5 When setting point is reached, carefully fold in the whipped cream or alternative.
6 Pour into individual moulds and place in the refrigerator to set.
7 When set, turn out onto plates and garnish each with half a poached pear, carefully fanned.
8 Mask with strawberry sauce.

HEALTHY EATING TIP

• Although avocado is rich in fat, this fat is unsaturated and a 'healthier' type of fat.
• Try using yoghurt or fromage frais in place of the cream.

* Using whipping cream

17 Bavarois: basic recipe (often referred to as a mousse)

Cal	Cal	Fat	Sat Fat	Carb	Sugar	Protein	Fibre	*
970 KJ	231 kcal	18.2 g	10.9 g	11.8 g	11.8 g	5.8 g	0.0 g	

6–8 portions

gelatine	10 g
medium eggs, separated	2
caster sugar	50 g
milk, whole or skimmed	¼ litre
whipping or double cream or	
non-dairy cream	125 ml

1 If using leaf gelatine, soak in cold water.
2 Cream the yolks and sugar in a bowl until almost white.
3 Whisk in the milk, which has been brought to the boil; mix well.
4 Clean the milk saucepan, which should be a thick-based one, and return the mixture to it.
5 Return to a low heat and stir continuously with a wooden spoon until the mixture coats the back of the spoon. The mixture must not boil.
6 Remove from the heat; add the gelatine and stir until dissolved.
7 Pass through a fine strainer into a clean bowl, leave in a cool place, stirring occasionally until almost at setting point.
8 Fold in the lightly beaten cream.
9 Fold in the stiffly beaten whites.
10 Pour the mixture into a mould or individual moulds (which may be very lightly greased with almond oil).
11 Allow to set in the refrigerator.
12 Shake and turn out on to a flat dish or plates.

Note: Bavarois may be decorated with sweetened, flavoured whipped cream (crème Chantilly). It is advisable to use pasteurised egg yolks and whites.

Variations
- *Chocolate bavarois:* dissolve 50 g chocolate couverture in the milk. Decorate with whipped cream and grated chocolate.
- *Coffee bavarois:* proceed as for bavarois, with the addition of coffee essence to taste.
- *Orange bavarois:* add grated zest and juice of 2 oranges and 1 or 2 drops orange colour to the mixture, and increase the gelatine by 2 leaves. Decorate with blanched, fine julienne of orange zest, orange segments and whipped cream.
- *Lemon bavarois:* as orange bavarois, using lemons in place of oranges.
- *Lime bavarois:* as orange bavarois, using limes in place of oranges.
- *Vanilla bavarois:* add a vanilla pod or a few drops of vanilla essence to the milk. Decorate with vanilla-flavoured sweetened cream (crème Chantilly).

* *Using whole milk and whipping cream*

18 Strawberry or raspberry bavarois (mousse)

Cal	Cal	Fat	Sat Fat	Carb	Sugar	Protein	Fibre	*
1102 KJ	265 kcal	17.7 g	10.0 g	19.0 g	19.0 g	8.5 g	0.6 g	

	4 portions	10 portions
fruit (picked, washed and sieved)	200 g	500 g
medium eggs	2	5
gelatine	10 g	25 g
milk, whole or skimmed	180 ml	500 ml
sugar, caster or unrefined	50 g	125 g
whipping or double cream or non-dairy cream	125 ml	300 ml

HEALTHY EATING TIP

• Use semi-skimmed milk and whipping cream to reduce the overall fat content.

* *Using whole milk and whipping cream*

1 Prepare as for the basic recipe (recipe 17).
2 When the custard is almost cool add the fruit purée.
3 Decorate with whole fruit and whipped cream.

19 Vanilla panna cotta served on a fruit compote

Cal	Cal	Fat	Sat Fat	Carb	Sugar	Protein	Fibre
1565 KJ	378 kcal	34.0 g	21.1 g	16.1 g	16.1 g	2.9 g	1.5 g

Andrew Bennett

	6 portions
milk	125 ml
double cream	375 ml
aniseeds	2
vanilla pod	½
leaf gelatine (soaked)	2 leaves
caster sugar	50 g
Fruit compote	
apricot purée	75 g
vanilla pod	½
peach	1
kiwi fruit	1
strawberries	75 g
blueberries	75 g
raspberries	50 g

1 Prepare the fruit compote by boiling the apricot purée and infusing with vanilla pod. Remove pod, allow purée to cool.
2 Finely dice the peach and the kiwi and quarter the strawberries. Mix, then add blueberries and raspberries.

3 Bind the fruit with the apricot purée. A little stock syrup (recipe 184) may be required to keep the fruit free flowing.
4 For the panna cotta, boil the milk and cream, add aniseeds, infuse with the vanilla pod, remove after infusion.
5 Add the soaked gelatine and caster sugar while warm. Strain through a fine strainer.
6 Place in a bowl set over ice and stir until it thickens slightly; this will allow the vanilla seeds to suspend throughout the mix instead of sinking to the bottom.
7 Fill individual dariole moulds.
8 Place the fruit compote with individual fruit plates, turn out the panna cotta, place on top of the compote, finish with a tuile biscuit.

* *Using blackcurrants for blueberries*

HEALTHY EATING TIP

• This dish will contribute to the recommended five portions of fruit and vegetables per day.

20 Chocolate panna cotta

Cal 2228 KJ	Cal 538 kcal	Fat 47.4 g	Sat Fat 29.4 g	Carb 25.2 g	Sugar 25.1 g	Protein 2.9 g	Fibre 0.2 g

	4–6 portions	10–12 portions
double cream	500 ml	1¼ litres
milk	125 ml	300 ml
caster sugar	100 g	250 g
vanilla essence, to taste		
Cointreau or brandy	1 tbsp	1½ tbsp
bitter chocolate, chopped	50 g	125 g
leaf gelatine (soaked in cold water)	2 leaves	5 leaves

1. Place the double cream and milk in a suitable saucepan, add the sugar and vanilla essence. Add the Cointreau or brandy.
2. Heat to just below boiling point.
3. Remove from heat, add the chopped chocolate, stir well.
4. Add the soaked and squeezed gelatine.
5. Strain through a fine strainer.
6. Allow to cool, stirring occasionally.
7. When cold, stir and pour into suitable individual moulds.
8. Cover and refrigerate for at least 8 hours.
9. To serve, loosen the sides of the moulds and turn out into suitable plates. Serve with a quenelle of mascarpone (soft Italian cheese with clotted cream) and segments of orange. Decorate with chocolate run-outs.

Ice creams and sorbets

Ice cream

Traditional ice cream is made from a basic egg custard sauce. The sauce is cooled and mixed with fresh cream. It is then frozen by a rotating machine where the water content forms ice crystals.

Ice cream should be served between –11°C and –8°C. This is the correct eating temperature, otherwise it is too hard. Long-term storage should be at between –18°C and –21°C.

Ice cream has, over the years, gone through many development stages, with savoury ice creams being the most controversial over the past five to six years.

The start of this section covers the traditional method of making ice cream using only egg yolks and sugar, and the traditional anglaise base. This is followed by a section on the more modern approach to making ice cream, with the use of stabilisers and different sugars. However, the most important part of the modern ice cream making process is the method of preparation. To simplify this new theory, the size of the fat micron and the stability of the water within the ice cream base are two of the most important factors. The modern version, made in a thermomix-style processor, somehow reduces the micron size from a peak of 5 microns down to an average size of 1.5 microns. This process allows the whole mix to homogenise and therefore offer a smoother mouth-feel; it also helps with the reduction of ice crystals. In addition, the use of egg whites in the mix prevents the high wastage of whites that might otherwise occur in the pastry section.

The Ice Cream Regulations

The Ice Cream Regulations 1959 and 1963 require ice cream to be pasteurised by heating to:

- 65°C for 30 minutes or
- 71°C for 10 minutes or
- 80°C for 15 seconds or
- 149°C for 2 seconds (sterilised).

After heat treatment, the mixture is reduced to 7.1°C within 1½ hours and kept at this temperature until the freezing process begins. Ice cream needs this treatment so as to kill harmful bacteria. Freezing without the correct heat treatment does not kill bacteria – it allows them to remain dormant. The storage temperature for ice cream should not exceed −2°C.

Any ice cream sold must comply with the following compositional standards.

- It must contain not less than 5 per cent fat and not less than 2.5 per cent milk protein (not necessary in natural proportions).
- It must conform to the Dairy Product Regulations 1995.

For further information contact the Ice Cream Alliance (see www.ice-cream.org).

The ice cream making process
1 **Weighing:** the requisite in our profession is weighing ingredients precisely in order to ensure optimum results and, what is more difficult, regularity and consistency.
2 **Pasteurisation:** without a doubt this is a vital stage in making ice cream. Its primary function is to minimise bacterial contamination by heating the mixture of ingredients to 85°C, then quickly cooling it to 4°C.
3 **Homogenisation:** high pressure is applied to cause the explosion of fats, facilitating their dissolution. This process makes ice cream more homogenous, creamier, smoother and much lighter. It is not usually done for home-made ice cream.
4 **Ripening:** this basic but optional stage refines flavour, further develops aromas and improves texture. This occurs during a rest period (4–24 hours), which gives the stabilisers and proteins time to act, improving the overall structure of the ice cream. This has the same effect on a crème anglaise, which is much better the day after it is made than it is on the same day.
5 **Churning:** here, the mixture is frozen while air is simultaneously incorporated. The ice cream is removed from the machine at about −10°C.

Functions and approximate percentages of the main components of ice cream
- Sucrose (common sugar) not only sweetens ice cream, but its solids also give it body. An ice cream that contains only sucrose (not recommended) has a higher freezing point.

- The optimum sugar percentage of ice cream is between 15 and 20 per cent.
- Ice cream that contains dextrose has a lower freezing point, and better taste and texture.
- As much as 50 per cent of the sucrose can be substituted with other sweeteners, but the recommended amount is 25 per cent.
- Glucose improves smoothness and prevents the crystallisation of sucrose.
- The quantity of glucose used should be between 25 and 30 per cent of the sucrose by weight.
- Atomised glucose is more water absorbent.
- The quantity of dextrose used should be between 6 and 25 per cent of the substituted sucrose (by weight).
- If we use inverted sugar in ice cream, it lowers the freezing point.
- Inverted sugar improves texture and delays crystallisation.
- The quantity of inverted sugar used should be a maximum of 33 per cent of the sucrose by weight. It has a high sweetening coefficient and gives the mix a low freezing point.
- Honey has more or less the same properties as inverted sugar.
- The purpose of cream in ice cream is to improve creaminess and taste.
- Egg yolks act as stabilisers for ice cream due to the lecithin they contain – that is, they facilitate the emulsion of fats in water.
- Egg yolks improve the texture and viscosity of ice cream.
- The purpose of stabilisers is to prevent crystal formation by absorbing the water contained in ice cream and making a stable gel.
- The quantity of stabilisers in ice cream should be between 3 and 5 g per kg of mix, with a maximum of 10 g.
- Stabilisers promote air absorption.

What you need to know about ice cream
- Maintaining hygiene with respect to materials, personnel, the kitchen and the pastry shop is essential while making ice cream.
- An excess of stabilisers in ice cream will make it sticky.

- Stabilisers should always be mixed with sugar before adding, to avoid lumps.
- Stabilisers should be added at 45°C, which is when they begin to act.
- Cold stabilisers have no effect on the mix, so the temperature must be raised to 85°C.
- Ice cream should be allowed to 'ripen' for 4–24 hours. This is a vital step that helps improve its properties.
- Ice cream should be cooled quickly to 4°C, because rapid micro-organism proliferation occurs between 20°C and 55°C.

Sorbets

Sorbets belong to the ice cream family; they are a mixture of water, sucrose, atomised glucose, stabiliser, fruit juice, fruit pulp or liqueurs.

What you need to know about sorbet
- Sorbet is always more refreshing and easier to digest than ice cream.
- Fruit for sorbets must always be of a high quality and perfectly ripe.
- The percentage of fruit used in sorbet varies according to the type of fruit, its acidity and the quality desired.
- The percentage of sugar is a function of the type of fruit used.
- The minimum sugar content in sorbet is about 13 per cent.
- As far as ripening is concerned, the syrup should be left to rest for 4–24 hours and never mixed with the fruit because its acidity would damage the stabiliser.
- Stabiliser is added in the same way as for ice cream.
- Sorbets are not to be confused with granitas, which are semi-solid.

Stabilisers

For what do we use gelling substances?
Within the realm of stabilisers are gelling substances, thickeners and emulsifiers. These are products we use regularly, each with its own specific function; but their main purpose is to retain water to make a gel. The case of ice cream is the most obvious, in which they are used to prevent ice crystal formation. They are also used to stabilise the emulsion, increase the viscosity of the mix and to give us a smoother product that is more resistant to melting. There are many stabilising substances, both natural and artificial.

Edible gelatine
Edible gelatine is extracted from animals' bones (pork and veal) and, more recently, fish skin. Sold in sheets of 2 g, it is easy to precisely control the amount used and manipulate it. The gelatine sheets must always be washed thoroughly with abundant cold water to remove impurities and any remaining odours. They must then be drained before use.

Gelatine sheets melt at 40°C and should be melted in a little of the liquid from the recipe before adding it to the base preparation.

Pectin
Pectin is another commonly used gelling substance because of its great absorption capacity. It comes from citrus peel (orange, lemon, etc.), though all fruits contain some pectin in their peel.

It is a good idea to always mix pectin with sugar before adding it to the rest of the ingredients.

Agar-agar
Agar-agar is a gelatinous marine algae found in Asia. It is sold in whole or powdered form and has a great absorption capacity. It dissolves very easily and, in addition to gelling, adds elasticity and resists heat (this is classified as a non-reversible gel).

Other stabilisers
- **Carob gum** comes from the seeds of the carob tree, makes sorbets creamier and improves heat resistance.
- **Guar gum** and **carrageen** are, like agar-agar, extracted from marine algae and are some of many other existing gelling substances available, but they are less often used.

Traditionally made ice cream

21 Vanilla ice cream (traditional) *(glace vanille)*

Cal	Cal	Fat	Sat Fat	Carb	Sugar	Protein	Fibre	*
616 KJ	147 kcal	8.1 g	4.2 g	15.8 g	15.8 g	3.5 g	0.0 g	

	8–10 portions
egg yolks	4
caster or unrefined sugar	100 g
milk, whole or skimmed	375 ml
vanilla pod or essence	
cream or non-dairy cream	125 ml

1 Whisk the yolks and sugar in a bowl until almost white.
2 Boil the milk with the vanilla pod or essence in a thick-based pan.
3 Whisk on to the eggs and sugar; mix well.
4 Return to the cleaned saucepan, place on a low heat.
5 Stir continuously with a spatula until the mixture coats the back of the spatula.
6 Pass through a fine strainer into a bowl.
7 Freeze in an ice cream machine, gradually adding the cream.

Variations
- *Coffee ice cream:* add coffee essence, to taste, to the custard after it is cooked.
- *Chocolate ice cream:* add 50–100 g of chopped couverture to the milk before boiling.
- *Strawberry ice cream:* add 125 ml of strawberry pulp in place of 125 ml of milk. The pulp is added after the custard is cooked.
- *Rum and raisin ice cream:* soak 50 g raisins in 2 tbsp rum for 3–4 hours. Add to mixture before freezing.

* *Using whole milk and single cream*

22 Baileys ice cream

Cal	Cal	Fat	Sat Fat	Carb	Sugar	Protein	Fibre
2179 KJ	524 kcal	36 g	16.4 g	36 g	36 g	6.4 g	0.0 g

	6 portions
milk	500 ml
double cream	250 ml
Baileys Irish Cream liqueur	250 ml
vanilla pod	1
egg yolks	6
caster sugar	125 g

1 Bring the milk, cream and Baileys with the vanilla pod to the boil. Remove from the heat.
2 Whisk the egg yolks and sugar, then cream well.
3 Pour a third of the milk mixture onto the egg yolks and sugar. Whisk well, add to the remainder of the milk, stir the custard over a low heat. Do not boil. When it coats the back of a spoon, strain.
4 Allow to cool, churn in an ice cream machine.

23 Peach Melba *(pêche Melba)*

Cal 607 KJ	Cal 145 kcal	Fat 2.6 g	Sat Fat 1.3 g	Carb 30.5 g	Sugar 30.2 g	Protein 1.6 g	Fibre 1.3 g

	4 portions	10 portions
peaches	2	5
vanilla ice cream	125 ml	300 ml
Melba sauce (recipe 69)	125 ml	300 ml

1 Dress the fruit on a ball of ice cream in an ice cream coupe and coat with Melba sauce.
2 Decorate with whipped cream if required.

Note: If using fresh peaches they should be dipped in boiling water for a few seconds, cooled by placing into cold water, then peeled and halved.

Variations
Fruit Melba can also be made using pear or banana instead of peach. Fresh pears should be peeled, halved and poached. Bananas should be peeled at the last moment.

24 Pear belle Hélène *(poire belle Hélène)*

1 Serve a cooked pear on a ball of vanilla ice cream in a coupe.
2 Decorate with whipped cream. Serve with a sauceboat of hot chocolate sauce (recipe 71 or 72).

25 Peach cardinal *(pêche cardinal)*

1 Place half a prepared peach on a ball of strawberry ice cream in a coupe.
2 Coat with Melba sauce; decorate with whipped cream and sprinkle with toasted almonds cut in slices, if required.

26 Coupe Jacques

1 Place some fruit salad in a coupe.
2 Arrange one scoop each of lemon and strawberry ice cream on top.
3 Decorate with whipped cream if required.

The modern approach

27 Ice cream base

Makes approx. 15 portions

large eggs	2
whipping cream	1360 g
full-fat milk	980 g
dextrose	85 g
Natracol (see note)	4 g
Velvet Gel	16 g
sugar	350 g
E471 (ice cream stabiliser)	6 g

1 Combine all the ingredients, excluding the sugar and stabiliser.
2 Place mix into a thermomix (see note) and heat on high speed to 70°C. At this point add the sugar and stabiliser.
3 Heat the mix up to 79.5°C. Remove immediately and pour into a cold container to arrest the cooking.

4 Leave to mature for at least 12 hours.
5 Churn and add up to 30 per cent over-run (volume increase). Over-run can only be achieved at -4°C or above. Below this temperature the ice cream mix is too stable to incorporate any air. Constant agitation of the mix at this temperature will only separate the fats, therefore whipping the air (over-run) while the mixture is still soft.
6 Store until required.

Note: Natrocol is a blend of hydrocolloids or stabilising gels that prevent any water molecules binding with other water molecules through a network of starch, thus preventing large ice crystals from forming in ice cream.

A thermomix is a food processor with different speeds, a high-powered blade and motor; a heat element is built into the unit that heats the jug while the food is being processed. It is great for making hollandaise and suchlike.

28 Coffee ice cream

Cal	Cal	Fat	Sat Fat	Carb	Sugar	Protein	Fibre	Salt
1088 KJ	260 kcal	16.9 g	9.8 g	24.5 g	22.6 g	4.0 g	0.0 g	0.1 g

Makes approx. 20 portions

Stage 1	
whole egg	400 g
whipping cream	680 g
milk	490 g
Velvet Gel	8 g
Stab 2000	3 g
Natracol	2 g
Stage 2	
dextrose	45 g
caster sugar	175 g
Stage 3	
dextrose	40 g
caster sugar	175 g
coffee paste (stocked by most pastry specialists)	70 g

Stage 1
1 Mix all the ingredients and heat to 70°C in the thermomix or heating food processor.

Stage 2
1 Add the dextrose and sugar and bring back to 70°C.

Stage 3
1 Add further dextrose and sugar, and the coffee paste, and bring up to 79.5°C for 15 seconds.
2 Pass and allow to cool over an ice bain-marie.
3 Place in the fridge and allow to cure over night before churning.
4 Cool on ice, allow to mature for 24 hours before churning.
5 Churn as normal and store in the usual manner.

29 Moscatel vinegar ice cream

Makes approx. 20 portions

Stage 1

whole egg	400 g
whipping cream	680 g
milk	270 g
Moscatel vinegar	220 g
Stab 2000	3 g
Velvet Gel	8 g
Natracol	2 g
Stage 2	
dextrose	45 g
caster sugar	175 g
Stage 3	
dextrose	40 g
caster sugar	175 g

1 Mix all the ingredients for stage 1 and heat to 70°C in a thermomix or heating food processor.
2 Add the ingredients for stage 2 and bring back to 70°C.
3 Add the ingredients for stage 3 and bring up to 79.5°C for 15 seconds.
4 Pass and allow to cool over an ice bain-marie.
5 Place in the fridge and allow to cure overnight before churning.
6 Cool on ice; allow to mature for 24 hours before churning.
7 Churn as normal and store in the usual manner.

30 Lemon sorbet *(sorbet au citron)*

Cal	Cal	Fat	Sat Fat	Carb	Sugar	Protein	Fibre
421 KJ	1000 kcal	0.0 g	0.0 g	26.3 g	26.3 g	0.4 g	0.0 g

	8–10 portions
sugar	200 g
water	½ litre
lemons	2
egg white, pasteurised	1

1 Bring the sugar, water and peeled zest of lemons to the boil.
2 Remove from the heat and cool. The saccarometer reading for the syrup should be 18–20° baumé.
3 Add the juice of the lemon.
4 Add the egg white and mix well.
5 Pass through a fine strainer and freeze.

31 Orange sorbet *(sorbet à l'orange)*

	8–10 portions
sugar	200 g
water	½ litre
large oranges	2
lemon	1
egg white, pasteurised	1

1 Prepare and freeze as for lemon sorbet (recipe 30); 18–20° baumé. (Baumé is the syrup density, measured with a saccharometer.)

HEALTHY EATING TIP
- Sorbet does not contain any fat, but nearly all the carbohydrate is from sugar.
- Garnish with exotic fruit.

32 Raspberry sorbet (sorbet à la framboise)

	8–10 portions
sugar	200 g
water	375 ml
lemon	1
raspberry purée	125 ml
egg white, pasteurised	1

1 Prepare and freeze as for lemon sorbet (recipe 30); 18–20° baumé.

Note: Passionfruit or mango sorbet can be made by substituting the relevant purée for raspberry.

33 Cucumber and lime sorbet

Cal 339 KJ	Cal 81 kcal	Fat 0.4 g	Sat Fat 0.2 g	Carb 19.6 g	Sugar 17.6 g	Protein 0.9 g	Fibre 0.2 g	Salt 0.04 g

	25 portions
Stage 1	
water	300 g
sugar	320 g
glucose	110 g
Super Neutrose	10 g
sugar	20 g
Stage 2	
cucumber juice, strained	700 g
natural yoghurt	300 g
limes, juice of	2

1 Bring all the ingredients for stage 1 to a rolling boil, excluding the Super Neutrose and 20 g of sugar.
2 Remove from the stove and allow to cool slightly, then add the Super Neutrose and 20 g of sugar.
3 Whisk in the ingredients for stage 2. Place in the fridge for 12 hours to mature, churn and store in the usual manner

Note: To juice the cucumber, quarter lengthways, deseed (skin on) and then place in a domestic juicer.

34 Mandarin sorbet

	18 portions
Stage 1	
water	250 g
sugar	180 g
glucose	75 g
Super Neutrose	10 g
Sugar	20 g
Stage 2	
mandarin purée	1000 g

1 Bring all the ingredients for stage 1 to a rolling boil, excluding the Super Neutrose and 20 g of sugar.
2 Remove from the stove and allow to cool slightly, then add the Super Neutrose and 20 g of sugar.
3 Whisk in the ingredients for stage 2. Place in the fridge for 12 hours to mature, churn and store in the usual manner

Note: Mandarin purée is available commercially as a ready-made product.

Soufflé puddings

35 Soufflé pudding: basic recipe (*pouding soufflé*)

Cal	Cal	Fat	Sat Fat	Carb	Sugar	Protein	Fibre	*
510 KJ	122 kcal	7.6 g	3.2 g	5.9 g	4.8 g	0.2 g	0.0 g	

	6 portions	10 portions
milk (whole or skimmed)	185 ml	375 ml
flour (white or wholemeal)	25 g	50 g
butter or margarine	25 g	50 g
caster or unrefined sugar	25 g	50 g
medium eggs, separated	3	6

1 Boil the milk in a sauteuse.
2 Combine the flour, butter and sugar.
3 Whisk into the milk and reboil.
4 Remove from heat, add the egg yolks one at a time, whisking continuously.
5 Stiffly beat the whites and carefully fold into the mixture.

6 Three-quarters fill buttered and sugared dariole moulds.
7 Place in a roasting tin, half full of water.
8 Bring to the boil and place in a hot oven at 230–250°C for 12–15 minutes.
9 Turn out on to a flat dish and serve with a suitable hot sauce, such as custard or sabayon sauce (recipe 7).

Note: Orange or lemon soufflé pudding is made by flavouring the basic mixture with the grated zest of an orange or lemon and a little appropriate sauce. Use the juice in the accompanying sauce.

* *Using white flour and hard margarine*

36 Vanilla soufflé (*soufflé à la vanille*)

Cal	Cal	Fat	Sat Fat	Carb	Sugar	Protein	Fibre
757 KJ	180 kcal	9.1 g	3.5 g	16.6 g	14.6 g	9.1 g	0.1 g

	4 portions	10 portions
butter	10 g	25 g
caster sugar, for soufflé case	50 g	125 g
milk	125 ml	300 ml
natural vanilla or pod		
medium eggs, separated	4	10
flour	10 g	25 g
caster sugar	50 g	125 g
icing sugar, to serve		

1 Lightly coat the inside of a soufflé case/dish with fresh butter.
2 Coat the butter in the soufflé case with caster sugar as needed, tap out surplus.
3 Boil the milk and vanilla in a thick-bottomed pan.
4 Mix half the egg yolks, the flour and sugar to a smooth consistency in a basin.
5 Add the boiling milk to the mixture, stir vigorously until completely mixed.
6 Return this mixture to a clean thick-bottomed pan and stir continuously with a wooden spoon over gentle heat until the mixture thickens, then remove from heat.

7 Allow to cool slightly. Add the remaining egg yolks and mix thoroughly.
8 Stiffly whip the egg whites and *carefully* fold into the mixture, which should be just warm. (An extra egg white can be added for extra lightness.)
9 Place the mixture into the prepared case(s) and level it off with a palette knife – do not allow it to come above the level of the soufflé case.
10 Place on a baking sheet and cook in a moderately hot oven – approx. 180–200°C – until the soufflé is well risen and firm to the touch – approx. 15–20 minutes. (For individual soufflés, reduce time by 5 minutes.)
11 Remove carefully from oven, dredge with icing sugar and serve at once. A hot soufflé must not be allowed to stand or it may sink.

Note: A pinch of egg white powder (merri-white) added when whisking the whites will strengthen them and assist in the aeration process.

37 Soufflé without flour: hot lemon curd soufflé

Cal	Cal	Fat	Sat Fat	Carb	Sugar	Protein	Fibre
1179 KJ	280 kcal	13.3 g	5.7 g	31.7 g	30.4 g	10.1 g	0.1 g

	4 portions	10 portions
eggs, medium	4	9
caster sugar	75 g	187 g
lemon, zest and juice	2	5
cream of tartar	pinch	large pinch
egg white powder	pinch	large pinch
icing sugar, to serve		
Lemon curd		
lemons, juice of	2	5
medium eggs	1	2
caster sugar	37 g	100 g
butter, unsalted	25 g	60 g
cornflour	6 g	15 g

1 Lightly grease the individual soufflé dishes with butter or margarine, and lightly dust with caster sugar.
2 Prepare the lemon curd by whisking the eggs with the caster sugar over a bain-marie of hot water, add the lemon juice, butter cut into small pieces and the cornflour. Whisk well until the mixture thickens.
3 Divide the lemon curd into the soufflé dishes.
4 Separate the egg whites and egg yolks. Mix the yolks with the caster sugar, the lemon zest and juice. Whisk well to thoroughly incorporate.
5 Carefully whisk the egg whites to soft peaks with a pinch of cream of tartar and egg white powder to strengthen.
6 Carefully fold the whites into the yolk and lemon mixture. Do not over-mix.
7 Divide the mixture into the soufflé dishes.
8 Place on a baking sheet and cook in a pre-heated oven (170°C) for approximately 12–16 minutes. Remove, dust with icing sugar and serve immediately.

Figure 14.7 Lemon curd soufflé

38 Cold lemon soufflé *(soufflé milanaise)*

Cal	Cal	Fat	Sat Fat	Carb	Sugar	Protein	Fibre
1385 KJ	330 kcal	18.6 g	10.6 g	36.2 g	36.2 g	6.7 g	0.0 g

	6 portions
leaf gelatine	10 g
lemons	2
pasteurised egg yolks	4
caster sugar	200 g
whipping or double cream, or	
non-dairy cream	¼ litre
pasteurised egg whites	4

1 Prepare a soufflé dish or individual dishes by tying an 8 cm wide strip of greaseproof paper around the outside top edge with string, so that it extends 2–4 cm above the top of the dish.
2 Soak the gelatine in cold water.
3 *Lightly* grate the zest of the lemons. Squeeze the juice of the lemons into a bowl.
4 Add the lemon zest, yolks and sugar, and whisk over a pan of hot water until the mixture thickens and turns a very light colour.
5 Dissolve the gelatine in a few drops of water over heat, mix in, remove from heat.
6 Lightly whisk the cream until three-quarters stiff.
7 Stiffly beat the egg whites.
8 Stir the basic mixture frequently until almost at setting point.
9 Gently fold in the cream. Gently fold in the egg whites.
10 Pour into the prepared dishes. Place in a refrigerator to set.
11 To serve, remove the paper collar and decorate the sides with green chopped almonds or pistachio nuts. The top may be similarly decorated or by using rosettes of sweetened vanilla-flavoured whipped cream.

Steamed puddings

39 Steamed currant roll

Cal 1997 KJ	Cal 476 kcal	Fat 22.7 g	Sat Fat 11.4 g	Carb 66.4 g	Sugar 25.2 g	Protein 5.5 g	Fibre 1.9 g	*

	6 portions	12 portions
flour	300 g	600 g
salt	pinch	large pinch
baking powder	10 g	20 g
or		
self-raising flour	300 g	600 g
suet, chopped	150 g	300 g
sugar, caster or unrefined	75 g	150 g
currants	100 g	200 g
water or milk	185 ml	375 ml

1 Sieve the flour, salt and baking powder (or replace the flour and baking powder with self-raising flour) into a bowl.
2 Mix in the suet. Mix in the sugar and currants.
3 Add sufficient water or milk to make a fairly firm dough.
4 Roll in greased greaseproof paper and a pudding cloth or foil. Tie with string at both ends. Steam for 1½ –2 hours.
5 Remove the cloth and paper and serve with a sauceboat of custard.

Note: Sultanas, raisins or dates may be used instead of currants. Vegetarian suet is available.

Variations
Using raisins, sultanas, and a pinch of mixed spice gives an old English pudding known as spotted dick, which can also be prepared in individual moulds and steamed for 1 hour.

* *Using water*

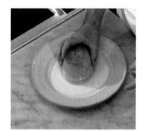

Figure 14.8 ✎ Preparation of steamed puddings

Figure 14.9 ✎ Selection of steamed puddings (left to right): fruit, chocolate and vanilla

40 Steamed dried fruit pudding

Cal	Cal	Fat	Sat Fat	Carb	Sugar	Protein	Fibre
1586 KJ	378 kcal	17.1 g	8.4 g	53.4 g	30.6 g	5.7 g	1.2 g

	6 portions	12 portions
flour	100 g	200 g
salt	pinch	large pinch
baking powder	10 g	20 g
or		
self-raising flour	100 g	200 g
breadcrumbs	100 g	200 g
suet, chopped	100 g	200 g
sugar, caster or unrefined	100 g	200 g
fruit (currants, raisins, dates or sultanas)	100 g	200 g
egg (medium), beaten	1	2
milk (whole or skimmed)	125 ml	250 ml

1 Mix all the dry ingredients together (use flour, salt and baking powder or replace the flour and baking powder with self-raising flour). Add the liquid and mix.
2 Place in a greased pudding basin or individual moulds (1 hour cooking time), cover and steam for 1½ –2 hours.
3 Serve with custard sauce or vanilla sauce.

41 Golden syrup or treacle pudding

Cal	Cal	Fat	Sat Fat	Carb	Sugar	Protein	Fibre
1315 KJ	313 kcal	13.0 g	5.9 g	47.8 g	26.6 g	4.3 g	0.9 g

	6 portions	12 portions
flour	150 g	300 g
salt	pinch	large pinch
baking powder	10 g	20 g
or		
self-raising flour	150 g	300 g
suet, chopped	75 g	150 g
caster or unrefined sugar	50 g	100 g
lemon, zest of	1	2
egg, beaten	1	2
milk (whole or skimmed)	125 ml	250 ml
golden syrup or light treacle	125 ml	250 ml

1 Sieve the flour, salt and baking powder (or replace the flour and baking powder with self-raising flour) into a bowl.
2 Mix the suet, sugar and zest.
3 Mix to a medium dough, with the beaten egg and milk.
4 Pour the syrup in a well-greased basin or individual moulds (1 hour cooking time). Place the pudding mixture on top.
5 Cover securely; steam for 1½ –2 hours.
6 Serve with a sauceboat of warm syrup containing the lemon juice, or with sauce anglaise or ice cream.

Note: Vegetarian suet is available for use in recipes 39–41.

42 Steamed sponge pudding: basic recipe

Cal	Cal	Fat	Sat Fat	Carb	Sugar	Protein	Fibre	*
1295 KJ	309 kcal	16.3 g	9.4 g	37.8 g	18.1 g	5.2 g	0.8 g	

	6 portions	12 portions
butter or margarine	100 g	200 g
caster or soft brown sugar	100 g	200 g
medium eggs, beaten	2	4
flour (white or wholemeal)	150 g	300 g
baking powder	10 g	20 g
milk	few drops	several drops

1 Cream the butter or margarine and sugar in a bowl until fluffy and almost white.
2 Gradually add the beaten eggs, mixing vigorously.
3 Sieve the flour and baking powder.
4 Gradually incorporate into the mixture as lightly as possible keeping to a dropping consistency by the addition of the milk.
5 Place in a greased pudding basin or individual moulds (45 minutes' cooking time).
6 Cover securely with greased greaseproof paper. Steam for 1–1½ hours.

Variations

Variations include the following (double the quantities for 12 portions).
- *Vanilla sponge pudding:* add a few drops of vanilla essence to the basic mixture and serve with a custard.
- *Chocolate sponge pudding:* add 25 g chocolate or cocoa powder in place of 25 g flour (that is 125 g flour, 25 g chocolate to basic recipe); serve with a chocolate sauce (page 579).
- *Lemon sponge pudding:* add the grated zest of one or two lemons, and a few drops of lemon essence to basic recipe; serve with a lemon sauce (page 576) or custard.
- *Orange sponge pudding:* proceed as for lemon pudding, but using oranges in place of lemons; serve with an orange sauce (page 576) or custard.
- *Cherry sponge pudding:* add 100 g chopped or quartered glacé cherries to basic recipe; serve with a custard (page 577) or almond sauce (page 577).
- *Sultana/currant/raisin sponge pudding:* add 100 g of washed, well-dried fruit to basic recipe; serve with custard sauce (page 577).

* *Using butter*

43 Christmas pudding

8–10 portions (1-litre basin)	
sultanas	100 g
raisins	100 g
currants	100 g
mixed chopped candied peel	25 g
barley wine	70 ml
Guinness (stout)	70 ml
rum	2 tbsp
self-raising flour	50 g
mixed spice	1 tsp
ground nutmeg	¼ tsp
cinnamon	1 tsp
breadcrumbs (white or brown)	100 g
suet, shredded	100 g
soft dark brown sugar	200 g
ground almonds	25 g
cooking apples, peeled and chopped	75 g
orange, grated zest of	½
lemon, grated zest of	½
eggs	2

1 Place all the dried fruit and candied peel in a mixing bowl; soak overnight with the barley wine, Guinness and rum.
2 Sift the flour with the mixed spice, nutmeg and cinnamon.
3 Add breadcrumbs, suet and sugar to the flour.
4 Drain the fruit from the alcohol. Add to the flour along with the almonds, apple and grated zest.
5 In a separate basin, beat the eggs with the alcohol.

6 Add the dried fruit to the flour, mix thoroughly.
7 Pack into a lightly greased basin (1 litre). Cover with a sheet of silicone and aluminium foil. Secure well.
8 Steam for 8 hours at normal atmospheric pressure.
9 Remove from steamer and allow to cool, remove foil and silicone, replace with fresh. Secure well.
10 Allow to mature for at least 2 months. Reheat by steaming for a further 2 hours.
11 Serve with rum and brandy sauce.

44 Sticky toffee pudding with butterscotch sauce

Cal	Cal	Fat	Sat Fat	Carb	Sugar	Protein	Fibre
4103.6 KJ	980 kcal	60.4 g	36.7 g	106.7 g	78.9 g	9.1 g	1.8 g

	4 portions	10 portions
Medjool dates, stoned and chopped	150 g	375 g
water	250 ml	625 ml
bicarbonate of soda	1 tsp	2½ tsp
unsalted butter	50 g	125 g
caster sugar	150 g	375 g
medium eggs	2	5
self-raising flour	150 g	375 g
vanilla essence	1 tsp	2½ tsp
Sauce		
double cream	250 ml	625 ml
butter	62 g	155 g
demerara sugar	100 g	250 g

1 For four portions, grease a baking tin approximately 28 × 18 cm in size (32 × 22 cm for 10 portions). (The modern version is to use individual pudding or dariole moulds.)
2 Boil the dates in the water for approximately 5 minutes until soft, then add the bicarbonate of soda.
3 Cream the butter and sugar together until light and white, gradually beat in the eggs.
4 Mix in the dates, flour and vanilla essence, stir well.
5 Form into the greased baking tin and bake in a pre-heated oven 180°C for approximately 30–40 minutes, until firm to the touch.
6 Carefully portion the sponge.
7 Make the sauce by boiling the cream, then whisk in the butter and sugar, simmer for 3 minutes. Carefully pour over the pudding.

Pancakes

45 Pancakes with lemon or orange (*crêpes au citron ou à l'orange*)

Cal	Cal	Fat	Sat Fat	Carb	Sugar	Protein	Fibre	*
1275 KJ	304 kcal	16.2 g	4.8 g	35.5 g	16.4 g	6.1 g	0.9 g	

	4 portions	10 portions
flour (white or wholemeal)	100 g	250 g
salt	pinch	large pinch
egg	1	2–3
milk (whole or skimmed)	¼ litre	625 ml
melted butter, margarine or oil	10 g	25 g
oil for frying		
sugar, caster or unrefined	50 g	125 g
lemon/orange quarters, to serve		

1 Sieve the flour and salt into a bowl, make a well in the centre.
2 Add the egg and milk, gradually incorporating the flour from the sides, whisk to a smooth batter.
3 Mix in the melted butter.
4 Heat the pancake pan, clean thoroughly.
5 Add a little oil; heat until smoking.
6 Add enough mixture to just cover the bottom of the pan thinly.
7 Cook for a few seconds until brown.
8 Turn and cook on the other side. Turn on to a plate.

9 Sprinkle with sugar. Fold in half then in half again.
10 Garnish with quarters of lemon or orange free from pips. Serve very hot, two pancakes per portion.

Note: When making a batch of pancakes it is best to keep them all flat, one on top of the other, on a plate. Sprinkle sugar between each. Fold them all when ready for service, sprinkle again with sugar and dress neatly overlapping on a serving dish or hot plates.

For a slightly thicker batter, add another 20 g of flour (50 g for 10 portions).

HEALTHY EATING TIP
• Use semi-skimmed milk to make the batter.

* Using white flour, whole milk, hard margarine and peanut oil

46 Pancakes with jam *(crêpes à la confiture)*

	4 portions	10 portions
pancakes (see recipe 45)		
warm jam	50 g	125 g
sugar	25 g	60 g

HEALTHY EATING TIP
• Use semi-skimmed milk to make the batter.

1 Prepare the pancakes as for recipe 45. Spread each with warm jam.
2 Roll up like a Swiss roll and trim the ends. Dredge with caster sugar and serve.

47 Pancakes with apple *(crêpes normande)*

Method 1
1 Cook as for the basic recipe (recipe 45).
2 Spread with hot purée of apple (page 617).
3 Roll up and sprinkle with caster sugar.

HEALTHY EATING TIP
• Use semi-skimmed milk to make the batter.

Method 2
1 Place a little cooked apple in a pan, add the pancake mixture and cook on both sides.
2 Turn out, sprinkle with caster sugar and roll up.

Meringues

48 Meringue (*meringue*)

Cal 3491 KJ	Cal 831 kcal	Fat 0.0 g	Sat Fat 0.0 g	Carb 210.0 g	Sugar 210.0 g	Protein 10.8 g	Fibre 0.0 g

	4 portions	10 portions
egg whites, pasteurised	4	10
caster sugar	200 g	500 g

1 Whip the egg whites stiffly.
2 Sprinkle on the sugar and carefully mix in.
3 Place in a piping bag with a large plain tube and pipe on to silicone paper on a baking sheet.
4 Bake in the slowest oven possible or in a hot plate (110°C). The aim is to dry out the meringues without any colour whatsoever.

Note: The reason egg whites increase in volume when whipped is because they contain so much protein (11 per cent). The protein forms tiny filaments, which stretch on beating, incorporate air in minute bubbles then set to form a fairly stable puffed-up structure expanding to seven times its bulk. To gain maximum efficiency when whipping egg whites, the following points should be observed.

- Because of possible weakness in the egg white protein it is advisable to strengthen it by adding a pinch of cream of tartar and a pinch of dried egg white powder. If all dried egg white powder is used no additions are necessary.
- Eggs should be fresh.
- When separating yolks from whites *no* speck of egg yolk must be allowed to remain in the white; egg yolk contains fat, the presence of which can prevent the white being correctly whipped.
- The bowl and whisk must be scrupulously clean, dry and free from any grease.
- When egg whites are whipped the addition of a little sugar (15 g to 4 egg whites) will assist the efficient beating and reduce the chances of over-beating.

Figure 14.10 Piping of meringues

Figure 14.11 Finished meringues

49 Meringue with whipped cream (meringue Chantilly)

1 Allow two meringues (see recipe 48) per portion.
2 Join together with a little sweetened, vanilla-flavoured whipped cream or non-dairy cream (known as crème Chantilly).
3 Decorate with whipped cream, glacé cherries and angelica, or crystallised violets or roses.

50 Meringue and ice cream (meringue glacée Chantilly)

1 Allow two meringues (see recipe 48) per portion.
2 Join together with a small ball of vanilla ice cream.
3 Serve in a coupe or ice cream dish.
4 Decorate with whipped cream.

51 Vacherin with strawberries and cream (vacherin aux fraises)

Cal	Cal	Fat	Sat Fat	Carb	Sugar	Protein	Fibre	*
1436 KJ	341 kcal	12.6 g	7.9 g	56.3 g	56.3 g	3.9 g	0.6 g	

	4 portions	10 portions
egg whites	4	10
caster sugar	200 g	500 g
strawberries, picked and washed)	100–300 g	250–750 g
cream (whipped and sweetened) or non-dairy cream	125 ml	300 ml

1 Stiffly whip the egg whites.
2 Carefully fold in the sugar.
3 Place the mixture into a piping bag with a 1 cm plain tube.
4 Pipe on to silicone paper on a baking sheet.
5 Start from the centre and pipe round in a circular fashion to form a base 16 cm then pipe around the edge 2–3 cm high.
6 Bake in a cool oven at 100°C until the meringue case is completely dry. Do not allow to colour.
7 Allow the meringue case to cool then remove from the paper.
8 Spread a thin layer of cream on the base. Add the strawberries.
9 Decorate with the remainder of the cream.

Note: A vacherin is a round meringue shell piped into a suitable shape so that the centre may be filled with sufficient fruit (such as strawberries, stoned cherries, peaches and apricots) and whipped cream to form a rich sweet. The vacherin may be prepared in one-, two- or four-portion sizes, or larger.

Variations

HEALTHY EATING TIP
• Try 'diluting' the fat in the cream with some low fat fromage frais.

• *Melba sauce* (recipe 69) may be used to coat the strawberries before decorating with cream. Refer to the notes in recipe 48 before whipping the egg whites.
• *Raspberries* can be used instead of strawberries.

* *Using 280 g strawberries and whipped cream*

52 Baked Alaska (omelette soufflée surprise)

Cal 2190 KJ	Cal 521 kcal	Fat 16.4 g	Sat Fat 7.3 g	Carb 91.3 g	Sugar 81.2 g	Protein 7.7 g	Fibre 0.6 g

	4 portions	10 portions
sponge cake	4 pieces	10 pieces
fruit syrup	60 ml	150 ml
vanilla ice cream	4 scoops	10 scoops
egg whites	4	10
caster sugar	200 g	500 g

1 Neatly arrange the pieces of sponge cake in the centre of a flat ovenproof dish or individual dishes.
2 Sprinkle the sponge cake with a little fruit syrup.
3 Place a flattened scoop of vanilla ice cream on each piece of sponge.
4 Meanwhile stiffly whip the egg whites and fold in the sugar.
5 Use half the meringue and completely cover the ice cream and sponge. Neaten with a palette knife.
6 Place the remainder of the meringue into a piping bag with a large tube (plain or star) and decorate over.

7 Place into a hot oven at 230–250°C and colour a golden brown or brown with a blowtorch. Serve immediately.

Note: The fruit syrup for soaking the sponge may be flavoured with rum, sherry, brandy, whisky, Tia Maria, curaçao or any other suitable liqueur.

Variations
Variations include the following.
- *Baked Alaska with peaches:* proceed as for the basic recipe, adding a little maraschino to the fruit syrup and using raspberry ice cream instead of vanilla; cover the ice cream with four halves of peaches.
- *Baked Alaska with pears:* proceed as for the basic recipe, adding a little kirsch to the fruit syrup and adding halves of poached pears to the ice cream.

Milk puddings

53 Baked rice pudding (pouding de riz)

Cal 1006 KJ	Cal 239 kcal	Fat 7.0 g	Sat Fat 3.9 g	Carb 40.7 g	Sugar 19.0 g	Protein 5.8 g	Fibre 0.6 g	*

	4 portions	10 portions
rice (short or whole grain)	50 g	125 g
sugar, caster or unrefined	50 g	125 g
milk (whole or skimmed)	½ litre	1¼ litres
butter or margarine	10 g	25 g
vanilla essence	2–3 drops	6–8 drops
grated nutmeg		

HEALTHY EATING TIP
• Use semi-skimmed milk.

* Using whole milk and hard margarine

1 Wash the rice, place in a pie dish or individual dishes.
2 Add the sugar and milk, mix well.
3 Add the butter, essence and nutmeg.
4 Place on a baking sheet; clean the rim of the pie dish.
5 Bake at 180–200°C, until the milk starts simmering.
6 Reduce the heat and allow the pudding to cook slowly, allowing 1½–2 hours in all (less time for individual dishes).

54 Rice pudding

Ingredients are as for baked rice pudding (recipe 53).

1 Boil the milk in a thick-based pan.
2 Add the washed rice, stir to the boil.
3 Simmer gently, stirring frequently until the rice is cooked.
4 Mix in the sugar, flavouring and butter (at this stage an egg yolk may also be added). A vanilla pod can be used in place of essence.
5 Pour into a pie dish or individual dishes, place on a baking tray and brown lightly under the salamander.

Note: Candied fruit and chopped nuts may be added for variety.

HEALTHY EATING TIP
• Use semi-skimmed milk.

55 Semolina pudding

Cal	Cal	Fat	Sat Fat	Carb	Sugar	Protein	Fibre	*
753 KJ	179 kcal	6.9 g	3.9 g	25.8 g	19.0 g	5.1 g	0.3 g	

	4 portions	10 portions
milk (whole or skimmed)	½ litre	1¼ litres
semolina	35 g	85 g
sugar, caster or unrefined	50 g	125 g
butter or margarine	10 g	25 g
lemon juice or lemon essence	2–3 drops	6–8 drops
egg yolk (optional)	1	3

1 Boil the milk in a thick-based pan.
2 Sprinkle in the semolina and stir to the boil.
3 Simmer for 15–20 minutes.
4 Add the sugar, butter, lemon juice or essence (and an egg yolk if desired).
5 Pour into a pie dish or individual dishes. Brown under the salamander.

Note: Sago, tapioca and ground rice pudding are made in the same way, using sago, tapioca or ground rice in place of semolina and vanilla essence for lemon essence.

* Using whole milk and hard margarine

Miscellaneous

56 Bread pudding

Cal	Cal	Fat	Sat Fat	Carb	Sugar	Protein	Fibre	*
2797 KJ	661 kcal	19.4 g	1.0 g	115.8 g	57.4 g	13.2 g	2.5 g	

	4 portions	10 portions
stale bread	½ kg	1¼ kg
sugar, caster or unrefined	125 g	300 g
currants or sultanas	125 g	300 g
mixed spice	½ tsp	1½ tsp
margarine	75 g	180 g
egg	1	3

1 Soak the bread in cold water or milk until soft.
2 Squeeze the bread dry and place in a bowl.
3 Mix in four-fifths of the sugar and the rest of the ingredients.
4 Place in a greased baking tray. Sprinkle with the remaining sugar.
5 Bake at 180°C for about 1 hour.

Note: Cut into suitable-sized pieces. It may be served cold or hot with a custard-type sauce.

* Using white bread

57 Trifle

Cal 2280 KJ	Cal 543 kcal	Fat 29.1 g	Sat Fat 17.1 g	Carb 66.2 g	Sugar 51.3 g	Protein 8.2 g	Fibre 1.9 g	*

6–8 portions

sponge (made with 3 eggs, medium)	1
jam	25 g
tinned fruit (pears, peaches, pineapple)	1
sherry (optional)	
Custard	
custard powder	35 g
milk (whole or skimmed)	375 ml
caster sugar	50 g
cream (½ whipped) or non-dairy cream	125 ml
whipped sweetened cream or non-dairy cream	¼ litre
angelica	25 g
glacé cherries	25 g

1 Cut the sponge in half, sideways, and spread with jam.
2 Place in a glass bowl or individual dishes and soak with fruit syrup drained from the tinned fruit; a few drops of sherry may be added.
3 Cut the fruit into small pieces and add to the sponge.
4 Dilute the custard powder in a basin with some of the milk, add the sugar.
5 Boil the remainder of the milk, pour a little on the custard powder, mix well, return to the saucepan and over a low heat and stir to the boil. Allow to cool, stirring occasionally to prevent a skin forming; fold in the three-quarters whipped cream.
6 Pour on to the sponge. Leave to cool.
7 Decorate with the whipped cream, angelica and cherries.

Variations
Other flavourings or liqueurs may be used in place of sherry (e.g. whisky, rum, brandy, Tia Maria).
For raspberry or strawberry trifle use fully ripe fresh fruit in place of tinned, and decorate with fresh fruit in place of angelica and glacé cherries.
A fresh egg custard may be used with fresh egg yolks (see recipe 1); a complete trifle recipe using fresh egg custard will be found in *Advanced Practical Cookery* (details at end of chapter).

* *Using whole milk and whipping cream*

58 Praline

Makes 800 g

Praline is a basic preparation used for flavouring items such as gâteaux, soufflés, ice creams and many other sweets.

almonds, shelled	100 g
hazelnuts, shelled	100 g
water	60 ml
sugar	200 g
lemon juice	1

1 Lightly brown the almonds and hazelnuts in an oven.
2 Cook the water, lemon juice and sugar in a copper or thick-based pan until the caramel stage is reached.
3 Remove the pan from the heat. Mix in the nuts.
4 Turn out the mixture on to a lightly oiled marble slab.
5 Allow to become quite cold.
6 Crush to a coarse texture using a rolling pin. Store in an airtight container.

Note: The addition of lemon juice inverts the sugar and prevents recrystallisation.

59 Chocolate fondant

Cal 2830 KJ	Cal 675 kcal	Fat 46.8 g	Sat Fat 29.6 g	Carb 55.9 g	Sugar 40.9 g	Protein 11 g	Fibre 0.6 g

	4 portions	10 portions
couverture chocolate	150 g	375 g
unsalted butter	125 g	312 g
eggs	3	7
yolks	2	5
caster sugar	75 g	182 g
flour	75 g	182 g

1 Lightly grease and flour individual dariole moulds.
2 Carefully melt the chocolate and butter in a suitable bowl, either in a microwave or over a pan of hot water (bain-marie).
3 In a separate bowl whisk the eggs, egg yolks and caster sugar until aerated to ribbon stage. Pour into the chocolate and butter mix, then whisk together.
4 Add the flour, then mix until smooth.
5 Pour into the moulds, bake in the oven at 200°C for 15 minutes.
6 Remove from the oven, leave for 5 minutes before turning out onto suitable plates.
7 Serve with a suitable ice cream (e.g. vanilla, pistachio, almond or Baileys).

60 Chocolate and griottine clafoutis

	6–8 portions
Cherry batter	
eggs	2
sugar	2½ tbsp
milk	180 ml
kirsch, from the griottines	2 tsp
plain flour	2½ tbsp
Chocolate batter	
plain chocolate	200 g
butter	100 g
eggs	2
sugar	2 tbsp
plain flour	tbsp
cornflour	tbsp
Chocolate sauce (optional)	
sugar	165 g
cocoa	55 g
water	125 ml
To finish	
drained griottines	220 g
icing sugar, for dusting	

Cherry batter
1 In a large bowl, beat the eggs and sugar together until smooth.
2 Add the milk and kirsch, then sieve in the flour.
3 Mix well, then strain the batter through a sieve and set aside.

Chocolate batter
1 Melt the chocolate and butter in a bowl placed over a pan of simmering water on a low heat.
2 Meanwhile, place the eggs and sugar in a mixing bowl or a mixer with a whisk attachment and whisk to a thick white foam.
3 Switch the machine to the slowest speed, add both flours and mix for 30–60 seconds.
4 Stir the chocolate and butter together then use a hand whisk to fold this mixture into the whisked egg mixture, ensuring total incorporation.
5 Carefully mix the two batters together to make one thick batter. This mixture can be stored in the refrigerator for up to 4 days.

Chocolate sauce (or follow recipe 72)
1 Place all the ingredients in a saucepan and bring to the boil, stirring to dissolve.
2 Remove from the heat, cool and store covered in the refrigerator until ready to serve, or for up to 1 month.

To complete
1 Preheat the oven to 180°C. Lightly, but thoroughly, butter some individual dishes. Alternatively use another ovenproof dish such as a gratin dish.
2 Place 10–12 griottine cherries in the base of each dish and divide the batter between them. Place the dishes on a baking shelf and bake for 8–10 minutes until just cooked.

3 Remove the clafoutis from the oven and allow it to cool slightly.
4 Dust with icing sugar and serve, with the chocolate sauce served separately if desired.

Note: Griottines are a type of cherry.

Sweet sauces

¼ litre = 4–8 portions, for all sauce recipes unless indicated otherwise

Use arrowroot instead of cornflour to give a clear finish to any of these sauces.

61 Jam sauce

Cal	Cal	Fat	Sat Fat	Carb	Sugar	Protein	Fibre
595 KJ	139 kcal	0.0 g	0.0 g	37.0 g	34.7 g	0.2 g	0.0 g

jam	200 g
water	100 ml
lemon juice	2–3 drops
cornflour	10 g

1 Boil the jam, water and lemon juice together.
2 Adjust the consistency with a little cornflour (or arrowroot) diluted with water.
3 Reboil until clear and pass through a conical strainer.

62 Apricot sauce *(sauce abricot)*

Cal	Cal	Fat	Sat Fat	Carb	Sugar	Protein	Fibre
595 KJ	139 kcal	0.0 g	0.0 g	37.0 g	34.7 g	0.2 g	0.0 g

apricot jam	200 g
water	100 ml
lemon juice	2–3 drops
cornflour	10 g

Proceed as for recipe 62.

63 Orange, lemon or lime sauce

Cal	Cal	Fat	Sat Fat	Carb	Sugar	Protein	Fibre	*
306 KJ	72 kcal	0.1 g	0.0 g	18.5 g	16.2 g	0.4 g	0.6 g	

sugar, caster or unrefined	50 g
water	250 ml
cornflour	10 g
oranges, lemons or limes	1–2

1 Boil the sugar and water.
2 Add the cornflour (or arrowroot) diluted with water, stirring continuously.
3 Reboil until clear, strain.
4 Add blanched julienne of orange zest and the strained orange juice.

Note: A little curaçao or Cointreau may be added for additional flavour.

* *Using oranges and cornflour*

64 Syrup sauce

Cal	Cal	Fat	Sat Fat	Carb	Sugar	Protein	Fibre	*
677 KJ	159 kcal	0.0 g	0.0 g	42.0 g	39.7 g	0.2 g	0.0 g	

syrup	200 g
water	125 ml
lemon, juice of	1
cornflour	10 g

1 Bring the syrup, water and lemon juice to the boil and thicken with diluted cornflour (or arrowroot).
2 Boil for a few minutes and strain.

* Using cornflour

65 Custard sauce

Cal	Cal	Fat	Sat Fat	Carb	Sugar	Protein	Fibre	*
1245 KJ	296 kcal	9.6 g	6.0 g	47.2 g	38.0 g	8.3 g	0.3 g	

custard powder	10 g
milk (whole or semi-skimmed)	250 ml
caster or unrefined sugar	25 g

1 Dilute the custard powder with a little of the milk.
2 Boil the remainder of the milk.
3 Pour a little of the boiled milk on to the diluted custard powder.

4 Return to the saucepan.
5 Stir to the boil and mix in the sugar.

Note: See also recipe 9, for fresh egg custard sauce.

* Using whole milk

66 Almond sauce

Cal	Cal	Fat	Sat Fat	Carb	Sugar	Protein	Fibre	*
314 KJ	75 kcal	2.5 g	1.6 g	11.7 g	9.4 g	2.1 g	0.0 g	

cornflour	10 g
milk (whole or skimmed)	250 ml
caster or unrefined sugar	25 g
almond essence	few drops

1 Dilute the cornflour with a little of the milk.
2 Boil the remainder of the milk. Whisk on to the cornflour.
3 Return to the pan, stir to the boil. Simmer for 3–4 minutes.
4 Mix in the sugar and essence. Pass through a strainer.

* Using whole milk and cornflour

67 Rum or brandy cream

Whipped, sweetened cream flavoured with rum or brandy.

68 Rum or brandy butter

Cream equal quantities of butter and sieved icing sugar together and add rum or brandy to taste.

69 Melba sauce (sauce Melba)

Cal	Cal	Fat	Sat Fat	Carb	Sugar	Protein	Fibre	*
558 KJ	131 kcal	0.0 g	0.0 g	34.7 g	34.7 g	0.2 g	0.0 g	

Method 1
raspberry jam	400 g
water	125 ml

Method 2
raspberries	400 g
water	125 ml
sugar, caster or unrefined	100 g

Method 3
raspberries	400 g
icing sugar	200 g
lemon juice	few drops

Method 1
1 Boil ingredients together and pass through a conical strainer.

Method 2
1 Boil ingredients together, cool, liquidise and strain.

Method 3
1 Liquidise ingredients, pass through a fine sieve and add a little lemon juice.

* Method 1. Method 2: 265 kJ/62 kcal Energy; 0.2 g Fat; 0.1 g Sat Fat; 15.4 g Carb; 15.4 g Sugar; 0.7 g Protein; 0.0 g Fibre. Method 3: 474 kJ/111 kcal Energy; 0.2 g Fat; 0.1 g Sat Fat; 28.5 g Carb; 28.3 g Sugar; 0.7 g Protein; 0.0 g Fibre

Note: Methods 2 and 3 are also known as raspberry cullis or coulis, which can be prepared using other fruits (e.g. peach, strawberry or mango).

70 Strawberry sauce

Cal	Cal	Fat	Sat Fat	Carb	Sugar	Protein	Fibre
350 KJ	83 kcal	0.0 g	0.0 g	16.5 g	16.5 g	0.3 g	0.4 g

	4 portions	10 portions
strawberry purée	200 g	500 g
water	60 ml	150 ml
caster sugar	50 g	125 g

1 Mix all the ingredients together and strain.

Note: Alternative fruit purées that can be used are peach, apricot, mango, pawpaw, strawberry and raspberry. Alternative sauces include raspberry, peach, apricot, lemon, orange and lime. For peach sauce, for example, proceed as for strawberry sauce, substituting peach purée for strawberry purée.

71 Chocolate sauce (sauce chocolat) 1- economy recipe

Cal 336 KJ	Cal 79 kcal	Fat 1.8 g	Sat Fat 1.1 g	Carb 15.1 g	Sugar 13.3 g	Protein 1.7 g	Fibre 0.2 g	*

cornflour	10 g
milk	250 ml
cocoa powder	10 g
or	
chocolate (block)	25 g
sugar	65 g
butter	5 g

With cocoa
1 Dilute the cornflour with a little of the milk, mix in the cocoa.
2 Boil the remainder of the milk.
3 Pour a little of the milk on to the cornflour.
4 Return to the saucepan.
5 Stir to the boil. Mix in the sugar and butter.

With chocolate
1 Shred the chocolate, add to the milk.
2 Proceed as above, omitting the cocoa.

Note: Chocolate sauce may be flavoured if desired with rum or crème de menthe.

* *Using cocoa; portion size 57 g*

72 Chocolate sauce (sauce chocolat) 2

Method 1

double cream	175 g
butter	40 g
milk or plain chocolate pieces	225 g

Method 2

caster sugar	40 g
water	120 ml
dark chocolate (75% cocoa solids)	160 g
unsalted butter	25 g
single cream	80 ml

Method 1
1 Place butter and cream in a saucepan and gently bring to a simmer.
2 Add the chocolate and stir well until the chocolate has melted and the sauce is smooth.

Method 2
1 Dissolve the sugar in the water over a low heat.
2 Remove from the heat. Stir in the chocolate and butter.
3 When everything has melted, stir in the cream and gently bring to the boil.

73 Sauce anglaise (fresh egg custard)

Makes 1 litre

milk	485 ml
cream	225 ml
vanilla pod, split	1
egg yolks	150 g
sugar	200 g

1 Boil the milk and cream with the vanilla pod.
2 In a bowl whisk together the egg yolks and sugar until pale, add the milk and mix together.
3 Return to a clean pan and, with a spatula, stir the custard until cooked out (it will coat the spoon and the froth will disappear). Do not boil or the eggs will scramble.
4 Place in a plastic container and leave to cool.

74 Fruit coulis

Makes 1500 ml

fruit purée	1 litre
caster sugar	500 g

1 Warm the purée.
2 Boil the sugar with a little water to soft-ball stage (121°C).

3 Pour the soft-ball sugar into the warm fruit purée while whisking vigorously.
4 This will then be ready to store.

Note: The reason the soft ball is achieved and mixed with the purée is that this stabilises the fruit and prevents separation once the coulis has been put onto the plate.

75 Rose petal syrup

Makes 740 ml

water	285 ml
caster sugar	455 g
large fragrant red roses	6
lemon, juice of	1

1 Heat the water and sugar until dissolved.
2 Add the rose petals and lemon juice, boil for 5 minutes, cool, cover and leave for 24 hours at room temperature.
3 Strain and store in an airtight container.

Variations
Lavender syrup: same as above, but substituting 16 heads of lavender or 4 tbsp of dried lavender.

Note: These syrups are used to finish sweets.

76 Caramel sauce

Makes 750 ml

caster sugar	100 g
water	80 ml
double cream	500 ml
egg yolks, lightly beaten (optional)	2

1 In a large saucepan, dissolve the sugar with the water over a low heat and bring to boiling point.
2 Wash down the inside of the pan with a pastry brush dipped in cold water to prevent crystals from forming.
3 Cook until the sugar turns to a deep amber colour. Immediately turn off the heat and whisk in the cream.

4 Set the pan back over a high heat and stir the sauce with the whisk. Let it bubble for 2 minutes, then turn off the heat.
5 You can now strain the sauce and use it when cooled, or, for a richer, smoother sauce, pour a little caramel onto the egg yolks, then return the mixture to the pan and heat to 80°C, taking care that it does not boil.
6 Pass the sauce through a conical strainer and keep in a cool place, stirring occasionally to prevent a skin from forming.

77 Boiled buttercream

medium eggs	2
icing sugar	50 g
granulated sugar or cube sugar	300 g
water	100 g
glucose	50 g
unsalted butter	400 g

1 Beat the eggs and icing sugar until at ribbon stage (sponge).
2 Boil the granulated or cube sugar with water and glucose to 118°C.
3 Gradually add the sugar at 118°C to the eggs and icing sugar at ribbon stage, whisk continuously and allow to cool to 26°C.
4 Gradually add the unsalted butter while continuing to whisk until a smooth cream is obtained.

Variations
Buttercream may be flavoured with numerous flavours and combinations of flavours:
* chocolate and rum
* whisky and orange
* strawberry and vanilla
* lemon and lime
* apricot and passionfruit
* brandy and praline
* coffee and hazelnut.

78 Buttercream

icing sugar	150 g
butter	200 g

1 Sieve the icing sugar.
2 Cream the butter and icing sugar until light and creamy.
3 Flavour and colour as required.

Variations
Variations include:
* *rum buttercream:* add rum to flavour and blend in
* *chocolate buttercream:* add melted chocolate, sweetened or unsweetened according to taste.

Fruit-based recipes

Quality requirements and purchasing points

Fresh fruit should be:

* whole and of fresh appearance (for maximum flavour the fruit must be ripe but not overripe)
* firm, according to type and variety
* clean, and free from traces of pesticides and fungicides
* free from external moisture
* free from any unpleasant foreign smell or taste
* free from pests or disease
* sufficiently mature; it must be capable of being handled and travelling without damage
* free from any defects characteristic of the variety in shape, size and colour
* free of bruising and any other damage due to weather conditions.

Soft fruits deteriorate quickly, especially if not sound. Care must be taken to see that they are not damaged or overripe when purchased. Soft fruits should look fresh; there should be no signs of wilting, shrinking or mould. The colour of certain soft fruits is an indication of their ripeness (e.g. strawberries or dessert gooseberries).

Food value

Fruit is rich in antioxidant minerals and vitamins. Antioxidants protect cells from damage by oxygen, which may lead to heart disease and cancer. The current recommendation is to eat five portions of fruit and vegetables each day.

Storage

Hard fruits, such as apples, are left in boxes and kept in a cool store. Soft fruits, such as raspberries and strawberries, should be left in their punnets or baskets in a cold room. Stone fruits are best placed in trays so that any damaged fruit can be seen and discarded. Peaches and citrus fruits are left in their delivery trays or boxes. Bananas should not be stored in too cold a place because their skins will turn black.

79 Apple charlotte (charlotte aux pommes)

Cal	Cal	Fat	Sat Fat	Carb	Sugar	Protein	Fibre	*
2163 KJ	515 kcal	22.3 g	9.3 g	74.5 g	23.4 g	9.4 g	6.1 g	

	4 portions	10 portions
stale bread	400 g	1¼ kg
margarine or butter	100 g	250 g
cooking apples	400 g	1¼ kg
sugar, caster or unrefined	50–75 g	125–150 g
breadcrumbs or		
cake crumbs	35 g	85 g

1 Use either one charlotte mould or four dariole moulds.
2 Cut the bread into 3 mm slices and remove the crusts.
3 Cut a round the size of the mould bottom, dip into melted butter or margarine on one side and place in the mould fat side down.
4 Cut fingers of bread 2–4 cm wide, and fit, overlapping well, to the sides of the mould after dipping each one in melted fat. Take care not to leave any gaps.
5 Peel, core and wash the apples, cut into thick slices and three parts cook in a little butter and sugar (a little cinnamon or a clove may be added), and add the breadcrumbs.
6 Fill the centre of the mould with the apple.
7 Cut round pieces of bread to seal the apple in.
8 Bake at 220°C for 30–40 minutes. Remove from the mould.
9 Serve with apricot (recipe 62) or custard (recipe 65) sauce.

* Using hard margarine

80 Apple fritters (beignets aux pommes)

Cal	Cal	Fat	Sat Fat	Carb	Sugar	Protein	Fibre	*
1034 KJ	246 kcal	10.2 g	1.9 g	38.9 g	25.0 g	2.1 g	3.0 g	

	4 portions	10 portions
cooking apples	400 g	1 kg
flour, as needed		
frying batter	150 g	375 g
apricot sauce	125 ml	300 ml

1 Peel and core the apples and cut into ½ cm rings.
2 Pass through flour, shake off the surplus.
3 Dip into the frying batter (page 187).
4 Lift out with the fingers, into fairly hot deep fat: 185°C.
5 Cook for about 5 minutes on each side.
6 Drain well on kitchen paper, dust with icing sugar and glaze under the salamander.
7 Serve with hot apricot sauce (recipe 62).

* Fried in peanut oil

Figure 14.12 ✎ Preparation of apple fritters

81 Banana fritters *(beignets aux bananes)*

Cal 1405 KJ	Cal 333 kcal	Fat 11.5 g	Sat Fat 1.4 g	Carb 57.9 g	Sugar 41.7 g	Protein 3.0 g	Fibre 1.6 g

	4 portions	10 portions
bananas	410	
frying batter	150 g	375 g
apricot sauce (recipe 62)	125 ml	300 ml

1 Peel and cut the bananas in half lengthwise, then in half across.
2 Cook and serve as for apple fritters (recipe 80).

Note: Bananas may be dipped in hot pastry cream flavoured with rum, allowed to cool on an oiled tray, before passing through flour and dipping in the frying batter.

82 Pineapple fritters *(beignets aux ananas)*

Cal 1082 KJ	Cal 257 kcal	Fat 11.2 g	Sat Fat 1.3 g	Carb 39.6 g	Sugar 25.7 g	Protein 1.9 g	Fibre 0.7 g

	4 portions
pineapple, rings	4
frying batter	150 g
apricot sauce (recipe 62)	125 ml

1 Cut the pineapple rings in half, cook and serve as for apple fritters (recipe 80).

Note: Pineapple fritters may also be dipped in hot pastry cream flavoured with liqueur, allowed to cool on an oiled tray before passing through flour and dipping in the frying batter.

83 Baked apple *(pommes bonne femme)*

Cal 663 KJ	Cal 156 kcal	Fat 5.1 g	Sat Fat 2.2 g	Carb 29.7 g	Sugar 29.5 g	Protein 0.4 g	Fibre 2.7 g	*

	4 portions	10 portions
medium-sized cooking apples	4	10
sugar, white or unrefined	50 g	125 g
cloves	4	10
butter or margarine	20 g	50 g
water	60 ml	150 ml

1 Core the apples and make an incision 2 mm deep round the centre of each. Wash well.
2 Place in a roasting tray or ovenproof dish.
3 Fill the centre with sugar and add a clove to each.
4 Place 5 g butter on each. Add the water.
5 Bake in a moderate oven at 200–220°C for 15–20 minutes.
6 Turn the apples over carefully.
7 Return to the oven until cooked, about 40 minutes in all.
8 Serve with a little cooking liquor and custard, cream or ice cream.

Note: For stuffed baked apple, proceed as for baked apples, but fill the centre with washed sultanas, raisins or chopped dates, or a combination of these.

* *Using hard margarine*

84 Apple crumble

Cal	Cal	Fat	Sat Fat	Carb	Sugar	Protein	Fibre	*
1993 KJ	470 kcal	10.9 g	6.6 g	94.9 g	66.4 g	4.2 g	3.6 g	

	4 portions	10 portions
Bramley apples	600 g	2 kg
sugar	100 g	250 g
cloves	1	2
Topping		
butter or margarine	50 g	125 g
plain flour	150 g	400 g
soft brown sugar	100 g	250 g

1 Peel, core and slice the apples.
2 Cook gently with a few drops of water, sugar and clove.
3 Place in a pie dish, then remove the clove(s).
4 For the topping, lightly rub the fat into the flour and combine with the sugar.

5 When the fruit is cool, add the topping and bake in a hot oven 190°C for about 30 minutes until lightly browned.
6 Serve with custard, cream or vanilla ice cream.

Variations
- Apple and blackberry, apple and gooseberry, rhubarb, rhubarb and ginger (all using cooked fruit); raspberry, blackcurrant, damson (using raw fruit).
- The topping can be varied by using wholemeal flour, self-raising flour – adding a little spice (e.g. cinnamon, nutmeg, mixed spice).
- Replacing a quarter of the flour with ground almonds or chopped almonds, walnuts or pecans.
- Use half the flour and half porridge oats.

* *Using butter*

85 Fresh fruit salad (*salade de fruits*)

Cal	Cal	Fat	Sat Fat	Carb	Sugar	Protein	Fibre
493 KJ	117 kcal	0.0 g	0.0 g	30.3 g	29.5 g	0.9 g	3.0 g

	4 portions	10 portions
orange	1	2–3
dessert apple	1	2–3
dessert pear	1	2–3
cherries	50 g	125 g
grapes	50 g	125 g
banana	1	2–3
Stock syrup		
caster sugar	50 g	125 g
water	125 ml	375 ml
lemon, juice of	½	1

  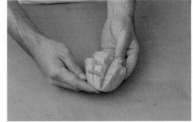

Figure 14.13 Peeling and preparing a mango – method 1: (a) slice through, keeping lateral to the stone; (b) score the flesh; (c) bend out the cubes

1 For the syrup, boil the sugar with the water and place in a bowl.
2 Allow to cool, add the lemon juice.
3 Peel and cut the orange into segments as for cocktail.
4 Quarter the apple and pear, remove the core, peel and cut each quarter into two or three slices, place in the bowl and mix with the orange.
5 Stone the cherries, leave whole.
6 Cut the grapes in half, peel if required, and remove the pips.
7 Mix carefully and place in a glass bowl in the refrigerator to chill.
8 Just before serving, peel and slice the banana and mix in.

Variations

All the following fruits may be used: dessert apples, pears, pineapple, oranges, grapes, melon, strawberries, peaches, raspberries, apricots, bananas, cherries. Kiwi fruit, plums, mangoes, pawpaws and lychees may also be used. Kirsch, Cointreau or Grand Marnier may be added to the syrup. All fruit must be ripe. Allow about 150 g unprepared fruit per portion. For the syrup, as an alternative to water and sugar a fruit juice (e.g. apple, orange, grape or passion fruit) can be used.

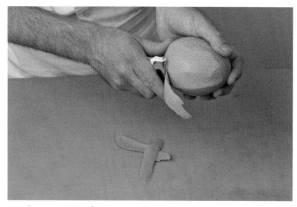

Figure 14.14 ✎ Peeling and preparing a mango – method 2

Figure 14.15 ✎ Fresh fruit salad

86 Tropical fruit plate

An assortment of fully ripe fruits – e.g. pineapple, papaya, mango (see above) – peeled, deseeded, cut into pieces and neatly dressed on a plate. An optional accompaniment could be yoghurt, vanilla ice cream, crème fraiche, fresh or clotted cream.

HEALTHY EATING TIP

• This colourful dessert helps to meet the recommended target of five portions of fruit and vegetables per day.

Figure 14.16 ✎ Tropical fruit plate

Figure 14.17 Tropical fruits (clockwise from top left): pineapple, papaya, coconut, kiwis, passion fruit

87 Fruit fool

Cal 942 KJ	Cal 222 kcal	Fat 2.6 g	Sat Fat 1.6 g	Carb 50.3 g	Sugar 44.5 g	Protein 2.4 g	Fibre 1.6 g	*

	4 portions	10 portions
Method 1		
fruit (apple, gooseberry, rhubarb, etc.)	400 g	1 kg
water	60 ml	150 ml
granulated or unrefined sugar	100 g	250 g
cornflour	25 g	60 g
milk (whole or skimmed)	¼ litre	625 ml
caster or unrefined sugar	25 g	60 g
Method 2		
fruit in purée (raspberries, strawberries, etc.)	400 g	1 kg
caster sugar	100 g	250 g
fresh whipped cream	¼ litre	625 ml
Method 3		
cornflour	35 g	85 g
water	375 ml	900 ml
sugar	100 g	250 g
fruit (as per method 2)	400 g	1¼ kg
cream	185 ml	500 ml

Method 1
1 Cook the fruit in water and granulated sugar, to a purée. Pass through a sieve.
2 Dilute the cornflour in a little of the milk, add the caster sugar.
3 Boil the remainder of the milk.
4 Pour on the diluted cornflour, stir well.
5 Return to the pan on a low heat and stir to the boil.
6 Mix with the fruit purée. The quantity of mixture should not be less than ½ litre.
7 Pour into four (or ten) glass coupes or suitable dishes and allow to set.
8 Decorate with whipped sweetened cream or non-dairy cream. The colour may need to be adjusted slightly with food colour.

Method 2
1 Mix the ingredients and serve in coupes.

Method 3
1 Dilute the cornflour in a little of the water.
2 Boil the remainder of the water with the sugar and prepared fruit until soft.
3 Pass through a fine sieve.
4 Return to a clean pan and reboil.
5 Stir in the diluted cornflour and reboil. Allow to cool.
6 Lightly whisk the cream and fold into the mixture.
7 Serve as for method 1.

Note: In methods 2 and 3 the fat content may be reduced by using equal quantities of cream and natural Greek-style yoghurt.

* Method 1 (using whole milk, apples). Method 2 (using strawberries): 1540 kJ/370 kcal Energy; 25.3 g Fat; 15.8 g Sat Fat; 35.7 g Carb; 35.7 g Sugar; 2.0 g Protein; 1.2 g Fibre. Method 3 (using raspberries and double cream): 1606 kJ/385 kcal Energy; 25.2 g Fat; 15.6 g Sat Fat; 40.0 g Carb; 31.9 g Sugar; 2.0 g Protein; 2.7 g Fibre

88 Poached fruits or fruit compote (compote de fruits)

Cal 531 KJ	Cal 126 kcal	Fat 0.0 g	Sat Fat 0.0 g	Carb 33.5 g	Sugar 33.5 g	Protein 0.2 g	Fibre 2.2 g	*

	4 portions	10 portions
stock syrup (recipe 184)	¼ litre	625 ml
fruit	400 g	1 kg
sugar	100 g	250 g
lemon, juice of	½	1

Apples, pears
1 Boil the water and sugar.
2 Quarter the fruit, remove the core and peel.
3 Place in a shallow pan in sugar syrup.
4 Add a few drops of lemon juice.
5 Cover with greaseproof paper.
6 Allow to simmer slowly, preferably in the oven, cool and serve.

Soft fruits (raspberries, strawberries)
1 Pick and wash the fruit. Place in a glass bowl.
2 Pour on the hot syrup. Allow to cool and serve.

Stone fruits (plums, damsons, greengages, cherries)
1 Wash the fruit, barely cover with sugar syrup and cover with greaseproof paper or a lid.
2 Cook gently in a moderate oven until tender.

Rhubarb
1 Trim off the stalk and leaf and wash. Cut into 5 cm lengths and cook as above, adding extra sugar if necessary. A little ground ginger may also be added.

Gooseberries, blackcurrants, redcurrants
1 Top and tail the gooseberries, wash and cook as for stone fruit, adding extra sugar if necessary.
2 The currants should be carefully removed from the stalks, washed and cooked as for stone fruits.

Dried fruits (prunes, apricots, apples, pears)
1 Dried fruits should be washed and soaked in cold water overnight.
2 Gently cook in the liquor with sufficient sugar to taste.

* Using pears

Figure 14.19 Stone fruits (clockwise from top): mango, plums, nectarines, dates

Figure 14.18 Hard fruits (clockwise from top left): Comice pears, quinces, William pears, Braeburn apples, crab apples, Red Delicious apples

Figure 14.20 Soft fruits (clockwise from top): redcurrants, raspberries, blackberries, strawberries

Variations

- A piece of cinnamon stick and a few slices of lemon may be added to the prunes or pears, one or two cloves to the dried or fresh apples.
- Any compote may be flavoured with lavender and/or mint.

HEALTHY EATING TIP
- Use fruit juice to poach the fruit.
- If dried fruits are used, no added sugar is needed.

89 Pear condé (*poire condé*)

Cal	Cal	Fat	Sat Fat	Carb	Sugar	Protein	Fibre	*
1299 KJ	309 kcal	4.9 g	3.1 g	64.5 g	48.3 g	5.7 g	2.4 g	

	4 portions	10 portions
rice (short or whole grain)	75 g	180 g
milk, whole or skimmed	½ litre	1¼ litres
sugar, caster or unrefined	50 g	125 g
vanilla essence or pod	3–4 drops	6–7 drops
ripe dessert pears	2	5
apricot glaze	125 ml	300 ml
angelica	10 g	25 g
glacé cherries	2	5

1 Cook the rice in the milk, sweeten and flavour. Allow to cool.
2 Peel, core and halve the pears; poach them carefully, leave to cool.
3 Dress the rice either in a glass bowl, on individual plates or a flat dish.
4 Drain the pears and neatly arrange them on top.
5 Coat with apricot glaze. Decorate with angelica and cherries.

Note: Many other fruits may be prepared as a condé: banana, pineapple, peach. The rice can be enriched with 10 g butter or margarine and an egg yolk (increase the quantities by 2½ for 10 portions).

* Using whole milk

90 Pears in red wine

Cal	Cal	Fat	Sat Fat	Carb	Sugar	Protein	Fibre
690 KJ	163 kcal	0.2 g	0.0 g	42.3 g	42.3 g	0.5 g	3.5 g

	4 portions	10 portions
whole ripe pears, medium	4	10
Cooking liquid		
water	250 ml	625 ml
sugar	100 g	250 g
red wine	125 ml	300 ml
cinnamon stick	1	2–3
lemon, zest of	1	2–3
cochineal	few drops	several drops

1 Boil all the ingredients for the cooking liquid.
2 Peel the pears. Use either whole, in which case the cores should be tunnelled out and half of the stalks left intact, or in halves or quarters with the cores and stalks removed.
3 Gently poach the pears covered with greaseproof paper in the cooking liquid.
4 The pears may be served hot or cold. An accompaniment might be cream (plain or whipped), ice cream (e.g. vanilla or pistachio), yoghurt or fromage frais.

Note: If the pears are cut up the amount of cooking liquid may be lessened. The amount of red wine can be varied according to taste. Pears in red wine may also be used as a garnish for other dishes (e.g. vanilla mousse or bavarois).

Other fruit-based recipes

There are numerous other recipes that include fruit. For example:

- baked Alaska (recipe 52)
- bavarois (recipe 17)
- cold lemon soufflé (recipe 38)
- Dutch apple tart (recipe 141)
- flans (recipe 124)
- ice cream (e.g. strawberry, raspberry) (recipe 27)
- kiwi slice (recipe 142)
- lemon meringue pie (recipe 131)
- meringue (recipe 48)
- pancakes (recipe 45)
- pies (recipe 119)
- sorbets (recipes 30–34)
- soufflé puddings (recipes 35–38)
- steamed sponge puddings (recipes 39–44)
- tartlets and barquettes (recipes 139 and 140)
- turnovers (recipe 152).

Many recipes also make use of dried fruit, For example:

- bread and butter pudding (recipe 3)
- bread pudding (recipe 56)
- Christmas pudding (recipe 43)
- mince pies (recipe 158).

Dough products

Bread and dough products basically contain wheat flour and yeast. Bread and bread products form the basis of our diet; it is not surprising, therefore, that bread is seen as a fundamental staple product in our society: 'Give us this day our daily bread.' We eat bread at breakfast, lunch and dinner, in sandwiches, as bread rolls, as croissants, as French sticks, etc. Bread is also used as an ingredient for many other dishes, either as slices or as breadcrumbs. The basic bread dough of wheat flour, yeast and water may be enriched with fat, sugar, eggs, milk and numerous other added ingredients.

Dough consists of strong flour, water, salt and yeast, which are kneaded together to the required consistency at a suitable temperature. When proving takes place the yeast produces carbon dioxide and water, which aerates the dough. When baked it produces a light digestible product with flavour and colour.

Some examples of enriched doughs or enriched breads are:

- buns
- savarins
- brioche
- croissants
- Danish pastries.

Croissants and Danish pastries are enriched doughs where the fat is added by layering or lamination; a softer eating quality is obtained because the fat in the dough insulates the water molecules, keeping the moisture level higher during baking.

Flour-based products provide us with variety, energy, vitamins and minerals. Wholemeal bread products also provide roughage, an essential part of a healthy diet.

Understanding fermentation

For dough to become leavened bread it must go through a fermentation process. This is brought about by the action of yeast, with enzymes in the yeast and dough; these convert sugar into alcohol, thus producing the characteristic flavour of bread. The action also produces carbon dioxide, which makes the bread rise.

Yeast requires ideal conditions for growth. These are as follows.

- **Warmth:** a good temperature for dough production is 22–30°C.
- **Moisture:** yeast requires moisture; the liquid should be added at approximately 38°C.
- **Food:** yeast requires food; this is obtained from the starch in the flour.
- **Time:** time is needed to allow the yeast to grow.

Yeast is a living single-cell micro-organism and, in the right conditions, with food, warmth and moisture, it ferments, producing carbon dioxide (see below) and alcohol while at the same time reproducing itself. It is rich in protein and vitamin B.

Yeast will not survive in a high concentration of

sugar or salt, and will slow down in a very rich dough with a high fat and egg content.

When mixing yeast in water or milk, make sure that the liquid is at the correct temperature, 38°C and disperse the yeast in the liquid. (As a living organism cannot be dissolved, the word disperse is used.)

Dried yeast has been dehydrated and requires creaming with a little water before use. It will keep for several months in its dry state.

Why does dough ferment?

The phenomenon of seeing dough ferment is extraordinary and very common in our profession. However, because it is so frequent, we do not pay much attention to how it happens. It is very interesting to know why doughs ferment and what the effects are on the end product. In order to understand why yeast dough rises, we must note that the main ingredients of natural leavening are water, air and, most importantly, sugar, which is transformed into carbon dioxide and causes the leavening. This carbon dioxide forms bubbles inside the dough and makes it rise. Fermentation is a transformation undergone by organic matter (sugars).

Points to remember

- Yeast should be removed from the refrigerator and used at room temperature.
- Check all ingredients are weighed carefully.
- Work in a clean and tidy manner to avoid cross-contamination.
- Check all temperatures carefully.
- All wholemeal doughs absorb more water than white doughs. The volume of water absorbed by flour also varies according to the strength (protein and bran content).
- When using machines, check that they are in working order.
- Always remember the health and safety rules when using machinery.
- Divide the dough with a dough divider, hard scraper or hydraulic cutting machine.
- Check the divided dough pieces for weight. When scaling, remember that doughs lose up to 12.5 per cent of water during baking; therefore

this needs to be taken into account when scaling.
- Keep the flour, bowl and liquid warm.
- Remember to knock the dough back carefully once proved, as this will expel the gas and allow the greater dispersion of the yeast. It will once again be in direct contact with the dough.
- Proving allows the dough to ferment; the second prove is essential for giving dough products the necessary volume and a good flavour.
- Time and temperature are crucial when cooking dough products.
- When using frozen dough products always follow the manufacturer's instructions. Contamination can occur if doughs are defrosted incorrectly.

Types of dough

Enriched doughs
- **Savarin:** a rich yeast dough used for savarins, babas and marignans.
- **Brioche:** a rich yeast dough with a high fat and butter content.

Laminated doughs
- **Croissants:** made from a dough in which the fat content has been layered (laminated) as in puff pastry.
- **Danish:** also a laminated dough; Danish pastries may be filled with fruit, frangipane, apple, custard, cherries and many other ingredients.

Speciality doughs
- **Blinis:** a type of pancake.
- **Naan bread:** unleavened bread, traditionally cooked in a tandoor (oven).
- **Pitta bread:** Middle Eastern and Greek bread, also unleavened.
- **Chapatti:** Indian unleavened bread made from a fine ground wholemeal flour.

Storage of cooked dough products

Crusty rolls and bread are affected by changes in storage conditions; they are softened by a damp environment and humid conditions. Always store in suitable containers at room temperature and in a freezer for longer storage. Do not store in a refrigerator unless you want the bread to stale quickly for use as breadcrumbs. Staling will also occur quickly in products that contain a high ratio of fat and milk. Many commercial dough products contain anti-staling agents.

Convenience dough products

There are many new different types of product on the market.
- Fresh and frozen preproved dough products: rolls; croissants; Danish pastries; French breads.
- Bake-off products. These are products ready for baking, either frozen or fresh, or in modified atmosphere-packaged forms (this method replaces most of the oxygen around the product to slow down spoilage). These products have to be kept refrigerated: garlic bread; rolls; Danish pastries.

Possible reasons for faults using yeast doughs

- Close texture:
  - insufficiently proved
  - insufficiently kneaded
  - insufficient yeast
  - oven too hot
  - too much water
  - too little water.
- Uneven texture:
  - insufficient kneading
  - oven too cool
  - over-proving.
- Coarse texture:
  - over-proofed, uncovered
  - insufficient kneading
  - too much water
  - too much salt.
- Wrinkled:
  - over-proved.

- Sour:
  - stale yeast
  - too much yeast.
- Broken crust:
  - under-proved at the second stage.
- White spots on crust:
  - not covered before second proving.

Breads

It is customary today in a restaurant to be offered a range of different flavoured breads. Internationally there is a wide variety available; different nations and regions have their own speciality breads. Bread plays an important part in many religious festivals, especially Christian and Jewish.

The traditional breadmaking process is known as the bulk fermentation process. This was used by many bakers before the introduction of high-speed mixing and dough conditioners, which both eliminate the need for bulk fermentation time. However, this traditional method produces a fine flavour due to the fermentation and is evident in the final product.

Bulk fermentation time (BFT)
This term is used to describe the length of time that the dough is allowed to ferment in bulk. BFT is measured from the end of the mixing method to the beginning of the scaling process. The length of BFT can be from 1 to 6 hours and is related to the level of salt and yeast in the recipe, as well as the dough temperature.

It is important during the bulk fermentation process that ideal conditions are adhered to:

- the dough must be kept covered to prevent the dough surface skinning
- the appropriate temperature is maintained to control the rate of fermentation.

91 Bread rolls

Cal 426 KJ	Cal 102 kcal	Fat 1.7 g	Sat Fat 0.7 g	Carb 19.5 g	Sugar 1.0 g	Protein 3.4 g	Fibre 1.1 g	*

	8 rolls	20 rolls
flour (strong)	200 g	500 g
yeast	5 g	12 g
liquid (half water, half milk)	125 ml	300 ml
butter or margarine	10 g	25 g
caster sugar	¼ tsp	½ tsp
salt		
eggwash		

1 Sieve the flour into a bowl; warm in oven or above the stove.
2 Cream the yeast in a small basin with a quarter of the liquid.
3 Make a well in the centre of the flour; add the dissolved yeast.
4 Sprinkle over a little of the flour, cover with a cloth, leave in a warm place until the yeast ferments (bubbles).
5 Add the remainder of the liquid (warm), the fat, sugar and the salt.
6 Knead firmly until smooth and free from stickiness.
7 Return to the basin, cover with a cloth and leave in a warm place until double its size. (This is called *proving* the dough.)
8 Knock back. Divide into even pieces.
9 Mould into the desired shape.
10 Place on a floured baking sheet. Cover with a cloth.
11 Leave in a warm place to prove (double in size).
12 Brush carefully with eggwash.
13 Bake in a hot oven at 220°C for about 10 minutes.

Note: At all times during preparation of the dough, extreme heat must be avoided as the yeast will be killed and the dough spoiled.

Variations
For variety (increase the quantities by 2½ for 10 portions):
● use all wholemeal flour, 1 tsp raw cane sugar in place of caster sugar, and all water and no milk
● Add 50 g each of chopped walnuts and sultanas.

* *Using white flour and hard margarine, 1 portion (2 rolls). Using wholemeal flour: 379 kJ/90 kcal; 1.6 g Fat; 0.5 g Sat Fat; 17.1 g Carb; 1.2 g Sugar; 3.4 g Protein; 2.3 g Fibre*

Figure 14.21 ✎ Assortment of bread rolls and loaves

92 Wholemeal bread

Makes 2 loaves

unsalted butter or oil	60 g
honey	3 tbsp
water, lukewarm	500 ml
fresh yeast	25 g
or	
dried yeast	18 g
salt	1 tbsp
unbleached strong white flour	125 g
stoneground wholemeal flour	625 g

1 Melt the butter in a saucepan.
2 Mix together 1 tbsp of honey and 4 tbsp of the water in a bowl.
3 Disperse the yeast into the honey mixture.
4 In a basin, place the melted butter, remaining honey and water, the yeast mixture and salt.
5 Add the white flour and half the wholemeal flour. Mix well.
6 Add the remaining wholemeal flour gradually, mixing well between each addition.
7 The dough should pull away from the side of the bowl and form a ball. The resulting dough should be soft and slightly sticky.
8 Turn out onto a floured work surface. Sprinkle with white flour, knead well.
9 Brush a clean bowl with melted butter or oil. Place in the dough, cover with a damp cloth and allow to prove in a warm place. This will take approximately 1–1½ hours.
10 Knock back and further knead the dough. Cover again and rest for 10–15 minutes.
11 Divide the dough into two equal pieces.
12 Form each piece of dough into a cottage loaf or place in a suitable loaf tin.
13 Allow to prove in a warm place for approximately 45 minutes.
14 Place in a pre-heated oven, 220°C and bake until well browned (approx. 40–45 minutes).
15 When baked, the bread should sound hollow and the sides should feel crisp when pressed.
16 Cool on a wire rack.

Variations
Alternatively, the bread may be divided into 50 g rolls, brushed with eggwash and baked at 200°C for approximately 10 minutes.

HEALTHY EATING TIP

• Only a little salt is necessary to 'control' the yeast. Many customers will prefer less salty bread.

93 Walnut and sultana rolls

Makes 16 rolls

wholemeal flour	400 g
fresh yeast	25 g
caster sugar	½ tsp
milk and water	250 ml
butter	25 g
salt	
sultanas	100 g
walnuts	100 g
eggwash	

1 Sieve the flour into a suitable bowl and warm in the oven or above the stove.
2 Cream the yeast and sugar together in a bowl, add a ½ of the liquid.
3 Make a well in the centre of the flour, add the dispersed yeast.
4 Sprinkle over a little flour, cover with a cloth and leave in a warm place until the yeast ferments.
5 Add the remainder of the liquid at 37°C, butter and salt.
6 Knead well until smooth and free from stickiness.
7 Return to the bowl, cover with a cloth and leave in a warm place until double in size.

8 Knock back gently, fold in the sultanas and walnuts.

9 Divide into 16 even pieces.

10 Mould into the desired shapes and place onto a lightly greased, floured baking sheet.

11 Cover with a cloth, allow to prove in a warm place until double in size.

12 Brush very carefully with eggwash and bake in a hot oven 220°C for approximately 12 minutes.

HEALTHY EATING TIP

• Only a little salt is necessary to 'control' the yeast. Many customers will prefer less salty bread.

94 Onion and walnut bread

Makes 1 crown loaf

milk	425 ml
fresh yeast	12 g
vegetable oil	30 ml
salt	10 g (2 tsp)
bread flour	500 g
onion, finely chopped	1 large
melted butter	
pepper	
walnut pieces, lightly toasted	50 g
eggwash	

1 Warm 60 ml (4 tbsp) of milk to 37°C.

2 Disperse the yeast into the milk.

3 Place the dispersed yeast, remaining milk, half the oil and salt into a large bowl.

4 Stir in half of the flour and mix well with your hand.

5 Gradually add the remaining flour, mixing well after each addition. Mix well until a smooth elastic dough is obtained. Adjust the consistency by adding more flour if necessary. The dough should be soft and slightly sticky.

6 Turn the dough out onto a floured work surface, knead well. Keep kneading until very smooth and elastic. This will take approximately 5–7 minutes.

7 Brush a large bowl with melted butter. Place the dough into the bowl, turn over so that it is covered with butter.

8 Cover with a damp cloth and allow to prove until double in size, approximately 1–1½ hours.

9 Heat the remaining oil in a frying pan. Sauté the finely chopped onion in the butter, season with salt and pepper. Sauté until lightly coloured. Allow to cool.

10 When proved, turn the dough out on to a lightly floured table and knock back for approximately 20 seconds, cover and allow to rest for approximately 5 minutes.

11 Knead the onion and walnuts into the dough. Cover and allow to rest for a further 5 minutes.

12 Mould the dough into a ball and form a ring approximately 25–30 cm in diameter.

13 Place ring on to a lightly greased baking sheet. Cover and allow to prove to double in size for approximately 45 minutes, preferably in a prover.

14 Brush with eggwash lightly. Using kitchen scissors, snip the top of the ring in a zig-zag fashion.

15 Bake in a pre-heated oven 200°C for 45–50 minutes.

16 When baked and golden brown place bread on a wire rack and allow to cool. If tapped, it should sound hollow and the sides should be crisp.

HEALTHY EATING TIP

• Only a little salt is necessary to 'control' the yeast. Many customers will prefer less salty bread.

95 Sundried tomato bread

Makes 2 × 450 g loaves

sundried tomatoes, chopped	100 g
water	300 ml
bread flour	500 g
salt	10 g
skimmed milk powder	12½ g
shortening	12½ g
yeast (fresh)	20 g
sugar	12½ g

1   Soak the sundried tomatoes in boiling water for 30 minutes.
2   Sieve the flour, salt and skimmed milk powder.
3   Add the shortening and rub through the dry ingredients.
4   Disperse the yeast into warm water, approximately 37°C. Add and dissolve the sugar. Add to the above ingredients.
5   Mix until a smooth dough is formed. Check for any extremes in consistency and adjust as necessary until a smooth elastic dough is formed.
6   Cover the dough, keep warm and allow to prove.

7   After approximately 30–40 minutes, knock back the dough and mix in the chopped sundried tomatoes (well drained).
8   Mould and prove again for another 30 minutes (covered).
9   Divide the dough into two and mould round.
10   Rest for 10 minutes. Keep covered.
11   Re-mould into ball shape.
12   Place the dough pieces into 15 cm diameter hoops laid out on a baking tray. The hoops must be warm and lightly greased.
13   With the back of the hand flatten the dough pieces.
14   Prove at 30–38°C in humid conditions, preferably in a prover.
15   Bake at 225°C for 25–30 minutes.
16   After baking, remove the bread from the tins immediately and place on a cooling wire.

HEALTHY EATING TIP

• Only a little salt is necessary to 'control' the yeast. Many customers will prefer less salty bread.

Rye

This is a prominent cereal in parts of Europe and Russia, mainly because it will grow better than wheat in poor soil and harsh weather conditions.

The grains are longer and thinner than wheat grains and yield a flour that is darker than wheat flour, having a low protein content. Its main use is for rye bread.

96 Rye bread with caraway seeds

Makes 1 medium-sized loaf

fresh yeast (or dried yeast may be used)	15 g
water	60 ml (4 tbsp)
black treacle	15 ml (1 tbsp)
vegetable oil	15 ml (1 tbsp)
caraway seeds	15 g
salt	15 g
lager	250 ml
rye flour	250 g
unbleached bread flour	175 g
polenta	
eggwash	

1 Disperse the yeast in the warm water (at approximately 37°C)
2 In a basin mix the black treacle, oil, two-thirds of the caraway seeds and the salt. Add the lager. Add the yeast and mix in the sieved rye flour. Mix well.
3 Gradually add the bread flour. Continue to add the flour until the dough is formed and it is soft and slightly sticky.
4 Turn the dough onto a lightly floured surface and knead well.
5 Knead the dough until it is smooth and elastic.
6 Place the kneaded dough into a suitable bowl that has been brushed with oil.
7 Cover with a damp cloth and allow the dough to prove in a warm place until it is double in size. This will take about 1½–2 hours.
8 Turn the dough onto a lightly floured work surface, knock back the dough to original size. Cover and allow to rest for approximately 5–10 minutes.
9 Shape the dough into an oval approximately 25 cm long.
10 Place onto a baking sheet lightly sprinkled with polenta.
12 Allow the dough to prove in a warm place, preferably in a prover, until double in size (approximately 45 minutes to 1 hour).
12 Lightly brush the loaf with eggwash, sprinkle with the remaining caraway seeds.
13 Using a small, sharp knife, make three diagonal slashes, approximately 5 mm deep into the top of the loaf.
14 Place in a pre-heated oven 190°C and bake for approximately 50–55 minutes.
15 When cooked, turn out. The bread should sound hollow when tapped and the sides should feel crisp.
16 Allow to cool.

HEALTHY EATING TIP

• Only a little salt is necessary to 'control' the yeast. Many customers will prefer less salty bread.

97 Olive bread

Makes 6 loaves

olive mother ferment	540 g
black olives, chopped	320 g
yeast	15 g
olive oil	150 ml
water	850 ml
no 4 flour (strong Canadian wheat flour)	1½ kg
salt	30 g
Maldon salt	

1 Place all the ingredients (three-quarters of the oil), except the flour and salt, into a large bowl. Mix the ingredients by hand.
2 Sprinkle the flour on top, then the salt, and stir to a slack dough, working in 6 turns of the bowl. Fold the edge into the centre and add a little more olive oil. Leave for 20 minutes.
3 Fold with the same method. The dough should resemble the shape of a doughnut with a dip in the centre.
4 Add a little more olive oil and leave in a warm place for 20 minutes.
5 Fold again and leave in a warm place for 20 minutes.

6 Divide the dough into approximately five 550 g balls.
7 Roll into slipper shapes divided by supported greaseproof paper.
8 Spray with water. Wrap with clingfilm and prove in the fridge overnight.
9 Remove from the fridge, unwrap and spray with water.
10 Place in a prover for approximately 30 minutes.
11 Remove, then spray again, removing greaseproof paper from the sides of the bread.
12 Divide onto oven board. Sprinkle with Maldon salt and dust with flour.
13 Cook on 230°C steaming five pulses for 4 minutes with the vent closed.

Figure 14.22 Olive bread

98 Olive bread with sage and oregano

Makes 1 large loaf

fresh yeast	12½ g
milk	310 ml
bread flour	825 g
sugar	5 g (1 tsp)
olive oil	80 ml
salt	5 g (1 tsp)
water	250 ml
black olives, de-stoned	150 g
fresh sage, chopped	2 tbsp
fresh oregano, chopped	2 tbsp

1 Disperse the yeast in the warm milk (approximately 37°C).
2 Whisk in the 300 g of the flour, sifted, and the sugar, stand in a warm place for approximately 30 minutes until the mixture is double in size.
3 Add the oil, the remainder of the sifted flour and salt. Mix well. Add a little more flour, or some water, if necessary, to form a smooth and elastic dough.
4 Turn out onto a floured surface and knead to form a smooth and elastic dough.
5 Place the dough into a large greased bowl, cover and allow to prove for approximately 1 hour until the dough has doubled in size.
6 Turn the dough onto a floured board, knock back and knead in remaining ingredients.
7 Roll dough into an oval 30 cm × 35 cm. Fold in almost half. Place onto a greased baking sheet, cover, stand in a warm place for about 45 minutes until double in size.
8 Dust with sifted flour and bake in a hot oven, approximately 200°C for 45 minutes.

99 Polenta soda bread with mixed seeds

Makes 1 loaf

strong flour	175 g
salt	6 g
bicarbonate of soda	1 tsp
polenta	150 g
pumpkin seeds	25 g
sunflower seeds	25 g
poppy seeds	12 g
fine oatmeal	25 g
caster sugar	1 tsp
egg	1
buttermilk	250 ml

1 Sift the flour, salt and bicarbonate of soda together in a large bowl.
2 Add the polenta and the seeds, oatmeal and caster sugar. Mix together well.
3 Whisk the egg and buttermilk together, add to the dry ingredients. Mix to form a smooth and slack dough.
4 Place into a lightly oiled loaf tin, sprinkle with poppy seeds.
5 Bake in a pre-heated oven, 190°C, for approximately 50–60 minutes.
6 Remove from oven, turn out, place on baking sheet and return to the oven for 5 minutes.
7 Remove, allow to cool on a wire rack.

Figure 14.23　Polenta soda bread

100 Soda bread with goats' cheese, potato and thyme

Makes 1 loaf

goats' cheese	110 g
self-raising flour	175 g
salt	1 tsp
cayenne pepper	pinch
potato, grated	175 g
spring onions, finely chopped	4
thyme, chopped	1 tsp
egg	1
milk	2 tbsp
grain mustard	1 tsp

1 Remove the rind from the goats' cheese, cut into ½ cm cubes
2 Sift the flour, salt and cayenne into a suitable bowl. Fold in the grated potato, chopped spring onions, chopped thyme (reserving a little for the topping) and two-thirds of the goats' cheese. Mix thoroughly.
3 Add the beaten egg, milk and mustard. Mix to a rough dough.
4 Mould into a round loaf tin (15 cm).
5 Place on a lightly greased baking sheet. Press the rest of the cheese evenly on top.
6 Lightly dust with flour and chopped thyme.
7 Place in a pre-heated oven, 190°C, for approximately 45–50 minutes until golden brown.
8 Remove from oven and serve immediately.

Variations
Rosemary, basil, oregano or tarragon may be used in place of thyme.

598

101 Focaccia

Makes 1 loaf

packages active dry yeast	2
sugar	1 tsp
lukewarm water (about blood temperature)	230 ml
extra virgin olive oil, plus extra to drizzle on the bread	70 g
salt	1½ tsp
unbleached all-purpose flour	725 g
coarse salt	
picked rosemary	

1 Dissolve the yeast and sugar in half of the lukewarm water in a bowl; let sit until foamy. In another bowl, add the remaining water, the olive oil, and the salt.
2 Pour in the yeast mixture.
3 Blend in the flour, a quarter at a time, until the dough comes together. Knead on a floured board for 10 minutes, adding flour as needed to make it smooth and elastic. Put the dough in an oiled bowl, turn to coat well, and cover with a towel.
4 Let rise in a warm draught-free place for 1 hour, until doubled in size.
5 Knock back the dough, knead it for a further 5 minutes, and gently roll it out in to a large disc or sheet to approx. 2 cm thick.
6 Let rise for 15 minutes, covered. Oil your fingers and make impressions with them in the dough, 3 cm apart. Let prove for 1 hour.
7 Preheat the oven to 210°C. Drizzle the dough with olive oil and sprinkle with coarse salt and picked rosemary.
8 Bake for 15–20 minutes in a very hot oven at 220°C, until golden brown. Sprinkle with additional oil if desired. Cut into squares and serve warm.

102 Kugelhopf bread with almonds, bacon and herbs

milk	250 ml
fresh yeast	25 g
or	
dried yeast	15 g
bread flour	500 g
salt	5 g (1 tsp)
eggs	3
unsalted butter, melted	150 g
sugar	15 ml (3 tsp)
streaky bacon, chopped	125 g
flaked almonds	50 g
fresh chopped sage	1 tsp
fresh chopped thyme	1 tsp

1 Take 60 ml (approximately 4 tbsp) of warm milk (37°C).
2 Disperse the yeast with the milk.
3 Sift the flour and salt into a suitable bowl.
4 Whisk the eggs and add to the flour with the dispersed yeast. Add the melted butter, sugar and remainder of the warm milk. Take special care that the butter does not exceed 37°C. It should be just melted.
5 Work well and mix thoroughly to a smooth dough.
6 Beat the dough well until it is very elastic. The dough should be very sticky, and reasonably wet.
7 Cover the bowl with a damp cloth and allow to prove in a warm place for 1–1½ hours.
8 Quickly fry the chopped streaky bacon in a pan for 3–4 minutes. Drain off all excess fat. Allow to cool.
9 Knock back the dough, mix in the bacon, almonds and chopped herbs. Mix well.
10 Fill the kugelhopf mould evenly with the dough. Cover with a damp cloth and allow to prove for 30–40 minutes, until double in size.
11 Bake in a pre-heated oven, 190°C, for approximately 45–50 minutes. Unmould onto a wire rack and allow to cool.

Note: This bread is baked in a kugelhopf mould, traditionally from the Alsace region of France.

Variations
Other nuts and different herbs may be used.

103 Bagels

Makes 12

water	125 ml
milk	250 ml
fresh yeast	12 g
or	
dried yeast	10 g
caster sugar	2 tbsp
bread flour	450 g
salt	15 g (3 tsp)
eggwash	
poppy seeds	1 tbsp
sea salt	10 g (2 tsp)

1 Warm the water and milk to 37°C, disperse the yeast in the water, add one tbsp of sugar, cover and leave to stand in a warm place for approximately 10 minutes.
2 Add the sifted flour and salt gradually, mixing into a firm dough. Add a little more flour, or some water, if necessary, to form a smooth and elastic dough.
3 Turn dough onto a floured surface. Knead well until dough is smooth and elastic. Place dough into a well-greased bowl, cover and leave to stand in a warm place in a prover for 1 hour or until the dough has doubled in size.
4 Turn dough out onto a floured surface, knead until smooth. Divide into 12, knead each into a ball. Make a hole in the centre of each.
5 Rotate each ball of dough with the finger until the hole is one-third of the size of the bagel.
6 Place bagels on a greased baking sheet approximately 3 cm apart. Cover and stand in a warm place or prover until double in size.
7 Drop bagels individually into a pan of boiling water. Do not allow them to touch. Turn bagels after 1 minute, simmer for a further 1 minute. Remove, drain well and place on greased baking sheet.
8 Brush each with eggwash, sprinkle with poppy seeds and sea salt. Bake in an oven 200°C for about 20 minutes. Remove, cool on a wire rack.

Note: Bagels are popular and are usually filled with a variety of fillings (e.g. smoked salmon and cream cheese) and served as a snack.

104 Bun dough: basic recipe

Cal	Cal	Fat	Sat Fat	Carb	Sugar	Protein	Fibre	*
656 KJ	157 kcal	6.4 g	2.7 g	22.6 g	4.0 g	3.6 g	1.2 g	

	8 buns	20 buns
flour (strong)	200 g	500 g
yeast	5 g	12 g
milk and water	60 ml	150 ml
	(approx.)	(approx.)
medium egg	1	2–3
butter or margarine	50 g	125 g
caster sugar	25 g	60 g

1 Sieve the flour into a bowl and warm.
2 Cream the yeast in a basin with a little of the liquid.
3 Make a well in the centre of the flour.
4 Add the dispersed yeast, sprinkle with a little flour, cover with a cloth, leave in a warm place until the yeast ferments (bubbles).
5 Add the beaten egg, butter or margarine, sugar and remainder of the liquid. Knead well to form a soft, slack dough, knead until smooth and free from stickiness.
6 Keep covered and allow to prove in a warm place. Use as required.

* *Using hard margarine, 1 portion (2 buns)*

105 Bun wash

sugar	100 g
water or milk	125 ml

1 Boil ingredients together until the consistency of a thick syrup.
2 Use as required.

106 Fruit buns

Cal 728 KJ	Cal 173 kcal	Fat 6.5 g	Sat Fat 2.7 g	Carb 26.9 g	Sugar 8.0 g	Protein 3.7 g	Fibre 1.7 g	*

1 Add 50 g washed, dried fruit (e.g. currants, sultanas) and a little mixed spice to the basic bun mixture (recipe 104).
2 Mould into eight round balls.
3 Place on a lightly greased baking sheet.
4 Cover with a cloth, allow to prove.

5 Bake in hot oven at 220°C (425°F) for 15–20 minutes.
6 Brush liberally with bun wash as soon as cooked.

Using hard margarine

107 Bath buns

1 Add to basic bun dough (recipe 104) 50 g washed and dried fruit (e.g. currants and sultanas), 25 g chopped mixed peel and 25 g sugar nibs.
2 Proceed as for fruit buns. Pull off into eight rough-shaped pieces.
3 Sprinkle with a little broken loaf sugar or nibs.
4 Cook as for fruit buns (recipe 106).

108 Chelsea buns

1 Take the basic bun dough (recipe 104) and roll out into a large square.
2 Brush with melted margarine or butter.
3 Sprinkle liberally with caster sugar.
4 Sprinkle with 25 g currants, 25 g sultanas and 25 g chopped peel.

5 Roll up like a Swiss roll, brush with melted margarine or butter.
6 Cut into slices across the roll 3 cm wide.
7 Place on a greased baking tray with deep sides.
8 Cover and allow to prove. Complete as for fruit buns.

109 Swiss buns

1 Divide basic bun dough (recipe 104) into eight pieces.
2 Mould into balls, then into 10 cm lengths.
3 Place on a greased baking sheet, cover with a cloth.

4 Allow to prove.
5 Bake at 220°C, for 15–20 minutes.
6 When cool, glaze with fondant or water icing.

110 Hot cross buns

1 Proceed as for fruit buns (recipe 106) using a little more spice.
2 When moulded, make a cross on top of each bun with the back of a knife, or make a slack mixture of

flour and water and pipe on crosses using a greaseproof paper cornet.
3 Allow to prove and finish as for fruit buns.

111 Water icing, glacé icing

Water icing is used to finish a number of cakes and pastries. For the basic icing simply take 400 g of icing sugar and add 60 ml (4 tbsp) of warm water; the icing should be thick enough to coat the back of a spoon. If necessary, add more water or icing sugar to adjust the consistency.

Variations
Water may be replaced with other liquids to add flavour to the icing – for example, orange juice, mango juice, lemon juice, apple juice, lime juice, grape juice, passionfruit juice – or use a combination of juices with Cointreau, kirsch, Grand Marnier, rum, Calvados, etc.

112 Doughnuts

Cal	Cal	Fat	Sat Fat	Carb	Sugar	Protein	Fibre	*
918 KJ	218 kcal	13.3 g	4.0 g	22.6 g	4.0 g	3.6 g	1.2 g	

1 Take the basic bun dough (recipe 104) and divide into eight pieces.
2 Mould into balls. Press a floured thumb into each.
3 Add a little jam in each hole. Mould carefully to seal the hole.
4 Cover and allow to prove on a well-floured tray.

5 Deep-fry in moderately hot fat, 175°C, for 12–15 minutes.
6 Lift out of the fat, drain and roll in a tray containing caster sugar mixed with a little cinnamon.

* *Using hard margarine and peanut oil*

113 Savarin paste: basic recipe

Cal	Cal	Fat	Sat Fat	Carb	Sugar	Protein	Fibre	*
700 KJ	167 kcal	7.4 g	3.9 g	21.5 g	2.5 g	4.9 g	0.8 g	

	8 portions	20 portions
flour (strong)	200 g	500 g
yeast	5 g	12 g
milk	125 ml	300 ml
medium eggs	2	5
butter, softened	50 g	125 g
sugar	10 g	25 g
salt	pinch	large pinch

1 Sieve the flour in a bowl and warm.
2 Cream the yeast with a little of the warm milk in a basin.
3 Make a well in the centre of the flour and add the dissolved yeast.
4 Sprinkle with a little of the flour from the sides, cover with a cloth and leave in a warm place until it ferments.
5 Add the remainder of the warm milk and the beaten eggs, knead well to a smooth elastic dough.
6 Replace in the bowl, add the butter in small pieces, cover with a cloth and allow to prove in a warm place.
7 Add the sugar and salt, mix well until absorbed.
8 Half fill a greased savarin mould, and prove.
9 Bake in a hot oven at 220°C for about 30 minutes.
10 Turn out when cooked, cool slightly.
11 Soak carefully in hot syrup (see recipe 115).
12 Brush over with apricot glaze (recipe 125).

* Using syrup, 1 portion of complete Savarin provides: 967 kJ/229 kcal Energy; 7.4 g Fat; 3.9 g Sat Fat; 38.2 g Carb; 19.1 g Sugar; 5.0 g Protein; 0.8 g Fibre

114 Rum baba (baba au rhum)

Cal	Cal	Fat	Sat Fat	Carb	Sugar	Protein	Fibre	*
797 KJ	190 kcal	7.6 g	4.2 g	25.4 g	6.4 g	4.9 g	1.4 g	

	8 portions	20 portions
flour (strong)	200 g	500 g
yeast	5 g	12 g
milk	125 ml	300 ml
currants	50 g	125 g
medium eggs	2	5
butter	50 g	125 g
sugar	10 g	25 g
salt	pinch	large pinch
small glass of rum	1	2–3

1 Sieve the flour in a bowl and warm.
2 Cream the yeast with a little of the warm milk in a basin.
3 Make a well in the centre of the flour and add the dispersed yeast.
4 Sprinkle with a little of the flour from the sides, cover with a cloth and leave in a warm place until it ferments.
5 Add the remainder of the warm milk and the washed, dried currants and the beaten eggs, knead well to a smooth elastic dough.
6 Replace in the bowl, add the butter in small pieces, cover with a cloth and allow to prove in a warm place.
7 Add the sugar and salt, mix well until absorbed.
8 Half fill greased dariole moulds, and allow to prove.
9 Bake in a hot oven at 220°C for about 20 minutes.
10 Turn out when cooked, cool slightly.
11 Soak carefully in hot syrup (recipe 115).
12 Sprinkle liberally with rum.
13 Brush all over with apricot glaze (recipe 125).

Note: Babas may also be decorated with whipped cream or crème Chantilly (whipped cream sweetened with caster sugar and flavoured with a little vanilla essence) and finished with a glacé cherry and angelica, or half walnuts or any glacéed fruit. Babas may also be flavoured with whisky or brandy in place of rum.

* Using butter

Points about use of cream (see also pages 541 and 543)

- Fresh cream must be cold when required for whipping.
- For preference it should be whipped in china or stainless steel bowls. If any other metal is used, the cream should be transferred to china bowls as soon as possible.

- If fresh cream is whipped too much, it turns to butter. This is more likely to happen in hot conditions. To prevent this, stand the bowl of cream in a bowl of ice while whisking.
- When adding cream to hot liquids dilute the cream with some of the liquid before adding to the main bulk. This helps to prevent the cream from separating.

115 Syrup for baba, savarin and marignans

Cal	Cal	Fat	Sat Fat	Carb	Sugar	Protein	Fibre
422 KJ	99 kcal	0.0 g	0.0 g	26.4 g	26.4 g	0.0 g	0.0 g

Serves 4

	4 babas	10 babas
sugar	100 g	250 g
bay leaf	1	2–3
rind and juice of lemon	1	2–3
water	¼ litre	600 ml
coriander seeds	2–3	6–7
small cinnamon stick	½	1–1½

1 Boil all the ingredients together and strain.
2 Use as required.

116 Savarin with fruit *(savarin aux fruits)*

Cal	Cal	Fat	Sat Fat	Carb	Sugar	Protein	Fibre
1224 KJ	292 kcal	13.5 g	7.7 g	39.1 g	20.6 g	00.0 5.9	1.0 g

1 Prepare the basic savarin mixture (recipe 113).
2 Prove and cook for about 30 minutes in a large greased savarin mould.

3 Complete in exactly the same way as rum baba (recipe 114) including the cream. The rum is optional for savarin.
4 Fill the centre with fruit salad.

117 Marignans Chantilly

Cal	Cal	Fat	Sat Fat	Carb	Sugar	Protein	Fibre
1202 KJ	286 kcal	13.4 g	7.7 g	38.0 g	19.5 g	5.8 g	0.8 g

1 Marignans are prepared from a basic savarin mixture (recipe 113) and cooked in barquette moulds.
2 After the marignans have been soaked, carefully make a deep incision along one side.

3 Decorate generously with whipped, sweetened vanilla-flavoured cream.
4 Brush with apricot glaze (recipe 125).

Pastry dishes: the principle building blocks

Flour

Flour is probably the most common commodity in daily use. It forms the foundation of bread, pastry and cakes and is also used in soups, sauces, batters and other foods. It is one of the most important ingredients in patisserie, if not *the* most important.

There are a great variety of high-quality flours made from cereals, nuts or legumes, such as chestnut flour, cornflour, and so on. They have been used in patisserie, baking, dessert cuisine and savoury cuisine in all countries throughout history. The king of all of them is without doubt wheat flour.

The composition of wheat flour

Wheat flour is basically composed of starch, gluten, sugar, fats, water and minerals.

Starch is the main component of flour. Another important element is gluten, which is elastic and impermeable. Found mainly in wheat, this is what makes wheat flour the most common flour used in bread making.

The quantity of sugar in wheat is very small and it plays a very important role in fermentation. Wheat contains only a maximum of 16 per cent water, but its presence is important. The mineral matter (ash), which is found mainly in the husk of the wheat grain and not in the kernel, determines the purity and quality of the flour.

From the ear to the final product, flour, wheat goes through several distinct processes. These are carried out in modern industrial plants, where wheat is subjected to the various treatments and phases necessary for the production of different types of flour. These arrive in perfect condition to our workplaces and are made into preparations like sponge cakes, yeast dough, puff pastries, cookies, pastries . . .

What you need to know about flour

- Flour is a particularly delicate living material, and it must be used and stored with special care. It must always be in the best condition, which is why storing large quantities is not recommended.
- It must be kept in a good environment: a clean, organised, disinfected and aerated storeroom.
- Warm and humid places must absolutely be avoided.

The production of flour

The endosperm of the wheat grain contains all the material used by the baker. It consists of numerous large cells of net-like form in which starch grains are tightly packed. In addition, the cells contain an insoluble gluten protein. When flour is mixed with water it is converted into a sticky dough. This characteristic is due to the gluten, which becomes sticky when moistened. The relative proportion of starch and gluten varies in different wheats, and those with a low percentage of gluten (soft flour) are not suitable for bread making. For this reason, wheat is blended.

In milling, the whole grain is broken up, the parts separated, sifted, blended and ground into flour. Some of the outer coating of bran is removed as is the wheatgerm, which contains oil and is therefore likely to become rancid and so spoil the flour. For this reason wholemeal flour should not be stored for more than 14 days.

Types of flour

White flour contains 72–85 per cent of the whole grain (the endosperm only). Wholemeal flour contains 100 per cent of the whole grain. Wheatmeal flour contains 85–95 per cent of the whole grain. Hovis flour contains 85 per cent of the whole grain. High-ratio or patent flour contains 40 per cent of the whole grain. Self-raising flour is white flour with the addition of baking powder. Semolina is granulated hard flour prepared from the central part of the wheat grain. White or wholemeal semolina is available.

Fats

Pastry goods may be made from various types of fat, either a single named fat or a combination. Examples of fats are:

- butter
- pastry margarine
- margarine

- shortening
- cake margarine
- lard.

Butter and other fats

Butter is the symbol of perfection in fats. It brings flowery smoothness, perfumes and aromas, and impeccable textures to our preparations. It is a point of reference for good gastronomy. Butter has a very long history, but its origin is unknown. Many books have been written about it, but we can only conclude that it was probably discovered by accident.

Butter is an emulsion – the perfect symbiosis of water and fat. It is composed of a minimum of 82 per cent fat, a maximum of 16 per cent water and 2 per cent dry extracts.

What you need to know about butter

- Butter is the most complete fat.
- It is a very delicate ingredient that can quickly spoil if a series of basic rules are not followed in its use.
- It has the property of absorbing odours very easily. It should always be stored far from anything that produces strong odours and it should be kept well covered.
- When kept at 15°C, butter is stable and retains all its properties: finesse, perfume and creaminess.
- It should not be kept too long: it is better to always work with fresh butter.
- Good butter has a stable texture, pleasing taste, fresh odour, homogenous colour and, most important, it must melt perfectly in your mouth.
- It softens preparations like cookies and petit fours, and keeps products like sponge cakes soft.
- Butter enhances flavour – as in brioches, for example.
- The melting point of butter is between 30°C and 35°C approximately.

Margarine

Margarine is often made from a blend of oils that have been hardened or hydrogenated (hydrogen gas is added). Margarine may contain up to 10 per cent butterfat.

Cake margarine

This is again a blend of oils, hydrogenated, to which is added an agent that helps combine water and fat together, an emulsifying agent. Cake margarine may contain up to 10 per cent butterfat.

Pastry margarine

This is used for puff pastry. It is a hard plastic or waxy fat that is suitable for layering.

Shortening (another name for fat used in pastry making)

This is made from oils and is 100 per cent fat, such as hydrogenated lard; another type of shortening is rendered pork fat.

Sugar

Sugar is extracted from sugar beet or sugar cane. The juice is crystallised by a complicated manufacturing process. It is then refined and sieved into several grades, such as granulated, caster or icing sugars.

Loaf or cube sugar is obtained by pressing the crystals while slightly wet, drying them in blocks, and then cutting the blocks into squares.

Syrup and treacle are produced during the production of sugar.

Fondant is a cooked mixture of sugar and glucose, which, when heated, is coloured and flavoured, and used for decorating cakes, buns, gâteaux and petits fours. Fondant is generally bought ready made.

Chemical properties of sucrose (common sugar, $C_{12}H_{22}O_{11}$)

Common sugar, or sucrose, consists of carbon (C_{12}), hydrogen (H_{22}) and oxygen (O_{11}), and is composed of two bonded molecules (in equal parts): glucose and fructose.

Inverted sugar

Inverted sugar is, after sucrose, one of the most commonly used sugars in the catering profession, thanks to its properties. It is a molecularly equal mix of the products obtained in the hydrolysis of sucrose (fructose and glucose) and is made from the hydrolysis of sugar in the presence of an enzyme. According to the hydrolysis and the dry material used, we end up with two types of inverted sugar: liquid inverted sugar and liquid inverted sugar syrup.

Inverted sugar syrup

This is a white, sticky paste and has no particular odour. It has no less than 62 per cent dry matter and more than 50 per cent inverted sugar. It is what we most frequently use. With equal proportions of dry matter and sucrose, its sweetening capacity is 25–30 per cent greater.

It has a constant moisture percentage – that is, it has hygroscopic properties.

Liquid inverted sugar

This is a yellowish liquid with no less than 62 per cent dry matter. It contains more than 3 per cent inverted sugar, but less than 50 per cent. It is used mainly in the commercial food industry.

Applications of inverted sugar
- It improves the aroma of products.
- It improves the texture of doughs.
- It prevents the dehydration of frozen products.
- It reduces or stops crystallisation.
- It is essential in ice cream making – it greatly improves it quality and lowers its freezing point.

Glucose

Glucose takes on various forms:

- the characteristics of a viscous syrup, called crystal glucose
- its natural state, in fruit and honey
- a dehydrated white paste (used mainly in the commercial food industry, but also used in our profession)
- 'dehydrated glucose' (atomised glucose) – a glucose syrup from which its water is evaporated; this is used in patisserie, but mainly in the commercial food industry.

Characteristics and properties of glucose syrup
- It is a transparent, viscous paste.
- It prevents the crystallisation of boiled sugars, jams and preserves.
- It delays the drying of a product.

- It adds plasticity and creaminess to ice cream and the fillings of chocolate bonbons.
- It prevents the crystallisation of ice cream.

Honey

Honey, a sweet composite that bees make with the nectar extracted from flowers, is without doubt the oldest known sugar. A golden-brown thick paste, its sweetness coefficient is 130 with respect to sucrose. It has the property of lowering the freezing point of ice cream.

It can be used like inverted sugar, but it is important to take into account that honey, unlike inverted sugar, will give flavour to the preparation. Also, it is inadequate for preparations that require long storage, since honey re-crystallises after some time.

Isomalt

Isomalt sugar is a sweetener that is still little known in the patisserie world, but it has been used for some time. It has properties distinct from those of the sweeteners already mentioned. It is produced through the hydrolysis of sugar, followed by hydrogenation (the addition of hydrogen). Produced through these industrial processes, this sugar has been used for many years in large industries, in candy and chewing gum production, and is now earning a place in gastronomy.

One of its most notable characteristics is that it can melt without the addition of water or another liquid. This is a very interesting property for making artistic decorations in caramel. Its appearance is like that of confectioners' sugar: a glossy powder. Its sweetening strength is half that of sucrose and it is much less soluble than sugar, which means that it melts less easily in the mouth.

Isomalt's main claim in gastronomy over the past five or six years has been the replacement of normal sugar or sucrose when making sugar decorations, blown sugar, pulled sugar or spun sugar as the hydroscopic properties are lower than normal sugar, therefore it will be less affected by atmospheric variance.

Raising agents

A raising agent is added to a cake or bread mixture to give lightness to the product. This lightness is based upon the principle that gases expand when heated. The gases used are air, carbon dioxide or water vapour. These gases are introduced before baking or are produced by substances added to the mixture before baking. When the product is cooked, the gases expand. These gases are trapped in the gluten content of the wheat flour. On further heating and cooking, the product, because of the pressure of the gluten, rises and sets.

Baking powder

Chemical raising agents cause a reaction between certain acidic and alkaline compounds, which produce carbon dioxide. The alkaline component is almost universally sodium bicarbonate or sodium acid carbonate, commonly known as baking soda. It is ideal because it is cheap to produce, easily purified, non-toxic and naturally tasteless. Potassium bicarbonate is available for those on low-sodium diets, but this compound tends to absorb moisture and react prematurely and gives off a bitter flavour.

Baking powder may be used without the addition of acid if the dough or batter is already acidic enough to react with it to produce carbon dioxide. Yoghurt and sour milk contain lactic acid, and often are used in place of water or milk in such products; sour milk can also be added along with the baking soda as a separate 'natural' component of the leavening.

Baking powder contains baking soda and an acid in the form of salt crystals that dissolve in water. Ground dry starch is also added to prevent premature reactions in humid air by absorbing moisture and to dilute the powder.

Most baking powders are 'double acting' – that is, they produce an initial set of gas bubbles upon mixing the powder into the batter and then a second set during the baking process. The first and smaller reaction is necessary to form many small gas cells in the batter or dough; the second, to expand these cells to a size appropriate to form the final light texture, but late enough in the baking so that the surrounding materials have set, preventing the escape of bubbles or the collapse of the product.

Different commercial baking powders differ mainly in the proportions of the acid salts. Cream of tartar is not normally used due to its high cost.

Carbon dioxide using baking powder

Alkali (bicarbonate of soda) + acid (cream of tartar (potassium hydrogen tartrate)).

Calcium phosphate and glucono-delta-lactose are now commonly used in place of cream of tartar.

Sodium aluminium sulphate is an acid that is active only at higher oven temperatures and has an advantage over other powders, which tend to produce gas too early.

Use of water vapour

This is produced during the baking process, from the liquid content used in the mixing. Water vapour has approximately 1600 times the original volume of the water. The raising power is slower than that of a gas. This principle is used in the production of choux pastry, puff pastry, rough puff, flaky and batter products.

Points to remember

- Always buy a reliable brand of baking powder.
- Store in a dry place in an airtight tin.
- Do not store for long periods of time, as the baking powder loses some of its residual carbon dioxide over time and therefore will not be as effective.
- Check the recipe carefully, making sure that the correct preparation for the type of mixture is used; otherwise, under- or over-rising may result.
- Sieve the raising agent with the flour and/or dry ingredients to give an even mix and thus an even reaction.
- Distribute moisture evenly into the mixture to ensure even action of the raising agent.
- If a large proportion of raising agent has been added to a mixture, and is not to be cooked immediately, keep in a cool place to avoid too much reaction before baking.

What happens if too much raising agent is used?
Too much raising agent causes:

- over-risen product that may collapse, giving a sunken effect
- a coarse texture
- poor colour and flavour
- fruit sinking to the bottom of the cake
- a bitter taste.

What happens if insufficient proportion of raising agent is used
Insufficient raising agent causes:

- lack of volume
- insufficient lift
- close texture
- shrinkage.

Eggs

Eggs are an important and versatile ingredient in pastry work. They act as enriching and emulsifying agents. Hens' eggs are graded in four sizes – small, medium, large, and very large. For the recipes in this chapter, use medium-sized eggs (approx. 50 g).

Eggs are used in pastry work because of their binding, emulsifying and coating properties. Eggs add both protein and fat, thus improving nutritional value and flavour.

Cream

See pages 541–543.

Techniques

Adding fat to flour
Fats act as a shortening agent. The fat coats the sub-proteins within the flour, which has the effect of shortening the gluten strands. These gluten strands are easily broken when eaten. The development of gluten in strong flour to the production of puff pastry is very important as long strands are needed to trap the expanding gases, and this is what makes the paste rise.

Ways of adding fat to flour are as follows.

- Rubbing in by hand: short pastry.
- Rubbing in by machine: short pastry.

- Creaming method by machine or by hand: sweet pastry.
- Flour batter method: slab cakes.
- Lamination: puff pastry.
- Boiling: choux pastry.

Terms

Folding
As in folding puff pastry.

Kneading
Used as a term when making dough or in the first stage of making puff pastry.

Blending
Mixing all the ingredients carefully by weight.

Relaxing
Keeping pastry covered with a damp cloth, clingfilm or plastic to prevent skinning. Relaxing allows the pastry to lose some of its resistance to rolling.

Cutting
- Always cut with a sharp, damp knife.
- When using cutters, always flour them before use by dipping in flour. This will give a sharp, neat cut.
- When using a lattice cutter, use only on firm pastry; if the pastry is too soft, you will have difficulty lifting the lattice.

Rolling
- Roll the pastry on a lightly floured surface; turn the pastry to prevent it sticking. Keep the rolling pin lightly floured and free from the pastry.
- Always roll with care, treat lightly, never apply too much pressure.
- Always apply even pressure when using a rolling pin.

Shaping
Shaping refers to producing flans, tartlets, barquettes and other such goods with the pastry. Shaping also refers to crimping with the back of a small knife using the thumb technique.

Docking
Piercing raw pastry with small holes to prevent rising during baking, as when cooking tartlets blind.

Glazing

Examples of glazing pastry dishes are as follows.

- Using a hot clear gel produced from a pectin source obtainable commercially for finishing flans and tartlets; always use while still hot. A cold gel is exactly the same except that it is used cold. The gel keeps a sheen on the goods and excludes all oxygen, which might otherwise cause discoloration.
- Using apricot glaze, produced from apricot jam, acts in the same way as gels.
- Using eggwash, prior to baking, to produce a rich glaze on removing from the oven.
- Dusting with icing sugar, then caramelising in the oven or under the grill.
- Using fondant to give a rich sugar glaze, which may be flavoured and/or coloured.
- Using water icing to give a transparent glaze, which may also be flavoured and/or coloured.

Finishing and presentation

It is essential that all products are finished according to the recipe requirements. Finishing and presentation is often a key stage in the process as failure at this point can affect sales. The way goods are presented is an important part of the sales technique. Each product of the same type must be of the same shape, size, colour and finish. The decoration should be attractive, delicate and in keeping with the product range. All piping should be neat, clean and tidy.

Some methods of finishing and presentation are as follows.

- **Dusting:** the sprinkling of icing sugar on to a product using a fine sugar dredger or sieve, or muslin cloth.
- **Piping:** done using fresh cream, chocolate or fondant.
- **Filling:** products may be finished by filling with fruit, cream, pastry cream, etc. Never overfill as this will often given the product a clumsy appearance.

Storage, health and safety

- Store all goods according to the Food Hygiene (Amendments) Regulations 1993/Food Safety Temperature Control Regulation 1995.
- Handle all equipment carefully to avoid cross-contamination.
- Take special care when using cream, and ensure that products containing cream are stored under refrigerated conditions.
- All piping bags must be sterilised after each use.
- Always make sure that storage containers are kept clean and returned ready for re-use. On their return they should be hygienically washed and stored.

Points to remember

- Check all weighing scales for accuracy.
- Follow the recipe carefully.
- Check all storage temperatures are correct.
- Fat is better to work with if it is 'plastic' (i.e. at room temperature). This will make it easier to cream.
- Always cream the fat and sugar well, before adding the liquid.
- Always work in a clean, tidy and organised way; clean all equipment after use.
- Always store ingredients correctly: eggs should be stored in a refrigerator, flour in a bin with a tight-fitting lid, sugar and other dry ingredients in closed storage containers.
- Ensure all cooked products are cooled before finishing.
- Understand how to use fresh cream; remember that it is easily over-whipped.
- Always plan your time carefully.
- Understand why pastry products must be rested or relaxed and docked. This will prevent excessive shrinkage in the oven, and docking will allow the air to escape through the product thus preventing any unevenness.
- Use silicone paper for baking in preference to greaseproof.
- Keep all small moulds clean and dry to prevent rusting.

Convenience pastry

Convenience mixes, such as short pastry, sponge mixes and choux pastry mixes, are now becoming increasingly used in a variety of establishments. These products have improved enormously over the last few years. Using such products gives the chef the opportunity to save on time and labour; and with skill, imagination and creativity, the finished products are not impaired.

The large food manufacturer dominates the frozen puff pastry market. Not surprisingly many caterers, including some luxury establishments, have turned to using frozen puff pastry. It is now available in 30 cm squares, ready rolled, thus avoiding the possibility of uneven thickness and the waste that can occur when rolling out yourself.

Manufactured puff pastry is available in three types, defined often by their fat content. The cheapest is made with the white hydrogenated fat, which gives the product a pale colour and a waxy taste. Puff pastry made with bakery margarine has a better colour and, often, a better flavour. The best-quality puff pastry is that which is made with all butter, giving a richer texture, colour and flavour.

Pastry bought in blocks is cheaper than pre-rolled separate sheets, but has to be rolled evenly to give an even bake. The sizes of sheets do vary with manufacturers; all are interleaved with greaseproof paper.

Filo pastry is another example of a convenient pastry product; it is available in frozen sheets of various sizes. No rolling out is required; once thawed, it can be used as required and moulded if necessary.

Brick paste is another widely used convenience pastry, similar to filo pastry.

Other convenience pastry products

Apart from convenience pastry mixes, there also exists on the market a whole range of frozen products suitable to serve as sweets and afternoon tea pastries. These include fruit pies, flans, gâteaux and charlottes. The vast majority are ready to serve once defrosted, but very often they do require a little more decorative finish. The availability of such products gives the caterer the advantage of further labour cost reductions, while permitting the chef to concentrate on other areas of the menu.

Short pastry

118 Short pastry (pâte à foncer)

Cal 6269 KJ	Cal 1493 kcal	Fat 92.6 g	Sat Fat 38.0 g	Carb 155.5 g	Sugar 3.1 g	Protein 18.9 g	Fibre 7.2 g	*

	5–8 portions	10–16 portions
flour (soft)	200 g	500 g
salt	pinch	large pinch
lard or vegetable fat	50 g	125 g
butter or margarine	50 g	125 g
water	2–3 tbsp	5–8 tbsp

1 Sieve the flour and salt.
2 Rub in the fat to achieve a sandy texture.
3 Make a well in the centre.
4 Add sufficient water to make a fairly firm paste.
5 Handle as little and as lightly as possible.

Note: The amount of water used varies according to:

- the type of flour (a very fine soft flour is more absorbent)
- the degree of heat (e.g. prolonged contact with hot hands, and warm weather conditions).

Variations
For wholemeal short pastry use ½ to ½ wholemeal flour in place of white flour.

Short pastry is used in fruit pies, Cornish pasties, etc.

Short pastry for sweet dishes such as baked jam roll (recipe 121) may be made with self-raising flour.

* *Using ½ lard, ½ hard margarine (5–8 portions)*

Possible reasons for faults in short pastry

- Hard:
  - too much water
  - too little fat
  - fat rubbed in insufficiently
  - too much handling and rolling
  - over-baking.
- Soft-crumbly:
  - too little water
  - too much fat.
- Blistered:
  - too little water
  - water added unevenly
  - fat not rubbed in evenly.
- Soggy:
  - too much water
  - too cool an oven
  - baked for insufficient time.
- Shrunken:
  - too much handling and rolling
  - pastry stretched whilst handling.

119 Fruit pies

Cal 6808 KJ	Cal 162 kcal	Fat 65.0 g	Sat Fat 26.6 g	Carb 260.0 g	Sugar 144.1 g	Protein 15.3 g	Fibre 15.0 g	*

	4–6 portions	10–15 portions
fruit (see note)	400 g	1½ kg
sugar	100 g	250 g
water	2 tbsp	5 tbsp
Short pastry		
flour (soft)	100 g	250 g
butter or margarine	25 g	60 g
lard or vegetable fat	25 g	60 g
water to mix		

1 Prepare the fruit, wash and place half in a ½-litre pie dish or individual dishes.
2 Add the sugar and water and the remainder of the fruit. (Place a clove in an apple pie.)
3 Make the pastry using the ingredients listed above. Roll out ½ cm thick to the shape of the pie dish, allow to relax. Damp the rim of the pie dish and edge the rim with a strip of the pastry.
4 Damp the edge of the pastry.
5 Carefully lay the pastry on the dish without stretching it and firmly seal the rim of the pie. Cut off any surplus pastry.
6 Brush with milk and sprinkle with caster sugar.
7 Place the pie on a baking sheet and bake in a hot oven at 220°C for about 10 minutes.
8 Reduce the heat or transfer to a cooler part of the oven and continue cooking for a further 30 minutes. If the pastry colours too quickly cover with a sheet of paper.
9 Clean the pie dish, and serve with a sauceboat of custard (½ litre), cream or ice cream.

Preparation of fruit for pies
- *Apples:* peeled, quartered, cored, washed, cut in slices.
- *Cherries:* stalks removed, washed.
- *Blackberries:* stalks removed, washed.
- *Gooseberries:* stalks and tails removed, washed.
- *Damsons:* picked and washed.
- *Rhubarb:* leaves and root removed, tough strings removed, cut into 2 cm pieces, washed.

For fruit crumbles see page 584.

Note: Fruit pies may be made with apple, blackberry, blackberry and apple, cherry, rhubarb, gooseberry, damson, damson and apple, etc.

* Using white flour and apple (4–6 portions). Using 50 per cent wholemeal flour and apple (4–6 portions): 6709 kJ/1598 kcal; 65.6 g Fat; 26.7 g Sat Fat; 251.1 g Carb; 144.5 g Sugar; 17.8 g Protein; 18.8 g Fibre

120 Treacle tart

Cal 1100 KJ	Cal 262 kcal	Fat 10.7 g	Sat Fat 5.8 g	Carb 41.1 g	Sugar 20.3 g	Protein 2.8 g	Fibre 0.8 g

	4 portions	10 portions
Short paste		
flour	100 g	250 g
lard, margarine or		
vegetable fat	25 g	60 g
butter or margarine	25 g	60 g
salt	pinch	large pinch
water, to mix		
Filling		
treacle	100 g	250 g
water	1 tbsp	2½ tbsp
lemon juice	3–4 drops	8–10 drops
fresh white bread or		
cake crumbs	15 g	50 g

1 Make pastry as in recipe 118, allow to rest in refrigerator.
2 Roll out to a 3 mm round.
3 Place onto a lightly greased, ovenproof plate.
4 Warm the treacle, water and lemon juice; add the crumbs.
5 Spread on the pastry and bake at 220°C for about 20 minutes.

Variations

This tart can also be made in a shallow flan ring. Any pastry debris can be rolled and cut into ½ cm strips and used to decorate the top of the tart before baking.

Treacle tarts can also be made in individual moulds.

121 Baked jam roll

Cal 1677 KJ	Cal 399 kcal	Fat 20.9 g	Sat Fat 8.9 g	Carb 50.6 g	Sugar 12.4 g	Protein 5.3 g	Fibre 2.2 g	*

	4 portions	10 portions
short paste (flour with baking powder added when sifting flour, or self-raising flour) (recipe 118)	200 g	500 g
jam	2–3 tbsp	5–7 tbsp

1 Roll out the pastry into a rectangle 30 × 16 cm.
2 Spread with jam, leaving 1 cm clear on all edges.
3 Fold over two short sides, 1 cm. Roll the pastry from the top.
4 Moisten the bottom edge to seal the roll.
5 Place edge down on a greased baking sheet.
6 Brush with eggwash or milk. Sprinkle with sugar.
7 Bake in a moderate oven at 200°C for about 40 minutes.
8 Serve with a sauceboat of jam or custard sauce separately.

Note: These can be made in individual portions.

* *Using white flour*

122 Baked apple dumplings

Cal	Cal	Fat	Sat Fat	Carb	Sugar	Protein	Fibre	*
1227 KJ	291 kcal	11.6 g	5.1 g	46.4 g	23.6 g	3.2 g	2.7 g	

	4 portions	10 portions
short paste (recipe 118)	200 g	500 g
small cooking apples	4	10
cloves	4	12
sugar	50 g	125 g

1 Roll out the pastry 3 mm thick into a square.
2 Cut into four even squares. Damp the edges.
3 Place a whole peeled, cored and washed apple in the centre of each square. Pierce the apple with a clove.
4 Fill the centre with sugar.
5 Fold over the pastry to completely seal the apple, without breaking the pastry.

6 Roll out any debris of pastry and cut neat 2 cm fancy rounds; place one on top of each apple.
7 Eggwash or milkwash and place on a lightly greased baking sheet.
8 Bake in a moderately hot oven at 200°C for about 30 minutes.
9 Serve with a sauceboat of custard, cream or ice cream.

Note: The centres of apples may also be filled with different mixtures of candied fruits, dried fruits, nuts and spices (e.g. cinnamon, ginger or nutmeg).

* *Using lard and margarine*

Sweet/sugar pastry

123 Sugar pastry (pâte à sucre)

Cal	Cal	Fat	Sat Fat	Carb	Sugar	Protein	Fibre	*
7864 KJ	1872 kcal	109.8 g	46.4 g	208.0 g	55.6 g	25.7 g	7.2 g	

	5–8 portions	10–16 portions
medium egg	1	2–3
sugar	50 g	125 g
margarine or butter	125 g	300 g
flour (soft)	200 g	500 g
salt	pinch	large pinch

Method 1

1 Taking care not to over-soften, cream the egg and sugar.
2 Add the margarine or butter, and mix for a few seconds.
3 Gradually incorporate the sieved flour and salt. Mix lightly until smooth.
4 Allow to rest in a cool place before using.

Method 2

1 Sieve the flour and salt. Lightly rub in the margarine to achieve a sandy texture.
2 Make a well in the centre. Add the sugar and beaten egg.
3 Mix the sugar and egg until dissolved.
4 Gradually incorporate the flour and margarine, and lightly mix to a smooth paste. Allow to rest before using.

Method 3 (machine method)

1 Mix the sugar and eggs on slow speed, emulsify for 2 minutes, add the butter and mix for 1–2 minutes.
2 Add the flour and mix on slow speed.

Note: Sugar pastry is used for flans, fruit tartlets, and so on; 50 per cent, 70 per cent or 100 per cent wholemeal flour may be used; the butter may be reduced from 125 to 100 g.

* *5–8 portions using hard margarine*

124 Flan

1 Allow 25 g flour per portion and prepare sugar pastry as per recipe 123.
2 Grease the flan ring and baking sheet.
3 Roll out the pastry 2 cm larger than the flan ring. The pastry may be rolled between greaseproof or silicone paper.
4 Place the flan ring on the baking sheet.
5 Carefully place the pastry on the flan ring, by rolling it loosely over the rolling pin, picking up and unrolling it over the flan ring.
6 Press the pastry into shape without stretching it, being careful to exclude any air.
7 Allow a ½ cm ridge of pastry on top of the flan ring.
8 Cut off the surplus paste by rolling the rolling pin firmly across the top of the flan ring.
9 Mould the edge with thumb and forefinger. Decorate (a) with pastry tweezers or (b) with thumbs and forefingers, squeezing the pastry neatly to form a corrugated pattern.

125 Apricot glaze

1 Prepare by boiling apricot jam with a little water.
2 Pass through a strainer. Glaze should be used hot.

Note: A flan jelly (commercial pectin glaze) may be used as an alternative to apricot glaze. This is usually a clear glaze to which food colour may be added.

Figure 14.24 ✐ Making a flan

126 Cherry flan, using fresh cherries (flan aux cerises)

Cal	Cal	Fat	Sat Fat	Carb	Sugar	Protein	Fibre	*
918 KJ	218 kcal	6.5 g	3.9 g	40.2 g	31.4 g	2.1 g	0.9 g	

	4 portions	10 portions
sugar paste (recipe 123)	100 g	250 g
cherries	200–300 g	500 g
sugar	50 g	125 g
red glaze (recipe 135)	2 tbsp	6 tbsp

1 Line the flan ring with sugar paste and pierce the bottom.
2 Stone the cherries. Arrange neatly in the flan case. Sprinkle with sugar.
3 Bake at 200–230°C for about 30 minutes.
4 Remove ring and eggwash sides. Complete the cooking.
5 Brush with hot red glaze (recipe 135).

Note: A ½ cm layer of pastry cream or thick custard may be placed in the flan case before adding the cherries.

* Using 250 g of fruit

127 Apple flan (flan aux pommes)

Cal	Cal	Fat	Sat Fat	Carb	Sugar	Protein	Fibre
1428 KJ	340 kcal	13.8 g	5.8 g	53.8 g	36 g	3.5 g	2.9 g

	4 portions	10 portions
sugar paste (recipe 123)	100 g	250 g
cooking apples	400 g	1 kg
sugar	50 g	125 g
apricot glaze (recipe 125)	2 tbsp	6 tbsp

1 Line a flan ring with sugar paste. Pierce the bottom several times with a fork.
2 Keep the best-shaped apple and make the remainder into a purée (see recipe 130).
3 When cool, place in the flan case.
4 Peel, quarter and wash the selected apple.
5 Cut into neat thin slices and lay carefully on the apple purée, overlapping each slice. Ensure that each slice points to the centre of the flan then no difficulty should be encountered in joining the pattern up neatly.
6 Sprinkle a little sugar on the apple slices and bake the flan at 200–220°C for 30–40 minutes.
7 When the flan is almost cooked, remove the flan ring carefully, return to the oven to complete the cooking. Mask with hot apricot glaze (recipe 125) or flan jelly.

Figure 14.25 ✎ Apple flan

128 Apple meringue flan (flan aux pommes meringué)

1 Cook as for apple flan, but without arranging the sliced apple.
2 Pipe with meringue (recipe 48) made using two egg whites.
3 Return to the oven at 200°C to cook and colour meringue (about 5 minutes).

Note: This may be finished with ordinary or Italian meringue (recipe 129).

Figure 14.26 ✎ Apple meringue flan

129 Italian meringue

granulated or cube sugar	200 g
water	60 ml
cream of tartar	pinch
egg whites	4

1 Boil the sugar, water and cream of tartar to hard ball stage 121°C.
2 Beat the egg whites to full peak and, while stiff, beating slowly, pour on the boiling sugar. Use as required.

130 Apple purée (marmalade de pomme)

	4 portions	10 portions
cooking apples	400 g	1 kg
butter or margarine	10 g	25 g
sugar	50 g	125 g

1 Peel, core and slice the apples.
2 Place the butter or margarine in a thick-bottomed pan; heat until melted.
3 Add the apples and sugar, cover with a lid and cook gently until soft.
4 Drain off any excess liquid and pass through a sieve or liquidise.

131 Lemon meringue flan: economic recipe

Cal	Cal	Fat	Sat Fat	Carb	Sugar	Protein	Fibre
1824 KJ	434 kcal	17.5 g	7.8 g	68.3 g	46.3 g	5.2 g	1.0 g

	8 portions	20 portions
sugar paste (recipe 123)	200 g	500 g
Lemon curd		
water	125 ml	300 ml
sugar	100 g	250 g
lemon	1	2½
cornflour	25 g	60 g
butter	25 g	60 g
yolks	1–2	3–5
Meringue		
egg whites	4	10
caster sugar	200 g	500 g

1 Line a flan ring with sugar paste and cook blind.
2 Prepare the lemon curd by boiling the water, sugar, and zest and juice of lemon to a syrup.
3 Thicken with diluted cornflour, remove from the heat, add the butter and whisk in yolks. Place in the flan case.
4 When set, pipe in the meringue (recipe 48) and colour in a hot oven at 220°C.

Note: This may also be finished with Italian meringue (recipe 129).

132 Lemon curd: alternative recipe

	8 portions	20 portions
medium eggs, separated, pasteurised	2	5
caster sugar	100 g	250 g
butter	100 g	250 g
lemon	1	2

1 Cream the egg yolks and sugar in a bowl with a whisk.
2 Add the butter, zest and juice of lemon.
3 Place in a bain-marie on a low heat and whisk continuously until it thickens (20–30 minutes).

133 Lemon tart (tarte au citron)

Cal	Cal	Fat	Sat Fat	Carb	Sugar	Protein	Fibre
1878 KJ	450 kcal	28.0 g	15.2 g	42.7 g	36.1 g	9.4 g	0.3 g

	8 portions
sugar paste (recipe 123)	150 g
lemons	juice of 3, zest from 4
medium eggs	8
caster sugar	300 g
double cream	250 ml

1 Prepare 150 g of sugar paste, adding the zest of 1 lemon to the mix.
2 Line a 16 cm flan ring with the paste.
3 Bake blind for approximately 15 minutes.
4 Prepare the filling: mix the eggs and sugar together until smooth, add the cream, lemon juice and zest. Whisk well.
5 Pour into the flan case, bake for 30–40 minutes at 150°C until set. (Take care when almost cooked as overcooking will cause the filling to rise.)
6 Remove from oven and allow to cool.
7 Dust with icing sugar and glaze under the grill or use a blowtorch. Portion and serve.

Note: The mixture will fill one 16 × 4 cm or two 16 × 2 cm flan rings. If using two flan rings, double the amount of pastry and reduce the baking time when the filling is added.

Variations
Limes may be used in place of lemons. If so, use the zest and juice of 5 limes or use a mixture of lemons and limes.

Figure 14.27 Lemon tart

134 Banana flan (flan aux bananes)

Cal 1549 KJ	Cal 369 kcal	Fat 16.0 g	Sat Fat 6.9 g	Carb 53.7 g	Sugar 30.3 g	Protein 6.0 g	Fibre 2.9 g

	4 portions	10 portions
sugar paste (recipe 123)	100 g	250 g
pastry cream or thick custard	125 ml	250 g
bananas	2	5
apricot glaze (recipe 125)	2 tbsp	5 tbsp

1 Line a flan ring with sugar paste. Cook blind and allow to cool.
2 Make pastry cream (recipe 10) or custard; pour while hot into the flan case.
3 Allow to set. Peel and slice the bananas neatly.
4 Arrange overlapping layers on the pastry cream. Coat with glaze.

Figure 14.28 Banana flan

Figure 14.29 Lattice cutters, pastry docker and straight and fluted cutters

135 Rhubarb flan (flan au rhubarbe)

Cal 955 KJ	Cal 226 kcal	Fat 6.5 g	Sat Fat 3.9 g	Carb 42.3 g	Sugar 33.5 g	Protein 2.3 g	Fibre 1.4 g	*

	4 portions	10 portions
rhubarb	300 g	1 kg
sugar paste (recipe 123)	100 g	250 g
sugar	100 g	250 g
apricot glaze (recipe 125) or red glaze (see below)	2 tbsp	5 tbsp

1 Trim the roots and leaves from the rhubarb and remove the tough string. Cut into 2 cm pieces, wash and dry thoroughly.
2 Line a flan ring with sugar paste and pierce.
3 Sprinkle with sugar.
4 Arrange the fruit neatly in the flan case.
5 Sprinkle with the remainder of the sugar.
6 Bake at 200–220°C.
7 When the flan is almost cooked, carefully remove the flan ring and return the flan to the oven to complete the cooking.
8 Mask with hot apricot or red glaze.

Red glaze
1 Boil the sugar and water or fruit syrup with a little red colour and thicken with diluted arrowroot or fecule, reboil until clear; strain.
2 Alternatively, use red jam and a little water boiled and passed through a strainer.

Note: A ½ cm layer of pastry cream or thick custard may be placed in the flan case before adding the rhubarb.

* *Using apricot glaze*

136 Plum or apricot flan *(flan aux prunes ou aux abricots)*

Cal 1028 KJ	Cal 243 kcal	Fat 6.5 g	Sat Fat 3.9 g	Carb 47.2 g	Sugar 38.4 g	Protein 2.0 g	Fibre 1.4 g	*

	4 portions	10 portions
sugar paste (recipe 123)	100 g	250 g
sugar	100 g	250 g
plums or apricots	200–300 g	500–700 g
apricot glaze (recipe 125)	2 tbsp	5 tbsp

1 Line a flan ring with sugar paste, and pierce. Sprinkle with sugar.
2 Quarter or halve the fruit. Arrange neatly in the flan case.
3 Sprinkle with the remainder of the sugar.
4 Bake at 200–220°C.
5 When the flan is almost cooked, carefully remove the flan ring and return the flan to the oven to complete the cooking.
6 Mask with hot apricot glaze.

Note: A ½ cm layer of pastry cream or thick custard may be placed in the flan case before adding the fruit.

* *Using 250 g plums and apricot glaze*

137 Soft fruit and tinned fruit flans

1 For soft fruit (e.g. strawberry, raspberry, banana) and tinned fruit (e.g. pear, peach, pineapple, cherry), the flan case is lined in the same way as for the above recipes, the bottom pierced and then cooked 'blind' (tear a piece of paper 2 cm larger in diameter than the flan ring, place it carefully in the flan case, fill the centre with dried peas, beans or small pieces of stale bread and bake at 200–220°C for about 30 minutes).
2 Remove the flan ring, paper and beans before the flan is cooked through, eggwash (including the inside) and return to the oven to complete the cooking.
3 Add pastry cream and sliced or whole drained fruit.
4 Mask with glaze. The glaze may be made with the fruit juice thickened with arrowroot (approximately 10 g to ¼ litre).

138 Strawberry or raspberry flan (flan aux fraises ou aux framboises)

Cal	Cal	Fat	Sat Fat	Carb	Sugar	Protein	Fibre
567 KJ	135 kcal	6.5 g	3.9 g	18.4 g	9.7 g	2.0 g	0.9 g

	4 portions	10 portions
sugar paste (recipe 123)	100 g	250 g
fruit	200 g	500 g
red glaze (recipe 135)	2 tbsp	5 tbsp

1 Cook the flan blind (as per recipe 137); allow to cool. Pick and wash the fruit, drain well.
2 Dress neatly in flan case. Coat with the glaze.

Note: A layer of pastry cream or thick custard may be placed in the flan case before adding the fruit.

139 Fruit tartlets

These are made from the same pastry and the same fruits as the fruit flans. The ingredients are the same. The tartlets are made by rolling out the pastry 3 mm thick and cutting out rounds with a fluted cutter and neatly placing them in greased tartlet moulds. Depending on the fruit used, they may sometimes be cooked blind (e.g. strawberries, raspberries).

140 Fruit barquettes

Certain fruits (e.g. strawberries, raspberries) are sometimes served in boat-shaped moulds. The preparation is the same as for tartlets. Tartlets and barquettes should be glazed and served allowing one large or two small per portion.

141 Dutch apple flan

Cal	Cal	Fat	Sat Fat	Carb	Sugar	Protein	Fibre
1628 KJ	386 kcal	13.0 g	7.7 g	67.8 g	50.3 g	3.8 g	2.6 g

	6–8 portions	15–20 portions
sugar paste (recipe 123)	200 g	500 g
cooking apples	400 g	1¼ kg
sugar	100 g	250 g
cinnamon	pinch	large pinch
lemon, zest of	1	3
sultanas	50 g	125 g

1 Roll out half the pastry 3 mm thick into a neat round and place on a greased plate, or line a flan ring.
2 Prick the bottom several times with a fork.
3 Peel, core, wash and slice the apples.
4 Place them in a saucepan with the sugar and a little water.
5 Partly cook the apples; add the cinnamon and zest of lemon.
6 Add the washed, dried sultanas and allow to cool.
7 Place on the pastry. Moisten the edges.
8 Roll out the other half of the pastry to a neat round and place on top.
9 Seal firmly, trim off excess pastry, mould the edges.
10 Brush with milk and sprinkle with caster sugar.
11 Place on a baking sheet, bake in a moderately hot oven at 200–220°C for about 40 minutes.
12 Remove from the plate carefully before serving.

142 Kiwi slice *(bande aux kiwis)*

1 Prepare as for recipe 141.
2 When cool add pastry cream.
3 Arrange slices of kiwi fruit on the pastry cream.
4 Coat with the apricot glaze (recipe 125).
5 Decorate with whipped cream.

Note: A whole variety of fruit may be used instead of or in combination with kiwi fruit, such as banana, apricots, raspberries, mango, strawberries, pawpaw, peaches, grapes or pears.

Figure 14.30 ✐ Kiwi slice

143 Mincemeat tart/pie

Cal	Cal	Fat	Sat Fat	Carb	Sugar	Protein	Fibre
1492 KJ	355 kcal	15.0 g	7.7 g	55.0 g	37.5 g	3.4 g	1.4 g

	4 portions	10 portions
sugar paste (recipe 123)	200 g	500 g
mincemeat (recipe 159)	200 g	500 g

1 Roll out half the pastry 3 mm thick into a neat round and place on a greased plate.
2 Prick the bottom several times with a fork.
3 Add the mincemeat. Moisten the edges.
4 Roll out the other half of the pastry to a neat round and place on top.
5 Seal firmly, trim off excess pastry, mould the edges.
6 Brush with milk and sprinkle with caster sugar.
7 Place on a baking sheet and bake at 200–220°C for about 40 minutes and serve.

144 Bakewell tart/flan

Cal 2105 KJ	Cal 501 kcal	Fat 28.8 g	Sat Fat 11.0 g	Carb 57.5 g	Sugar 33.7 g	Protein 6.7 g	Fibre 2.2 g	*

	8 portions
sugar paste (using 227 g flour)	
(recipe 123)	200 g
raspberry jam	50 g
eggwash	
apricot glaze (recipe 125)	50 g
icing sugar	35 g
Frangipane (make as for recipe 157)	
butter or margarine	100 g
ground almonds	50 g
medium eggs	2
caster sugar	100 g
flour	50 g
almond essence	

1 Line a flan ring using three-quarters of the paste 2 mm thick.
2 Pierce the bottom with a fork.
3 Spread with jam and the frangipane.
4 Roll the remaining paste, cut into neat ½ cm strips and arrange neatly criss-crossed on the frangipane; trim off surplus paste. Brush with eggwash.
5 Bake in a moderately hot oven at 200–220°C for 30–40 minutes. Brush with hot apricot glaze.
6 When cooled brush over with very thin water icing.

* *Using hard margarine*

145 Baked chocolate tart (aero)

Makes 830 g, 1 flan cooked blind
(200 mm diameter × 35 mm height)

eggs	3
egg yolks	3
caster sugar	60 g
butter	200 g
chocolate pistoles (55% cocoa, unsweetened)	300 g

1 Whisk the eggs, yolks and sugar together.
2 Bring butter to the boil, remove and mix in chocolate pistoles until it is all melted.
3 Once sabayon is light and fluffy, fold in chocolate and butter mix very carefully, so as not to beat out the air.
4 Pour into cooked flan case (baked blind) and place in a deck oven at 150°C until the edge crusts (approx. 5 minutes). Chill.
5 Once set, remove from fridge.
6 Serve at room temperature.

Figure 14.31　Baked chocolate tart (aero)

Puff pastry

Puff pastry is one of the most interesting creations of our profession. It brings many tastes and textures to our products. It is a dough with a centuries old origin. Basically, it consists of making layers by folding a flour paste and a fat of the same texture.

Its applications are infinite, as much in patisserie as in cooking. Its exquisite texture, soft and crunchy, is a real pleasure to the palate, and it can be combined with all types of food in sweet and savoury dishes. One of the differences of making it is in the fat used. There is no comparison between the taste and texture of a puff pastry made with butter and one made with any other fat.

When the flour paste and the fat are laid in successive folds and rolled between each turn, rather than kneaded, the two elements do not bind completely. The fat forms a separating layer which, when cooked, retains the steam generated by the water in the dough and produces the layer separation effect. The flour paste, which includes part of the fat, becomes crunchy and takes on a nice golden tone rather than becoming hard and dry.

146 Puff pastry (feuilletage)

Cal 8997 KJ	Cal 2142 kcal	Fat 164.8 g	Sat Fat 70.9 g	Carb 150.8 g	Sugar 3.0 g	Protein 23.2 g	Fibre 7.4 g	*

	5–8 portions	10–16 portions
flour (strong)	200 g	500 g
salt		
margarine or butter	200 g	500 g
ice-cold water	125 ml	300 ml
lemon juice, ascorbic or tartaric acid	few drops	several drops

1 Sieve the flour and salt (50 per cent wholemeal flour may be used).
2 Rub in one-quarter of the butter or margarine.
3 Make a well in the centre.
4 Add the water and lemon juice (to make the gluten more elastic), and knead well into a smooth dough in the shape of a ball.
5 Relax the dough in a cool place for 30 minutes.
6 Cut a cross halfway through the dough and pull out the corners to form a star shape.

7 Roll out the points of the star square, leaving the centre thick.
8 Knead the remaining butter or margarine to the same texture as the dough. This is very important: if the fat is too soft it will melt and ooze out, if too hard it will break through the paste when being rolled.
9 Place the butter or margarine on the centre square, which is four times thicker than the flaps.
10 Fold over the flaps.
11 Roll out to 30 × 15 cm, cover with a cloth or plastic and allow to rest for 5–10 minutes in a cool place.
12 Roll out 60 × 20 cm, fold both the ends to the centre, fold in half again to form a square. (This is one double turn.)
13 Allow to rest in a cool place for 20 minutes.
14 Half turn the paste to the right or the left.

Figure 14.32 ✎ Preparation of puff pastry

15 Give one more double turn; allow to rest for 20 minutes.
16 Give two more double turns, allowing to rest between each.
17 Allow to rest before using.

Note: Care must be taken when rolling out the paste to keep the ends and sides square. The lightness of the puff pastry is mainly due to the air that is trapped when folding the pastry during preparation. The addition of lemon juice (acid) works to strengthen the gluten in the flour, thus helping to make a stronger dough so that there is less likelihood of the fat oozing out; 3 g (7½ g for 10 portions) ascorbic or tartaric acid may be used in place of lemon juice. The rise is caused by the fat separating layers of paste and air during rolling. When heat is applied by the oven, steam is produced, causing the layers to rise and give the characteristic flaky formation.

Puff pastry is used for meat pies, sausage rolls, jam puffs, etc.

HEALTHY EATING TIP
• Add the minimum amount of salt.
• Puff pastry is very high in fat and should be rolled out thinly.

* *Using hard margarine (5–8 portions)*

Possible reasons for faults in puff pastry

• Not flaky:
  – fat too warm thus preventing the fat and paste remaining in layers during rolling
  – excessively heavy use of rolling pin.
• Fat oozes out:
  – fat too soft
  – dough too soft
  – edges not sealed
  – uneven folding and rolling
  – oven too cool.
• Hard:
  – too much water
  – flour not brushed off between rolling
  – over-handling.

• Shrunken:
  – insufficient resting between rolling
  – overstretching.
• Soggy:
  – under-baked
  – oven too hot.
• Uneven rise:
  – uneven distribution of fat
  – sides and corners not straight
  – uneven folding and rolling.

147 Rough puff pastry

Cal 7464 KJ	Cal 1777 kcal	Fat 124.3 g	Sat Fat 53.2 g	Carb 150.8 g	Sugar 3.0 g	Protein 23.3 g	Fibre 0.0 g	*

	5–8 portions	10–16 portions
flour (strong)	200 g	500 g
salt		
butter or margarine	150 g	375 g
ice-cold water	125 ml	300 ml
lemon juice, ascorbic or tartaric acid	squeeze	large squeeze

1 Sieve the flour and salt (50 per cent wholemeal flour may be used).
2 Cut the fat into 10 g pieces and lightly mix them into the flour without rubbing in.
3 Make a well in the centre.
4 Add the liquid and mix to a fairly stiff dough.
5 Turn on to a floured table and roll into an oblong strip, about 30 × 10 cm, keeping the sides square.
6 Give one double turn as for puff pastry.
7 Allow to rest in a cool place, covered with cloth or plastic for 30 minutes.
8 Give three more double turns, resting between each. Allow to rest before using.

* Using hard margarine (5–8 portions)

148 Puff pastry slice (mille-feuilles)

Cal 1158 KJ	Cal 369 kcal	Fat 10.9 g	Sat Fat 1.3 g	Carb 67.7 g	Sugar 52.3 g	Protein 4.9 g	Fibre 0.1 g

Makes 6–8 slices

puff pastry (recipe 146)	200 g
pastry cream	¼ litre
apricot jam	100 g
fondant or water icing	200 g

1 Roll out the pastry 2 mm thick into an even-sided square.
2 Roll up carefully on a rolling pin and unroll onto a greased, dampened baking sheet.
3 Using two forks, pierce as many holes as possible in the paste.
4 Cut in half with a large knife then cut each half in two to form four even-sized rectangles.
5 Bake in a hot oven at 220°C for 15–20 minutes; turn the strips over after 10 minutes. Allow to cool.
6 Keep the best strip for the top. Spread pastry cream on one strip.
7 Place another strip on top and spread with jam.
8 Place the third strip on top and spread with pastry cream.
9 Place the last strip on top, flat side up.
10 Press down firmly with a flat tray.
11 Decorate by feather-icing as follows:
12 Warm the fondant to blood heat and correct the consistency with sugar syrup if necessary.
13 Separate a little fondant into two colours and place in paper cornets.
14 Pour the fondant over the mille-feuilles in an even coat.
15 Immediately pipe on one of the colours lengthwise in strips 1 cm apart.
16 Quickly pipe on the second colour between each line of the first.

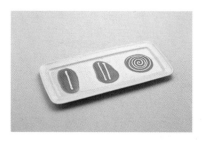

Figure 14.33 ✒ Feathering

17 With the back of a small knife, wiping after each stroke, mark down the slice at 2 cm intervals.
18 Quickly turn the slice around and repeat in the same direction with strokes in between the previous ones.
19 Allow to set and trim the edges neatly.
20 Cut into even portions with a sharp thin-bladed knife, dip into hot water and wipe clean after each cut.

Variations
At steps 15 and 16 baker's chocolate or tempered couverture may be used for marbling. Whipped fresh cream may be used as an alternative to pastry cream. Also a variety of soft fruits may be incorporated in the layers, such as raspberries, strawberries, canned well-drained pears, peaches or apricots, kiwi fruit or caramelised poached apple slices. The pastry cream or whipped cream may also be flavoured with a liqueur if so desired, such as curaçao, Grand Marnier or Cointreau.

Figure 14.34 Puff pastry slice (Parisienne slice)

149 Fruit slice (bande aux fruits)

Cal	Cal	Fat	Sat Fat	Carb	Sugar	Protein	Fibre
767 KJ	183 kcal	7.8 g	3.4 g	28.6 g	21.3 g	1.3 g	1.6 g

8–10 portions

puff pastry (recipe 146)	200 g
fruit (see note)	400 g
pastry cream	250 ml approx.
sugar, to sweeten	
appropriate glaze	2 tbsp

1 Roll out the pastry 2 mm thick in a strip 12 cm wide.
2 Place on a greased, dampened baking sheet.
3 Moisten two edges with eggwash; lay two 1½ cm-wide strips along each edge.
4 Seal firmly and mark with the back of a knife. Prick the bottom of the slice.
5 Then, depending on the fruit used, either put the fruit (such as apple) on the slice and cook together, or cook the slice blind and afterwards place the pastry cream and fruit (such as tinned peaches) on the pastry. Glaze and serve as for flans.

Note: Fruit slices may be prepared from any fruit suitable for flans.

Variations
Alternative methods are:
• to use short or sweet pastry for the base and puff pastry for the two side strips
• to use sweet pastry in a slice mould.

150 Cream horns

Cal	Cal	Fat	Sat Fat	Carb	Sugar	Protein	Fibre	*
735 KJ	176 kcal	14.9 g	8.6 g	9.8 g	6.3 g	1.2 g	0.2 g	

Makes 16

puff pastry (page 630)	200 g
eggwash	
icing sugar, to sprinkle	
jam	50 g
caster sugar	50 g
vanilla essence	few drops
cream	½ litre

1 Roll out the pastry 2 mm thick, 30 cm long.
2 Cut into 1½ cm-wide strips. Moisten on one side.
3 Wind carefully round lightly greased cream horn moulds, starting at the point and carefully overlapping each round slightly.
4 Brush with eggwash on one side and place on a greased baking sheet.
5 Bake at 220°C for about 20 minutes.

6   Sprinkle with icing sugar and return to a hot oven for a few seconds to glaze.
7   Remove carefully from the moulds and allow to cool.
8   Place a little jam in the bottom of each.
9   Add the sugar and essence to the cream and whip stiffly.
10 Place in a piping bag with a star tube and pipe a neat rose into each horn.

Variations

These may also be partially filled with pastry cream, to which various flavourings or fruit may be added. For example:
* praline
* chocolate
* coffee
* lemon
* raspberries

* strawberries
* mango
* orange segments.

* *Using whipping cream*

Figure 14.35 ✎ Cream horns and palmiers

151 Eccles cakes

Cal 691 KJ	Cal 164 kcal	Fat 8.6 g	Sat Fat 3.7 g	Carb 22.1 g	Sugar 17.3 g	Protein 1.1 g	Fibre 1.4 g

Makes 12 cakes

puff or rough puff pastry (recipe 146 or 147)	200 g
egg white, to brush	
caster sugar, to coat	
Filling	
butter or margarine	50 g
raisins	50 g
demerara sugar	50 g
currants	200 g
mixed spice (optional)	pinch

1   Roll out the pastry 2 mm thick.
2   Cut into rounds 10–12 cm diameter. Damp the edges.
3   Mix together all the ingredients for the filling and place a tbsp of the mixture in the centre of each round.
4   Fold the edges over to the centre and completely seal in the mixture.
5   Brush the top with egg white and dip into caster sugar.
6   Place on a greased baking sheet.
7   Cut two or three incisions with a knife so as to show the filling.
8   Bake at 220°C for 15–20 minutes.

152 Apple turnovers (*chausson aux pommes*)

Makes 12

puff pastry (recipe 146)	200 g
dry, sweetened apple purée	100 g
egg white, to brush	
caster sugar, to coat	

1   Roll out the pastry 2 mm thick.
2   Cut into 8 cm diameter rounds.
3   Roll out slightly oval, 12 × 10 cm.
4   Moisten the edges, place a little apple purée in centre of each.
5   Fold over and seal firmly.

6 Brush with egg white and dip in caster sugar.
7 Place sugar side up on a dampened baking sheet.
8 Bake in hot oven, 220°C for 15–20 minutes.

Note: Other types of fruit may be included in the turnovers, such as apple and mango, apple and blackberry, apple and passionfruit, and apple, pear and cinnamon.

153 Palmiers

1 Roll out puff pastry (recipe 146), 2 mm thick, into a square.
2 Sprinkle liberally with caster sugar on both sides and roll into the pastry.
3 Fold into three from each end so as to meet in the middle; brush with eggwash and fold in two.
4 Cut into strips approximately 2 cm thick; brush with eggwash and dip one side in caster sugar.
5 Place on a greased baking sheet, sugared side down, leaving a space of at least 2 cm between each.

6 Bake in a very hot oven for about 10 minutes.
7 Turn with a palette knife, cook on the other side until brown and the sugar is caramelised.

Note: Puff pastry trimmings are suitable for these. Palmiers may be made in all sizes. Two joined together with a little whipped cream may be served as a pastry, small ones for petits fours. They may be sandwiched together with soft fruit, whipped cream and/or ice cream and served as a sweet.

154 Puff pastry cases (bouchées and vol-au-vents)

Makes 12 bouchées or 6 vol-au-vent cases

puff pastry (recipe 146)	200 g

1 Roll out the pastry approximately ½ cm thick.
2 Cut out with a round, fluted 5 cm cutter.
3 Place on a greased, dampened baking sheet; eggwash.
4 Dip a plain 4 cm diameter cutter into hot fat or oil

and make an incision 3 mm deep in the centre of each.
5 Allow to rest in a cool place.
6 Bake at 220°C for about 20 minutes.
7 When cool, remove the caps or lids carefully and remove all the raw pastry from inside the cases.

Note: Bouchées are filled with a variety of savoury fillings and are served hot or cold. They may also be

Figure 14.36   Vol-au-vents and bouchées (empty)

Figure 14.37   Vol-au-vents and bouchées (filled)

filled with cream and jam or lemon curd as a pastry. Large bouchées are known as vol-au-vents. They may be produced in one-, two-, four- or six-portion sizes; a single-sized vol-au-vent would be approximately twice the size of a bouchée. When preparing one- and two-portion sized vol-au-vents, the method for bouchées

may be followed. When preparing larger-sized vol-au-vents, it is advisable to have two layers of puff pastry each ½ cm thick, sealed together with eggwash. One layer should be a plain round, and the other of the same diameter with a circle cut out of the centre.

Figure 14.38 ✎ Preparation of vol-au-vents

155 Jalousie

Cal 1178 KJ	Cal 282 kcal	Fat 17.8 g	Sat Fat 5.1 g	Carb 27.2 g	Sugar 17.5 g	Protein 3.8 g	Fibre 0.8 g

	8–10 portions
puff pastry (recipe 146)	200 g
mincemeat (recipe 159), jam or frangipane (recipe 157)	200 g

1 Roll out one-third of the pastry 3 mm thick into a strip 25 × 10 cm and place on a greased, dampened baking sheet.
2 Pierce with a fork. Moisten the edges.
3 Spread on the desired filling, leaving 2 cm free all the way round.
4 Roll out the remaining two-thirds of the pastry to the same size.

5 Fold in half lengthwise and, with a sharp knife, cut slits across the fold about ½ cm apart to within 2 cm of the edge.
6 Carefully open out this strip and neatly place on to the first strip.
7 Neaten and decorate the edge. Brush with eggwash.
8 Bake at 220°C for 25–30 minutes.
9 Sprinkle with icing sugar and return to a very hot oven to glaze.

156 Gâteau pithiviers

Cal 928 KJ	Cal 222 kcal	Fat 15.6 g	Sat Fat 3.8 g	Carb 18.5 g	Sugar 8.9 g	Protein 3.8 g	Fibre 0.5 g

	8–10 portions	20 portions
puff pastry (recipe 146)	200 g	500 g
apricot jam	1 tbsp	3 tbsp
frangipane (recipe 157)	½ the recipe	1½ times the recipe

1 Roll out one-third of the pastry into a 20 cm round, 2 mm thick; moisten the edges and place on a greased, dampened baking sheet; spread the centre with jam.
2 Prepare the frangipane as per recipe 157, by creaming the margarine and sugar in a bowl, gradually adding the beaten eggs, and folding in the flour and almonds.
3 Spread on the frangipane, leaving a 2 cm border round the edge.
4 Roll out the remaining two-thirds of the pastry and cut into a slightly larger round.
5 Place neatly on top, seal and decorate the edge.
6 Using a sharp-pointed knife, make curved cuts 2 mm deep, radiating from the centre to about 2 cm from the edge. Brush with eggwash.
7 Bake at 220°C for 25–30 minutes.
8 Glaze with icing sugar as for jalousie (recipe 155).

Figure 14.39 Gâteau pithiviers

157 Frangipane

	8 portions
butter	100 g
caster sugar	100 g
medium eggs	2
ground almonds	100 g
flour	10 g

1 Cream the butter and sugar.
2 Gradually beat in the eggs.
3 Mix in the almonds and flour (mix lightly).
4 Use as required.

158 Mince pies

Cal 718 KJ	Cal 171 kcal	Fat 10.2 g	Sat Fat 4.5 g	Carb 17.7 g	Sugar 10.2 g	Protein 1.3 g	Fibre 1.0 g

Makes 8–12 pies

puff pastry (recipe 146)	200 g
mincemeat (recipe 159)	200 g

1 Roll out the pastry 3 mm thick.
2 Cut half the pastry into fluted rounds 6 cm diameter.
3 Place on a greased, dampened baking sheet.
4 Moisten the edges.
5 Place a little mincemeat in the centre of each.
6 Cut the remainder of the pastry into fluted rounds, 8 cm diameter.
7 Cover the mincemeat, seal the edges. Brush with eggwash.
8 Bake at 220°C for about 20 minutes.
9 Sprinkle with icing sugar and serve warm. Accompany with a suitable sauce (e.g. custard, brandy sauce, brandy cream).

Variations
Mince pies may also be made with short or sugar/sweet pastry.

159 Mincemeat (for mince pies)

Cal 330 KJ	Cal 78 kcal	Fat 2.7 g	Sat Fat 1.5 g	Carb 12.1 g	Sugar 11.7 g	Protein 0.3 g	Fibre 0.4 g	*

suet, chopped	100 g
mixed peel, chopped	100 g
currants	100 g
sultanas	100 g
raisins	100 g
apples, chopped	100 g
Barbados sugar	100 g
mixed spice	5 g
lemon, grated zest and juice of	1
orange, grated zest and juice of	1
rum	60 ml
brandy	60 ml

1 Mix the ingredients together.
2 Seal in jars and use as required.

* per 28 g

160 Sausage rolls

Cal 799 KJ	Cal 190 kcal	Fat 15.9 g	Sat Fat 5.8 g	Carb 7.9 g	Sugar 0.2 g	Protein 4.3 g	Fibre 0.4 g

	12 rolls
puff pastry (recipe 146)	200 g
sausage meat	400 g
eggwash	

1 Roll out the pastry 3 mm thick into a strip 10 cm wide.
2 Make the sausage meat into a roll 2 cm in diameter.
3 Place on the pastry. Moisten the edges of the pastry.
4 Fold over and seal. Cut into 8 cm lengths or leave whole to be cut after baking.
5 Mark the edge with the back of a knife. Brush with eggwash.
6 Place on to a greased, dampened baking sheet.
7 Bake at 220°C for about 20 minutes.

161 Tatin of apple (tarte tatin)

Makes 10 portions

caster sugar	100 g
glucose	10 g
water	200 ml
unsalted butter, diced	100 g
Granny Smith's apples, peeled and cored	7
lemon, juice	½
puff pastry (recipe 146)	175 g

1 Cook the sugar, glucose and water in a thick-bottomed copper (bear in mind that the tatin will be cooked in this so it will need to be ovenproof) until it reaches a pale, amber colour, which is pre-caramel.
2 Remove from the heat and add the diced butter.
3 While the butter is melting, cut the apples into eighths, lightly sprinkle with lemon juice and place on top of the caramel/butter.
4 Place in the oven for 25 minutes until the apples are half-cooked and starting to caramelise.
5 Meanwhile, roll out the puff pastry, 3–4 mm thick, and slightly larger than the diameter of the pan.
6 Cover the apples with the pastry and bake for a further 15–20 minutes, until the pastry is golden.
7 Remove from the oven and leave to cool slightly before turning out.
8 Serve with vanilla ice cream or crème fraîche.

Note: This is the name given to an apple tart that is cooked under a lid of pastry, but then served with the pastry underneath the fruit. This is a delicious dessert in which the taste of caramel is combined with the flavour of the fruit, finished with a crisp pastry base; it was the creation of the Tatin sisters, who ran a hotel-restaurant in Lamotte-Beuvron at the beginning of the last century. Having been made famous by the Tatin sisters the dish was first served at Maxim's in Paris, as a house speciality. It is still served there to this day.

Figure 14.40 🥄 Tatin of apple

Suet pastry

162 Suet paste

Cal 6402 KJ	Cal 1524 kcal	Fat 89.3 g	Sat Fat 40.6 g	Carb 171.3 g	Sugar 3.0 g	Protein 19.3 g	Fibre 7.2 g	*

	5–8 portions	10 portions
flour (soft) or self-raising flour	200 g	500 g
baking powder	10 g	25 g
salt	pinch	large pinch
prepared beef suet	100 g	250 g
water	125 ml	300 ml

1 Sieve the flour, baking powder and salt.
2 Mix in the suet. Make a well. Add the water.
3 Mix lightly to a fairly stiff paste.

Note: Suet paste is used for steamed fruit puddings, steamed jam rolls, steamed meat puddings and dumplings. Vegetarian suet is also available.

* 5–8 portions

Possible reasons for faults in suet paste

- Heavy and soggy:
  – cooking temperature too low.
- Tough:
  – too much handling, over-cooking.

163 Steamed fruit puddings

Cal 967 KJ	Cal 230 kcal	Fat 7.4 g	Sat Fat 3.4 g	Carb 41.5 g	Sugar 27.1 g	Protein 1.9 g	Fibre 3.0 g	*

	6 portions
suet paste (recipe 162)	200 g
fruit	¾–1 kg
sugar	100 g
water	2 tbsp

1 Grease a basin.
2 Line, using three-quarters of the paste.
3 Add prepared and washed fruit and the sugar. (Add 1–2 cloves in an apple pudding.)
4 Add water. Moisten the edge of the paste.
5 Cover with the remaining quarter of the pastry. Seal firmly.
6 Cover with greased greaseproof paper, a pudding cloth or foil.
7 Steam for about 1½ hours and serve with custard.

Note: Steamed fruit puddings can be made with apple, apple and blackberry, rhubarb, rhubarb and apple, and so on.

* Using apple

164 Steamed jam roll

Cal 673 KJ	Cal 160 kcal	Fat 7.0 g	Sat Fat 3.9 g	Carb 24.3 g	Sugar 11.7 g	Protein 1.5 g	Fibre 0.5 g

	6 portions	15 portions
suet paste (recipe 162)	200 g	400 g
jam	100 g	200 g

1 Roll out the paste into a rectangle 3 × 16 cm.
2 Spread with jam, leaving 1 cm clear on all edges.
3 Fold over the two short sides, 1 cm. Roll the pastry from the top.

4 Moisten the bottom edge to seal the roll.
5 Wrap in buttered greaseproof paper and a pudding cloth or foil; tie both ends. Steam for 1½ –2 hours. Serve with jam or custard sauce.

Note: The jam may be sprinkled with finely chopped nuts (e.g. walnuts, hazelnuts, pecan, almonds). The jam roll may be made in individual portions.

Choux pastry

165 Choux paste (pâte à choux)

Cal 6248 KJ	Cal 1488 kcal	Fat 106.6 g	Sat Fat 43.3 g	Carb 99.3 g	Sugar 4.1 g	Protein 38.9 g	Fibre 4.5 g	*

	5–8 portions	10–16 portions
water	¼ litre	625 ml
sugar	pinch	large pinch
salt	pinch	large pinch
butter, margarine or oil	100 g	250 g
flour (strong)	125 g	300 g
eggs	4	10

1 Bring the water, sugar, salt and fat to the boil in a saucepan. Remove from heat.
2 Add the sieved flour and mix in with a wooden spoon (50 per cent, 70 per cent or 100 per cent wholemeal flour may be used).

3 Return to a moderate heat and stir continuously until the mixture leaves the sides of the pan.
4 Remove from the heat and allow to cool.
5 Gradually add the beaten eggs, beating well. Do not add all the eggs at once – check the consistency as you go. The mixture may not take all the egg. It should just flow back when moved in one direction.

Note: Choux paste is used for éclairs, cream buns and profiteroles.

* Using hard margarine (5–8 portions)

Figure 14.41 Preparation of choux paste

Possible reasons for faults in choux paste

- Greasy and heavy:
  - basic mixture over-cooked.
- Soft, not aerated:
  - flour insufficiently cooked; eggs insufficiently beaten in the mixture; oven too cool; under-baked.

166 Chocolate éclairs *(éclairs au chocolat)*

Cal 516 KJ	Cal 123 kcal	Fat 9.5 g	Sat Fat 5.7 g	Carb 8.8 g	Sugar 7.3 g	Protein 1.1 g	Fibre 0.1 g

Makes 12 éclairs

choux paste (recipe 165)	125 ml
whipped cream	¼ litre
fondant	100 g
chocolate couverture	25 g

1 Place the choux paste into a piping bag with a 1 cm plain tube.
2 Pipe into 8 cm lengths onto a lightly greased, dampened baking sheet.
3 Bake at 200–220°C (less in a convection oven) for about 30 minutes.
4 Allow to cool. Slit down one side, with a sharp knife.
5 Fill with sweetened, vanilla-flavoured whipped cream, using a piping bag and small tube. The continental fashion is to fill with pastry cream.
6 Warm the fondant, add the finely cut chocolate, allow to melt slowly, adjust the consistency with a little sugar and water syrup if necessary. *Do not overheat or the fondant will lose its shine.*
7 Glaze the éclairs by dipping them in the fondant; remove the surplus with the finger. Allow to set.

Note: Traditionally, chocolate éclairs were filled with chocolate pastry cream.

Figure 14.42 ✎ Chocolate éclairs, cream choux buns, profiteroles and chocolate sauce

Figure 14.43 ✎ Piping éclairs

Figure 14.44 ✎ Glazing chocolate éclairs

167 Coffee éclairs (éclairs au café)

1 Proceed as for recipe 166, but add a few drops of coffee essence instead of chocolate to the fondant.

Variations
Coffee éclairs may be filled with coffee-flavoured pastry cream (recipe 10) or whipped non-dairy cream.

168 Profiteroles

These are small choux paste buns that can be made in a variety of sizes:

- pea size, for consommé garnish
- double pea size (stuffed) for garnish
- half cream bun size (recipe 169), filled with cream and served with chocolate sauce.

169 Cream buns (choux à la crème)

Makes 8 buns

choux paste (recipe 165)	125 ml
chopped almonds	25 g
whipped cream	¼ litre
icing sugar, to serve	

1 Place the choux paste into a piping bag with a 1 cm plain tube.
2 Pipe out on to a lightly greased, dampened baking sheet into pieces the size of a walnut.
3 Sprinkle each with chopped almonds. Cook, allow to cool, split and fill as for éclairs (recipe 166).
4 Sprinkle with icing sugar and serve.

170 Profiteroles and chocolate sauce (profiteroles au chocolat)

Cal	Cal	Fat	Sat Fat	Carb	Sugar	Protein	Fibre
919 KJ	219 kcal	16.2 g	9.7 g	16.4 g	12.8 g	2.9 g	0.2 g

8 portions	
choux paste (recipe 165)	125 ml
chocolate sauce (recipe 71 or 72)	¼ litre
whipped, sweetened, vanilla-flavoured cream	¼ litre
icing sugar, to serve	

1 Proceed as for cream buns (recipe 169), but pipe out half the size and omit the almonds. Fill with cream and dredge with icing sugar.
2 Serve with a sauceboat of cold chocolate sauce.

Variations
Alternatively, coffee sauce may be served and the profiteroles filled with non-dairy cream. Profiteroles may also be filled with chocolate-, coffee- or rum-flavoured pastry cream.

171 Choux paste fritters (beignets soufflés, sauce abricot)

Cal	Cal	Fat	Sat Fat	Carb	Sugar	Protein	Fibre
344 KJ	82 kcal	3.9 g	1.3 g	11.5 g	8.8 g	0.9 g	0.2 g

	8 portions
choux paste (recipe 165)	125 ml
icing sugar, to serve	
apricot sauce (recipe 62) , to serve	125 ml

1 Using a tbsp and the finger, break the paste off into pieces the size of a walnut into a moderately hot deep fat 170°C.
2 Allow to cook gently for 10–15 minutes.
3 Drain well, sprinkle liberally with icing sugar.
4 Serve with a sauceboat of hot apricot sauce (recipe 62).

Filo pastry

172 Filo paste

Makes 1 kg of paste	
strong flour	1 kg
water	250–375 ml
vinegar	1 tbsp
salt	2 tsp
olive oil	4 tbsp

1 Sift the flour into a bowl.
2 Add the water, vinegar and salt, and mix to a thick paste.
3 Slowly add the oil while working the mixture.
4 Knead until the dough is smooth and elastic.

5 Split the dough into suitable-sized pieces.
6 Roll out with an ordinary rolling pin, then continue rolling using a pasta machine or a very thin rolling pin to make the paste wafer thin.
7 The pastry is now ready for use and should be covered with a damp or oiled cloth when not being rolled out or before use. If this is not done the pastry will dry out and be difficult to handle.

Note: Ready-made filo pastry is available. Brick paste/pastry is similar to filo pastry and is bought as a commercial product from specialist suppliers.

Cakes and biscuits

Cake mixtures

There are three basic methods of making cake mixtures, also known as cake batters. The working temperature of cake batter should be 21°C.

Sugar batter method

For this method, the fat (cake margarine, butter or shortening) is blended in a machine with caster sugar. This is the basic or principal stage; the other ingredients are then usually added in the order shown in Figure 14.45.

Flour batter method

For this method the eggs and sugar are whisked to a half sponge; this is the basic or principal stage, which aims to foam the two ingredients together until half the maximum volume is achieved. Other ingredients are added as shown in Figure 14.46.

A humectant such as glycerine may be added to assist with moisture retention; if so, add at stage 2.

Blending method

Used for high-ratio cake mixtures. This uses high-ratio flour specially produced so that it will absorb more liquid. For this method also use a high-ratio

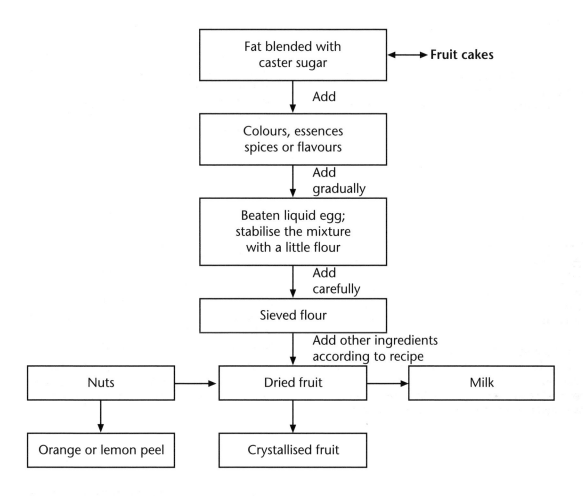

Figure 14.45 ✎ The sugar batter method

fat. This is made from oil, to which a quantity of emulsifying agent has been added, enabling the fat to take up a greater quantity of liquid.

High-ratio cakes contain more liquid and sugar, resulting in a fine stable crumb, extended shelf life, good eating and excellent freezing qualities.

The principal or basic stage is the mixing of the fat and flour to a crumbling texture. It is essential that each stage of the batter is blended into the next to produce a smooth batter, free from lumps.

When using mixing machines, it is important to remember to:

* blend on a slow speed
* beat on a medium speed, using a paddle attachment.

When blending, always clear the mix from the bottom of the bowl to ensure that any first- or second-stage butter does not remain in the bowl.

Baking powder

Baking powder may be made from one part sodium bicarbonate to two parts cream of tartar. In commercial baking the powdered cream of tartar may be replaced by another acid product, such as acidulated calcium phosphate.

When used under the right conditions it produces carbon dioxide gas; to produce gas, a liquid and heat are needed. As the acid has a delayed action, only a small amount being given off when the liquid is added, the majority of the gas is released when the mixture is heated. Therefore cakes when mixed do not lose the property of the baking powder if they are not cooked right away.

Possible reasons for faults in cakes

- Uneven texture:
  – fat insufficiently rubbed in
  – too little liquid
  – too much liquid.
- Close texture:
  – too much fat
  – hands too hot when rubbing in
  – fat to flour ratio incorrect.
- Dry:
  – too little liquid
  – oven too hot.
- Bad shape:
  – too much liquid
  – oven too cool
  – too much baking powder.
- Fruit sunk:
  – fruit wet
  – too much liquid
  – oven too cool.
- Cracked:
  – too little liquid
  – too much baking powder.

Biscuit mixtures

Biscuits may be produced by the following methods:

- rubbing in
- flour batter
- foaming
- blending
- sugar batter.

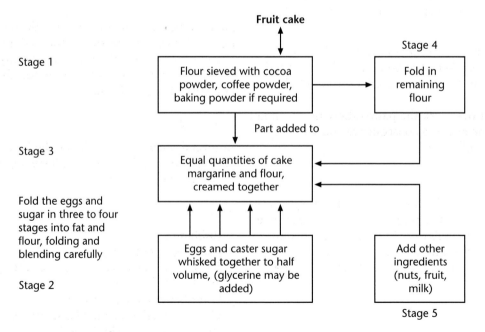

Fruit cake

Stage 1 — Flour sieved with cocoa powder, coffee powder, baking powder if required

Stage 4 — Fold in remaining flour

Part added to

Stage 3 — Equal quantities of cake margarine and flour, creamed together

Fold the eggs and sugar in three to four stages into fat and flour, folding and blending carefully

Stage 2 — Eggs and caster sugar whisked together to half volume, (glycerine may be added)

Stage 5 — Add other ingredients (nuts, fruit, milk)

Figure 14.46 ✎ The flour batter method

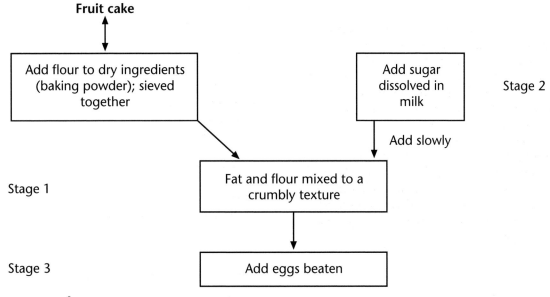

Fruit cake

| Add flour to dry ingredients (baking powder); sieved together | | Add sugar dissolved in milk | Stage 2 |

Add slowly

Stage 1

| Fat and flour mixed to a crumbly texture |

Stage 3

| Add eggs beaten |

Figure 14.47 ✐ The blending method

Rubbing in

This is probably the best-known method and is used in producing some of the most famous types of biscuits, such as shortbread. The method is exactly the same as that for producing short pastry.

- Rub the fat into the flour, by hand or by machine, adding the liquid and the sugar and mixing in the flour to produce a smooth biscuit paste.
- Do not overwork the paste otherwise it will not combine and as a consequence you will not be able to roll it out.

Foaming

This is where a foam is produced from egg whites, egg yolks or both. Sponge fingers are an example of a two-foam mixture. Meringue is an example of a single-foam mixture using egg whites. Great care must be taken not to over-mix the product.

Sugar batter method

Fat and sugar are mixed together to produce a light and fluffy cream. Beaten egg is added gradually. The dry ingredients are then carefully folded in.

Flour batter method

Half the sieved flour is creamed with the fat. The eggs and sugar are beaten together before they are added to the fat and flour mixture. Finally, the remainder of the flour is folded in, together with any other dry ingredients.

Blending method

In several biscuit recipes, the method requires the chef only to blend all the ingredients together to produce a smooth paste.

Production methods and examples

- **Rubbing in:** shortbread.
- **Foaming:** sponge fingers.
- **Sugar batter method:** cats' tongues (langues de chat), sablé biscuits.
- **Flour batter method:** cookies.
- **Blending method:** almond biscuits (using basic almond commercial mixture).

Batters and whisked sponges

Batters and sponges allow us to make a large assortment of desserts and cakes. Basically, they are a mix of eggs, sugar, flour and the air incorporated when these are beaten. Certain other raw materials can be combined – for example, almonds, hazelnuts, walnuts, chocolate, butter, fruit, ginger, anise, coffee and vanilla.

Sponge mixtures are produced from a foam of eggs and sugar. The eggs may be whole eggs or separated. Examples of sponge products are gâteaux, sponge fingers and sponge cakes.

The egg white traps the air bubbles by forming a semi-rigid membrane structure. When eggs and sugar are whisked together, they thicken until maximum volume is reached; then flour is carefully folded in by a method known as cutting in. This is the most difficult operation as the flour must not be allowed to sink to the bottom of the bowl, otherwise it becomes lumpy and difficult to clear. However, the mixture must not be stirred as this will disturb the aeration and cause the air to escape, resulting in a much heavier sponge. If butter, margarine or oil is added, it is important that this is added at about 36°C, otherwise overheating will cause the fat or oil to act on the flour and create lumps, which are difficult, often impossible, to dispense.

Stabilisers are often added to sponges to prevent them from collapsing. The most common are ethylmethyl cellulose and glycerol monostearate; these are added to the eggs and sugar on the commencement of mixing.

What you need to know about sponge cakes

- You should never add flour or ground dry ingredients to a batter until the end because they impede the air absorption in the first beating stage.
- When making sponge cakes, we must always sift the dry ingredients (flour, cocoa powder, ground nuts, etc.) to avoid clumping.
- Mix in the flour as quickly and delicately as possible, because a rough addition of dry ingredients acts like a weight on the primary batter and can remove part of the air already absorbed.
- Flours used in sponge cakes are low in gluten content. In certain sponge cakes, a portion of the flour can be left out and substituted with cornstarch. This yields a softer and more aerated batter.
- The eggs used in sponge cake batters should be fresh and at room temperature so that they take in air faster.
- Adding separately beaten egg whites produces a lighter and fluffier sponge cake.
- Once sponge cake batters are beaten and poured into moulds or baking trays, they should be baked as soon as possible. Otherwise, the batter loses volume.

Methods of making sponges

Foaming method
Whisking eggs and sugar together to ribbon stage; folding in/cutting flour.

Melting method

As with foaming, adding melted butter, margarine or oil to the mixture. The fat content enriches the sponge, improves the flavour, texture and crumb structure, and will extend shelf life.

Boiling method

Sponges made by this method have a stable crumb texture that is easier to handle than Genoese sponge, crumbling less when cut. This method will produce a sponge that is suitable for dipping in fondant. The stages are shown in Figure 14.48.

Blending method

High-ratio sponges follow the same principles as high-ratio cakes. As with cakes, high-ratio goods produce a fine, stable crumb, an even texture, excellent shelf life and good freezing qualities.

Creaming method

This is the traditional method and is still used today for Victoria sandwich and light fruit cakes.

The fat and sugar are creamed together, beaten egg is added and, finally, the sieved flour is added with the other dry ingredients as desired.

Separate yolk and white method

This method is used for sponge fingers (recipe 187).

Possible reasons for faults in sponges

- Close texture:
  - under-beating
  - too much flour
  - oven too cool or too hot.
- 'Holey' texture:
  - flour insufficiently folded in
  - tin unevenly filled.
- Cracked crust:
  - oven too hot.
- Sunken:
  - oven too hot
  - tin removed during cooking.
- White spots on surface:
  - insufficient beating.

Possible reasons for faults in Genoese sponges

- Close texture:
  - eggs and sugar overheated
  - eggs and sugar under-beaten
  - too much flour
  - flour insufficiently folded in
  - oven too hot.
- Sunken:
  - too much sugar
  - oven too hot
  - tin removed during cooking.
- Heavy:
  - butter too hot
  - butter insufficiently mixed in
  - flour over-mixed.

Points to remember

- Check all ingredients carefully.
- Make sure scales are accurate; weigh all ingredients carefully.
- Check ovens are at the right temperature and that the shelves are in the correct position.
- Check that all work surfaces and equipment are clean.
- Check that all other equipment required, such as cooling wires, is within easy reach.
- Always sieve flour to remove lumps and any foreign material.
- Make sure that eggs and fats are at room temperature.
- Check dried fruits carefully; wash, drain and dry if necessary.
- Always follow the recipe carefully.
- Always scrape down the sides of the mixing bowl when creaming mixtures.

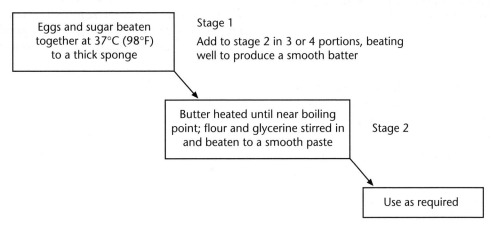

Stage 1

Eggs and sugar beaten together at 37°C (98°F) to a thick sponge

Add to stage 2 in 3 or 4 portions, beating well to produce a smooth batter

Stage 2

Butter heated until near boiling point; flour and glycerine stirred in and beaten to a smooth paste

Use as required

Figure 14.48 ✎ The boiling method

- Always seek help if you are unsure, or lack understanding.
- Try to fill the oven space when baking by planning production carefully; this saves time, labour and money.
- Never guess quantities. Time and temperature are important factors; they too should not be guessed.
- The shape and size of goods will determine the cooking time and temperature: the wider the cake, the longer and more slowly it will need to cook.
- Where cakes contain a high proportion of sugar in the recipe, this will caramelise the surface quickly before the centre is cooked. Therefore cover the cake with sheets of silicone or wetted greaseproof and continue to cook.
- When cake tops are sprinkled with almonds or sugar, the baking temperature needs to be lowered slightly to prevent over-colouring of the cake crust.
- When glycerine, glucose and invert sugar, honey or treacle is added to cake mixtures, the oven temperature should be lowered as these colour at a lower temperature than sugar.
- Always work in a clean and hygienic way; remember the hygiene and safety rules, in particular the Food Safety Act.
- All cakes and sponges benefit from being allowed to cool in their tins as this makes handling easier. If sponges need to be cooled quickly, place a wire rack over the top of the tin and invert, then remove the lining paper and cool on a wire rack.

The introduction of steam or moisture

Because they become too dry while baking due to oven temperature producing a dry atmosphere, some cakes require the injection of steam. Combination ovens are ideally suited for this purpose. The steam delays the formation of the crust until the cake batter has become fully aerated and the proteins have set. Alternatively, add a tray of water to the oven while baking. If the oven is too hot the cake crust will form early and the cake batter will rise into a peak.

Convenience cake, biscuit and sponge mixes

There is now available on the market a vast range of prepared mixes, as well as frozen goods. Premixes enable the caterer to calculate costs more effectively, reduce labour costs (with less demand for highly skilled labour) and limit the range of stock items to be held.

Every year more and more convenience products are introduced on to the market by food manufacturers large and small. The caterer should be encouraged to investigate these products, and to experiment in order to assess their quality.

Decorating and finishing for presentation

Filling
Cakes, sponges and biscuits may be filled or sandwiched together with a variety of different types of filling. Some examples are presented below.

- Creams:
  - buttercream (plain), flavoured and/or coloured
  - pastry cream, flavoured and/or coloured
  - whipped cream
  - clotted cream.
- Fruit:
  - fresh fruit purée
  - jams
  - fruit pastries
  - fruit mousses
  - preserves
  - fruit gels.
- Pastes and spreads:
  - chocolate
  - praline
  - nut
  - curds.

Spreading and coating to finish
This is where smaller cakes and gâteaux are covered top and sides with any of the following:

- fresh whipped cream
- fondant
- chocolate
- royal icing

- buttercream
- water icing
- meringue
- ordinary
- Italian
- Swiss
- commercial preparations.

Piping

Piping is a skill that takes practice. There are many different types of piping tube available. The following may be used for piping:

- royal icing
- meringue
- chocolate
- boiled sugar
- fondant
- fresh cream.

Dusting, dredging, sprinkling

These techniques are used to give the product a final design or glaze during cooking using sugar.

- **Dusting:** a light, even finish.
- **Dredging:** heavier dusting with sugar.
- **Sprinkling:** a very light sprinkle of sugar.

The sugar used may be icing, caster or granulated white; demerara, Barbados or dark brown sugar.

The product may be returned to the oven for glazing, or glazed under the salamander.

Remember that decorating is an art form and there is a range of equipment and materials available to assist you in this work. Some examples of decorative media are as follows.

- Glacé and crystallised fruits:
  - cherries
  - lemons
  - oranges
  - pineapple
  - figs.
- Crystallised flowers:
  - rose petals
  - violets
  - mimosa
  - lilac.
- Crystallised stems:
  - angelica.
- Nuts:
  - almonds (nibbed, flaked)
  - coconut (fresh slices, desiccated)
  - hazelnuts
  - brazil nuts
  - pistachio.
- Chocolate:
  - rolls
  - vermicelli
  - flakes
  - chocolate piping
  - chips.

Biscuit pastes

Piped biscuits can be used for decoration. For example:

- piped sablé paste (recipe 191)
- cats' tongues (recipe 188)
- almond biscuits (recipe 192).

Cakes

173 Scones

Cal 678 KJ	Cal 162 kcal	Fat 5.8 g	Sat Fat 2.5 g	Carb 26.3 g	Sugar 7.5 g	Protein 2.7 g	Fibre 1.0 g	*

	8 scones	20 scones
self-raising flour	200 g	500 g
baking powder	5 g	12 g
salt	pinch	large pinch
butter or margarine	50 g	125 g
caster sugar	50 g	125 g
milk or water	95 ml	250 ml

1 Sieve the flour, baking powder and salt.
2 Rub in the fat to achieve a sandy texture. Make a well in the centre.
3 Dissolve the sugar in the liquid.
4 Gradually incorporate the flour; mix lightly.
5 Roll out two rounds, 1 cm thick. Place on a greased baking sheet.
6 Cut a cross halfway through the rounds with a large knife.
7 Milkwash and bake at 200°C for 15–20 minutes.

Note: The comparatively small amount of fat, rapid mixing to a soft dough, quick and light handling are essentials to produce a light scone.

Variations
- Add 50 g (125 g for 20 scones) washed and dried sultanas to the scone mixture for fruit scones; 50 per cent wholemeal flour may be used.
- For precisely formed scones, roll out the dough to approx. 2 cm thick and cut out scones with a 4–5 cm cutter.

* Using hard margarine

Figure 14.49 ✎ Scones

174 Small cakes: basic mixture

Cal 947 KJ	Cal 225 kcal	Fat 11.6 g	Sat Fat 4.8 g	Carb 28.8 g	Sugar 13.4 g	Protein 3.3 g	Fibre 0.7 g	*

	10 medium or 20 small cakes
flour (soft) or self-raising	200 g
baking powder (with plain flour)	1 level tsp
salt (optional)	pinch
margarine or butter	125 g
caster sugar	125 g
medium eggs	2–3

Method 1: rubbing in
1 Sieve the flour, baking powder and salt (if using).
2 Rub in the butter or margarine to achieve a sandy texture. Add the sugar.
3 Gradually add the well-beaten eggs and mix as lightly as possible until combined.

Method 2: creaming
1 Cream the margarine and sugar in a bowl until soft and fluffy.
2 Slowly add the well-beaten eggs, mixing continuously and beating really well between each addition.
3 Lightly mix in the sieved flour, baking powder and salt (if using).

Note: In both cases the consistency should be a light dropping one, and if necessary it may be adjusted with the addition of a few drops of milk.

* Using hard margarine

Variations

- *Cherry cakes:* add 50 g glacé cherries cut in quarters and 3–4 drops vanilla essence to the basic mixture (method 2) and divide into 8–12 lightly greased cake tins or paper cases. Bake in a hot oven at 220°C for 15–20 minutes.
- *Coconut cakes:* in place of 50 g flour, use 50 g desiccated coconut and 3–4 drops vanilla essence to the basic mixture (method 2) and cook as for cherry cakes.

- *Raspberry buns:* divide basic mixture (method 1) into 8 pieces. Roll into balls, flatten slightly, dip tops into milk then caster sugar. Place on a greased baking sheet, make a hole in the centre of each, add a little raspberry jam. Bake in a hot oven at 200°C for 15–20 minutes.
- *Queen cakes:* to the basic mixture (method 2) add 100 g washed and dried mixed fruit and cook as for cherry cakes.

175 Rock cakes

Cal	Cal	Fat	Sat Fat	Carb	Sugar	Protein	Fibre	*
913 KJ	217 kcal	8.7 g	3.6 g	33.6 g	14.3 g	3.4 g	1.3 g	

	8 cakes	20 cakes
flour (soft) or self-raising	200 g	500 g
dried fruit (e.g. currants, sultanas)	50 g	125 g
baking powder (with plain flour)	5 g	12 g
salt	pinch	large pinch
margarine or butter	75 g	180 g
caster sugar	75 g	180 g
large egg	1	2–3

1 Use method 1 (recipe 174), adding the dried fruit at the same time as the flour. Keep the mixture slightly firm.
2 Fashion roughly with a fork into 8–12 shapes on a greased baking sheet; milkwash or eggwash.
3 Bake in a fairly hot oven at 220°C for about 20 minutes.

Variations
Add a small pinch of mixed spice.

* *Using hard margarine*

176 Rich fruit cake

	16 cm dia, 8 cm deep	21 cm dia, 8 cm deep	26 cm dia, 8 cm deep	31 cm dia, 8 cm deep
butter or margarine	150 g	200 g	300 g	550 g
caster or soft brown sugar	150 g	200 g	300 g	550 g
eggs	4	6	8	10
glycerine	2 tsp	3 tsp	1 tbsp	2 tbsp
soft flour	125 g	175 g	275 g	500 g
nutmeg	¾ tsp	1 tsp	1¼ tsp	2 tsp
mixed spice	¾ tsp	1 tsp	1¼ tsp	2 tsp
cinnamon	¾ tsp	1 tsp	1¼ tsp	2 tsp
ground almonds	75 g	100 g	125 g	200 g
salt	6 g	8 g	10 g	12 g
currants	150 g	200 g	300 g	550 g
sultanas	150 g	200 g	300 g	550 g
raisins	125 g	150 g	225 g	400 g
mixed peel	75 g	100 g	125 g	200 g
glacé cherries	75 g	100 g	125 g	200 g
lemon, grated rind of	½	½	1	2
oven temperature	150°C	150°C	130°C	110°C
time (approx.)	3 hours	3½ hours	4½ hours	6–7 hours

1 Cream the butter or margarine and sugar until light and fluffy.
2 Gradually beat in the eggs, creaming continuously.
3 Add the glycerine.
4 Sift the flour, nutmeg, mixed spice and cinnamon. Add the ground almonds and salt, mix well.
5 Carefully fold in the flour, nutmeg, mixed spice, cinnamon, ground almonds and salt into the eggs and sugar.
6 Fold in the dried fruit, mixed peel, glacé cherries and lemon rind.
7 Place the mixture into a prepared cake tin lined with silicone. The outside of the tin should also be well protected with paper. Bake at the required temperature for the required time.
8 To test, insert a needle into the centre of the cake; when cooked, it should come out clean and free of uncooked mixture.
9 Remove from the oven and allow to cool.
10 Wrap in tin foil and allow to mature for 2–3 weeks before coating with marzipan (recipe 177) and icing (recipe 178).

Note: The dried fruit may be soaked in brandy for 12 hours. Allow 3 tbsp of brandy for a 16 cm diameter cake; 4 tbsp for 21 cm diameter; 5 tbsp for 26 cm diameter, etc. Alternatively, instead of soaking the fruit before baking, the brandy may be poured over the cake once it leaves the oven after baking.

177 Marzipan or almond paste (cooked)

Makes 400 g of paste

water	250 ml
caster sugar	1 kg
ground almonds	400 g
yolks	3
almond essence	2–3 drops

1 Place the water and sugar in a pan and boil. Skim as necessary.
2 When the sugar reaches 116°C, draw aside and mix in the ground almonds; then add the yolks and essence and mix in quickly to avoid scrambling.
3 Knead well until smooth.

178 Royal icing

icing sugar	400 g
whites of egg, pasteurised	3
lemon, juice of	1
glycerine	2 tsp

1 Mix well together in a basin the sieved icing sugar and the whites of egg, with a wooden spoon.
2 Add a few drops of lemon juice and glycerine and beat until stiff.

Note: Modern practice is to use egg white substitute or dried egg whites. Always follow the manufacturer's instructions for quantities.

Sponges

To improve the shelf life of a sponge, substitute 5 g of every 100 g of sugar with 1 teaspoon of glycerine.

179 Victoria sandwich

Cal	Cal	Fat	Sat Fat	Carb	Sugar	Protein	Fibre	*
6866 KJ	164 kcal	94.3 g	39.3 g	184.7 g	106.6 g	23.3 g	3.6 g	

	single sponge	double sponge
butter or margarine	100 g	250 g
caster sugar	100 g	250 g
medium eggs	2	5
flour (soft)	100 g	250 g
baking powder	5 g	12 g

1 Cream the fat and sugar until soft and fluffy.
2 Gradually add the beaten eggs.
3 Lightly mix in the sieved flour, and baking powder.
4 Divide into two 18 cm greased sponge tins.
5 Bake at 190–200°C for 12–15 minutes.
6 Turn out on to a wire rack to cool.
7 Spread one half with jam, place the other half on top.
8 Dust with icing sugar.

* Using hard margarine

180 Genoese sponge (génoise)

Cal	Cal	Fat	Sat Fat	Carb	Sugar	Protein	Fibre	*
5978 KJ	1423 kcal	65.8 g	25.6 g	182.8 g	106.6 g	36.5 g	3.6 g	

	single sponge	double sponge
medium eggs	4	10
caster sugar	100 g	250 g
flour (soft)	100 g	250 g
butter, margarine or oil	50 g	125 g

1 Whisk the eggs and sugar with a balloon whisk in a bowl over a pan of hot water.
2 Continue until the mixture is light and creamy, and has doubled in bulk.
3 Remove from the heat and whisk until cold and thick (ribbon stage). Fold in the flour very gently.
4 Fold in the melted butter very gently.
5 Place in a greased, floured Genoese mould.
6 Bake in a moderately hot oven, at 200–220°C, for about 30 minutes. (More quickly and cooler in a convection oven.)

* Using hard margarine (4 portions)

181 Chocolate Genoese (génoise au chocolat)

Cal	Cal	Fat	Sat Fat	Carb	Sugar	Protein	Fibre
1518 KJ	362 kcal	17.6 g	8.8 g	43.5 g	26.6 g	10.1 g	0.9 g

	single sponge	double sponge
flour (soft)	75 g	180 g
cocoa powder	10 g	25 g
cornflour	10 g	25 g
medium eggs	4	10
caster sugar	100 g	250 g
butter, margarine or oil	50 g	125 g

1 Sift the flour and the cocoa together with the cornflour.
2 Proceed as for Genoese sponge (recipe 180).

182 Chocolate gâteau

Cal 20113 KJ	Cal 4789 kcal	Fat 260.9 g	Sat Fat 148.7 g	Carb 606.0 g	Sugar 533.2 g	Protein 41.6 g	Fibre 4.8 g	*

	single gâteau	double gâteau
chocolate Genoese sponge (recipe 181)		
egg	4	10
chocolate vermicelli or flakes	50 g	125 g
stock syrup (recipe 184), as required		
Buttercream		
unsalted butter	200 g	500 g
icing sugar	150 g	375 g
block chocolate (melted in a basin in a bain-marie)	50 g	125 g

1 Cut the Genoese into three slices crosswise.
2 Prepare the buttercream as for recipe 78, and mix in the melted chocolate.
3 Lightly moisten each slice of Genoese with stock syrup, which may be flavoured with kirsch, rum, etc.
4 Lightly spread each slice of Genoese with buttercream and sandwich together.
5 Lightly coat the sides with buttercream, then cover with chocolate vermicelli or flakes.
6 Neatly smooth the top using a little more buttercream if necessary.

Variations
Many variations can be used in decorating this gâteau; chocolate fondant may be used on the top, and various shapes of chocolate can be used to decorate the top and sides.

* *Using hard margarine and butter (4 portions)*

Figure 14.50 🍴 Chocolate gâteau

183 Coffee gâteau (gâteau moka)

Cal 4046 KJ	Cal 963 kcal	Fat 65.5 g	Sat Fat 36.0 g	Carb 86.0 g	Sugar 66.2 g	Protein 13.1 g	Fibre 1.7 g

	single gâteau	double gâteau
chocolate Genoese sponge (recipe 181)		
egg	4	10
stock syrup (recipe 184), as required		
toasted, flaked or nibbed almonds	50 g	125 g
Buttercream		
unsalted butter	200 g	500 g
icing sugar	150 g	375 g
coffee essence	2–3 drops	5–8 drops

1 Cut Genoese into three slices crosswise.
2 Prepare the buttercream as for recipe 78, and flavour with coffee essence.
3 Lightly moisten each slice of Genoese with stock syrup, which may be flavoured with Tia Maria, brandy, etc.
4 Lightly spread each slice with buttercream and sandwich together.
5 Lightly coat the sides with buttercream and coat with almonds.
6 Smooth the top using a little more buttercream if necessary.
7 Decorate by piping the word 'MOKA' in buttercream.

Variations
Coffee-flavoured fondant may be used in place of buttercream for the topping.

184 Stock syrup

	4 portions	10 portions
water	500 ml	1¼ litres
granulated sugar	150 g	375 g
glucose	50 g	125 g

1 Boil the water, sugar and glucose together.
2 Strain and cool.

Note: Glucose helps to prevent crystallising.

185 Swiss roll

Cal	Cal	Fat	Sat Fat	Carb	Sugar	Protein	Fibre	*
4445 KJ	1058 kcal	25.3 g	8.0 g	182.7 g	106.5 g	36.5 g	3.6 g	

	4 portions	10 portions
Method 1		
medium eggs	4	10
caster sugar	100 g	250 g
flour (soft)	100 g	250 g
jam, as required		
Method 2		
medium eggs	250 ml	625 ml
caster sugar	175 g	425 g
flour (soft)	125 g	300 g
jam, as required		

1 Whisk the eggs and sugar with a balloon whisk in a bowl over a pan of hot water, using the ingredients specified for either method 1 or 2.
2 Continue until the mixture is light, creamy and double in bulk.
3 Remove from the heat and whisk until cold and thick (ribbon stage).
4 Fold in the flour very gently.
5 Grease a Swiss roll tin and line with greased greaseproof or silicone paper.
6 Pour in the mixture and bake at 220°C for about 6 minutes.
7 Turn out on to a sheet of paper sprinkled with additional caster sugar.
8 Remove the paper from the Swiss roll, spread with warm jam.
9 Roll into a fairly tight roll, leaving the paper on the outside for a few minutes.
10 Remove the paper and allow to cool on a wire rack.

* *4 portions*

Biscuits and tarts

186 Shortbread biscuits

Cal	Cal	Fat	Sat Fat	Carb	Sugar	Protein	Fibre	*
507 KJ	121 kcal	7.0 g	4.4 g	14.1 g	4.6 g	1.2 g	0.5 g	

Makes 12 biscuits

Method 1

flour (soft)	150 g
salt	pinch
butter or margarine	100 g
caster sugar	50 g

Method 2

soft flour (white or wholemeal)	100 g
rice flour	100 g
butter or margarine	100 g
caster or unrefined sugar	100 g
medium egg, beaten	1

Method 3

butter or margarine	100 g
icing sugar	100 g
medium egg	1
flour (soft)	150 g

Method 1

1 Sift the flour and salt.
2 Mix in the butter or margarine and sugar with the flour.
3 Combine all the ingredients to a smooth paste.
4 Roll carefully on a floured table or board to the shape of a rectangle or round, ½ cm thick. Place on a lightly greased baking sheet.
5 Mark into the desired size and shape. Prick with a fork.
6 Bake in a moderate oven at 140°C for 15–20 minutes.

Method 2

1 Sieve the flour and rice flour into a basin.
2 Rub in the butter until the texture of fine breadcrumbs. Mix in the sugar.
3 Bind the mixture to a stiff paste using the beaten egg.
4 Roll out to 3 mm using caster sugar, prick well with a fork and cut into fancy shapes. Place the biscuits on a lightly greased baking sheet.
5 Bake in a moderate oven at 140°C for 15 minutes or until they have a little colour.
6 Remove with a palette knife on to a cooling rack.

Method 3

1 Cream the butter or margarine and sugar thoroughly.
2 Add the egg and mix in. Mix in the flour.
3 Pipe on to lightly greased and floured baking sheets using a large star tube.
4 Bake at 140°C, for approximately 15 minutes.

* *Using butter*

187 Sponge fingers (biscuits à la cuillère)

Cal 145 KJ	Cal 34 kcal	Fat 0.9 g	Sat Fat 0.2 g	Carb 5.7 g	Sugar 3.3 g	Protein 1.3 g	Fibre 0.1 g

Makes 32 fingers

medium eggs	4
caster sugar	100 g
flour (soft)	100 g
icing sugar, to sprinkle	

1 Cream the egg yolks and sugar in a bowl until creamy and almost white.
2 Whip the egg whites stiffly.
3 Add a little of the whites to the mixture and cut in.
4 Gradually add the sieved flour and remainder of the whites alternately, mixing as lightly as possible.

5 Place in a piping bag with 1 cm plain tube and pipe in 8 cm lengths on to baking sheets lined with greaseproof or silicone paper.
6 Sprinkle liberally with icing sugar. Rest for 5 minutes, repeat, then bake.
7 Bake in a moderate hot oven at 200–220°C for about 10 minutes.
8 Remove from the oven, lift the paper on which the biscuits are piped and place upside down on the table.
9 Sprinkle liberally with water. This will assist the removal of the biscuits from the paper. (No water is needed if using silicone paper.)

Petits fours

These are an assortment of small biscuits, cakes and sweets served with coffee after special meals. There is a wide variety of items that can be prepared and, when serving petits fours, as large an assortment as possible should be offered.

Basically petits fours fall into two categories: dry and glazed. Dry includes all manner of biscuits, macaroons, meringue (see recipe 48) and marzipan items. Glazed includes fruits (recipe 190) dipped in sugar, fondants, chocolates, sweets and small pieces of neatly cut Genoese sponge (see recipe 180) covered in fondant.

188 Cats' tongues (langues de chat)

Makes approx. 40

icing sugar	125 g
butter	100 g
vanilla essence	3–4 drops
egg whites	3–4
soft flour	100 g

1 Lightly cream the sugar and butter, add the vanilla essence.
2 Add the egg whites one by one, continually mixing and being careful not to allow the mixture to curdle.
3 Gently fold in the sifted flour and mix lightly.
4 Pipe on to a lightly greased baking sheet using a 3 mm plain tube, 2½ cm apart.
5 Bake at 230–250°C, for a few minutes.
6 The outside edges should be light brown and the centres yellow.
7 When cooked, remove on to a cooling rack using a palette knife.

Figure 14.51 ✎ Making cornets and *langues de chat*: (a) spreading for cornets; (b) piping for *langues de chat*; (c) moulding cornets; (d) finished cornets and *langues de chat*

189 Cornets (*cornets*)

	Makes approx. 30
icing sugar	125 g
butter	100 g
vanilla essence	3–4 drops
egg whites	3–4
soft flour	100 g

1 Proceed as for steps 1–3 of recipe 188 (cats' tongues).
2 Using a 3 mm plain tube, pipe out the mixture onto a lightly greased baking sheet into rounds approximately 2½ cm in diameter.
3 Bake at 230–250°C, until the edges turn brown and the centre remains uncoloured.
4 Remove the tray from the oven.
5 Work quickly while the cornets are hot and twist them into a cornet shape using the point of a cream horn mould. (For a tight cornet shape it will be found best to set the pieces tightly inside the cream horn moulds and leave them until set.)

190 Glazed fruits

- Dates stoned, stuffed with marzipan (left yellow or lightly coloured pink or green) and rolled in caster sugar
- Grapes (in pairs left on the stalk) or tangerine in segments, passed through a syrup and prepared as outlined below

Syrup	
sugar	400 g
glucose	50 g
water	250 ml
lemon, juice of	1

1 Boil the sugar, glucose and water to 160–165°C.
2 Add the lemon juice, shake in thoroughly, remove from the heat.
3 Pass the fruits listed above through this syrup using a fork, then place them on to a lightly oiled marble slab to cool and set.

Note: Marzipan (recipe 177) can be coloured and moulded into a variety of shapes. These can then be either rolled in caster sugar or glazed by dipping in a syrup as described in this recipe.

Figure 14.52 Piping sablé biscuits

Figure 14.53 Sablé biscuits

191 Piped biscuits (sablés à la poche)

	20–30 biscuits
caster or unrefined sugar	75 g
butter or margarine	150 g
medium egg	1
vanilla essence	3–4 drops
or	
grated lemon zest	
soft flour, white or wholemeal	200 g
ground almonds	35 g

1 Cream the sugar and butter until light in colour and texture.
2 Add the egg gradually, beating continuously, add the vanilla essence or lemon zest.
3 Gently fold in the sifted flour and almonds, mix well until suitable for piping. If too stiff, add a little beaten egg.
4 Pipe on to a lightly greased and floured baking sheet using a medium-sized star tube (a variety of shapes can be used).
5 Some biscuits can be left plain, some decorated with half almonds or neatly cut pieces of angelica and glacé cherries.
6 Bake in a moderate oven at 190°C for about 10 minutes.
7 When cooked, remove on to a cooling rack using a palette knife.

192 Almond biscuits (biscuits aux amandes)

Cal 3361 KJ	Cal 800 kcal	Fat 53.5 g	Sat Fat 4.2 g	Carb 62.4 g	Sugar 62.4 g	Protein 21.2 g	Fibre 14.4 g

	16–20 biscuits
egg whites	1½
ground almonds	100 g
caster or unrefined sugar	50 g
almond essence	3–4 drops
sheet rice paper	1
glacé cherries or angelica	

1 Whisk the egg whites until stiff.
2 Gently stir in the ground almonds, sugar and almond essence. Place the rice paper on a baking sheet.
3 Pipe the mixture, using a medium star tube, into shapes.
4 Decorate with neatly cut diamonds of angelica and glacé cherries.
5 Bake at 180–200°C, for 10–15 minutes.
6 Trim with a small knife to cut through the rice paper; place on to a cooling rack using a palette knife.

193 Tuiles

	Makes 15–20
butter	100 g
icing sugar	100 g
flour	100 g
egg whites	2

1 Mix all ingredients; allow to rest for 1 hour.
2 Spread to the required shape and size.
3 Bake at approx. 200–210°C.
4 While hot, mould the biscuits to the required shape and leave to cool.

194 Madeleines

Makes 585 g, 45 portions

caster sugar	125 g
eggs	3
vanilla pod, seeds from	1
flour	150 g
baking powder	1 tsp
beurre noisette	125 g

1 Whisk the sugar, eggs and vanilla seeds to a hot sabayon.
2 Fold in the flour and the baking powder.
3 Fold in the beurre noisette and chill for up to 2 hours.
4 Pipe into well buttered madeleine moulds and bake in a moderate oven.
5 Turn out and allow to cool.

Figure 14.54 Madeleines

Advanced techniques

For those who may wish to study the advanced pastry technique of sugar work, marzipan, chocolate work and pastillage, an introduction to these subjects can be found in the authors' *Advanced Practical Cookery* (see reference, below).

Reference

Campbell, J., Foskett, D. and Ceserani, V. (2006) *Advanced Practical Cookery: A Textbook For Education and Industry* (4th edn). London: Hodder.

Sandwiches (page 673) with
game chips (page 524)

Wraps (page 674)

A type of club sandwich (page 673)

chapter 15

SNACKS, LIGHT MEALS, SAVOURIES AND CONVENIENCE FOODS

VRQ

Unit 214   **Prepare and cook bakery products**

NVQ

Unit 650 (2FPC15)   **Prepare and present food for cold preparation**

Practical skills
The candidate will be able to:
1 Demonstrate the correct use of tools and equipment to prepare a range of snacks and light meals
2 Prepare a range of snacks, light meals and savouries according to dish specifications
3 Demonstrate a range of skills and techniques to prepare and serve snacks, light meals and savouries
4 Demonstrate skills in the use of convenience foods
5 Demonstrate safe and hygienic practice
6 Evaluate a range of snacks, light meals, savouries and convenience foods

Underpinning knowledge
The candidate will be able to:
1 Identify a range of dishes suitable for use as snacks, light meals and savouries
2 Describe a range of dishes suitable for use as snacks, light meals and savouries
3 Identify suitable equipment for the preparation of snacks, light meals and savouries
4 Describe the range of skills required to prepare snacks, light meals and savouries
5 Describe the use of convenience foods
6 State the correct holding and storage procedures for snacks, light meals and savouries

Snacks, light meals and savouries

Snacks (to be held in the hand) and light meals are a popular form of catering at any time of day or night; a wide variety of foods may be offered, as outlined below.

Snacks

- Sandwiches made with fresh bread or toasted (page 673), accompanied with potato or vegetable crisps and a little salad.
- Rolls, baps, French bread, croissants, pitta bread, cut through and filled with a variety of fillings.
- Cornish pasties (page 291).
- Fried or grilled chicken pieces (pages 343 and 344).
- Hamburgers (page 291).
- Potato chips, crisps and other shapes (page 524).
- Sausage rolls (page 633).
- Fruit fritters (e.g. apple, banana, pineapple) (pages 582–3).
- Samosas (page 407).
- Tortillas (page 415).

Light meals

- Soup served with a warm roll or bread.
- Selection of hors d'oeuvre (page 110).
- Selection of salad greens served with pâté, cheese, shellfish (e.g. crab, lobster, prawns, shrimps) or smoked fish (e.g. mackerel fillet, salmon, trout, eel).
- Cold meat and poultry, quiche or pie with or without salad.
- Any composed salad.
- Plate of assorted smoked fish.
- Plate of assorted preserved meats.
- An egg dish (omelette, boiled, poached, fried or scrambled eggs) (page 133).
- A small dish of pasta (page 143).
- Poached smoked haddock (page 197).
- Kedgeree (page 211).
- A small portion of any fish dish.
- Kebabs (page 248).
- Barbecued spare ribs (page 315).
- Burritos (page 416).
- A small portion of any vegetarian dish (page 440).
- Baked beans on toast.
- Fried egg and chips.
- Pizza (page 666).

Savouries

Many savouries can be served as a snack or light meal. They are sometimes offered as the last course for lunch, dinner or supper (although this is not so much the case these days and is practised mainly in places such as London clubs). A variety of savouries served on hot buttered toast include the following.

- **Angels on horseback:** raw oysters wrapped in thinned streaky bacon, skewered and grilled.
- **Devils on horseback:** well-cooked, stoned prunes filled with chopped chutney, rolled in thinned streaky bacon, skewered and grilled.
- **Chicken liver and bacon (canapé Diane):** trimmed pieces of chicken liver, wrapped in thinned bacon, skewered and grilled.

- **Mushroom:** peeled open mushrooms, brushed with oil and grilled.
- **Soft herring roes:** floured and fried or grilled on both sides.
- **Soft roes and mushrooms:** cooked roes and grilled mushrooms.
- **Haddock:** lightly grilled pieces of smoked haddock fillet cut to the shape of the pieces of toast.
- **Haddock and bacon:** wrapped pieces of fish in thinned bacon and grilled.
- **Creamed haddock and cheese:** cooked, flaked smoked haddock mixed with béchamel or cream, piled on toast, sprinkled with grated cheese and lightly browned under the grill. After toasting the bread, remove crusts and leave the slices whole or cut into halves.

Convenience foods

What makes a food or product convenient? What constitutes a convenience food? The word 'convenience' encompasses a wide range of prepared and part-prepared food. This means that certain stages or steps in the process have been eliminated, thus less labour is required in their preparation.

Convenience foods can be categorised into: fresh convenience; dried; canned; bottled; frozen; chilled; vacuum packed; and portion controlled food (e.g. butter portions, jam portions).

The range of convenience foods available to the caterer is expanding all the time, as new technology becomes available to the food manufacturer, and there continues to be an increased demand for a wide variety of products from the caterer.

Convenience foods require a range of skills in their preparation and service. The caterer must make a full assessment of what products will be suitable to use in specific situations; will the customer accept the product you intend to use? The equipment required for preparation and service will also have to be reviewed. How is this assessment going to be carried out?

Basic level of convenience

This is where the basic stages have been completed, such as in peeled potatoes or carrots, but any slicing, chopping or dicing still has to be carried out.

Pre-assembly convenience

These are products where all the basic stages have been completed, together with the dicing, chopping, slicing, etc.

Pre-cooking convenience

This is where the constituents have only to be assembled prior to cooking.

Pre-service convenience

This is where the products have only to undergo minimal processing prior to service, such as defrosting prior to service (gâteaux), or defrosting followed by cooking and service. The products may simply have to be cooked for a relatively short period in a conventional or microwave oven.

Full-service convenience

This is where all the products are ready to be
served, when nothing more in certain cases is
required than opening a box or can. A brief guide
to convenience foods is given in Table 15.1.

Table 15.1 ✎ A guide to convenience foods

Type	Packaged items where food is cooked or prepared	Beverages	Packaged items where food is not cooked or fully prepared
Full convenience	butter portions jam portions sliced bread potted shrimps gâteaux salad dressings	fruit juices	frozen fruit
Pre-service convenience	ice cream canned fruit canned meats canned soup fruit pies	tea bags liquid coffee	frozen fruit
Pre-cooking convenience	canned steak dehydrated soup sausage rolls fish fingers croquettes		uncooked frozen pies/pastries breadcrumbed scampi scallops portioned meat/suprêmes of chicken
Pre-assembly convenience	canned steak frozen pastry fruit pie fillings pastry products	ground coffee	sponge mixes pastry mixes unfrozen scampi fish fillets/portioned meat
Basic convenience		coffee beans (to be ground)	peeled vegetables dried fruit jointed meats minced meat, sausages

Snacks, light meals and savouries recipes

1 Fried ham and cheese savoury (croque monsieur)

Cal	Cal	Fat	Sat Fat	Carb	Sugar	Protein	Fibre	*
1554 KJ	370 kcal	23.0 g	14.1 g	22.8 g	2.7 g	19.1 g	1.7 g	

	4 portions	10 portions
slices cooked ham	4	10
slices Gruyère cheese	8	20
slices thin toast	8	20
clarified butter,		
margarine or sunflower oil	50 g	125 g

1 Place each slice of ham between two slices of cheese, then between two slices of lightly toasted bread.
2 Cut out with a round cutter.
3 Gently fry on both sides in clarified butter or oil and serve.

* Using butter

2 Scotch woodcock

Cal	Cal	Fat	Sat Fat	Carb	Sugar	Protein	Fibre	*
611 KJ	145 kcal	10.6 g	4.2 g	8.1 g	0.5 g	5.1 g	0.8 g	

	4 portions	10 portions
medium eggs	2–3	6–8
salt, pepper		
butter or margarine	35 g	85 g
slices toast	2	5
anchovy fillets	5 g	12 g
capers	5 g	12 g

1 Break the eggs into a basin. Season with salt and pepper.
2 Thoroughly mix with a fork or whisk.
3 Place 25 g of butter in a small thick-based pan.

4 Allow to melt over a low heat.
5 Add the eggs and cook slowly, stirring continuously until lightly scrambled. Remove from the heat.
6 Spread on four rectangles or round-cut pieces of buttered toast.
7 Decorate each with two thin fillets of anchovy and four capers; serve.

Note: Adding 1 tbsp cream or milk when the eggs are almost cooked will help to prevent overcooking.

* Using hard margarine

3 Welsh rarebit

Cal	Cal	Fat	Sat Fat	Carb	Sugar	Protein	Fibre	*
1074 KJ	256 kcal	18.6 g	9.7 g	11.9 g	2.4 g	10.1 g	0.7 g	

	1 portion
butter or margarine	25 g
flour	10 g
milk, whole or skimmed	125 ml
Cheddar cheese	100 g
egg yolk	1
beer	4 tbsp
salt, cayenne	
Worcester sauce	
English mustard	
butter or margarine	10 g
slices toast	2

1 Melt the butter or margarine in a thick-based pan.
2 Add the flour and mix in with a wooden spoon.
3 Cook on a gentle heat for a few minutes without colouring.
4 Gradually add the cold milk and mix to a smooth sauce.
5 Allow to simmer for a few minutes.
6 Add the grated or finely sliced cheese.
7 Allow to melt slowly over a gentle heat until a smooth mixture is obtained.
8 Add the yolk to the hot mixture, stir in and immediately remove from the heat.

9 Meanwhile, in a separate pan boil the beer and allow it to reduce to half a tablespoon.
10 Add to the mixture with the other seasonings.
11 Allow the mixture to cool.
12 Spread on the buttered toast.
13 Place on a baking sheet and brown gently under the salamander; serve.

Note: Cheese contains a large amount of protein, which will become tough and strong if heated for too long or at too high a temperature.

HEALTHY EATING TIP
- A low-fat Cheddar may be used instead of the traditional full-fat variety.
- Use sunflower margarine and semi-skimmed milk to make the sauce.
- No added salt is needed as the cheese has salt in it.

* Using hard margarine

4 Buck rarebit

1 Prepare as for Welsh rarebit (recipe 3).
2 Place a well-drained poached egg on each portion.

Variations
Variations include:
- lightly cooked slices of tomato and/or mushrooms put on the toast before adding the mixture
- grilled back rashers or sliced, cooked ham put either under or on top of the mixture
- the mixture spread on portions of smoked haddock, a little milk added then baked in the oven; thinly sliced cooked tomato or mushroom can also be added.

5 Cheese and ham savoury flan (quiche lorraine)

Cal	Cal	Fat	Sat Fat	Carb	Sugar	Protein	Fibre
2955 KJ	704 kcal	48.4 g	22.6 g	38.1 g	6.5 g	31.6 g	1.8 g

	4 portions	10 portions
rough puff, puff or short pastry	100 g	250 g
ham, chopped	50 g	125 g
cheese, grated	25 g	60 g
medium egg	1	2
milk	125 ml	300 ml
cayenne, salt		

1 Lightly grease four (or ten) good-size barquette or tartlet moulds. Line thinly with pastry.
2 Cook in a hot oven at 230–250°C for 3–4 minutes or until the pastry is lightly set.
3 Remove from the oven; press the pastry down if it has tended to rise.
4 Add the chopped ham and grated cheese.

5 Mix the egg, milk, salt and cayenne thoroughly. Strain into the barquettes.
6 Return to the oven at 180–190°C and bake gently for 15–20 minutes or until nicely browned and set.

Note: A variation is to line a 12 cm flan ring with short paste and proceed as above. The filling can be varied by using lightly fried lardons of bacon (in place of the ham), chopped cooked onions and chopped parsley.

Variations
A variety of savoury flans can be made by using imagination and experimenting with different combinations of food (e.g. Stilton and onion; salmon and cucumber; sliced sausage and tomato).

6 Cheese straws (paillettes au fromage)

Cal	Cal	Fat	Sat Fat	Carb	Sugar	Protein	Fibre
2562 KJ	610 kcal	48.1 g	24.1 g	28.7 g	0.6 g	17.4 g	1.4 g

	4 portions	10 portions
puff or rough puff paste	100 g	250 g
cheese, grated	50 g	125 g
cayenne		

1 Roll out the pastry to 60 × 15 cm.
2 Sprinkle with the cheese and cayenne.
3 Give a single turn – that is, fold the paste one-third the way over so that it covers the first fold.
4 Roll out to 3 mm thick.
5 Cut out four circles 4 cm in diameter.
6 Remove the centre with a smaller cutter leaving a circle ½ cm wide.
7 Cut the remaining paste into strips 8 × ½ cm.
8 Twist each once or twice.
9 Place on a lightly greased baking sheet.
10 Bake in a hot oven at 230–250°C for 10 minutes or until a golden brown.
11 To serve, place a bundle of straws into each circle.

Note: 50 per cent white and 50 per cent wholemeal flour can be used for the pastry.

7 Cheese soufflé (soufflé au fromage)

Cal	Cal	Fat	Sat Fat	Carb	Sugar	Protein	Fibre	*
3223 KJ	767 kcal	60.2 g	28.2 g	17.6 g	6.1 g	39.7 g	0.5 g	

	4 portions	10 portions
butter or margarine	25 g	60 g
flour	15 g	50 g
milk	125 ml	300 ml
egg yolks	3	8
salt, cayenne		
cheese, grated	50 g	125 g
egg whites	4	10

1 Melt the butter in a thick-based pan.
2 Add the flour and mix with a wooden spoon.
3 Cook out for a few seconds without colouring.
4 Gradually add the cold milk and mix to a smooth sauce.
5 Simmer for a few minutes.
6 Add one egg yolk, mix in quickly; immediately remove from the heat.
7 When cool, add the remaining yolks. Season with salt and cayenne.
8 Add the cheese.
9 Place the egg whites and a pinch of salt (a pinch of egg white powder will help strengthen the whites) in a scrupulously clean bowl, preferably copper, and whisk until stiff.
10 Add one-eighth of the whites to the mixture and mix well.
11 Gently fold in the remaining seven-eighths of the mixture, mix as lightly as possible. Place into a buttered soufflé case.
12 Cook in a hot oven at 220°C for 25–30 minutes.
13 Remove from the oven, place on a round flat dish and serve immediately.

HEALTHY EATING TIP

- Use sunflower margarine and semi-skimmed milk to make the sauce.
- No added salt is needed as the cheese has salt in it.

* *Using hard margarine*

8 Cheese fritters *(beignets au fromage)*

Cal	Cal	Fat	Sat Fat	Carb	Sugar	Protein	Fibre
1409 KJ	340 kcal	28.4 g	11.2 g	11.8 g	0.4 g	9.9 g	0.5 g

	4 portions	10 portions
water	125 ml	300 ml
butter or margarine	50 g	125 g
flour, white or wholemeal	60 g	200 g
medium eggs	2	5
Parmesan cheese, grated	50 g	125 g
salt, cayenne		

1 Bring the water and butter or margarine to the boil in a thick-based pan. Remove from the heat.
2 Add the flour, mix with a wooden spoon.
3 Return to a gentle heat and mix well until the mixture leaves the sides of the pan. Remove from the heat. Allow to cool slightly.
4 Gradually add the eggs, beating well. Add the cheese and seasoning.

5 Using a spoon, scoop out the mixture in pieces the size of a walnut; place into deep hot fat at 185°C.
6 Allow to cook, with the minimum of handling, for about 10 minutes.
7 Drain and serve sprinkled with grated Parmesan.

HEALTHY EATING TIP
• Use sunflower margarine for the fritters.
• No extra salt is needed as the cheese has salt in it.
• Fry in hot sunflower oil and drain on kitchen paper.

9 Pizza

Cal	Cal	Fat	Sat Fat	Carb	Sugar	Protein	Fibre	*
3956 KJ	941 kcal	46.3 g	13 g	114.4 g	20.1 g	23.6 g	8.4 g	

flour, strong white	200 g
pinch of salt	
margarine	12 g
yeast	5 g
water or milk at 24°C	125 ml
caster sugar	5 g
onions	100 g
cloves garlic, crushed	2
sunflower oil	60 ml
canned plum tomatoes	200 g
tomato purée	100 g
oregano	3 g
basil	3 g
sugar	10 g
cornflour	10 g
mozzarella cheese	100 g

1 Sieve the flour and the salt. Rub in the margarine.
2 Disperse the yeast in the warm milk or water; add the caster sugar. Add this mixture to the flour.
3 Mix well, knead to a smooth dough, place in a basin covered with a damp cloth and allow to prove until doubled in size.

4 Knock back, divide into two and roll out into two 18 cm discs. Place on a lightly greased baking sheet.
5 Sweat the finely chopped onions and garlic in the oil until cooked.
6 Add the roughly chopped tomatoes, tomato purée, oregano, basil and sugar. Bring to the boil and simmer for 5 minutes.
7 Dilute the cornflour in a little water, stir into the tomato mixture and bring back to the boil.
8 Take the discs of pizza dough and spread 125 g of filling on each one.
9 Sprinkle with grated mozzarella cheese or lay the slices of cheese on top.
10 Bake in a hot oven at 220°C, for about 10 minutes.

Note: The pizza dough may also be made into rectangles so that it can be sliced into fingers for buffet work.

Pizza is a traditional dish originating from southern Italy. In simple terms it is a flat bread dough that can be topped with a wide variety of ingredients and baked quickly. The only rule is not to add wet ingredients, such as tomatoes, which are too juicy, otherwise the pizza will become soggy. Traditionally pizzas are baked in a wood-fired brick oven, but they can be baked in any type of hot oven for 8–15 minutes depending on the ingredients. The recipe given here is a typical one.

Variations
Oregano is sprinkled on most pizzas before baking. This is a basic recipe and many variations exist, some have the addition of olives, artichoke bottoms,

prawns, mortadella sausage, garlic sausage or anchovy fillets. Other combinations include:

- mozzarella cheese, anchovies, capers and garlic
- mozzarella cheese, tomato and oregano
- ham, mushrooms, egg and parmesan cheese
- prawns, tuna, capers and garlic
- ham, mushrooms and olives.

* Using 100 per cent strong white flour

10 Bruschetta

Bruschetta is a thick slice of toasted or grilled bread rubbed with a fresh clove of garlic and sprinkled with extra virgin olive oil. It can then be embellished with tomato, basil, anchovies, ricotta cheese or almost any type of topping. The recipe given here is a typical one.

Recipe 1
1 Toast or grill the slices of bread and rub them with garlic cloves while hot.
2 Cook the raw ingredients for the topping (see 'Variations', below) in olive oil and pile on to the bread.
3 Add any final ingredients desired, such as cheese, anchovies and/or herbs.

Recipe 2
1 As mentioned above, one of the most popular ways of serving bruschetta is to toast or grill thick slices of ciabatta and rub with garlic cloves while hot.

2 Then add a generous topping of diced cheese (e.g. ricotta or mozzarella) and diced tomato flesh (skin and deseed the tomatoes).
3 Sprinkle with a good-quality olive oil and finely chopped onion or chives; serve.

HEALTHY EATING TIP
- Use a little olive oil to cook the topping ingredients.
- Ricotta cheese contains less fat than mozzarella.

Variations
Toppings include mushrooms, aubergine, onions, spinach, tomatoes, ham, rocket, olives, Parmesan, mozzarella and anchovies. Traditionally an Italian-type bread (e.g. ciabatta) is used.

11 Bocconcini and tomato bruschetta

1 Cut small rounds of bruschetta the size of a 50p piece, then lightly toast.
2 Place a basil leaf on each slice, arrange slices of bocconcini cheese and tomato.
3 Drizzle with garlic-flavoured olive oil, season with salt and black pepper.

Note: See recipe 10 for more information.

12 Canapés

A wide variety of cold canapés can be offered. Just a few examples are presented here.

- Cherry tomatoes, scooped out, filled with crab meat, seasoned and bound with mayonnaise.
- Avocado pear purée with lime juice, mixed with a fine dice of yellow peppers.
- Slices of rye bread with a slice of lobster, topped with asparagus, garnished with lobster eggs.
- Smoked duck on slices of rye bread, garnished with mango.
- Small new potatoes, cooked, scooped out, filled with sour cream and chives, garnished with caviar or lumpfish roe.
- Small choux pastry éclairs filled with liver pâté.
- Brioche croûtes with apricot chutney and Gorgonzola.
- Marinated and smoked salmon twisted onto the end of silver forms with a mustard dip. The marinade can be a combination of different flavours, e.g. beetroot and soya, lime juice and coriander.
- Various types of sushi.
- Profiteroles filled with prawns in cocktail sauce.

Some examples of hot canapés are as follows.

- Small Yorkshire puddings with a slice of beef topped with horseradish cream.
- Oyster beignets, garlic mayonnaise.
- Aubergine and goats' cheese tartlet.
- Monkfish spring rolls, remoulade sauce.
- Chicken and risotto croquettes.
- Small pizzas.
- Small pieces of chicken on skewers with bacon.
- Satay (peanut) sauce.
- Angels on horseback (page 661).
- Vegetable samosas (page 407).
- Latkes (page 421).

Dips for hot canapés:

- garlic mayonnaise
- yoghurt, cucumber and mint
- apricot chutney.

Figure 15.1 ✐ Selection of cold canapés

At some receptions, small finger pastries are requested. Some examples of what can be offered are:

- fruit tartlets, Bakewell tarts, lemon meringue tartlets
- éclairs
- palmiers with strawberries and cream
- scones filled with tropical fruit
- cornets made of brandy snaps filled with cream and stem ginger
- small scoops of ice cream dipped in white and dark chocolate
- lemon meringue tartlets
- various tuille shapes, caskets filled with lemon mousse.

13 Cocktail canapés (traditional)

These are small items of food, hot or cold, served at cocktail parties or buffet receptions, and may be offered as an accompaniment to drinks before any meal (luncheon, dinner or supper). Typical items for cocktail parties and light buffets are as follows.

- Hot savoury pastry patties or bouchées of lobster, chicken, crab, salmon, mushroom, ham, etc. Small pizzas, quiches, brochettes, hamburgers.

- Hot sausages (chipolatas), various fillings, such as chicken livers, prunes, mushrooms, tomatoes, gherkins, etc., wrapped in bacon, skewered and cooked under the salamander. Fried goujons of fish.
- Game chips, gaufrette potatoes, fried fish balls, celery stalks spread with cheese.

14 Lamb satay

Makes 20

lamb fillets or loin of lamb	500 g
clove of garlic, crushed and chopped	3
Thai fish sauce	2 tsp
sweet chilli sauce	2 tbsp
fresh ginger, grated	2 tsp
lime juice	62 ml
peanut butter (coarse)	2 tbsp
ground cumin	1 tsp
ground turmeric	1 tsp
Sauce	
white vinegar	62 ml
caster sugar	2 tbsp
sweet chilli sauce	1 tbsp
unsalted, roasted peanuts	1 tbsp
fresh coriander leaves, finely chopped	1 tbsp

1 Prepare the lamb, cutting it into thin strips.
2 In a bowl place the garlic, sauces, ginger, lime juice, peanut butter and spices. Mix well.
3 Place the marinade over the lamb and put in refrigerator for 3 hours or overnight.
4 Meanwhile, prepare some bamboo skewers in water for about an hour to prevent scorching.
5 Thread the lamb onto the skewers. Grill the lamb skewers, turning once until cooked and nicely coloured.
6 Prepare the sauce. Place the vinegar and sugar in a small pan, stir until the sugar has dissolved. Bring to the boil, simmer for 2 minutes. Stir in the remaining ingredients.
7 Serve the lamb on a suitable platter on banana leaves with the sauce in a bowl in the centre.

15 Crab cakes with chilli lime dipping sauce

Makes 30–40

crab meat	350 g
uncooked prawns, shelled and de-veined	650 g
red curry paste	1 tbsp
egg	1
spring onions	2
fresh coriander, finely chopped	2 tbsp
lemon grass, finely chopped	2 tsp
red Thai chilli, deseeded and chopped	1
vegetable oil	2 tbsp
Dipping sauce	
lime juice	2 tbsp
water	2 tbsp
fish sauce	2 tsp
kaffir lime leaf, chopped	1
red Thai chilli, deseeded, finely chopped	1

1 In a food processor, place the crab, prawns, curry paste, egg, onion, coriander, lemon grass and chilli. Combine all ingredients until all mixed together.
2 Shape into small cakes.
3 Heat the oil in a shallow pan and stir-fry the crab cakes on both sides until golden brown. Drain, place on a suitable dish with the dipping sauce (see below).

Dipping sauce
1 Combine all ingredients in a suitable bowl.
2 Stir well.

16 Potato wedges with tomato chilli salsa

Makes 40

large potatoes	5
sea salt	1 tsp
coarse black pepper	1 tsp
Tomato chilli salsa	
large beef tomato, peeled, seeded and finely chopped	1
red onion	1
chilli, finely chopped	1
lime juice	1 tbsp
chopped fresh basil leaves	1 tbsp

1 Wash the potatoes and cut into wedges.
2 Heat a little oil in a suitable roasting tray, add the wedges skin side down. Sprinkle with salt and pepper.
3 Bake in a hot oven until brown and crisp.
4 Prepare the salsa: place all ingredients into a suitable bowl and mix well.
5 When the potatoes are cooked, place on a suitable serving platter, arranged around a bowl of sour cream and a bowl of the salsa.

17 Pork and corn Thai cakes

Makes 20

minced pork	500 g
red curry paste	1 tbsp
egg, lightly beaten	1
spring onions, finely chopped	6
cooked sweetcorn	100 g
breadcrumbs	50 g
coriander leaves, finely chopped	1 tbsp

1 Place the minced pork into a bowl, add the curry paste, egg, onion, sweetcorn and breadcrumbs, and mix well. Add coriander leaves, give a further mix.
2 Divide into 20 small balls, then flatten into cakes.
3 Place on an oiled tray, bake in a hot oven until cooked and golden brown, turn once.
4 To serve, place on a suitable dish garnished with coriander leaves and in the centre a suitable dipping sauce (e.g. tomato and chilli salsa – see recipe 15).

Variations
Veal may be used in place of pork.

18 Honey prawns

large uncooked prawns	20
honey	60 ml
soy sauce	60 ml
hoi sin sauce	1 tbsp
garlic, crushed and chopped	2 cloves
small chilli, deseeded and chopped	1
toasted sesame seeds, to serve	2 tsp

1 Shell and de-vein the prawns, leaving the tails intact.
2 Cut along prawn backs lengthways without separating halves.
3 In a suitable bowl, add the honey, soy sauce, hoi sin sauce, garlic and chilli. Mix well.
4 Pour over the prawns and allow to marinate for at least 3 hours or overnight.
5 Flatten the prawns and grill on both sides.
6 Serve on a suitable platter sprinkled with sesame seeds.

19 Lemon grass prawns

uncooked prawns	32
lemons	2
lemon grass, finely chopped	2
sambal ulek (chilli paste)	2 tsp
honey	60 ml
lemon juice	2 tbsp
cloves of garlic	2
fresh lemon grass stems	4

1 Shell and de-vein the prawns, leaving the tails intact.
2 Peel the lemons, remove the pith from the rind and cut the rind into a short julienne. Place this in a basin with the chopped lemon grass, sambal ulek, honey, lemon juice and garlic. Mix well.
3 Pour this mixture over the prawns and marinate for at least 3 hours or overnight.
4 Cut off 1 cm from the base of the lemon grass stems and discard. Peel away the coarse inner layers. Cut each in half crossways; cut one end into a sharp point.
5 Thread 2 prawns onto each lemon grass skewer. Grill each skewer gently on both sides.
6 Serve on pieces of coconut shell on a reel of finely sliced cucumber.

20 Pumpernickel rounds with smoked salmon, sour cream and dill

1 Cut small rounds of pumpernickel and pipe on top
  a rosette of sour cream flavoured with chopped dill.
2 Arrange smoked salmon on top.
3 Garnish with lemon and dill.

21 Fresh mussels with tomato and cheese

1 Prepare mussels by removing the beards.
2 Place in a pan, surface covered with white wine or
  fish stock.
3 Add the mussels and cook over fierce heat until
  they open. Drain and discard the liquid.

4 Place each mussel in a half-shell. Place on a tray,
  cover mussels with cooked tomato concassée,
  sprinkle with mozzarella cheese and grill until it is
  melted.

22 Mini poppadoms

These may be filled with a variety of different foods
(e.g. curried eggs, spiced tuna and lime dressing,
chicken tikka, curried fish).

23 Deep-fried pork noodles

Makes 36–40

dried egg noodles	50 g
minced pork	250 g
onion, finely chopped	100 g
garlic, crushed and chopped	2
fresh ginger, grated	2 tsp
coriander, chopped	1 tsp
egg yolk	1
flour	50 g
sambal ulek (chilli paste)	1 tsp
fish sauce	1 tsp
Dip	
sweet chilli sauce	62 ml
lime juice	2 tbsp

1 Crush the noodles, place in a suitable bowl, cover
  with boiling water, stand for 5 minutes, then drain.
2 Add the pork, onion, garlic, ginger, coriander, egg
  yolk, flour, sambal ulek and fish sauce.
3 Mix well. Divide into small balls, deep-fry until
  golden brown and cooked through. Drain. Serve
  with the dipping sauce of sweet chilli and lime juice.

24 Tuna nori rolls

Makes 36–40

koshi hikari rice (small round-grain white rice)	400 g
rice vinegar	60 ml
sugar	2 tbsp
salt	pinch
toasted nori*	6 sheets
sashimi tuna	125 g
Lebanese cucumber	125 g
avocado pear	200 g
pickled ginger slices	2 tbsp
wasabi (Japanese white radish)	½ tsp

* dried seaweed sold in paper-thin sheets

1 Cook the rice in boiling salted water until tender, drain well and allow to stand for 5 minutes. Stir in the vinegar, sugar and salt. Allow to cool.
2 Place one sheet of nori, rough side up, on a bamboo sushi mat. Spread one-sixth of the rice mixture over the nori, leaving 4 cm on the short side. Press the rice firmly in place.
3 Make a lengthways hollow across the centre of the rice. Place one-sixth of each of the tuna, cucumber, avocado, ginger slices and wasabi in the hollow in the centre of the rice.
4 Use the bamboo mat to roll the tuna nori, pressing firmly as you roll.
5 Cut each into the desired number of pieces (approx. 6) and place on a serving dish. Repeat with each piece of nori.
6 Serve with soy sauce.

25 Sandwiches

For speed of production, sandwiches are made in bands by cutting the bread rectangularly. When filled, the crusts are removed and the sandwiches cut into fingers.

Today bakers will bake the bread to your specification and slice it ready for use. The specification may also include speciality breads like tomato, basil, walnut and olive bread.

Sandwiches may also be cut into small cubes and a variety placed on a cocktail stick like a mini kebab.

Sandwiches may be made from every kind of bread, fresh or toasted, in a variety of shapes, and with an almost endless assortment of fillings. They may be garnished with potato or vegetable crisps and a little salad.

Toasted sandwiches

These are made by inserting a variety of savoury fillings between two slices of hot, freshly buttered toast (e.g. scrambled egg, bacon, fried egg, scrambled egg with chopped ham) or by inserting two slices of buttered bread with the required filling into a sandwich toaster.

Club sandwich

This is made by placing between three slices of hot buttered toast a filling of lettuce, tomato, grilled bacon, slices of hard-boiled egg, mayonnaise and slices of chicken.

Bookmaker sandwich

This is an underdone minute steak between two slices of bloomer toast.

Double-decker and treble-decker sandwiches

Toasted and untoasted bread can be made into double-decker sandwiches, using three slices of bread with two separate fillings. Treble- and quadro-decker sandwiches may also be prepared. They may be served hot or cold.

Open sandwich or Scandinavian smorgasbord

These are prepared from a buttered slice of any bread, garnished with any type of meat, fish, eggs, vegetables, salads, etc. The varieties of open sandwich include the following:

● smoked salmon, lettuce, potted shrimps, slice of lemon
● cold sliced beef, sliced tomato, fans of gherkins

- shredded lettuce, sliced hardboiled egg, mayonnaise, cucumber
- pickled herring, chopped gherkin, capers (sieved), hardboiled egg.

 Further information

For further information contact the British Sandwich Association, 8 Home Farm, Ardington, Wantage, Oxfordshire OX12 8PN, www.sandwich.org.uk.

26 Wraps

These are made enclosing various fillings wrapped in tortillas (plain or flavoured – e.g. tomato, herbs) (see page 415). Any of a wide variety of fillings can be used – for example, chicken and roasted vegetables; beans and red pepper salad with guacamole (a well-flavoured avocado pulp). Flat breads (e.g. pitta, ciabatta) can be used with various fillings (e.g. chicken tikka).

27 Bagels

Bagels are ring doughnut-shaped rolls of leavened bread that are boiled before being baked, giving them a hard texture. They are traditionally filled with smoked salmon and cream cheese (a Jewish speciality).

Glossary of culinary terms

à la In the style of

à la française In the French style

à la minute Cooked to order

à la carte Dishes prepared to order and priced individually

Abatis de volaille Poultry offal, giblets, etc.

Abats Offal, heads, hearts, liver, kidney, etc.

Accompaniments Items offered separately with a dish of food

Agar-agar A vegetable gelling agent obtained from seaweed, used as a substitute for gelatine

Aile Wing of poultry or game birds

Aloyau de boeuf Sirloin of beef

Ambient Room temperature, surrounding atmosphere

Amino acid Organic acids found in proteins

Antibiotic Drug used to destroy disease-producing germs within human or animal bodies

Antiseptic Substance that prevents the growth of bacteria and moulds, specifically on or in the human body

Aromats Fragrant herbs and spices

Arroser To baste, as in roasting

Ascorbic acid Known as vitamin C, found in citrus fruits and blackcurrants, necessary for growth and the maintenance of health

Aspic A savoury jelly mainly used for decorative larder work

Assorti An assortment

Au bleu When applied to meat it means very underdone

Au beurre With butter

Au four Baked in the oven

Au gratin Sprinkled with cheese or breadcrumbs and browned

Au vin blanc With white wine

Bactericide Substance that destroys bacteria

Bacterium (pl. bacteria) Single-celled micro-organisms; some are harmful and cause food poisoning; others are useful, such as those used in cheese making

Bain-marie
- A container of water to keep foods hot without fear of burning
- A container of water for cooking foods to prevent them burning
- A deep, narrow container for storing hot sauces, soups and gravies

Barder To bard = to cover breasts of birds with thin slices of bacon

Barquette A boat-shaped pastry case

Basting Spooning melted fat over food during cooking to keep it moist

Bat out To flatten slices of raw meat with a cutlet bat

Bean curd Also known as tofu (see below); a curdled, soft, cheese-like preparation made from soybean milk; a good source of protein

Beansprouts Young shoots of dried beans – e.g. mung beans, alfalfa and soybean

Beurre manié Equal quantities of flour and butter used for thickening sauces

Blanc A cooking liquor of water, lemon juice, flour and salt; also applied to the white of chicken (breast and wings)

Blanch
- To make white, as with bones and meat
- To retain colour, as with certain vegetables
- To skin, as for tomatoes
- To make limp, as for certain braised vegetables
- To cook without colour, as for the first frying of fried (chip) potatoes

Blanquette A white stew cooked in stock from which the sauce is made

Blitz to rapidly purée or foam a light sauce, generally using an electric hand blender at the last moment before service

Bombay duck Small, dried,

salted fish; fried, it is used as an accompaniment to curry dishes

Bombe An ice cream speciality of different flavours in a bomb shape

Bone out To remove the bones

Botulism Rare form of food poisoning

Bouchée A small puff paste case, literally 'a mouthful'

Bouillon Unclarified stock

Bouquet garni A faggot of herbs (e.g. parsley stalks, thyme and bay leaf), tied in pieces of celery and leek

Brine A preserving solution of water, salt, saltpetre and aromats used for meats (e.g. silverside, brisket, tongue)

Brunoise Small dice

Butter
- Black butter (*beurre noir*)
- Brown butter/nut brown butter (*beurre noisette*)
- Melted butter (*beurre fondu*)
- Parsley butter (*beurre maître d'hôtel*)

Buttermilk Liquid remaining from the churning of butter

Calcium A mineral required for building bones and teeth, obtained from cheese and milk

Calorie A unit of heat or energy, known as a kilocalorie

Canapé A cushion of bread on which are served various foods, hot or cold

Carbohydrate A nutrient that has three groups – sugar, starch and cellulose; the first

two provide the body with energy; cellulose provides roughage (dietary fibre)

Carbon dioxide A gas produced by all raising agents

Carrier A person who harbours and may transmit pathogenic organisms without showing signs of illness

Carte du jour Menu for the day

Casserole An earthenware fireproof dish with a lid

Cellulose The coarse structure of fruit, vegetables and cereals that is not digested but is used as roughage (dietary fibre)

Châteaubriand The head of the fillet of beef

Chaud-froid A demi-glace or creamed velouté with gelatine or aspic added, used for masking cold dishes

Chiffonade Fine shreds, e.g. of spinach, lettuce

Chinois A conical strainer

Chlorophyll The green colour in vegetables

Ciseler To make slight incisions in the surface of a thick fillet of fish, on or off the bone, to allow even cooking

Civet A brown stew of game, usually hare

Clarification To make clear such as stock, jelly, butter

Clostridium perfringens Food-poisoning bacterium found in the soil, vegetables and meat

Coagulation The solidification of protein that is

irreversible (e.g. fried egg, cooking of meat)

Cocotte Porcelain or earthenware fireproof dish

Collagen/elastin Proteins in connective tissue (e.g. gristle)

Compote Stewed (e.g. stewed fruit)

Concassée Coarsely chopped (e.g. parsley, tomatoes)

Confit A cooked meat, poultry or game preserved in good fat or oil

Consommé Basic clear soup

Contamination Occurrence of any objectionable matter in food

Contrefilet Boned-out sirloin of beef

Cook out The process of cooking flour in a roux, soup or sauce

Cordon A thread or thin line of sauce

Correcting Adjusting the seasoning, consistency and colour

Côte A rib or chop

Côtelette A cutlet

Coupe An individual serving bowl

Couper To cut

Court-bouillon A well-flavoured cooking liquor for fish

Crème fraiche Whipping cream and buttermilk heated to 24–29°C

Crêpes Pancakes

Credit notes Issued when an invoice contains incorrect details; credit is therefore given

Croquettes Cooked foods moulded into a cylinder shape, coated in flour and egg, crumbed and deep-fried

Cross-contamination The transfer of micro-organisms from contaminated to uncontaminated hands, utensils or equipment

Croutons Cubes of fried or toasted bread served with soup; also triangular pieces served with spinach, and heart-shaped with certain vegetables and entrées

Crudités Small neat pieces of raw vegetables served with a dip as an appetiser

Cuisse de poulet Chicken leg

Cullis (coulis) Sauce made of fruit or vegetable purée (e.g. raspberry, tomato)

Danger zone of bacterial growth Temperature range within which the multiplication of pathogenic bacteria is possible; from 10–63°C

Dariole A small mould, as used for crème caramel

Darne A slice of round fish (e.g. salmon) on the bone

Déglacer To swill out a pan in which food has been roasted or fried, with wine, stock or water, in order to use the sediment for the accompanying sauce or gravy

Dégraisser To skim fat off liquid

Delivery note Form sent by supplier with delivery of goods

Demi-glace Brown stock reduced to a light consistency

Désosser To bone out meat

Detergent Substance that dissolves grease

Dilute To mix a powder (e.g. cornflour) with a liquid

Dish paper A plain dish paper

Disinfectant Substance that reduces the risk of infection

Doily A fancy dish paper

Drain Placing food in a colander, allowing liquid to seep out

Duxelle Finely chopped mushrooms cooked with chopped shallots

Eggwash Beaten egg with a little milk or water

Emulsion A mixture of oil and liquid (such as vinegar), which does not separate on standing (e.g. mayonnaise, hollandaise)

Entrecôte A steak cut from a boned sirloin

Enzymes Chemical substances produced from living cells

Escalope A thin slice such as escalope of veal

Farce Stuffing

Fecule Fine potato flour

Feuilletage Puff pastry

Fines herbes Chopped fresh herbs (e.g. parsley, tarragon, chervil)

First-aid materials Suitable and sufficient bandages and dressings, including waterproof dressings and antiseptic; all dressings to be individually wrapped

Flake To break into natural segments (e.g. fish)

Flan Open fruit tart

Fleurons Small crescent-shaped pieces of puff pastry

Flute A 20 cm diameter French bread used for soup garnishes

Food-borne Bacteria carried on food

Food handling Any operation in the storage, preparation, production, processing, packaging, transportation, distribution and sale of food

Frappé Chilled (e.g. melon frappé)

Freezer burn Affects frozen items, which are spoiled due to being left unprotected for too long

Friandises Sweetmeats, petits fours

Fricassée A white stew in which the meat, poultry or fish is cooked in the sauce

Friture A pan that contains deep fat

Fumé Smoked (e.g. saumon fumé = smoked salmon)

Garam masala A combination of spices

Garnish Served as part of the main item; trimmings

Gastroenteritis Inflammation of the stomach and intestinal tract that normally results in diarrhoea

Gâteau A cake of more than one portion

Ghee The Indian name for clarified butter; ghee is pure butter fat

Gibier Game

Glace Ice or ice cream from which all milk solids have been removed

Glaze To glaze
- To colour a dish under the salamander (e.g. fillets of sole bonne femme)
- To finish a flan or tartlet (e.g. with apricot jam)
- To finish certain vegetables (e.g. glazed carrots)

Gluten This is formed from protein in flour when mixed with water

Gratin A thin coating of grated cheese and/or breadcrumbs on certain dishes then browned under the grill or in an oven

Haché Finely chopped or minced

hors d'oeuvre Appetising first course dishes, hot or cold

Humidity Amount of moisture in the air

Incubation period Time between infection and first signs of illness

Infestations Insects breeding on the premises

Insecticide Chemical used to kill insects

Invoice Bill listing items delivered, with costs of items

Jardinière Vegetables cut into batons

Julienne Cut into fine strips

Jus-lié Thickened gravy

Larding Inserting strips of fat bacon into meat

Lardons Batons of thick streaky bacon

Liaison A thickening or binding

Macédoine
- A mixture of fruit or vegetables
- Cut into ? cm dice

Magnetron Device that generates microwaves in a microwave oven

Marinade A richly spiced pickling liquid used to give flavour and assist in tenderising meats

Marmite Stock pot

Mascarpone An Italian cheese resembling clotted cream

Menu List of dishes available

Micro-organisms Very small living plants or animals (bacteria, yeasts, moulds)

Mignonette Coarsely ground pepper

Mildew Type of fungus, similar to mould

Mineral salts Mineral elements, small quantities of which are essential for health

Mirepoix Roughly cut onions and carrots, a sprig of thyme and a bay leaf

Mise-en-place Basic preparation prior to serving

Miso Seasoning made from fermented soybeans

Monosodium glutamate (MSG) A substance added to food products to increase flavour

Moulds Microscopic plants (fungi) that may appear as woolly patches on food

Mousse A dish of light consistency, hot or cold

Napper To coat or mask with sauce

Natives A menu term for English oysters

Navarin Brown stew of lamb

Niacin Part of vitamin B, found in liver, kidney, meat extract, bacon

Noisette (nut) A cut from a boned-out loin of lamb

Nutrients The components of food required for health (protein, fats, carbohydrates, vitamins, mineral salts, water)

Optimum Best, most favourable

Palatable Pleasant to taste

Pané Floured, egg and crumbed

Panettone A very light traditional Italian Christmas cake

Parsley butter Butter containing lemon juice and chopped parsley

Pass To cause to go through a sieve or strainer

Pathogen Disease-producing organism

Paupiette A stuffed and rolled strip of fish or meat

Paysanne Cut in even, thin triangular, round or square pieces

Persillé Finished with chopped parsley

Pesticide Chemical used to kill pests

Pests e.g. cockroaches, flies, silverfish

Petits fours Very small pastries, biscuits, sweets, sweetmeats

pH value A scale indicating acidity or alkalinity in food

Phosphorus A mineral element found in fish; required for building bones and teeth

Piquant Sharply flavoured

Piqué Studded clove in an onion

Plat du jour Special dish of the day

Poppadoms Dried, thin, large, round wafers made from lentil flour, used as an accompaniment to Indian dishes

Printanier Garnish of spring vegetables

Protein The nutrient needed for growth and repair

Prove To allow a yeast dough to rest in a warm place so that it can expand

Pulses Vegetables grown in pods (peas and beans) and dried; source of protein and roughage

Quark Salt-free soft cheese made from semi-skimmed milk

Ragout Stew (ragout de boeuf); brown beef stew

Rare When applied to meat, it means underdone

Réchauffer To reheat

Reduce To concentrate a liquid by boiling

Refresh To make cold under running cold water

Residual insecticide Insecticide that remains active for a considerable period of time

Riboflavin Part of vitamin B known as B2; sources in yeast, liver, eggs, cheese

Rissoler To fry to a golden brown

Rodents Rats and mice

Roux A thickening of cooked flour and fat

Sabayon Yolks of eggs and a little water or wine cooked until creamy

Saccharometer An instrument for measuring the density of sugar

Salamander Type of grill; heat from above

Salmonella Food-poisoning bacterium found in meat and poultry

Sanitiser Chemical agent used for cleaning and disinfecting surfaces and equipment

Sauté
- Toss in fat (e.g. pommes sautées)
- Cook quickly in a sauté pan or frying pan
- A brown stew of a specific type (e.g. veal sauté)

Seal To set the surface of meat in a hot oven or pan to colour and retain the juices

Seared Cooked quickly on both sides in a little hot fat or oil

Seasoned flour Flour seasoned with salt and pepper

Set
- To seal the outside surface
- To allow to become firm or firmer (e.g. jelly)

Shredded Cut in fine strips (e.g. lettuce, onion)

Silicone paper Non-stick paper (e.g. siliconised paper)

Singe To brown or colour

Smetana A low-fat product; a cross between soured cream and yoghurt

Sodium Mineral element in the form of salt (sodium chloride); found in cheese, bacon, fish, meat

Soufflé A very light dish, sweet or savoury, hot or cold

Soy sauce Made from soybeans and used extensively in Chinese cookery

Spores Resistant resting phase of bacteria, protecting them against adverse conditions such as high temperatures

Staphylococcus Food-poisoning bacterium found in the human nose and throat, and also in septic cuts

Starch A carbohydrate found in cereals, certain vegetables and farinaceous foods

Sterile Free from all living organisms

Sterilisation Process that destroys living organisms

Steriliser Chemical used to destroy all living organisms

Stock rotation Sequence of issuing goods: first into store = first to be issued

Strain To separate the liquid from the solids by passing through a strainer

Sweat To cook in fat under a lid without colour

Syneresis The squeezing out of liquid from an overcooked protein and liquid mixture (e.g. scrambled egg, egg custard)

Table d'hôte A meal at a fixed price; a set menu

Tahini A strong-flavoured sesame seed paste

Tartlet A small round pastry case

Terrine An earthenware dish used for cooking and serving pâté; also used as a name for certain products

Thiamine Part of vitamin B known as B1, it assists the nervous system; sources in yeast, bacon, wholemeal bread

Timbale A double serving dish

Tofu Low-fat bean curd made from soybeans (see also bean curd)

Tourné Turned, shaped in barrels or large olives

Tranche A slice

Trichinosis Disease caused by hair-like worms in the muscles of meat (e.g. pork)

Tronçon A slice of flat fish on the bone (e.g. turbot)

TVP Texturised vegetable protein, derived from soybeans

Vegan A person who does not eat fish, meat, poultry, game, dairy products, honey and eggs, and who does not use any animal products (e.g. leather)

Vegetarian A person who does not eat meat, poultry or game

Velouté
- Basic sauce
- A soup of velvet or smooth consistency

Viruses Microscopic pathogens that multiply in the living cells of their host

Vitamins Chemical substances that assist the regulation of body processes

Vol-au-vent A large puff pastry case

Wok A round-bottomed pan used extensively in Chinese cooking

Yeast extract A mixture of brewer's yeast and salt, high in flavour and protein

Yoghurt An easily digested fermented milk product